ZAGAT®

America's Top Restaurants

2011

STAFF EDITOR
Bill Corsello

Published and distributed by
Zagat Survey, LLC
4 Columbus Circle
New York, NY 10019
T: 212.977.6000
E: americastop@zagat.com
www.zagat.com

ACKNOWLEDGMENTS

We thank Claudia Alarcon, Alicia Arter, Olga Boikess, Nikki Buchanan, Suzi Forbes Chase, Ann Christenson, Bill Citara, Jeanette Foster, Mary Ann Castronovo Fusco, Rona Gindin, Meesha Halm, Lynn Hazlewood, Edie Jarolim, Valerie Jarvie, Marty Katz, Elizabeth Keyser, Michael Klein, Rochelle Koff, Naomi Kooker, Gretchen Kurz, Sharon Litwin, Lori Midson, David Nelson, Jan Norris, Jenny Pavlasek, Joe and Ann Pollack, Laura Putre, Virginia Rainey, Laura Reiley, Mike Riccetti, Heidi Knapp Rinella, Julia Rosenfeld, Shelley Skiles Sawyer, Helen Schwab, Merrill Shindler, Jane Slaughter, Kelly Stewart, Eryn Swanson, Pat Tanner, John Turiano, Alice Van Housen, Carla Waldemar, Amanda Boyd Walters, Kate Washington and Kay Winzenried, as well as the following members of our staff: Caitlin Eichelberger (associate editor), Brian Albert, Sean Beachell, Maryanne Bertollo, Danielle Borovoy, Jane Chang, Sandy Cheng, Reni Chin, Larry Cohn, John Deiner, Carol Diuguid, Alison Flick, Jeff Freier, Curt Gathje, Michelle Golden, Matthew Hamm, Justin Hartung, Karen Hudes, Anna Hyclak, Cynthia Kilian, Natalie Lebert, Mike Liao, James Mulcahy, Josh Rogers, Jacqueline Wasilczyk, Art Yaghci, Yoji Yamaguchi, Sharon Yates, Anna Zappia and Kyle Zolner.

This guide is based on public opinion surveys of regular restaurant-goers like you. The ratings reflect the average scores given by the survey participants who voted on each establishment. The text is based on quotes from, or paraphrasings of, the surveyors' comments. Phone numbers, addresses and other factual data were correct to the best of our knowledge when published in this guide.

© 2010 Zagat Survey, LLC
ISBN-13: 978-1-60478-308-7
ISBN-10: 1-60478-308-7
Printed in the
United States of America

Contents

Ratings & Symbols	4
About This Survey	5
What's New	6
Top Food by Area	7
Most Popular by Area	10

RESTAURANT DIRECTORY

Names, Locations, Contact
   Info, Ratings & Reviews

Atlanta	14
Atlantic City	24
Austin	28
Baltimore/Annapolis	33
Boston	38
Charlotte	48
Chicago	53
Cincinnati	63
Cleveland	68
Columbus	73
Connecticut	77
Dallas/Ft. Worth	86
Denver/Mtn. Resorts	95
Detroit	104
Ft. Lauderdale	109
Honolulu	114
Houston	118
Kansas City	126
Las Vegas	131
Long Island	140
Los Angeles	149
Miami	158
Milwaukee	167
Minneapolis/St. Paul	172
Naples, FL	177
New Jersey	181
New Orleans	190
New York City	199
Orange County, CA	209
Orlando	214
Palm Beach	223
Philadelphia	228
Phoenix/Scottsdale	237
Portland, OR	242
Sacramento	247
Salt Lake City/Mtn. Resorts	252
San Antonio	257

San Diego	262
San Francisco Bay Area	267
Seattle	277
St. Louis	286
Tampa/Sarasota	291
Tucson	296
Washington, DC	301
Westchester/Hudson Valley	311

INDEXES

Alpha Page Index	321
Wine Chart	348

Ratings & Symbols

Zagat Top Spot	Name	Symbols		Cuisine	Zagat Ratings			
					FOOD	DECOR	SERVICE	COST

Area, Address & Contact	🅩 **Tim & Nina's** ◐ *American* ▽ 23 | 9 | 13 | $101
	W 50s | 4 Columbus Circle (8th Ave.) | 212-977-6000 | www.zagat.com
Review, surveyor comments in quotes	"T&N take sustainability to exciting new heights" at their "tasty", "costly" Columbus Circle rooftop New American where "they grow all the produce" and "raise chickens too"; but respondents wonder "why is the staff so sanctimonious?" – and "couldn't they have covered up the air-conditioning units?"

Ratings **Food, Decor** and **Service** are rated on the Zagat 0 to 30 scale.

0 – 9	poor to fair
10 – 15	fair to good
16 – 19	good to very good
20 – 25	very good to excellent
26 – 30	extraordinary to perfection
▽	low response | less reliable

Cost Our surveyors' estimated price of a dinner with one drink and tip. Lunch is usually 25 to 30% less. For unrated **newcomers** or **write-ins,** the price range is shown as follows:

I	$25 and below	E	$41 to $65
M	$26 to $40	VE	$66 or above

Symbols

◐	serves after 11 PM
Ⓢ	closed on Sunday
Ⓜ	closed on Monday
⊅	no credit cards accepted

About This Survey

Here are the results of our **2011 America's Top Restaurants Survey,** covering 1,552 eateries in 45 major markets across the country. Like all our guides, this one is based on input from avid local consumers – over 153,000 all told. Our editors have synopsized this feedback, highlighting representative comments (in quotation marks within each review). To read full surveyor comments – and share your own opinions – visit **ZAGAT.com,** where you'll also find the latest dining news plus menus, photos and lots more, all for free.

THREE SIMPLE PREMISES underlie our ratings and reviews. First, we believe that the collective opinions of large numbers of consumers are more accurate than those of any single person. (Consider that our surveyors bring some 25 million annual meals' worth of experience to this Survey. They also visit restaurants year-round, anonymously – and on their own dime.) Second, food quality is only part of the equation when choosing a restaurant, thus we ask surveyors to separately rate food, decor and service and report on cost. Third, since people need reliable information in a fast, easy-to-digest format, we strive to be concise and we offer our content on every platform. For the best of the best in this guide, see Top Food Rankings by Area (pages 7-9) and Most Popular by Area (pages 10-12), as well as lists by Food ranking at the beginning of each city section.

ABOUT ZAGAT: In 1979, we started asking friends to rate and review restaurants purely for fun. The term "user-generated content" had not yet been coined. That hobby grew into Zagat Survey; 32 years later, we have over 375,000 surveyors and cover airlines, bars, dining, fast food, entertaining, golf, hotels, movies, music, resorts, shopping, spas, theater and tourist attractions in over 100 countries. Along the way, we evolved from being a print publisher to a digital content provider, e.g. **ZAGAT.com, ZAGAT.mobi** (for web-enabled mobile devices), **ZAGAT TO GO** (for smartphones) and **nru** (for Android phones). We also produce customized gifts and marketing tools for a wide range of corporate clients. And you can find us on Twitter (twitter.com/zagatbuzz), Facebook and other social media networks.

THANKS: We're grateful to editor, Bill Corsello, as well as our data collectors and in-house and local contributors for their hard work over the years. Thank you, guys. We also sincerely thank the thousands of surveyors who participated – this guide is really "theirs."

JOIN IN: To improve our guides, we solicit your comments; it's vital that we hear your opinions. Just contact us at **nina-tim@zagat.com.** We also invite you to join our surveys at **ZAGAT.com.** Do so and you'll receive a choice of rewards in exchange.

New York, NY
October 27, 2010

Nina and Tim Zagat

What's New

As you'd expect, people are more price-sensitive in these tough economic times. Naturally, they're eating out less (3.1 times per week, down from 3.3 pre-recession), reading their menus from right to left (i.e. prices first) and cutting back on appetizers, dessert and/or alcohol (given the normal markups, anyone who spends over $50 on a bottle of wine in a restaurant is throwing money away). On a more positive note, 55% of respondents feel they're getting better deals via prix fixe meals and other discounts, 41% suspect their patronage is more appreciated and 33% say that reservations are easier to come by. As for the national average price of a meal, it rose 2.2% in the past year to $35.37 (and it's up 2.2% to $78.07 at the most expensive places). New Orleans has the lowest average meal cost ($28.36), while Las Vegas, at $44.44, has the priciest.

BACK TO THE BIG TIME: In the last few years, many major restaurateurs and chefs bowed to the economic times and opened casual, affordable eateries. But this year, there was a return to pricey form, signaling that high-end dining is far from dead. Among the many upscale premieres from culinary luminaries: **Simon Prime Steaks & Martinis** in Atlantic City; **Uchiko** in Austin; **Bistro Alex** and **Valentino** in Houston; **BLT Steak** in Honolulu; **Sage** in Las Vegas; **Bouchon** and **WP24** in Los Angeles; **Eos** in Miami; **ABC Kitchen** and **The Mark** in New York; **Spruce** in the Salt Lake City area; and **Benu, Frances, Morimoto Napa, RN74** and **Wayfare Tavern** in the San Francisco Bay Area.

MAKING THE GRADE: Similar to a Los Angeles system that's been in place for years, New York City restaurants are now required to prominently display letter grades (A, B or C) from their health-department inspections; 80% of our surveyors nationwide favor this practice.

CODES OF CONDUCT: Thirteen percent of surveyors take smartphone pictures of their dishes – but another 11% deem it rude . . . 63% consider texting, e-mailing or talking on the phone at the table inappropriate . . . When seated next to a noisy party, 34% ask to be moved, 9% ask management to talk to the noisemakers, 4% talk to them themselves and 53% simply ignore them, i.e. sit and suffer in silence.

SURVEY ALSO SAYS: Twenty-four percent report eating out less than they did six months ago, 13% say more . . . 67% call service the No. 1 restaurant irritant . . . Average tip: 19.2% . . . Regarding cash-only eateries: 37% avoid them, 13% spend less at them . . . Favorite cuisines: Italian (26%), American (17%), Japanese (11%), French (11 %), Mexican (10%) . . . 60% would pay more for food that's locally sourced, organic or sustainable, while 31% seek out restaurants specializing in such 'green' cuisine . . . The Internet as a reservations tool continues to gain popularity, with 26% booking online.

New York, NY
October 27, 2010

Nina and Tim Zagat

Menus, photos, voting and more - free at ZAGAT.com

Top Food Rankings by Area

ATLANTA

29 Bacchanalia
28 Quinones Room
   Aria
   McKendrick's
   Bone's

ATLANTIC CITY

27 SeaBlue
   Chef Vola's
26 Il Mulino
   White House
   Old Homestead

AUSTIN

28 Uchi
27 Eddie V's
   Wink
   Torchy's Tacos
   Vespaio*

BALTIMORE/ ANNAPOLIS

28 Charleston
   Volt
27 Prime Rib
   Samos
   Di Pasquale's

BOSTON

28 L'Espalier
   Oleana
   O Ya
   La Campania
   No. 9 Park

CHARLOTTE

28 Barrington's
27 McNinch House
26 Capital Grille
   Carpe Diem
   Fig Tree

CHICAGO

29 Les Nomades
   Alinea
   Schwa
28 Arun's
   Topolobampo
   Michael
   Tallgrass
   Tru
27 L2O
   Blackbird

CINCINNATI

28 Boca
   Nicola's
27 Daveed's
   Jeff Ruby's Precinct
   Orchids

CLEVELAND

29 Chez François
28 Johnny's Bar
   Parallax
   Lola
   Crop

COLUMBUS

28 L'Antibes
27 Refectory
   Akai Hana
   Cameron's
   G. Michael's

CONNECTICUT

28 Thomas Henkelmann
   Ibiza
   Le Petit Cafe
   Cavey's
   Jean-Louis

DALLAS/FT. WORTH

29 Bonnell's
28 York Street
   Saint-Emilion
   French Room
   Cacharel

DENVER AREA

28 Fruition
   Frasca
   Matsuhisa
   Splendido
   Mizuna

DETROIT

28 Lark
   Bacco
27 Common Grill
   Zingerman's
   Café Cortina

FT. LAUDERDALE

27 LaSpada's
   Eduardo de San Angel
   Casa D'Angelo

---

* Indicates a tie with restaurant above

La Brochette
26 Canyon

HONOLULU
28 Alan Wong's
Sushi Sasabune
27 La Mer
Le Bistro
26 Nobu Waikiki

HOUSTON
28 Le Mistral
Kanomwan
Pappas Bros. Steak
Mark's
27 Da Marco

KANSAS CITY
29 Justus Drugstore
28 Bluestem
Michael Smith
27 Oklahoma Joe's
Le Fou Frog

LAS VEGAS
28 L'Atelier/Joël Robuchon
Joël Robuchon
Rosemary's
Nobu
Todd's Unique Dining

LONG ISLAND
28 Kitchen A Bistro
North Fork Table
Maroni
Chachama
27 Lake House

LOS ANGELES
29 Sushi Zo
28 Matsuhisa
Mélisse
Brandywine
Shiro
Providence
Angelini Osteria
Sushi Nozawa
27 Asanebo
Wa

MIAMI
28 Palme d'Or
27 Romeo's Cafe
Pascal's
Michy's
Nobu Miami Beach

MILWAUKEE
29 Roots
Sanford
Eddie Martini's
28 Lake Park Bistro
Osteria del Mondo

MINNEAPOLIS/ST. PAUL
28 La Belle Vie
112 Eatery
27 Vincent
Alma
Bar La Grassa

NAPLES, FL
26 Truluck's
Chops City Grill
Ruth's Chris
Bleu Provence
25 Roy's

NEW JERSEY
28 Nicholas
Lorena's
Ajihei
Cafe Panache
Saddle River Inn

NEW ORLEANS
28 Bayona
Stella!
Brigtsen's
27 Clancy's
Royal China

NEW YORK CITY
29 Le Bernardin
28 Per Se
Daniel
Jean Georges
Sushi Yasuda
La Grenouille
Gramercy Tavern
Eleven Madison Park
27 Bouley
Blue Hill

ORANGE COUNTY, CA
28 Marché Moderne
Basilic
Tradition by Pascal
Hobbit
27 Studio

ORLANDO
28 Victoria & Albert's
Le Coq au Vin

27. Primo
Chatham's Place
Enzo's

PALM BEACH

28. 11 Maple St.
27. Marcello's La Sirena
Chez Jean-Pierre
Café Boulud
Casa D'Angelo

PHILADELPHIA

28. Vetri
Fountain
Birchrunville Store
Amada
Gilmore's

PHOENIX/ SCOTTSDALE

28. Kai
Binkley's
27. Pizzeria Bianco
26. Atlas
T. Cook's

PORTLAND, OR

28. Painted Lady
27. Apizza Scholls
Beast
Toro Bravo
Nuestra Cocina

SACRAMENTO

29. La Bonne Soupe
28. Kitchen
Waterboy
27. Mulvaney's
Biba

SALT LAKE CITY AREA

28. Mariposa
Forage
27. Takashi
Mandarin
Tree Room

SAN ANTONIO

28. Dough
27. Il Sogno
Bohanan's
Frederick's
Bistro Vatel

SAN DIEGO

28. Sushi Ota
WineSellar
27. El Bizcocho

Karen Krasne's
Pamplemousse

SAN FRANCISCO AREA

29. Gary Danko
French Laundry
28. Cyrus
Sierra Mar
Acquerello
La Folie
Erna's Elderberry
Hana
Chez Panisse
27. Kaygetsu

SEATTLE

28. Cafe Juanita
Paseo
Mashiko
Spinasse
Herbfarm

ST. LOUIS

28. Niche
27. Stellina
Sidney St. Cafe
Trattoria Marcella
Tony's

TAMPA/SARASOTA

28. Cafe Ponte
Beach Bistro
27. Mise en Place
Restaurant B.T.
26. Bern's

TUCSON

27. Vivace
Cafe Poca Cosa
Janos
26. Le Rendez-Vous
Feast

WASHINGTON, DC

29. Marcel's
Inn at Little Washington
Komi
28. CityZen
Rasika

WESTCHESTER/ HUDSON VALLEY

29. Xaviars at Piermont
28. Freelance Cafe
Serevan
Il Cenàcolo
Blue Hill at Stone Barns

Most Popular by Area

ATLANTA

1. Bacchanalia
2. Bone's
3. Buckhead Diner
4. Rathbun's
5. Canoe

ATLANTIC CITY

1. Ruth's Chris
2. P.F. Chang's
3. Bobby Flay
4. Buddakan
5. Morton's

AUSTIN

1. Salt Lick
2. Eddie V's
3. Uchi
4. Fonda San Miguel
5. Chuy's

BALTIMORE/ANNAPOLIS

1. Woodberry Kitchen
2. Charleston
3. Volt
4. Cinghiale
5. Prime Rib

BOSTON

1. Legal Sea Foods
2. Blue Ginger
3. L'Espalier
4. No. 9 Park
5. Hamersley's

CHARLOTTE

1. Barrington's
2. Capital Grille
3. Upstream
4. P.F. Chang's
5. Carpe Diem

CHICAGO

1. Frontera Grill
2. Alinea
3. Topolobampo
4. Charlie Trotter's
5. Gibsons
6. Joe's Sea/Steak/Crab
7. Blackbird
8. Wildfire
9. Morton's
10. Tru

CINCINNATI

1. Boca
2. Montgomery Inn
3. Jeff Ruby's Precinct
4. Nicola's
5. Dewey's

CLEVELAND

1. Lola
2. Blue Point Grille
3. L'Albatros
4. Chez François
5. Johnny's Bar

COLUMBUS

1. Lindey's
2. Refectory
3. Hyde Park
4. Rigsby's
5. Barcelona

CONNECTICUT

1. Frank Pepe Pizzeria
2. Barcelona
3. Cheesecake Factory
4. Coromandel
5. Thomas Henkelmann

DALLAS/FT. WORTH

1. Abacus
2. Fearing's
3. Del Frisco's
4. French Room
5. Stephan Pyles

DENVER AREA

1. Frasca
2. Sweet Basil
3. Rioja
4. Mizuna
5. Elway's

DETROIT

1. Zingerman's
2. Lark
3. Beverly Hills Grill
4. Bacco
5. Capital Grille

FT. LAUDERDALE

1. Casa D'Angelo
2. Blue Moon
3. Capital Grille
4. Bonefish Grill
5. Anthony's

HONOLULU

1. Alan Wong's
2. Roy's
3. La Mer
4. Sansei
5. Duke's Canoe Club

HOUSTON

1. Da Marco
2. Mark's
3. Tony's
4. Pappas Bros. Steak
5. Pappadeaux

KANSAS CITY

1. Fiorella's Jack Stack
2. Arthur Bryant's
3. Oklahoma Joe's
4. Lidia's
5. Bristol

LAS VEGAS

1. Picasso
2. Bouchon
3. Delmonico
4. Bellagio Buffet
5. Aureole

LONG ISLAND

1. Peter Luger
2. Cheesecake Factory
3. Bryant & Cooper
4. Kotobuki
5. Besito

LOS ANGELES

1. Pizzeria Mozza
2. Bazaar/José Andrés
3. Spago
4. Osteria Mozza
5. Angelini Osteria
6. Café Bizou
7. Mélisse
8. A.O.C.
9. Mastro's
10. Bouchon

MIAMI

1. Joe's Stone Crab
2. Prime One Twelve
3. Michael's
4. Michy's
5. Barton G.

MILWAUKEE

1. Sanford
2. Lake Park Bistro
3. Coquette Cafe
4. Eddie Martini's
5. Bacchus

MINNEAPOLIS/ST. PAUL

1. 112 Eatery
2. Manny's
3. La Belle Vie
4. Kincaid's
5. Alma

NAPLES, FL

1. Campiello
2. Chops City Grill
3. Truluck's
4. Roy's
5. Bleu Provence

NEW JERSEY

1. Nicholas
2. River Palm
3. Cafe Panache
4. Ruth's Chris
5. Cheesecake Factory

NEW ORLEANS

1. Commander's Palace
2. Galatoire's
3. Bayona
4. August
5. Acme Oyster

NEW YORK CITY

1. Gramercy Tavern
2. Le Bernardin
3. Eleven Madison Park
4. Peter Luger
5. Union Square Cafe
6. Babbo
7. Daniel
8. Gotham B&G
9. Balthazar
10. Jean Georges

ORANGE COUNTY, CA

1. Marché Moderne
2. Napa Rose
3. In-N-Out
4. Charlie Palmer
5. Five Crowns

ORLANDO

1. California Grill
2. Seasons 52
3. Victoria & Albert's
4. Emeril's Orlando
5. Jiko

PALM BEACH

1. Abe & Louie's
2. Café Boulud
3. Bonefish Grill
4. Chops Lobster Bar
5. 32 East

PHILADELPHIA

1. Amada
2. Buddakan
3. Le Bec-Fin
4. Osteria
5. Vetri

PHOENIX/SCOTTSDALE

1. T. Cook's
2. Binkley's
3. Lon's
4. P.F. Chang's
5. Eddie V's

PORTLAND, OR

1. Jake's
2. Higgins
3. Heathman
4. Andina
5. Paley's Place

SACRAMENTO

1. Mikuni
2. Biba
3. Waterboy
4. Ella
5. Mulvaney's

SALT LAKE CITY AREA

1. Market Street
2. Red Iguana
3. Cucina Toscana
4. Bambara
5. Takashi

SAN ANTONIO

1. Boudro's
2. Biga
3. Rudy's
4. Silo
5. Paesanos

SAN DIEGO

1. George's Ocean Terrace
2. Pamplemousse
3. Prado
4. Sammy's
5. Roppongi

SAN FRANCISCO AREA

1. Gary Danko
2. Boulevard
3. Slanted Door
4. French Laundry
5. Cyrus
6. Chez Panisse
7. Zuni Café
8. Kokkari Estiatorio
9. Chez Panisse Café
10. A16

SEATTLE

1. Wild Ginger
2. Dahlia Lounge
3. Canlis
4. Cafe Juanita
5. Rover's

ST. LOUIS

1. Sidney St. Cafe
2. 1111 Mississippi
3. Niche
4. Annie Gunn's
5. Tony's

TAMPA/SARASOTA

1. Bern's
2. Bonefish Grill
3. Columbia
4. Roy's
5. Mise en Place

TUCSON

1. Grill at Hacienda del Sol
2. Cafe Poca Cosa
3. Vivace
4. El Charro
5. Janos

WASHINGTON, DC

1. Zaytinya
2. 2 Amys
3. Central Michel Richard
4. Citronelle
5. Inn at Little Washington

WESTCHESTER/ HUDSON VALLEY

1. X2O Xaviars
2. Blue Hill at Stone Barns
3. Xaviars at Piermont
4. Crabtree's Kittle House
5. Harvest on Hudson

RESTAURANT
DIRECTORY

Atlanta

TOP FOOD RANKING

	Restaurant	Cuisine
29	Bacchanalia	American
28	Quinones Room	American
	Aria	American
	McKendrick's	Steak
	Bone's	Steak
27	Kevin Rathbun	Steak
	di Paolo	Italian
	La Grotta	Italian
	Chops Lobster Bar	Seafood/Steak
	Hal's on Old Ivy	Steak
	Rathbun's	American
	MF Buckhead	Japanese
	Nan	Thai
	Kyma	Greek/Seafood
26	Dogwood	American
	MF Sushibar	Japanese
	Pura Vida	Pan-Latin
	Busy Bee Cafe	Soul Food
	New York Prime	Steak
	Atmosphere	French

OTHER NOTEWORTHY PLACES

Abattoir	American
Atlanta Fish Market	Seafood
Babette's Cafe	European
BLT	French/Steak
BluePointe	American
Buckhead Diner	American
Cakes & Ale	American
Canoe	American
Craft	American
Ecco	Continental
Floataway Cafe	French/Italian
4th & Swift	American
Holeman and Finch	American
JCT. Kitchen & Bar	Southern
Muss & Turner's	American/Deli
Pricci	Italian
Sotto Sotto	Italian
Tierra	Pan-Latin
Watershed	Southern
Woodfire Grill	American

	FOOD	DECOR	SERVICE	COST

Abattoir ⓈⓂ *American* | 23 | 23 | 22 | $43 |

Westside | White Provision | 1170 Howell Mill Rd. (14th St.) |
404-892-3335 | www.starprovisions.com

"Not as scary as the name implies", this "relaxed" Westside American
housed in a former "meatpacking house" is a "worthy addition" to the
Bacchanalia "'stable'", offering "affordable", locally sourced variety
meats that are an "offal lover's dream", plus "approachable" selections for the "faint of heart – and those who fear eating them", backed
by a "whimsical wine list" and "handcrafted cocktails" that are "works
of art"; the "open", "rustic Frenchy" space boasts a "lovely patio"
"overlooking the train tracks", and while opinions of the service range
widely, at its best, it's "superlative."

Aria Ⓢ *American* | 28 | 25 | 26 | $58 |

Buckhead | 490 E. Paces Ferry Rd. NE (Maple Dr.) | 404-233-7673 |
www.aria-atl.com

"Bravo" bellow boosters who "can't get enough" of this "flawless" New
American "well situated" in the heart of Buckhead, offering "fantastic"
fare, "glamorous cocktails" and selections from a "superior" wine list,
as well as "impeccable" service complete with "smiles" ("even when the
tab arrives"); the "showstopper" space begins with a "cool, beaded
(curtain) entry" into a "transporting" dining room, and includes a "romantic" wine cellar that's a "favorite" for "special occasions" or "intimate dinners"; in sum, it's "everything a fine restaurant should be."

Atlanta Fish Market *Seafood* | 23 | 19 | 21 | $41 |

Buckhead | 265 Pharr Rd. NE (Peachtree Rd.) | 404-262-3165 |
www.buckheadrestaurants.com

"Seafood fanatics" report a "wonderful" experience at this Buckhead
"piscatorial palace" offering a "wide variety" of fin fare "so fresh it
practically splashes you in the face" plus "wonderful" service; it can get
"boisterous" in the "barn" of a space (regulars opt for the "fish shack
feel" of the cozier Geechee Lounge bar), and though detractors find the
cuisine "unexciting", the service "pushy" and the decor "tired", many
others consider it a "reliable" choice, which is why it's "always busy."

Atmosphere Ⓜ *French* | 26 | 23 | 25 | $38 |

Midtown | 1620 Piedmont Ave. (Morningside Dr. NE) | 678-702-1620 |
www.atmospherebistro.com

"To call it a bistro shortchanges the experience" at this "refined", but
"relaxing" Midtown French aver aficionados, who praise its "superb"
cuisine and "fantastic brunch" (the signature "escargots are delicious"), "wonderful" service and "great location" "right on Piedmont";
"affordable" prices, including "remarkable $25" prix fixe dinners on
Tuesdays and Wednesdays, boost the *très bon* factor, and the
"warm" atmosphere in the "cozy" cottage with a "dog-friendly" patio
rounds out a "truly pleasant experience" "worth repeating."

Babette's Cafe Ⓜ *European* | 25 | 21 | 25 | $38 |

Poncey-Highland | 573 N. Highland Ave. (Freedom Pkwy.) | 404-523-9121 |
www.babettescafe.com

Fans get all "warm and fuzzy" about this "unpretentious" "Poncey-
Highland mainstay" that "always lives up to expectations" with "superb" European cuisine, "well-priced wines", "honest cocktails" and

FOOD DECOR SERVICE COST

an "incomparable Sunday brunch" – all "without the fancy prices"; an "impeccable" staff that "has been there for years" "really cares" about its "valued customers", and the "comfortable", "quaint" "old cottage" with "lighted outdoor deck" and "pretty little bar" "complete the experience."

Bacchanalia ⊠ American — 29 | 25 | 27 | $89

Westside | Westside Mktpl. | 1198 Howell Mill Rd. (bet. 14th St. & Huff Rd.) | 404-365-0410 | www.starprovisions.com

This "pantheon" of "perfection" "reigns supreme" as Atlanta's No. 1 for Food and Most Popular, thanks to the "sheer gourmet firepower" of its "divine" New American "delectables" that'll "bring tears to your eyes", made better by "excellent" "wine pairings" and "impeccable" service; the "phenomenal" Westside "warehouse setting" has a "romantic" "urban vibe" (though some find it "dreary") and casual sorts can "sit at the bar" in "shorts and flip-flops" and order à la carte; wallet-watchers warn of "car payment"–size tabs, but for foodies it's a "fantasy come true."

BLT Steak French/Steak — 24 | 23 | 23 | $68

Downtown | W Atlanta-Downtown | 45 Ivan Allen Jr. Blvd. NW (Spring St. NW) | 404-577-7601 | www.bltsteak.com

"Pillowy" popovers "start the magic" at Laurent Tourondel's Downtown "power steakhouse scene", located "inside the ultra-Zen W Hotel" "near Centennial Park", which "mesmerizes" meat eaters with an "amazing selection" of "prime" *boeuf* served "French brasserie–style", at tabs that are "for daddy or the expense account" (though "lunch is a bargain", relatively speaking); though detractors deem it "overrated and overpriced", fans say the "exceptional service" and "sleek" "NYC atmosphere" make it "heaven on earth" for those "looking for something extra."

BluePointe American — 23 | 25 | 22 | $51

Buckhead | 3455 Peachtree Rd. (Lenox Rd.) | 404-237-9070 | www.buckheadrestaurants.com

Things are "always jumping" at the Buckhead Life group's "high-end" New American located between Phipps Plaza and Lenox Square Mall, where a "dressed-to-the-nines", *Real Housewives of Atlanta* crowd matches the "stylish", "dramatic multilevel" space with a "magnificent Murano glass chandelier"; "outstanding sushi" and "impeccable fish" dishes highlight a "fantastic" menu that "has stood the test of time", as has the "top-notch service", and while detractors dub it "cougarville" and declare that it's "not as trendy as it once was", for many others it's "still an experience", "stockbrokers" and "Spandex" notwithstanding.

Bone's Restaurant Steak — 28 | 23 | 27 | $66

Buckhead | 3130 Piedmont Rd. (Peachtree Rd.) | 404-237-2663 | www.bonesrestaurant.com

"You can almost taste the prestige" at this "marvelous" "carnivore's castle" and "Buckhead boys' hangout" that's been serving "beautifully prepared steaks" "like buttah", "phenomenal martinis" and a "fantastic wine list" for more than 30 years, delivered by "extraordinary" servers who "treat you like a regular even if you're not one"; "major deals are consummated" and "special" "parties go on" in the "clubby", "masculine" dining room and "semi-private rooms", so "expense-account" prices notwithstanding, most agree this "comfortable" "Atlanta classic" "never gets old."

	FOOD	DECOR	SERVICE	COST

Buckhead Diner ● *American*

23 | 21 | 23 | $36

Buckhead | 3073 Piedmont Rd. NE (Paces Ferry Rd.) | 404-262-3336 | www.buckheadrestaurants.com

"Ball gowns, blazers and blue jeans" are "all welcome" at this "perennial favorite" from the Buckhead Life Group offering a "broad menu" of "wonderful" New American "comfort food" at "reasonable prices", served in a "retro-glam dining room" that's a "wonderful step back in time"; the "no-reservations policy" makes for "lengthy waits" (they do have a call-ahead system), but service is usually "quick and crisp", and though critics pan it as "loud", "expensive" and "totally overrated", most are "still crazy for this place after all these years."

Busy Bee Cafe *Soul Food*

26 | 13 | 22 | $15

Downtown | 810 Martin Luther King Jr. Dr. SW (bet. Paschal Blvd. & Raymond St. SW) | 404-525-9212 | www.busybeeatl.com

"One of a vanishing line of truly Southern restaurants", this "family-friendly" Downtown haunt has boosters buzzing over its "shockingly good fried chicken" and other "soulful" fare "to die for", doled out by a "staff rich with character"; you can scope out some "great church hats" in the otherwise no-frills digs that are "always packed" with "native Atlantans" and tourists alike.

Cakes & Ale ⑤Ⓜ *American*

25 | 22 | 24 | $37

Decatur | 254 W. Ponce de Leon Ave. (bet. Commerce Dr. & Ponce de Leon Pl.) | 404-377-7994 | www.cakesandalerestaurant.com

Inside this "charming little hole-in-the-wall in Downtown Decatur" is a "destination dining place" showcasing a "chalkboard" menu of chef-owner Billy Allin's "soul-satisfying", "ultracreative" New American "farm-to-table" fare, "killer artisan cocktails" and "thoughtful wine and beer list", and pastry chef Cynthia Wong's "phatty cakes", which alone are "worth the price of admission" for many; "dim lighting" lends a "sexy vibe" to the "smart", "cozy" (read: "small") space, and "warm" service from a "knowledgeable", "entertaining" staff rounds out the "quintessential neighborhoody" experience.

Canoe *American*

25 | 26 | 26 | $51

Vinings | Vinings on the River | 4199 Paces Ferry Rd. NW (bet. Garraux Rd. & Northside Pkwy.) | 770-432-2663 | www.canoeatl.com

Making a "comeback" after "epic floods" shut it down in 2009, this Vinings New American helps fans "get away from it all" with its "fantastic" "gardens" and what some say is the "No. 1 patio in town", amid a "picturesque setting on the Chattahoochee River"; the "superb" staff "does a phenomenal job catering" to every whim of "regulars" and "out-of-town guests" while serving chef Carvel Grant Gould's "inventive, seasonal" cuisine, which includes "lots of game" and is backed by a "terrific wine list"; what's more, the "very reasonable prices" make it a "fantastic value."

Chops Lobster Bar *Seafood/Steak*

27 | 25 | 26 | $59

Buckhead | Buckhead Plaza | 70 W. Paces Ferry Rd. (Peachtree Rd.) | 404-262-2675 | www.buckheadrestaurants.com

A "rock-solid" "classic" from the Buckhead Life Group, this "clubby beef and fish palace" attracts a "good mix of businesspeople and plain (rich!) folks" with "perfectly prepared beef" and some of the "best inland seafood in the Southeast", served by a staff that "knows what you need before you realize it"; downstairs is a "unique 'tiled cave'" setting, while upstairs is a "carnivore"-centric space that can get "loud", and while some find it "overpriced", most deem it "money well spent" for a "perfect power" meal or "romantic" "evening out."

Craft *American*
23 | 25 | 21 | $65

Buckhead | Mansion on Peachtree | 3376 Peachtree Rd. NE (Stratford Rd. NE) | 404-995-7580 | www.craftrestaurant.com

This "imported NYC hot spot" from *Top Chef*'s Tom Colicchio shows "all the potential of putting down roots" "in the heart of Buckhead", where it offers "terrific" New American fare "served family-style" with a "team approach" in a "beautiful space" highlighted by "warm woods" and "lush fabrics"; "zaftig prices" knock this one into the "special-occasion" category for many, and while critics who find it "overrated" and "uninspired" jeer "Tom, pack your knives and go", others deem it a "gustatory delight" that's "worth every penny."

di Paolo Ⓜ *Italian*
27 | 23 | 25 | $40

Alpharetta | Rivermont Sq. | 8560 Holcomb Bridge Rd. (Nesbit Ferry Rd.) | 770-587-1051 | www.dipaolorestaurant.com

Though this Italian can be "a little on the expensive side", some fanatics "would pay triple" for chef-owner Darin Hiebel's "superb", "seasonally changing" fare and "first-class wine pairings"; the "wonderful" servers "can't do enough for you" in the "warm", "comfortable" space with a "cozy" bar, and despite its "bizarre location" in an "ugly Alpharetta strip mall", it's an "unbeatable" experience that "never gets old", even for the "loyal base" that goes there "once a week."

Dogwood Ⓢ Ⓜ *American*
26 | 26 | 26 | $46

Midtown | The Reynolds | 565 Peachtree St. (bet. Linden & North Aves. NE) | 404-835-1410 | www.dogwoodrestaurant.com

"They try so hard, and it shows" say fans of this "doggone good" newcomer in Midtown, where chef-owner Shane Touhy creates "superb", "elegantly presented" American fare with an "upscale", "nouveau-Southern" "twist" (the "grits bar" is "perfect") for a clientele that includes an "older crowd", "pre-theater" diners, "Southern natives" and those celebrating a "big deal"; the "serene", "elegant space" with "pastel decor" is "conducive to talking" and the cozy bar offers a "great city skyline view", while the "welcoming staff" provides "inspired service" to round out an "amazing" experience.

Ecco *Continental*
25 | 24 | 24 | $43

Midtown | 40 Seventh St. NE (Cypress St.) | 404-347-9555 | www.fifthgroup.com

This Midtown "foodie paradise" is "worth repeating over and over" "echo" fans who "go ga-ga" over the "phenomenally creative" Continental menu featuring "stunning small plates" that make it the "perfect place" for "sharing with a group" or a "romantic date", while a "well-thought-out wine list" with some "terrific" "values" helps make it "one of the best upscale bargains in town"; "knowledgeable servers" provide "sincere service with no pretense", and "superb bartending" helps infuse some "energy" into the "warm" space highlighted by a "visible kitchen", "divine" patio and "classic charm."

	FOOD	DECOR	SERVICE	COST

Floataway Cafe 🗟Ⓜ *French/Italian* | 25 | 22 | 24 | $47 |

Emory | Floataway Bldg. | 1123 Zonolite Rd. NE (bet. Briarcliff & Johnson Rds.) | 404-892-1414 | www.starprovisions.com

Drew Belline's "sublime" "farm-to-table" Italian-French cuisine showcased at this "sophisticated", yet "down-to-earth" sibling of Bacchanalia and Quinones "more than makes up for the geography quiz" of finding it in an "industrial park" near Emory, and the wine list is also "worth exploring"; though some critics claim service can be "flighty", others find it "impeccable", while the "calming" decor and "beautiful bar area" help make it a "dependable" "date or business dinner" choice; though it's "expensive", many consider it a "bargain for what you get."

4th & Swift *American* | 25 | 24 | 24 | $46 |

Old Fourth Ward District | 621 North Ave. NE (Glen Iris Dr.) | 678-904-0160 | www.4thandswift.com

"It's not dinner unless a pig dies" at this "phenomenal" pork-centric New American in the Old Fourth Ward, where almost "everything is better with bacon" and chef-owner Jay Swift's "spectacular" "farm-to-table fare" "never disappoints", nor do the "fantastic cocktails" or "superb wine list"; the "attentive" staff "rocks" in the "sleek" "converted commercial dairy space", which critics complain "can be noisy when crowded" ("thank goodness earplugs don't affect your ability to taste"), but decibels notwithstanding, most agree you get "a lot of bang for your buck here."

Hal's on Old Ivy 🗟 *Steak* | 27 | 19 | 25 | $55 |

Buckhead | 30 Old Ivy Rd. NE (Piedmont Rd.) | 404-261-0025 | www.hals.net

There's "no denying the steaks are A+" at this Buckhead chophouse that's "retro in the right ways" with its *Mad Men*-era menu of "outstanding" fare including "French Quarter classics" (e.g. "exquisite crawfish tails", "incredible bread pudding"); "perfect waiters" navigate the "intimate" (some say "cramped") dining room, while the "packed", smoker-friendly "piano bar" pulses with "preppy-but-aging" singles clutching "big drinks."

Holeman and Finch ● *American* | 26 | 22 | 23 | $34 |

South Buckhead | 2277 Peachtree Rd. (Peachtree Memorial Dr.) | 404-948-1175 | www.holeman-finch.com

Cognoscenti liken this midpriced "gastropub supreme" in South Buckhead to a "college bar packed with grown-up foodies" and "chefs" who "swoon with delight" over "exceptional" American "small plates" brimming with "whole-animal enthusiasm" and "legendary" "'10 PM' burgers" that "get the house rocking"; "crazy good cocktails" are "handcrafted in front of you" by "genius mixologists", and waiters provide "outstanding" service (though some could do with "less attitude") in the "tiny" but "comfortable" space where fans are "willing to wait" (they "don't take reservations").

JCT. Kitchen & Bar *Southern* | 24 | 22 | 21 | $38 |

Westside | 1198 Howell Mill Rd. (bet. 14th St. & Huff Rd.) | 404-355-2252 | www.jctkitchen.com

Those in search of "comfort-food heaven" seek out this "shining star" on the Westside for its "reasonably priced", "fantastic" Southern fare, including "first-rate specials" and some of the "best fried chicken in town", and a "wonderful wine list" that may "force you to drink too much"; service is "super", in the "perfect" "rooftop bar" overlooking the tracks as well as downstairs in the "gorgeous", "minimalist" dining room, and though some grouse that it gets "loud" when things get "lively", many consider it a "treasure" "not to be missed."

Kevin Rathbun Steak ⑤ *Steak*   27 | 25 | 25 | $60

Inman Park | 154 Krog St. (Lake Ave.) | 404-524-5600 | www.kevinrathbunsteak.com

"Prime beef" "aged perfectly and cooked within an inch of amazing" is the star at this "cool" steakhouse "off the beaten track" in Inman Park from "congenial" "celebrity chef" Kevin Rathbun (Rathbun's), with a supporting cast of "imaginative" apps, sides that "really shine", "superlative desserts" and service that "rocks"; even if some quip it's so "dark" you need a "head lamp" to see, there's "high energy" emanating from the "modern" "wood"-centric space and "Beltline patio", and sure, it's "expensive", but "what steakhouse isn't?"

Kyma *Greek/Seafood*   27 | 25 | 25 | $51

Buckhead | 3085 Piedmont Rd. NE (Paces Ferry Rd.) | 404-262-0702 | www.buckheadrestaurants.com

This "chic" Greek from the Buckhead Life Group earns "rave reviews" for its "large selection" of "fabulous" fin fare and other "excellent" dishes so "deliciously authentic" "you'll likely overlook" the fact that it "seems to be priced in euros" quip commentators, who consider it "worth the splurge" for a "celebration" or that "special someone"; "hunky Mediterranean guys" provide "polished" service in the "stunning" space where "whitewashed walls" and a "fresh seafood display" set the stage for a "lively" scene that makes people think they're by the "Aegean", "not Piedmont."

La Grotta ⑤ *Italian*   27 | 22 | 27 | $54

Buckhead | 2637 Peachtree Rd. NE (bet. Lindbergh Dr. & Wesley Rd.) | 404-231-1368

La Grotta Ravinia ⑤ *Italian*

Dunwoody | Crowne Plaza Ravinia Hotel | 4355 Ashford Dunwoody Rd. (Hammond Dr.) | 770-395-9925
www.lagrottaatlanta.com

"Spectacular service" from "old-world–style waiters" coupled with "superb Italian cuisine" that "loyalists" laud as a "benchmark" in the city makes this "elegant" Buckhead "classic" and its Dunwoody "sister" a "Rome away from Rome" that's "highly recommended" for "special occasions"; the "inviting", "comfortable" settings are "like stepping back in time" – and the original sports a "lovely patio" reminiscent of a "private garden in Italy", so the "civilized crowd" "doesn't mind the prices."

McKendrick's Steak House *Steak*   28 | 24 | 25 | $62

Dunwoody | Park Place Shopping Ctr. | 4505 Ashford Dunwoody Rd. (Perimeter Ctr.) | 770-512-8888 | www.mckendricks.com

For a "business lunch" or a "special occasion", Dunwoody denizens are "blown away" by this "beltway" bastion of beef "near Perimeter Mall" that "hits the spot" (and has improved scores to show it) with "perfect steaks", seafood that "shines" and a "great wine selection", all delivered by a "first-rate" staff that "understands customer service"; even though the "old-time men's club" dining room can get "noisy", it's still "classy" and "worth the price."

MF Buckhead *Japanese* | 27 | 26 | 24 | $66 |

Buckhead | 3280 Peachtree Rd. (Piedmont Rd.) | 404-841-1192 | www.mfbuckhead.com

"Mouths water just thinking about" the "transporting" experience at this "fancy-schmancy" Buckhead Japanese that comes "highly recommended" for "world-class sushi" and other "deliciousness" from the "fantastic robata grill"; a "helpful" staff and "opulent" decor "impress" "business-lunchers" and other "high-maintenance" types (read: "not the place for flip-flops"), and while critics cry "overpriced", devotees declare it a "culinary destination well worth" the "sticker shock"; P.S. a late-night lounge opened post-Survey.

MF Sushibar *Japanese* | 26 | 22 | 22 | $48 |

Midtown | 265 Ponce de Leon Ave. (Penn Ave.) | 404-815-8844 | www.mfsushibar.com

"The 'M' is for 'magic'" remind regulars of this Midtown "decadent" "delight" from the Kinjo Brothers (of MF Buckhead fame) where "perfect sushi" crafted from the "freshest" fish exudes the "essence of sea"; the digs are "high on the hip factor", though the staff can be "aloof" (even as it "grates fresh wasabi" at your table), and while detractors decry the "dent in your wallet", waves of "enthusiasts" who don't mind "paying handsomely" shrug "why compromise with raw fish?"

Muss & Turner's *American/Deli* | 26 | 19 | 23 | $25 |

Smyrna | 1675 Cumberland Pkwy. (Atlanta Rd.) | 770-434-1114 | www.mussandturners.com

Smyrna surveyors sum up "the fuss with Muss" as "fine dining in a casual environment" on "reasonably priced", "shockingly" "delicious" deli sandwiches by day and "seasonal" American entrees by night; a "thoughtful wine selection" and "superb" beer list (complete with an "in-house expert") complement the meal in a setting "upscale" enough for "out-of-town guests" yet "welcoming" to "kids", and the "hospitable" staff just "keeps getting better."

Nan Thai Fine Dining *Thai* | 27 | 27 | 26 | $48 |

Midtown | 1350 Spring St. NW (17th St.) | 404-870-9933 | www.nanfinedining.com

This "exotic trip for the senses" is "both a culinary and visual delight" with "pricey", "artfully prepared" Thai fare so "exceptional" "you'll be tempted to lick the bowl", served in a "gorgeous" Midtown setting with gold columns, a sunken bar and "destination" "restrooms that feel like a spa"; a "beautiful", "gracious" staff blends in with the "sophisticated" scene, and while a few regulars rally for "some new specialties", most "wouldn't change a thing."

New York Prime *Steak* | 26 | 22 | 24 | $62 |

Buckhead | Monarch Tower | 3424 Peachtree Rd. NE (Lenox Rd.) | 404-846-0644 | www.newyorkprime.com

"Red meat, red wine and tobacco" equal "man-night defined" at this "old-school steakhouse" in the heart of Buckhead where "excellent steaks" are accompanied by "ridiculous-size side dishes" plus "lots of smoke"; "friendly, service-oriented bartenders" who "pour a stiff

	FOOD	DECOR	SERVICE	COST

drink" add to the "noisy", rather "mature scene", and while critics carp it's "pre-recession overpriced", others who "bring an expense account" deem it "worth every penny."

Pricci *Italian* 25 | 22 | 24 | $50

Buckhead | 500 Pharr Rd. NE (Maple Dr.) | 404-237-2941 | www.buckheadrestaurants.com

"Prom couples" and "older" but still "boisterous" diners are "never disappointed" at this "standout in the Buckhead Life Restaurant Group", thanks to chef Piero Premoli's "superb" Italian fare, including a regional menu that's a "huge hit", complemented by a "drop-dead" Boot-centric wine list that's "half price on Thursdays"; the "well-trained staff" provides "outstanding service" "even at the busiest of times" when things can get "too loud", and while trendy types claim the terrazzo-floored space is "outdated", recently added patent leather walls add a touch of modern "style."

Pura Vida Ⓢ *Pan-Latin* 26 | 20 | 23 | $34

Poncey-Highland | 656 N. Highland Ave. NE (bet. North Ave. & Ponce de Leon Blvd.) | 404-870-9797 | www.puravidatapas.com

At this "innovative" Poncey-Highland Pan-Latin, "celebrity chef" Hector Santiago's "out-of-this-world" tapas will "get your taste buds really going", while "killer mojitos", "consistently attentive service" and "fabulous tango-ing" (live dancers perform bi-weekly) make it a "kicky" choice to "have a celebration" whether in "a group or a date"; it's a "wonderful" scene that's "full of life" – but cognoscenti point out it's "not cheap."

Quinones Room at Bacchanalia Ⓢ Ⓜ *American* 28 | 27 | 28 | $104

Westside | Courtyard of Bacchanalia | 1198 Howell Mill Rd. (bet. 14th St. & Huff Rd.) | 404-365-0410 | www.starprovisions.com

At this "marvelous" Westside sibling of Bacchanalia, "your every need is anticipated" by a "stellar staff" as you're "pampered and plied" with a "simply stunning" tasting menu of "off-the-chart" New American fare exhibiting a "decidedly Southern influence", plus "excellent wine pairings" that are "worth" the "splurge"; the "beautiful room" resembles an "elegant home", setting the stage for an "undeniably flawless" experience that is "unbeatable" "for the price."

Rathbun's Ⓢ *American* 27 | 23 | 25 | $53

Inman Park | Stove Works | 112 Krog St. NE (bet. Edgewood Ave. NE & Irwin St. NE) | 404-524-8280 | www.rathbunsrestaurant.com

This "top-of-the-crop" New American in Inman Park is "deserving of its ratings" declare devotees dazzled by its "devilishly delicious" offerings, from the "incredible" "small and large plates" to the "awesome" desserts, backed by a "fab" wine list; "congenial celebrity chef" Kevin Rathbun and his "skilled", "happy" staff "make you feel special" in a "spirited", "electric" setting, with a "jumping" "bar scene" as well as a "quieter" "wine room" and "lovely outdoor patio"; sure, the "price is high" but most conclude it's "well worth it."

Sotto Sotto *Italian* 26 | 19 | 23 | $47

Inman Park | 313 N. Highland Ave. NE (Elizabeth St.) | 404-523-6678 | www.sottosottorestaurant.com

Aficionados insist this "charming" Northern Italian in "eclectic" Inman Park is "head-and-shoulders above" the rest, thanks to "flawlessly executed", "phenomenal" cuisine ("risotto from heaven", "out-of-this-world chocolate soup") and a "lovely wine list", "served with care" by "vigilant", "black-garbed waiters"; the "comfortable neighborhood" setting is "ideal" for "impressing your date, your colleagues or your mom", though some find it "cramped", and there's a "cool" bar scene where you can chill "while you wait", which you will without a "reservation."

Tierra 🖼 Ⓜ *Pan-Latin*   26 17 24 $34

Midtown | 1425B Piedmont Ave. NE (Westminster Dr.) | 404-874-5951 | www.tierrarestaurant.com

A "fantastic" find near the Botanical Gardens in Midtown, this Pan-Latin is run by an "energetic" couple that "scours Latin America" for inspiration for its "frequently varied" menu of "exquisite" eats, including "to-die-for tres leches" cake that'll "make a non-dessert person a member of the clean plate club"; service is "prompt and friendly" and the white-tablecloth space is "small but workable", albeit in a "strange location" that "always looks closed" according to some, all of which add up to a "dream-come-true" experience for many.

Watershed *Southern*   24 20 22 $35

Decatur | 406 W. Ponce de Leon Ave. (Commerce Dr.) | 404-378-4900 | www.watershedrestaurant.com

You'll "get a belly full of yummy" no "matter what you order" at this "unpretentious" "star of the South" in Decatur serving "consistently awesome" "comfort food", including "divine fried chicken" that some would "sit on broken glass to eat"; the staff "stays on top of things" in the "former garage" space, a "charming spot with bad acoustics", which a few find "uncomfortable", and while cynics say it's "overrated", others insist "you'll leave with a smile"; P.S. chef Scott Peacock's post-Survey departure may not be reflected in the above Food score.

Woodfire Grill 🖼 Ⓜ *American*   26 22 24 $47

Cheshire Bridge | 1782 Cheshire Bridge Rd. (Piedmont Rd.) | 404-347-9055 | www.woodfiregrill.com

"Just the scent" from the eponymous grill is "worth the visit" to this "magnificent" Cheshire Bridge "charmer" where "*Top Chef*" "celebrity" Kevin Gillespie creates "consistently delicious farm-to-table" American fare, including a "wine-pairing prix fixe" that "delighted" devotees describe as a "religious experience"; an "energetic, knowledgeable" staff mans the "comfortable" space that's "great for a group" or a "date", and the bar sets a "cozy" stage for "awesome seasonal cocktails."

Atlantic City

TOP FOOD RANKING

	Restaurant	Cuisine
27	SeaBlue	Seafood
	Chef Vola's	Italian
26	Il Mulino	Italian
	White House	Sandwiches
	Old Homestead	Steak
	Dock's	Seafood
	Capriccio	Italian
25	Bobby Flay	Steak
	Buddakan	Asian
	Morton's	Steak

OTHER NOTEWORTHY PLACES

Continental	American
Girasole	Italian
izakaya	Japanese
Little Saigon	Vietnamese
Mia	Italian
Palm	Steak
P.F. Chang's	Chinese
Ruth's Chris	Steak
Simon	Steak
Wolfgang Puck	American

Bobby Flay Steak Ⓜ *Steak*   25 | 25 | 24 | $70

Atlantic City | Borgata Hotel, Casino & Spa | 1 Borgata Way (Huron Ave.) | 866-692-6742 | www.bobbyflaysteak.com

"A winner – even if you don't win in the casino" brag boosters of this "Borgata babe of beef" that's "worth every penny" for its "perfectly cooked" steaks with "Southwest flair"; the AC "namesake" of the celeb chef gets further flay-re from an "impressive" wine selection, "super" service and "high-energy decor" by David Rockwell.

Buddakan *Asian*   25 | 27 | 23 | $58

Atlantic City | Pier at Caesars | 1 Atlantic Ocean (Arkansas Ave.) | 609-674-0100 | www.buddakanac.com

Stephen Starr "has done it again" with this "sumptuous" third incarnation of his Philly and NYC Pan-Asian "experience" at The Pier at Caesars; "belly up" to the 10-ft. golden Buddha at the "beautiful" communal table, dine in a curtained nook or "celebrate" at a regular table, enjoying "food just adventurous enough to be innovative", topped off by "above-average service"; P.S. "your wallet will know you've been there."

Capriccio *Italian*   26 | 23 | 25 | $62

Atlantic City | Resorts Atlantic City Casino & Hotel | 1133 Boardwalk (North Carolina Ave.) | 609-340-6789 | www.resortsac.com

It's like "dining in a villa" at this "high-end" Italian now in its third decade in Resorts Casino & Hotel that's "still one of Atlantic City's best";

with "ocean views" from window tables and an "experienced, courteous staff" adding to its allure, the "casino prices" can be forgiven.

Chef Vola's ⊠⼝ *Italian* 27 | 13 | 23 | $53

Atlantic City | 111 S. Albion Pl. (Pacific Ave.) | 609-345-2022 | www.chefvolas.com

Veterans plead "don't tell anyone", but the word is out – ditto the once-secret reservations number – on this "hard to find, hard to get into and even harder to resist" "ageless" Italian with "superlative" "eats" "like mama's", served in the "cramped", "low-ceiling basement" "of a house on a side street in Atlantic City"; P.S. "they don't take walk-ins", and it's "cash only" at this BYO "gem."

Continental *American* 23 | 24 | 22 | $44

Atlantic City | Pier at Caesars | 1 Atlantic Ocean (Arkansas Ave.) | 609-674-8300 | www.continentalac.com

This "fun place to graze" on the Pier at Caesars has Stephen Starr's signature "cool atmosphere" plus "terrific" ocean views that its "Philly cousins" lack; the slate of "consistently good" small plates features "modern takes" on American "classic comfort foods" ("three words: lobster-mashed potatoes"), and the "signature drinks" and service earn kudos as well, making it a "satisfying" stop for Atlantic City visitors.

Dock's Oyster House *Seafood* 26 | 21 | 23 | $52

Atlantic City | 2405 Atlantic Ave. (Georgia Ave.) | 609-345-0092 | www.docksoysterhouse.com

"Venture off the boardwalk" and "skip the overpriced casino restaurants" for this "beloved" AC "institution", a "seafood standout" with "fabulous", "fresh" fish, a "pleasing wine list", "excellent" service and "wonderful hosts"; it's been evincing "charm" since 1897 and is "worth the pricey prices" to experience real "old-time class"; P.S. there's piano music almost every night.

Girasole *Italian* 25 | 22 | 21 | $57

Atlantic City | Ocean Club Condos | 3108 Pacific Ave. (bet. Chelsea & Montpelier Aves.) | 609-345-5554 | www.girasoleac.com

Escape the AC casino "glitz" and "crowds" at this "comfy and classy" Versace-designed Southern Italian located between the Tropicana and the Hilton; supporters cite "high-quality food served with old-world charm" – "if you can afford it" and need "a break" from gambling, check it out.

Il Mulino New York *Italian* 26 | 22 | 24 | $68

Atlantic City | Trump Taj Mahal | 1000 Boardwalk at Virginia Ave. (bet. Pacific & Pennsylvania Aves.) | 609-449-6006 | www.ilmulino.com

"Ahhh, Italia" sigh those enamored by this AC Taj Mahal outpost of the famed NYC original; so what if it's "pricey" – the food is "magnificent" ("be prepared to eat big"), the decor "elegant yet fun" and "courteous" servers "treat you like royalty"; P.S. the adjacent Marketplace vends signature sauces, coffee and more.

izakaya *Japanese* ∇ 26 | 25 | 25 | $62

Atlantic City | Borgata Hotel, Casino & Spa | 1 Borgata Way (Huron Ave.) | 609-317-1000 | www.theborgata.com

Celeb chef Michael Schulson is behind this "sleek", "excellent" Japanese "gastropub" in AC's Borgata; the "exceptional" sushi and robatayaki (from an open-hearth grill) are "to die for" (though portions "are small"), and the room and staff are equally "beautiful"; P.S. there's a late-night DJ.

Little Saigon   *Vietnamese*   25 | 10 | 17 | $29

Atlantic City | 2801 Arctic Ave. (Iowa Ave.) | 609-347-9119
The "spartan" appearance of this small Atlantic City BYO belies the "authentic" Vietnamese cuisine served within – "priced right and always fresh", it's "a treat" for those who step away from the casinos; since the "nice" owner and his wife "are the staff", service can be "slow", so "sit back, relax and enjoy."

Mia ⌧ Ⓜ *Italian*   25 | 24 | 24 | $68

Atlantic City | Caesars on the Boardwalk | 2100 Pacific Ave. (Arkansas Ave.) | 609-441-2345 | www.miaac.com
"Thank you, Georges Perrier" (and Chris Scarduzio) extol fans of Philly's favorite restaurant team and their "high-quality", high-price venue at Caesars on the Boardwalk, whose "wonderful", "classy" Italian fare comes in "cavernous", "over-the-top" quarters complete with "impressive" "Roman-style columns"; a "well-trained" staff adds to the overall appeal, leaving only the "noise" from its "open-area" locale near the casino floor to detract; P.S. check out the "value"-oriented midweek prix fixe dinner.

Morton's The Steakhouse   *Steak*   25 | 22 | 24 | $68

Atlantic City | Caesars on the Boardwalk | 2100 Pacific Ave. (Atlantic Ave.) | 609-449-1044 | www.mortons.com
"Magnificent" steaks at "over-the-top" prices lure meat lovers looking to "show off" at this Atlantic City link of the "classic" "carnivorium" chain manned by a "superb" staff; a few find its tradition of "bringing raw, plastic-wrapped" cuts to the table "a useless exercise", but to most it's all part of the "old-fashioned steakhouse experience."

Old Homestead   *Steak*   26 | 24 | 24 | $72

Atlantic City | Borgata Hotel, Casino & Spa | 1 Borgata Way (Huron Ave.) | 609-317-1000 | www.theoldhomesteadsteakhouse.com
A "paradise for the steak lover", this Borgata chophouse is a "close copy" of the legendary NYC original, complete with "handsome" setting, "professional, polished" servers and "epic", "easily shared" portions that entail a tab that's "heavy" but for most, "worth the splurge."

Palm, The   *Steak*   25 | 21 | 24 | $70

Atlantic City | Quarter at the Tropicana | 2801 Pacific Ave. (Iowa Ave.) | 609-344-7256 | www.thepalm.com
"Reliable as the sun rising", this "representative of the classic steak tradition" at the Quarter at the Tropicana in AC is home to "succulent", "dinosaur-sized" steaks and lobsters as well as the chain's signature celeb-caricature decor; it's "bustling" and "energetic", with "pro" service that helps soften the "big bucks" expended.

P.F. Chang's China Bistro ◐ *Chinese*   20 | 21 | 19 | $34

Atlantic City | Quarter at the Tropicana | 2801 Pacific Ave. (Iowa Ave.) | 609-348-4600 | www.pfchangs.com
"It may be a chain", but it's a "well-oiled" one and "always busy" thanks to "tasty", "reliable", "modern" Chinese fare ("check out the lettuce

wraps") served in a relatively "upscale", "loud" but "fun" environment at the Quarter at the Tropicana; just be aware that service "varies", and the wise advise "make reservations or you will wait."

Ruth's Chris Steak House *Steak*   25 | 22 | 23 | $64

Atlantic City | The Walk | 2020 Atlantic Ave. (bet. Arkansas & Michigan Aves.) | 609-344-5833 | www.ruthschris.com

It "might be a chain", but the "sizzling" butter-topped steaks and "white-linen" service at this "classic" chophouse at The Walk offer "pure bliss" to carnivores who also appreciate the "huge" sides – and say the similarly sized tabs are "worth the splurge"; P.S. decor is "polished, if standardized."

SeaBlue *Seafood*   27 | 26 | 26 | $77

Atlantic City | Borgata Hotel, Casino & Spa | 1 Borgata Way (Huron Ave.) | 609-317-8220 | www.theborgata.com

Michael Mina is "the man", and his "beautiful" Tihany-designed AC seafooder in the Borgata "has few equals", what with its "amazing" "world-class" fare ("art that dances in your mouth"), "superb" wine list, "well-versed", "friendly" staff and "soothing" multiple-screened virtual aquarium; although a few carp over the "noise from the casino floor", to most it's a "magical eating experience" and "so worth" the "pricey" tabs.

Simon Prime Steaks & Martinis Ⓜ *Steak*   – | – | – | E

Atlantic City | Atlantic City Hilton | The Boardwalk (Boston Ave.) | 609-340-7453 | www.hiltonac.com

West Coast celebrity chef Kerry Simon adds steaks to his repertoire of upscale comfort food at this stylish newcomer at the recently renovated Hilton on the AC boardwalk; servers in jeans and sneakers, music-related artwork, bare tabletops and specialty cocktails inform the cool, sexy vibe, which remains casual despite the special-occasion pricing.

White House ⑰ *Sandwiches*   26 | 9 | 16 | $14

Atlantic City | 2301 Arctic Ave. (Mississippi Ave.) | 609-345-1564

It's "hoagie heaven" at this "legendary" 60-plus-years-old AC "land-mark", a "sandwich" "icon" that may not "be good for your cholesterol – but is very satisfying"; credit the "lines-out-the-door" to the bread that's delivered multiple times daily from a nearby bakery to this "small", "worn" "time warp" where all overlook the decor ("there isn't any") and "pushy" but efficient staff.

Wolfgang Puck American Grille *American*   24 | 23 | 23 | $57

Atlantic City | Borgata Hotel, Casino & Spa | 1 Borgata Way (Huron Ave.) | 609-317-1000 | www.theborgata.com

Wolfgang Puck's AC Borgata New American is "a joy every time" for its "delicious" "typical Puck" fare, which ranges from burgers and pizza in the "casual" tavern up front to "high-end" "gourmet" offerings in the rear dining room of its "exciting", Tony Chi–designed space; "well-trained" service is one more reason it's a "solid" bet.

Austin

TOP FOOD RANKING

	Restaurant	Cuisine
28	Uchi	Japanese
27	Eddie V's	Seafood/Steak
	Wink	American
	Torchy's Tacos	Mexican
	Vespaio*	Italian
	Driskill Grill	American
	Bistro 88	Asian
26	Gumbo's	Cajun/Creole
	Hudson's	American
	TRIO	American

OTHER NOTEWORTHY PLACES

Aquarelle	French
Carillon	American
Chuy's	Tex-Mex
Fonda San Miguel	Mexican
La Condesa	Mexican
Olivia	French/Italian
Paggi House	American
Perla's	Seafood
Salt Lick	BBQ
Uchiko	Japanese

Aquarelle ⊠Ⓜ *French* | 24 | 24 | 24 | $62 |

Downtown | 606 Rio Grande St. (6th St.) | 512-479-8117 |
www.aquarellerestaurant.com

This "classy", "romantic" Downtown French with a "lovely" modern look provides "*très bon*" cuisine and "carefully selected" wines in a "charming little cottage" with a patio; factor in near-"impeccable" service, and it's easy to see why it's "a favorite" despite the high prices.

Bistro 88 *Asian* | 27 | 20 | 23 | $46 |

West Lake Hills | 2712 Bee Caves Rd. (bet. Edgegrove Dr. & Mo-Pac Expwy.) | 512-328-8888 | www.bistro88.com

"Hidden" in a West Lake strip mall, this "superb" Asian-European fusion eatery is "worth a visit" for its "uniformly excellent" dishes from miso cod to crispy quail; it's not inexpensive, but pays off with smooth service and a "quiet", "elegant" atmosphere.

Carillon, The *American* | – | – | – | E |

Campus | AT&T Executive Education and Conference Center | 1900 University Ave. (MLK Blvd.) | 512-404-3655 | www.thecarillonrestaurant.com

Rising star chef Josh Watkins (ex Driskill Grill) mans the stoves at this elegant Campus-area spot in the AT&T Executive Education and

---

* Indicates a tie with restaurant above

Conference Center spotlighting his signature New American creations like coffee-rubbed strip steak; it's not quite priced for student budgets, but the cushy lounge area features well-priced small plates to go along with specialty cocktails; N.B. lunchtime is reserved for UT faculty and hotel guests only.

Chuy's *Tex-Mex*   21 | 19 | 19 | $19

North Austin | 10520 N. Lamar Blvd. (Meadows Dr.) | 512-836-3218
North Austin | 11680 Research Blvd. (Duval Rd.) | 512-342-0011
Round Rock | 2320 N. I-35 (Old Settlers Blvd.) | 512-255-2211
South Austin | Shops at Arbor Trails | 4301 W. William Cannon Dr. (Mo-Pac Expwy.) | 512-899-2489
Zilker | 1728 Barton Springs Rd. (Lamar Blvd.) | 512-474-4452
www.chuys.com

The "gold standard" for chain Mex chow, this "quirky" franchise "always hits the spot" with "tasty", "dependable" fare – "and lots of it" – washed down with margaritas that really "pack a punch"; perhaps the food "won't wow any diehards", but "speedy" service, "cheap" bills and a "zany", "high-kitsch" atmosphere mean it's "too fun to miss."

Driskill Grill 🅂🅼 *American*   27 | 28 | 27 | $56

Downtown | Driskill Hotel | 604 Brazos St. (6th St.) | 512-391-7162 | www.driskillgrill.com

"The picture of Texas elegance", this "grand" dining room in the historic Driskill Hotel Downtown boasts a "clubby", antiques-filled setting that just oozes "old-school charm"; "wonderful" New American cuisine, "fabulous wines" and "gracious", "unobtrusive service" make it the "perfect place" for a "special occasion."

Eddie V's Prime Seafood *Seafood/Steak*   27 | 26 | 25 | $53

Arboretum | 9400 Arboretum Blvd. (Capital of Texas Hwy.) | 512-342-2642
Downtown | 301 E. Fifth St. (San Jacinto Blvd.) | 512-472-1860
www.eddiev.com

A "class act", this Austin-bred chainlet in Arboretum and Downtown offers a "first-rate experience on all counts", from the "fabulous" steaks and seafood (including "amazing fresh oysters" and crab) to the "professional" service and "modern", leather-trimmed quarters; given the "expense-account" pricing, many seek out the "half-price apps" deals during happy hour.

Fonda San Miguel *Mexican*   26 | 27 | 25 | $37

Highland Park | 2330 W. North Loop Blvd. (Hancock Dr.) | 512-459-4121 | www.fondasanmiguel.com

A taste of "San Miguel de Allende" in Highland Park, this hacienda decked out with terra-cotta tile and colorful "Kahlo"-esque art features "intelligent" interior Mexican dishes "prepared with care" and served by a "courteous" staff at moderate prices; especially "memorable" is Sunday's bounteous buffet brunch – a long-standing "tradition."

Gumbo's *Cajun/Creole*   26 | 23 | 25 | $36

Downtown | Brown Bldg. | 710 Colorado St. (8th St.) | 512-480-8053 | www.gumbosaustin.com 🅂
Round Rock | 901 Round Rock Ave. (Chisholm Trail) | 512-671-7925 | www.gumbosroundrock.com

For "a taste of New Orleans without the humidity" diners rely on these independently owned outposts for "reliable" renditions of Cajun-Creole classics like crawfish étouffée and gumbo (natch); both boast a similar Southern panache/hospitality and upmarket pricing, but the Round Rock locale earns special nods for its "beautiful" old cottage setting on the Chisholm Trail.

Hudson's on the Bend American
26 | 23 | 24 | $58

Lakeway | 3509 Ranch Rd. 620 N. (Hudson Bend Rd.) | 512-266-1369 | www.hudsononthebend.com

"Adventurous" eaters "go wild" for this "ranch-style bistro" in Lakeway famed for its "over-the-top" New American menu highlighting "beautifully cooked game" and other "exotic" fare like rattlesnake; indeed, it's "pricey", but the majority insists it's also "one of Austin's best for special occasions."

La Condesa Mexican
∇ 29 | 25 | 24 | $38

Second Street District | 400A W. Second St. (Guadalupe St.) | 512-499-0300 | www.lacondesaaustin.com

"Innovative takes on Mexican street food" make up the menu at this Second Street District destination pairing taquitos, tuna tostadas and the like with "top-notch" cocktails courtesy of "famed New York mixologist" Junior Merino; a "see-and-be-seen" crowd and "attractive" modern design may just take your mind off the upper-end prices ("$4 for chips and salsa?").

Olivia French/Italian
∇ 22 | 24 | 23 | $49

South Lamar | 2043 S. Lamar Blvd. (Oltorf St.) | 512-804-2700 | www.olivia-austin.com

"It's hard to deny the charms" of this South Lamar spot sporting a "breathtaking" modern look by Michael Hsu and a sleek open kitchen; an "attentive" staff ferries generally "excellent" French-Italian cuisine based on local ingredients, though "uneven" execution is an issue, as are the "pretty pricey" tabs.

Paggi House American
∇ 26 | 24 | 22 | $49

Downtown South | 200 Lee Barton Dr. (Riverside Dr.) | 512-473-3700 | www.paggihouse.com

An Austin "classic" with "contemporary" decor, this Downtown venue housed in a historic home prepares a "pricey", "original" New American menu; the patio overlooking Lady Bird Lake is quite the "hot spot" at happy hour, and equally "lovely" for a "nightcap under the stars."

Perla's Seafood
∇ 22 | 22 | 22 | $46

SoCo | 1400 S. Congress Ave. (Gibson St.) | 512-291-7300 | www.perlasaustin.com

This "Cape Cod-style" seafood house in SoCo boasts a "huge selection of oysters", "exemplary" fish platters and imaginative cocktails delivered by a staff "straight out of a J. Crew catalog"; though it's usually packed to the rafters, the mood is "serene", especially under the oak-cloaked patio; P.S. there's also a "wonderful" weekend brunch.

Salt Lick BBQ
25 | 19 | 19 | $21

Round Rock | 3350 E. Palm Valley Blvd. (Harrell Pkwy.) | 512-386-1044
Driftwood | 18300 FM 1826 (FM 967) | 512-858-4959 ⊅
www.saltlickbbq.com

Meat lovers "make the pilgrimage" to these "legendary" BBQers – ranked tops for Popularity in Austin – for "superb" "open-pit" brisket and ribs so "messy" and "mouthwatering", even a vegetarian might be tempted to "fall off the wagon"; both branches boast a "rustic", "ranch mess hall"–style atmosphere kicked up by live music on weekends; P.S. it's cash only and BYO at the Driftwood original.

Torchy's Tacos *Mexican* | 27 | 13 | 18 | $11 |

Bouldin Creek | South Austin Trailer Pk. | 1311 S. First St. (bet. Elizabeth & Gibson Sts.) | 512-366-0537
Bouldin Creek | 2809 S. First St. (El Paso St.) | 512-444-0300
Campus | 2801 Guadalupe St. (bet. 28th & 29th Sts.) | 512-494-8226
Northwest Hills | 4211 Spicewood Springs Rd. (Mesa Dr.) | 512-291-7277
www.torchystacos.com

Boosters are "blown away" by the "imaginative" overstuffed tacos loaded with fried avocado and other "unusual" items at this ever-growing local Mexican chain; the original trailer on 1311 South First Street - a pioneer in the local "food-truck phenomenon" - is chock-full of "Austin" atmosphere with picnic tables overrun with "hordes" of fans, while the indoor offshoots have a/c and plenty of seating, but feature no frills otherwise, except the same "cheap" tabs.

TRIO *American* | 26 | 25 | 27 | $59 |

Downtown | Four Seasons Hotel | 98 San Jacinto Blvd. (Cesar Chavez) | 512-685-8300 | www.trioaustin.com

An "impeccable" service staff ("blink and they'll come see what you need") is at the forefront of this "superlative" New American in the Four Seasons Downtown; "fabulous" "seasonal" dishes, "inspiring" wines and "beautiful views of Lady Bird Lake" make it "de rigueur for a business lunch or tourists", but "hold onto your wallets, boys", this one isn't cheap; P.S. happy hour and Sunday's brunch buffet are especially popular.

Uchi *Japanese* | 28 | 24 | 25 | $61 |

Zilker | 801 S. Lamar Blvd. (Juliet St.) | 512-916-4808 |
www.uchiaustin.com

"Every detail is perfect" at "passionate" chef Tyson Cole's "elegant", "modern" Zilker Japanese, from the absolutely "swoon-worthy" dishes - once again ranked No. 1 for Food in Austin - to the near-"flawless" service from a "knowledgeable" staff; perpetual "waits" hardly deter the faithful, but brace yourself for a bill that "mounts up fast."

Uchiko *Japanese* | - | - | - | E |

Rosedale | 4200 N. Lamar Blvd. (bet. 42nd & 43rd Sts.) | 512-916-4808 |
www.uchikoaustin.com

Chef Tyson Cole follows up his acclaimed Uchi with this Rosedale sibling, offering highly inventive seasonal Japanese fare and sushi prepared with fresh local ingredients plus unique items from around the globe; sommelier June Rodil's wine and sake lists are also impressive, as is the setting, a modern take on Asian simplicity, and while tabs are steep, that hasn't deterred the crowds, so make reservations.

Vespaio *Italian* | 27 | 22 | 24 | $45 |

SoCo | 1610 S. Congress Ave. (Monroe St.) | 512-441-6100 |
www.austinvespaio.com

"Delectable", "authentic" Italian fare and "exceptional" wines join up with some of the "best people-watching" in town at this midpriced

SoCo "standout"; the "professional" staff makes all feel "well taken care of", though an "open kitchen", convivial bar and limited reservations policy signal "long waits" and a somewhat "frenetic" atmosphere.

Wink ●☒ *American*   27 | 21 | 24 | $57

Old West Austin | 1014 N. Lamar Blvd. (W. 11th St.) | 512-482-8868 | www.winkrestaurant.com

"True foodies" tout this Old West Austin New American delivering "bold", "dazzlingly delicious" dishes from a daily changing lineup (try the "tasting menu" with pairings); an "attentive", "knowledgeable" staff treats diners "like special guests", so in spite of an "awkward" strip-mall locale and overly "intimate" seating, most "keep coming back again and again"; P.S. the adjacent wine bar vends small plates and vinos.

Baltimore/Annapolis

TOP FOOD RANKING

Restaurant	Cuisine
28 Charleston	American
Volt	American
27 Prime Rib	Steak
Samos	Greek
Di Pasquale's	Italian
Tasting Room	American
Thai Arroy	Thai
Peter's Inn	American
Linwoods	American
Salt	American

OTHER NOTEWORTHY PLACES

Chameleon Cafe	American
Cinghiale	Italian
Clementine	American
Dogwood	American
Faidley's	Seafood
Mr. Bill's Terrace Inn	Crab House
Paul's Homewood Café	American/Greek
Petit Louis Bistro	French
Woodberry Kitchen	American
Zorba's	Greek

Chameleon Cafe 🈺Ⓜ *American* | 27 | 17 | 25 | $42 |

Northeast Baltimore | 4341 Harford Rd. (bet. Montebello Terr. & Overland Ave.) | Baltimore | 410-254-2376 | www.thechameleoncafe.com

"Hurray!" cheer champions of this "unexpected treasure" in a converted Northeast Baltimore row house, a "top-flight" showcase for chef/co-owner Jeffrey Smith's "dedication" to "seasonal, local" gustation via an "elegantly prepared" New American menu that's like "a symphony for the taste buds" accompanied by "excellent wines"; a "knowledgeable and attentive" team monitors the "simple" but "cozy" setting, and despite "all the buzz" over the "sublime dining", the "price is right."

Charleston 🈺 *American* | 28 | 27 | 27 | $85 |

Harbor East | 1000 Lancaster St. (Exeter St.) | Baltimore | 410-332-7373 | www.charlestonrestaurant.com

"The hype is all true" at this "top-of-the-line" Harbor East "jewel" – rated No. 1 for Food in the Baltimore Survey – which "raises the bar" with the "incomparable" Cindy Wolf's "stellar" New American cuisine, presented on a diner's-choice tasting menu paired with "outstanding wines"; the "impeccable" service and "sheer elegance" of the setting will "sweep you off your feet", so even if you "need to take out a second mortgage", "you won't care."

	FOOD	DECOR	SERVICE	COST

Cinghiale *Italian*
24 | 26 | 25 | $57

Harbor East | 822 Lancaster St. (Exeter St.) | Baltimore | 410-547-8282 | www.cgeno.com

Charleston owners Cindy Wolf and Tony Foreman "work their magic" at this Baltimore Harbor East Northern Italian, where the "inspired" cooking, "highly attentive" service and "cosmopolitan" atmosphere go "so well together"; the "dressed-down" enoteca serves "quality meats and cheeses" from the in-house salumeria while the "more formal" osteria matches its "memorable" dishes with an "exceptional" wine list, and if it all comes at a "steep price", "you get what you pay for."

Clementine ⓜ *American*
23 | 19 | 21 | $30

Northeast Baltimore | 5402 Harford Rd. (bet. Echodale & Hamilton Aves.) | Baltimore | 410-444-1497 | www.bmoreclementine.com

After an "expansion", it's now "easier to get in" to this Northeast Baltimore New American "hot spot", the darling of "boomers" and "hipsters gone to parenting" thanks to chef-owner Winston Blick's "super" seasonal "fusion of comfort and trendy foods" (including "homemade charcuterie" and desserts from his pastry-chef mom); the "bohemian setting" and "pleasant" staff lend an "inviting" "local" feel, now enhanced by "a full bar"; P.S. Tuesday's $10-per-platter "taco nights" are a "bargain."

Di Pasquale's Italian Market ⓢ *Italian*
27 | 14 | 19 | $16

East Baltimore | 3700 Gough St. (Dean St.) | Baltimore | 410-276-6787 | www.dipasquales.com

"One hundred percent authentic", this "family-run" Italian grocery in East Baltimore dispenses "awesome", "well-priced" deli faves (subs, "brick-oven pizza", "housemade lasagna" etc.) over the counter with "no fuss, no muss"; there's bare-bones seating for a "homey" lunch "in the neighborhood", but you "go for the great food not the atmosphere", so feel free to "take it home"; P.S. closes at 6 PM.

Dogwood ⓢⓜ *American*
25 | 18 | 22 | $39

Hampden | 911 W. 36th St. (Roland Ave.) | Baltimore | 410-889-0952 | www.dogwoodbaltimore.com

"Thank goodness it's back!" cheer fans of this refurbished and recently reopened Hampden New American, where chef Galen Sampson and wife Bridget merge their "farm-to-table philosophy" with a "social mission" "of providing reentry employment" for "ex-offenders" into an "unexpected" culinary "treat" showcasing "inspired dishes" devised from "organic and local ingredients"; with a "funky" basement space, "excellent service" and "reasonable prices" to "add to the enjoyment", it's "a keeper" "with a conscience"; P.S. a street-level lunch bar opened post-Survey.

Faidley's Seafood ⓢ *Seafood*
27 | 10 | 17 | $20

Downtown West | Lexington Mkt. | 203 N. Paca St. (Lexington St.) | Baltimore | 410-727-4898 | www.faidleyscrabcakes.com

"Go lump or go home" at this "legendary" Lexington Market "mecca for seafood devotees" that opened in 1886 and remains stuck in some sort of "miraculous time warp"; "you eat standing up" at high-top tables amid seafood counters, but since its "fantastic "crab cakes (broiled please)" are the "standard by which all other Baltimore crab cakes are judged", few seem to care; P.S. "freshly shucked oysters" from its "excellent raw bar" make a "cheap lunch."

Linwoods *American* | 27 | 26 | 26 | $56 |

Owings Mills | 25 Crossroads Dr. (McDonogh & Reisterstown Rds.) | 410-356-3030 | www.linwoods.com

With its "well-heeled clientele" and "stylish" setting, there's a "New York feeling" in the air at this "long-term" Owings Mills "treat" that remains one of the region's "best and most consistent places"; chef/co-owner Linwood Dame's "luscious" New American fare puts "innovative twists on old favorites" ("this guy can cook!"), and while you may wish someone else were "paying the bill", a "charming staff" ensures the experience is "always superb."

Mr. Bill's Terrace Inn Ⓜ *Crab House* | ▽ 26 | 11 | 19 | $38 |

Essex | 200 Eastern Blvd. (Helena Ave.) | 410-687-5996

"There's no Bill, no terrace and no inn", but "you know you're in Bawlmer, hon", when you step through the doors of this "noisy" Essex seafooder and start hammerin' piles of some of the "best crabs in town" alongside "old Colts and Orioles"; "go early or wait a long time" (tip: it's less "busy" Tuesdays–Thursdays), though whenever you arrive you'll "always feel welcome."

Paul's Homewood Café *American/Greek* | 21 | 21 | 24 | $31 |

Annapolis | 919 West St. (Taylor Ave.) | 410-267-7891 | www.paulscafe-annapolis.com

"Homestyle Greek cooking" and "excellent" New American cuisine share top billing at this "family-run" Annapolis cafe, a "nice little spot" that's retained its charm despite a recent refurb that resulted in "a lot more room"; add in an "everybody-knows-your-name" vibe, and it's "not hard to see why it's lasted" more than 60 years; P.S. "do the impossible and save room for dessert."

Peter's Inn ⓈⓂ *American* | 27 | 18 | 22 | $33 |

Fells Point | 504 S. Ann St. (Eastern Ave.) | Baltimore | 410-675-7313 | www.petersinn.com

Perhaps "Baltimore's worst-kept secret", this "former biker bar" draws Fells Point foodies who vow it's "worth the wait" to sample its "short" "weekly menu" of "spectacular" New American cuisine and "great wines by the glass"; "friendly" servers navigate the "tight", "quirky" quarters featuring decor "right out of [your] father's basement", which somehow all seems so "hip" it begs the question "are you cool enough to eat here?"

Petit Louis Bistro *French* | 25 | 22 | 23 | $46 |

Roland Park | 4800 Roland Ave. (Upland Rd.) | Baltimore | 410-366-9393 | www.petitlouis.com

For a "fabulous little taste of France" "without the jet lag", Francophiles pack into this "bustling" Roland Parker featuring "perfectly executed bistro classics", an "excellent French wine list" and "first-class" service ("I tip my beret to the staff"); *oui*, "extremely close" tables lead to rampant "eavesdropping" and "deafening" noise levels, but regulars retort "bring an appetite . . . and earplugs"; P.S. euro-pinchers sidestep "pricey" tabs with a $20 lunch prix fixe.

	FOOD	DECOR	SERVICE	COST

Prime Rib *Steak* | 27 | 25 | 27 | $68

Downtown North | 1101 N. Calvert St. (Chase St.) | Baltimore | 410-539-1804 | www.theprimerib.com

In Downtown Baltimore, the "godfather of steakhouses" mixes "old-world elegance" with "just the right touch of film-noir decadence", live music and "dynamite food" – the "best slab-o-meat in town", "first-rate" crab and "huge" sides – to make each "expensive" meal an "event"; the "retro-classy" digs are attended by "tuxedoed waiters" (there's a "dress code" for customers too), while the "bar scene will hurt your eyes if you're married."

Salt *American* | 27 | 22 | 25 | $43

East Baltimore | 2127 E. Pratt St. (Collington St.) | Baltimore | 410-276-5480 | www.salttavern.com

Smitten surveyors "kinda love" this "top-notch" "neighborhood secret" crammed into a "tiny" East Baltimore row house, where a "reliable kitchen" turns out an "ever-changing menu" of "beyond-the-norm" New American fare ("mmm, duck-fat fries"); it's all washed down with "imaginative" cocktails and served by a "comfortably attentive" staff, and if "difficult parking" is a deterrent for some, most say "by all means, go."

Samos ⊠⇎ *Greek* | 27 | 12 | 20 | $22

Greektown | 600 S. Oldham St. (Fleet St.) | Baltimore | 410-675-5292 | www.samosrestaurant.com

They "come from miles away and wait for hours" to sample the "real-deal" Hellenic eats at this "well-priced" Greektown "institution", where chef-owners Nick and Mike Georgalas greet you with a "warm smile and open arms" and ensure no one "leaves unsatisfied"; it's "small, cramped" and "nothing fancy", but "quick" service and a BYO policy that "makes it even better" means most "would go back in a flash"; P.S. "bring cash" and, on weekends, "your patience."

Tasting Room ⊠ *American* | 27 | 21 | 24 | $48

Frederick | 101 N. Market St. (Church St.) | 240-379-7772 | www.tastetr.com

The "big windows let everyone see what you're eating" at this "sophisticated" New American, an "upscale" "gem" whose "fantastic" "seasonal" cuisine, "creative martinis" and vino off one of the "best wine lists for miles around" are "professionally" served "at a Frederick pace"; the decor has a "chic, modern" edge, but seating that's a "little cramped" means there's little "privacy" and no lack of "noise"; P.S. wallet-watchers can opt for "great lunch deals."

Thai Arroy Ⓜ *Thai* | 27 | 15 | 23 | $21

South Baltimore | 1019 Light St. (bet. Cross & Hamburg Sts.) | Baltimore | 410-385-8587 | www.thaiarroy.com

Lines "often extend outside the door" for tables at this South Baltimore Thai, and for good reason: though portions are "massive", folks just "can't get enough" of its "exceptionally tasty" fare ("some spicy, some not"); a "lovely" staff oversees a dining room "small on space, huge on flavor", while a BYO policy that "makes it acceptable to have a 12-pack at your feet" also makes a "bargain" spot even "cheaper."

	FOOD	DECOR	SERVICE	COST

Volt Ⓜ *American*

28 | 26 | 27 | $73

Frederick | Houck Mansion | 228 N. Market St. (bet. 2nd & 3rd Sts.) | 301-696-8658 | www.voltrestaurant.com

He lost *Top Chef,* but Bryan Voltaggio has a "winner" in this "electrifying" Frederick New American, where the "astonishing", "locally sourced" cuisine packed with "sensational flavors" is eclipsed only by the bounty of 'Table 21', at which the "culinary star" himself presents a "delectable" "21-course tasting menu"; set in a "lovely" 1890 mansion awash in "modern" trappings and "over-the-top" service, it's "one of the best dining experiences" around – but "good luck getting a reservation"; P.S. the $20 lunch prix fixe and $15 bar lunch may be the "biggest bargains ever"; P.S. closed Tuesdays.

Woodberry Kitchen *American*

26 | 26 | 24 | $47

Hampden | 2010 Clipper Park Rd. (Clipper Rd.) | Baltimore | 410-464-8000 | www.woodberrykitchen.com

It's in a "hard-to-find" "old foundry" west of Hampden, but there's no doubt chef/co-owner Spike Gjerde's "elegant, farm-to-table" New American "has been discovered", inasmuch as it's Baltimore's Most Popular restaurant; expect "crowds" of "beautiful people" poring over an "ever-changing menu" of "stunning" fare made from "local, sustainable" ingredients, all paired with "interesting wines" and "creative cocktails" and served by a "polished" staff; just know that the "rustic-urban" space is "noisy when full" (i.e. almost always) and "reservations are a must."

Zorba's Bar & Grill ◐ *Greek*

21 | 11 | 17 | $22

Greektown | 4710 Eastern Ave. (Oldham St.) | Baltimore | 410-276-4484

For a "true sense of Greektown" and "some of the best lamb chops" in town, make tracks to this "small", "no-frills" taverna turning out "amazing charcoal spit-roasted meats", 20 types of "grilled fish" and other "traditional dishes" "prepared with love"; it gets "noisy and crowded" (sit upstairs to avoid), but "friendly" service and "reasonable prices" lead many to conclude it's "worth the effort."

Boston

TOP FOOD RANKING

	Restaurant	Cuisine
28	L'Espalier	French
	Oleana	Mediterranean
	O Ya	Japanese
	La Campania	Italian
	No. 9 Park	French/Italian
27	Ten Tables	American/European
	Bistro 5	Italian
	Clio/Uni	French
	Neptune Oyster	Seafood
	Troquet	American/French
	Oishii	Japanese
	Hamersley's	French
	EVOO	Eclectic
	Meritage	American
	Taranta	Italian/Peruvian
	Sorellina	Italian
	Hungry Mother	American
	Lumière	French
	Il Capriccio	Italian
	Delfino	Italian

OTHER NOTEWORTHY PLACES

Restaurant	Cuisine
Abe & Louie's	Steak
Basho	Japanese
Blue Ginger	Asian
Coppa	Italian
Craigie on Main	French
Eastern Standard	American/European
Gargoyles	American
Ginger Park	Asian
Il Casale	Italian
Legal Sea Foods	Seafood
Market	American
Myers + Chang	Asian
Petit Robert Bistro	French
Prezza	Italian
Rendezvous	Mediterranean
Rialto	Italian
Sam's	American/French
Sel de la Terre	French
Toro	Spanish
Towne	American

	FOOD	DECOR	SERVICE	COST

Abe & Louie's *Steak*
26 | 22 | 25 | $61

Back Bay | 793 Boylston St. (Fairfield St.) | 617-536-6300 |
www.abeandlouies.com

"You'll swear you died and went to fat-cat heaven" at this "manly"
Back Bay steakhouse where the "melt-on-your-tongue" beef served
with "all the bells and whistles" is "worth every penny", especially if
you "go on someone else's expense account"; while the "'in' crowd"
downs "fantastic wines" at the bar, others enjoy the "elegant" (if
"noisy") dining room where "top-notch", "seasoned" staffers help
make any meal feel "celebratory."

Basho Japanese Brasserie *Japanese*
- | - | - | M

Fenway | 1338 Boylston St. (bet. Jersey & Kilmamock Sts.) | 617-262-1338 |
www.bashosushi.com

From the glass-enclosed robata grill to the dozen or so seats at the
sushi bar, this arrival not far from Fenway Park provides a casual shrine
to Japanese cuisine, including signature rolls, sushi, sashimi, lunch
specials, entrees and raw-bar specialties; the cavernous, minimalist
setting hosts a lounge area with high-top tables and banquettes, a
communal table, private and semi-private dining, and a sidewalk terrace in warm weather.

Bistro 5 🗷Ⓜ *Italian*
27 | 24 | 26 | $50

West Medford | 5 Playstead Rd. (High St.) | 781-395-7464 | www.bistro5.com
An "unprepossessing exterior" hides this West Medford "jewel" where
chef-owner Vittorio Ettore takes "great pride" in his "consistently
wonderful" "gourmet" Northern Italian dishes bolstered by "local" ingredients with "explosive" flavors (he also "frequents" the "elegant"
dining room to "chat" with his guests); adding to the "amazing" – and
yes, "pricey" – experience are "fabulous" staffers who "offer great
pairing" ideas from the "well-chosen wine list."

Blue Ginger *Asian*
26 | 23 | 25 | $58

Wellesley | 583 Washington St. (Church St.) | 781-283-5790 |
www.ming.com

"As good as the hype" suggests, this "Wellesley wonder" stars Ming
Tsai's "palate-popping" "East-meets-West" Asian-fusion "miracles" –
and the best part is that the "gifted" "star chef" is "actually there"
("what a novelty!"), further rendering it "well worth" the "expensive"
tabs; the "calming blue" environs feature a "phenomenal" bar area
where folks can "drop in for a light meal without having made a reservation a month in advance."

Clio/Uni *French*
27 | 26 | 26 | $81

Back Bay | Eliot Hotel | 370A Commonwealth Ave. (Mass. Ave.) |
617-536-7200 | www.cliorestaurant.com

Within the "gracious confines" of the Back Bay's Eliot Hotel, this "tranquil enclave" continues to make foodies "swoon" over both the "bold,
complex flavors" of chef Ken Oringer's "exceptional" New French fare
("with touches of molecular gastronomy") and the "heavy blow dealt
to the wallet"; "more casual" yet just as "outrageously expensive",
neighbor Uni does "spectacular" sashimi, and if a few find the staffers
throughout to be "snooty", most cheer them as "professional" escorts
to "ethereal" "heights of expectation fulfillment."

	FOOD	DECOR	SERVICE	COST

Coppa ◐ *Italian*

| - | - | - | M |

South End | 253 Shawmut Ave. (Milford St.) | 617-391-0902 |
www.coppaboston.com

Housemade charcuterie, pasta and wood-oven pizza, plus an extensive menu of small plates, define this midpriced Italian enoteca in the
South End run by chef-partners Ken Oringer and Jamie Bissonnette;
the space is romantic and rustic with reclaimed wood floors, high ceilings, subway tile and a small wooden bar where beer, wine and inventive cocktails made from cordials are served.

Craigie on Main Ⓜ *French*

| 27 | - | 25 | $64 |

(fka Craigie Street Bistrot)

Central Square | 853 Main St. (Allen St.) | Cambridge | 617-497-5511 |
www.craigieonmain.com

"Knowledgeable, serious" chef Tony Maws knows what his fans want –
"wildly inventive", "truly adventurous" French cuisine "emphasizing
local ingredients", fashioned into "innovative presentations" and conveyed by "helpful, cheerful" servers – and now he delivers it in Central
Square, having moved from the old "tiny" Harvard Square "basement"
post-Survey; nervous Nellies who "hope he can maintain the quality"
in "bigger digs" most likely have nothing to worry about, but dollar-
watchers who "pray for lower prices" shouldn't bet on it.

Delfino Ⓜ *Italian*

| 27 | 17 | 24 | $37 |

Roslindale | 754 South St. (bet. Belgrade Ave. & Washington St.) |
617-327-8359 | www.delfinorestaurant.com

Regulars of this "casual" Roslindale Italian spot "treasure" its "generous portions" of "fresh and delightful" fare as much as they do the "accommodating" staff; indeed, the "drawbacks" of a "no-reservations
policy" ("call ahead and put your name on the list"), "long waits",
"crowds", "noise" and "tight seating" are "small prices to pay", especially considering the "quite reasonable" tabs.

Eastern Standard ◐ *American/European*

| 22 | 24 | 22 | $40 |

Kenmore Square | Hotel Commonwealth | 528 Commonwealth Ave.
(Brookline Ave.) | 617-532-9100 | www.easternstandardboston.com

From a "wonderful breakfast" to a "casual, inexpensive" American
lunch complemented by "intriguing", "innovative" cocktails (the "mixologists are geniuses") to an "elegant, pricey" European dinner paired
with "well-chosen wines", there's "something for everyone" at this
"cavernous", "glamorous" Kenmore Square "grande cafe" with a "gorgeous marble bar", "high ceilings" and an "excellent heated patio"; always "buzzing", it's especially "noisy" on "game day" – "like the Gare
du Nord filled with Sox fans."

EVOO *Eclectic*

| 27 | 22 | 26 | $47 |

Kendall Square | 350 Third St. (Potter St.) | Cambridge | 617-661-3866 |
www.evoorestaurant.com

At this "gem", which relocated from Somerville to Kendall Square in
March 2010 (thereby outdating the Decor score), devoted regulars
say the "sophisticated" Eclectic fare with "great emphasis on local
ingredients" "scores every time", particularly with the assistance of
the "stellar" servers' "helpful" explanations of the "unique combinations" and "wonderful wine" pairings; for "this caliber", the prices

are "completely reasonable", especially the "incredible-bargain" three-course prix fixe.

Gargoyles on the Square Ⓜ *American* | 24 | 21 | 22 | $43 |

Somerville | 219 Elm St. (Grove St.) | 617-776-5300 | www.gargoylesrestaurant.com

"Always creative" and "sometimes sublime" cheer fans of the New American fare served at this "hip", "intimate" Davis Square spot where every "fairly priced" dish contains "an unusual ingredient" and "extraordinary flair"; a minority decries that the "over-ambitious" combinations "don't always work" while falling "short on value" – but at least they "outshine the strangely curtained decor"; P.S. don your "halter top" for the Sunday disco brunch – "the funnest!"

Ginger Park *Asian* | - | - | - | M |

South End | 1375 Washington St. (Union Park St.) | 617-451-0077 | www.gingerparkboston.com

NYC expat chef Patricia Yeo has brought her Southeast Asian street food to the South End, where she's serving a midpriced menu of small plates accompanied by wine and sake; the expansive, elegant setting includes an undulating wood ceiling and a bar backed by windows that offer a view of the bustling cityscape.

Hamersley's Bistro *French* | 27 | 23 | 25 | $61 |

South End | 553 Tremont St. (Clarendon St.) | 617-423-2700 | www.hamersleysbistro.com

"Maestro" Gordon Hamersley remains "very visible" at this "light, airy" South End "institution", just as his "not-trendy", "seasonally changing" country French fare "still lives up to its well-deserved reputation", particularly the "luscious" "signature roast chicken" (rumored to trigger "out-of-body experiences"); the "top-notch" fare and "superior service" command upper-tier pricing, but the "thoughtful wine list" displays "some good buys."

Hungry Mother Ⓜ *American* | 27 | 22 | 25 | $41 |

Kendall Square | 233 Cardinal Medeiros Ave. (Binney St.) | Cambridge | 617-499-0090 | www.hungrymothercambridge.com

Settle in for some "high-end Southern comfort" at this "terrific" Kendall Square spot where a "small, innovative menu" of "elegant" New American cuisine gets a "Virginia spin" courtesy of "great", "dedicated" chef Barry Maiden (ex Lumière); but don't try it "without a reservation", because the "chic, homey" and "cramped" space gets "insanely busy" with folks keen on the "unique whiskey-based cocktails", "appreciable wine list" and "knowledgeable", "energetic staff."

Il Capriccio Ⓔ *Italian* | 27 | 22 | 25 | $58 |

Waltham | 888 Main St. (Prospect St.) | 781-894-2234 | www.ilcappricciowaltham.com

"Waltham's foodie paradise" "impresses" with "luxurious", "magical-at-times" Northern Italian cuisine ("don't miss" the "incredible" mushroom soufflé) – but it's "incomparable" sommelier Jeannie Rogers' "superb", "voluminous wine list" that really "makes the evening special"; some dub the setting a "cold", "tight" "maze", but most say it's "sophisticated", just like the "intelligent service" – "as you should expect for a restaurant in this [upper] price range."

	FOOD	DECOR	SERVICE	COST

Il Casale ▣ Italian

| - | - | - | M |

Belmont | 50 Leonard St. (Moore St.) | 617-209-4942 |
www.ilcasalebelmont.com

Chef Dante de Magistris draws inspiration from his childhood summers spent in Southern Italy for small plates and family-style dinners served in a renovated 1899 Belmont firehouse, where handcrafted Vermont wood tables and hand-blown Venetian glass lanterns evoke the restaurant's name (*casale* means 'rural home'); the dining room features a communal table overlooking the open kitchen, and there's sidewalk seating in warmer months.

La Campania ▣▣ Italian

| 28 | 25 | 26 | $59 |

Waltham | 504 Main St. (bet. Cross & Heard Sts.) | 781-894-4280 |
www.lacampania.com

For a "special" "event", "reserve well in advance" for this "sublime" Waltham "experience" where "wonderfully flavorful, well-plated and inventive Italian cuisine" is conveyed by "exquisite, unobtrusive" staffers in a "charmingly rustic", "romantic" dining room; a "stellar wine list" completes the nearly "flawless package", and though you may be "surprised at how expensive" it is, this is one "splurge" that's "worth every penny."

Legal Sea Foods Seafood

| 22 | 18 | 20 | $41 |

Back Bay | Copley Pl. | 100 Huntington Ave. (bet. Dartmouth & Exeter Sts.) |
617-266-7775

Back Bay | Prudential Ctr. | 800 Boylston St. (Fairfield St.) | 617-266-6800

Park Square | 26 Park Plaza (Columbus Ave.) | 617-426-4444

Waterfront | Long Wharf | 255 State St. (Atlantic Ave.) | 617-227-3115

Harvard Square | 20 University Rd. (Eliot St.) | Cambridge | 617-491-9400

Kendall Square | 5 Cambridge Ctr. (bet. Ames & Main Sts.) | Cambridge |
617-864-3400

Chestnut Hill | Chestnut Hill Shopping Ctr. | 43 Boylston St.
(Hammond Pond Pkwy.) | 617-277-7300

Peabody | North Shore Mall | 210 Andover St./Rte. 114 (Rte. 128) |
978-532-4500

Burlington | Burlington Mall | 75 Middlesex Tpke. (Rte. 128) | 781-270-9700

Framingham | 50-60 Worcester Rd./Rte. 9 (bet. Concord & Speen Sts.) |
508-766-0600

www.legalseafoods.com

Additional locations throughout the Boston area

"Chain shmain!" – this seafood "institution" again earns Boston's Most Popular restaurant title not (only) due to its "ubiquity", but because of its "consistent" delivery of "guaranteed-fresh, well-prepared" fish, from the "basic" to the "ambitious", plus a "surprisingly decent wine list"; the "big, bustling" settings swing from "plain-Jane" to "upscale" ("service varies" too), and while even admirers admit it's "perhaps a little overpriced", it's "worth it" for such "quality."

L'Espalier French

| 28 | - | 28 | $95 |

Back Bay | 774 Boylston St. (bet. Exeter & Fairfield Sts.) | 617-262-3023 |
www.lespalier.com

"An extraordinary culinary adventure" awaits at this Back Bay "legend" where the "unforgettable textures, flavors and scents" of its "inventive" New French cuisine – once again "soaring above the rest" to earn Boston's No. 1 Food rating – are "matched" to "world-class wines" by "extremely well-informed", equally highly ranked staffers; post-Survey, it moved into "more spacious", "modern" digs connected to the Mandarin Oriental, and while "the jury's out as to how it translates" ("can a hotel have the warmth and charm of the old brownstone?"), "as long as" "genius" chef Frank McClelland is "in the kitchen", long-time fans with "fat wallets" will "be in the dining room."

Lumière *French*

| 27 | 23 | 26 | $57 |

Newton | 1293 Washington St. (Waltham St.) | 617-244-9199 | www.lumiererestaurant.com

Demonstrating "what can be done with a few exceptional ingredients", Michael Leviton's West Newton "destination restaurant" offers an "ever-changing" menu of "consistently superb" New French dishes with an "emphasis on local produce" (you can "feel the love with each bite"); the "classy white", "modernist" setting, "impeccable" service and "quiet" sophistication make it a natural for "special-occasion" dining, and even though it's "a little dear" pricewise, it "never fails to please."

Market *American*

| – | – | – | M |

Theater District | W Boston | 100 Stuart St. (Tremont St.) | 617-310-6790 | www.marketbyjgboston.com

For this New American in the Theater District's W Hotel, renowned chef Jean-Georges Vongerichten has put together a moderately priced menu of 'greatest hits' from his other restaurants, featuring dishes peppered with French, Asian and Italian influences and served in sexy brown, gray and black environs overlooking Tremont Street; P.S. an adjacent lounge serves small plates from the restaurant.

Meritage ☑ *American*

| 27 | 27 | 26 | $68 |

Waterfront | Boston Harbor Hotel | 70 Rowes Wharf (Atlantic Ave.) | 617-439-3995 | www.meritagetherestaurant.com

"Fabulous harbor views" are only part of the package at this "special" Waterfront "wine-lover's paradise" via chef Daniel Bruce, whose "in-novative" New American dishes are available in "small and large" por-tions ("enabling those with smaller appetites to sample more") and designed to be paired with a "perfect" selection of "terrific" *vini*; true, it's "expensive, but totally worth it" given the "polished service", "sumptuous surroundings" and overall "exquisite dining experience."

Myers + Chang *Asian*

| 23 | 19 | 20 | $34 |

South End | 1145 Washington St. (E. Berkeley St.) | 617-542-5200 | www.myersandchang.com

Asian dining goes "trendy" at this "chic diner" in the South End from restaurateur Christopher Myers, where "fashionable" folks dig into chef Joanne Chang's "modern" Chinese, Thai and Vietnamese spe-cialties; sure, it's "loud" and the "family-style small-plates" approach means the "bill can add up quickly", but ultimately most say this eat-ing "adventure" is one "highly entertaining experience."

Neptune Oyster *Seafood*

| 27 | 20 | 22 | $42 |

North End | 63 Salem St. (Cross St.) | 617-742-3474 | www.neptuneoyster.com

"Escape the typical Italian fare in the North End" at this "sardine"-sized, perennially "packed" seafooder famed for its "magnificent" raw bar se-lection and "vaunted hot lobster roll", served in a "little-bit-of-Paris" setting; the "cramped conditions" aren't helped by the "no-reservations" policy, so savvy shuckers snag seats by "arriving early" and "checking their bank account" before digging in (it's on the "pricey" side).

No. 9 Park 🖪 *French/Italian*   28 | 24 | 27 | $75

Beacon Hill | 9 Park St. (bet. Beacon & Tremont Sts.) | 617-742-9991 | www.no9park.com

Barbara Lynch still "dazzles" at her "jewel box"-esque Beacon Hill flagship where "movers and shakers" for whom "money is no object" "celebrate in style" with "elegant", "intriguing" French-Italian creations that "marry unexpected tastes and textures" with "decadent, heavenly" results; if the "smaller-than-small portions" are occasional balloon-bursters, the "savvy", "polished" "service team" and "superior" bartenders ("mixology is an art here", as is wine selection) "heighten the experience" – right on up to "cloud 9."

Oishii 🖻 *Japanese*   27 | 17 | 21 | $55

Chestnut Hill | 612 Hammond St. (Boylston St.) | 617-277-7888
Sudbury | Mill Vill. | 365 Boston Post Rd./Rte. 20 (Concord Rd.) | 978-440-8300

Oishii Boston ●🖻 *Japanese*

South End | 1166 Washington St. (E. Berkeley St.) | 617-482-8868 | www.oishiiboston.com

"Pristine" "flavors come shining through" thanks to "chefs who care about the fundamentals" at this "sublime" sushi set that provides "aesthetic" as well as "culinary treats" with "fantastical", "innovative presentations"; the staffers can be "quite helpful" in their "recommendations" at all locations, whether at the original Chestnut Hill "shoebox" ("always a wait", "expensive"), the more "modern" Sudbury branch (less "frenetic", "expensive") or the "hoity-toity" South End offshoot ("dark, romantic", "insanely expensive").

Oleana *Mediterranean*   28 | 23 | 25 | $52

Inman Square | 134 Hampshire St. (bet. Elm & Norfolk Sts.) | Cambridge | 617-661-0505 | www.oleanarestaurant.com

"Attention to detail" is the hallmark of this "compelling" Inman Square "foodie attraction", where a "coveted reservation" allows the opportunity to sample chef-owner Ana Sortun's "unrivaled" Arabic-Mediterranean cooking (and simultaneously get an "education in spices" from the "enthusiastic" staffers); though seating is a little "cramped" and the pricing decidedly "upscale", diehards declare "there's no other restaurant like it"; P.S. a meal on the "first-come, first-served" patio is as "close to heaven" as you'll find in these parts.

O Ya 🖪🖻 *Japanese*   28 | 23 | 26 | $112

Leather District | 9 East St. (South St.) | 617-654-9900 | www.oyarestaurantboston.com

"Oh yeah", "the accolades are warranted!" – this "tiny" Leather District firehouse-turned-"sleek" izakaya provides culinary "transcendence" via "wildly creative Japanese-fusion morsels" bursting with "extraordinary" "flavors not found elsewhere"; "put yourself in the capable hands" of the "enthusiastic" staff by ordering the "knockout omakase" – but bear in mind those 15 or so courses yield about "17 bites of food", which causes the "still hungry" to cry "o ya gotta be kidding me" when handed the "mortgage payment"-worthy, "nosebleed"-triggering bill.

	FOOD	DECOR	SERVICE	COST

Petit Robert Bistro *French* | 24 | 20 | 22 | $39 |

Kenmore Square | 468 Commonwealth Ave. (W. Charlesgate) | 617-375-0699
South End | 480 Columbus Ave. (Rutland Sq.) | 617-867-0600
Needham | 45 Chapel St. (Highland Ave.) | 781-559-0532
www.petitrobertbistro.com

"Almost perfect replicas of French bistros" can be found at these "un-pretentious", "cozy" sibs in Kenmore Square and the South End, where "authentic" "comfort fare for Francophiles" is paired with "suitable wines"; "respectful service" from "accented" staffers earns cheers, but it's the "great bang for the buck" that really gets fans to cry *"c'est magnifique!"*; P.S. suburbanites are "excited for the Needham location", which opened post-Survey.

Prezza *Italian* | 27 | 22 | 24 | $57 |

North End | 24 Fleet St. (Moon St.) | 617-227-1577 | www.prezza.com

"Not your typical North End" eatery, this "classy" spot puts a "unique", even "edgy" spin on Italian with "flavorful" results quite different from "typical red-sauce fare"; a "vast wine list", "helpful, charming" staff and "stylish", "intimate", "quite romantic" setting add to a night out that's a "heavenly" "treat" – "when you can afford it."

Rendezvous *Mediterranean* | 26 | 19 | 24 | $47 |

Central Square | 502 Massachusetts Ave. (Brookline St.) | Cambridge | 617-576-1900 | www.rendezvouscentralsquare.com

Central Square suppers "pray to the altar" of "restaurateur par excellence" Steve Johnson at his "whopper" of a "casual" restaurant, a "jazzed-up" "former Burger King" where he "creatively combines" "locally sourced ingredients" to yield "glorious, distinctive" Mediterranean fare ("quite well priced", just like the "fantastic wine list"); "friendly, helpful service" keeps the "comfort level high", especially during Sunday's prix fixe service, featuring the same "wonderful food for a little less cash."

Rialto *Italian* | 26 | 25 | 25 | $63 |

Harvard Square | Charles Hotel | 1 Bennett St. (Eliot St.) | Cambridge | 617-661-5050 | www.rialto-restaurant.com

At Jody Adams' "beautiful", "modern", "stylish" Harvard Square establishment, the culinary "goddess" works with "creative", "incredible combinations" of "the freshest ingredients" that "layer flavor after flavor" into her "regional Italian specialties"; like the menu, the "impressive wine list" contains several "wallet-busters", so "bring the wealthy in-laws" and succumb to the "savvy suggestions" of the staffers, "exemplars of stellar service" all.

Sam's *American/French* | - | - | - | M |

Seaport District | 60 Northern Ave., 2nd fl. (Courthouse Way) | 617-295-0191 | www.samsatlouis.com

Restaurant veteran Esti Parsons is behind this midpriced American-French bistro (think seafood, steak and roast chicken) perched on the second floor of the new Louis Boston clothier in the Seaport District; the space exudes hospitable warmth despite the modern industrial decor, and an outside deck and 180-degree views of Boston Harbor help sweeten the deal.

	FOOD	DECOR	SERVICE	COST

Sel de la Terre ● *French* | 23 | 21 | 22 | $46 |

Back Bay | Mandarin Oriental | 774 Boylston St. (Fairfield St.) | 617-266-8800
Waterfront | 255 State St. (Atlantic Ave.) | 617-720-1300
www.seldelaterre.com

Originally opened on the Waterfront, with a spin-off in the Back Bay, this "notable" French chainlet (itself a more casual spin-off of L'Espalier) offers "high-quality" Provençal cuisine in "stylish" but "rustic" settings; the "skilled" cooking is paired with a "wine list to suit all pocketbooks" served by a "quick", "down-to-earth" team, while "phenomenal" breads from on-site bakeries ice the cake; the only quibble: there's "nothing country about the prices."

Sorellina *Italian* | 27 | 28 | 26 | $65 |

Back Bay | 1 Huntington Ave. (Dartmouth St.) | 617-412-4600 | www.sorellinaboston.com

"Luxurious", "modern", "perfectly lit" and "visually stunning" are some of the accolades bestowed upon the highly rated black-and-white decor at this "awesome experience" in the Back Bay – while just as "wow"-worthy is Jamie Mammano's Italian fare filled with "contemporary" "twists" and "sumptuous combinations of fresh ingredients"; "caring, professional service" helps to create a "terrific ambiance" overall that leaves admirers "wishing" they "could afford to go more often."

Taranta *Italian/Peruvian* | 27 | 21 | 23 | $44 |

North End | 210 Hanover St. (Cross St.) | 617-720-0052 | www.tarantarist.com

A "breath of fresh air" blows through the North End courtesy of chef-owner José Duarte's "creative" "fusion" of Peruvian and Southern Italian cuisines (gourmands report that the "surprising mix of flavors works incredibly well") at this "charming" spot with three "lovely", "traditional" levels and a "lively", "knowledgeable" staff; it's "a little expensive, but worth it", especially to environmentalists who award it bonus points for having "gone completely green."

Ten Tables *American/European* | 27 | 20 | 25 | $43 |

Jamaica Plain | 597 Centre St. (Pond St.) | 617-524-8810
Harvard Square | 5 Craigie St. (Berkeley St.) | Cambridge | 617-576-5444
www.tentables.net

"Locals are lucky" to have this "homey" spot in Jamaica Plain, as its European–New American fare is "prepared with love", served with "gusto" by a "knowledgeable" staff and loaded with "spectacular", "surprising tastes and textures"; those "loathe to give it a good review" because, "true" to its name, there are just 10 tables – and it's "10 times as good as" many more expensive competitors – now send their friends to Harvard Square, where a slightly larger offshoot opened post-Survey.

Toro *Spanish* | 26 | 21 | 20 | $43 |

South End | 1704 Washington St. (Mass. Ave.) | 617-536-4300 | www.toro-restaurant.com

"Bullfight-level noise" emanates from this "rustic", "tiny" South End Spaniard, giving the "droves of people clamoring for a cramped table" an accurate idea of the "wild" time "famed chef Ken Oringer" has in store for them via his "mouthwateringly delicious" tapas, which "range from authentic to trendy" ("you have to try" the "decadent" grilled corn specialty); "no reservations" mean "excruciating" lines, and "all those small plates" lead to "big bills", but is it "worth it? - absolutely."

Towne *American*   – | – | – | M ·

Back Bay | 900 Boylston St. (Gloucester St.) | 617-247-0400 | www.towneboston.com

Two powerhouse chefs – Lydia Shire and Jasper White – are the culinary directors behind this newcomer adjacent to the Hynes Convention Center in the Back Bay, where an all-day menu of seasonal American fare is prepared in an exhibition kitchen set behind glass on the second floor; the expansive upstairs dining rooms are replete with oak, antiqued mirrors, artisan chandeliers, horseshoe booths and Shire-designed chairs (plus art from her personal collection), while downstairs an LED-lit resin bar offers corner views of passersby.

Troquet Ⓢ Ⓜ *American/French*   27 | 22 | 25 | $63

Theater District | 140 Boylston St. (bet. Charles & Tremont Sts.) | 617-695-9463 | www.troquetboston.com

"Amazing by-the-glass pairings" in either "2- or 4-oz. servings" from a "deep wine list" that's "priced to enjoy" make this "classy" Theater District haunt "an oenophile's delight" – and the French–New American cuisine, featuring "incredible cheeses", "rises to the occasion" with "fantastic, creative" preparations (this is where the "expense" comes in); while the bi-level space gets "noisy" "when full", "great views of the Common" appeal to "romantics", as do staffers who "anticipate every need without being obtrusive."

Charlotte

TOP FOOD RANKING

	Restaurant	Cuisine
28	Barrington's	American
27	McNinch House	Continental
26	Capital Grille	Steak
	Carpe Diem	American
	Fig Tree	Continental
	Toscana	Italian
	Luce	Italian
	Upstream	Seafood
25	Dolce	Italian
	Sullivan's	Steak

OTHER NOTEWORTHY PLACES

Bentley's	American/French
Blue	Mediterranean
Fiamma	Italian
Good Food	American
Ilios Noche	Greek/Italian
Liberty	American
P.F. Chang's	Chinese
Sonoma	American
Soul	Eclectic
Zebra	French

Barrington's ⊠ *American*   28 | 22 | 26 | $53

SouthPark | Foxcroft Shopping Ctr. | 7822 Fairview Rd.
(bet. Carmel & Colony Rds.) | 704-364-5755 |
www.barringtonsrestaurant.com

"Quite simply the best" in Charlotte is the ruling on this "intriguing" SouthPark New American, with voters yet again declaring it No. 1 for both Food and Popularity due to "genius" chef-owner Bruce Moffett's "perfectly prepared" "locally sourced" seasonal fare with "beautifully layered flavors"; though the "cozy" digs are "not good for sensitive conversation", they do ensure you'll "get great attention from your server"; P.S. "call way in advance for reservations."

Bentley's on 27 ⊠ *American/French*   24 | 27 | 24 | $55

Uptown | Charlotte Plaza Bldg. | 201 S. College St., 27th fl. (bet. 3rd & 4th Sts.) | 704-343-9201 | www.bentleyson27.com

"Tremendous views of the city" through "floor-to-ceiling windows" help to make this "luxurious" American-French aerie perched on the 27th floor of the Charlotte Plaza Building in Uptown "one of the most romantic places" in town; "service fit for royalty" – including "old-school, white-apron, tableside service" of "classic" "throwbacks" like steak Diane and bananas Foster ("expensive" but "well worth it") – keeps the dining room feeling "classy", while the "fun lounge" draws a "lively crowd."

	FOOD	DECOR	SERVICE	COST

Blue Restaurant & Bar ☒ *Mediterranean* | 24 | 25 | 23 | $51 |

Uptown | Hearst Plaza | 214 N. Tryon St. (bet. 5th & 6th Sts.) | 704-927-2583 | www.bluecharlotte.com

"Chase your blues away" at this "lush" Mediterranean "hot spot" Uptown, where a "vibrant bar" sits off a main room with a "fabulous '30s-style nightclub ambiance" with "great live music" (Wednesday-Saturday nights); the service is as "well-orchestrated" as the "adventurous cuisine" is "delicious and beautiful" – just "prepare to open your wallet wide" to experience them.

Capital Grille *Steak* | 26 | 25 | 26 | $58 |

Downtown | IJL Financial Ctr. | 201 N. Tryon St. (5th St.) | 704-348-1400 | www.thecapitalgrille.com

"For an extravagant night", "take out a loan", then head Downtown to this "consummate" steakhouse chain, where the "melt-in-your-mouth" cuts are "the size of manhole covers", the "sides are bountiful" and even the "seafood is wonderful" ("the calamari is a must-have"); the "impressive wine list", "tremendously accommodating" service and "pleasing atmosphere" further make for a "memorable" dinner, but it's also a "hot lunch place", especially with "business and political heavies."

Carpe Diem ☒ *American* | 26 | 25 | 25 | $44 |

Elizabeth | 1535 Elizabeth Ave. (Hawthorne Ln.) | 704-377-7976 | www.carpediemrestaurant.com

This "unique" Elizabeth "jewel" is all about "beauty", from the "gorgeous" art nouveau decor to the "artful", "imaginative" and "consistently amazing" New American fare, including "tasty vegetarian options" ("hard-to-find in Charlotte"); "professional, personable servers" and a "well-thought-out" wine list are two more reasons why the "popularity" of this "institution" is "well-deserved."

Dolce ☒ *Italian* | 25 | 19 | 23 | $34 |

Dilworth | Kenilworth Commons | 1710 Kenilworth Ave. (East Blvd.) | 704-332-7525 | www.dolceristorante.net

"Gnocchi Tuesdays" (the only day the "fluffy potato pillows of paradise" are offered) are a "must-do" at this "cozy" Dilworth Italian "hidden treasure", but no matter when you come, you're sure to find the "authentic" fare – from "divine" pastas to "pure-delight" gelati – "superb"; its "shopping-center location" is "nothing to rave about", but owners and staff that "make you feel like a part of their family" certainly are.

Fiamma *Italian* | 25 | 17 | 23 | $37 |

Dilworth | Park Square Shopping Ctr. | 2418 Park Rd. (Ordermore Ave.) | 704-333-3062

If you "never expect divine Italian" in the South, this Dilworth "neighborhood go-to" "surprises" with "outstanding" "homemade pastas and sauces" and "sublime", "creative" specials – and all at "midlevel prices" no less; though the "run-down" strip-mall setting "bores", the "welcoming", "attentive" staffers "never fail to impress."

Fig Tree *Continental* | 26 | 25 | 26 | $54 |

Elizabeth | 1601 E. Seventh St. (Louise Ave.) | 704-332-3322 | www.charlottefigtree.com

"Rare combinations" of "magnificent" seasonal Continental cuisine (French and Italian in particular) loaded with "sophisticated sauces" and "prepared with the freshest ingredients" keep devotees "coming back" to this "beautiful Craftsman-style house" with a "wonderful porch for alfresco dining" in "historic Elizabeth"; a "wine list innovative enough to stand up to the chef's creative flavors" and "outstanding service" further make it "perfect for a special-occasion" "splurge."

Good Food on Montford ☒ American   - | - | - | M

SouthPark | 1701 Montford Dr. (Park Rd.) | 704-525-0881 | www.goodfoodonmontford.com

Brothers Kerry and Bruce Moffett (of top-rated Barrington's) craft dynamic New American–style small plates (alongside noodle dishes and a few entrees) at this moderately priced SouthPark scene; to complement the seasonal eats is modern-rustic decor, with exposed-brick walls, sconces made from flatware and funky artwork.

Ilios Noche ☒ Greek/Italian   24 | 17 | 23 | $29

South Charlotte | 11508 Providence Rd. (I-485) | 704-814-9882 | www.iliosnoche.com

A "good bang for the buck", which is rare in South Charlotte, wins kudos for this "cool", "family-friendly" "surprise" in a strip mall offering a "frequently updated menu" of Greek-Italian eats (including "amazing" wood-grilled entrees) that "never disappoint"; the "minimal", "diner-ish" digs aren't off-putting thanks to the "friendly, attentive staff" and owners who stay "very involved" even when it's "mobbed", which is often.

Liberty, The American   - | - | - | M

South End | 1812 South Blvd. (East Blvd.) | 704-332-8830 | www.thelibertycharlotte.com

Chef Tom Condron's rethought New American comfort plates are the draw at this affordable South End gastropub where the fare's prepared with the hearty selection of U.S. craft draft and bottled beers in mind (there are some rare imports too); also putting it in the Destination category is the cool, industrial setting, with columns made from kegs and walls and ceilings fashioned from crates.

Luce ☒ Italian   26 | 24 | 24 | $47

Uptown | Hearst Plaza | 214 N. Tryon St. (bet. 5th & 6th Sts.) | 704-344-9222 | www.luceristorante.net

A "romantic date place" "in the heart" of Uptown, this "intimate" Northern Italian from restaurateur Augusto Conte envelops love birds in "an oasis of calm" even as the "elegant decor" reminds them of "a grand old-hotel lobby in Italy"; "food you can tell is made especially for you" and an "excellent" Tuscan-centric wine list are not only "worth the bucks", but even more "delectable" on the patio.

McNinch House ☒Ⓜ Continental   27 | 27 | 28 | $102

Uptown | 511 N. Church St. (bet. 8th & 9th Sts.) | 704-332-6159 | www.mcninchhouserestaurant.com

A "unique dining experience" is "beautifully presented" at this "special-occasion restaurant", an "elegant" restored Queen Anne residence Uptown, where "dressed-up" folks are "pampered" by "wonderful" servers ferrying seven "fabulous" Continental courses paired, if desired, with "outstanding wines"; all sittings are prix fixe (you choose the entree when making the requisite reservation), and each one is an "event that unfolds over three hours" – is it any wonder it may necessitate a "second mortgage"?

P.F. Chang's China Bistro *Chinese*
21 | 20 | 19 | $29

SouthPark | Phillips Pl. | 6809-F Phillips Place Ct. (Charlton Ln.) | 704-552-6644

Northlake | 10325 Perimeter Pkwy. (bet. Reames Rd. & Perimeter Woods Dr.) | 704-598-1927

www.pfchangs.com

"Always great" "American-style" Chinese food with "bright, imaginative flavor" "twists" keeps this chain with locations in SouthPark and Northlake "always busy" – indeed, you will "always wait for a table" in the "loud", "vaguely Asian" dining rooms, but once you get seated, you can count on "good service for the price point"; sure, it's "predictable", but that's one of the reasons it's so "popular."

Sonoma Modern American ⓈＡＮ *American*
23 | 22 | 22 | $47

Uptown | Bank of America Corporate Ctr. | 100 N. Tryon St. (Trade St.) | 704-332-1132 | www.sonomarestaurants.net

This Uptown New American is "always a treat" – if "a bit pricey"; the "sleek", "chic", "European" setting can get "loud" with "Bank of America executives" ordering from the "intelligent wine list" "after work", but you "can't beat its location" next to the Blumenthal Performing Arts Center for pre- and post-performance eats; P.S. a new chef premiered a new menu post-Survey, outdating the Food score.

Soul Gastrolounge ● *Eclectic*
- | - | - | I

Plaza-Midwood | 1500 Central Ave. (Pecan Ave.) | 704-348-1848 | www.soulgastrolounge.com

At this hip Plaza-Midwood nook, Eclectic tapas, sushi, cocktails and even cupcakes are served to a varying soundtrack of beats from live DJs, and at mostly inexpensive price points; the cool, casual, lounge-like setting featuring exposed brick, hardwood floors and teal mirrors is just right for the nightlife, but a sweet-and-savory brunch makes it a daytime destination on weekends.

Sullivan's Steakhouse *Steak*
25 | 23 | 24 | $57

South End | 1928 South Blvd. (Tremont Ave.) | 704-335-8228 | www.sullivansteakhouse.com

In a city "crowded with high-end chains", this "sophisticated" yet "not-so-stuffy" South End franchise "holds status as a go-to" thanks to "amazing steaks and seafood" "well worth" the "expensive" tabs; "consistent" staffers with "impressive energy levels", "cool" live jazz, "knockout martinis" and an "extensive wine list" further make it what most deem a "winner."

Toscana Ⓢ *Italian*
26 | 21 | 23 | $45

SouthPark | Specialty Shops on the Park | 6401 Morrison Blvd. (Roxborough Rd.) | 704-367-1808 | www.toscana-ristorante.net

Evoking "a trattoria in a small Italian town", this "class act" from restaurateur Augusto Conte in SouthPark serves "dependable", "*delizioso*" pasta, meats and fish from the North Boot in "cozy quarters" and a "charming courtyard"; it's "not cheap", but a "terrific wine list", servers that "treat every table as family" and a generally "romantic" vibe make it "perfect" "for impressing dates."

	FOOD	DECOR	SERVICE	COST

Upstream *Seafood*   26 | 24 | 24 | $54

SouthPark | Phillips Pl. | 6902 Phillips Place Ct. (bet. Colony & Sharon Rds.) | 704-556-7730 | www.upstreamit.com

"Imaginative" "twists on fish" – including "succulent" sushi – are the stars of seasonal menus that "change faster than Clark Kent" at this "heavenly" SouthPark "seafood mecca"; a "fat wallet" is required, but it's "worth every penny", especially factoring in the "efficient service", the "upscale", "chic" decor and the "exciting bar" where "outstanding martinis" are the tipples of choice; P.S. the "steal" of a Sunday buffet brunch is "a particular treasure."

Zebra Restaurant & Wine Bar 🅩 *French*   25 | 23 | 23 | $58

SouthPark | 4521 Sharon Rd. (bet. Fairview Rd. & Morrison Blvd.) | 704-442-9525 | www.zebrarestaurant.net

"Innovation" hunters find it in chef-owner Jim Alexander's "artful", "delightful" New French fare at this "big splurge" in SouthPark (for "an incredible experience", try the "fabulous" tasting menu with pairings culled from the "awesome" 900-label wine list); the "intimate setting", festooned with "warm woods" and a zebra mural, is made doubly "inviting" by staffers who leave "no stone unturned to ensure you're satisfied"; FYI, open for breakfast, lunch and dinner.

Chicago

TOP FOOD RANKING

	Restaurant	Cuisine
29	Les Nomades	French
	Alinea	American
	Schwa	American
28	Arun's	Thai
	Topolobampo	Mexican
	Michael	French
	Tallgrass	French
	Tru	French
27	L2O	Seafood
	Blackbird	American
	Oceanique	French/Seafood
	Carlos'	French
	Naha	American
	Vie	American
	Charlie Trotter's	American
	mk	American
	Katsu	Japanese
	Spring	American/Seafood
	Everest	French
	sushi wabi	Japanese

OTHER NOTEWORTHY PLACES

Avec	Mediterranean
Avenues	American
Frontera Grill	Mexican
Gibsons	Steak
Green Zebra	Vegetarian
Hot Doug's	Hot Dogs
Joe's Sea/Steak/Crab	Seafood/Steak
Kith & Kin	American
Kuma's Corner	American
Lou Malnati's	Pizza
Lula Cafe	Eclectic
Mercat a la Planxa	Spanish
Morton's	Steak
NoMI	French
one sixtyblue	American
Publican	American
Shanghai Terrace	Asian
Spiaggia	Italian
Wildfire	Steak
XOCO	Mexican

	FOOD	DECOR	SERVICE	COST

Alinea ⓜ *American* `29` `27` `28` `$199`

Lincoln Park | 1723 N. Halsted St. (bet. North Ave. & Willow St.) | 312-867-0110 | www.alinearestaurant.com

"World-famous for its vision and creativity", "genius" Grant Achatz's "progressive" New American "gastronirvana" provides "amazing" "avant-garde food" in a "labor-intensive" multicourse "wild ride" that "incorporates all the senses" and includes cleverly "engineered" serving pieces ("acupuncture needles", "trapezes", "pillows", "branches", "rubber tablecloths"); *Get Smart* "automatic doors" give way to the "luxurious, minimalistic" Lincoln Park setting where a "professional" staff provides "personal" attention "with some humor", completing an "unforgettable", "shock-and-awe experience" – albeit a "fiscally challenging" one that's "not for the faint of culinary heart"; P.S. "if you can afford it", choose the "incredible wine pairings."

Arun's ⓜ *Thai* `28` `23` `27` `$96`

Northwest Side | 4156 N. Kedzie Ave. (bet. Irving Park Rd. & Montrose Ave.) | 773-539-1909 | www.arunsthai.com

"Who says Thai can't be upscale?" ask admirers of Arun Sampanthavivat's "unforgettable" Northwest Side jewel where a "top-notch" staff rolls out "exquisite" prix fixe meals composed of "unusual", "delicious little dishes" that "just keep on coming"; it's set in "simple" digs, although more than a few "wish they'd upgrade the space" to match the "splurge"-worthy prices.

avec ◑ *Mediterranean* `26` `21` `23` `$44`

West Loop | 615 W. Randolph St. (Jefferson St.) | 312-377-2002 | www.avecrestaurant.com

Blackbird's vino-focused "casual yet classy" next-door cafe is a West Loop "chef hangout" where surveyors say Koren Grieveson's "imaginative", "chef-driven" Mediterranean small plates and "gourmet charcuterie" feature "flavor combinations that make you rethink life"; while some who "wish the prices were as minimal as the portions" "could do without cuddling up to a stranger" in the "uncomfortable", "communal" setting reminiscent of a "Swedish sauna", "extroverts" "squeeze in and have a ball" with "wonderful wine experiences" prompted by "savvy servers."

Avenues ⓩⓜ *American* `26` `27` `27` `$102`

River North | Peninsula Hotel | 108 E. Superior St. (bet. Michigan Ave. & Rush St.) | 312-573-6754 | www.peninsula.com

Curtis Duffy's "superb, creative" New American "cuisine with artful design and surprising flavor combinations" meets "sublime service" in the "beautifully serene atmosphere" of the Peninsula Hotel's "formal" dining room at this "understated, elegant" River North "special-occasion" place; an "excellent view" featuring the historic Water Tower and "impressive wine list" add to an "experience" that's "simply stunning" and "tremendously expensive"; P.S. jackets are suggested.

Blackbird ⓩ *American* `27` `22` `25` `$66`

West Loop | 619 W. Randolph St. (bet. Desplaines & Jefferson Sts.) | 312-715-0708 | www.blackbirdrestaurant.com

The West Loop's "bold" "destination" "flagship of the [Paul] Kahan empire" flies an "outstanding", "ever-changing menu" from chef Mike

	FOOD	DECOR	SERVICE	COST

Sheerin that's "crafted in the finest tradition of New American" cuisine and coupled with an "unbelievable wine list" and "skillful service" in "sleek, stark" surroundings; while "priced for a special occasion", it delivers a vaunted "value-quality ratio" (wallet-watchers might "come for lunch"), and if the other "diners are so close you're practically wearing each other's clothes", the "high noise and energy level is part of the plan", so just "eat" and "talk later."

Carlos' *French*

27 | 26 | 27 | $92

Highland Park | 429 Temple Ave. (Waukegan Ave.) | 847-432-0770 | www.carlos-restaurant.com

"Still near the top of the charts" after some 30 years, Highland Park's New French "destination" offers "amazing, approachable gourmet" cuisine and an "incredible, if pricey, wine list" accompanied by service "with grace and a sense of humor"; the "conversation-friendly", "intimate space" adds to the feeling of "understated elegance" (jackets are required) and "you pay a premium", but it's "perfect" for even the "most special of occasions."

Charlie Trotter's 🖼 🅼 *American*

27 | 25 | 27 | $140

Lincoln Park | 816 W. Armitage Ave. (bet. Dayton & Halsted Sts.) | 773-248-6228 | www.charlietrotters.com

Regulars revere "the original celebrity chef's palace of haute cuisine" as the "pinnacle" of "precision", where a "memorable" "three-hour homage" to New American "gastronomic bliss" "showcases flavors in new intensities and sometimes surprising combinations" alongside selections from an "encyclopedic wine list"; "formal", "professional service" befits the "staid" Lincoln Park setting, and though some patrons are "put off" by "pretense" and "petite portions", the faithful insist "go at least once in your lifetime", especially if you can "find someone with an expense account."

Everest 🖼 🅼 *French*

27 | 27 | 27 | $106

Loop | One Financial Pl. | 440 S. LaSalle St., 40th fl. (Congress Pkwy.) | 312-663-8920 | www.everestrestaurant.com

"High expectations" (and "stratospheric prices") "reflect the name" of this Loop "special-occasion" French perched on the 40th floor of the Chicago Stock Exchange that surveyors hail as the "summit" for "sublime", "classic white-linen" dining on the "inventive menus" of Jean Joho; an "unbelievable" ("in size and price") "wine binder" with "excellent half-bottles" enhances an experience that's completed with "pomp", "formal" service and a "view that seems to stretch to Iowa"; P.S. jacket suggested.

Frontera Grill 🖼 🅼 *Mexican*

27 | 22 | 23 | $45

River North | 445 N. Clark St. (bet. Hubbard & Illinois Sts.) | 312-661-1434 | www.fronterakitchens.com

"Magnificent" Mexican cuisine from celebrity chef Rick Bayless is a "revelation" at this River North "temple", voted Chicago's Most Popular and touted for its "bold", "complex flavors" ("he won *Top Chef Masters* for a reason"), "drinks as spectacular as" the fare and "colorful decor" with "museum-quality artwork"; the "first-come, first-served" "crowds can be daunting, but it's worth the wait" to a "cultish following" that boasts "you have to believe Mexico is jealous" and calls the prices "totally reasonable"; P.S. "hint: sit at the bar for the same food but faster service."

Gibsons Bar & Steakhouse ● *Steak*　26 | 21 | 24 | $64
Gold Coast | 1028 N. Rush St. (Bellevue Pl.) | 312-266-8999
Rosemont | Doubletree O'Hare | 5464 N. River Rd. (bet. Balmoral & Bryn Mawr Aves.) | 847-928-9900
www.gibsonssteakhouse.com
"Waiters show you the slabs before they're cooked" at these "brash" city and suburban "speakeasy-styled steakhouses" serving "big", "succulent" steaks, "big side dishes" and "big desserts" at "big prices"; the "professional service" is "terrific" and "they pour a righteous drink", while the "people-watching" is peppered with "celebrities", "pro athletes", "cougars and sugar daddies" (especially in the "piano bar"), and if the Rosemont offshoot is "not quite the same" as the "Rush Street cornerstone", on the plus side it's also open till midnight most nights.

Green Zebra *Vegetarian*　26 | 23 | 24 | $53
West Town | 1460 W. Chicago Ave. (Greenview Ave.) | 312-243-7100 |
www.greenzebrachicago.com
"No one will miss the meat" with the "best vegetarian dining in Chicago" at Shawn McClain's "brilliant" West Town "innovator" where the "high-end", "creative, edgy" small plates are "almost totally veggie" and boast "plenty of flavors, a variety of influences" and "seasonal ingredients"; specialty "libations", "excellent brunch" and a "lovely staff" complete the "satisfying" supping in this "soothing", "subdued" sage-colored modern setting.

Hot Doug's 🗷🗟 *Hot Dogs*　27 | 13 | 20 | $12
Northwest Side | 3324 N. California Ave. (Roscoe St.) | 773-279-9550 |
www.hotdougs.com
"Believe what you read" woof hot-dog hounds hooked on the "mind-boggling" "gourmet" "encased meat" and "amazing fries" (sometimes "fried in duck fat") at this Northwest Sider dispensing everything from the "classic" Chicago-style to "adventures in sausageology" including specials such as spicy alligator; "Doug [Sohn] is a mini-celebrity who still mans" the cash-only counter "with a smile", and though "lines are incredibly long" at this colorful space with Elvis memorabilia and outdoor seating, "they keep it moving" and "it's worth the wait"; P.S. open till 4 PM.

Joe's Seafood,　26 | 22 | 25 | $64
Prime Steak & Stone Crab *Seafood/Steak*
River North | 60 E. Grand Ave. (Rush St.) | 312-379-5637 | www.joes.net
Surveyors "look forward to" meals at Lettuce Entertain You's "sophisticated", "supper club"-like River Norther that emulates the "famous" "Miami original" by serving "extra-fresh seafood in traditional and contemporary dishes" (of course, "stone crabs are the showstopper", even if they're "frozen" when "out of season") but also "outstanding steaks" and "Key lime pie for dessert"; "spot-on service" is "well trained" to handle "families and businessmen alike", and "it's jumping every night" due to "large crowds", the "high density of tables" and the "busy bar" - all in all, "a real treat and worth every wildly expensive penny."

	FOOD	DECOR	SERVICE	COST

Katsu Japanese Ⓜ *Japanese* | 27 | 16 | 23 | $52 |

Northwest Side | 2651 W. Peterson Ave. (bet. Talman & Washtenaw Aves.) | 773-784-3383

Fish fanatics "skip the tony and more-publicized sushi boutiques and head" to the Northwest Side's "hidden gem", the "best Japanese restaurant in Chicago" where "caring owners" offer the "freshest", "most delectable" seafood and "traditional" hot fare that's "often exquisite", accompanied by "attentive service" and an "excellent sake selection" in a "conversation-friendly", "elegant, traditional" atmosphere; cost is also "top of the line" but most maintain it's "worth the money."

Kith & Kin ◑ *American* | - | - | - | E |

Lincoln Park | 1119 W. Webster Ave. (bet. Clifton & Seminary Aves.) | 773-472-7070 | www.kithandkinchicago.com

Cognoscenti concur this Lincoln Park New American "neighborhood find" "is going to go far" thanks to "outstanding" cuisine from Grant Achatz protégé David Carrier that's "reasonably priced" given the "high quality"; "attentive" "servers are quite knowledgeable", and the space has a clean, "casual" feel with a tin ceiling and a working fireplace.

Kuma's Corner ◑ *American* | 26 | 15 | 17 | $20 |

Logan Square | 2900 W. Belmont Ave. (Francisco Ave.) | 773-604-8769 | www.kumascorner.com

You'll find "about the best" "mind-blowing" burgers in Chicago (and a mac 'n' cheese that some call the real "star") at this Logan Square "heavy metal bar – really!" where the staff is "as friendly as it is tattooed" and "body-pierced", and the "rock-star atmosphere" includes "way too loud" music and "crazy", "long lines"; luckily, the "tables turn quickly", and in summer, you can "sit outside" and escape the noise.

Les Nomades Ⓢ Ⓜ *French* | 29 | 27 | 28 | $113 |

Streeterville | 222 E. Ontario St. (bet. Fairbanks Ct. & St. Clair St.) | 312-649-9010 | www.lesnomades.net

"One of the last bastions of haute cuisine", the No. 1 for Food in Chicago is Streeterville's French "crème de la crème" of "very formal" "fine dining", where chef Chris Nugent's "sophisticated", "beautifully prepared and presented" fare "is en pointe" as is the "extremely attentive service" and "remarkable", "francocentric" wine selection; the "quietly elegant", "clubby townhouse" ("once a private dining club") is a "place out of time and space" with "white linens", an "upstairs fireplace" and "gorgeous flowers", and though it's "*très pricey*", it's "perfect for a special, romantic occasion."

Lou Malnati's Pizzeria *Pizza* | 24 | 14 | 19 | $21 |

River North | 439 N. Wells St. (Hubbard St.) | 312-828-9800
Lincoln Park | 958 W. Wrightwood Ave. (Lincoln Ave.) | 773-832-4030
Southwest Side | 3859 W. Ogden Ave. (Cermak Rd.) | 773-762-0800
Evanston | 1850 Sherman Ave. (University Pl.) | 847-328-5400
Lincolnwood | 6649 N. Lincoln Ave. (bet. Devon & Pratt Aves.) | 847-673-0800
Buffalo Grove | 85 S. Buffalo Grove Rd. (Lake Cook Rd.) | 847-215-7100
Elk Grove Village | 1050 E. Higgins Rd. (bet. Arlington Heights & Busse Rds.) | 847-439-2000
Schaumburg | 1 S. Roselle Rd. (Schaumburg Rd.) | 847-985-1525

(continued)

(continued)

Lou Malnati's Pizzeria

Naperville | 131 W. Jefferson Ave. (bet. Main & Webster Sts.) | 630-717-0700
Naperville | 2879 W. 95th St. (Rte. 59) | 630-904-4222 ●▣
www.loumalnatis.com
Additional locations throughout the Chicago area

Legions of loyalists swear by these "deep-dish joints" where the "authentic", "home-grown" Chicago-style pizzas are built with "the right amount of everything" including a "flaky", "buttery crust" and "quality ingredients"; just know that service and surroundings vary by location, the latter from "classic" to "sports bar" to "minimal", and the pies are "cooked to order" so you may have to "wait"; P.S. for "yearners" who "live far away", "life will never be the same" since most surveyors say the "in-restaurant" version outshines the "frozen", "shipped" option.

L2O *Seafood*

27 | 28 | 27 | $142

Lincoln Park | Belden-Stratford Hotel | 2300 N. Lincoln Park W. (Belden Ave.) | 773-868-0002 | www.l2orestaurant.com

It's "nothing but superlatives" for "Chicago's finest seafooder", Lincoln Park's "inventive, seductive" "artistic triumph" from restaurateurs Lettuce Entertain You and chef Laurent Gras, featuring "amazing taste sensations" and "surprising techniques" (there's no shortage of "powders and foam"); add "eye-popping" decor that's "smart and modern without formality" and "scrupulous" service, and it amounts to a "truly divine" "escape from everyday life", especially if you "have the wine pairings" and "don't look at the tab"; P.S. gentlemen, "jackets are preferred."

Lula Cafe *Eclectic*

26 | 19 | 21 | $31

Logan Square | 2537-41 N. Kedzie Blvd. (bet. Fullerton Ave. & Logan Blvd.) | 773-489-9554 | www.lulacafe.com

Logan Square's "semi-secret" "neighborhood gem" confers "creative, market-driven" Eclectic dishes "with fresh, local organic ingredients" for breakfast, lunch and dinner in an "unpretentious", "arty environment" with a "quirky staff" that "adds to the milieu"; there are no reservations, so you may encounter a "long wait."

Mercat a la Planxa *Spanish*

26 | 24 | 22 | $53

South Loop | Blackstone Hotel | 638 S. Michigan Ave. (Balbo Ave.) | 312-765-0524 | www.mercatchicago.com

"Upbeat and swank", this "soaring space" "reminiscent of Barcelona" revitalizes the "former ballroom" of the South Loop's historic Blackstone Hotel thanks to Jose Garces' "dizzying array" of "adventurous" Catalan tapas (a "cut above the usual" in both "selection and price") and entrees including "roast pig for a large group"; "gracious service", "outstanding" wine selections and "unusual sangrias" please patrons who praise the "beautiful", "Gaudí"-esque setting with a "busy bar scene" and an "amazing view" of Grant Park.

Michael Ⓜ *French*

28 | 23 | 27 | $67

Winnetka | 64 Green Bay Rd. (Fisher Ln.) | 847-441-3100 | www.restaurantmichael.com

Namesake chef and "personality" Michael Lachowicz is "always there, interacting with his guests" at this Winnetka "winner" where his "exceptional", "delicate and flavorful" New French fare with "spot-on wine

| | FOOD | DECOR | SERVICE | COST |

pairings" is served in an "elegant but casual", "conversation-friendly" room by a staff that "works well together"; it's admittedly "pricey", but "worthwhile for celebrating, relaxing or rewarding a good client."

mk *American* 27 | 24 | 26 | $72

Near North | 868 N. Franklin St. (bet. Chestnut & Locust Sts.) | 312-482-9179 | www.mkchicago.com
It's continuing "kudos" for Michael Kornick's "classy", "happening" Near North haunt that's "stood the test of time" and still "shines" with "honest", "outstanding", "seasonal" New American cuisine "minus the fussiness"; expect "knockout desserts", a "stellar wine list" and "excellent service all around" in the "spare", "urban-cool", "renovated warehouse" space – in other words, it "meets high expectations" "from start to finish."

Morton's The Steakhouse *Steak* 26 | 22 | 25 | $70

Loop | 65 E. Wacker Pl. (bet. Michigan & Wabash Aves.) | 312-201-0410
Gold Coast | Newberry Plaza | 1050 N. State St. (Maple St.) | 312-266-4820
Rosemont | 9525 Bryn Mawr Ave. (River Rd.) | 847-678-5155
Northbrook | 699 Skokie Blvd. (Dundee Rd.) | 847-205-5111
Schaumburg | 1470 McConnor Pkwy. (bet. Golf & Meacham Rds.) | 847-413-8771
Naperville | 1751 Freedom Dr. (Diehl Rd.) | 630-577-1372
www.mortons.com
Carnivores who crown the late Arnie Morton's "old-school" "class act" the "king of the national steakhouse chains" say they're "incredibly consistent" for "fabulous", "prime" "aged beef Chicago-style"; the "ridiculous prices" are offset by "insane amounts of food", a solid wine cellar and "elaborately staged demonstrations" from a staff that "knows how to read the customer", plus the "masculine spaces – especially at the "original", "clubby" State Street basement – are "classic" "business" settings.

Naha ⊠ *American* 27 | 24 | 25 | $64

River North | 500 N. Clark St. (Illinois St.) | 312-321-6242 | www.naha-chicago.com
Locals find "the total package" at this "upscale" River North New American where chef Carrie Nahabedian serves up "perfection on a plate" with a "world-class" yet "accessible" fusion of "contemporary styling" and "organic produce" at its "absolute peak"; beyond that, there's a staff that "anticipates your needs" and a "refined atmosphere" in a "cool, modern" space, so even those bothered by the "noise" "get over it" given the "spectacular" value.

NoMI *French* 27 | 28 | 26 | $75

Gold Coast | Park Hyatt Chicago | 800 N. Michigan Ave. (Chicago Ave.) | 312-239-4030 | www.nomirestaurant.com
This "romantic" Gold Coast "fine-dining" destination is "first class all the way"; each item on "amazing chef" Christophe David's New French menu is "a work of art", the "wine list is excellent", "service is beautifully executed" and the "gorgeous", "sophisticated" setting includes a "cool" rooftop deck in summer, but the "million-dollar" Mag Mile view comes with a tab that makes it best for a "memorable" "splurge"; P.S. there's a sushi station and a "to-die-for" brunch that some say is even "better than dinner."

	FOOD	DECOR	SERVICE	COST

Oceanique ⌧ *French/Seafood*

| 27 | 22 | 27 | $63 |

Evanston | 505 Main St. (bet. Chicago & Hinman Aves.) | 847-864-3435 | www.oceanique.com

Mark Grosz's "memorable", "magnifique" Evanston eatery offers some of the "best seafood in the city", serving "superb new fusion and old-school dishes" with "unique" "combinations of French and Asian flavors" along with a "fantastic wine list"; the "fancy", "formal" setting and "top-notch service" further elevate the experience (and the prices), but "you get what you pay for" – though you can pay less at the weeknight prix fixe.

one sixtyblue ⌧ *American*

| 26 | 24 | 25 | $66 |

West Loop | 1400 W. Randolph St. (Ogden Ave.) | 312-850-0303 | www.onesixtyblue.com

Fans of this "first-class" West Loop "favorite", owned in part by former basketball star Michael Jordan, cite chef Michael McDonald's "exceptional" and "unique" New American dishes, the "expansive wine list" and the "helpful, but not intrusive, service", deeming it "modern-chic but warm", "gourmet but comfortable" and "tucked-away but accessible"; sure, it's also "pricey", so look for "bargains on various nights"; P.S. perfect for "dinner on the way to United Center."

Publican, The *American*

| 25 | 20 | 22 | $47 |

West Loop | 837 W. Fulton Mkt. (Green St.) | 312-733-9555 | www.thepublicanrestaurant.com

Those who "do swine and brew totally dig" this "unique" West Loop "pork paradise" "from the team that brought us avec and Blackbird", an "offal good place" that "caters to the well-heeled hipster" willing to "get out of the comfort zone and try something new" from a "wonderfully innovative" New American pub menu paired with an "extensive" "beer selection like no other"; be prepared for a "loud atmosphere" with "European flair" in the farmhouse-style setting with "communal tables" (or "swinging-door pens" "for more privacy"), and know that the "knowledgeable staff" is "overwhelmed at times."

Schwa ⌧Ⓜ *American*

| 29 | 15 | 25 | $105 |

Wicker Park | 1466 N. Ashland Ave. (Le Moyne St.) | 773-252-1466 | www.schwarestaurant.com

Zealots call Michael Carlson a "god among men" for his "fascinating" New American cuisine with "bright, surprising flavors" and a "side of wit"; the prix fixe menu is "served by the chefs", adding to an "unforgettable" experience that unfolds in a "relaxed", "small" Wicker Park BYO storefront; though it's "not inexpensive", fans contend it offers a "wonderful value", and if a few gripe that this "quirky" place comes off as "too complicated for its good", the fact that you must "persevere" to "secure a reservation" proves they're outvoted.

Shanghai Terrace ⌧ *Asian*

| 25 | 28 | 27 | $66 |

River North | Peninsula Hotel | 108 E. Superior St., 5th fl. (bet. Michigan Ave. & Rush St.) | 312-573-6744 | www.chicago.peninsula.com

A "stunning", '30s-style Asian supper club setting sets the stage at this expensive, "elegant" and "tranquil" respite in the Peninsula Hotel in River North, where acolytes claim they've had some of the "best Chinese meals outside of China"; "wonderful" Michigan Avenue views from the "outdoor terrace" in summer add to the appeal, as does "knowledgeable" service, though the less-smitten are "disappointed" that the former "chef is gone"; N.B. hours vary by season.

Spiaggia *Italian*
27 | 27 | 27 | $93

Gold Coast | One Magnificent Mile Bldg. | 980 N. Michigan Ave., 2nd fl. (Oak St.) | 312-280-2750 | www.spiaggiarestaurant.com

"It may be cheaper to fly to Rome" than to dine at Tony Mantuano's Gold Coast "destination", but surveyors succumb to the "breathtaking" cheese selection, "delicate, handmade pastas", "velvety sauces" and entrees that "sing your name" matched by a "superb", "extensive Italian wine list"; the "quiet", "elegant", "multilevel" dining room offering "exquisite views of the lake" – alone "an experience" – has "attentive" yet "unobtrusive" service, but "as astounding as it is", some favor the less "formal" "cafe next door"; N.B. jackets are required.

Spring 🅜 *American/Seafood*
27 | 24 | 26 | $59

Wicker Park | 2039 W. North Ave. (Damen Ave.) | 773-395-7100 | www.springrestaurant.net

Acolytes attest "it's criminal that they make you choose" since all the fare is "superb" at Shawn McClain's "serene, spare" Asian-tinged New American seafooder in a converted Wicker Park bathhouse, where the fish is so "divine" "there's no reason to get anything else", though the "creative" menu proves "all-around satisfying" with "fabulous cocktails" and an "awesome" "wine list to match"; the "elegant" minimalist setting "allows for privacy" and the service is "outstanding", adding up to an "absolutely wonderful", "unique experience" surveyors call "reasonably priced" for the "quality."

sushi wabi *Japanese*
27 | 18 | 20 | $44

West Loop | 842 W. Randolph St. (bet. Green & Peoria Sts.) | 312-563-1224 | www.sushiwabi.com

"Sushi snobs" regard this modern West Loop Japanese as "one of the best" spots to "belly up" for "inventive" maki ("it's like buttah"); just "plan to spend a few bucks", and keep in mind that "service lacks often" and tables in the "industrial"-looking setting afford little "privacy from your neighbors" – most notably during "prime time" when it's "crowded" and "high-energy (translate: loud)."

Tallgrass 🅜 *French*
28 | 23 | 24 | $74

Lockport | 1006 S. State St. (10th St.) | 815-838-5566 | www.tallgrassrestaurant.com

It's "well worth the drive from Downtown" gush groupies of this "relaxed", "romantic" French in a "beautiful" vintage building, where "decades of culinary experience" "shows" in the modern prix fixe–only menu; it's "still a value" after all these years, with a "knowledgeable" staff and "fantastic" wine list that's "extremely fairly" priced sealing its status as a "special night out" in the Southwest Suburbs; P.S. jackets are suggested.

Topolobampo 🅢🅜 *Mexican*
28 | 24 | 26 | $68

River North | 445 N. Clark St. (bet. Hubbard & Illinois Sts.) | 312-661-1434 | www.rickbayless.com

"Converts" call Rick Bayless' "modern", "refined" River North standout "the best" "gourmet Mexican" "in the country", declaring the "remarkable" "regional" flavors "expensive but worth it"; the art-adorned, "white-tablecloth" setting – plus the "fine wine service" and a "skilled", "professional" staff – makes patrons "forget" preconceptions about "south-of-the-border" cuisine (just be sure to reserve "long in advance"); P.S. "value"-hunters might try the chef's "casual Frontera Grill" next door or grab a torta from nearby XOCO.

Tru 🗷 *French* | 28 | 27 | 28 | $130 |

Streeterville | 676 N. St. Clair St. (bet. Erie & Huron Sts.) | 312-202-0001 | www.trurestaurant.com

Streeterville's jacket-required, "world-class" New French from Rick Tramonto and Gale Gand stays "true to its reputation" with "flawless" "super-luxury" tastings and famed, "expense account"–required "crystal steps of caviar"; while perhaps "a little stuffy", this "adult-only" go-to for "anniversaries" and "special occasions" is capped by a "wonderful wine selection", "serene", art-adorned dining room and "extraordinary" service that resembles "heaven on earth."

Vie 🗷 *American* | 27 | 25 | 28 | $68 |

Western Springs | 4471 Lawn Ave. (Burlington Ave.) | 708-246-2082 | www.vierestaurant.com

Locavores "drive from the city" and beyond to Paul Virant's "deservedly respected" New American "haven" in Western Springs, where "magical" dishes are crafted using "simple", "sustainable" ingredients (including house-"pickled garnishes" and "great charcuterie"); the "lovely" 1940s-era, French-inspired interior, the "wonderful" service and the high prices – though "lower than Downtown" – place it in the "special-occasion category", but admirers could "eat [here] every day."

Wildfire *Steak* | 23 | 21 | 21 | $43 |

River North | 159 W. Erie St. (bet. LaSalle Blvd. & Wells St.) | 312-787-9000
Lincolnshire | 235 Parkway Dr. (Milwaukee Ave.) | 847-279-7900
Glenview | 1300 Patriot Blvd. (Lake Ave.) | 847-657-6363
Schaumburg | 1250 E. Higgins Rd. (National Pkwy.) | 847-995-0100
Oak Brook | Oakbrook Center Mall | 232 Oakbrook Ctr. (Rte. 83) | 630-586-9000
www.wildfirerestaurant.com

"Consistent" from "location to location", these "always packed" River North and suburban steakhouses from the Lettuce Entertain You group have a "broad", if pricey, menu of "superb" wood-grilled meat ("love the trio of filets"), "solid sides" and "excellent seafood" – all in "huge portions"; still, the sometimes "mediocre service", "unpleasantly noisy" environs and "clubby", "1940s"-ish decor make it feel a bit "like a chain" for some; P.S. "reservations are a must."

XOCO 🗷🅼 *Mexican* | 25 | 16 | 18 | $20 |

River North | 449 N. Clark St. (Illinois St.) | 312-334-3688 | www.xocochicago.com

Master Chef Rick Bayless' LEED-certified "counter-service"-meets-"haute"-style River North Mexican cultivates *pasión* among "street food" enthusiasts, who brave the "cosmic waits" for "outstanding" tortas ("especially any with pork"), "giant bowls of caldos", "addictive churros" and cacao bean-to-cup hot chocolate; "what it lacks in comfort" – an "odd" ordering protocol, "cramped", communal seating – is forgiven once the "awe-inspiring" eats arrive, hot from a wood-burning oven.

Cincinnati

TOP FOOD RANKING

	Restaurant	Cuisine
__28__	Boca	Italian
	Nicola's	Italian
__27__	Daveed's	Eclectic
	Jeff Ruby's Precinct	Steak
	Orchids	American
	BonBonerie	Bakery/Tearoom
__26__	Palace	American
	Jeff Ruby's Steakhouse	Steak
	Jeff Ruby's Carlo & Johnny	Seafood/Steak
	Cumin	Eclectic

OTHER NOTEWORTHY PLACES

Brown Dog Cafe	American
Chalk Food + Wine	American
China Gourmet	Chinese
Dewey's	Pizza
Montgomery Inn	BBQ
Morton's	Steak
Nada	Mexican
Palomino	American/Mediterranean
Trio	American
Via Vite	Italian

Boca ⧈Ⓜ *Italian* | 28 | 25 | 26 | $67 |

Oakley | 3200 Madison Rd. (bet. Brazee St. & Ridge Rd.) | 513-542-2022 | www.boca-restaurant.com

"Seemingly simple dishes" soar thanks to chef/co-owner David Falk's "inventive" takes on "seasonal" ingredients at this "high-energy" Oakley Italian, voted No. 1 for Food and the Most Popular restaurant in the Cincinnati area; set in a "casual but upscale" space and featuring an "outstanding wine list", it's a "splurge" for sure, but most maintain it's "amazing", and the "impeccable" staff is the "frosting on the cake."

BonBonerie *Bakery/Tearoom* | 27 | 19 | 20 | $16 |

O'Bryonville | 2030 Madison Rd. (bet. O'Bryan & Cinnamon Sts.) | 513-321-3399 | www.thebonbon.com

It's "all about dessert" at this "lovely" O'Bryonville bakery, where the "palate-perfect" confections include an "opera cream cake that hits every high note"; then again, a "recent cafe addition" with a midpriced selection of "soup, sandwiches and quiche" ensures that the "ladies who lunch" don't go hungry, plus it's a "fun place for a mother-daughter tea."

Brown Dog Cafe ⧈ *American* | 25 | 17 | 23 | $40 |

Blue Ash | Pfeiffer Commons | 5893 Pfeiffer Rd. (bet. I-71 & Kenwood Rd.) | 513-794-1610 | www.browndogcafe.com

"Don't let let the strip-mall location fool you" – chef-owner Shawn McCoy's "relaxed" Blue Ash "surprise" offers a "wonderfully creative"

New American menu flush with "healthy options and various game dishes" that provide a "constant source of culinary inspiration" (with service to match); sure, the "small" space is "nothing to write home about" and some consider tabs a tad "expensive", but it's a "comeback place for foodies" nonetheless.

Chalk Food + Wine ☒ *American*   23 | 21 | 21 | $37

Covington | 318 Greenup St. (bet. E. 3rd St. & Park Pl.) | 859-643-1234 | chalkfoodwine.com

"What's not to like?" ponder partisans of this "reasonably priced" Covington American where "up-and-coming" chef Mark Bodenstein's seasonal menu is "always changing", so there's "always something adventurous to try"; it's lodged in a "quirky" century-old building with a "terrific bar", and though service gets mixed marks ("attentive" vs. a bit of "attitude"), most maintain it's a "gem worth looking for."

China Gourmet ☒ *Chinese*   23 | 19 | 24 | $34

Hyde Park | 3340 Erie Ave. (Marburg Ave.) | 513-871-6612 | www.thechinagourmet.com

Members of the Moy family "attend to every customer" at their "premier" Hyde Park Chinese, a "friendly" "favorite" praised for its "fresh ingredients, inventive preparations" ("can't beat the whole fresh fish") and willingness to "customize any menu item"; while the "upscale" ambiance is reflected in "pricey" tabs, "fervent fans" insist that with this "winner" in town, it's ok to "forget the chains."

Cumin ☒ *Eclectic*   26 | 24 | 24 | $41

Hyde Park | 3520 Erie Ave. (Pinehurst Ave.) | 513-871-8714 | www.cuminrestaurant.com

The "fusion fare gets better every year" at this "change-of-pace" Hyde Park Eclectic, where the "snappy decor sets the tone" for "imaginative" chef Owen Maass' "unique" dishes tinged with "Indian flavors"; add in a "fantastic" staff that treats you "like family", a lovely patio and a selection of "up-and-coming wines", and you may wonder "am I actually in Cincinnati?"

Daveed's at 934 ☒ Ⓜ *Eclectic*   27 | 22 | 26 | $61

Mt. Adams | 934 Hatch St. (St. Gregory St.) | 513-721-2665 | www.daveeds.net

"Nestled" atop Mt. Adams, this "French-inspired" Eclectic has "no view", but chef/co-owner David Cook's "fresh, creative seasonal cooking" infused with "unusual ingredients" gives patrons plenty to admire nonetheless – including duck breast that'll have you "licking your plate"; "unparalleled service" from a "knowledgable" staff and a "bright, arty" space sweeten the deal, making it a "favorite celebration spot" or a "place to impress a date."

Dewey's Pizza *Pizza*   24 | 17 | 21 | $19

Clifton | 265 Hosea Ave. (Clifton Ave.) | 513-221-0400
Oakley | Oakley Sq. | 3014 Madison Rd. (Markbreit Ave.) | 513-731-7755
Crestview Hills | Crestview Hills Town Ctr. | 2949 Dixie Hwy. (Rosemont Dr.) | 859-341-2555
Newport | Newport on the Levee | 1 Levee Way (Monmouth St.) | 859-431-9700
Kenwood | 7767 Kenwood Rd. (Montgomery Rd.) | 513-791-1616

(continued)

Dewey's Pizza

Symmes | Shops at Harper's Point | 11338 Montgomery Rd.
(bet. E. Kemper Rd. & Harper Point Dr.) | 513-247-9955
West Chester | 7663 Cox Ln. (University Dr.) | 513-759-6777
www.deweyspizza.com

For "pizza the way it should be" – i.e. a "just-thick-enough crust"
topped with "piquant sauce" and a "robust selection of toppings" –
pie-seekers pack into this local chain where even the "house salads
are delicious"; true, the "generic" digs can get "stupidly loud", but
"solid" service and a "family-friendly" vibe (kids "watch the dough being tossed" while adults quaff "craft beers") offer ample compensa-
tion for those who "love" the place.

Jeff Ruby's Carlo & Johnny ⊠ *Seafood/Steak*

| 26 | 25 | 24 | $63 |

Montgomery | 9769 Montgomery Rd. (Remington Rd.) | 513-936-8600 |
www.jeffruby.com

"Oh, those steaks" sigh carnivores sated by the "high-quality" main
attraction at this Montgomery "special-occasion restaurant" where
waiters who "know what they're doing" also serve up "excellent" seafood and "great sides" you can "share"; the "1930s motif" and "refined, comfortable" setting in a "historic mansion" give it the feel of
"Capone's old Chicago", while 21st-century prices have some sug-
gesting an "unlimited expense account" comes in handy here.

Jeff Ruby's Precinct *Steak*

| 27 | 22 | 26 | $61 |

Columbia Tusculum | 311 Delta Ave. (Columbia Pkwy.) | 513-321-5454 |
www.jeffruby.com

Insiders insist it'd be a crime to skip Jeff Ruby's "always-busy" chophouse, a "clubby" Columbia Tusculum "institution" housed in an "old
brick police station" with a lineup of "melt-in-your-mouth" steaks and
seafood options; it's "not cheap" and "you have to like close-set tables", but the "attentive" staff "makes you feel special", and the "huge
portions" ensure you'll leave "full"; P.S. jacket suggested.

Jeff Ruby's Steakhouse ⊠ *Steak*

| 26 | 25 | 26 | $64 |

Downtown | 700 Walnut St. (7th St.) | 513-784-1200 | www.jeffruby.com

"Mouthwatering" steaks "sized for a linebacker", "excellent (but rich)
sides" and an "extensive wine list" headline a "great menu" at this
"over-the-top" Downtown "favorite" with a "super-masculine atmosphere", "terrific live music" and "see-and-be-seen" clientele; even if
"inviting" service makes it "less uptight" than some of its peers, you'll
still "dine lavishly", so take note: it's "not a place for dieters or those
with a thin wallet."

Montgomery Inn *BBQ*

| 22 | 19 | 21 | $33 |

Downtown | 925 Riverside Dr. (Eggleston Ave.) | 513-721-7427
Ft. Mitchell | 400 Buttermilk Pike (I-75) | 859-344-5333
Montgomery | 9440 Montgomery Rd. (bet. Cooper & Remington Rds.) |
513-791-3482
www.montgomeryinn.com

"Come for the ribs, stay for everything else" at these Cincy 'cue "classics" where the "irresistible" babybacks "can't be contained on one
plate" and vets ask for "extra BBQ sauce" (and "buy it by the case");
whether you visit Downtown's Boathouse branch with its "spectacu-

lar" river view, the Montgomery "mother ship" packed with "local sports memorabilia" or the newer Ft. Mitchell outpost, expect "friendly" – and efficient – staffers who "herd 'em in, feed 'em up, head 'em out."

Morton's The Steakhouse *Steak* | 25 | 24 | 26 | $67 |

Downtown | Carew Tower | 441 Vine St. (5th St.) | 513-621-3111 | www.mortons.com

For everything from "business dinners" to "celebrations", Downtowners descend upon this Carew Tower Arcade link of the "consistent" chain, whose "impeccable" staff delivers "perfectly aged and cooked" steaks and "excellent" seafood along with "ridiculously portioned side dishes"; though a few naysayers balk at "pricey" tabs ("go on someone's expense account") and detect a "corporate vibe", they're outvoted by those who declare they "will return."

Nada *Mexican* | 24 | 24 | 22 | $34 |

Downtown | 600 Walnut St. (6th St.) | 513-721-6232 | www.eatdrinknada.com

Downtowners who "want some spice in their lives" flock to Boca owner David Falk's "cool, modern" Mexican, which serves "upscale takes on traditional dishes" (the "fish tacos are a must") to a "young, lively crowd"; "fantastic cocktails", "skilled" staffers and a primo location "next to the Aronoff" are other reasons it gets "crazy busy", and though a few grouse it "doesn't live up to the hype", most maintain that's nada concern.

Nicola's 🅢 *Italian* | 28 | 23 | 26 | $59 |

Downtown | 1420 Sycamore St. (Liberty St.) | 513-721-6200 | www.nicolasrestaurant.com

"Even the bread basket is a work of art" at this "real-deal" Northern Italian, a "treasure" north of Downtown spotlighting "inventive" chef Joel Malloy's "tempting" menu of "sublime" Tuscan fare – including "amazing housemade pastas" – and an "extensive, varied" wine list; it's a bit "off the beaten track" in a "changing neighborhood" (and "expensive" to boot), but the "warm" service and "romantic" vibe may have you vowing to "never go to chains again."

Orchids at Palm Court *American* | 27 | 28 | 25 | $54 |

Downtown | Hilton Cincinnati Netherland Plaza | 35 W. Fifth St. (Race St.) | 513-421-9100 | www.orchidsatpalmcourt.com

The "room is worth the price of dinner" declare enthusiasts enchanted by this "art deco wonderland" in Downtown's "historic" Hilton Netherland Plaza, where "wonderful" chef Todd Kelly's cooking lives up to the "grandeur of the spectacular space" – prepare to be "totally blown away" by New American dishes like a "food-gasmic lobster salad"; add in "top-flight" service and a "wine list to match", and you're in for an "experience to be savored."

Palace, The *American* | 26 | 24 | 26 | $62 |

Downtown | Cincinnatian Hotel | 601 Vine St. (6th St.) | 513-381-6006 | www.palacecincinnati.com

Expect "over-the-top everything" at this "stellar" New American nestled in a "beautiful" Downtown hotel, from the "personable" service and "plush" space – think white tablecloths and dark wood – to the "scrumptious" fare that "hits the high notes flawlessly" (e.g. "to-die-for Dover sole"); naturally, the "upscale" atmosphere is reflected in the prices, but wallet-watchers note that the prix fixe menu is a "nice option"; P.S. there's live jazz Fridays and Saturdays.

Palomino *American/Mediterranean* `22` `22` `21` `$37`

Downtown | Fountain Pl. | 505 Vine St. (5th St.) | 513-381-1300 | www.palomino.com

"Get a table overlooking Fountain Square" (with its "stretch limos, prom-goers and buggy riders") and you're likely to agree that this "happening" Downtown New American–Med "doesn't feel like a chain at all", and the "dependable" menu with "something for everyone" and "proficient service" certainly don't hurt; a "fabulous" all-day happy hour and "kid-friendly" vibe seal the deal.

Trio *American* `23` `19` `22` `$37`

Kenwood | 7565 Kenwood Rd. (Orchard Ln.) | 513-984-1905 | www.triobistro.com

There's "always something new on the menu" at this "busy, dependable" New American serving up everything from "pizza to fancy items" – e.g. filet mignon and "wonderful" fish – in a "clubby atmosphere"; if some snarl it's "short on character" and a bit "pricey", "seamless service" ensures "repeat visits"; P.S. its location across from Kenwood Towne Centre means there's "plenty of parking."

Via Vite *Italian* `24` `24` `22` `$38`

Downtown | Fountain Sq. | 524 Vine St. (5th St.) | 513-721-8483 | www.viaviterestaurant.com

"Order anything with Bolognese sauce" at this "little sister of Nicola's", an "always-packed" Downtown trattoria in the "middle of Fountain Square" where chef Cristian Pietoso's "modern Italian food" (and the equally "modern decor") attracts a "young", "fashionable" crowd; a "fabulous rooftop bar" and "wonderful" service provide further enticement, even if it can all get a "bit pricey", "loud" and "cramped"; P.S. there's a late-night menu.

Cleveland

TOP FOOD RANKING

	Restaurant	Cuisine
29	Chez François	French
28	Johnny's Bar	Italian
	Parallax	Eclectic/Seafood
	Lola	American
	Crop	American
	Downtown 140	American
	Red The Steakhouse	Steak
27	Dante	American
	Flying Fig	American/Eclectic
	L'Albatros	French

OTHER NOTEWORTHY PLACES

Blue Point	Seafood
Chinato	Italian
Fahrenheit	American
Fire Food & Drink	American
Greenhouse Tavern	American
Lolita	American/Mediterranean
Luxe Kitchen	Mediterranean
Momocho	Mexican
Sérgio's	Eclectic
Three Birds	American

Blue Point Grille *Seafood*   `27` `25` `25` `$48`

Warehouse District | 700 W. St. Clair Ave. (6th St.) | 216-875-7827 | www.hrcleveland.com

Expect "no surprises" at this "elegant" Warehouse District anchor, only "consistently excellent" seafood "so fresh you can almost hear the waves", plus "high-quality" servers who whisk it to tables; it's "not cheap" and the slightly "corporate" feel makes it "good for grown-ups talking rate of return" (read: "business meals"), but most everyone "remembers the experience for a long time" – especially if they "sit downstairs and enjoy the view" through the floor-to-ceiling windows.

Chez François Ⓜ *French*   `29` `27` `28` `$66`

Vermilion | 555 Main St. (Liberty Ave.) | 440-967-0630 | www.chezfrancois.com

"Isn't it great to be spoiled?" swoon surveyors smitten with this "out-standing" French restaurant "hidden on the banks of the Vermilion River", where the "classic" cuisine steeped in "fresh Ohio products" ("almost everything on the menu is rich") earns it the No. 1 Food rating in the Cleveland area; it may be "in the middle of nowhere", but factor in the "impeccable" service, "extraordinary" wine list and "breathtaking" patio, and no wonder some say "if money were no object, I'd move in"; P.S. jacket required.

Chinato ⊠ *Italian*

26 | 24 | 25 | $40

Downtown | 2079 E. Fourth St. (Prospect Ave.) | 216-298-9080 |
www.chinatocleveland.com

At his "classy" new Italian on the "hippest street in town", "creative"
chef Zack Bruell (L'Albatros) once again proves he "knows what to do
with food and unusual pairings", hence the "smartly updated regional
dishes" in which "red sauces don't rule" ("mama's cooking has nothing on this place"); the "casually upscale" Downtown space includes a
bar with a "nice neighborhood feeling", all enhanced by "professional"
service and relatively "reasonable" prices.

Crop ⓜ *American*

28 | 26 | 26 | $43

Warehouse District | 1400 W. Sixth St. (bet. Frankfort & St. Clair Aves.) |
216-696-2767 | www.cropbistro.com

A "rustic yet elegant" space sets the scene for "startlingly flavorful
food" at this "laid-back" Warehouse District New American, where the
"inventive" fare "made from fresh, local" ingredients "proves that all
chefs are slightly insane" (e.g. "balsamic popcorn", "jalapeño ice
cream"); while it's a tad "too experimental" for some, most agree the
"vivacious" staff serves up one of "Cleveland's best dining experiences"; P.S. "go on Sundays" for the three-course $25 bargain.

Dante ⊠ *American*

27 | 26 | 26 | $46

Tremont | 2247 Professor Ave. (Literary Rd.) | 216-274-1200 |
www.restaurantdante.us

Set in a "restored bank building" in Tremont, this "exciting" Med-
inflected New American proffers chef-owner Dante Bocuzzi's "inventive", "flavorful" fare, but with a twist: patrons "choose the size and
price point of the dish they order" (i.e. "small plates, appetizer-size
portions" and full entrees); alas, "high ceilings and hard surfaces"
make the otherwise "handsome" space "rather noisy", but an "enthusiastic" staff and the fact that "you can eat at 10 PM and not be the
person closing the restaurant" placate most.

Downtown 140 *American*

28 | 25 | 26 | $56

Hudson | 140 N. Main St. (Rte. 303) | 330-656-1294 |
www.downtown140.com

A "cozy dining room, small plates, great wines and a cool crowd" converge at this "upscale" "treasure" tucked into a Hudson storefront; the
"well-choreographed menu" of "elegant" New American dishes (with
French and Asian tinges) is "prepared and presented with precision"
by a "knowledgeable staff", causing converts to concur "you may be in
a basement, but the food is on top of the world."

Fahrenheit ⊠ *American*

26 | 23 | 24 | $45

Tremont | 2417 Professor Ave. (Jefferson Ave.) | 216-781-8858 |
www.fahrenheittremont.com

Within this "hectic" Tremont "staple", "larger-than-life" chef-owner
Rocco Whalen cooks up "innovative" New American fare – including
"great gourmet pizzas" – that infuses "fresh ingredients" with a "modern twist"; the "handsome" dining room (think dark wood and white
tablecloths) is a "good place for grown-ups to go and feel cool", but it
gets "loud", so consider "sitting on the patio"; P.S. check out the
"happy-hour specials" in the "cozy bar."

	FOOD	DECOR	SERVICE	COST

Fire Food & Drink Ⓜ American
26 | 23 | 25 | $45

Shaker Square | 13220 Shaker Sq. (Moreland Blvd.) | 216-921-3473 | www.firefoodanddrink.com

Chef-owner Doug Katz really "knows how to fire it up" at this "casually elegant" Shaker Square destination for American "haute-comfort" cuisine, where locally sourced, "high-quality ingredients" are "skillfully subjected to high heat" ("any meat that comes out of the tandoor is amazing"); since the "place is always packed" and "sometimes noisy", regulars advise trying to "snag a table outdoors" – a particular "delight" during the "inspired Sunday brunch."

Flying Fig Ⓜ American/Eclectic
27 | 22 | 25 | $41

Ohio City | 2523 Market Ave. (W. 25th St.) | 216-241-4243 | www.theflyingfig.com

At her "lovely" "neighborhood joint" in Ohio City, "rock star" chef-owner Karen Small "continues to deliver a fabulous food experience" by turning "fresh, local ingredients" into "consistently delicious" New American–Eclectic fare that "works on all levels"; while the "cool vibe", "modern-chic decor" and "understated service" are widely applauded, frugal types gripe about "small plates and big prices", which is why the "awesome happy-hour specials" may be one of the "best deals" around.

Greenhouse Tavern ❶ American
25 | 22 | 24 | $39

Downtown | 2038 E. Fourth St. (bet. Euclid & Prospect Aves.) | 216-443-0511 | www.thegreenhousetavern.com

It's "all about sustainability" at "clever" chef-owner Jonathon Sawyer's "cutting-edge" Downtowner, from the "remarkable" New American fare made from "farm-fresh, organic" ingredients to the "simple" decor "completely crafted" from "repurposed/recycled" materials; if a few "don't understand the hype" and rip "rising prices", the "attentive" service and "cool bartenders creating cool cocktails" at Ohio's first "certified green restaurant" offer further enticement, leading devotees to decree that the competition "should be green with envy."

Johnny's Bar Ⓧ Italian
28 | 22 | 26 | $58

West Boulevard | 3164 Fulton Rd. (Trent Ave.) | 216-281-0055 | www.johnnyscleveland.com

At this "perennial favorite" west of Downtown, "upscale" Northern Italian fare – off an "exhausting list" of "excellent specials" or from a "never-changing menu" of near-"perfect classics" – is enjoyed in a "retro-cool interior" reminiscent of "old Hollywood" ("David Lynch and Martin Scorsese would love" it); maybe it's "not in the greatest section" of town, but regulars "show up in jeans or black tie" nevertheless to be spoiled by staffers who "cater to their every whim", albeit at "prices justified by the superb food."

L'Albatros Ⓧ French
27 | 25 | 25 | $43

University Circle | 11401 Bellflower Rd. (bet. Ford Dr. & 115th St.) | 216-791-7880 | www.albatrosbrasserie.com

A "bright spot on the University Circle horizon", chef/co-owner Zack Bruell's "contemporary" brasserie in a "romantic" "converted carriage house" offers "fantastic reinterpretations of French classics" that are "expertly prepared" with "much attention to detail" – and "reasonably priced" to boot; a "spectacular" wine and cheese selection, "top-grade" service and one of the "best patios in Cleveland" round out the picture, leaving most in a state of "l'ecstasy."

Lola ☒ *American*   28 | 27 | 26 | $55

Downtown | 2058 E. Fourth St. (Prospect Ave.) | 216-621-5652 | www.lolabistro.com

"Who would've thought you'd find heaven in Cleveland?" coo connoisseurs of this "prime spot on trendy East Fourth", where chef Michael Symon's "artful presentations" of "nothing-less-than-brilliant" New American fare compete for attention with a "gorgeous", "NYC-loud" space (including an "inner-lit bar"); "off-the-chart" service is another reason diners "won't get in on short notice without a reservation", not a surprise considering it's voted the area's Most Popular restaurant.

Lolita Ⓜ *American/Mediterranean*   27 | 24 | 25 | $40

Tremont | 900 Literary Rd. (Professor Ave.) | 216-771-5652 | www.lolabistro.com

It's "less expensive" and "more intimate" than its Downtown sib, but "Lola's little sister still knows how to shake her stuff" thanks to celeb chef Michael Symon's "sumptuous" take on New American–Med fare, including "must-try" Brussels sprouts ("if you never liked them, you will now"); with its "friendly" staff and "comfortable" vibe that befits the setting in "eclectic" Tremont, no wonder acolytes aver it's "always a treat"; P.S. "don't miss the $5 happy hour."

Luxe Kitchen *Mediterranean*   23 | 21 | 22 | $34

Gordon Square | 6605 Detroit Ave. (65th St.) | 216-920-0600 | www.luxecleveland.com

"Somewhere between neighborhood restaurant and haute cuisine", this "down-home" Gordon Square Med from chef-owner Marlin Kaplan features an "inventive" menu of small plates, family-style dinners and "thin-crust pizzas" that ensures there's "something for everyone"; so what if "service can be slow" – the "excellent" prices, large wine list and "eclectic-chic" decor (e.g. a salvaged art deco bar alongside "crystal chandeliers and animal-print booths") keeps the "youngish crowd" "coming back."

Momocho Ⓜ *Mexican*   27 | 22 | 23 | $32

Ohio City | 1835 Fulton Rd. (Bridge Ave.) | 216-694-2122 | www.momocho.com

"Prepare to say *adios*" to typical south-of-the-border grub at this mid-priced Ohio City storefront whose "tiny kitchen" churns out an "ever-changing menu" of "*muy delicioso*" mod-Mexican morsels, including a "guacamole sampler that leaves you licking the bowls"; it's a "little snug" and can get "loud" as the tequila flows, but the "amusingly dark decor" brightened by convivial "tattooed-and-pierced servers" makes it a "great place to go with friends" nonetheless.

Parallax ☒ *Eclectic/Seafood*   28 | 25 | 26 | $48

Tremont | 2179 W. 11th St. (Fairfield Ave.) | 216-583-9999 | www.parallaxtremont.com

A "light hand in the kitchen" and "acute attention to detail" distinguish this "classy" Eclectic, a "Tremont star" spotlighting chef-owner Zack Bruell's "ability to transform the traditional to the unusual", including "some of Cleveland's best seafood" ("sushi is wonderful"); the "intimate", "minimalist" and frequently "crowded" space is manned by "accommodating" staffers who "really take care of their customers", adding to the overall vibe of a "neighborhood restaurant gone fabulous."

Red The Steakhouse *Steak*   28 | 24 | 25 | $63

Beachwood | 3355 Richmond Rd. (Chagrin Blvd.) | 216-831-2252 | www.redthesteakhouse.com

There's no need to ask "where's the beef?" at this Beachwood "class act" – "you can't miss" the "delicious prime cuts grilled with care" and "terrific side dishes" being savored throughout the "sleek, contemporary" space; it all comes with "service that's attentive but not cloying", an "excellent" wine list, a "patio cigar bar" and "pricey" tabs, so "if steak is your thing, then this is the place."

Sérgio's in University Circle 🗷 *Eclectic*   25 | 21 | 25 | $39

University Circle | 1903 Ford Dr. (Bellflower Rd.) | 216-231-1234 | www.sergioscleveland.com

Set in a "quaint" former gatehouse in "Cleveland's cultural district", this "intimate" University Circle "oasis" is attended by a "professional, attentive" team; while the "inventive" Eclectic cuisine has undergone a recent shift from Brazilian to Italian accents (which may not be reflected in the Food score), the "exotic" Latin American drinks remain unchanged, as does the "pleasant patio that's often filled with jazz musicians" and "cozy" if "tight" interior ("if you want to feel tall, eat here").

Three Birds 🗷 *American*   26 | 25 | 25 | $46

Lakewood | 18515 Detroit Ave. (Riverside Dr.) | 216-221-3500 | www.3birdsrestaurant.com

Plant yourself on the "enchanting patio" ("definitely a summer favorite") and "you'll never want to leave" this "hidden treasure" in Lakewood, which serves up "marvelous" New American fare and "surprising" specialty cocktails mixed by "outstanding bartenders"; an "airy, comfortable" interior and "consistently excellent" service are other pluses, though regulars suggest its "far-from-glam" location may be why it "doesn't get the hype it deserves."

Columbus

TOP FOOD RANKING

	Restaurant	Cuisine
28	L'Antibes	French
27	Refectory	French
	Akai Hana	Japanese
	Cameron's	American
	G. Michael's	American
	Alana's	Eclectic
26	Basi Italia	Italian
	Moretti's	Italian
	Lindey's	American
	Rigsby's	Italian

OTHER NOTEWORTHY PLACES

Barcelona	Spanish
Columbus Fish Market	Seafood
DeepWood	American
Eddie Merlot's	American
Hyde Park	Steak
M	American
Mitchell's	Steak
Top Steak House	Steak
Worthington Inn	American
Z Cucina	Italian

Akai Hana *Japanese*   27 | 19 | 23 | $29

Northwest | Kenny Ctr. | 1173 Old Henderson Rd. (Kenny Rd.) |
614-451-5411 | www.akaihanaohio.com

"Don't expect any kind of hipster scene" at this "premier" Japanese in
Northwest, just a "continental crowd" enjoying some of the "best sushi
in town" ("try the spicy scallop roll") and "top-notch" cooked fare; perhaps it's "not the fanciest place", but a "polite, professional" staff and
modest prices more than compensate, so it's no surprise it's "popular."

Alana's Food & Wine 🄢🅜 *Eclectic*   27 | 20 | 24 | $42

University | 2333 N. High St. (bet. Oakland & Patterson Aves.) |
614-294-6783 | www.alanas.com

A "flavor queen with an edge", chef/co-owner Alana Shock lures locavores to her "relaxed" University-area "destination" with a "constantly
changing menu" of "spectacular" Eclectic fare enhanced by "fantastic", "fairly priced" wines and "personalized" service; if some consider
the art-filled digs a bit "cluttered", once the "food comes, you forget."

Barcelona *Spanish*   24 | 25 | 23 | $37

German Village | 263 E. Whittier St. (Jaeger St.) | 614-443-3699 |
www.barcelonacolumbus.com

You'll feel as if you've "strolled down Las Ramblas" after a night out at
this "warm, upscale" Spaniard in the "heart of German Village";
"friendly" servers add to a "hopping" atmosphere fueled by "excellent"

tapas, paella and "pitchers of peach sangria", and if you think it "doesn't get better than this", you haven't checked out the "best patio in town."

Basi Italia ☒ *Italian* | 26 | 22 | 24 | $37

Victorian Village | 811 Highland St. (Buttles Ave.) | 614-294-7383 | www.basi-italia.com

"Cozy doesn't even begin to cover" how "tiny" this "romantic Italian get-away" in a Victorian Village "alley" is; surveyors swoon over the "remarkable", "innovative" cooking and the "reasonably priced" wines, while an "engaging" staff "makes you feel like part of the family", even if limited seating (the "perfect" seasonal patio more than doubles capacity) and "nonexistent" parking means reservations and the valet are a "must."

Cameron's American Bistro *American* | 27 | 23 | 26 | $39

Worthington | 2185 W. Dublin-Granville Rd. (Linworth Rd.) | 614-885-3663 | www.cameronmitchell.com

The "original remains one of his best" say supporters of restaurateur Cameron Mitchell's "dependable" Worthington American, where "meticulous" staffers deliver "seasonal", "mouthwatering" fare harboring "unique twists"; "inviting" decor and "good bartenders" add to the allure, so even if a few find it a "bit noisy", most just "love this place."

Columbus Fish Market *Seafood* | 25 | 21 | 23 | $36

Grandview Heights | 1245 Olentangy River Rd. (bet. 3rd & 5th Aves.) | 614-291-3474

Worthington | Crosswoods | 40 Hutchinson Ave. (Rte. 270) | 614-410-3474 www.columbusfishmarket.com

For a "nice piece of fish" in the "flatlands", diners dive into this "delicious" duo offering "generous portions" of "tasty" seafood at tabs that won't require a "second mortgage"; they're "not the most romantic" spots, but "well-trained" servers help make them "winners."

DeepWood ☒ *American* | 26 | 23 | 25 | $45

Short North | 511 N. High St. (Goodale St.) | 614-221-5602 | www.deepwoodrestaurant.com

At this Short North "surprise", chef/co-owner Brian Pawlak's "innovative", "often sinful" New American dishes are "crafted with care" and "impeccably" served in a choice of two "beautiful" dining spaces (white linen or a less "pricey" tavern atmosphere); an "extensive" wine/cocktail list offers further enticement.

Eddie Merlot's *Steak* | 23 | 24 | 24 | $48

Polaris | 1570 Polaris Pkwy. (Lyra Dr.) | 614-433-7307 | www.eddiemerlots.com

Promises of "bourbon-marinated rib-eyes" and a "see-and-be-seen" lounge have beef eaters and hipsters heading for Polaris to dine at this "haven for carnivores", a "cozy" "breath of fresh air" among "steakhouse chains" (so "no dark gloomy lighting, no boys' club decor"); though even a few fans fret it's "not a great value", most agree the "attentive" service and "elegant" atmosphere make it ideal for a "special occasion."

G. Michael's Bistro & Bar *American* | 27 | 23 | 25 | $44

German Village | 595 S. Third St. (Willow St.) | 614-464-0575 | www.gmichaelsbistro.com

Expect a "fabulous feast for the palate" ("if duck's on the menu, try it") at this "divine" New American housed in an "intimate", brick-walled

German Village space; it's "definitely not cheap", but an "outstanding wine list", "attentive" service and "romantic" patio ensure that just about everyone "leaves happy"; P.S. the $30 Monday prix fixe is a "bargain."

Hyde Park Prime Steakhouse *Steak*

| 25 | 23 | 24 | $50 |

Short North | 569 N. High St. (Goodale St.) | 614-224-2204
Dublin | 6360 Frantz Rd. (161st St.) | 614-717-2828 ☒
Upper Arlington | 1615 Old Henderson Rd. (Larwell Rd.) | 614-442-3310
Worthington | 55 Hutchinson Ave. (I-270) | 614-438-1000 ☒
www.hydeparkrestaurants.com

"Bring a hearty appetite and a stuffed wallet" to these "lively" chophouses that broke ground long "before the chains invaded" and continue to proffer "well-executed" beef and seafood, plus "top-notch" sides; "elegant" decor and "friendly" servers who "expertly assist you in navigating" the menu complete the picture.

L'Antibes ☒ Ⓜ *French*

| 28 | 22 | 26 | $49 |

Short North | 772 N. High St. (Warren St.) | 614-291-1666 |
www.lantibes.com

"If you can't afford a trip to Paris", this "romantic" (and tiny) Short North French "has it going on" with a "thoughtfully constructed" menu of "exceptional" Gallic dishes that once again earns it the No. 1 ranking for Food in the Columbus area; a "top-notch" staff and "tasteful" if "minimal" decor further its rep as a "special place."

Lindey's *American*

| 26 | 25 | 26 | $39 |

German Village | 169 E. Beck St. (Mohawk St.) | 614-228-4343 |
www.lindeys.com

"Catch a glimpse of Columbus' movers and shakers" at restaurateur Sue Doody's German Village "landmark", once again voted the area's Most Popular restaurant thanks to its "fabulous, worth-the-price" American fare, "top-drawer" service and "chic", brass-and-hardwoodheavy setting; factor in the "gorgeous patio with its lovely outdoor bar", and it's no surprise it's "still going strong after 25-plus years."

M ☒ *American*

| 25 | 28 | 23 | $52 |

Downtown | 2 Miranova Pl. (W. Mound St.) | 614-629-0000 |
www.cameronmitchell.com

With New American fare that's "lovely to look at and even better to eat", Cameron Mitchell's "wonderful" Downtown flagship has become a "destination for foodies", while "romantic" types are drawn to the "beautiful" digs (complete with "gilded ceiling" and "unforgettable patio"); it's predictably "pricey" and a bit "out of the way", but "creative cocktails" and fine service seal its status as a "must-go."

Mitchell's Steakhouse *Steak*

| 25 | 24 | 26 | $49 |

Downtown | 45 N. Third St. (bet. Gay & Lynn Sts.) | 614-621-2333
Polaris | Polaris Fashion Pl. | 1408 Polaris Pkwy. (Lyra Dr.) | 614-888-2467
www.mitchellssteakhouse.com

"For a fancy night out" or an "intimate" "business lunch", carnivores head to these "elegant" steakhouses – at the Downtown site, diners "sit elbow to elbow with lobbyists and legislators" while slicing into "dry-aged beef at its best", and in Polaris, suburbanites enjoy a "place to be seen" with free parking (but less of an "ooh-and-ahh" factor); both are praised for their "professional" staffs, if not their "costly" tabs.

	FOOD	DECOR	SERVICE	COST

Moretti's of Arlington *Italian*

26 | 20 | 23 | $30

Upper Arlington | 2124 Tremont Ctr. (Tremont Rd.) | 614-486-2333 |
www.morettisofarlington.com

"A taste bud's best friend" is how Upper Arlington eaters describe the "memorable", even "addictive" fare at chef-owner Tim Moretti's "quaint family Italian", where an "exceptional" staff serves up his "outstanding" "housemade pastas"; a "pleasant" patio belies its "minimall" setting, and the "value" pricing makes it "worth the trip."

Refectory ⓈＩ *French*

27 | 26 | 27 | $52

Northwest | 1092 Bethel Rd. (Kenny Rd.) | 614-451-9774 |
www.refectory.com

"You know you've done something good when you find yourself" at this "top-notch" French set in a "dramatic renovated church", a Northwest "veteran" revered for its "inventive" dishes infused with "sublime flavors", "gracious", "tuxedo-clad" servers and "amazing wine list" ("pure heaven"); it's "expensive, but worth it", though frugal gourmets can indulge in a "more reasonably priced" bistro prix fixe.

Rigsby's Kitchen *Italian*

26 | 24 | 25 | $42

Short North | 698 N. High St. (bet. Buttles Ave. & Lincoln St.) |
614-461-7888 | www.rigsbyskitchen.com

This "vibrant" North Italian "gem" "helped start the rebirth of Short North", and after 25 years chef/co-owner Kent Rigsby's kitchen is still "delivering the goods" (including "divine" "housemade bread") to the "sophicated and fashionable set"; the "airy" space gives off a "Tuscan" vibe, enhanced by "knowledgeable" servers who "know your name", "generous quartini of wine" and "fair prices."

Top Steak House *Steak*

25 | 19 | 23 | $44

Bexley | 2891 E. Main St. (Chesterfield Rd.) | 614-231-8238 |
www.thetopsteakhouse.com

"All aboard the wayback machine" for a Bexley steakhouse experience reminiscent of a time "before anyone cared about cholesterol"; from the "swinging" piano bar to the Naugahyde booths, the "1950s atmosphere" is as "old school" as the "been-there-forever" staff, and while a few quibble over the "21st-century" prices, most concur it's "still a classic."

Worthington Inn *American*

25 | 23 | 25 | $38

Worthington | 649 High St. (W. New England Ave.) | 614-885-2600 |
www.worthingtoninn.com

"Beautifully prepared" American cuisine with French and Italian accents keeps diners returning to this "well-priced" Worthington "gem" set in "historic" Victorian digs; service is "excellent" and the cooking is "modern", but the decor is strictly "traditional", and while most maintain the "old-world" ambiance "feels good", others advise hitting the "bar or patio to be freed from the 1800s."

Z Cucina ⓈＩ *Italian*

21 | 22 | 23 | $37

Grandview Heights | 1368 Grandview Ave. (3rd Ave.) | 614-486-9200 |
www.zcucina.com

Like its ultra-"hip" address, this "lively" Grandview Heights haven for "creative" Italian is the kind of place "you return to without thinking"; some cite an owner who "aims to please", others the "comfortable" decor and "great" staff – either way, it results in a "wonderful evening."

Connecticut

TOP FOOD RANKING

Restaurant	Cuisine
28 Thomas Henkelmann	French
Ibiza	Spanish
Le Petit Cafe	French
Cavey's	French/Italian
Jean-Louis	French
27 Bernard's	French
Carole Peck's	American
Union League	French
Harvest Supper	American
Max Downtown	American/Steak
Valencia Luncheria	Venezuelan
26 Paci	Italian
Elizabeth's Cafe	American
Woodward House	American
Frank Pepe Pizzeria	Pizza
Bistro Bonne Nuit	French
Meigas	Spanish
Frank Pepe's The Spot	Pizza
Feng	Asian
Métro Bis*	American

OTHER NOTEWORTHY PLACES

Barcelona	Spanish
Boathouse	American
Cheesecake Factory	American
Columbus Park	Italian
Community Table	American
Coromandel	Indian
DaPietro's	French/Italian
Firebox	American
Le Farm	American
Match	American
Max's Oyster Bar	Seafood
Mayflower Inn	American
Napa & Co.	American
Pasta Nostra	Italian
Rebeccas	American
Schoolhouse	American
Still River	American
Stonehenge	Continental
Thali	Indian
Winvian	American

* Indicates a tie with restaurant above

	FOOD	DECOR	SERVICE	COST

Barcelona Restaurant & Wine Bar *Spanish* | 23 | 21 | 20 | $41 |

Fairfield | Hi Ho Hotel | 4180 Black Rock Tpke. (Rte. 15) | 203-255-0800

Greenwich | 18 W. Putnam Ave. (Greenwich Ave.) | 203-983-6400

New Haven | Omni Hotel | 155 Temple St. (Chapel St.) | 203-848-3000

South Norwalk | 63 N. Main St. (bet. Ann & Marshall Sts.) | 203-899-0088

Stamford | 222 Summer St. (Broad St.) | 203-348-4800 ◗

West Hartford | 971 Farmington Ave. (Main St.) | 860-218-2100

www.barcelonawinebar.com

"Bring on the sangria" and "to-die-for mojitos" cheer amigos of this "ultrachic" mini-chain boasting "terrific" vini and "outstanding Spanish tapas" packing "intense" flavors; while the "kickin' bar scene" lures both "upscale singles" "looking for a little action" and "desperate housewives" "dressed for a night on the town", distressed diners dis the "glaringly loud" din and say prices can "add up quickly" (though recessionistas revel in the "half-price wines on Sundays").

Bernard's Ⓜ *French* | 27 | 25 | 26 | $67 |

Ridgefield | 20 West Ln./Rte. 35 (High Ridge Ave.) | 203-438-8282 | www.bernardsridgefield.com

"They do everything right" at chef-owner Bernard Bouissou's *magnifique* French "gem", the "clear winner in Ridgefield for imagination and taste"; the "excellent food (and it should be for the price)", "superior" wines, "romantic" "country inn" setting and "attentive" service mean most consider it tailor-made for "special occasions"; P.S. Sarah's Wine Bar upstairs has a "bistro feel" and a separate menu.

Bistro Bonne Nuit *French* | 26 | 20 | 22 | $55 |

New Canaan | 12 Forest St. (bet. East & Locust Aves.) | 203-966-5303 | www.culinarymenus.com/bistrobonnenuit.htm

Francophiles almost "expect Edith Piaf to flit through" this "exquisite" bistro, where reservations are needed "to beat New Canaanites to a table" – and it's no wonder, since the "excellent wine list" and "sophisticated food served with aplomb" will leave you "craving cassoulet" for some time; *oui*, "cramped" quarters and "rising prices" are downers, but consider that part of the "Parisian feel."

Boathouse at Saugatuck Ⓜ *American* | - | - | - | E |

Westport | Saugatuck Rowing Club | 521 Riverside Ave. (Bridge St.) | 203-227-3399 | www.saugatuckrowing.com

Lidia Bastianich protégé John Holzwarth is making a splash at this nautical-themed Westport New American anchored above the Saugatuck Rowing Club, particularly among locavores lured by such farm-to-table treats as pasture-raised chicken, terrine of local rabbit and a sustainable fish of the day; it's not inexpensive, but the clubby yet casual atmosphere and panoramic river vistas seem likely to float many a boat; P.S. also closed Tuesdays.

Carole Peck's Good News Cafe *American* | 27 | 20 | 24 | $49 |

Woodbury | Sherman Village Plaza | 694 Main St. S./Rte. 6 (Rte. 64) | 203-266-4663 | www.good-news-cafe.com

It's a "godsend in the bleak landscape of CT restaurants" exult enthusiasts of this Woodbury New American whose namesake chef "uses locally grown organic foods" to create "cuisine for cultivated palates" in "fresh, delicious" ways (e.g. "wonderful onion rings that go with

	FOOD	DECOR	SERVICE	COST

anything"); patrons part ways over the "funky" art, which some call "quirky" and others say "might improve if they threw plates of spaghetti on it"; P.S. closed Tuesdays.

Cavey's Restaurants ⊠ Ⓜ *French/Italian*

| 28 | 25 | 26 | $60 |

Manchester | 45 E. Center St. (Main St.) | 860-643-2751 |
www.caveysrestaurant.com

At this two-in-one "treasure" in Manchester, you're in for a "memorable dining experience" whether you choose the "special occasion"-worthy downstairs French or the "less formal", "more affordable" street-level Italian; the "delicious" duo shares "sophisticated" service, a "wonderful" 20,000-bottle wine cellar (with "options in different price ranges") and an "ambiance conveying warmth and luxury."

Cheesecake Factory *American*

| 18 | 18 | 17 | $30 |

Hartford | 71 Isham Rd. (Raymond Rd.) | 860-233-5588 |
www.thecheesecakefactory.com

It's a "suburbanite" "mob scene" at this "line-out-the-door" chain link in Hartford, where the "endless" American options arrive in equally "colossal" portions; despite an "ordinary" setting, "spotty" staffing and "lots of commotion", the "well-oiled machine" is so "busy, busy, busy" that it's best accessed "off-hours" to avoid a "long wait."

Columbus Park Trattoria ⊠ *Italian*

| 25 | 19 | 22 | $44 |

Stamford | 205 Main St. (Washington Blvd.) | 203-967-9191 |
www.columbusparktrattoria.com

Owner Maria Marchetti makes the pasta "fresh each morning" and "boy, does it show" at this "old world–style" Stamford Italian, which dishes up "nearly flawless" food (including "amazing" osso buco) coupled with "impeccable" service; sure, it's "pricey" and can get a "little cramped", but most agree the "only complaint is when the meal is over."

Community Table *American*

| - | - | - | M |

Washington | 223 Litchfield Tpke. (Wilbur Rd.) | 860-868-9354 |
www.communitytablect.com

At this New American bistro in tony Washington, weekending celebs and mere mortals gather 'round the table to graze on locally sourced fare as light and fresh as the spare interior of this 36-seater where sustainability rules (from the solar panels on the roof to the tables crafted from area trees); happily, the moderate prices on the ever-changing menu are as rejuvenating as the food; P.S. closed Tuesdays and the month of February.

Coromandel *Indian*

| 26 | 18 | 22 | $34 |

Darien | Goodwives Shopping Ctr. | 25-11 Old Kings Hwy. N. (Sedgewick Ave.) | 203-662-1213
Orange | 185 Boston Post Rd. (Lindy St.) | 203-795-9055
South Norwalk | 86 Washington St. (bet. Main & Water Sts.) | 203-852-1213
Stamford | 68 Broad St. (Summer St.) | 203-964-1010
www.coromandelcuisine.com

"Like dining first-class on the night train to Mumbai", these "top-notch" Indians take "lovers of exotic comfort food" on a "tour of the subcontinent" while managing to "outclass others" of their ilk with "standout culinary artistry" and "stellar service"; the weekend buffet brunches are a "steal" - just "don't let the dated decor scare you off."

	FOOD	DECOR	SERVICE	COST

DaPietro's ⌷ *French/Italian* — 26 | 20 | 24 | $65

Westport | 36 Riverside Ave. (Post Rd.) | 203-454-1213 | www.dapietros.com

"Reservations are a must" at this "fabulous" 28-seat Westport "shoebox" where for more than two decades "master chef" Pietro Scotti's "outstanding" French–Northern Italian cuisine and "excellent wine list" have provided "memorable experiences for true foodies"; some surveyors find the "intimate" atmosphere "romantic", but critics carp about a "dining room built for Lilliputians" and prices that are so "high" they should include "a limousine ride home."

Elizabeth's Cafe at Perfect Parties *American* — 26 | 18 | 24 | $51

Madison | 885 Boston Post Rd. (bet. Scotland Ave. & Wall St.) | 203-245-0250 | www.perfectparties.com

"From its take-out origins", this "casual" Madison New American has blossomed into an "absolute gem" with "delicious", "imaginative dishes" and "excellent Sunday brunches"; "cottagey antiques and castoffs" create a "charming" (if "tight") space that's "homey but stylish", and while it's still the local "savior when you need catered food in a hurry", there's "one caveat: it ain't cheap"; P.S. closed Tuesdays.

Feng Asian Bistro *Asian* — 26 | 25 | 23 | $47

Hartford | 93 Asylum St. (bet. Main & Trumbull Sts.) | 860-549-3364 | www.fengrestaurant.com

Downtown Hartford "really needed something like this" "stunning" Pan-Asian "paradise" declare devotees, who say that "everything" – "from the sushi to the Kobe beef" – is "fresh and full of flavor"; coupled with "awesome drinks", "solicitous service" and "sleek, modern" decor (banquettes, polished wood, stainless steel), it's no surprise it can be "expensive", but few fuss.

Firebox *American* — 25 | 25 | 24 | $46

Hartford | Billings Forge | 539 Broad St. (bet. Capitol Ave. & Russ St.) | 860-246-1222 | www.fireboxrestaurant.com

So "hot", yet so "chill": this "farm-to-table" New American in Downtown Hartford's Billings Forge complex has boosters buzzing, as much for its "masterful" "seasonal fare" derived mostly from "organic, local ingredients" as its "breathtaking decor" (including the "funky" bar's 30-ft. vaulted ceiling) and "attentive service"; true, it's "a bit off the beaten path", but since "you really can't go wrong" once you arrive, "don't let the location keep you away."

Frank Pepe Pizzeria *Pizza* — 26 | 11 | 15 | $20

Fairfield | 238 Commerce Dr. (bet. Berwick Ct. & Brentwood Ave.) | 203-333-7373
Manchester | 233 Buckland Hills Dr. (bet. Buckland & Deming Sts.) | 860-644-7333
New Haven | 157 Wooster St. (Brown St.) | 203-865-5762
www.pepespizzeria.com

"Bury me with a slice in my hand" declare devotees of this New Haven "pinnacle of pizzerias" and its offshoots, voted Most Popular in the Connecticut Survey for its "always perfect fresh tomato" pizzas, "transcendent" white clam pies and other offerings on a menu that "hasn't changed in 85 years because it hasn't had to"; cognos-

| | FOOD | DECOR | SERVICE | COST |

centi caution that service can be "bipolar when it gets crowded", which is often, and the waits can be "intolerable" – but all the same, to most it's "worth it anytime."

Frank Pepe's The Spot Ⓜ *Pizza* `26` `10` `15` `$20`

New Haven | 163 Wooster St. (Brown St.) | 203-865-7602 | www.pepespizzeria.com

The "lines are usually shorter and the pace a little less rushed" at this "no-frills" "original location" of New Haven's pizza "standard-bearer", serving the "same delicious" pies as the "parent across the alley"; some find the "interior a little bleak" and say "don't expect to be pampered", but in the end, "your stomach won't be disappointed."

Harvest Supper Ⓢ Ⓜ *American* `27` `20` `26` `$56`

New Canaan | 15 Elm St. (Main St.) | 203-966-5595

The "tiny, tempting" dishes "salute the seasons" and "burst with flavor" at this "classy" New Canaan New American that's "like being in Manhattan", which makes sense since it's owned by NYC restaurateurs Jack and Grace Lamb (she's also the "gracious" hostess); chef Michael Campbell's menu is "inventive" "without making diners squeamish" and so "delicious" "you'll want to order everything", but those with "slender wallets" might want to show restraint.

Ibiza Ⓢ *Spanish* `28` `24` `25` `$53`

New Haven | 39 High St. (bet. Chapel & Crown Sts.) | 203-865-1933 | www.ibizanewhaven.com

New Haven's "premier Spanish" "might as well be in a little villa in Spain" attest amigos agog over the "exquisite", "authentic" cuisine, including a weeknight $59 six-course tasting menu "worth fasting for"; the "well-coordinated" staff "manages to be both meticulous and warm" in the "comfortable, spare" contemporary space, all of which makes it an "experience to savor – and especially to repeat."

Jean-Louis Ⓢ *French* `28` `23` `26` `$83`

Greenwich | 61 Lewis St. (bet. Greenwich Ave. & Mason St.) | 203-622-8450 | www.restaurantjeanlouis.com

Chef-owner Jean-Louis Gerin helps you "discover taste buds you never knew you had" at his "first-rate" Greenwich French, where the "imaginative, adventurous" cuisine is complemented by a "beautifully appointed dining room" and the "most courteous service imaginable"; *oui*, you may need "to get that second mortgage" or have "someone else pick up the tab", but for a "special occasion" the experience will be "hard to duplicate anywhere" ("including NYC").

Le Farm Ⓢ Ⓜ *American* `-` `-` `-` `E`

Westport | 256 Post Rd. E. (bet. Compo Rd. & Imperial Ave.) | 203-557-3701 | www.lefarmwestport.com

Chef-owner Bill Taibe (ex Napa & Co.) raises the bar again at this pricey Westport New American where his farm-to-table approach encompasses unique relationships with local growers plus 12 acres of his own on which he's growing rare veggies; surprising the palate seems to be the goal of the ever-evolving menu – as in the signature dessert, cornbread with candied bacon and maple chile gelato – while simpatico service and modern farmhouse decor heighten the experience; P.S. with only 34 seats, reservations are a must.

	FOOD	DECOR	SERVICE	COST

Le Petit Cafe ⓜ French — 28 | 23 | 27 | $55

Branford | 225 Montowese St. (Main St.) | 203-483-9791 |
www.lepetitcafe.net

"Personable" chef-owner Roy Ip "turns out exquisite French food"
"presented elegantly" in his "sophisticated", "tiny" Branford bistro, including "homemade truffle butter on warm bread"; even better, the
"extraordinary" "four-course prix fixe menu" ($48.50) is an "unbeliev-
able bargain", leading a legion of loyalists to declare it's "one of the
best meals you'll eat on the shoreline – at any price."

Match American — 24 | 22 | 21 | $49

South Norwalk | 98 Washington St. (bet. Main & Water Sts.) |
203-852-1088 | www.matchsono.com

"There's no match for this" "always-evolving" New American in South
Norwalk, where co-owner/chef Matt Storch's "inventive" touch is evident "from appetizer to dessert"; take note that the "Manhattan-type
atmosphere" comes with "Manhattan-level prices" – and a "cool" crowd
nursing "fancy drinks" that can really ratchet up the decibel level.

Max Downtown American/Steak — 27 | 24 | 26 | $53

Hartford | City Place | 185 Asylum St. (bet. Ann & Trumbull Sts.) |
860-522-2530 | www.maxrestaurantgroup.com

Considered by connoisseurs to be the "crown jewel of the Max group",
this "Downtown Hartford power spot" "consistently delivers" "heaven
on a plate" in the form of "awesome steaks" and "terrific" New American
fare coupled with "inspired cocktails" and "fine wines"; "top-notch
service" "without snobbery" and "elegant" yet "comfortable" environs
are two more reasons why it's "totally worth" the "pricey" tabs.

Max's Oyster Bar Seafood — 25 | 23 | 23 | $50

West Hartford | 964 Farmington Ave. (S. Main St.) | 860-236-6299 |
www.maxrestaurantgroup.com

"Often filled to the max", this "sublime" seafooder in West Hartford
features a "loud", "happening" bar where "yupscale singles" slurp "exotic" cocktails and a "grand choice of oysters"; in the dining area, bur-
gundy booths help create a "Rat Pack"-like atmosphere, while
"attentive" staffers "guide you to what's best" among the "expensive",
"extra-fresh" fish; P.S. "outdoor dining in the summer is a plus."

Mayflower Inn & Spa American — 25 | 27 | 25 | $73

Washington | The Mayflower Inn & Spa | 118 Woodbury Rd./Rte. 47
(Rte. 199) | 860-868-9466 | www.mayflowerinn.com

"Dress your best here, folks, otherwise you'll feel like the help" at this
"over-the-top" "dining experience" in Washington's "plush" Relais &
Châteaux inn/spa, where "pampering and primping" meet "outstanding"
New American cuisine; an "attentive" staff makes you "feel royal" in
the "exquisite surroundings", and while a few find all the fuss "too precious for words" and the menu "in need of some spark", the majority
says it's worth the "astronomic prices" for a "treat with all the frills."

Meigas Spanish — 26 | 22 | 24 | $57

Norwalk | 10 Wall St. (bet. High & Knight Sts.) | 203-866-8800 |
www.meigasrestaurant.com

"Superb", "creative" Spanish cuisine and "an equally outstanding wine
list" are conveyed by "gracious", "experienced" servers at this Norwalk

| | FOOD | DECOR | SERVICE | COST |

"sophisticate" – and while it's "not cheap", the $64-per-couple, 10-course tapas tasting proves to be a relatively economical option; some aesthetes "can't get away from the feeling" that they're "in an office building", but the majority finds the "lovely setting" "suitable for both business and romance."

Métro Bis 🗷 *American*

| 26 | 21 | 25 | $47 |

Simsbury | Simsburytown Shops | 928 Hopmeadow St./Rte. 10 (bet. Massaco St. & Plank Hill Rd.) | 860-651-1908 | www.metrobis.com

Chef-owner Christopher Prosperi is Simsbury's "epicurean star", and his "cozy" New American bistro boasts a "loyal following" that returns often to sample the "creative", locally sourced fare; its strip-mall setting is "not ideal", but if you can get over that, you're in for a "gourmet" "meal with superb service" (and it's only "a little pricey").

Napa & Co. *American*

| 25 | 23 | 21 | $56 |

Stamford | Courtyard Marriott Hotel | 75 Broad St. (bet. Bedford & Summer Sts.) | 203-353-3319 | www.napaandcompany.com

Known for its "farm-to-fork philosophy", this "transporting" Stamford New American has won raves from respondents for its "terrific", "ever-evolving menu", "amazing cheese selection" and "wall of wine"; yes, it's in a Courtyard Marriott, but "don't let the location" or "uneven service" dissuade you, because devotees declare it's almost a "pleasure to spend money here"; P.S. the post-Survey departure of founding chef Bill Taibe places the above Food rating in question.

Paci 🗷 Ⓜ *Italian*

| 26 | 25 | 23 | $62 |

Southport | 96 Station St. (Pequot Ave.) | 203-259-9600 | www.pacirestaurant.com

"Impressed" surveyors "haven't seen a slowdown in the economy" at this "steeply priced" Italian in a converted Southport train station, as it's always filled with folks enjoying the "outstanding", "inventive" fare and "large variety of wines"; the "modern", brick-lined downstairs "with a big clock projection" is quite "open" (hence, it "can get loud"), while the upstairs is more "intimate" and the "barroom is cozy."

Pasta Nostra 🗷 Ⓜ *Italian*

| 25 | 15 | 20 | $54 |

South Norwalk | 116 Washington St. (bet. Main & Water Sts.) | 203-854-9700 | www.pastanostra.com

"If you can get into" this South Norwalk Italian, you're in for "*stupendo*" fare that "changes weekly" based on "seasonally available ingredients and chef Joe Bruno's imagination" (he "knows what he's doing", but he's got "peculiarities" – "try making substitutions" at your own peril); the "diligent, long-employed staff" helps pair the "wonderful wines", and while the whole shebang is "expensive", it's "worth it", even if it comes with "not much atmosphere."

Rebeccas 🗷 Ⓜ *American*

| 25 | 20 | 22 | $79 |

Greenwich | 265 Glenville Rd. (bet. Pemberwick & Riversville Rds.) | 203-532-9270 | www.rebeccasgreenwich.com

At his Greenwich "foodie mecca", Reza Khorshidi's New American menu "abounds with nonpareil culinary delights" such as "heaven-sent" foie gras dumplings in black truffle broth, and his wife, Rebecca, "runs a tight ship"; you can "rub elbows with the super-elite" in the "ultramodern" (read: "very minimal") space, but nitpickers note it can get "excruciatingly noisy", and as one might expect from the "parking lot full of hedge-fund trophy cars", the "prices are over the top."

Schoolhouse at Cannondale ▣ American
(aka Cannondale)

- | - | - | E

Wilton | 34 Cannon Rd. (Seeley Rd.) | 203-834-9816 |
www.schoolhouseatcannondale.com

Housed in one of Wilton's most treasured historic buildings (an 1872 schoolhouse overlooking the Norwalk River), this intimate New American establishment focuses on farm-fresh produce that's locally grown, with chef-owner Tim LaBant contributing to the bounty with his own gardens; expect a decidedly French slant to the weekly evolving menu that showcases the best the season has to offer; P.S. also closed Tuesdays.

Still River Café ▣ American

▽ 26 | 26 | 24 | $58

Eastford | 134 Union Rd./Rte. 171 (Centre Pike) | 860-974-9988 |
www.stillrivercafe.com

True, this 27-acre Eastford farm and its 150-year-old "restored barn" are "in the middle of nowhere", but once you sample the "brilliant" New American cuisine "you feel as if you've died and gone to paradise"; co-owners Robert and Kara Brooks share responsibilities, and kudos: he "grows most of the [organic] produce", she "turns out magic" in the kitchen with her "inspired 'trios'" (as in duck prepared three ways); pricey, perhaps, but "worth every penny"; P.S. open for dinner only Friday–Saturday, plus Sunday brunch.

Stonehenge ▣▣ Continental

24 | 25 | 24 | $63

Ridgefield | Stonehenge Inn | 35 Stonehenge Rd. (Rte. 7) | 203-438-6511 |
www.stonehengeinn-ct.com

"Expensive but exquisite", this Continental on 11 acres in Ridgefield is "still the queen of Fairfield County inns" according to respondents, who rave that the "indulgent service" and "beautiful" setting "will transport you to millionaires' row"; while some think it's "passé" and no longer "matches its reputation of yesteryear", for many it's a "wonderful" experience that "warrants a trip to the boonies."

Thali Indian

26 | 22 | 23 | $39

New Canaan | 87 Main St. (bet. East & Locust Aves.) |
203-972-8332
New Haven | 4 Orange St. (George St.) | 203-777-1177
Ridgefield | Ridgefield Motor Inn | 296 Ethan Allen Hwy./Rte. 7
(Florida Hill Rd.) | 203-894-1080
www.thali.com

Thali Too Indian

New Haven | Yale University campus | 65 Broadway (Elm St.) |
203-776-1600 | www.thalitoo.com

These "innovative Indians" make you "come back again" for their "wonderful variety of dishes" singing with "sensuous spices", complemented by "generous cocktails" and a "surprisingly good wine list"; the digs are "cool" and "unusual", especially in New Canaan, with its "suspended waterfall in a high-ceiling room", and while some lament that it's "expensive", the $16.95 Sunday brunch is a real "buy"; P.S. New Haven's vegetarian outlet, Thali Too, opened post-Survey.

	FOOD	DECOR	SERVICE	COST

Thomas Henkelmann 🗷Ⓜ *French* 28 | 28 | 28 | $86

Greenwich | Homestead Inn | 420 Field Point Rd. (bet. Bush Ave. & Merica Ln.) | 203-869-7500 | www.thomashenkelmann.com

Voted No. 1 for Food in the CT Survey, this "extraordinary" Greenwich New French helmed by "master" chef Thomas Henkelmann and "charming" wife/hostess Theresa is where the "incredible is the usual" – "ethereal" cuisine, "uncompromised" service and "richly textured decor" reminiscent of a "European country manor"; the prices can "intimidate", but most insist it's "worth" the "splurge" – it "doesn't get any better than this"; P.S. jacket required.

Union League Cafe 🗷 *French* 27 | 26 | 25 | $57

New Haven | 1032 Chapel St. (bet. College & High Sts.) | 203-562-4299 | www.unionleaguecafe.com

"Despite a down economy", "sophisticated" Yalies and "high-society" types shell out "hefty" payments for "well-trained" chef Jean-Pierre Vuillermet's "perfectly prepared classic French cuisine" (augmented with "some twists, so it never bores") at this "grande dame of New Haven"; vintage stained glass, mahogany and other "elegant" appointments lend it the feeling of a "formal" "private club", while the "remarkable service" comes generally "without pomposity."

Valencia Luncheria 🗷 *Venezuelan* 27 | 10 | 18 | $19

Norwalk | 172 Main St. (bet. Catherine St. & Plymouth Ave.) | 203-846-8009 | www.valencialuncheria.com

With "breakfasts worth waking up for", "amazing lunches" ("try the heavenly empanadas") and "delicious" dinners featuring a "dizzying list of specials", this "teeny-tiny", cash-only Venezuelan "hole-in-the-wall" in Norwalk hits "extraordinary" heights; "enormous portions" for "cheap" and a BYO policy make it "one of the best values" around – no wonder there's often "a long wait" for a table.

Winvian Ⓜ *American* - | - | - | E

Morris | 155 Alain White Rd. (bet. County & E. Shore Rds.) | 860-393-3004 | www.winvian.com

Inside an elegant Colonial-style former home recently opened to the public, this Traditional American eatery is part of a Relais & Châteaux resort featuring whimsically themed cottages hidden in the Litchfield Hills town of Morris; diners feast within three intimate, crackling fireplace-equipped rooms, or out on the lovely porch (at lunch only), enjoying sumptuous fare such as the signature beef duo (tenderloin and braised short rib) or frisée salad with pigeon and foie gras; P.S. the $90 three-course prix fixe seems almost economical given all the opulence.

Woodward House Ⓜ *American* 26 | 28 | 28 | $64

Bethlehem | 4 The Green (West Rd.) | 203-266-6902 | www.thewoodwardhouse.com

This "outstanding" New American housed in "everyone's dream of a picturesque 18th-century Colonial" boasts four small dining rooms, each "decorated in its own style" (including one "with funky Peter Max original artwork"); chef-owner Jerry Reveron's cuisine is "sumptuous", "innovative and excellent", his wife, Adele, is a "gracious, pleasing hostess" and both are "visibly engaged in running" things to ensure a "wonderful" (albeit "pricey") dining experience.

Dallas/Ft. Worth

TOP FOOD RANKING

Restaurant	Cuisine
29 Bonnell's	Southwestern
28 York Street	American
Saint-Emilion	French
French Room	American/French
Cacharel	French
Pappas Bros. Steak	Steak
Teppo Yakitori	Japanese
Yao Fuzi	Chinese
Yutaka*	Japanese
Amici	Italian
27 Café Pacific	Seafood
Bijoux	French
Abacus	Eclectic
Nick & Sam's	Seafood/Steak
Lonesome Dove	Southwestern
Eddie V's	Seafood/Steak
Ellerbe	American
Fearing's	Southwestern
Lanny's Alta Cocina*	Eclectic
Tei Tei Robata Bar	Japanese

OTHER NOTEWORTHY PLACES

Angelo's	BBQ
Bolsa	American
Charlie Palmer	American
Craft	American
Del Frisco's	Steak
Five Sixty	American
Grace	American
Hattie's	American
Jasper's	American
Joe T. Garcia's	Tex-Mex
Lambert's	Steak
Mansion	American
Mia's	Tex-Mex
Mi Cocina	Tex-Mex
Nana	American
Neighborhood Services	American
Shinsei	Asian
Stephan Pyles	Southwestern
Tei An	Japanese
Tillman's	American

---

* Indicates a tie with restaurant above

Abacus 🅱 *Eclectic*
27 | 26 | 26 | $70

Knox-Henderson | 4511 McKinney Ave. (Armstrong Ave.) | Dallas | 214-559-3111 | www.kentrathbun.com

Chef Kent Rathbun's "top-tier" "culinary mecca" in Knox-Henderson is once again Dallas/Ft. Worth's Most Popular restaurant, catering to a "who's who" of society types with "haute" Eclectic cuisine in "inspired presentations" ("the lobster shooters are a must"); all comes served in a "sleek", cream leather-trimmed interior by an "impressive" staff that "really knows its stuff", so despite a bill that "hurts", for many it ranks as "close to perfect."

Amici 🅱🅼 *Italian*
28 | 17 | 24 | $39

Carrollton | 1022 S. Broadway St. (Belt Line Rd.) | 972-245-3191 | www.amicisignature.com

Oenophiles applaud the BYO policy with an "absurdly low $4.50 corkage fee" on top of the "truly remarkable" Italian cooking at this "quaint" second-floor restaurant set in a "historic building in Old Carrollton"; customers who "can't get enough" also say the "attentive" staff alone makes it well worth the trip.

Angelo's Barbecue 🅱 *BBQ*
24 | 15 | 16 | $15

Near West | 2533 White Settlement Rd. (bet. Henderson St. & University Dr.) | Ft. Worth | 817-332-0357 | www.angelosbbq.com

"You can smell the BBQ cooking from a mile away" at this "true Texas" "icon" in Near West Ft. Worth where "succulent" brisket and "meaty" ribs are served cafeteria-style with "ice-cold" schooners of beer; it's been open since 1958, so perhaps the "roadhouse"-style setting has "seen better days", yet it remains a "must-visit" in the area.

Bijoux 🅱 *French*
27 | 26 | 26 | $77

West Lovers Lane | Inwood Vill. | 5450 W. Lovers Ln. (Inwood Rd.) | Dallas | 214-350-6100 | www.bijouxrestaurant.com

"Prepare yourself" for a "top-of-the-line" "two-and-a-half-hour meal" at Scott Gottlich's "enchanting" West Lovers Lane destination whipping up "heavenly" prix fixe meals of New French cuisine that's "absolutely worth the splurge"; it follows through with an "attractive", chandelier-lit interior and "impeccable", "unstuffy" service, so most conclude they "couldn't recommend it more."

Bolsa *American*
26 | 23 | 22 | $33

Oak Cliff | 614 W. Davis St. (Cedar Hill Ave.) | Dallas | 214-367-9367 | www.bolsadallas.com

"Nothing misses" at this "hip" gas station–turned–"local hangout" in the heart of Oak Cliff cooking up "clever" New American creations that rely on "local and organic" ingredients; an "easygoing" staff and relatively "inexpensive" prices suit the overall "unpretentious" vibe; P.S. on Sundays it hosts a farmer's market featuring fresh local produce and cheese.

Bonnell's 🅱🅼 *Southwestern*
29 | 26 | 28 | $53

Southwest | 4259 Bryant Irvin Rd. (Southwest Blvd.) | Ft. Worth | 817-738-5489 | www.bonnellstexas.com

"Master" chef, and "one of the nicest [guys] in town", Jon Bonnell is behind this Southwest Ft. Worth "destination" that's rated No. 1 for Food – with a rare 29 – in the Dallas/Ft. Worth Survey thanks to his "brilliant"

	FOOD	DECOR	SERVICE	COST

brand of "modern Texas cuisine" starring loads of "local game" (elk tacos, anyone?); factor in "flawless" service and an "understated" Western-style setting – not to mention relatively understated prices – and you've got a "class act" all around.

Cacharel ⊠ *French* | 28 | 26 | 27 | $52 |

Arlington | Brookhollow Tower Two | 2221 E. Lamar Blvd., 9th fl. (Ballpark Way) | 817-640-9981 | www.cacharel.net

"First-class" all the way, this Arlington entry "overlooking the new Cowboys dome" delivers true "fine dining", from the "marvelous" French fare and steaks down to the "wonderful" Grand Marnier soufflé; it's certainly not inexpensive, but with a "posh" cream-colored setting and "charming" service, it's the "perfect spot for a quiet, romantic dinner."

Café Pacific *Seafood* | 27 | 25 | 26 | $51 |

Park Cities | 24 Highland Park Vill. (Preston Rd.) | Dallas | 214-526-1170 | www.cafepacificdallas.com

A Park Cities "institution", this "clubby" seafooder is where "elegant ladies and dapper gents" savor "wonderful" dishes prepared "with flair" plus some of the "best martinis in town"; it's all a bit "old school", with "watchful, expert service" making for a "memorable" meal at prices that well-heeled regulars can well afford; P.S. "tables are tough to get on weekends", so reserve in advance.

Charlie Palmer at the Joule *American* | 25 | 27 | 23 | $72 |

Downtown Dallas | Joule Hotel | 1530 Main St. (bet. Akard & Ervay Sts.) | Dallas | 214-261-4600 | www.charliepalmer.com

A "jewel" in the "luxury" Joule Hotel Downtown, this entry from celeb chef Charlie Palmer "lives up to the hype" with "deliciously different" New American cuisine and an "impressive" array of wines accessed on an electronic touch pad; with a "gorgeous" room brimming with "celebrities" and an "expert" staff that "always delivers", admirers insist it's "one of Dallas' finest" – but you'll need that extra "credit line" to afford it.

Craft Dallas *American* | 26 | 27 | 25 | $70 |

Victory Park | W Hotel | 2440 Victory Park Ln. (Olive St.) | Dallas | 214-397-4111 | www.craftdallas.com

Simply "outstanding" laud fans of *Top Chef* Tom Colicchio's stylish outpost in the W Hotel in Victory Park, featuring "delectable" New American dishes that make "incredible use" of "fresh, seasonal and local ingredients"; though the "first-class" service and luxe, "modern" digs are "beyond reproach", some customers chide the "extremely high prices."

Del Frisco's Double Eagle Steak House *Steak* | 26 | 25 | 25 | $67 |

North Dallas | 5251 Spring Valley Rd. (Dallas N. Tollway) | Dallas | 972-490-9000

Downtown Ft. Worth | 812 Main St. (8th St.) | Ft. Worth | 817-877-3999

www.delfriscos.com

"When you want to impress" – especially "on the company dime" – this high-end chophouse chain in North Dallas and Downtown Ft. Worth fits the bill with "top-flight steaks", a well-stocked wine cellar and "spectacular" desserts; "handsome" digs done up in "dark, rich woods" with "lots of brass" make for a "consistent", if somewhat predictable, experience.

Eddie V's Prime Seafood *Seafood/Steak*   27 | 26 | 25 | $53

Cultural District | 3100 W. Seventh St. (Bailey Ave.) | Ft. Worth |
817-336-8000 | www.eddiev.com

A "class act", this Austin-bred chainlet in Ft. Worth's Cultural District
offers a "first-rate experience on all counts", from the "fabulous"
steaks and seafood (including "amazing fresh oysters" and crab) to
the "professional" service and "modern", leather-trimmed quarters;
given the "expense-account" pricing, many seek out the "half-price
apps" deals during happy hour.

Ellerbe Fine Food 🗷🅼 *American*   27 | 21 | 22 | $44

Hospital District | 1501 W. Magnolia Ave. (7th Ave.) | Ft. Worth |
817-926-3663 | www.ellerbefinefoods.com

Ft. Worth's increasingly "hip" Hospital District is home to this "very
LA" venue spotlighting chef/co-owner Molly McCook's "highly imaginative" American cuisine rooted in "Southern" tradition and based on
"local, seasonal" ingredients; factor in moderate prices and a "pleasant" converted gas station setting, and it's no wonder locals are laud-
ing this "find" as "fabulous."

Fearing's *Southwestern*   27 | 28 | 28 | $79

Uptown | Ritz-Carlton Hotel | 2121 McKinney Ave. (Pearl St.) | Dallas |
214-922-4848 | www.fearingsrestaurant.com

Smitten fans "have nothing but superlatives" for Dean Fearing's venue
in Uptown's Ritz-Carlton Hotel, where "everything shines bright",
from the "memorable" Southwestern meals to the "power-broker" clientele; "impeccable" service (including "tableside visits" from the
man himself) in the "maze" of "beautiful" dining spaces elevates it to
among "Dallas' finest" – if there's one place to "go bust", this is it.

Five Sixty Wolfgang Puck 🗷 *American*   25 | 27 | 22 | $63

Downtown Dallas | Reunion Tower | 300 E. Reunion Blvd. (Houston St.) |
Dallas | 214-741-5560 | www.wolfgangpuck.com

Set in the Reunion Tower's glowing glass ball above Downtown Dallas,
this "memorable" venture features a menu that reads like a "best-of-
Wolfgang-Puck compilation", with his "exciting" Asian-inflected New
American signatures like Shanghai-style lobster and Chinois chicken
salad; a "professional" staff and "panoramic" views from the "revolving"
dining room are perks, even if a few leave feeling "queasy" about the tab.

French Room 🗷🅼 *American/French*   28 | 29 | 29 | $88

Downtown Dallas | Hotel Adolphus | 1321 Commerce St. (Field St.) |
Dallas | 214-742-8200 | www.hoteladolphus.com

It's "like eating at Versailles" at this "opulent" rococo showpiece in the
landmark Hotel Adolphus Downtown, with a "luxurious" setting and
"discreet" staff that "tends to you like royalty"; factor in "superb", "sophisticated" French–New American cuisine and it all adds up to an
"over-the-top" experience that's "close to perfection", and priced ac-
cordingly; P.S. jackets required.

Grace 🗷 *American*   23 | 27 | 25 | $62

Downtown Ft. Worth | 777 Main St. (7th St.) | Ft. Worth | 817-877-3388 |
www.gracefortworth.com

This "cosmopolitan" venture in Downtown Ft. Worth "blazes a bold
trail" with "creative" American cuisine; the setting is "stunning" and

service "hits its mark", adding up to a "superlative" experience, but "you pay for it."

Hattie's *American*
26 | 24 | 23 | $38

Oak Cliff | 418 N. Bishop Ave. (8th St.) | Dallas | 214-942-7400 | www.hatties.net

A "real find" in Oak Cliff, this "bright and cheery" "gem" dispenses "elegantly prepared" American fare steeped in Low Country tradition (think fried green tomatoes or shrimp and grits); the "charming", light-filled space is all awash with Southern hospitality that makes you "feel like dining in a friend's home", and the tab is equally easygoing.

Jasper's *American*
24 | 24 | 23 | $45

West Plano | Shops at Legacy | 7161 Bishop Rd. (Legacy Dr.) | Plano | 469-229-9111 | www.jaspers-restaurant.com

"Über-chef" Kent Rathbun (of Abacus) is behind this "attractive" West Plano canteen turning out "sophisticated" takes on "homestyle" Americana headlined by "divine" blue-cheese potato chips and slow-smoked ribs; a "savvy", "tuned-in" staff increases the appeal, though a few find the bills a touch "overpriced" for "backyard" fare.

Joe T. Garcia's ⊘ *Tex-Mex*
20 | 23 | 21 | $22

North Side | 2201 N. Commerce St. (22nd St.) | Ft. Worth | 817-626-4356 | www.joets.com

"What they do, they do very well" profess fans of this "venerable" Tex-Mex "institution" on the North Side of Ft. Worth turning out a "limited", "no-surprises" menu (fajitas or enchiladas) capped by "killer 'ritas"; yet despite a "beautiful", "historic" setting with a "heavenly" poolside garden, an "underwhelmed" contingent is content to cede it "to the tourists"; P.S. cash only.

Lambert's *Steak*
23 | 20 | 23 | $41

Near West | 2731 White Settlement Rd. (Foch St.) | Ft. Worth | 817-882-1161 | www.lambertsfortworth.com

This Near West Ft. Worth steakhouse trades in "delicious" fare like oak-grilled, all-natural meats and "Southwestern-style" entrees; an "unobtrusive" staff and gussied-up rustic decor create an ambiance that's upmarket without feeling "overdone or fussy"; P.S. live music on Saturday nights.

Lanny's Alta Cocina Mexicana Ⓢ Ⓜ *Eclectic*
27 | 24 | 25 | $55

Cultural District | 3405 W. Seventh St. (Boland St.) | Ft. Worth | 817-850-9996 | www.lannyskitchen.com

"Perfect for a date", this "beautifully-appointed" Cultural District mainstay showcases "palate-pleasing" "Mexican-inspired" Eclectic plates from chef-owner Lanny Lancarte (a "maestro" in the kitchen); "personal" service and a "chic", "casually elegant" setting account in part for the "expensive" cost; P.S. the tasting menu with wine pairings is "highly recommended."

Lonesome Dove
Western Bistro Ⓢ *Southwestern*
27 | 23 | 24 | $53

Stockyards | 2406 N. Main St. (24th St.) | Ft. Worth | 817-740-8810 | www.lonesomedovebistro.com

Diners declare themselves "blown away" by celebrity chef-owner Tim Love's "terrific" "modern takes" on cowboy cuisine ("love the buffalo!") at his "chic" Southwestern flagship set on the edge of the Ft. Worth Stockyards; despite "splurge"-worthy pricing and a few "gaps in service", "out-of-towners" especially find it "hard to beat"; P.S. "reservations a must."

Mansion, The *American*

| 26 | 26 | 26 | $79 |

Uptown | Rosewood Mansion on Turtle Creek | 2821 Turtle Creek Blvd. (Gillespie St.) | Dallas | 214-559-2100 | www.mansiononturtlecreek.com

This Uptown Dallas "icon" turns out an "haute" American menu in glossy, "modern" digs; a "thrilling" wine list and "seamless" service that "makes you feel like an oil baron" mean it's still a "top" pick for special occasions.

Mia's *Tex-Mex*

| 23 | 13 | 17 | $21 |

Lemmon Avenue | 4322 Lemmon Ave. (Wycliff Ave.) | Dallas | 214-526-1020 | www.miastexmex.com

"Two words: brisket tacos" sum up much of the appeal of this Lemmon Avenue *cocina*, a "longtime favorite" for "wonderful", "no-fuss" Tex-Mex eats, as evidenced by the perpetual "lines" out front; no, there's "not much decor" or "elbow room" either, but bargain prices compensate.

Mi Cocina *Tex-Mex*

| 20 | 19 | 20 | $25 |

Galleria | Galleria | 13350 N. Dallas Pkwy. (Lyndon B. Johnson Frwy.) | Dallas | 972-239-6426

Lake Highlands | 7201 Skillman St. (Walnut Hill Ln.) | Dallas | 214-503-6426

Park Cities | Highland Park Vill. | 77 Highland Park Vill. (Preston Rd.) | Dallas | 214-521-6426

Preston Forest | Preston Forest Vill. | 11661 Preston Rd. (bet. Forest Ln. & Preston Haven Dr.) | Dallas | 214-265-7704

West Village | West Vill. | 3699 McKinney Ave. (Lemmon Ave.) | Dallas | 469-533-5663

North Dallas | 18352 Dallas Pkwy. (Frankford Rd.) | Dallas | 972-250-6426

West Plano | Lakeside Mkt. | 4001 Preston Rd. (Lorimar Dr.) | Plano | 469-467-8655

West Plano | Shops at Legacy | 5760 Legacy Dr. (Bishop Rd.) | Plano | 972-473-8745

Sundance Square | Sundance Sq. | 509 Main St. (bet. 4th & 5th Sts.) | Ft. Worth | 817-877-3600

Southlake | Southlake Town Sq. | 1276 Main St. (Carroll Ave.) | 817-410-6426 www.mcrowd.com

Additional locations throughout the Dallas/Ft. Worth area

The high-profile departure of founder Mico Rodriguez hasn't muffled the buzz at these "tony" Tex-Mex chain cantinas favored by the "young and beautiful" for their "dependable" grub and "killer" Mambo Taxi 'ritas ("after two you'll want to mambo and need a taxi"); detractors decry "overrated" eats, "too-expensive" tabs and variable service, though the primo "people-watching" keeps the "crowds" coming back.

Nana *American*

| 27 | 28 | 26 | $69 |

Market Center | Hilton Anatole Hotel | 2201 Stemmons Frwy., 27th fl. (Market Center Blvd.) | Dallas | 214-761-7470 | www.nanarestaurant.com

"High-quality dining in many senses" can be found at this "top-shelf" New American on the 27th floor of the Hilton Anatole in Market Center, offering "fantastic" views to accompany the "stellar" cuisine by chef Anthony Bombaci; thoughtfully curated Asian art on display and a "lovely" staff enhance the experience, justifying the "expensive" tabs.

	FOOD	DECOR	SERVICE	COST

Neighborhood Services Ⓢ *American* | 23 | 20 | 23 | $46 |

Knox-Henderson | 2405 N. Henderson St. (Capital Ave.) | Dallas | 214-827-2405
West Lovers Lane | 5027 W. Lovers Ln. (Inwood Rd.) | Dallas | 214-350-5027
www.neighborhoodservicesdallas.com

"Haute blue-plate specials" headline chef Nick Badovinus' "ingredient-driven" New American menu delivering "creative twists on homestyle food" at this "hip" West Lovers Lane "favorite"; the servers (dressed "like Ivy League cheerleaders") are "impressive", and while some critics cite "extremely long waits" (due to a no-reservations policy), others take the opportunity for a little "social networking" at the "trendy bar", or "call ahead to get their name on the list"; P.S. the Knox-Henderson branch opened post-Survey.

Nick & Sam's *Seafood/Steak* | 27 | 25 | 26 | $69 |

Uptown | 3008 Maple Ave. (bet. Carlisle & Wolf Sts.) | Dallas | 214-871-7444 | www.nick-sams.com

"You can feel the power" in this Uptown steakhouse known for "over-the-top" meals of "fabulous meat", seafood and "amazing sides"; the "dark", "old-fashioned" setting, brightened up by a "piano player in the kitchen", is the kind of place where regulars request their favorite table and "superb" waiter, so get in the swing and "bring the corporate AmEx or a Brinks truck."

Pappas Bros. Steakhouse Ⓢ *Steak* | 28 | 25 | 26 | $63 |

Love Field | 10477 Lombardy Ln. (Northwest Hwy.) | Dallas | 214-366-2000 | www.pappasbros.com

Smitten carnivores swear "it doesn't get any better" than this Pappas family "flagship" located in Love Field, where the "luscious", "perfectly marbled" steaks "melt in your mouth"; the "memorable" meals are enhanced by "outstanding" wines, "fawning" service and a "lavish" 1920s-inspired setting – just "be prepared to shell out the big bucks."

Saint-Emilion ⓈⓂ *French* | 28 | 26 | 28 | $51 |

Cultural District | 3617 W. Seventh St. (Montgomery St.) | Ft. Worth | 817-737-2781 | www.saint-emilionrestaurant.com

"Always a winner for a special occasion" or "date night", this petite restaurant in Ft. Worth's Cultural District serves "amazing", "authentic" Gallic food "prepared with love and care" in a "romantic" country French setting; ever-present co-chef/owner Bernard Tronche "oversees every little detail", ensuring "outstanding" service and maintaining flexibility in the "high-end", prix fixe-only format.

Shinsei Ⓢ *Asian* | 23 | 21 | 21 | $48 |

West Lovers Lane | 7713 Inwood Rd. (bet. Newmore Ave. & W. Lovers Ln.) | Dallas | 214-352-0005 | www.shinseirestaurant.com

A vibrant "buzz" surrounds this pricey "people-watching place" on West Lovers Lane hosted by Lynae Fearing and Tracy Rathbun (wives of Dean and Kent), where Pan-Asian cuisine shares top billing with "gorgeous, fresh sushi"; though some would like "more room", the space's sexy earth tones, loungey accents and "warm" service are certainly appealing; P.S. lunch is served only on Fridays.

	FOOD	DECOR	SERVICE	COST

Stephan Pyles Ⓢ *Southwestern* — 26 | 26 | 26 | $65

Arts District | 1807 Ross Ave. (St. Paul St.) | Dallas | 214-580-7000 |
www.stephanpyles.com

"Legendary", "charming" chef Stephan Pyles turns out another hit with this "must-do" Southwestern in the Arts District whose "rock-star" roster includes "spectacular" ceviche, "top-notch" turf items and an "impressive" wine list; though a few critics huff there's "too much hype", fans affirm the "vibrant" atmosphere, "stylish" decor and "wonderful" service all add to a "memorable experience" that's worth the big bucks; P.S. dine at the bar for a prime view of the kitchen in action.

Tei An Ⓢ *Japanese* — ▽ 28 | 27 | 26 | $49

Arts District | One Arts Plaza | 1722 Routh St. (bet. Flora St. & Ross Ave.) |
Dallas | 214-220-2828

Pioneering chef-owner Teiichi Sakurai is a "master of his genre", showcasing "fresh handmade" soba noodles (as well as more "esoteric" specials and sushi) at this "unique, cutting-edge" Japanese atelier in the Arts District that never fails to "delight palates of the adventurous"; authentic touches from the "stoneware and wicker mats" to the "spot-on service" make it a "culinary must", so fans only wish they could "afford it more often"; P.S. there's also a rooftop cocktail bar.

Tei Tei Robata Bar Ⓜ *Japanese* — 27 | 21 | 24 | $55

Knox-Henderson | 2906 N. Henderson Ave. (Willis Ave.) | Dallas |
214-828-2400 | www.teiteirobata.com

Enthusiasts exalt the "uncompromising quality" of the "top-notch" sushi, "Tokyo"-style robata and "fantastic sake menu" at this Japanese "marvel" in Knox-Henderson; "everything is served elegantly and simply" in a contemporary, warmly lit space, though a few aren't so keen on the "scene", the "long wait" and the price/portion ratio.

Teppo Yakitori & Sushi Bar Ⓜ *Japanese* — 28 | 22 | 27 | $46

Greenville Avenue | 2014 Greenville Ave. (Prospect Ave.) | Dallas |
214-826-8989 | www.teppo.com

"Who knows how they get such fresh fish, but it's wonderful" attest admirers of the "brilliant" sushi, while grill-lovers laud the "stellar" yakitori by "chefs who take pride in their work" at this "comfortable" Japanese standout on Greenville Avenue; the slightly upscale tabs are further justified by a "knowledgeable" staff that always "recognizes" return customers.

Tillman's Roadhouse *American* — 23 | 24 | 23 | $35

Oak Cliff | 324 W. Seventh St. (N. Bishop Ave.) | Dallas |
214-942-0988 ⓈⓂ
Near West | 2933 Crockett St. (bet. Currie & Norwood Sts.) | Ft. Worth |
817-850-9255
www.tillmansroadhouse.com

"Metrosexuals meet cowboys" at this "unique" "Western-chic" venue in Oak Cliff, where "faux deer heads, chandeliers" and "old black-and-white movies in the lounge", plus the warm personality of "queen-of-the-place" owner Sara Tillman, set a "magical" tone for feasting on "fantastic", "gourmeted-up roadhouse" cuisine (topped off by "tableside s'mores"); with a moderate bill to boot, fans are "blown away"; N.B. the Near West branch opened post-Survey.

Yao Fuzi Cuisine *Chinese*

| 28 | 24 | 25 | $30 |

West Plano | 4757 W. Park Blvd. (bet. Ohio Dr. & Preston Rd.) | Plano |
214-473-9267 | www.yaofuzi.com

Customers "crave" the "exceptional" Shanghainese cuisine (featuring both "Americanized" dishes and "authentic" discoveries) at this "lovely" family-owned "gem" in a West Plano strip mall, a "big step above the typical joint" boasting a "calm, beautiful" ambiance along with "congenial" service; it's "not too expensive" either, making it a "top" choice all around.

York Street 🅈 🅜 *American*

| 28 | 23 | 27 | $62 |

East Dallas | 6047 Lewis St. (Skillman St.) | Dallas | 214-826-0968 |
www.yorkstreetdallas.com

Set in a "minimalist" white storefront, this tiny East Dallas destination from chef Sharon Hage is "sure to wow" with an "intelligent" ever-changing New American menu that emphasizes "the freshest, seasonal ingredients" in "flawless" dishes; factor in a tightly edited wine list and "impeccable service", and it's easy to see why it's "worth every penny"; P.S. dinner only, with lunch service on Wednesdays.

Yutaka Sushi Bistro 🅈 *Japanese*

| 28 | 21 | 26 | $52 |

Uptown | 2633 McKinney Ave. (Boll St.) | Dallas | 214-969-5533 |
www.yutakasushibistro.com

"Perfection in execution and presentation" sets apart this "popular" Uptown Japanese where "freaking genius" chef-owner Yutaka Yamato "makes everything look effortless" as he prepares the "finest" sushi and small plates; "warm service" and an adjacent sake lounge help ease the "waits" inside the "Lilliputian setting", and help the "pricey" tabs go down easier too; P.S. reservations accepted for six or more.

Denver & Mountain Resorts

TOP FOOD RANKING

Restaurant	Cuisine
28 Fruition	American
Frasca	Italian
Matsuhisa	Japanese
Splendido	American
Mizuna	American
27 Sushi Sasa	Japanese
Sushi Den	Japanese
Virgilio's	Italian
Rioja	Mediterranean
L'Atelier	French
Six89	American
Del Frisco's	Steak
Luca d'Italia	Italian
Z Cuisine	French
26 Izakaya Den	Asian
Grouse Mountain	American
Montagna	American
Kitchen	Eclectic
Keystone Ranch	American
Tables	American

OTHER NOTEWORTHY PLACES

Argyll	British
Barolo Grill	Italian
Black Cat	American
Cafe Brazil	South American
Colt & Gray	American
Duo	American
Elway's	Steak
Flagstaff House	American
Jax Fish House	Seafood
La Tour	French
Marco's	Pizza
Olivéa	Mediterranean
Opus	American
Palace Arms	American
Panzano	Italian
Squeaky Bean	American
Sweet Basil	American
TAG	Eclectic
Venue	American
Vesta	American

Argyll ● *British*

21 **19** **22** **$30**

Cherry Creek | 2700 E. Third Ave. (Clayton St.) | Denver | 720-382-1117 | argyllpub.com

Just "smashing" say supporters of this "trendy, innovative", British-style gastropub in Cherry Creek, whose menu highlights include the "great food of Scotland", "decadent mac 'n' cheese" and "awesome craft beers"; an "enthusiastic staff" and "killer patio" are two more reasons why the "amusing crowd" that comes here calls it "money well spent."

Barolo Grill ☒Ⓜ *Italian*

26 **23** **26** **$55**

Cherry Creek | 3030 E. Sixth Ave. (bet. Milwaukee & St. Paul Sts.) | Denver | 303-393-1040 | www.barologrilldenver.com

"Surviving trends and busts", this rustic, "comfortable" Cherry Creek "mainstay" delivers an "ever-changing menu" of "tremendous", "imaginative" Northern Italian dishes alongside an "incomparable wine list"; the "charming", "eager-to-please" staff's much-ballyhooed "yearly trip to Italy" "seems to pay off" in "loyalty and knowledge" – but "it's gonna cost ya!"; P.S. "ask for the table by the fireplace for a romantic dinner."

Black Cat *American*

24 **21** **23** **$53**

Boulder | 1964 13th St. (Pearl St.) | 303-444-5500 | www.blackcatboulder.com

For the "ultimate farm-to-table experience", forage no further than this "quaint" Boulder bistro where chef-owner "Eric Skokan rocks your world" with "innovative", "sophisticated" New American cuisine (many of the ingredients are "grown on his own farm") served "without pretense" by a "knowledgeable" staff; just like the regular *carte*, the "fabulous tasting menus" and "lovely wine list featuring more than just the usual suspects" are "well worth" the "pricey" charges.

Cafe Brazil ☒Ⓜ *S American*

24 **17** **22** **$36**

North Denver | 4408 Lowell Blvd. (44th Ave.) | Denver | 303-480-1877 | www.cafebrazildenver.com

North Denver denizens "can't get enough" of the "extensive", "delicious mix" of "bold" South American flavors whipped up at this "relaxed" yet "lively" "tropical food vacation", which is also lauded for its "staggering rum selection"; the colorful setting is "a wee bit tacky" for some tastes, but hey, at least it's "something to talk about."

Colt & Gray *American*

25 **25** **23** **$44**

Platte River Valley | 1553 Platte St. (bet. 15th & 16th Sts.) | Denver | 303-477-1447 | www.coltandgray.com

"Intriguing" New American dishes "you will not find anywhere else" make this "fabulous new addition" to the Platte River Valley "worth repeat trips" – or so says its "chic clientele", which also toasts the "clever cocktails" mixed by "superb bartenders"; the "small space" is reminiscent of a "glam lodge" that's "warm and inviting on snowy winter evenings" ("cozy up to the fireplace") and "fun" in summer when the patio beckons.

Del Frisco's Double Eagle Steak House *Steak*

27 **24** **26** **$68**

Greenwood Village | Denver Tech Ctr. | 8100 E. Orchard Rd. (I-25, exit 198) | 303-796-0100 | www.delfriscos.com

"Businessmen on expense accounts" join the "glitterati", e.g. "Broncos", at this Greenwood Village "power scene" known for its "generous" portions of "outstanding steaks", "impressive wine list" and "big bills"; a "knowledgeable, attentive staff" helps set a "relaxed" tone in the "warm, sumptuous" room, but be warned if you're seated close to the "hot bar": it's "sometimes too noisy"; P.S. there's also a "super" cigar lounge.

Duo *American*

26 | 21 | 24 | $41

Highlands | 2413 W. 32nd Ave. (Zuni St.) | Denver | 303-477-4141 | www.duodenver.com

"A fantastic escape from suburban monotony", this "hip", "lively" Highlands "gathering place" turns out "exquisite" "farm-to-table" New American cuisine that "won't break the bank"; "superb service" sets a "warm, friendly" tone, but the setting's "hard surfaces" ("wood floors, brick walls") make it "typically loud" – then again, all those "delicious cocktails" should probably share the blame.

Elway's *Steak*

24 | 24 | 23 | $57

Cherry Creek | 2500 E. First Ave. (University Blvd.) | Denver | 303-399-5353
Downtown Denver | Ritz-Carlton Denver | 1881 Curtis St. (19th St.) | Denver | 303-312-3107
www.elways.com

"Big John" "scores big" at this "always hopping" "place to meet and greet in Cherry Creek" (with a "sophisticated, welcoming" Downtown sibling), a "masculine", "classy environment" where "superb" servers present a "diverse menu" starring "flat-out outstanding", "beautifully seasoned slabs of grilled beef" alongside an "impressive wine list"; the "lively" bar scene is "truly spectacular", plus it offers its own "nightly special": "cougar"; P.S. though it's "expensive", "compared to the competition, prices are reasonable."

Flagstaff House *American*

26 | 27 | 27 | $72

Boulder | 1138 Flagstaff Rd. (on Flagstaff Mtn.) | 303-442-4640 | www.flagstaffhouse.com

At this "time-tested classic" "up the mountain", it's hard to decide what's most "over-the-top": the "million-dollar views" of "Boulder and beyond", the "exquisite", "gourmet" New American fare with "fancy presentations" or the "formal" service from the "superb" staff "in tuxedos"; it could be the "amazing", "novel"-sized wine list – but it's most likely the "crazy expensive" prices (still, everyone should "experience it at least once").

Frasca Food and Wine 🄔 *Italian*

28 | 24 | 28 | $70

Boulder | 1738 Pearl St. (18th St.) | 303-442-6966 | www.frascafoodandwine.com

"Believe the hype!" – this "beautiful little place" in Boulder is voted Colorado's Most Popular restaurant thanks to chef Lachlan Mackinnon-Patterson's "incredibly innovative", "ethereal" cuisine from the Friuli region of Northern Italy and "consummate host"/"outstanding sommelier" Bobby Stuckey's "killer wine list" and "unbelievable pairings"; it's "expensive", "yet feels like a bargain" considering it's such a "'wow' experience"; in fact, "the only flaws are the cramped seating" and "difficulty getting reservations", so if you haven't booked "the prescribed 30 days in advance", "go early and sit at the bar" or the salumi counter.

Fruition *American* | 28 | 22 | 27 | $55 |

Country Club | 1313 E. Sixth Ave. (bet. Lafayette & Marion Sts.) | Denver | 303-831-1992 | www.fruitionrestaurant.com

"A not-to-be-missed adventure" sums up this "shining diamond" between Country Club and Capitol Hill, where chef Alex Seidel creates "innovative", "beautifully plated", "ever-changing" New American cuisine that earns Denver's No. 1 Food rating (and gets a boost from "excellent wine pairings"); the "tables are cramped" in the "tight quarters" ("plan ahead to get in"), but the "warmth" of "witty" host Paul Attardi and his "exceptional" staff creates a "cozy feel", which also helps to make the "expensive-side" tabs "seem more reasonable."

Grouse Mountain Grill *American* | 26 | 24 | 24 | $65 |

Beaver Creek | Pines Lodge Beaver Creek Resort | 141 Scott Hill Rd. (Village Rd.) | 970-949-0600 | www.grousemountaingrill.com

Settle in for a "delightful" evening in the "elegant", "warm" dining room of Beaver Creek Resort's Pines Lodge, where "attentive" servers ferry "spectacular", "innovative" New American fare; or you might choose the "great piano bar" to listen to jazz (Thursdays–Saturdays in season) while getting "Rocky Mountain high" via pours from the "dictionary-thick wine list" – just be warned: like the food, the vino's "exceptionally expensive" (but most find everything "worth it").

Izakaya Den Ⓜ *Asian* | 26 | 26 | 23 | $44 |

Platt Park | 1518 S. Pearl St. (Florida Ave.) | Denver | 303-771-0691 | www.izakayaden.net

"Just as good" as Sushi Den across the street, this "fabulous" Platt Park offshoot is "a bit more creative", as it offers its "fantastic fresh fish" and "delicious rolls" alongside "innovative" Asian fusion "cooked small plates" boasting "amazing presentations and flavors" (there are "great cocktails" too, and everything's delivered by "accommodating" staffers); in addition, the "trendy" space is "bigger" than its "overcrowded" sibling, which "means less wait time" and an overall "more serene" experience.

Jax Fish House *Seafood* | 24 | 19 | 21 | $43 |

LoDo | 1539 17th St. (Wazee St.) | Denver | 303-292-5767 | www.jaxfishhousedenver.com
Boulder | 928 Pearl St. (bet. 9th & 10th Sts.) | 303-444-1811 | www.jaxfishhouseboulder.com

"Even at a mile high, you can taste the salty sea" at these "friendly", "trendy" LoDo and Boulder seafooders dishing out "expertly prepared", "unique" fish dishes and "out-of-this-world oysters", the latter the star of the "exceptional-deal happy hour" at the "hopping bar"; other times, the fare's "a bit pricey", but the place is always "crowded", resulting in "decibel levels" that "could wake the dead."

Keystone Ranch Ⓢ Ⓜ *American* | 26 | 27 | 27 | $73 |

Keystone | Keystone Ranch Golf Course | 1437 Summit County Rd. 150 (Rd. D) | 970-496-4161 | www.keystoneresort.com

"The Old West never tasted so good" crow supporters of the "creative" New American dishes served at this "rustic", "beautiful, historic" Keystone "mountain hideaway", whose "magical" atmosphere is bolstered by an "extensive wine list" and an "incredible view"; "charming" staffers serving "desserts and after-dinner drinks by the roaring fire" make for "happy memories", but just "make sure your credit limit is high" before you go (not to worry, it's "worth" the "expensive" tabs).

Kitchen, The *Eclectic*
26 | 21 | 23 | $45

Boulder | 1039 Pearl St. (bet. 10th & 11th Sts.) | 303-544-5973 | www.thekitchencafe.com

You can spot everyone from "Boulder royalty" to students at this "lively", "casual" "staple", which bases its "innovative" Eclectic cuisine on "fabulously fresh" "farm-to-table" ingredients (the whole endeavor is "environmentally conscientious", and there are "quite a few values" on the menu to boot); what's more, the "friendly", "energetic staff" can steer you toward the most "wonderful wine picks" and "amazing drinks", either in the "unassuming" downstairs dining room or "fantastic" upstairs vino bar, featuring a "great happy hour."

L'Atelier *French*
27 | 24 | 25 | $57

Boulder | 1739 Pearl St. (18th St.) | 303-442-7233 | www.latelierboulder.com

"Clever" chef-owner Radek Cerny is "a master of creating inventive dishes" (with "impeccable sauces"), which are "beautifully presented" alongside an "extensive wine list" by "exceptionally attentive", "warm" staffers at this Boulder French with Eclectic influences; though it's "elbow-to-elbow", the "lovely", "little" digs feel "warm", and while it's somewhat pricey, the "half-priced wine" special on Tuesdays is a "wonderful" deal, just like the "bargain" "gourmet lunches."

La Tour *French*
25 | 23 | 25 | $64

Vail | 122 E. Meadow Dr. (I-70) | 970-476-4403 | www.latour-vail.com

"Consistently wonderful", "refined" French fare is matched by an impressive, "large wine list" at this "upscale" "gem" in Vail, boasting a "pretty", "cozy atmosphere" with "little nooks for romantic dining", "complemented by outstanding bronze sculptures at every table" (each for sale) plus a "most gracious staff"; yes, it's a real "splurge", but "watch for early and late season specials when the prices descend from the stratosphere."

Luca d'Italia ☒ Ⓜ *Italian*
27 | 21 | 26 | $55

Capitol Hill | 711 Grant St. (bet. 7th & 8th Aves.) | Denver | 303-832-6600 | www.lucadenver.com

"Another dazzling restaurant" from chef-owner Frank Bonanno (Mizuna), this "first-class tour of Italy" in "minimalist" Capitol Hill digs "impresses" with "delicious pastas" and "deftly prepared" secondi; the "warm" servers and sommeliers are "knowledgeable" to boot (the latter overseeing an "excellent wine list"), all of which conspires to create a "wonderful" "culinary adventure" that's "expensive" but "worth every penny."

Marco's Coal-Fired Pizzeria *Pizza*
25 | 20 | 23 | $24

Ballpark | 2129 Larimer St. (bet. 21st & 22nd Sts.) | Denver | 303-296-7000 | www.marcoscoalfiredpizza.com

"Definitely a home run for the Ballpark neighborhood", this "urban pie palace" churns out "divine pizzas" with "heavenly" "charred" crusts topped with "imported, quality ingredients", plus "amazing salads" and "ridiculously tasty" limoncello chicken wings; "friendly, attentive servers" who "never rush you" and a "hip", "vibrant scene" complete the "must-go" experience.

Matsuhisa *Japanese* | 28 | 22 | 24 | $73 |

Aspen | 303 E. Main St. (Monarch St.) | 970-544-6628 | www.matsuhisaaspen.com

"Every bit as good" as famed NYC sibling Nobu, this "hip" spot in "see-and-be-seen" Aspen offers "exquisite presentations" of "phenome-nal" sushi that's "worth every penny – and you will spend many of them"; a "professional staff" and a "wonderful" "zen atmosphere" add appeal (that the main dining room's in a "basement keeps few people away, so book as early as possible"), plus there's an "amazing" up-stairs bar whipping up "great saketinis that pack a punch."

Mizuna 🗷 Ⓜ *American* | 28 | 23 | 27 | $64 |

Capitol Hill | 225 E. Seventh Ave. (bet. Grant & Sherman Sts.) | Denver | 303-832-4778 | www.mizunadenver.com

"Another of Frank Bonanno's masterpieces", this "stellar" Capitol Hill New American "will knock your socks off" with its "innovative" dishes (consider the "heavenly tasting menu" with "great wine pairings", but definitely get the "legendary lobster mac 'n' cheese"); the environs are criticized for being "tight" and possibly "dated", but the "gracious", "impeccable service" helps to make it a "worry-free evening" that's "worth saving up for."

Montagna *American* | 26 | 25 | 26 | $77 |

Aspen | The Little Nell Hotel | 675 E. Durant Ave. (Spring St.) | 970-920-6330 | www.thelittlenell.com

What may be the "best wine list in the West" – a "superb", "thick book" ranging from "well priced" to "expensive" – complements chef Ryan Hardy's "astounding" New American cuisine at this "pinnacle of fine dining" in Aspen's Little Nell Hotel; the "elegant, timeless" environs are fittingly "luxurious" for the "formal" experience, and the ser-vice is expectedly "exceptional."

Olivéa *Mediterranean* | 24 | 20 | 22 | $45 |

Uptown | 719 E. 17th Ave. (Clarkson St.) | Denver | 303-861-5050 | www.olivearestaurant.com

Chef John Broening plies a "trendy crowd" with "intriguing", "season-ally driven", "reasonably priced" Mediterranean mains at this "chic", "charming" Uptown "gem", while his wife, Yasmin Lozada-Hissom, turns out "amazing confections" for dessert; despite the "somewhat noisy and cramped" setting, most folks "can't wait to go back" to eat, engage with the "relaxed but attentive" servers and sample more of the "excellent, off-the-beaten-path wines."

Opus *American* | 26 | 23 | 24 | $56 |

Littleton | 2575 W. Main St. (Curtice St.) | 303-703-6787 | www.opusdine.com

"Crazy-talented kitchen genius" Michael Long "beautifully composes" "artful", "remarkable" New American fare – attuned with "splendid wine pairings" – at this "delight" in Downtown Littleton; the "spacious, comfortable dining room" makes it suitable for "impressing a date or celebrating a special occasion", as do the "attentive, pleasant" staff-ers and "expensive tabs."

Palace Arms ⊠ *American* | 25 | 26 | 26 | $67

Downtown Denver | Brown Palace Hotel | 321 17th St. (Tremont Pl.) | Denver | 303-297-3111 | www.brownpalace.com

"You're treated like royalty" by "formal", "old-school" staffers at this "definition of elegant fine dining" "in a classy old hotel" Downtown, where "gorgeous Napoleonic trappings and antique flags" are highlights of the "sumptuous surroundings" and the "quality" New American cuisine comes at predictably high prices; maybe it's "dated" and "a little stuffy", but that's "part of the attraction" for folks who want to "feel like they have been transported back in time."

Panzano *Italian* | 25 | 22 | 23 | $50

Downtown Denver | 909 17th St. (Champa St.) | Denver | 303-296-3525 | www.panzano-denver.com

The majority of surveyors say they've "never been disappointed" by this "Downtown jewel" specializing in "solid, reliable" Northern Italian cuisine, complemented by "interesting wine selections" and conveyed by an "attentive, never overbearing staff" in "lovely" environs; the "wide range" of prices swings from "reasonable" to "bring a few gold bars", but the daily happy hour (2:30–6 PM) is always a "superb bargain."

Rioja *Mediterranean* | 27 | 24 | 25 | $49

Larimer Square | 1431 Larimer St. (bet. 14th & 15th Sts.) | Denver | 303-820-2282 | www.riojadenver.com

"Every detail is executed to perfection" at this "hit" in "trendy" Larimer Square, from "master of taste and design" Jennifer Jasinski's "outside-the-box" Mediterranean cuisine (particularly the "to-die-for homemade breads and pastas") to the "outstanding service" to the "hip, urban", "glassware"-bedecked decor; there is "one beef" though: the "terrible acoustics", exacerbated by the fact that it's "usually crowded"; P.S. tabs "can be expensive", but the "decadent" brunch is a "great value."

Six89 Ⓜ *American* | 27 | 21 | 26 | $50

Carbondale | 689 Main St. (7th St.) | 970-963-6890 | www.six89.com

For "outstanding" "big-city food" at "'down-valley' prices", Carbondale foodies flock to this "charming" venue where chef-owner Mark Fischer turns out "seasonal, imaginative", "beautifully presented" New American fare in a "homelike setting"; add "a great range of wines for all tastes and budgets", "exceptional service" and "memorable summer patio dining", and it's easy to see why nonlocals deem it "worth the journey."

Splendido at the Chateau Ⓜ *American* | 28 | 28 | 27 | $74

Beaver Creek | Beaver Creek Resort | 17 Chateau Ln. (Scott Hill Rd.) | 970-845-8808 | www.splendidobeavercreek.com

"It's like stepping into another world" at this "one-of-a-kind" "treat" in "posh Beaver Creek", where executive chef David Walford's New American fare is a "brilliantly executed" "feast for the eyes and palate" (matched by "fantastic wines"); the "stratospheric prices" are easier to swallow given the "accomplished" service, "plush", European-style surroundings with a "fireplace and a piano" and "beautiful mountain views" – no wonder the smitten suggest it should be "renamed 'Perfetto.'"

Squeaky Bean *American* | 24 | 18 | 22 | $31 |

Highlands | 3301 Tejon St. (33rd Ave.) | Denver | 303-284-0053 | www.thesqueakybean.net

"Such a deal!" cheer bargain-hunters about the "wonderful", "innovative" "farm-to-table" New American dishes served at this "funky" all-day "neighborhood spot" in the Highlands; "service can be spotty" and "tables are jammed" into the "small" "bistro"-like setting, but a "lovely patio" makes dining here in good weather "especially enjoyable."

Sushi Den *Japanese* | 27 | 23 | 23 | $48 |

South Denver | 1487 S. Pearl St. (E. Florida Ave.) | Denver | 303-777-0826 | www.sushiden.net

Come "early" or endure a "painful wait" at the "sushi capital" of South Denver, which is "crowded" "no matter the day of the week" with "fashionable", "trendy" types indulging in "the freshest fish" ("all the usuals, plus many inventive" rolls), in addition to scads of "amazing" cooked fare; unsurprisingly, the "contemporary" room is "really noisy" and the checks are "expensive", but all in all, it's "well worth it."

Sushi Sasa *Japanese* | 27 | 23 | 23 | $51 |

Highlands | 2401 15th St. (Platte St.) | Denver | 303-433-7272 | www.sushisasadenver.com

"Artful" presentations of "sumptuous" "fish so fresh it's still quivering on your plate" is the deal at this "heaven on earth" in the Highlands, where sushi mavens suggest you go for "genius" chef-owner Wayne Conwell's "startlingly original omakase"; indeed, those with "adventurous palates" (not to mention deep pockets) "have a ball" in environs that are "modern", "upscale" and "intimate" (though less so after a post-Survey expansion, which most likely outdates the Decor score).

Sweet Basil *American* | 26 | 23 | 24 | $57 |

Vail | 193 E. Gore Creek Dr. (Bridge St.) | 970-476-0125 | www.sweetbasil-vail.com

"End a powder day" at Vail's "extraordinary" "old faithful" that "lives up to its reputation" with "inventive", "exceptional" New American vittles boasting "bright, intense flavors", "excellent wines" and service with "not a whiff of pretension"; "ask for a window table" for "priceless views" of Gore Creek, or sit in the thick of things, soak up the "marvelous ambiance" and check out all the "interesting", lively diners "visiting their friends at the next table"; P.S. "lunch is wonderful, and more affordable than dinner."

Tables 🅢🅜 *American* | 26 | 17 | 22 | $43 |

Park Hill | 2267 Kearney St. (23rd Ave.) | Denver | 303-388-0299 | www.tablesonkearney.com

"Tons of personality" distinguishes this "treasure tucked away in Park Hill", where the "creative, delectable" New American cuisine boasts "flavors that are as bright as the chairs are mismatched" in the "shabby-chic" space; "friendly service" makes it "easy to feel at home", but it's "pretty small", so "be sure to make reservations."

TAG *Eclectic*   25 | 24 | 23 | $47

Larimer Square | 1441 Larimer St. (14th St.) | Denver | 303-996-9985 |
www.tag-restaurant.com

"Troy Guard is a magician in the kitchen" at this "expensive" Larimer Square "urban" "hot spot" conjuring "phenomenal", "adventurous", "ever-changing" Eclectic plates, which are "served with panache and a sense of humor" by "knowledgeable" staffers; the "stylish" dining room befits the "trendy" crowd, and the "inventive drinks" concocted with "fresh herbs and fruits" even more so.

Venue *American*   24 | 18 | 22 | $40

Highlands | 3609 W. 32nd Ave. (Lowell Blvd.) | Denver | 303-477-0477 |
www.venuebistro.com

Though the milieu is a somewhat "austere", "small rectangular room", the "unique interpretations" of "farm-to-table" New American fare from chef James Rugile "elevate the mood" at this moderately priced "standout" in "lively" Highlands; also "injecting a bit of fun" is the "cool" owner, who "happily greets guests", "works as a server and makes sure everything is perfect."

Vesta Dipping Grill *American*   24 | 23 | 23 | $45

LoDo | 1822 Blake St. (bet. 18th & 19th Sts.) | Denver | 303-296-1970 |
www.vestagrill.com

"Exciting from start to finish", this "distinctive" "LoDo favorite" takes "energetic crowds" on a "fun" "culinary journey" in which each New American plate is served with a choice of "wonderful dipping sauces" "ranging from subtle to in-your-face spicy"; "unique cocktails and wines" pair well with the "hip" space featuring "gorgeous exposed brick, wood beams" and "deafening" noise levels, and though tabs are "a little pricey", it's "still a treat" – for which you definitely "need reservations."

Virgilio's Pizzeria Napoletana *Italian*   27 | 16 | 21 | $20

Lakewood | Lakewood Commons | 7986 W. Alameda Ave.
(Wadsworth Blvd.) | 303-985-2777 | www.virgiliospizzeria.com

"Authentic" "New York" pizza comes "to 5,280 ft." via this Lakewood strip-mall spot tossing "wonderful" pies with "perfect crusts", "rich, spicy sauce" and "fresh toppings", plus other Italian staples ("awesome garlic twists", "amazing salads"); there's "little atmosphere" in the "little space" ("be prepared to wait", no reservations taken), but "that's ok", especially since it offers such good "value."

Z Cuisine A Côté 🅢🅜 *French*   27 | 22 | 22 | $51

Highlands | 2239 W. 30th Ave. (Wyandot St.) | Denver | 303-477-1111 |
www.zcuisineonline.com

"Highfalutin Francophiles" "can't believe" the "authentic", "gorgeous French feasts" served by a "knowledgeable staff" alongside "unpretentious wines" at this "adorable restaurant in the heart of the Highlands"; "sadly, it does not take reservations, seats only a handful of people" ("show up early" or "you risk dying of old age" waiting for a table), is open only Wednesday–Saturday and is "expensive" – but still, "it's worth the hassle."

Detroit

TOP FOOD RANKING

	Restaurant	Cuisine
28	Lark	Continental
	Bacco	Italian
27	Common Grill	American
	Zingerman's	Deli
	Café Cortina	Italian
26	Beverly Hills Grill	American
	Saltwater	Seafood
	West End Grill	American
	Streetside	Seafood
	Logan	American

OTHER NOTEWORTHY PLACES

Assaggi	Mediterranean
Atlas	Eclectic
Capital Grille	Steak
Earle	French/Italian
Eve	French
Hong Hua	Chinese
Rattlesnake Club	Seafood/Steak
Roast	Steak
Rugby Grille	American/Continental
Whitney	American

Assaggi Bistro Ⓜ *Mediterranean* 25 | 20 | 24 | $40

Ferndale | 330 W. Nine Mile Rd. (bet. Allen Rd. & Planavon St.) | 248-584-3499 | www.assaggibistro.com

"Caring, always-on-site owners" set the "warm, welcoming" tone at this Ferndale bistro serving "diverse", "well-prepared" Mediterranean dishes with "fabulous" "twists here and there", alongside "affordable wines and generous drinks"; if the interior's "a little pedestrian" for some, everyone raves about the "beautiful" dining garden, where some of the menu's "fresh veggies and herbs" are grown.

Atlas Global Bistro *Eclectic* 24 | 22 | 21 | $37

Orchestra Hall Area | 3111 Woodward Ave. (Charlotte St.) | 313-831-2241 | www.atlasglobalbistro.com

At this "cool, urban", "upscale but not stuffy" eatery near Orchestra Hall, "interesting takes" on Eclectic fare are offered "at a range of prices", just like the "plethora of wines"; it's "terrific before the symphony, etc.", as the "well-trained staff" "can handle a rush of diners" and there's "free van transportation" to nearby events.

Bacco Ristorante Ⓩ *Italian* 28 | 24 | 26 | $58

Southfield | 29410 Northwestern Hwy. (bet. Franklin & Inkster Rds.) | 248-356-6600 | www.baccoristorante.com

Though "not for the faint of wallet", this "gorgeous", "upscale", "see-and-be-seen" Italian in Southfield is "worth it" for "superb" fare matched by "exceptional wines" from The Boot, and the "experienced staff" can offer "great help" in choosing among the latter (occasionally in a "condescending" manner); it's "too small" for its popularity and diners are "sandwiched in like sardines", so if the weather's nice, ask for the "lovely" patio for more elbow room.

Beverly Hills Grill   American
26 | 20 | 25 | $35

Beverly Hills | 31471 Southfield Rd. (bet. Beverly & 13 Mile Rds.) | 248-642-2355 | www.beverlyhillsgrill.com

"White-tablecloth food at casual prices" is the deal at this "intimate", "sophisticated yet casual" "icon" in Beverly Hills, which whips its "creative", "ever-changing", "something-for-everyone" New American fare into "fabulous breakfasts", "marvelous lunches" and "delicious dinners" ("love the fish specials!"); the staff of "seasoned professionals" also earns kudos, and while "no reservations mean a long wait", habitués say it "isn't bad if you snuggle up to the bar."

Café Cortina ☒ Italian
27 | 25 | 26 | $59

Farmington Hills | 30715 W. 10 Mile Rd. (Orchard Lake Rd.) | 248-474-3033 | www.cafecortina.com

"For a special occasion", Farmington Hills folk head for this "cozy", "family-owned" Italian, where the *"fantastico"* fare – including provender "from the owner's garden" and "wonderful homemade pastas" – is conveyed by "meticulous" servers in three "beautiful", "romantic" rooms ("ask for a table by the fireplace"), plus a "heavenly" patio; yes, it's "expensive", but "you won't forget a meal you've eaten here."

Capital Grille   Steak
25 | 25 | 25 | $62

Troy | Somerset Collection-North | 2800 W. Big Beaver Rd. (bet. Coolidge Hwy. & Lakeview Dr.) | 248-649-5300 | www.thecapitalgrille.com

"A capital experience" exalt the "movers and shakers" who use their "large expense accounts" (the "big", "fabulous" chops "ain't cheap") at this chain steakhouse in Troy's "tony Somerset Collection"; "knowledgeable" staffers work the "beautiful" room, and even though "stuffiness"-shunners liken it to an "old-men's club", "give them credit – you don't feel like you're in a mall."

Common Grill Ⓜ American
27 | 22 | 25 | $39

Chelsea | 112 S. Main St. (bet. Middle & South Sts.) | 734-475-0470 | www.commongrill.com

Detroit gourmets say it's "worth the drive" to "charming Chelsea" for this "value"-venue's "uncommonly good" New American fare, especially the "wonderful range" of "contemporary, creative seafood"; no advance reservations are taken (you can call ahead and put your name on a list) and it's "always packed", which equals a "high noise level" in the "casual", "hardwood" setting – but on the upside, the acoustics are "great" for the jazz brunch held every third Sunday of the month.

Earle, The   French/Italian
23 | 21 | 22 | $47

Ann Arbor | 121 W. Washington St. (bet. Ashley & Main Sts.) | 734-994-0211 | www.theearle.com

The "brilliant", "deep, varied" wine list and "wealth-of-knowledge sommelier" get the most laurels at this "reliable" "standby" in Ann Arbor, but the "well-cooked and -presented" "classical" French-Italian fare holds its own; so, even if the world has possibly "passed it by cuisinewise", and the "cozy", "dark cellar setting" (often with "nice live jazz") could be "getting a bit dated", most of its customers wouldn't call it old – "comforting, maybe, but not old."

Eve 🅼 *French*

26 | 23 | 23 | $49

Kerrytown | 415 N. Fifth Ave. (on Kingsley St., bet. 4th & 5th Aves.) | Ann Arbor | 734-222-0711 | www.evetherestaurant.com

"Adventuresome" eclectic influences in New French fare prepared with "passion and precision" by "an innovative chef" who's an advocate of the Slow Food movement make this Kerrytown spot "a true delight" for foodies; "hip" staffers patrol the "chic", "urban setting" with exposed-brick walls, while pours from the "terrific wine list" help numb the "sting" of the "quite expensive" tabs.

Hong Hua *Chinese*

25 | 20 | 22 | $35

Farmington Hills | 27925 Orchard Lake Rd. (bet. Barlow St. & Twelve Mile Rd.) | 248-489-2280 | www.honghuafinedining.com

For an "authentic" Cantonese experience, supporters of this Farmington Hills haunt recommend you "let the staff suggest" some of the "exotic offerings on the separate menu published in Chinese only" – though whatever your order, expect "superb" fare (Peking duck prepared tableside is "a top choice") and prices that are just a "little" more "expensive" than the norm; "not the usual decor" ("spacious", "pleasant") entices folks to dine in, but "takeout is done well" also.

Lark, The 🅩🅼 *Continental*

28 | 27 | 28 | $90

West Bloomfield | 6430 Farmington Rd. (W. Maple Rd.) | 248-661-4466 | www.thelark.com

"Still the top of the heap", this "old-school elegant" (like a "posh" "country inn") destination in West Bloomfield again earns the Detroit Survey's No. 1 Food score for its "positively phenomenal" Continental prix fixe meals, which are bookended by appetizer and dessert carts conveying a "variety" of "outstanding" goodies; an "eager-to-please staff" and "stellar wine list" with "over 1,000 offerings" add to the "guaranteed memorable" experience, as does the "heavy bill" – however, "for what you get" ("huge quantities" plus "more of whatever you want" from the menu), it feels like a "relative bargain."

Logan 🅩🅼 *American*

26 | 21 | 24 | $52

Ann Arbor | 115 W. Washington St. (bet. Ashley & Main Sts.) | 734-327-2312 | www.logan-restaurant.com

"Delicious, inventive" New American dishes boasting "interesting presentations" come with "charming service" and a "polished" wine list at this "chic, upscale" option in Downtown Ann Arbor; it's "on the pricier side" for the area, but the "nice portions make the high tabs a little less painful", and the tasting menu is a "special-occasion treat."

Rattlesnake Club 🅩🅼 *Seafood/Steak*

24 | 25 | 24 | $58

River Place | Stroh's River Pl. | 300 River Place Dr. (Joseph Campau St.) | 313-567-4400 | www.rattlesnakeclub.com

Chef-owner "Jimmy Schmidt is still on his game" at this River Place "treasure", which serves "contemporary" steak and seafood with "interesting ingredients and preparations" in "beautiful surroundings", including alfresco seating boasting an "awesome view"; there's a "nice

selection of wines" as well, plus "attentive, courteous service" that
befits the "posh" pricing.

Roast *Steak* | 25 | 24 | 24 | $55 |

Downtown | Westin Book Cadillac Hotel | 1128 Washington Blvd.
(Michigan Ave.) | 313-961-2500 | www.roastdetroit.com

"If it walked on hooves", chef-owner Michael Symon "knows how to
serve it up with panache", especially the "innovative" 'roast beast of
the day' special ("a fantastic idea"), at this "celebration of meat"
Downtown; though tabs are "costly", you also get "professional service" and a "slick" "boardroom-meets-techno" setting in the 1924
Westin Book Cadillac Hotel, which after its "magnificent refurbishment" has "never looked better."

Rugby Grille ● *American/Continental* | 25 | 24 | 26 | $60 |

Birmingham | Townsend Hotel | 100 Townsend St. (bet. Henrietta &
Pierce Sts.) | 248-642-5999 | www.townsendhotel.com

A "throwback to different times" (long "before the collapse"), this "expensive" American-Continental inside Birmingham's "classy" Townsend
Hotel "continues to impress" with "well-prepared", "formal"-leaning
cuisine, including "wonderful breakfast" and "lovely high tea" "elegantly served" by an "impeccable" staff; "you might even see some famous faces" if you dine in the "warm, clubby" main room (the "overflow
seating" in "a hallway" "leaves something to be desired").

Saltwater ⊠Ⓜ *Seafood* | 26 | 27 | 26 | $67 |

Downtown | MGM Grand Casino | 1777 Third St. (bet. Bagley St. &
Grand River) | 313-465-1646 | www.mgmgranddetroit.com

MGM Grand gamblers are "amazed by the preparation and presentation" of executive chef Michael Mina's seafood at this "delightful"
Downtowner, even now that the "original menu's been scaled down" (it's
"cheaper" too, but you'll still need to "win" lots of "chips to pay the
tab"); the staff "pampers", and the glittery decor is "spectacular" – "if
only you didn't have to walk through the smoky casino to get there."

Streetside Seafood *Seafood* | 26 | 20 | 25 | $38 |

Birmingham | 273 Pierce St. (Maple Rd.) | 248-645-9123 |
www.streetsideseafood.com

Its "neighborhood-favorite" status and no-reservations policy mean
this "small", "happening", brick-walled Birmingham spot with a "tight"
back room and a "small bar" is "always crowded" (and "cacophonous") with folks dining on "fantastic seafood", including "spectacular
specials"; "lengthy waits" are de rigueur, but so are "great wines" and
cocktails, a "friendly staff" and "fair prices."

West End Grill ⊠Ⓜ *American* | 26 | 23 | 25 | $55 |

Ann Arbor | 120 W. Liberty St. (Main St.) | 734-747-6260 |
www.westendgrillannarbor.com

To visit this "perennial Ann Arbor favorite", "make reservations well in
advance", as its "charming, romantic, candlelit room" is "filled every
night" with folks seeking "high-end dining" in an "informal", "bistro"-
like atmosphere; once you're seated, staffers "recite the entire menu"
of "skillfully prepared", "fabulous" New American fare, which is
matched by "safe but well-chosen wine selections"; BTW, "the bar is
a great place to meet interesting folks."

	FOOD	DECOR	SERVICE	COST

Whitney, The Ⓜ *American*　　　　21 | 27 | 23 | $58

Wayne State | 4421 Woodward Ave. (Canfield St.) | 313-832-5700 |
www.thewhitney.com

"Dine like royalty" – or at least like the lumber baron who built the "gorgeous 19th-century mansion" housing this "upscale" New American restaurant in the Wayne State area, offering "many dining rooms" adorned with Tiffany chandeliers, stained-glass windows, marble fireplaces and "unequaled workmanship" in the woodwork; other attractions include live music on some nights, a "pretty garden" and an "interesting top-floor bar" – "if only the food were as good as the place looks."

Zingerman's Delicatessen *Deli*　　27 | 16 | 22 | $22

Ann Arbor | 422 Detroit St. (Kingsley St.) | 734-663-3354 |
www.zingermansdeli.com

Voted the Detroit area's Most Popular eatery, this Ann Arbor "institution" is "mecca for foodies" who don't mind "waiting" on "long lines" for an "endless choice" of "zing-tastic" deli sandwiches "overstuffed" with "superb ingredients", plus "gourmet treats" like "world-class cheeses", "olive oils, balsamic vinegars", "coffees, teas", "exceptional breads", "awesome desserts" and other "exotic specialty foods"; a lot of folks "bitch about paying so much", but in the end, "who cares?" – "you get the best quality" available; P.S. cheers to the "generous free-sample policy."

Ft. Lauderdale

TOP FOOD RANKING

	Restaurant	Cuisine
27	LaSpada's	Deli
	Eduardo de San Angel	Eclectic/Mexican
	Casa D'Angelo	Italian
	La Brochette	Mediterranean
26	Canyon	Southwestern
	Valentino's	Italian
	Cafe Maxx	American/Eclectic
	Rainbow Palace	Chinese
	Capital Grille	Steak
	Thai Spice	Thai

OTHER NOTEWORTHY PLACES

Anthony's	Pizza
Blue Moon	Seafood
Bonefish Grill	Seafood
Cafe Martorano	Italian
Chima	Brazilian/Steak
Da Campo	Italian
Grille 66	Seafood/Steak
Josef's	Italian
Steak 954	Steak
3030 Ocean	American/Seafood

Anthony's Coal Fired Pizza *Pizza*   23 | 16 | 20 | $21

Ft. Lauderdale | 2203 S. Federal Hwy. (SE 22nd St.) | 954-462-5555
Pompano Beach | 1203 S. Federal Hwy. (SE 12th St.) | 954-942-5550
Coral Springs | Magnolia Shops | 9521 Westview Dr. (University Dr.) |
954-340-2625
Cooper City | Home Depot Shopping Ctr. | 11037 Pines Blvd. (Hiatus Rd.) |
954-443-6610
Weston | Weston Commons | 4527 Weston Rd. (Griffin Rd.) | 954-358-2625
Plantation | 512 N. Pine Island Rd. (bet. Broward & Cleary Blvds.) |
954-474-3311
www.anthonyscoalfiredpizza.com

"It's smokin'!" declare devotees of the "tasty" coal-fired-oven pizza at
this "no-frills" chain whose "limited menu" also features "wings with
pizzazz" and "salads big enough for two"; even if the "well-done" pies
are deemed "burnt" by some, most salute the "crispest crusts imaginable" and happily brave "daunting waits" to savor them.

Blue Moon Fish Co. *Seafood*   25 | 23 | 23 | $48

Lauderdale-by-the-Sea | 4405 W. Tradewinds Ave. (Commercial Blvd.) |
954-267-9888
Coral Springs | 10317 Royal Palm Blvd. (Coral Springs Dr.) | 954-755-0002 Ⓜ
www.bluemoonfishco.com

Voted Broward's Most Popular, this "romantic" Lauderdale-by-the-
Sea fish house on the Intracoastal (with a "quieter", view-free, sepa-

rately owned sib in Coral Springs) continues to hook patrons with its "fabu seafood", "outstanding Sunday brunch" and "service with a smile"; it's "pricey", for sure, but "get a seat outside" and "you'll have a piece of heaven" – as well as a "gorgeous" vista of the "über-rich motoring by" on "mega-yachts."

Bonefish Grill *Seafood*   22 | 20 | 21 | $35

Ft. Lauderdale | 6282 N. Federal Hwy. (NE 62nd St.) | 954-492-3266
Coral Springs | 1455 N. University Dr. (Shadow Wood Blvd.) | 954-509-0405
Davie | Weston Commons | 4545 Weston Rd. (Griffin Rd.) | 954-389-9273
Plantation | 10197 W. Sunrise Blvd. (Nob Hill Rd.) | 954-472-3592
www.bonefishgrill.com

You can almost "feel the sea breeze" at these "upscale yet casual" chain seafooders whose "broad selection" of "consistently delicious", "always-fresh" fish ("if it swims, they have it") has habitués "hooked"; "fair prices" and "courteous", "well-trained" servers help explain why they're usually "jam-packed "with a "loud" crowd, so "be prepared to wait"; P.S. "the bang-bang shrimp is to die-die for."

Cafe Martorano *Italian*   25 | 17 | 19 | $68

Ft. Lauderdale | 3343 E. Oakland Park Blvd. (N. Ocean Blvd.) | 954-561-2554
Hollywood | Seminole Paradise at Hard Rock Hotel & Casino | 1 Seminole Way (bet. Griffin & Stirling Rds.) | 954-584-4450 ●Ⓜ
www.cafemartorano.com

"Always a scene", this Ft. Lauderdale "destination" "where you can wait for hours" ("no reservations") is a "mix of [mobster] movies, disco balls and great food" courtesy of "larger than life" chef-owner Steve Martorano, who turns out "old-school South Philly" Italian dishes like "baseball-size meatballs that melt in your mouth"; it's a "real love-it-or-hate-it experience", with fans raving it's "fun, fun, fun" while foes rant it's "crowded, noisy" and "crazy expensive" – in any event, it's "not to be forgotten"; P.S. the Hollywood branch opened post-Survey.

Cafe Maxx *American/Eclectic*   26 | 20 | 24 | $58

Pompano Beach | 2601 E. Atlantic Blvd. (NE 26th Ave.) | 954-782-0606 | www.cafemaxx.com

After more than 25 years, this "sophisticated" New American–Eclectic in Pompano Beach is "still wonderful" – and still attracting droves of devotees thanks to chef Oliver Saucy's "creative" menu, an "outstanding" wine list and "polished but not stuffy" service; nitpickers nag that the decor "needs updating" (the "dumpy strip-mall" locale doesn't help) and bemoan "out-of-sight prices", but aficionados contend it delivers "Maxx-a-yum enjoyment" that's "worth every penny."

Canyon *Southwestern*   26 | 22 | 23 | $52

Ft. Lauderdale | 1818 E. Sunrise Blvd. (N. Federal Hwy.) | 954-765-1950 | www.canyonfl.com

A "hip vibe" pervades this "sophisticated" Southwestern in Ft. Lauderdale, a "relatively small", often "crowded" nook featuring "killer" cuisine with "unique flavor combos", "helpful" staffers and "intimate" booths with "drawn curtains"; the "no-reservations policy is a pain", but "sublime prickly pear margaritas" ("in a class by themselves") from the "shwanky bar" ease "long waits."

	FOOD	DECOR	SERVICE	COST

Capital Grille *Steak*

| 26 | 25 | 26 | $65 |

Ft. Lauderdale | 2430 E. Sunrise Blvd. (Bayview Dr.) | 954-446-2000 | www.thecapitalgrille.com

Sure, "it's part of a chain", but this "swank" Ft. Lauderdale "meat lover's paradise" attracts a "well-heeled" horde of "movers and shakers" jonesing for "generous portions" of "superb beef" (including a Kona-crusted sirloin) and "to-die-for sides"; it's all accented by an "extensive wine list", "clubby" atmosphere and service that "makes you feel like royalty", which you may have to be to afford the "prime prices", but partisans proclaim you "get what you pay for."

Casa D'Angelo *Italian*

| 27 | 22 | 25 | $59 |

Ft. Lauderdale | Sunrise Square Plaza | 1201 N. Federal Hwy. (bet. E. Sunrise Blvd. & NE 13th St.) | 954-564-1234 | www.casa-d-angelo.com

"*Magnifico*" rave regulars who say "master chef" Angelo Elia turns out some of the "best" and most "authentic" Italian cuisine in Ft. Lauderdale; "generous servings" of "homemade pasta" star in "dishes so out of this world it's hard to choose", all paired with a "world-class" wine list and "ready-to-please" service; yes, securing a seat can be a "challenge" ("even with reservations") and it's "expensive", "crowded and loud", but "go anyway."

Chima Brazilian Steakhouse *Brazilian/Steak*

| 24 | 24 | 24 | $59 |

Ft. Lauderdale | 2400 E. Las Olas Blvd. (SE 25th Ave.) | 954-712-0580 | www.chima.cc

It's "Valhalla for carnivores" at this "high-end" Ft. Lauderdale rodizio where gaucho-garbed waiters "waltz around" a "gorgeous space" (Brazilian pottery, "cool lighting", courtyard with waterfalls, etc.) delivering a "never-ending" parade of "well-prepared" meat and seafood; it's easy to "overeat", so "pace yourself" – starting with the "overwhelming salad bar" that's a "meal in itself."

Da Campo Osteria *Italian*

| 24 | 24 | 23 | $62 |

Ft. Lauderdale | Il Lugano Hotel | 3333 NE 32nd Ave. (bet. Oakland Park Blvd. & NE 34rd Ave.) | 954-226-5002 | www.dacampofl.com

"Todd [English] has done it again" sigh fans of the celeb chef's "terrific" Ft. Lauderdale debut in a "comfortable" if "small" space in the Il Lugano Hotel, where the "true gourmet" Northern Italian fare "can be as stunning as the Intracoastal view"; if a few fret it "doesn't live up to the hype", most agree it's a "welcome addition" – particularly when "friendly" servers "make mozzarella at your table" ("showtime!").

Eduardo de San Angel ☒ *Eclectic/Mexican*

| 27 | 22 | 26 | $56 |

Ft. Lauderdale | 2822 E. Commercial Blvd. (bet. Bayview Dr. & NE 28th Ave.) | 954-772-4731 | www.eduardodesanangel.com

Don't expect the "typical tacos and tamales" at this "high-end" hacienda in Ft. Lauderdale, but rather "divine" Eclectic-Mexican fare steeped in "incredible flavors"; chef-owner Eduardo Pria's "commitment to excellence" extends to his "gracious" team of staffers, who are "helpful but not obtrusive" as they navigate the "cozy", "romantic" quarters; all in all, it's a "rare find" that's "always at the top of its game."

	FOOD	DECOR	SERVICE	COST

Grille 66 *Seafood/Steak* — 25 | 25 | 24 | $63

Ft. Lauderdale | Hyatt Regency Pier 66 | 2301 SE 17th St. (23rd Ave.) |
954-728-3500 | www.grille66andbar.com

Sit on the "heavenly terrace" and "watch the yachts" float by on Ft.
Lauderdale's Intracoastal Waterway at this "elegant" Hyatt complex eatery where "out-of-town visitors will be wowed" by the "outstanding" surf 'n' turf, "superb" 800-label wine list and "high-end service"; "arm-and-a-leg" prices startle some, but the majority "keeps going back."

Josef's 🅱🅼 *Italian* — 25 | 20 | 23 | $54

Plantation | Central Park Pl. | 9763 W. Broward Blvd. (Nob Hill Rd.) |
954-473-0000 | www.josefsplantation.com

"Those who find this wonderful place" "hidden" in a Plantation strip mall "return time and again" say surveyors smitten by chef-owner Josef Schibanetz's "hearty", "consistently interesting" Northern Italian dishes reflecting his Austrian heritage; it's all bolstered by a "fascinating (and reasonable) wine list" and service so "warm" "you'll really feel like a guest."

La Brochette Bistro 🅼 *Mediterranean* — 27 | 20 | 26 | $46

Cooper City | Embassy Lakes Plaza | 2635 N. Hiatus Rd. (Sheridan St.) |
954-435-9090 | www.labrochettebistro.com

"You'll be blown away" by this "tiny" Med secreted in a Cooper City "strip mall" predict partisans who implore "don't even look at the menu" until you hear chef-owner Aboud Kobaitri's "wonderful specials" (including "amazing fresh fish"); add in a "top-notch staff", "reasonable prices" and a "lovely", "romantic" space, and you've got a "local find" where "reservations are a must."

LaSpada's Original Hoagies *Deli* — 27 | 8 | 22 | $11

Lauderdale-by-the-Sea | 4346 Seagrape Dr. (Commercial Blvd.) |
954-776-7893
Coral Springs | 7893 W. Sample Rd. (bet. Riverside & Woodside Drs.) |
954-345-8833
Davie | Shoppes of Arrowhead | 2645 S. University Dr. (Nova Dr.) |
954-476-1099
www.laspadashoagies.com

"Meat goes flying through the air" and "lands on fresh-cut rolls" as "pros" "put on a show" at this veteran sandwich trio, voted Broward's No. 1 for Food by bang-for-the-buck-loving enthusiasts who exclaim "these are the best, biggest, baddest subs in town" (just "try eating a whole Monster yourself"); sure, they're "short on decor" and "out-the-door lines" are the norm, but "service is fast" and the "wait is worth it" for the "holy grail of hoagies."

Rainbow Palace *Chinese* — 26 | 23 | 26 | $57

Ft. Lauderdale | 2787 E. Oakland Park Blvd. (Bayview Dr.) | 954-565-5652 |
www.rainbowpalace.com

"Make no mistake", this "elegant" Ft. Lauderdale "splurge" "is no ordinary Chinese restaurant", as evident by the "mouthwatering" cuisine (including "out-of-this-world dumplings"), "tuxedo-clad servers" who are "as professional as they come" and extensive wine list; natch, the "terrific-all-around" experience may give you "sticker shock", but loyalists agree it's "worth" the "big bucks."

	FOOD	DECOR	SERVICE	COST

Steak 954 *Steak*

	▽ 24	28	20	$76

Ft. Lauderdale | W Ft. Lauderdale | 401 N. Ft. Lauderdale Beach Blvd. (Bayshore Dr.) | 954-414-8333 | www.steak954.com

If you "want to impress your date", grab the "gold Amex card" and head to this "romantic" spot in the oceanfront W Ft. Lauderdale for "impressive" steak and seafood; it's part of Stephen Starr's empire (Buddakan and Morimoto in Philly and NYC, et al.), so expect memorable decor inside and out, including a "15-ft.-long jellyfish tank that's pretty wicked."

Thai Spice *Thai*

	26	21	24	$36

Ft. Lauderdale | 1514 E. Commercial Blvd. (bet. NE 13th Ave. & NE 15th Terr.) | 954-771-4535 | www.thaispicefla.com

"When they say hot, they mean hot" at this "upscale" Ft. Lauderdale strip-maller that heat-seekers turn to for some of the "best Thai food in town"; patrons choose from a "varied menu" or a "long list of daily specials", whisked to tables by "attentive" staffers who dart among three "pretty" dining rooms and "colorful fish tanks."

3030 Ocean *American/Seafood*

	25	22	24	$55

Ft. Lauderdale | Harbor Beach Marriott Resort & Spa | 3030 Holiday Dr. (Seabreeze Blvd.) | 954-765-3030 | www.3030ocean.com

"In a sea of generic hotel restaurants", this "elegant" New American in the Marriott on Ft. Lauderdale beach "stands out" with its "inventive", "consistently excellent" seafood from chef Dean Max and "professional service"; if a few aesthetes aver its "lobby" locale "leaves a lot to be desired", most deem it a "good catch."

Valentino's Cucina Italiana 🅂🅼 *Italian*

	26	16	24	$60

Ft. Lauderdale | 1145 S. Federal Hwy. (bet. Davie Blvd. & SE 11th St.) | 954-523-5767 | www.valentinoscucinaitaliana.com

Once you find it, devotees decree "you'll fall in love" with this "innovative Italian" secreted in a "nondescript" Ft. Lauderdale strip mall; "exquisitely prepared, flavorful" fare is paired with "great service", and if "tight quarters" irk a few, overall it's "set the bar so high you'll need a cushion when you land on the other side."

Honolulu

TOP FOOD RANKING

	Restaurant	Cuisine
28	Alan Wong's	Hawaii Regional
	Sushi Sasabune	Japanese
27	La Mer	French
	Le Bistro	French
26	Nobu Waikiki	Japanese
	Helena's	Hawaiian
	Hiroshi	Eurasian
	Chef Mavro	French/Hawaii Regional
	Sansei	Japanese/Pacific Rim
	Orchids	Pacific Rim

OTHER NOTEWORTHY PLACES

Restaurant	Cuisine
Azure	Seafood
Beachhouse	American/Steak
BLT	Steak
Duke's Canoe Club	American
Hoku's	Pacific Rim
Michel's	French
Pineapple Room	Hawaii Regional
Roy's	Hawaii Regional
Taormina	Italian
3660 on the Rise	Pacific Rim

Alan Wong's Hawaii Reg. 28 | 22 | 27 | $67

McCully | 1857 S. King St. (bet. Hauoli & Pumehana Sts.) | 808-949-2526 | www.alanwongs.com

Voted No. 1 for Food and Most Popular in Honolulu, this "ingenious" Hawaii Regional offers dishes by the namesake chef "prepared to perfection" and "artfully presented" by a "superbly trained" staff; "understated decor" and an "unusual setting" in an "inconspicuous" building in McCully keep the "clear focus on the food" – and it's simply "sensational", if expensive; P.S. no surprise, "reservations are a must."

Azure Seafood - | - | - | E

Waikiki | Royal Hawaiian | 2259 Kalakaua Ave. (Royal Hawaiian Ave.) | 808-923-7311 | www.azurewaikiki.com

Candlelit beachfront cabanas make this intimate seafooder in the Royal Hawaiian hotel one of Waikiki's most romantic destinations; the freshest fish and fruits de mer are served by an attentive team (for a pretty penny), and insiders say getting either the five- or eight-course tasting menu is the way to go.

Beachhouse at the Moana American/Steak 21 | 25 | 20 | $50

Waikiki | Moana Surfrider | 2365 Kalakaua Ave. (Kaiulani Ave.) | 808-921-4600 | www.moana-surfrider.com

Waikiki's Moana Surfrider resort is home to this "pricey" New American steakhouse boasting an "elegant", "old Hawaii" setting enhanced with an "open veranda" and "spectacular ocean views"; fans call it a "wonderful splurge", though nitpickers note occasionally "slow" service.

BLT Steak *Steak*

| – | – | – | E |

Waikiki | Trump International | 223 Saratoga Rd. (Kalia Rd.) | 808-683-7440 | www.bltsteak.com

Chef-restaurateur extraordinaire Laurent Tourondel brings his chic chophouse franchise to the ground floor of the elegant Trump International Hotel on Waikiki; French technique abounds in the expensive prime steaks, sides and signature Gruyère popovers, and luxury proliferates in the setting, highlighted by dark leather booths, rich walnut floors, interesting artwork and trellised lanais.

Chef Mavro 🍽Ⓜ *French/Hawaii Reg.*

| 26 | 23 | 26 | $90 |

Moiliili | 1969 S. King St. (McCully St.) | 808-944-4714 | www.chefmavro.com

Chef George Mavrothalassitis "elevates dining in paradise to a higher level" at his namesake Hawaii Regional–French where the "first-class" tasting menus with paired wines are "brilliantly prepared" and "outstandingly presented" by "informative" servers in a "subtly sophisticated" space; even if the McCully/Moiliili location is a little out of the way and the fare so "sinfully expensive" that you may "melt down a credit card", connoisseurs consider it a "must" experience.

Duke's Canoe Club *American*

| 19 | 23 | 20 | $33 |

Waikiki | Outrigger Waikiki | 2335 Kalakaua Ave. (bet. Duke's Ln. & Kaiulani Ave.) | 808-922-2268 | www.dukeswaikiki.com

"Nostalgia" rules at the original Outrigger Waikiki Beach location of this "popular", "crowded" island institution named for "surfing legend" Duke Kahanamoku; it's more about the "laid-back Hawaiian experience", enhanced by specialty drinks and "nightly music", than the "typical", moderately priced American bar food.

Helena's Hawaiian Food 🍽Ⓜ⊄ *Hawaiian*

| 26 | 8 | 19 | $17 |

Kalihi | 1240 N. School St. (Houghtailing St.) | 808-845-8044 | www.helenashawaiianfood.com

The late Helen Chock may no longer be in the kitchen at this family-run Hawaiian "hole-in-the-wall", but "you can still feel her presence" inside the Kalihi space where her grandson now mans the stoves; since you can also taste her touch in the "broke da mouth" fare, loyalists advise "go early to beat the crowds"; P.S. it's BYO and cash-only.

Hiroshi Eurasion Tapas *Eurasian*

| 26 | 21 | 25 | $53 |

Restaurant Row | 500 Ala Moana Blvd. (bet. Punchbowl & South Sts.) | 808-533-4476 | www.hiroshihawaii.com

Chef Hiroshi Fukui's "delightfully creative" tapas are "small treasures" at this "casual-upscale" Eurasian on Restaurant Row; though a few find the tabs "too expensive for the bite-sized portions", fans say the "only thing better" than the food is sommelier Chuck Furuya's wine list; P.S. the kaiseki dinners (call for schedule) are "a must."

Hoku's *Pacific Rim*

| 25 | 26 | 25 | $73 |

Kahala | Kahala Hotel & Resort | 5000 Kahala Ave. (Kealaolu Ave.) | 808-739-8780 | www.kahalaresort.com

Set in a "romantic" locale with "jaw-dropping" ocean views, this "insanely expensive" Pacific Rim "classic" at the Kahala Hotel &

Resort is known for its "fresh" seafood and "outstanding Sunday brunch buffet"; the "impeccable", "unfailingly friendly" service also draws applause, though detractors deem the atmosphere "a little formal for Hawaii."

La Mer *French*

27 | 28 | 28 | $96

Waikiki | Halekulani | 2199 Kalia Rd. (Lewers St.) | 808-923-2311 | www.halekulani.com

This "remarkable" New French "indulgence" in Waikiki's "famed Halekulani Hotel" is set in a "tasteful" room filled with "elegant Asian art" and staffed by an "exceptional" team that "treats you like royalty"; the fare features "flavors that will linger in your mind's eye forever", and while it's "frighteningly expensive", an "evening in paradise" "isn't supposed to be economical"; P.S. jackets or long-sleeve collared shirts are required for gentlemen.

Le Bistro *French*

27 | 20 | 24 | $54

Niu Valley | Niu Valley Shopping Ctr. | 5730 Kalanianaole Hwy. (Halemaumau St.) | 808-373-7990

Reaching culinary "levels unheard of in a neighborhood restaurant", this "quaint" bistro "hidden" in the Niu Valley Shopping Center serves "glorious" French fare and is "always crowded" with "locals"; the "sunny-yellow" setting is just as "warm" as the "knowledgeable staff", and though it's "a little pricey", "large portions" compensate.

Michel's *French*

25 | 26 | 26 | $76

Waikiki | Colony Surf | 2895 Kalakaua Ave. (Poni Moi Rd.) | 808-923-6552 | www.michelshawaii.com

"Old-style" "sophistication" thrives at this "ritzy", "romantic" venue at the Colony Surf, where a harpist or "guitarist serenades" as a "tux-edoed" staff serves "superb" Classic French dishes, some with "table-side preparations"; many "dine early" to catch the "gorgeous sunset" from the terrace, but the "fabulous" after-dark "lights of Waikiki" are equally "worth skipping your next mortgage payment" for.

Nobu Waikiki *Japanese*

26 | 25 | 25 | $80

Waikiki | Waikiki Parc Hotel | 2233 Helumoa Rd. (Lewers St.) | 808-237-6999 | www.noburestaurants.com

Sample "ambrosial" Japanese-Peruvian fusion at this "stylish" outpost of Nobu Matsuhisa's restaurant empire in the Waikiki Parc Hotel, where diners ready for an "all-out splurge" dig into "amazing" "edible art"; though a few find the room "raucous" and the "innovative" menu too "complicated", the staff is "more than happy to recommend" one of the "mouthwatering" selections and suggest a "lovely pairing of sake" to boot.

Orchids *Pacific Rim*

26 | 28 | 27 | $65

Waikiki | Halekulani | 2199 Kalia Rd. (Lewers St.) | 808-923-2311 | www.halekulani.com

Appropriately decorated with the namesake flower, the Halekulani's "elegant", "oceanfront" Pacific Rim venue in Waikiki is famed for its "legendary Sunday brunch" (don't miss the "famous coconut cake") and "fabulous views of Diamond Head"; the "fantastic" service, "re-laxing" vibe and "prix fixe lunch" also earn kudos, though given the "splurge" pricing, many reserve dinner for "special occasions only."

	FOOD	DECOR	SERVICE	COST

Pineapple Room *Hawaii Reg.*

25 | 19 | 23 | $39

Ala Moana | Macy's, Ala Moana Ctr. | 1450 Ala Moana Blvd.
(bet. Atkinson Dr. & Piikoi St.) | 808-945-6573 | www.alanwongs.com
You "can't go wrong" with this "innovative" Hawaii Regional "pleaser"
via Alan Wong in the Ala Moana Center Macy's, where the "expert"
chef's "gustatory delights" are available at lower prices than his namesake flagship; an "elegant" setting and "lovely wine list" seal the deal.

Roy's *Hawaii Reg.*

26 | 22 | 24 | $54

Hawaii Kai | 6600 Kalanianaole Hwy. (Keahole St.) | 808-396-7697
Kapolei | Ko Olina Resort & Marina | 92-1220 Aliinui Dr. (Kamoana Pl.) |
808-676-7697
Waikiki | Waikiki Beach Walk | 226 Lewers St. (Kalia Rd.) | 808-923-7697
www.roysrestaurant.com
"Absolutely the best" is the word on chef Roy Yamaguchi's Hawaii
Regional eateries; it's a "bit of a drive" to the longtime Hawaii Kai original, but the Kapolei and Waikiki Beach Walk iterations boast the
same "outstanding" fare; most praise the "lively" settings, but a "disappointed" handful complains of "rushed service" and "lost excitement"; P.S. "nothing compares" to his melting hot chocolate soufflé.

Sansei *Japanese/Pacific Rim*

26 | 19 | 21 | $44

Waikiki | Waikiki Beach Marriott Resort & Spa | 2552 Kalakaua Ave.
(bet. Ohua & Paoakalani Aves.) | 808-931-6286 | www.sanseihawaii.com
Fans call this Waikiki location of the contemporary Japanese chainlet a
"favorite", contending there "aren't enough superlatives" for its "mouthwatering" "new wave" sushi and Pacific Rim fare; kudos also go to the
"inventive rolls", "excellent" sashimi and "plate-lickin'" sauces, but
some are less enthused about the occasionally "chaotic atmosphere."

Sushi Sasabune 🗷 *Japanese*

28 | 15 | 22 | $87

Ala Moana | 1419 S. King St. (Keeaumoku St.) | 808-947-3800 |
www.sasabunehawaii.com
This "out-of-this-world" Japanese eatery set on a "nondescript street"
in Ala Moana offers sushi "carefully prepared by master" chef Seiji
Kumagawa, whose signature command to diners is 'trust me'; aficionados advise "sit at the bar" for the omakase and "do exactly as in-
structed or you'll be asked to leave", but critics contend that for "all the
hype" and those "sky-high prices", the "setting needs serious attention."

Taormina *Italian*

- | - | - | E

Waikiki | 227 Lewers St. (Kalakaua Ave.) | 808-926-5050 |
www.taorminarestaurant.com
The buzz continues to build for the Sicilian cuisine served at this tri-
level Waikiki trattoria, with a menu created by an Italophile Japanese
chef; the furnishings inside and on the patio are contemporary yet
comfortable, while the prices are on par for an upscale resort area.

3660 on the Rise 🅼 *Pacific Rim*

25 | 20 | 24 | $52

Kaimuki | 3660 Waialae Ave. (Wilhelmina Rise) | 808-737-1177 |
www.3660.com
Chef Russell Siu's flagship Pacific Rim specialist is known for "locally
sourced", "artfully presented" dishes served by a "pleasant" staff; it's
"popular" with locals for "special occasions and parties" despite its
"bland decor" and "unimpressive" location in a Kaimuki office building.

Houston

TOP FOOD RANKING

	Restaurant	Cuisine
28	Le Mistral	French
	Kanomwan	Thai
	Pappas Bros. Steak	Steak
	Mark's	American
27	Da Marco	Italian
	Chez Nous	French
	Masraff's	Continental
	Damian's	Italian
	Eddie V's	Seafood/Steak
	Tony's	Continental/Italian
	Glass Wall	American
	Catalan	American/Spanish
26	Shade	American
	Indika	Indian
	Hugo's	Mexican
	Tony Mandola's	Seafood
	Vic & Anthony's	Steak
	Café Rabelais	French
	Au Petit Paris	French
	Morton's	Steak

OTHER NOTEWORTHY PLACES

Américas	South American
Backstreet Café	American
Bistro Alex	Creole
Branch Water	American
Brennan's	Creole/Southwestern
Chez Roux	French
Churrascos	South American
Del Frisco's	Steak
Dolce Vita	Italian
Feast	British
Haven	American
Ibiza	Mediterranean
Kiran's	Indian
Mockingbird	American
Pappadeaux	Cajun/Seafood
Reef	Seafood
RDG/Bar Annie	American
t'afia	American
Valentino	Italian
Zelko	American

	FOOD	DECOR	SERVICE	COST

Américas *S American*
24 | **26** | **23** | **$47**

Galleria | The Pavilion | 1800 Post Oak Blvd. (bet. San Felipe St. & Westheimer Rd.) | 713-961-1492
The Woodlands | 21 Waterway Ave. (Timberloch Pl.) | 281-367-1492
www.cordua.com

The "wow factor" is high at this upmarket South American duo where the "innovative" fare is bested only by the "fabulous" decor featuring a "rainforest"-inspired motif at the Galleria original and a "dark", "rich" "contemporary" look at the newer Woodlands offshoot; the "celebratory" atmosphere means the din can be "deafening" at both branches, yet they remain a "favorite" for "impressing out-of-towners."

Au Petit Paris ⌧ *French*
26 | **20** | **23** | **$46**

Lower Shepherd | 2048 Colquitt St. (Shepherd Dr.) | 713-524-7070 | www.aupetitparisrestaurant.com

"*Très charmant*" purr fans of this Lower Shepherd "gem" famed for its "truly French" fare served in a rehabbed bungalow; whether it's "cozy" or just plain "cramped" is up for debate, though all agree it has a "homey", "pleasant" vibe, aided by a "welcoming" staff and prices that are moderate for the area.

Backstreet Café *American*
25 | **23** | **24** | **$40**

River Oaks | 1103 S. Shepherd Dr. (Clay St.) | 713-521-2239 | www.backstreetcafe.net

"There's always something to tickle the imagination" at this "cute River Oaks cottage" – a local "favorite" for over a quarter century – turning out "creative", moderately priced American cuisine complemented by "excellent", "well-priced" wines; "gracious" service ups the "charming" atmosphere, and in warm weather, "nothing beats" lunch on the "tranquil", "oak-shaded" patio.

Bistro Alex *Creole*
- | **-** | **-** | **E**

Memorial | Hotel Sorella | 800 W. Sam Houston Pkwy. (Queensbury Ln.) | 713-827-3545 | www.bistroalex.com

The scion of the Brennan restaurant family puts his name on this fine-dining entry in the relatively new Hotel Sorella in Memorial, offering Texan-inflected Creole cuisine like turtle soup, plus lots of beef; the thoroughly modern interior sports rough-hewn wood accents, navy booths and soaring wine walls encasing an impressive array of vino.

Branch Water Tavern ◑ Ⓜ *American*
- | **-** | **-** | **M**

Heights | 510 Shepherd Dr. (bet. Blossom & Gibson Sts.) | 713-863-7777 | www.branchwatertavern.com

Despite the watering-hole moniker, this Heights newcomer serves some serious New American cooking, from dressed-up bar snacks like duck fat popcorn to meaty mains constructed with locally sourced ingredients; all are washed down with whiskeys, microbrews and creative cocktails in an atmospheric space with hardwood floors, brick walls, leather club chairs and antique light fixtures lending it a neo-speakeasy vibe.

Brennan's *Creole/Southwestern*
- | **-** | **-** | **E**

Midtown | 3300 Smith St. (Stuart St.) | 713-522-9711 | www.brennanshouston.com

The grande dame of the Houston restaurant scene has reopened in Midtown after a lengthy hiatus stemming from Hurricane Ike; despite

	FOOD	DECOR	SERVICE	COST

a full refurbishment of the interior, the most iconic elements of the 1930s Vieux Carré–style structure have been maintained (including the courtyard), and the pricey, locally attuned Creole-inflected menu still features favorites like turtle soup and bananas Foster.

Café Rabelais ☒ *French* | 26 | 21 | 23 | $40 |

Rice Village | 2442 Times Blvd. (bet. Kelvin & Morningside Drs.) | 713-520-8841 | www.caferabelais.com

"Tiny", "elegant" and oh-so-"very French", this "true bistro" in Rice Village features an ever-changing chalkboard menu of "terrific" Gallic cuisine complemented by "well-priced" wines; perpetually "packed" conditions mean it can get "a little noisy", but "attentive service" keeps the ambiance "charming."

Catalan Food and Wine Ⓜ *American/Spanish* | 27 | 24 | 25 | $46 |

Heights | 5555 Washington Ave. (TC Jester Blvd.) | 713-426-4260 | www.catalanfoodandwine.com

An "intriguing" array of "cutting-edge tapas" is at the forefront of Chris Shepherd's "chic" Spanish-inspired American in the Heights where the "inventive" nibbles pair up with "excellent, well-priced" wines, also available in tasting-size pours; the candlelit space with an open kitchen is brimming with energy – just brace yourself for "noisy" acoustics and prices some deem "a tad expensive"; P.S. "reservations a must."

Chez Nous ☒ *French* | 27 | 22 | 23 | $59 |

Humble | 217 S. Ave. G (bet. Granberry & Staitti Sts.) | 281-446-6717 | www.cheznousfrenchrestaurant.com

Those who "don't mind driving out to Humble" are rewarded with this Gallic "gem" where "country French" cuisine is crafted using fresh-from-the-garden ingredients; "everything is first class", from the prices to the "professional" service and the "cozy" ambiance that's "old-fashioned in a good way" (think "your great aunt's living room"); P.S. jackets suggested.

Chez Roux ☒Ⓜ *French* | - | - | - | VE |

Montgomery | La Torretta Del Lago | 600 La Torretta Blvd. (Del Lago Blvd.) | 936-448-4400 | www.latorrettalakeresort.com

"Superlative in every category (including price)" sums up this French spot in the ritzy La Torretta Del Lago Resort & Spa on Lake Conroe from legendary London-based chef Albert Roux; it features a contemporary seasonal menu in a modern, waterside setting whose centerpiece is a glass-enclosed wine cellar showcasing a stellar collection of bottles.

Churrascos *S American* | 26 | 22 | 24 | $42 |

Lower Shepherd | 2055 Westheimer Rd. (Shepherd Dr.) | 713-527-8300

Southwest Houston | 9705 Westheimer Rd. (Gessner Rd.) | 713-952-1988 www.cordua.com

Offering a "different take on the Texas steakhouse", these South American grills from the Cordúa family furnish "über-flavorful" meats ("so tender you can cut them with a butter knife") capped with "excellent" cocktails and a "tremendous" tres leches cake for dessert; they're somewhat "pricey", but a "polished", "modern" look and "welcoming" hospitality mean they never fail to "impress."

	FOOD	DECOR	SERVICE	COST

Da Marco ☒Ⓜ *Italian* — 27 | 22 | 25 | $61

Montrose | 1520 Westheimer Rd. (bet. Ridgewood & Windsor Sts.) | 713-807-8857 | www.damarcohouston.com

"Simply outstanding" praise patrons of chef/co-owner Marco Wiles' Montrose "classic" – and Houston's Most Popular restaurant – where a well-heeled crowd sups on "exciting", "sophisticated" Northern Italian cuisine in an "understated" former home; "yes, it's crowded, noisy and expensive", but service is "well tuned", if occasionally "rushed", and "the food never lets you down"; P.S. don't miss the "chalkboard specials."

Damian's Cucina Italiana ☒ *Italian* — 27 | 21 | 26 | $44

Midtown | 3011 Smith St. (bet. Anita & Rosalie Sts.) | 713-522-0439 | www.damians.com

"Steady as she goes", this "old-school" Midtown Italian lures "business", "social" and theatergoing types with "consistently excellent" renditions of red-sauce favorites; a few find it "a little stuffy", but "excellent" service compensates and supporters swear "you can always count on it" for a special meal.

Del Frisco's Double Eagle Steak House *Steak* — 26 | 25 | 25 | $67

Galleria | 5061 Westheimer Rd. (bet. Post Oak Blvd. & Sage Rd.) | 713-355-2600 | www.delfriscos.com

"When you want to impress" – especially "on the company dime" – this high-end chophouse chain in the Galleria fits the bill with "top-flight steaks", a well-stocked wine cellar and "spectacular" desserts; "handsome" digs done up in "dark, rich woods" with "lots of brass" make for a "consistent", if somewhat predictable, experience.

Dolce Vita Pizzeria Enoteca Ⓜ *Italian* — 25 | 18 | 18 | $29

Montrose | 500 Westheimer Rd. (Whitney St.) | 713-520-8222 | www.dolcevitahouston.com

Piezani praise this Montrose Italian – and "less-expensive" sib of Marco Wiles' Da Marco – firing up "extremely thin" pizzas matched by "delicious" antipasti and well-chosen wines; it's bustling most nights with a "see-and-be-seen" clientele, but most find it's "worth rubbing elbows with the Botox crowd" for such "fabulous" food.

Eddie V's Prime Seafood *Seafood/Steak* — 27 | 26 | 25 | $53

Memorial | CityCentre Complex | 12848 Queensbury Ln. (I-10) | 832-200-2380 | www.eddiev.com

A "class act", this Austin-bred chainlet in Memorial offers a "first-rate experience on all counts", from the "fabulous" steaks and seafood (including "amazing fresh oysters" and crab) to the "professional" service and "modern", leather-trimmed quarters; given the "expense-account" pricing, many seek out the "half-price apps" deals during happy hour.

Feast *British* — 23 | 19 | 21 | $43

Montrose | 219 Westheimer Rd. (Bagby St.) | 713-529-7788 | www.feasthouston.com

"A must for any self-respecting foodie", this "funky" Montrose venue serves a "ballsy" British menu featuring "bold, seriously delicious" "snout-to-tail" dishes including some "unusual offal-based" items (think pork tongue with chutney and guinea fowl liver mousse); prices are "reasonable", while a "down-to-earth" staff and a "cute and cozy" Arts and Crafts setting complete the package; P.S. closed Tuesdays.

	FOOD	DECOR	SERVICE	COST

Glass Wall 🅱️ Ⓜ *American* — 27 | 22 | 25 | $44

Heights | 933 Studewood St. (10th St.) | 713-868-7930 |
www.glasswalltherestaurant.com

A "stunning mix" of "fresh", local ingredients turns up in the "sophisticated" New American dishes (think "higher-end comfort food") at this Heights "favorite" where the fare is bolstered by "daring", "spot-on" wine pairings from sommelier/co-owner Shepard Ross; add in "a simple, yet elegant" modern setting with an open kitchen, and "the only negative is the noise level."

Haven 🅱️ *American* — - | - | - | M

Upper Kirby District | 2502 Algerian Way (Kirby Dr.) | 713-581-6101 |
www.havenhouston.com

Randy Evans (ex Brennan's) heads up this Upper Kirby District arrival – the first certified-green restaurant in the area, designed with recycled materials, open ceilings and energy-efficient lighting; the eco-friendly ethos is also reflected in the midpriced New American menu, with farm-to-table takes on Texas classics.

Hugo's *Mexican* — 26 | 22 | 25 | $40

Montrose | 1600 Westheimer Rd. (Mandell St.) | 713-524-7744 |
www.hugosrestaurant.net

This upscale Montrose Mexican is known for its "sophisticated, nuanced" dishes plated with an "innovative, elegant twist"; the contemporary space is "loud", but "polished service" plus premium margaritas and plenty of "fine wines" keep most patrons happy; P.S. be sure to reserve ahead for Sunday's "fabulous brunch."

Ibiza Ⓜ *Mediterranean* — 26 | 23 | 24 | $43

Midtown | 2450 Louisiana St. (McGowen St.) | 713-524-0004 |
www.ibizafoodandwinebar.com

"The small plates steal the show" at chef Charles Clark's "stylish" Midtowner where "clean-flavored" modern Med dishes gain a lift from a "superb" 500-bottle wine list (highlighted on an eye-popping display wall); the "high-energy" setting is perpetually overflowing with "beautiful people", but an "experienced" staff keeps the mood "pleasant", no matter how "jammed and noisy" it gets.

Indika Ⓜ *Indian* — 26 | 22 | 24 | $42

Montrose | 516 Westheimer Rd. (Whitney St.) | 713-524-2170 |
www.indikausa.com

"Nouvelle" spins on traditional recipes distinguish this "delightful" lower Montrose Indian from chef-owner Anita Jaisinghani who sends out "beautiful", "bright-flavored" dishes, some with "enough spice to make you swoon"; an "upscale" contemporary setting, "knowledgeable" service and an "inspired" cocktail list are clues that it's "not cheap", but certainly "worth making a habit of."

Kanomwan 🅱️ *Thai* — 28 | 8 | 13 | $18

Neartown | 736½ Telephone Rd. (S. Lockwood St.) | 713-923-4230
Gastronomes gush over this Neartown BYO Thai (aka 'Telephone Thai') whipping up "fabulous" food at "unbeatable" prices; you'll have to "put up with" no-frills decor and somewhat "surly" service, although longtime customers claim the endearingly "cranky" owner "actually cracks a smile every once in a while."

	FOOD	DECOR	SERVICE	COST

Kiran's ⊠ *Indian*
▽ 27 | 24 | 25 | $39

Galleria | 4100 Westheimer Rd. (Midlane St.) | 713-960-8472 |
www.kiranshouston.com

"Terrific" Indian fusion plates are prepared with a "delicate" touch at this Galleria-area "fine-dining" venue also famed for its "remarkable" stash of wines; "it's a little high priced" in comparison to more "traditional" spots, but fans find the upscale English colonial-style setting and "exceptional" service "worth every penny."

Le Mistral *French*
28 | 26 | 25 | $49

West Houston | 1400 Eldridge Pkwy. (Briar Forest Dr.) | 832-379-8322 |
www.lemistralhouston.com

"Spectacular" sums up this West Houston French rated the city's No. 1 for Food, where the Denis brothers roll out "beautiful" Provençal-accented plates in a "lovely" white-tablecloth setting; prices are high, but "superior" service sets the stage for a "special meal."

Mark's American Cuisine *American*
28 | 27 | 27 | $67

Montrose | 1658 Westheimer Rd. (bet. Dunlavy & Ralph Sts.) |
713-523-3800 | www.marks1658.com

Housed in a "splendid" "old church" in Montrose, this New American from chef Mark Cox delivers a "heavenly" experience, with an "outstanding", "unfussy" menu based on seasonal ingredients, a "deep wine list" and service that's "unobtrusive", but always at the ready; indeed, even if the prices can feel a bit "hellish", most surveyors swear it's "not to be missed."

Masraff's ⊠ *Continental*
27 | 25 | 25 | $54

Uptown | 1753 S. Post Oak Ln. (bet. San Felipe St. & Westheimer Rd.) |
713-355-1975 | www.masraffs.com

"They take good care of their customers" at this family-owned "gem" where the "personal touch" shows in the "wonderful" Continental cooking and coddling service "from beginning to end"; as for the bill, it's appropriately "expensive"; P.S. post-Survey, it moved within Uptown, outdating the Decor score.

Mockingbird Bistro Wine Bar *American*
26 | 23 | 26 | $52

River Oaks | 1985 Welch St. (McDuffie St.) | 713-533-0200 |
www.mockingbirdbistro.com

This "cozy bistro" "tucked into a quiet neighborhood" near River Oaks is an "all-time favorite" for "locals" thanks to chef-owner John Sheely's "excellent" seasonal American dishes and extensive array of wines by the glass; "hospitable" service and a low-lit Gothic setting provide a "pleasant atmosphere", even if tabs can feel a little "high" for what you get.

Morton's The Steakhouse *Steak*
26 | 23 | 25 | $67

Downtown | 1001 McKinney St. (bet. Fannin & Main Sts.) | 713-659-3700
Galleria | Centre at Post Oak | 5000 Westheimer Rd. (Post Oak Blvd.) |
713-629-1946
www.mortons.com

"Corporate types" clamor for the "massive" steaks and "wonderful" sides and wines at these "manly" Downtown and Galleria outposts of the nationwide chophouse chain; they're "consistent", from the "top-notch" service to the "dark", "noisy" settings and premium prices, and if some find them "nothing special", they're "rarely disappointing" either.

	FOOD	DECOR	SERVICE	COST

Pappadeaux *Cajun/Seafood* — 22 | 19 | 20 | $31

Medical Center | 2525 S. Loop W. (bet. Buffalo Spdwy. & Kirby Dr.) | 713-665-3155

Champions | 7110 FM 1960 W. (Cutten Rd.) | 281-580-5245

FM 1960 | 2226 FM 1960 Rd. W. (Kuykendahl Rd.) | 281-893-0206

Galleria | 6015 Westheimer Rd. (Greenridge Dr.) | 713-782-6310

Memorial | 10499 Katy Frwy. (bet. Attingham Dr. & Town & Country Blvd.) | 713-722-0221

Northwest Houston | 13080 Hwy. 290 (bet. Hollister St. & Northwest Central Dr.) | 713-460-1203

Upper Kirby District | 2410 Richmond Ave. (Kirby Dr.) | 713-527-9137

West Houston | 12109 Westheimer Rd. (Houston Center Blvd.) | 281-497-1110

Conroe | 18165 I-45 S. (Shenandoah Park Dr.) | 936-321-4200

Stafford | 12711 Southwest Frwy. (bet. Hwy. 90A & Kirkwood Rd.) | 281-240-5533

www.pappas.com

Additional locations throughout the Houston area

Though it's certainly "popular", opinions are split on this "N'Awlins"-inspired chain; while it pleases the "masses" with "accessible" renditions of all the Cajun "classics", from gumbo to étouffée, and earns points for "value" pricing and portions that "guarantee leftovers", detractors dis "blah" fare and "cookie-cutter" "faux" Louisiana looks.

Pappas Bros. Steakhouse ☒ *Steak* — 28 | 25 | 26 | $63

Galleria | 5839 Westheimer Rd. (bet. Augusta & Bering Drs.) | 713-780-7352 | www.pappasbros.com

Smitten carnivores swear "it doesn't get any better" than this Pappas family "flagship" in the Galleria, where the "luscious", "perfectly marbled" steaks "melt in your mouth"; the "memorable" meals are enhanced by "outstanding" wines, "fawning" service and a "lavish" 1920s-inspired setting – just "be prepared to shell out the big bucks."

RDG + Bar Annie *American* — 21 | 26 | 20 | $72

Galleria | 1800 Post Oak Blvd. (Ambassador Way) | 713-840-1111 | www.rdgbarannie.com

From culinary legend Robert Del Grande, this "happening" three-in-one concept in the Galleria lures "lots of flashy people" with its cushy lounge, "noisy" bar area and "innovative" American-Southwestern menu presented in a "cool" cedar-accented dining room; still, some are "disappointed" by "inattentive" service and high prices.

Reef ☒ *Seafood* — 26 | 21 | 24 | $49

Midtown | 2600 Travis St. (McGowen St.) | 713-526-8282 | www.reefhouston.com

"Flawless seafood" gets top billing at this "popular" Midtown boîte where "hands-on" chef-owner Bryan Caswell whips up "as fresh as it gets" fish at prices that feel "fair for the quality"; it boasts a "gorgeous" blue-hued interior, but "lively" is putting it mildly when it comes to the ambiance – "take earplugs, and forget table conversation."

Shade *American* — 26 | 21 | 24 | $39

Heights | 250 W. 19th St. (bet. Rutland & Yale Sts.) | 713-863-7500 | www.shadeheights.com

A pioneer in bringing "sophistication to the Heights", this "casually elegant" spot draws a "fab-looking" crowd for "flavorful" New American cooking; with an "efficient staff" and an "inviting" modern setting done up in neutral hues, the "only problem is the noise."

t'afia ☒Ⓜ *American* 24 | 18 | 23 | $42

Midtown | 3701 Travis St. (bet. Alabama & Winbern Sts.) | 713-524-6922 | www.tafia.com

An "ever-changing" lineup of "innovative" "local and organic foods" is "cooked with love" at chef-owner Monica Pope's "memorable" Midtown New American that "shines"; given its relative affordability, the one complaint is that many "wish" the modern digs "were more welcoming."

Tony Mandola's Gulf Coast Kitchen *Seafood* 26 | 21 | 25 | $40

River Oaks | River Oaks Ctr. | 1962 W. Gray St. (Driscoll St.) | 713-528-3474 | www.tonymandolas.com

"Regulars abound" at this longtime River Oaks seafooder from the "ubiquitous" Mandola family mixing up "excellent" Gulf Coast-style classics and a smattering of Italian standards; tabs are somewhat "pricey", but with an experience this "reliable", no one seems to mind.

Tony's ☒ *Continental/Italian* 27 | 27 | 27 | $71

Greenway Plaza Area | 3755 Richmond Ave. (Timmons Ln.) | 713-622-6778 | www.tonyshouston.com

"La crème de la crème" of the local dining scene, this 45-year-old Greenway Plaza charmer shows that Tony Vallone "hasn't lost his touch" with "top-notch" Italian-Continental cuisine made even better by a "four-star" staff and "stunning" art-filled setting; though it certainly sets the "gold standard" in the area, many find "you need to be a regular" with deep pockets to best appreciate it.

Valentino ☒ *Italian* - | - | - | VE

Galleria | Hotel Derek | 2525A W. Loop S. (Westheimer Rd.) | 713-850-9200 | www.pieroselvaggio.com

Piero Selvaggio presents this branch of his venerable Santa Monica-born Italian in the Galleria-area's sleek Hotel Derek; extravagant multicourse meals are dished out in a modern, cushy setting done up in dark tones and crimson, while the adjacent less-formal space is home to the stylish Vin Bar spotlighting a wide range of small plates, crudo and wines.

Vic & Anthony's *Steak* 26 | 25 | 26 | $63

Downtown | 1510 Texas Ave. (La Branch St.) | 713-228-1111 | www.vicandanthonys.com

This "high-end" Downtown steakhouse near Minute Maid Park "hits a home run" with "cooked-to-perfection" meats, "generous" sides and an "extensive" wine collection priced "for Enron executives who haven't been caught yet"; "elegant service" and a dark "modern bordello" setting increase the appeal – if you don't mind "having to empty your wallet", it doesn't get "much better than this."

Zelko Bistro Ⓜ *American* - | - | - | M

Heights | 705 E. 11th St. (Studewood St.) | 713-880-8691 | www.zelkobistro.com

Co-owners Jamie Zelko and Jeb Stuart (ex Shade) are chef and wine director, respectively, at this Heights arrival offering comfort-leaning New American fare at wallet-friendly prices; the cozy bungalow setting is artfully adorned with leather banquettes, mason jar lighting and a recycled wood-paneled bar, all spot-on for the neighborhood.

Kansas City

		FOOD	DECOR	SERVICE	COST

TOP FOOD RANKING

	Restaurant	Cuisine
29	Justus Drugstore	American
28	Bluestem	American
	Michael Smith	American
27	Oklahoma Joe's	BBQ
	Le Fou Frog	French
	Capital Grille	Steak
	American Restaurant	American
	Piropos	Argentinean/Steak
26	Extra Virgin	Mediterranean
	Starker's	American

OTHER NOTEWORTHY PLACES

Restaurant	Cuisine
Arthur Bryant's	BBQ
Bristol	Seafood
Lidia's	Italian
Fiorella's Jack Stack	BBQ
Jasper's	Italian
Korma Sutra	Indian
R Bar	Eclectic
Room 39	American
Thai Place	Thai
Webster House	Eclectic

American Restaurant, The ⊠ *American* 27 | 24 | 27 | $72

Crown Center | 200 E. 25th St. (E. Pershing Rd.), MO | 816-545-8001 | www.theamericankc.com

"Celebrated chef" Debbie Gold "continues to serve up wonderful" New American cuisine "on the cutting edge" at this Crown Center "landmark" with a "fabulous skyline view", "extensive wine cellar" and "highly trained" staff; just "bring your gold card" and "dress well", though some suggest the dining room itself "needs a makeover."

Arthur Bryant's *BBQ* 25 | 12 | 17 | $16

18th & Vine | 1727 Brooklyn Ave. (18th St.), MO | 816-231-1123 | www.arthurbryantsbbq.com

"Forget about Memphis and Texas": since 1930, this "real-deal" "BBQ heaven" in the Historic Jazz District has had "every segment of the KC community", "presidents and celebrities" queuing for "incredible sandwiches", "fabulous ribs" and "giant piles of fries"; true, the "disheveled" decor and "Army-mess-line" service is an "acquired taste" (not unlike its trademark "vinegary sauce"), but insiders insist it "can't be missed."

Bluestem Ⓜ *American* 28 | 24 | 26 | $65

Westport | 900 Westport Rd. (Roanoke Rd.), MO | 816-561-1101 | www.bluestemkc.com

For a "world-class meal", Westporters turn to this "true gem" from "culinary rock star" Colby Garrelts, whose "progressive" New American cuisine – crafted from "locally grown produce and meats" – is "fresh, balanced" and "beautifully presented"; enhanced by "informed service", it's "expensive" but "worth it", though a "comfy" adjacent bar that draws both "blue bloods and people in blue jeans" offers "substantial tastes at a fraction of the price."

Bristol Seafood Grill *Seafood*
25 | 25 | 24 | $40

Downtown KCMO | Power & Light District | 51 E. 14th St. (Main St.), MO | 816-448-6007
Leawood | Town Ctr. Plaza | 5400 W. 119th St. (Nall Ave.), KS | 913-663-5777
www.bristolseafoodgrill.com

They may be "as far from an ocean as you can get", but this "adult respite" in Leawood and its Downtown KC outpost feature a "constantly evolving" menu of "scrumptious" seafood prepared with "care and imagination"; a "superior staff" supplements the "elegant atmosphere", and while tabs can be "pricey", wallet-watchers fishing for deals note that lunch is a "real bargain."

Capital Grille *Steak*
27 | 26 | 27 | $59

Country Club Plaza | Country Club Plaza | 4740 Jefferson St. (bet. W. 47th & 48th Sts.), MO | 816-531-8345 | www.thecapitalgrille.com

In this "steak town", "you have to be good" to succeed (especially if you're a "national chain") – and this Country Club Plaza destination "keeps pace" with "outstanding" chops and an "excellent wine list"; the "oaky" interior is "perfect for power dinners or special occasions" and overseen by a "professional", "pampering" staff, which makes it easier to swallow tabs that "aren't for the light of wallet."

Extra Virgin ⊠ *Mediterranean*
26 | 23 | 24 | $33

Crossroads | 1900 Main St. (19th St.), MO | 816-842-2205 | www.extravirginkc.com

Michael Smith's "innovative" small plates – an "exceptional" mélange of Med flavors "geared toward the more adventurous diner" – "bring Europe to the Crossroads" at this "casual" "must-visit" next to the chef's namesake flagship; even better, the "bountiful libations" and "generous samples" of "haute cuisine without the haute attitude" (enjoyed in the "bar-centric" dining room or on the patio) can be had "without dropping a chunk of change."

Fiorella's Jack Stack *BBQ*
26 | 22 | 23 | $26

Crossroads | Freight House | 101 W. 22nd St. (Wyandotte St.), MO | 816-472-7427
Country Club Plaza | 4747 Wyandotte St. (bet. 47th St. & Ward Pkwy.), MO | 816-531-7427
Overland Park | 9520 Metcalf Ave. (95th St.), KS | 913-385-7427
Martin City | 13441 Holmes Rd. (135th St.), MO | 816-942-9141
www.jackstackbbq.com

"KC BBQ goes upscale" "without losing its soul" at this "fab" foursome featuring "smokin' good" grub, from "burnt ends and beans" to lamb ribs and "cheesy corn bake" ("how I love thee"); even if the "lovely surroundings" make some "feel bad about eating with their fingers", they're still "noisy and crowded", which makes sense since they're voted the area's Most Popular restaurants.

	FOOD	DECOR	SERVICE	COST

Jasper's ⓩ *Italian*

| 26 | 22 | 25 | $43 |

South KC | Watts Mill | 1201 W. 103rd St. (State Line Rd.), MO | 816-941-6600 | www.jasperskc.com

It's in a South KC "strip center", but step inside this "family-owned" "classic" and you'll feel like a "welcome guest in their home", and the "outstanding" Italian fare "makes it even better"; whether you're "entertaining out-of-town guests" or having a "romantic evening", it "never fails to please", especially if you nab a seat on the "screened-in porch"; P.S. thrifty types can nosh for "under $20" in the on-site deli.

Justus Drugstore: A Restaurant Ⓜ *American*

| 29 | 21 | 25 | $57 |

Smithville | 106 W. Main St. (169 Spur), MO | 816-532-2300 | www.drugstorerestaurant.com

Even the "pickiest foodies" agree it's "worth the drive" to this Smithville "locavore heaven" to sample chef/co-owner Jonathan Justus' "exceptional" New American fare, which draws on "French and Napa influences" and earns the No. 1 Food rating for the KC area; there's also "attentive service with a leisurely pace" (so "don't go if you're in a rush"), "house-recipe cocktails" and a "pleasant", somewhat "funky" setting in an old drugstore, prompting partisans to proclaim "my prescription can be filled here anytime."

Korma Sutra *Indian*

| 24 | 15 | 22 | $19 |

Westport | 4113 Pennsylvania Ave. (Westport Rd.), MO | 816-931-7775 Ⓜ
Overland Park | 7212 W. 110th St. (Metcalf Ave.), KS | 913-345-8774 | www.kckormasutra.com

"You can taste the love" in the "wide variety" of "excellent" fare at these reasonably priced Overland Park and Westport Indians where the "spice is right", the lunch buffet is "flavorful and filling" and the "warm staff remembers your regular order"; true, they're "sparsely decorated", but a "family-friendly" vibe means you can "take the kids and introduce them to new foods."

Le Fou Frog Ⓜ *French*

| 27 | 20 | 24 | $50 |

River Market | 400 E. Fifth St. (Oak St.), MO | 816-474-6060 | www.lefoufrog.com

A "true cast of characters" "with a sense of humor" serves up "fantastic" French fare at this "charming" River Market bistro that simply "swirls with joie de vivre"; the "tiny" place is "crowded, noisy", "dark" and "not cheap", but no matter: it's "as close to France as you'll find in KC – and worth the investment."

Lidia's *Italian*

| 25 | 26 | 24 | $38 |

Crossroads | 101 W. 22nd St. (Baltimore Ave.), MO | 816-221-3722 | www.lidias-kc.com

"Still a favorite in KC", this Crossroads "mainstay" from celeb chef Lidia Bastianich offers "superb" Italian cuisine infused with "sublime flavor combinations" and complemented by "knock-your-socks-off" wines that are "easy on the pocketbook" (the food's "reasonably priced" too); you can "dine outdoors" and "watch the trains go by" (it's across from Union Station) or let the "exemplary" staff pamper you in a "gorgeous space" adorned with "magnificent" chandeliers and a towering "slate fireplace."

	FOOD	DECOR	SERVICE	COST

Michael Smith ☒Ⓜ *American* | 28 | 24 | 26 | $55

Crossroads | 1900 Main St. (19th St.), MO | 816-842-2202 |
www.michaelsmithkc.com

"Pedigreed chef" Michael Smith "crafts dishes that are exciting, even daring" at his eponymous Crossroads New American, a "moderately expensive" "special-occasion spot" serving up "complex yet elemental" food "you can't make at home"; "much quieter" than adjacent sib Extra Virgin, it features "elegant" decor and "attentive" service, all the more reason to "eat here before New York kidnaps the place."

Oklahoma Joe's Barbecue ☒ *BBQ* | 27 | 15 | 19 | $15

Rosedale | 3002 W. 47th Ave. (Mission Rd.), KS | 913-722-3366
Olathe | 11950 S. Strang Line Rd. (119th St.), KS | 913-782-6858
www.oklahomajoesbbq.com

The "kitschy" "gas station location is part of the charm" of this KCKS "BBQ icon" that fuels 'cue-noisseurs with "championship-quality" vittles, including some of the "best pulled pork in town"; it all comes with "order-it-pick-it-up" service, "long lines" and "reasonable prices"; P.S. the Olathe venue features a more traditional restaurant atmosphere.

Piropos *Argentinean/Steak* | 27 | 26 | 25 | $47

Northland | Briarcliff Vill. | 4141 N. Mulberry Dr. (Briarcliff Pkwy.),
MO | 816-741-3600 | www.piroposkc.com

"Awesome steaks" with a "South American twist" make the cut at this "worth-a-trip" Argentinean venue in Northland; it's a "little expensive", but with "amazing service", "scrumptious desserts" and a "breathtaking view" of the skyline, just about everyone "wants to go back."

R Bar & Restaurant ☒Ⓜ *American* | ▽ 22 | 23 | 20 | $37

West Bottoms | 1617 Genessee St. (bet. 16th & 17th Sts.), MO |
816-471-1777 | www.rbarkc.com

Whatever you do, "use your GPS if you haven't been" to the West Bottoms or you'll never find this "perfect mix of historic bar, trendy hangout" and "music venue" serving up "inventive" New American cuisine and "fantastic" libations; while admirers advise to "stay for the entertainment", take note: it can become a "zoo" Thursday–Saturday when live performances pervade the "small space."

Room 39 ☒ *American* | 26 | 21 | 25 | $38

39th Street | 1719 W. 39th St. (bet. Bell & Genessee Sts.), MO |
816-753-3939
Leawood | Mission Farms | 10561 Mission Rd. (bet. I-435 & 103rd St.),
KS | 913-648-7639
www.rm39.com

"Local from the stock in the saucepans to the art on the walls", this "small" "neighborhood gem" on "eclectic" 39th Street puts "considerable thought" into its "ever-changing menu" of "robust", "farm-fresh" American comfort food; "quaint" decor and "caring" staffers add to the allure; P.S. Leawood has less "atmosphere" but is still "worth a trip."

Starker's Restaurant ☒ *American* | 26 | 25 | 26 | $56

Country Club Plaza | 201 W. 47th St. (Wyandotte St.), MO | 816-753-3565 |
www.starkersrestaurant.com

"What a wine list" sigh sippers who frequent this "intimate" Country Club Plaza "treat" spotlighting the "creative" concoctions of chef-owner John McClure; perhaps prices for the "fresh", "seasonal" New American dishes run "in the high range", but "personal service" helps ensure you're in for a "special evening."

Thai Place *Thai*   25 | 19 | 21 | $22

Westport | 4130 Pennsylvania Ave. (Westport Rd.), MO | 816-753-8424
Overland Park | 11838 Quivira Rd. (W. 119th St.), KS | 913-451-8424
Overland Park | Louisburg Square | 9359 W. 87th St. (Grant St.), KS | 913-649-5420
www.kcthaiplace.com

A "shockingly good dining experience" awaits at this "unassuming" Thai trio with a "large menu" of "fresh, tasty" fare that's "properly spiced" (ok, heat-seekers warn even the "medium-hot will kill you"); a "pleasant atmosphere", "gracious" staff and "excellent" prices complete the picture; P.S. Westport sports a "nice outdoor patio."

Webster House ☒ *Eclectic*   26 | 27 | 25 | $39

Crossroads | 1644 Wyandotte St. (17th St.), MO | 816-221-4713 | www.websterhousekc.com

Set on the second floor of a "converted schoolhouse" (with an antiques shop downstairs), this "sedate" Crossroads "destination" serves up "imaginatively prepared" Eclectic fare to everyone from "ladies who lunch" to culture vultures bound for the "opera or symphony"; if the "lovely" vintage furnishings and stained-glass windows are a "treat" for the eyes, "flawless service" makes it even better; P.S. it's likely to become "hugely popular" when a new performing arts center opens nearby.

Las Vegas

TOP FOOD RANKING

	Restaurant	Cuisine
28	L'Atelier/Joël Robuchon	French
	Joël Robuchon	French
	Rosemary's	American
	Nobu	Japanese
	Todd's Unique Dining	Eclectic
	Guy Savoy	French
27	Picasso	French
	Lotus of Siam	Thai
	Alex	French
	Tableau	American
	Michael Mina	Seafood
26	Del Frisco's	Steak
	André's	French
	B&B	Italian
	Prime	Steak
	Alizé	French
	Le Cirque	French
	Sterling Brunch	Eclectic
	SW Steak	Steak
	Ferraro's	Italian

OTHER NOTEWORTHY PLACES

Restaurant	Cuisine
Aureole	American
Bartolotta	Italian/Seafood
Bellagio Buffet	Eclectic
Botero	Steak
Bouchon	French
Burger Bar	Burgers
Craftsteak	Seafood/Steak
Delmonico	Steak
Eiffel Tower	French
Firefly	Spanish
Mix	American/French
Nobhill Tavern	Californian
Ping Pang Pong	Chinese
Raku	Japanese
Sage	American
Silk Road	Mediterranean
Simon	American
Switch	Steak
Veloce Cibo	Eclectic

	FOOD	DECOR	SERVICE	COST

Alex 🛇Ⓜ French

27	28	27	$200

Strip | Wynn Las Vegas | 3131 Las Vegas Blvd. S. (bet. Desert Inn & Spring Mountain Rds.) | 702-248-3463 | www.wynnlasvegas.com

"No detail is left undone" at "genius" chef Alessandro Stratta's "foodie fantasy come true" in the Wynn, where "achingly delicious" prix fixe meals of New French cuisine "hit their mark perfectly", "exceptional" servers "treat everyone like a high roller" and "even your purse gets a fancy chair"; from the first step "down the grand staircase" into the "opulent" room to the last "sublime" bite of dessert, it's a "luxurious" "over-the-top experience" that has some "big spenders" swearing it's "worth repeating"; next time, "skip the gambling and invest your money here."

Alizé French

26	27	26	$86

W of Strip | Palms Casino Hotel | 4321 W. Flamingo Rd. (Arville St.) | 702-951-7000 | www.alizelv.com

"Ooh-la-la – fine dining with magnificent views to boot" enthuse fans of this "sophisticated" André Rochat–owned French perched atop the Palms Hotel west of the Strip where the "phenomenal" dishes are best enjoyed when "day turns into night" and you can "watch the city come alive"; "impeccable" service from the "surprisingly unpretentious" staff and an "elegant" room that oozes with "romance" mean that most have no regrets about "offloading some winnings" here.

André's Ⓜ French

26	24	26	$80

Strip | Monte Carlo Resort | 3770 Las Vegas Blvd. S. (Harmon Ave.) | 702-798-7151 | www.andrelv.com

"Old Las Vegas" is alive at this Strip spot where "excellent", "rich" French fare ("even the butter is sautéed in butter") is served in "elegant", "Louis XIV-style" quarters; "impeccably polite service" further makes it "worth the splurge"; P.S. the Decor score does not reflect a post-Survey spruce-up.

Aureole American

25	27	24	$101

Strip | Mandalay Bay Resort | 3950 Las Vegas Blvd. S. (Hacienda Ave.) | 702-632-7401 | www.charliepalmer.com

"It feels like walking into a dream" swoon surveyors "wowed" by chef Charlie Palmer's "NYC transplant" in Mandalay Bay where a "dramatic entranceway" opens into a "beautiful" room with a multistory wine tower famously attended to by "harnessed" "angels" who "elegantly ascend" to retrieve vintages from a "tremendous" collection; "first-class" New American cuisine "rises to new heights" as well in a "superb" prix fixe menu while near "flawless" service "makes you feel like a million bucks"; in all, it's an experience of "sensory overload" that "more than satisfies", especially if "someone else is paying" the "insanely expensive" bill.

B&B Ristorante Italian

26	24	24	$75

Strip | Venetian Hotel | 3355 Las Vegas Blvd. S. (bet. Flamingo & Spring Mountain Rds.) | 702-266-9977 | www.bandbristorante.com

"Finally", "just what Vegas was missing" declare "foodies" "delighted" with Mario Batali's pricey Venetian venture that mirrors the experience of NYC's Babbo with "phenomenal wines" and "ingenious" "twists on classic Italian dishes" like the "amazing" signature beef cheek ravioli; a "knowledgeable" staff and "intimate" digs decked out in dark woods also win raves, and if a few find "they still have a few kinks to work out", the majority is convinced this "exciting" experience "will only get better."

Bartolotta *Italian/Seafood*
24 | 26 | 24 | $91

Strip | Wynn Las Vegas | 3131 Las Vegas Blvd. S. (bet. Desert Inn & Spring Mountain Rds.) | 702-770-3305 | www.wynnlasvegas.com
Connoisseurs claim they're "transported to a seaside village" thanks to a "unique assortment" of "fantastically fresh fish" from the Mediterranean at chef Paul Bartolotta's "simply outstanding" Italian seafooder at the Wynn with "romantic" lakefront seating available in one of the private cabanas; "top-notch" staffers "aim to please" with "superb" service (including "tableside presentations"), making this local "treasure" a "memorable" experience, and one that's "way worth" the "truly outrageous" final bill.

Bellagio Buffet *Eclectic*
24 | 19 | 19 | $34

Strip | Bellagio Hotel | 3600 Las Vegas Blvd. S. (Flamingo Rd.) | 702-693-7223 | www.bellagio.com
"A certain diet destroyer" say the legions of surveyors who endure almost "constant lines" for what they call the "mac daddy" of all buffets, with a "vast" spread of Eclectic dishes from "Buffalo wings to wild boar", "bountiful quantities" of seafood, plus a "fantastic" brunch on Saturdays and Sundays, where the champagne "flows like the Bellagio fountains themselves"; some contend it's more "expensive" than competitors, though defenders justify the "high" prices, declaring "it's the only meal you need for the day."

Botero *Steak*
- | - | - | VE

Strip | Encore Hotel | 3121 Las Vegas Blvd. S. (Sands Ave.) | 702-248-3463 | www.encorelasvegas.com
Works by the namesake himself adorn the walls at this steakhouse close to the shops and theater in the Encore on the Strip, but natural art is in evidence as well with two garden and pool areas viewed from an expanse of glass that opens wide in pleasant weather; expect dishes like brioche-crusted rack of lamb at prices as voluptuous as the master's works.

Bouchon *French*
25 | 24 | 24 | $60

Strip | Venetian Hotel | 3355 Las Vegas Blvd. S., 9th fl. (bet. Flamingo & Spring Mountain Rds.) | 702-414-6200 | www.bouchonbistro.com
Thomas Keller's "relatively affordable" "outpost of gastronomy" in the Venetian is "true to his Yountville original" with "perfectly executed French bistro fare", from "heavenly breakfasts" ("light-as-a-feather waffles", a cheese Danish "to dream about") to "indescribably delicious" dinners; the "beautiful" Adam Tihany–designed dining area includes "relaxing" patio seating "overlooking a quiet, well-shaded pool" that "makes you forget where you are", so even if service is sometimes "a little lacking", patrons proclaim it all "thoroughly enjoyable" nonetheless.

Burger Bar *Burgers*
23 | 17 | 18 | $26

Strip | Mandalay Place | 3930 Las Vegas Blvd. S. (Hacienda Ave.) | 702-632-9364 | www.burgerbarlv.com
From the "Zen-like simplicity" of a plain patty to the "baroque opulence" of "Kobe beef with foie gras and black truffles", the "possibilities are unlimited" for "building your own" version of that "old American favorite" at this "great concept" in Mandalay Place; not only can you

choose from "an array of tasty toppings", but the burgers themselves come in a "huge variety" – at a "wide range of prices"; beyond monitors broadcasting sports events, the "casual" place isn't nearly as well dressed as the namesakes.

Craftsteak *Seafood/Steak*

| 25 | 23 | 24 | $79 |

Strip | MGM Grand Hotel | 3799 Las Vegas Blvd. S. (Tropicana Ave.) | 702-891-7318 | www.mgmgrand.com

"Truly exceptional" steaks and "marvelously simple" sides showcasing "artisanal" ingredients are the hallmarks of chef Tom Colicchio's "exorbitantly priced" surf 'n' turfer in the MGM Grand where the "fantastic food" is supported by an "unbelievable wine list" and a selection of 120 single-malt scotches; surroundings are "sleek" and "nontraditional", while "ever-so-attentive" servers ensure an experience so "outstanding" it makes any night "feel like an occasion."

Del Frisco's Double Eagle Steak House *Steak*

| 26 | 23 | 25 | $67 |

E of Strip | 3925 Paradise Rd. (Corporate Dr.) | 702-796-0063 | www.delfriscos.com

"A mix of locals and tourists" puts this east of the Strip chain beef bonanza "at the top of the list", saying "you can't go wrong" with its "divine" steaks, "extraordinary wines" and "remarkable" service even if prices nearly "break the bank"; diners, however, take opposing sides on the mahogany wood and white-tablecloth decor, with some deeming it "classy" and others insisting it's "bland" and in need of an "update."

Delmonico Steakhouse *Steak*

| 26 | 23 | 25 | $76 |

Strip | Venetian Hotel | 3355 Las Vegas Blvd. S. (bet. Flamingo & Spring Mountain Rds.) | 702-414-3737 | www.emerils.com

"Emeril has it all together here" gush groupies of celebrity chef Lagasse, whose "absolute hunk-o-meat perfection" in the Venetian pleases with "fabulous cuts" of beef (including a "primo" bone-in rib-eye), "wonderful Caesar salad" prepared tableside and an "amazing", "unending" wine list; in spite of a few "lapses", servers "take care of your every need", so the only complaint is the "monastery-like" atmosphere, which some say needs to be "kicked up a notch" – most would "prefer a little more grandeur" given the "high prices."

Eiffel Tower *French*

| 22 | 26 | 22 | $76 |

Strip | Paris Las Vegas | 3655 Las Vegas Blvd. S. (bet. Flamingo Rd. & Harmon Ave.) | 702-948-6937 | www.eiffeltowerrestaurant.com

Those expecting "a gimmick" may be "surprised" by the "fine" French fare (including "perfectly executed soufflés") served in a "spectacular" "romantic" setting with vistas of the city and the Bellagio fountains at this Paris Las Vegas destination; the staff is "knowledgeable" if a bit "stiff", and though the whole experience strikes most as "*magnifique*", a minority claims it wasn't "blown away", citing "pedestrian" eats and "hefty price tags" as cause for complaint.

Ferraro's ◑ *Italian*

| 26 | 19 | 26 | $52 |

E of Strip | 4480 Paradise Rd (Harmon Ave.) | 702-364-5300 | www.ferraroslasvegas.com

Though it moved from the West Side to east of the Strip post-Survey (outdating the Decor score), it's still "worth the trip" to this stalwart joint that "jumps" on most nights with "live piano", setting the scene for "fabulous" meals of "old-world" Italian cuisine; despite a few grumbles about "high prices", most find it a "delightful" experience enhanced by a "friendly" chef and "superb" service.

Firefly *Spanish*

24 | 18 | 21 | $28

Downtown | The Plaza Hotel and Casino | 1 Main St. (Ogden St.) | 702-380-1352
E of Strip | 3900 Paradise Rd. (bet. Flamingo Rd. & Twain Ave.) | 702-369-3971 ◐
www.fireflylv.com

"Tasty little plates" of "easy-to-share" tapas "keep on comin'" to your table thanks to "helpful" servers at this East Side Spaniard that's "nowhere near as stuffy or expensive" as its Strip counterparts, and does without those "ringing slot machines" too; decorwise it may be a bit "blasé" inside, so "sit on the patio" instead, where pitchers of "dangerous" sangria go down easier; P.S. the Downtown offshoot debuted post-Survey.

Guy Savoy 🅼 *French*

28 | 26 | 27 | $195

Strip | Caesars Palace | 3570 Las Vegas Blvd. S. (Flamingo Rd.) | 702-731-7731 | www.caesarspalace.com

"How do you say 'beyond perfect' *en français*?" ask acolytes of "genius" chef Guy Savoy, who has "outdone himself" with this "gastronomic adventure" in Caesars Palace, which some say is "better than the three-star Paris original" with "brilliantly presented" New French cuisine served à la carte or from an "exquisite" tasting menu plus a "terrific" wine list with 1,500 labels; also "memorable" is "impeccable", "unpretentious" service (ladies like the "purse perches") and a "stylish" setting done up in dark, rich woods, while "breathtaking prices" are commensurate with the "once-in-a-lifetime" experience; P.S. the Bubbles Bar inside the restaurant offers a small-bites menu.

Joël Robuchon *French*

28 | 27 | 28 | $251

Strip | MGM Grand Hotel | 3799 Las Vegas Blvd. S. (Tropicana Ave.) | 702-891-7925 | www.mgmgrand.com

"Truly an experience for the ages" swoon surveyors "savoring each moment" of chef Joël Robuchon's "life-altering" New French in the MGM Grand, where the "exquisite" tasting menus "build to a crescendo of amazing intensity", rendering "all other [meals] a mere blur"; so don a jacket, "buckle in" and revel in the "elegant lavender and cream interior" and "pampering" treatment – and if you're daunted by the "three-hour-plus" meal (not to mention the "stratospheric prices"), gastronomes advise "pace yourself, breathe deeply and keep looking at the dessert cart for motivation."

L'Atelier de Joël Robuchon *French*

28 | 24 | 26 | $118

Strip | MGM Grand Hotel | 3799 Las Vegas Blvd. S. (Tropicana Ave.) | 702-891-7358 | www.mgmgrand.com

This downscaled (but still "staggeringly" expensive) sister to Joël Robuchon in the MGM Grand is "a less stuffy way" for "hard-core foodies" to experience "the master's" "stunning" New French cuisine, which earns the No. 1 Food score in Las Vegas thanks to "memorable" small plates best appreciated from the U-shaped bar where "you can marvel at the action" in the open kitchen; refreshingly "unpretentious" service makes the black-and-red interior feel both "sleek" and "casual" at the same time, setting the scene for "one of the single best dining experiences in Vegas" – just bring your "sense of adventure."

Le Cirque ▣ *French*　　　　26 | 27 | 26 | $96

Strip | Bellagio Hotel | 3600 Las Vegas Blvd. S. (Flamingo Rd.) | 702-693-7223 | www.bellagio.com

"A class act", this "extravagant" New York offshoot in the Bellagio is "delightful in every way" say those savoring "exceptional" repasts of New French cuisine, "smooth service" from waiters who "anticipate your every desire" and "spectacular views of the fountains" from the "playful" silk-tented dining room; in short, "it's simply one of the best" – just bring a fat wallet.

Lotus of Siam *Thai*　　　　27 | 10 | 20 | $28

E Side | Commercial Ctr. | 953 E. Sahara Ave. (bet. Joe Brown Dr. & Maryland Pkwy.) | 702-735-3033 | www.lotusofsiamlv.com

"Hitchhike if you have to", but "don't leave town" without a stop at this "local treasure" east of the Strip that intrepid eaters rank as the "best Thai restaurant in the country", with a "dazzling" "affordable" array of "complex" dishes including "exquisite" Northern-style "gems" like jackfruit curry that pair well with sips from an "excellent list of German Rieslings"; "friendly service" helps you forget all about the "strip-mall" setting and nondescript decor; P.S. it underwent a post-Survey expansion.

Michael Mina *Seafood*　　　　27 | 24 | 26 | $93

Strip | Bellagio Hotel | 3600 Las Vegas Blvd. S. (Flamingo Rd.) | 702-693-7223 | www.michaelmina.net

"Easily the best seafood on the Strip" rave regulars who savor tastings that "tickle the senses" at chef/co-owner Michael Mina's "romantic", "beautiful and relaxing" Bellagio destination; a "superb" wine list and "marvelous" service help justify the "third mortgage required to fund the extravagance."

Mix *American/French*　　　　23 | 27 | 22 | $89

Strip | Mandalay Bay Resort | 3950 Las Vegas Blvd. S., 64th fl. (Hacienda) | 702-632-9500 | www.chinagrillmgt.com

"Killer views" from "64 floors up" are "hard to beat" at Alain Ducasse's "gem" in THEhotel at Mandalay Bay, where the "gorgeous" *Austin Powers* interior with a chandelier of 15,000 blown-glass bubbles suggests "sitting in a glass of champagne"; the New American–New French menu is "memorable" too, and while the "amiable" staff is sometimes "spotty", fans call it "one of the few places that can almost justify the price"; P.S. "reserve an outside table and watch the sun set over the Strip."

Nobhill Tavern *Californian*　　　　26 | 24 | 25 | $88

Strip | MGM Grand Hotel | 3799 Las Vegas Blvd. S. (Tropicana Ave.) | 702-891-7337 | www.michaelmina.net

One of the "culinary treasures" of MGM Grand on the Strip, this "exquisite" Californian by chef/co-owner Michael Mina features "innovative cuisine of the high-calorie kind", complemented by "freshly baked" breads; an "exceptional" staff works the dining room whose savviest guests "book early to reserve one of the private booths", but also warn that dining here can "drain your wallet faster than the high-roller tables"; P.S. the scores do not reflect a post-Survey revamp, which introduced tavern-style menu items and more casual furnishings.

Nobu *Japanese* | 28 | 23 | 24 | $80 |

E of Strip | Hard Rock Hotel | 4455 Paradise Rd. (bet. Flamingo Rd. & Harmon Ave.) | 702-693-5090 | www.noburestaurants.com

"Exceptional raw fish in the desert" attracts seekers of the "absolute freshest" "sushi and sashimi creations" as well as "amazing cooked dishes" ("love the miso cod"), all served by a "superb" staff at Nobu Matsuhisa's outpost in the Hard Rock Hotel east of the Strip; sure, "they blast music like eardrums are going out of style" and you can expect a "flabbergasting bill", but many advise "just say omakase", "watch the masters at work at the bar" and "enjoy the ride."

Picasso *French* | 27 | 29 | 27 | $149 |

Strip | Bellagio Hotel | 3600 Las Vegas Blvd. S. (Flamingo Rd.) | 702-693-7223 | www.bellagio.com

"Perfection on a grand scale" comes via chef Julian Serrano's "lavish" New French palace in the Bellagio (voted Most Popular in Las Vegas) where "high rollers" "live the luxe life" "surrounded by original Picassos" and an "abundance of fresh flowers" while tasting "transcendent" prix fixe meals paired with "fantastic" wines from an "extensive" European list; "polished" servers exhibit "pure finesse", making for a "sublime" experience that's sure to "break you out of your blue period" – at least until you get the check.

Ping Pang Pong ◐ *Chinese* | ∇ 21 | 11 | 14 | $25 |

W Side | Gold Coast Hotel | 4000 W. Flamingo Rd. (bet. Valley View Blvd. & Wynn Rd.) | 702-367-7111 | www.goldcoastcasino.com

"The won ton soup is won-derful" and all of the "creative Chinese" dishes are "not to be expected in such simple" "cafeteria decor", but here they are at this "real surprise" on the West Side; open till 3 AM, it's "good for a late-night snack", if you can deal with the staff: "either the waiters won't leave you alone, or they won't come back."

Prime Steakhouse *Steak* | 26 | 27 | 26 | $92 |

Strip | Bellagio Hotel | 3600 Las Vegas Blvd. S. (Flamingo Rd.) | 702-693-7223 | www.bellagio.com

"Now *this* is what it's like in the lap of luxury" purr proponents of Jean-Georges Vongerichten's "posh" 1930s-style chophouse in the Bellagio that's "straight out of a movie set", with velvet drapes and Baccarat chandeliers setting the scene for a "high-rolling" "celebrity crowd" sipping "well-poured drinks" and nibbling "perfectly cooked" steaks; from the "superb" service to the "hard-to-beat" views of the fountains outside, it's a "prime" contender for "one of the most elegant dining experiences" in town.

Raku ◐🗷 *Japanese* | - | - | - | M |

W Side | 5030 Spring Mountain Rd. (Decatur Blvd.) | 702-367-3511 | www.raku-grill.com

During their time off, some of the city's chefs gather at this tiny Japanese housed in a shopping center on the West Side for tapaslike dishes, robata grill items and made-fresh-daily tofu; its sleek, wood-accented decor is enlivened by touches like a woven wall.

	FOOD	DECOR	SERVICE	COST

Rosemary's *American*

| 28 | 20 | 26 | $58 |

W Side | West Sahara Promenade | 8125 W. Sahara Ave. (bet. Buffalo Dr. & Cimarron Rd.) | 702-869-2251 | www.rosemarysrestaurant.com

"A winner" that "hasn't lost its special touch", this West Sider proves "a tough act to follow", with chef-owners Michael and Wendy Jordan's "simply outstanding" New American cuisine showcasing "delicate flavors" and served à la carte or in an "excellent" $55 prix fixe meal available with "inspired" beer and wine pairings; "stellar" service makes the "pretty" (some say "dowdy") decor all the more "inviting", and though it's "quite a trip" from the Strip, most maintain they'd "go back in a heartbeat"; P.S. on Fridays the "$25 three-course lunch may be the best deal in town."

Sage ⑤ *American*

| - | - | - | E |

Strip | Aria | 3730 Las Vegas Blvd. S. (Harmon Ave.) | 877-230-2742 | www.arialasvegas.com

Chef Shawn McClain, of Chicago's highly rated Green Zebra and Spring, gambles on Sin City at this upscale venue in the Strip's Aria resort and casino, where he creates a seasonal New American menu jazzed up with Mediterranean accents; the interior is a sexy homage to Old Vegas lushness, with large curved booths amid plum and brass accents; P.S. at the bar, cutting-edge mixology is the star.

Silk Road *Mediterranean*

| - | - | - | E |

Strip | Vdara, CityCenter | 2600 W. Harmon Ave. (Las Vegas Blvd. S.) | 866-745-7767 | www.vdara.com

Vibrant yellows and oranges whose brightness dims with the daylight festoon an undulating sculptural partition at this cafe in the Vdara Hotel and Spa (at the Strip's City Center), where the dramatic design also includes shimmering golds, plush purples and walls of glass; though fundamentally Mediterranean (e.g. meze, tagines), the pricey, petite breakfast, lunch and dinner menus are laden with Middle Eastern and Asian influences, reflecting the eatery's namesake trade route.

Simon Restaurant & Lounge *American*

| - | - | - | M |

W of Strip | Palms Place | 4381 W. Flamingo Rd. (Arville St.) | 702-944-3292 | www.palmsplace.com

Lots of wood, glass and vaguely '70s decor accents characterize this hip, happening American overlooking the pool at Palms Place west of the Strip; the servers are as sexy as the view, and the coolness factor extends to Kerry Simon's midpriced menu of updated comfort classics like pizza, meatloaf and short ribs; P.S. breakfast, lunch and sushi are also offered.

Sterling Brunch Ⓜ *Eclectic*

| 26 | 22 | 25 | $71 |

Strip | Bally's Las Vegas | 3645 Las Vegas Blvd. S. (Flamingo Rd.) | 702-967-7999 | www.ballyslasvegas.com

"Decadence" is the theme of Bally's "ritzy" Sunday brunch featuring an "over-the-top" Eclectic spread with "abundant lobsters" and "caviar aplenty" and where you'll "never lack for champagne", thanks to waiters in "tuxes and white gloves" who keep the bubbly "flowing"; "reservations" are a must, and while it may be "expensive", some wallet-watchers insist it's a relative deal – at least "you won't need dinner."

	FOOD	DECOR	SERVICE	COST

Strip House *Steak*

-	-	-	E

Strip | Planet Hollywood Resort | 3667 Las Vegas Blvd. S. (Harmon Ave.) | 702-737-5200 | www.striphouse.com

Crimson decor and prints of Victorian-era hussies set a tone of decadence at this outpost of the NY–based steakhouse in Planet Hollywood; the à la carte menu boasts lusty dishes like porterhouses and goose-fat potatoes, while stiff drinks make the steep tabs go down easier.

Switch Steak *Steak*

-	-	-	VE

Strip | Encore Hotel | 3121 Las Vegas Blvd. S. (Sands Ave.) | 702-248-3463 | www.encorelasvegas.com

It's a moveable feast, literally, at this steak spot in Encore on the Strip, where the art, ceiling and walls shift and morph throughout the meal; there's plenty of action in the kitchen as well, which churns out a luxe menu that features its fair share of seafood and French flair.

SW Steakhouse *Steak*

26	26	25	$90

Strip | Wynn Las Vegas | 3131 Las Vegas Blvd. S. (bet. Desert Inn & Spring Mountain Rds.) | 702-248-3463 | www.wynnlasvegas.com

"SW stands for 'swanky'" at this Wynn steakhouse "splurge" offering up "fabulous" food and bottles from a "dazzling wine list"; it may not be "as hip as other spots in town", but "incredible views" of the nightly fountain shows plus "expert" service keep it "crowded", just beware of occasional "waits, even with reservations."

Tableau *American*

27	25	27	$82

Strip | Wynn Las Vegas | 3131 Las Vegas Blvd. S. (bet. Desert Inn & Spring Mountain Rds.) | 888-352-3463 | www.wynnlasvegas.com

"Exceptional breakfasts" and "civilized lunches" await at this French-influenced New American whose "exclusive" south tower location in the Wynn makes it feel like an "elegant" "private dining room", with poolside views and "flawless service" adding to the "appeal"; diehards decree that it "deserves more attention", though insiders insist the fact that it's "not so well known" is exactly what makes it "special."

Todd's Unique Dining 🗷 *Eclectic*

28	16	25	$47

Henderson | 4350 E. Sunset Rd. (Green Valley Pkwy.) | 702-259-8633 | www.toddsunique.com

One of Henderson's "best-kept secrets", chef-owner Todd Clore's "valley favorite" "shines" with "serious", "sophisticated" seasonal Eclectic dishes plus a wine list with "phenomenal values" (and no pouring charge on Wednesdays, should you decide to bring your own); factor in "accommodating service" and enthusiasts appraise it's "as good as any on the Strip", but at "half the price"; even if the decor "could use sprucing up", everything else "just keeps getting better."

Veloce Cibo *Eclectic*

-	-	-	M

S of Strip | M Resort | 12300 Las Vegas Blvd. S. (St. Rose Pkwy.) | 702-797-1000 | www.themresort.com

The Eclectic menu at this midpriced venture in the M Resort (South of the Strip on the outskirts of Henderson) is nothing if not contemporary, mixing sushi and tapas with more conventional entrees, while the view from its 16th-floor rooftop perch can only be called timeless; that also describes much of the decor, which evokes the Italian Riviera with lemon-tree motifs and hand-blown glass bottles.

Long Island

TOP FOOD RANKING

	Restaurant	Cuisine
28	Kitchen A Bistro	French
	North Fork Table	American
	Maroni	Eclectic/Italian
	Chachama	American
27	Lake House	American
	Aji 53	Japanese
	Dario's	Italian
	Kotobuki	Japanese
	Peter Luger	Steak
	Vine Street Café	American
	Le Soir	French
26	Stone Creek	French/Mediterranean
	Mosaic	American
	Mirko's	Eclectic
	Piccolo	American/Italian
	Vintage Prime	Steak
	Panama Hatties	American
	Barney's	American/French
	Plaza Cafe	American
	Nagahama	Japanese

OTHER NOTEWORTHY PLACES

Restaurant	Cuisine
Besito	Mexican
Bravo Nader!	Italian
Bryant & Cooper	Steak
Cheesecake Factory	American
Dave's Grill	Continental/Seafood
Della Femina	American
Harvest on Fort Pond	Italian/Mediterranean
Il Mulino	Italian
La Plage	Eclectic
Limani	Mediterranean/Seafood
Mirabelle	French
Nick & Toni's	Italian/Mediterranean
Nisen Sushi	Japanese
Orient	Chinese
Rialto	Italian
1770 House	Continental
Siam Lotus	Thai
Starr Boggs	American/Seafood
Tellers	Steak
Toku	Asian

	FOOD	DECOR	SERVICE	COST

Aji 53 *Japanese*

| 27 | 24 | 24 | $39 |

Bay Shore | 53 E. Main St. (3rd Ave.) | 631-591-3107 | www.aji53.com

Admirers say *"arigato"* for the "spectacular presentations" of "outstanding" sushi ("Manhattan rolls without the train trip") and "beyond delicious" cooked Japanese dishes at this "Bay Shore jewel" whose owner's "Nobu pedigree" also shows in the "hip" surroundings and "steep" but "tasty" cocktails; with "convivial" service to boot, the "secret is out" – so "definitely call ahead for reservations."

Barney's Ⓜ *American/French*

| 26 | 23 | 25 | $63 |

Locust Valley | 315 Buckram Rd. (Bayville Rd.) | 516-671-6300 | www.barneyslv.com

"There's no better place on a chilly autumn night" "when the fireplace is aglow" than this "snug" Locust Valley "charmer" where the New American–French cooking is as "delectable as the atmosphere"; a "fine wine list" (with "affordable" options) and "superb" service make it "outstanding in every way", so no wonder it's still "hot with the chichi set."

Besito *Mexican*

| 23 | 23 | 21 | $46 |

Roslyn | Harborview Shoppes | 1516 Old Northern Blvd. (bet. Northern Blvd./Rte. 25A & Remsen Ave.) | 516-484-3001
Huntington | 402 New York Ave. (bet. Carver & Fairview Sts.) | 631-549-0100
www.besitomex.com

"Vibrant" Mexican food with a "modern flair" (including "must-have" guac made tableside) "kisses the palate" at this "hip" Huntington and Roslyn duo that also boasts "boutique margaritas", "beautiful people" and "dark", "gorgeous" ambiance ("candles lit against the back wall make it look phenomenal"); despite some complaints of "upselling", most maintain the "terrific" service suits the "sophisticated" meal.

Bravo Nader! *Italian*

| 26 | 14 | 23 | $55 |

Huntington | 9 Union Pl. (bet. New York Ave. & Wall St.) | 631-351-1200 | www.bravonader.com

Though the name may resemble a chant for an all-star soccer forward, this "shoebox" Huntington haunt is "beloved" for the "marvelous", "worth-every-penny" Southern Italian food ("specials are the sweet spot") crafted by "amazing" chef-owner Nader Gebrin, who "works magic in the kitchen" and "makes you feel at home"; even if the space often gets so "crammed" "you could eat off your neighbor's plate by mistake", fans love that the "wine is flowing and loud conversations abound"; P.S. closed Tuesday.

Bryant & Cooper Steakhouse *Steak*

| 26 | 20 | 23 | $67 |

Roslyn | 2 Middle Neck Rd. (Northern Blvd.) | 516-627-7270 | www.bryantandcooper.com

The prime cuts are "consistently tops" and the "seafood and sides are terrific too" at this "steakhouse extraordinaire" on the "corridor of carnivores" in Roslyn; while the "old-time" dining room can be a "tight squeeze", it's tended to by "professional, witty waiters", and loyalists love that it's "loud, full of testosterone" and a "fun scene" with a crowd "six-deep" at the bar – just be sure to "check your 401(k)" before footing the bill; P.S. don't miss the butcher and retail shop next door.

	FOOD	DECOR	SERVICE	COST

Chachama Grill *American*   28 | 20 | 26 | $49

East Patchogue | Swan Nursery Commons | 655 Montauk Hwy.
(Country Rd.) | 631-758-7640 | www.chachamagrill.com

"Dinner is nothing short of a magical experience" for ardent fans of the "artistic" New American fare by chef Elmer Rubio that's a "true treat for the palate" at this "surprising" "storefront extraordinaire" in East Patchogue; featuring a "wonderful" staff, "reasonably priced wine list" and prix fixe deals, it's one of the "best bets" on the island.

Cheesecake Factory *American*   20 | 19 | 17 | $30

Westbury | Mall at the Source | 1504 Old Country Rd. (Evelyn Ave.) | 516-222-5500 ◑

Huntington Station | Walt Whitman Mall | 160 Walt Whitman Rd. (Weston St.) | 631-271-8200

Lake Grove | Smith Haven Mall | 610 Smith Haven Mall (bet. Middle Country Rd. & Nesconsett Hwy.) | 631-361-6600
www.thecheesecakefactory.com

The menu's "mammoth" – and "so are the crowds" – at these "family-pleasing" chain links where the "endless" American options arrive in equally "colossal" portions (ironically, "they give you so much there's no room" for their "heavenly" namesake desserts); despite "ordinary" settings, "spotty" staffing and "lots of commotion", these "well-oiled machines" are so "busy, busy, busy" that they're best accessed "off-hours" to avoid a "long wait."

Dario's Ⓩ *Italian*   27 | 18 | 26 | $57

Rockville Centre | 13 N. Village Ave. (bet. Merrick Rd. & Sunrise Hwy.) | 516-255-0535

"You can eat simply or elaborately – just let them feed you" at this Rockville Centre "winner" known for Northern Italian cuisine "at its finest" and a "cordial" staff that "sets the standard for service"; even though the decor and ambiance are "not comparable" to the food, most agree it's "pricey but worth it" for a "fabulous" meal.

Dave's Grill *Continental/Seafood*   26 | 17 | 21 | $59

Montauk | 468 W. Lake Dr. (bet. Flamingo Ave. & Soundview Dr.) | 631-668-9190 | www.davesgrill.com

Fans effuse "the fish practically flop onto your plate straight off the dock out back" at this Montauk mainstay that cooks up a "memorable", "high-end" Continental menu of "outstanding" seafood; the dining room may be "cramped" and "stuck in the '80s" and there's a chorus of complaints about the "frustrating" same-day reservation policy (it's "tough unless you get there or phone right at opening"), but most conclude it's "always worth it."

Della Femina *American*   24 | 22 | 22 | $67

East Hampton | 99 N. Main St. (Cedar St.) | 631-329-6666 | www.dellafemina.com

Still the "place to be seen on a Saturday night" in East Hampton, this "hot ticket" rewards its "tony" clientele with "spectacular" New American fare "emphasizing fresh, local seasonal ingredients that never fail to please"; service is "smooth" (if a touch "smug"), and the "light, airy setting" designed with "well-spaced tables" and celebrity caricatures creates an "elegant" atmosphere that's especially inviting on "quieter" (and more affordable) winter nights.

	FOOD	DECOR	SERVICE	COST

Harvest on Fort Pond *Italian/Mediterranean* | 25 | 21 | 21 | $50 |

Montauk | 11 S. Emery St. (Euclid Ave.) | 631-668-5574 |
www.harvest2000.com

"Bring some friends" as the "gigantic" Mediterranean-Tuscan plates
are "meant to be shared" – and so "delicious" "it's tough to pick just a
few" – at this "best-for-the-money" Montauk "must" where revelers
"sit outside in the garden", "catch a sunset" over Fort Pond and "love
life"; "packed" and "happening", it's a "tough reservation", but even
those who have "waited two hours" say it's "worth it."

Il Mulino New York *Italian* | 26 | 22 | 24 | $78 |

Roslyn Estates | 1042 Northern Blvd. (bet. Cedar Path & Searingtown Rd.) |
516-621-1870 | www.ilmulino.com

"Quintessential" Northern Italian dining awaits at this Roslyn Estates
chain link spun off from the "superb" NYC original and featuring the
same "excellent" cooking and "great service"; granted, the mood can
be "stuffy" and the pricing "exorbitantly high", but ultimately they'll
"feed you so much" – the meal comes with "lots of extras" "before you
even order" – that a "good walk afterward" is recommended; P.S. the
prix fixe Sunday supper is slightly less steep.

Kitchen A Bistro ⊄ *French* | 28 | - | 23 | $44 |

St. James | 404 N. Country Rd. (Edgewood Ave.) | 631-862-0151 |
www.kitchenabistro.com

"Phenomenal" fare "continues to astound" at this St. James French
bistro, voted No. 1 for Food on Long Island, where "genius" chef-owner
Eric Lomando "pays attention to detail in every dish", achieves "poetry" in seafood and changes the menu "at his whim"; it relocated
post-Survey, but is still quite "intimate", and the no-corkage BYO policy means "you can't beat the price"; P.S. "make your reservations
waaay in advance" and "bring cash."

Kotobuki Ⓜ *Japanese* | 27 | 18 | 20 | $40 |

Roslyn | Harborview Shoppes | 1530 Old Northern Blvd. (Bryant Ave.) |
516-621-5312
Babylon | 86 Deer Park Ave. (Main St.) | 631-321-8387
Hauppauge | 377 Nesconset Hwy. (Hauppauge Rd.) | 631-360-3969
www.kotobukinewyork.com

"All hail" the "exceptional", "über-fresh" sushi and other "succulent"
dishes offering "amazing value" at this "top" Japanese trio with a
"huge following"; it's generally "impossible to get a table without a
minimum 30-minute wait" (no reservations are taken), the interior is
"tight" and service "needs improving", so savvy souls recommend
"sitting at the sushi bar if you want some peace and quiet."

Lake House Ⓜ *American* | 27 | 24 | 25 | $61 |

Bay Shore | 240 W. Main St. (bet. Garner Ln. & Lawrence Ave.) |
631-666-0995 | www.thelakehouserest.com

"Delectable" New American creations by "truly talented" chef/co-
owner Matthew Connors are "nothing short of superlative" at this "extraordinary" "find" that boasts a "tranquil lake setting" in Bay Shore; enthused epicures say a "cocktail by the fire pit" is a fine way to start, and
"first-rate" service keeps them "delighted" all the way to the "expensive
but worth-it" check; P.S. open for lunch Tuesday–Friday in season.

	FOOD	DECOR	SERVICE	COST

La Plage *Eclectic* | 26 | 18 | 23 | $59 |

Wading River | 131 Creek Rd. (Sound Rd.) | 631-744-9200 | www.laplagerestaurant.net

Guests feel like they've "stumbled onto a secret" at this "laid-back", "rustic" "gem" on the north shore of Wading River, where the "fabulous", "artfully presented" Eclectic fare via chef Wayne Wadington continues to impress; though a handful takes issue with the "cramped" setting and a "beach view that's across a parking lot", most focus on the "inspired" dishes served by an "efficient" staff.

Le Soir Ⓜ *French* | 27 | 20 | 24 | $52 |

Bayport | 825 Montauk Hwy. (Bayport Ave.) | 631-472-9090

Devotees are still drawn to this "landmark" Bayport bistro for chef/co-owner Michael Kaziewicz's "impeccable" French dinners, from "homemade soups" to "magnificent desserts, one better than the next"; though some feel the "dimly lit" room "could use a makeover", both the staff and the Sunday–Thursday prix fixe specials are more than "welcoming."

Limani *Mediterranean/Seafood* | - | - | - | VE |

Roslyn | 1043 Northern Blvd. (bet. Middle Neck Rd. & Port Washington Blvd.) | 516-869-8989 | www.limaniny.com

Theatrical and grand, this Roslyn Mediterranean follows the Greek concept of selling fish by the pound and allowing guests to make their selection from a huge iced display; tall ceilings, teak floors, mosaic tile and touches of marble all contribute to the high-end atmosphere, while a glass-enclosed floor-to-ceiling wine display separates private parties from the main dining room.

Maroni Cuisine Ⓢ Ⓜ ⊟ *Eclectic/Italian* | 28 | 16 | 25 | $97 |

Northport | 18 Woodbine Ave. (bet. Main St. & Scudder Ave.) | 631-757-4500 | www.maronicuisine.com

"Prepared to exquisite standards" by "one-of-a-kind" chef-owner Michael Maroni, the "incredible" Eclectic-Italian tasting menu "has to be eaten to be believed" at this cash-only Northport "blast" requiring "reservations exactly a month in advance"; despite its "tight" interior with "classic rock" playing, it feels "close to the best cocktail party ever" - "you'll leave stuffed and satisfied and not care about what you spent", so "sit back and enjoy the ride" (and "take home some meatballs in a pot"); P.S. the space has been upgraded post-Survey with a new courtyard and chic private party room.

Mirabelle, Restaurant Ⓜ *French* | - | - | - | VE |

Stony Brook | Three Village Inn | 150 Main St. (Shore Rd.) | 631-751-0555 | www.threevillageinn.com

Chef Guy Reuge's acclaimed French has relocated from St. James to a space carved out of several former event rooms in Stony Brook's Three Village Inn; elegant soft rose and ivory walls, tall ceilings, fireplaces and fresh flowers set the stage for rarefied meals, with à la carte options as well as seasonal prix fixe and tasting menus.

Mirko's Ⓜ *Eclectic* | 26 | 23 | 24 | $71 |

Water Mill | Water Mill Sq. | 670 Montauk Hwy. (bet. Cobb & Old Mill Rds.) | 631-726-4444 | www.mirkosrestaurant.com

"Masterfully prepared" Eclectic fare with "Eastern European flair" is the hallmark of this "highly recommended" Water Mill eatery where the "warm" "husband-and-wife team doesn't miss a trick"; its "inviting" country interior with a fireplace is always packed (there's also seasonal outdoor seating), but "if you can secure a table", it's worth the "expense"; P.S. closed January to mid-February.

Mosaic ⊠Ⓜ *American*
26 | 21 | 25 | $56

St. James | 418 N. Country Rd. (Edgewood Ave.) | 631-584-2058 | www.eatmosaic.com

The skilled chefs can "put food together (or take it apart) in ways one would not typically imagine", then "beautifully plate it" and couple it with "inspired wine pairings" at this "wonderful" New American whose nightly tasting menu (with an à la carte option) gives locals "something to get excited about" in "sleepy St. James"; "impeccable" service in an "intimate", pale-green space adorned with black-and-white photos completes the "experience."

Nagahama *Japanese*
26 | 15 | 21 | $35

Long Beach | 169 E. Park Ave. (bet. Long Beach & Riverside Blvds.) | 516-432-6446 | www.nagahamasushi.com

Devotees insist "nothing else compares locally" to chef/co-owner Hide Yamamoto's Long Beach Japanese where "fabulous sushi" is crafted from the "freshest" fish; even "cramped quarters" and "ridiculous waits" don't detract from the allure, as "smiling waitresses" deliver "prompt" service.

Nick & Toni's *Italian/Mediterranean*
23 | 21 | 22 | $68

East Hampton | 136 N. Main St. (bet. Cedar St. & Miller Terrace) | 631-324-3550 | www.nickandtonis.com

"Inspired" yet "not overly fussy" rustic Italian-Med dishes and wood-fired specialties live up to the "hype and hustle" at this star-studded East Hampton "staple"; "knowledgeable" servers and surprisingly intimate rooms round out what fans call "one of the best dining experiences in the Hamptons", which explains why the "price almost doesn't matter" and it's so packed that the big question is "how do you get a reservation?"; P.S. closed Monday–Tuesday in the winter.

Nisen Sushi *Japanese*
26 | 27 | 22 | $59

Woodbury | Woodbury Village Shopping Ctr. | 7967 Jericho Tpke. (Southwoods Rd.) | 516-496-7000 | www.nisensushi.com

"Exquisite" raw and cooked Japanese cuisine sates discriminating diners who "aren't sure which is more mouthwatering, the innovative sushi or the trendy crowd" at this "hip" Woodbury "scene" with "gorgeous" surroundings; yes, it will cost you an "arm and a leg", but the atmosphere delivers "a bit of Manhattan" "chic" – just "make sure you have reservations"; P.S. DJs and live music stir up extra excitement Thursday–Saturday nights.

North Fork Table & Inn *American*
28 | 25 | 27 | $71

Southold | North Fork Table & Inn | 57225 Main Rd./Rte. 25 (bet. Boisseau & Laurel Aves.) | 631-765-0177 | www.northforktableandinn.com

"A true star in the fork" by NYC expats who "know how to do it", this "sublime" Southolder "lives up to the hype" – and the "expense" – with a "marvelous" New American menu by Gerry Hayden showcasing "plentiful local" ingredients with "astonishing twists that work", as well as "irresistible desserts" by Claudia Fleming (ex Gramercy

Tavern); it's set in a "glowing dining room with a country house feel" and tended by a "warm, youthful" and "knowledgeable" staff; P.S. hours vary in the off-season.

Orient, The *Chinese*   26 | 10 | 19 | $26

Bethpage | 623 Hicksville Rd. (bet. Courtney & Fiddler Lns.) | 516-822-1010

For "wonderfully prepared, fresh" Cantonese, Hunan and Sichuan fare, "gracious host Tommy" Tan's Bethpage Chinese is the "undisputed" choice say aficionados who "get over the lack of decor" and "let the waiter recommend a special dish or two" from the "extensive menu"; though it's "always crowded" and "rushed" ("especially on weekends"), the "price is great", so there's "no need to trudge into Chinatown" – even for "terrific dim sum."

Panama Hatties *American*   26 | 22 | 25 | $70

Huntington Station | Post Plaza | 872 E. Jericho Tpke. (bet. Cooper Ave. & Emerald Ln.) | 631-351-1727 | www.panamahatties.com

"Don't be fooled by the outside, it's definitely worth" seeking out this "oasis" in a Huntington Station strip mall enthuse epicures enthralled with chef-owner Matthew Hisiger's "out-of-this-world", "perfectly prepared" New American cuisine; "very professional, friendly service" augments the "culinary experience", as does an "elegant" interior with pressed-tin ceilings – and not surprisingly, "it will really cost you."

Peter Luger *Steak*   27 | 17 | 21 | $71

Great Neck | 255 Northern Blvd. (bet. Jayson Ave. & Tain Dr.) | 516-487-8800 | www.peterluger.com

Reigning as the Most Popular restaurant on Long Island for the 17th year running, this "mecca of beef" in Great Neck (spun off from the Brooklyn original) serves up "superb", "melt-in-your-mouth" steaks and "delicious" sides in a "masculine" setting – and some even claim the "waiters aren't as grumpy as people say"; indeed, "they pour a healthy drink to make you forget" the hefty tab, and now they accept credit cards.

Piccolo *American/Italian*   26 | 21 | 24 | $57

Huntington | Southdown Shopping Ctr. | 215 Wall St. (bet. Mill Ln. & Southdown Rd.) | 631-424-5592 | www.piccolorestaurant.net

Customers crave the "stellar" dishes on the "inventive" New American-Italian menu accompanied by a "surprising wine list" at this "warm, inviting" Huntington "favorite" with a "fantastic" staff that makes "you feel like you're being served by friends"; a piano player (Sunday-Thursday) adds a "nice touch" to the "expensive" meal, which is so "transporting", "reservations are a must."

Plaza Cafe *Seafood*   26 | 21 | 25 | $71

Southampton | 61 Hill St. (bet. 1st Neck & Windmill Lns.) | 631-283-9323 | www.plazacafe.us

"It's not just a celebrity hangout" exclaim enthusiasts who thrill to the "outstanding", "imaginative" menu showcasing "wonderful seafood" at chef-owner Douglas Gulija's "sophisticated" Southampton "treat"; the staff is "attentive and knowledgeable" and the atmosphere "spacious" and "subdued", so even though it's "quite expensive", nobody is complaining.

	FOOD	DECOR	SERVICE	COST

Rialto ⓜ *Italian* | 26 | 20 | 25 | $57

Carle Place | 588 Westbury Ave. (bet. Glen Cove Rd. & Post Ave.) | 516-997-5283 | www.rialtorestaurantli.com

An "absolutely fabulous" meal awaits at this "pricey" Carle Place Italian where the "whole fish is prepared to perfection" and the "gnocchi pesto is out of this world"; "gracious" servers treat the "well-heeled patrons" like "kings", so it's only the "stodgy" setting that needs help.

1770 House Restaurant & Inn *Continental* | 25 | 25 | 24 | $65

East Hampton | 1770 House | 143 Main St. (Dayton Ln.) | 631-324-1770 | www.1770house.com

"Dark and romantic" with "fireplaces warming the rooms", this "beautifully appointed" Continental in a "historic" East Hampton inn provides a "sanctuary" for feasting on "fine cooking" served by a "polished" staff; many "make it a point to visit the old speakeasy bar downstairs", boasting a more "relaxed", "convivial" atmosphere and "delicious" pub menu option, while others savor the "savings" of the early prix fixe dinner in the "garden on a summer evening."

Siam Lotus Thai ⓜ *Thai* | 26 | 15 | 24 | $33

Bay Shore | 1664 Union Blvd. (bet. 4th & Park Aves.) | 631-968-8196 | www.siamlotus.info

"Artfully presented", "outstanding" Thai specialties are spiced to "delight any palate" (though "even adventure-seekers need to think twice before asking for native Thai heat") at this "brilliant" Bay Shore "gem" offering lots of daily specials; while there's "not much ambiance", most visitors assure that it's "more than made up for" by the "caring family owners" who make an effort to keep "everyone happy."

Starr Boggs *American/Seafood* | 25 | 22 | 22 | $68

Westhampton Beach | 6 Parlato Dr. (Library Ave.) | 631-288-3500 | www.starrboggsrestaurant.com

"Who cares about traffic on the LIE when you know dinner awaits?" at this Westhampton Beach "blast" ask Starr-struck fans of the chef's "uniquely satisfying" seafood and New American fare served amid "lovely", "clubby" surroundings; while the check can be sizable, "top-notch" service and perks like the "don't-miss" Monday lobster bake in the summer keep it "jumping"; P.S. closed January to mid-April.

Stone Creek Inn *French/Mediterranean* | 26 | 24 | 24 | $65

East Quogue | 405 Montauk Hwy. (bet. Carter Ln. & Wedgewood Rd.) | 631-653-6770 | www.stonecreekinn.com

"A serious restaurant where you can enjoy yourself", this French-Med in East Quogue "excites the palate" with "expertly prepared" seasonal fare served amid "simple yet elegant" surroundings by a "professional, accommodating" staff; connoisseurs conclude it's the "complete package", though the high cost keeps it a "special-occasion" place for some.

Tellers American Chophouse *Steak* | 26 | 26 | 24 | $66

Islip | 605 Main St. (bet. Locust & Nassau Aves.) | 631-277-7070 | www.tellerschophouse.com

"Who needs bulls and bears when you have steers like this?" ask sanguine steak lovers smitten by the "first-class" filets and rib-eyes "like butter" (not to mention "amazing" seafood) "served with style" in this "soaring" space, a former Islip bank building that "makes you feel like a VIP"; the "inviting" bar, walk-in "wine cellar vault" and a staff "at your beck and call" add to the "luxurious" meal, so most don't mind shelling out the "big bucks."

Toku *Asian*   24 | 27 | 22 | $63

Manhasset | The Americana | 2014C Northern Blvd. (Searingtown Rd.) | 516-627-8658 | www.tokumodernasian.com

"God arrived, and he made Toku" aver hip habitués of this "trendy", "urbane" addition to the Miracle Mile in Manhasset's The Americana, whose "stunning", temple-influenced surroundings create a "sparkling" backdrop for "wonderful" sushi and "decadent", "not-your-usual" Asian fusion plates; a "courteous" staff navigates the "chichi" scene of "beautiful, well-dressed" people, so "bring your Benjamins" to fit right in.

Vine Street Café *American*   27 | 20 | 23 | $63

Shelter Island | 41 S. Ferry Rd. (Cartwright Rd.) | 631-749-3210 | www.vinestreetcafe.com

Wayfarers wax ecstatic about the "novel", "exquisite" American dishes at this "expensive" "Manhattan-quality" "destination" that "makes Shelter Island a happening place"; while the "Jaguars lined up outside" can be "a little daunting", the "bustling", "bistro-type" space (renovated post-Survey) with a "lovely porch" is "unpretentious" and tended in "relaxed" style, rewarding a "trip on the ferry"; P.S. closed Tuesday–Wednesday in the winter.

Vintage Prime Steakhouse *Steak*   26 | 22 | 24 | $65

St. James | 433 N. Country Rd. (Clinton Ave.) | 631-862-6440

A "rare find" in St. James, this "meat-eaters' heaven" provides "mouth-watering mains" and sides in an atmosphere suited to an "intimate dinner or a group of eight"; "professional" service enhances the meal, so while "the more Western decor may throw you off a little" and prices are "steep", most affirm it's "well worth it."

Los Angeles

TOP FOOD RANKING

	Restaurant	Cuisine
29]	Sushi Zo	Japanese
28]	Matsuhisa	Japanese
	Mélisse	American/French
	Brandywine	Continental
	Shiro	French/Japanese
	Providence	American/Seafood
	Angelini Osteria	Italian
	Sushi Nozawa	Japanese
27]	Asanebo	Japanese
	Wa	Japanese
	Saam/The Bazaar	Eclectic
	Hatfield's	American
	Leila's	Californian
	Babita	Mexican
	Sushi Sasabune	Japanese
	Saddle Peak	American
	Lucques	Californian/Mediterranean
	Water Grill	Seafood
	Mori Sushi	Japanese
	Spago	Californian

OTHER NOTEWORTHY PLACES

Restaurant	Cuisine
A.O.C.	Californian/French
Bazaar/José Andrés	Spanish
Bouchon	French
BP Oysterette	Seafood
Café Bizou	Californian/French
Chego!	Korean/Mexican
Chinois on Main	Asian/French
Delphine	French/Mediterranean
Din Tai Fung	Chinese
Gorbals	Eclectic
In-N-Out	Burgers
Lazy Ox	Eclectic
Mastro's	Steak
Noir	Eclectic
Osteria Mozza	Italian
Pizzeria Mozza	Pizza
Red O	Mexican
Tar Pit	Eclectic
Waterloo & City	British
WP24	Chinese

Angelini Osteria ▣ *Italian*

28 | 18 | 24 | $53

Beverly Boulevard | 7313 Beverly Blvd. (bet. N. Fuller Ave. & N. Poinsettia Pl.) | 323-297-0070 | www.angeliniosteria.com

"Dazzling" dishes from chef-owner Gino Angelini – such as "salt-crusted branzino" "to die for" and lasagna that's a "Proustian experience" – are accompanied by "exquisite wines" at this "tiny" Beverly Boulevard Italian; surveyors say "solicitous service" and a "warm, inviting" vibe help to ensure such an "overall excellent dining experience" that no one much "cares" about the "sardine" seating or the fact that it can be a bit "pricey."

A.O.C. *Californian/French*

27 | 23 | 24 | $54

Third Street | 8022 W. Third St. (bet. Crescent Heights Blvd. & Fairfax Ave.) | 323-653-6359 | www.aocwinebar.com

"A rare treat for the senses", this food-lovers' "mainstay" on Third Street from Suzanne Goin (Lucques) offers a "remarkable roster of wines by the glass" coupled with "brilliant", "farm-driven" Cal-French small plates, including "tremendous" charcuterie and cheese; "professional, savvy" servers add to the overall "delight", so even if tables in the "elegant, simple" space are a bit "close" and it's all too "easy to rack up a substantial bill", "there's no other place quite like it in LA"; P.S. if you're feeling "lucky", try for a spot at the wine bar – no reservations required.

Asanebo ▣ *Japanese*

27 | 16 | 23 | $69

Studio City | 11941 Ventura Blvd. (bet. Carpenter & Radford Aves.) | 818-760-3348

It might be a "hole-in-the-wall" on Studio City's "Sushi Row", but "genius" chef-owner Tetsuya Nakao's "top-notch" Japanese presents sushi and sashimi that's "sublime", along with "perfectly flavored cooked fish dishes", for an omakase experience that is "one incredible course after another"; though it could almost be "less expensive to actually fly to Japan", fans say "it never fails to amaze" and is "worth the cost."

Babita Mexicuisine ▣ *Mexican*

27 | 16 | 24 | $41

San Gabriel | 1823 S. San Gabriel Blvd. (Norwood Pl.) | 626-288-7265

Don't let the "dive" exterior "fool you", this San Gabriel Mexican is "adored" for its "exceptional" "haute cuisine" as well as its "gracious" chef-owner Roberto Berrelleza, who ensures a "friendly, warm" experience; it's "small" and "not cheap", but for fans "there's nothing comparable" and it's "well worth the trip getting here."

Bazaar by José Andrés, The *Spanish*

26 | 27 | 24 | $77

Beverly Hills | SLS at Beverly Hills | 465 S. La Cienega Blvd. (Clifton Way) | 310-247-0400 | www.thebazaar.com

Prepare to be "blown away" by chef José Andrés' "crazy-brilliant molecular gastronomy" – "cotton candy foie gras", "liquid olives" – that's "balanced" by more traditional yet no less "magical" tapas at this Beverly Hills Spaniard in the SLS Hotel; Philippe Starck's "deliciously outrageous" "high-concept decor" provides a variety of backdrops including a *blanco* room ("quiet"), *rojo* room ("noisier"), pink patisserie and a "chic" bar; surveyors are split on service ("attentive" vs. "casual"), but the majority agrees "it's worth every penny" for such a "memorable", "over-the-top" experience; afterwards, pick up a "unique souvenir" from the Moss retail store also on-site.

	FOOD	DECOR	SERVICE	COST

Bouchon *French*

| 24 | 26 | 25 | $68 |

Beverly Hills | 235 N. Cañon Dr., 2nd fl. (bet. Dayton Way & Wilshire Blvd.) | 310-271-9910 | www.bouchonbistro.com

"Commando chef" "Thomas Keller has done it again" with this "long-awaited" Beverly Hills bistro ("sister" to the Yountville original) that "lives up to its reputation" with "perfectly prepared", "quintessential" French classics like "exquisite roast chicken", "impressive *fruits de mer*" and "divine desserts"; service is "meticulous" and "well trained", though the "spacious, airy" decor gets mixed reviews ("transporting" and "beautiful" vs. "faux Paris" à la "Vegas"), and naturally such a "glam scene" does not come "cheap", but most say "it's worth every cent."

BP Oysterette *Seafood*

| 22 | 17 | 21 | $36 |

Santa Monica | 1355 Ocean Ave. (Santa Monica Blvd.) | 310-576-3474 | www.blueplatesantamonica.com

Santa Monicans take a "trip to New England" at this "upscale clam shack" (whose initials stand for Blue Plate) offering an "array" of oysters and other seafood so "fresh" "you could have picked it out of the ocean yourself"; "helpful" servers and a "cozy" space featuring a "great raw bar" give it a "been-here-forever feel", all leading most to agree it's "worth shelling out for."

Brandywine ☒ *Continental*

| 28 | 20 | 27 | $64 |

Woodland Hills | 22757 Ventura Blvd. (Fallbrook Ave.) | 818-225-9114

"Elegant" Continental cuisine "priced for perfection" is the forte of this "romantic" Woodland Hills "gem" overseen by a "husband-and-wife team" who "bend over backwards" to please patrons; though the "cozy" French country-inn decor strikes some as too "'70s"-style, loyalists still consider it "one of the best places in the Valley for that special date", adding "they just don't make 'em like this anymore."

Café Bizou *Californian/French*

| 23 | 19 | 22 | $32 |

Pasadena | 91 N. Raymond Ave. (Holly St.) | 626-792-9923
Sherman Oaks | 14016 Ventura Blvd. (bet. Costello & Murietta Aves.) | 818-788-3536

Bizou Grill ☒ *Californian/French*

Santa Monica | Water Gdn. | 2450 Colorado Ave. (26th St.) | 310-453-8500 www.cafebizou.com

"High-quality" "gourmet food at a reasonable price" is the raison d'être of these "charming", wildly popular Cal-French bistros dishing up "solid" pastas and other "comfort" classics that "never fail to satisfy"; with $2 corkage and "gracious service", it's a "terrific" pick for "date night", but downsides include a "noisy" setting with tables "so close" you can practically "kiss" your neighbors.

Chego! ☒Ⓜ *Korean/Mexican*

| - | - | - | I |

Palms | 3300 Overland Ave. (Rose Ave.) | 310-287-0331 | www.eatchego.com

This Palms mini-mall spot provides a permanent home for a popular food-truck chef's Korean-Mexican rice bowls, plus other affordable items including fried meatballs, charred asparagus with blueberry jalapeño salsa and a glazed pork belly bowl (but no tacos); the wildly busy, counter-serve setting includes wood tables with red chairs and walls decorated with giant letters that spell out the name.

	FOOD	DECOR	SERVICE	COST

Chinois on Main *Asian/French*　26 | 20 | 23 | $63

Santa Monica | 2709 Main St. (Hill St.) | 310-392-9025 |
www.wolfgangpuck.com

"Phenomenal" Asian-French flavors ferried by "fabulous" servers are
the hallmark of this "Puck empire" spot in Santa Monica that's "still
going strong" after more than 25 years; you may "need earplugs" and
a shoehorn to handle its "jammed", "dated" (think *Miami Vice*) dining room, but nonetheless it remains a "memorable experience" – "if
you've got the dough."

Delphine *French/Mediterranean*　20 | 23 | 22 | $43

Hollywood | W Hollywood Hotel | 6250 Hollywood Blvd. (Vine St.) |
323-798-1355 | www.restaurantdelphine.com

A "young" crowd "dressed in black" flocks to this upscale "hot spot" in
the W Hollywood Hotel where a "well-trained staff" delivers "seriously
good" French-Mediterranean dishes in a "beautiful interior" conjuring
the South of France; the location is "convenient for the Pantages", and
there's also a "comfortable adjacent lounge" for a "post-dinner drink."

Din Tai Fung *Chinese*　25 | 15 | 16 | $21

Arcadia | 1088 S. Baldwin Ave. (Arcadia Ave.) | 626-446-8588
Arcadia | 1108 S. Baldwin Ave. (bet. Arcadia Ave. & Duarte Rd.) |
626-574-7068
www.dintaifungusa.com

Despite "brusque" (if "efficient") service, "basic decor" and "pricey
for the area" tabs, "massive crowds" gather every weekend to experience the "holy grail" of "juicy pork dumplings" at these neighboring
Arcadia links in a Taipei-based chain; though there are other "fresh"
Chinese dishes on the menu, their trademark "mouthwatering" "morsels from heaven" are the real stars here.

Gorbals, The ●🅩 *Eclectic*　21 | 13 | 19 | $35

Downtown | Alexandria Hotel | 501 S. Spring St. (5th St.) | 213-488-3408 |
www.thegorbalsla.com

"Interesting" is how surveyors describe *Top Chef* Ilan Hall's "quirky",
"inventive" Eclectic in Downtown's renovated "historic Alexandria
Hotel", where "gourmet" "Scottish-Jewish fusion" is the "oddly winning combination" behind seasonal "small bites" such as the "highly
touted bacon-wrapped matzo balls"; though some find the relatively
"easy-on-the-wallet" menu and service "uneven", the "friendly hipster
crowd" filling the communal tables amid "bare-bones industrial-type
decor" agrees it's "an experience."

Hatfield's *American*　27 | 24 | 26 | $66

Melrose | 6703 Melrose Ave. (Citrus Ave.) | 323-935-2977 |
www.hatfieldsrestaurant.com

"Better than ever" swoon supporters of this "jewel in the crown" of LA
eateries, where husband-and-wife team Quinn and Karen Hatfield are
"outdoing themselves" with "meticulous", "pricey" American cuisine
(including a "fabulous" chef's tasting menu) in a new, "expansive" and
"prettier" setting on Melrose; factor in "impeccable" service and most
"can't wait to go back."

In-N-Out Burger ● *Burgers*　24 | 11 | 20 | $9

Hollywood | 7009 Sunset Blvd. (Orange Dr.)

(continued)

In-N-Out Burger

Culver City | 13425 Washington Blvd. (bet. Glencoe & Walnut Aves.)
West LA | 9245 W. Venice Blvd. (S. Canfield Ave.)
Westwood | 922 Gayley Ave. (Levering Ave.)
Westchester | 9149 S. Sepulveda Blvd. (bet. 92nd St. & Westchester Pkwy.)
North Hollywood | 5864 Lankershim Blvd. (bet. Califa & Emelita Sts.)
Sherman Oaks | 4444 Van Nuys Blvd. (Moorpark St.)
Studio City | 3640 Cahuenga Blvd. (Fredonia Dr.)
Van Nuys | 7930 Van Nuys Blvd. (bet. Blythe & Michaels Sts.)
Woodland Hills | 19920 Ventura Blvd. (bet. Oakdale & Penfield Aves.)
800-786-1000 | www.in-n-out.com
Additional locations throughout the Los Angeles area

This "legendary" West Coast bang-for-the-buck hamburger chain inspires a widespread "cult following", with converts to the "church of In-N-Out" swearing that the "cooked-to-order" "never-frozen" patties, "freshly cut french fries" ("order them crispy") and "off-menu" "customizing" options are so "phenomenal" they must have been "created on the eighth day"; yes, they're always "mobbed" and drive-thru "lines are interminable", but "it's the food of the gods."

Lazy Ox Canteen ● *Eclectic* | 24 | 18 | 22 | $45 |

Little Tokyo | 241 S. San Pedro St. (bet. 2nd & 3rd Sts.) | 213-626-5299 | www.lazyoxcanteen.com

Culinary "wizard" Josef Centeno "effortlessly incorporates" international influences into his "wildly innovative" Eclectic menu at this Little Tokyo canteen, "an instant favorite" for its "impressive" meat-centric small plates, "gracious staff" and "reasonable prices"; the "cool but casual setting" with bare bulbs swinging from the ceiling stays "welcoming" into the late hours (doors usually close at midnight).

Leila's Ⓜ *Californian* | 27 | 20 | 24 | $47 |

Oak Park | Oak Park Plaza | 706 Lindero Canyon Rd. (Kanan Rd.) | 818-707-6939 | www.leilasrestaurant.com

"Gourmet fare in a suburban strip mall" attracts "well-deserved" "attention" to this Oak Park Californian, hailed as the "crown jewel of the Conejo Valley" for its "fabulous" menu (focused on "imaginative" small plates) and "incredibly diverse" wine list, all "superbly served" at relatively "reasonable prices"; "tucked" into a "cute" space, it's a "destination" that "can compete with the best."

Lucques *Californian/Mediterranean* | 27 | 24 | 25 | $62 |

West Hollywood | 8474 Melrose Ave. (La Cienega Blvd.) | 323-655-6277 | www.lucques.com

"Sensational" chef Suzanne Goin is "still the queen of the hill" at this WeHo Cal-Med "standard-bearer", a "charming" carriage house where a "sublime", oft-"changing menu" featuring "the freshest ingredients" is paired with a "thoughtful" wine list curated by co-owner Caroline Styne; "impeccable" service and a "lovely courtyard" add to an "essential" experience, and the prix fixe Sunday suppers are an "amazing" "bargain."

Mastro's Steakhouse *Steak* | 26 | 23 | 25 | $73 |

Beverly Hills | 246 N. Cañon Dr. (bet. Clifton & Dayton Ways) | 310-888-8782

(continued)

(continued)

Mastro's Steakhouse

Thousand Oaks | 2087 E. Thousand Oaks Blvd. (bet. Conejo School Rd. & Los Feliz Dr.) | 805-418-1811
www.mastrosrestaurants.com

"Still the king" of carnivorous consumption, this "über-steakhouse" chain hosts "wheeler dealer" types "paying a fortune" for "generous" cuts of "mouthwatering" "prime meat", "extravagant" seafood towers and "sinful" sides, all matched with "world-class" service; the Beverly Hills branch comprises a "vibrant", "Vegas"-like piano bar and a toned-down dining room while Thousand Oaks flaunts a "classic" "dark" look.

Matsuhisa *Japanese*

28 | 17 | 24 | $83

Beverly Hills | 129 N. La Cienega Blvd. (bet. Clifton Way & Wilshire Blvd.) | 310-659-9639 | www.nobumatsuhisa.com

"Oh my!" cry "enchanted" "sushi lovers" as "consummate" chef Nobu Matsuhisa continues to "wow", crafting "spectacular" Japanese fare "with Peruvian flair" at this much-"imitated" Beverly Hills fusion "temple"; don't be fooled by the "non-stuffy" service and "dated" decor, you'll still need to "drop off your wallet at the door", especially for "exquisite" omakases that connoisseurs consider "the only way to go."

Mélisse ☒Ⓜ *American/French*

28 | 26 | 27 | $105

Santa Monica | 1104 Wilshire Blvd. (11th St.) | 310-395-0881 | www.melisse.com

"Josiah Citrin is still at the top of his game" gush fans of his Santa Monica fine-dining room that continues to "hit on all cylinders" with "flawlessly composed" French–New American cuisine backed by an "incredible" 800-bottle wine list; it follows through with "almost worshipful service" in a "beautiful", "formal" platinum room, adding up to an experience so "exquisite", even "the bill will take your breath away."

Mori Sushi ☒ *Japanese*

27 | 17 | 22 | $76

West LA | 11500 W. Pico Blvd. (Gateway Blvd.) | 310-479-3939 | www.morisushi.org

"Sublime" sums up this "exquisite, little" Japanese in West LA where "master" chef Morihiro Onodera crafts "divine" slabs of fish and serves them up with "real wasabi" and homegrown rice on his "original" handmade ceramics; acolytes gladly "pay a lot" for the experience, even if it's all a little too "precious" for some.

Noir Food & Wine *Eclectic*

25 | 20 | 25 | $46

Pasadena | 40 N. Mentor Ave. (Colorado Blvd.) | 626-795-7199 | www.noirfoodandwine.com

The "innovative" roster of small plates by chef Claud Beltran is bested only by the "terrific wine selection" at this Pasadena Eclectic, also "impressing" with "on-the-ball" service and an "intimate", low-lit setting; in spite of "minuscule" portions and not-so-minuscule prices, the majority of locals labels it a "great addition" to the area.

Osteria Mozza *Italian*

27 | 23 | 24 | $65

Hollywood | 6602 Melrose Ave. (Highland Ave.) | 323-297-0100 | www.mozza-la.com

"Heaven" for "foodies", this big-ticket Batali-Silverton collaboration in Hollywood is the site of "truly memorable" "Roman feasts" starring "sublime" secondi, "sensuous cheeses" from the in-house mozzarella bar and a "gorgeous" egg-filled raviolo that could make you "tear up" just thinking about it; cap it off with a "killer" vino list and a "dark", "celeb"-heavy room "abuzz" with "New York energy" and most are willing to overlook the "deadly sound level", "difficult-to-get reservations" and staff that could sometimes "use a little less 'tude."

Pizzeria Mozza ◐ *Pizza*   27 | 19 | 21 | $38

Hollywood | 641 N. Highland Ave. (Melrose Ave.) | 323-297-0101 | www.mozza-la.com

Still one of "the hottest places in town", this "beloved" Hollywood pizzeria from Mario Batali and Nancy Silverton – LA's Most Popular restaurant – turns a mere slice into a true "gastronomic experience" with "delectable" pies supported by "deliciously charred" crusts cooked to a "bubbly, chewy perfection"; no surprise, "getting in is a challenge", service is "iffy" and the "jammed", "noisy" quarters have the feel of "a high-end bus station", but even so, "no one should miss it."

Providence *American/Seafood*   28 | 25 | 27 | $98

Hollywood | 5955 Melrose Ave. (Cole Ave.) | 323-460-4170 | www.providencela.com

"Simply sublime" sigh fans of this Hollywood New American "paragon of fine dining" showcasing "genius" chef/co-owner Michael Cimarusti's "matchless" hand with seafood, best experienced via the "utterly blissful" tasting menu featuring 16 "meticulously considered" courses; whether the ambiance is "civilized" or just "somber" is up for debate, but all agree the service is "pitch-perfect" and the overall experience "expensive", but "worth every penny."

Red O *Mexican*   - | - | - | M

Melrose | 8155 Melrose Ave. (Kilkea Dr.) | 323-655-5009 | www.redorestaurant.com

Rick Bayless (Chicago's Frontera Grill, Topolobampo, Xoco) created the menu at this Melrose Nouvelle Mexican offering a seasonally based selection of 'savory snacks' in an ultrastylish space – including a tequila lounge entered through a glass tunnel – designed by the ubiquitous Dodd Mitchell; in a city where south-of-the-border fare is the lingua franca, it should still manage to make its mark.

Saam at The Bazaar by   27 | 26 | 25 | $156
José Andrés ⚏Ⓜ *Eclectic*

Beverly Hills | SLS at Beverly Hills | 465 S. La Cienega Blvd. (Clifton Way) | 310-247-0400 | www.thebazaar.com

Devotees "delight in the brilliance of José Andrés" at this "stunning" chef's table restaurant at The Bazaar in Beverly Hills delivering 22 "bite-sized" Eclectic courses of pure "deliciousness" showcasing "fanciful" molecular techniques; add in "expert" service and a "secluded" setting in the "trippy" Philippe Starck–designed space, and it all adds up to an experience that's "expensive", but truly "unique."

Saddle Peak Lodge Ⓜ *American*   27 | 27 | 26 | $71

Calabasas | 419 Cold Canyon Rd. (Piuma Rd.) | 818-222-3888 | www.saddlepeaklodge.com

"Spectacular in every way" swoon admirers of this "rustic log cabin" "set on a wooded hillside" between Malibu and Calabasas where the "incredibly romantic" surroundings and "delicious" "exotic game dishes" make it the "ultimate" place to "pop the "question" – "unless she's a vegetarian"; the "staff goes above and beyond, and so do the prices", although the "excellent" brunch is much more reasonable.

Shiro ⓂFrench/Japanese

| 28 | 21 | 26 | $53 |

South Pasadena | 1505 Mission St. (bet. Fair Oaks & Mound Aves.) | 626-799-4774 | www.restaurantshiro.com

Putting a "unique spin" on Asian cooking is this South Pasadena "favorite", a "go-to" for a "truly amazing" signature deep-fried catfish among other "superb" French-Japanese items backed by an "extensive" wine list; perhaps the "grand" decor feels "straight out of 1992", but service is "impeccable" and longtime fans profess they've "never had a bad meal here"; P.S. closed Mondays and Tuesdays.

Spago Californian

| 27 | 25 | 26 | $77 |

Beverly Hills | 176 N. Cañon Dr. (Wilshire Blvd.) | 310-385-0880 | www.wolfgangpuck.com

"The place where Wolfgang Puck started it all", this Beverly Hills "classic" "sets the bar high" with his brand of "superb" "no-holds-barred" Californian cuisine that still "exceeds expectations" "after all these years"; "impeccable" service (including "frequent" tableside visits from Puck himself), a "splashy" room "full of dealmakers" and a garden that's "pure bliss" make it "worth every penny", even if you have to drain "your kid's college fund" to afford it.

Sushi Nozawa 🖂 Japanese

| 28 | 9 | 15 | $62 |

Studio City | 11288 Ventura Blvd. (bet. Arch & Tropical Drs.) | 818-508-7017 | www.sushinozawa.com

"Whatever you do, don't ask for soy sauce" at this "expensive", "traditional" Studio City Japanese helmed by famously "grouchy" "master" chef Kazunori Nozawa that "rewards" purists with "exceptional", "top-flight" fish in "clean, straightforward" preparations; acolytes insist it's "worth enduring" the "fluorescent-lit" strip-mall digs and "rushed" pace because the omakase "rocks"; P.S. closed Saturdays and Sundays.

Sushi Sasabune 🖂 Japanese

| 27 | 13 | 22 | $66 |

West LA | 12400 Wilshire Blvd. (Centinela Ave.) | 310-268-8380

Sushi-Don Sasabune Express Japanese

Pacific Palisades | 970 Monument St. (bet. Bashford St. & Sunset Blvd.) | 310-454-6710 | www.sushidonppl.com

"Sit at the bar", "splurge" on the omakase and let the chef "feed you like Flipper" instruct fans of this "traditional" West LA Japanese known for its ultra-"fresh", "melt-in-your-mouth" cuts; a "sterile", "cafeteria-like" setting is part of the package, but that's no matter since "you'll leave happy"; P.S. there's an express outlet in Pacific Palisades with takeout and a handful of tables.

Sushi Zo 🖂 Japanese

| 29 | 13 | 21 | $104 |

West LA | 9824 National Blvd. (bet. Castle Heights Ave. & Shelby Dr.) | 310-842-3977

"Enter with a willing palate and an empty stomach" at this "omakase-only" West LA Japanese where "every bite is exquisite" thanks to "stern" chef-owner Keizo Seki's "brilliant" yet "subtle" cuisine, ranked No. 1 for Food in Los Angeles; "shockingly expensive" prices and an "austere" strip-mall setting near the freeway hardly deter those seeking sushi that's "as good as it gets in LA."

Tar Pit, The ● *Eclectic*

| 20 | 27 | 23 | $52 |

La Brea | 609 N. La Brea Ave. (Melrose Ave.) | 323-965-1300

"One tar pit worth getting stuck in", this La Brea newcomer from chef/co-owner Mark Peel channels a "glamorous" art deco "supper club" where "dreamy" decor sets the stage for "inventive" mixology and an "excellent" Eclectic menu featuring faves from "years gone by" like steak Diane and chicken à la king; with a "solicitous staff" and a "noisy", "tons-of-fun" "bar scene", it's "deservedly" "a hit."

Wa Ⓜ *Japanese*

| 27 | 12 | 22 | $52 |

West Hollywood | La Cienega Plaza | 1106 N. La Cienega Blvd. (Holloway Dr.) | 310-854-7285

There's "no glitz, no glam" just "high-quality" sushi that's "as authentic as it gets" at this West Hollywood "gem", "hidden" away on the second floor of a strip mall; acolytes insist it's like "Nobu" "without the crowds or attitude", although the "high" prices can sometimes feel at odds with the "nonexistent" atmosphere.

Water Grill *Seafood*

| 27 | 25 | 26 | $68 |

Downtown | 544 S. Grand Ave. (bet. 5th & 6th Sts.) | 213-891-0900 | www.watergrill.com

"Still top-notch after all these years" sigh fans of this 20-year-old Downtown respite that remains "in a class of its own" with chef David LeFevre's "exceptional", "artfully prepared" seafood backed by a "wonderful selection of fine wines"; impeccable" service and a "quiet", "clubby" setting make it perfect for a "power lunch" or "pre-theater" dinner, and "worth every penny" of the whale of a tab.

Waterloo & City *British*

| - | - | - | M |

Culver City | 12517 W. Washington Blvd. (Venice Blvd.) | 310-391-4222 | www.waterlooandcity.com

This Culver City gastropub gets its name from the London Underground stop near the childhood home of chef-owner Brendan Collins (ex Mélisse), and his midpriced Modern British menu includes the likes of Manchester quail with chopped liver on toast and pig's trotter with sweetbreads and salsa; the whimsical space features church pews painted pink and orange in the lounge, overstuffed suede banquettes, antique mirrors, a communal table and a patio.

WP24 *Chinese*

| - | - | - | E |

Downtown | Ritz-Carlton | 900 W. Olympic Blvd., 24th fl. (Figueroa St.) | 213-743-8824 | www.wolfgangpuck.com

Situated on the 24th floor of Downtown's newly opened Ritz-Carlton, Wolfgang Puck's latest harks back to early Puckian concepts like Chinois on Main, though in this case, the dim sum is offset by sushi and other Asian fare, plus dishes finished tableside; a view of Nokia Theatre and the Staples Center dominates the setting, while its shiny, floor-to-ceiling metal tubes are like a bit of Las Vegas come to LA.

Miami

TOP FOOD RANKING

	Restaurant	Cuisine
28	Palme d'Or	French
27	Romeo's Cafe	Italian
	Pascal's	French
	Michy's	American/French
	Nobu Miami Beach	Japanese
	Hy-Vong	Vietnamese
	OLA*	Pan-Latin
	Matsuri	Japanese
	Joe's Stone Crab	Seafood
	Azul	Mediterranean
26	Il Gabbiano	Italian
	Francesco	Peruvian
	Osteria del Teatro	Italian
	Prime One Twelve	Seafood/Steak
	Michael's	American
	Spiga	Italian
	Red Light	American
	Ortanique	Caribbean/New World
	Graziano's	Argentinean/Steak
	Palm	Steak

OTHER NOTEWORTHY PLACES

Area 31	Seafood
Barton G.	American
BLT	Steak
Blue Door	Brazilian/French
Bourbon Steak	Steak
Canyon Ranch	Health Food
Eos	Mediterranean
Fratelli Lyon	Italian
Gotham Steak	Steak
Hakkasan	Chinese
Hiro's Yakko San	Japanese
Meat Market	Steak
Naoe	Japanese
Por Fin	Mediterranean/Spanish
Sardinia	Italian
Scarpetta	Italian
Sra. Martinez	Spanish
Sugarcane	Eclectic
Timo	Italian/Mediterranean
Versailles	Cuban

---

* Indicates a tie with restaurant above

	FOOD	DECOR	SERVICE	COST

Area 31 *Seafood*
22 | 24 | 20 | $55

Downtown | Epic Hotel | 270 Biscayne Boulevard Way (Brickell Ave.) | 305-424-5234 | www.area31restaurant.com

Boasting "power views" that make you "feel like you're in a tropical Times Square", this "upscale" Downtown seafooder atop the Epic Hotel is "swank, sexy and scrumptious"; true, a few find the service a bit "lacking", but chef John Critchley's "interesting" cuisine and the "sophisticated atmosphere" hook most.

Azul 🖫 *Mediterranean*
27 | 26 | 25 | $74

Brickell Area | Mandarin Oriental Hotel | 500 Brickell Key Dr. (SE 8th St.) | 305-913-8358 | www.mandarinoriental.com

It "all comes together" at this "stunningly decorated" "gem" in the Mandarin Oriental – a "perfect combination" of "impeccable service", "excellent wines" and "stupendous" Med cuisine that "blends Asian flavors with European"; "one of the best views in Miami" adds to an atmosphere that's "sooo romantic", "even for those of us who've been married 50 years", and while it may be "made for those on an endless expense account", few deny that it's "worth every penny."

Barton G. The Restaurant *American*
23 | 26 | 23 | $71

South Beach | 1427 West Ave. (14th Ct.) | Miami Beach | 305-672-8881 | www.bartong.com

"Gaudí meets the Ringling Brothers" at this "unique" SoBe New American in a "festive tropical setting" where "charming" waiters lug "oversized portions" of "elaborately presented" food "so far over the top you need a ladder to eat"; cynics shrug it's "all flash, no substance" and "more show than restaurant", but vets insist that "seeing is believing" – just "close your eyes when paying the bill."

BLT Steak *Steak*
24 | 23 | 23 | $70

South Beach | The Betsy Hotel | 1440 Ocean Dr. (bet 14th & 15th Sts.) | Miami Beach | 305-673-0044 | www.bltsteak.com

Chef-restaurateur Laurent Tourondel's "chic" chophouse in SoBe's Betsy Hotel wins praise for its "perfectly cooked" steaks, "amazing sauces and phenomenal sides", not to mention "fabulous" signature popovers; the "no-attitude" service enhances a "civilized" ambiance that's "at once casual and refined", though a few find the lobby setting a little "weird", and wallet-watchers balk at the "big bill."

Blue Door at Delano ➋ *Brazilian/French*
23 | 27 | 23 | $73

South Beach | Delano Hotel | 1685 Collins Ave. (17th St.) | Miami Beach | 305-674-6400 | www.chinagrillmgt.com

"Cool and sleek like the tan young things at the pool", this Delano Hotel "treasure" remains the "scene of all scenes", where an "attentive" staff makes "everyone feel like one of the beautiful people" as they down consulting chef Claude Troisgros' "delish" New French–Brazilian fare and "rub shoulders with SoBe celebs"; if some say it's "pretentious and pricey", more insist it's still the "place to be" "after all these years."

Bourbon Steak 🖫 *Steak*
25 | 27 | 24 | $84

Aventura | Fairmont Turnberry Isle Resort & Club | 19999 W. Country Club Dr. (Aventura Blvd./NE 199th St.) | 786-279-6600 | www.michaelmina.net

Celebrity chef-restaurateur Michael Mina "has done it again" crow carnivores about this "swank" Aventura chophouse, where the "killer" cuts, "superb" wine list and "exceptional" "city-chic" decor by Tony Chi combine to "give new meaning to the American steakhouse"; service is "marvelous" too, but brace yourself for a "breathtaking" experience, "especially when you get the bill."

Canyon Ranch Grill Health Food
23 | 23 | 22 | $53

Miami Beach | Canyon Ranch Living | 6801 Collins Ave. (bet. 67th & 69th Sts.) | 305-514-7474 | www.canyonranch.com

Partisans proclaim that the "yummy" "organic" fare at this "upscale but unstuffy" health-fooder in the oceanfront Canyon Ranch Miami Beach "tastes of real ingredients" and will "almost make you forget it's good for you" (and it's relatively "affordable" at that); still, a few critics sniff that the grub and service "don't live up to the beautiful space", though the "nutritional information on the menu" is a "big plus."

Eos Mediterranean
- | - | - | E

Brickell Area | The Viceroy Hotel | 485 Brickell Ave., 15th fl. (SE 5th St.) | 305-503-4400 | www.viceroymiami.com

Famed New York duo chef Michael Psilakis and telegenic restaurateur Donatella Arpaia come south to create this sophisticated Mediterranean stunner in Brickell's Viceroy Hotel; dressed in Aegean opulence (lots of gray marble) and tropical elegance (splashes of flowery color), it boasts impressive 15th-floor views that help soften the not-exactly-cheap prices on its tapas-style menu.

Francesco ⊠ Peruvian
26 | 17 | 24 | $53

Coral Gables | 325 Alcazar Ave. (bet. SW 42nd Ave. & Salzedo St.) | 305-446-1600 | www.francescorestaurant.com

If you "crave" "quality seafood" and "ceviche that'll blow your socks (and everything else) off", surveyors swear "this place is for you" – a "small, crowded" Coral Gables "knockout" awash in "awesome" "Peruvian flavors"; the "decor is lacking", but "you'll forget about [that] once you start eating", and the "welcoming" staff and "solid" wine list don't hurt; all that, and a "bang for your buck" too.

Fratelli Lyon Italian
23 | 21 | 19 | $48

Design District | Driade | 4141 NE Second Ave. (bet. 41st & 42nd Sts.) | 305-572-2901 | www.fratellilyon.com

"You can taste Italy in every bite" of the "delicious" trattoria fare drawn from grass-fed meats and sustainable seafood at this "sophisticated" – and "high-priced" – Design District "breath of fresh air"; despite "inconsistent service" and a "love it or hate it" "über-modern" space in the Driade furniture showroom, the majority maintains it "never disappoints."

Gotham Steak Steak
22 | 24 | 20 | $79

Miami Beach | Fontainebleau Miami Beach | 4441 Collins Ave. (off Hwy. 195) | 305-674-4780 | www.fontainebleau.com

"Beautiful people and beautiful food" unite at this "sexy" spot from chef-owner Alfred Portale, who brings a Manhattan flair to the "extravagant" Fontainebleau Miami Beach; "melt-in-your-mouth steaks" and other chophouse standards vie for attention with a "gorgeous" space highlighted by a "showcase kitchen" and "dazzling" bi-level "wine reserve"; if "insane" tabs and service that can be "off" fire up some, more maintain it's "worth a special evening."

	FOOD	DECOR	SERVICE	COST

Graziano's Restaurant *Argentinean/Steak* | 26 | 21 | 23 | $47 |

Brickell Area | 177 SW Seventh St. (bet. 1st & 2nd Aves.) |
305-860-1426
Coral Gables | 394 Giralda Ave. (42nd Ave.) | 305-774-3599
Hialeah | 5993 W. 16th Ave. (60th St.) | 305-819-7461
Westchester | 9227 SW 40th St./Bird Rd. (92nd Ave.) | 305-225-0008
www.parrilla.com

"If you love a perfect steak" and "can't afford the flight to Argentina", consider this trio of "authentic" *parrillas* (grills) offering an "excellent" variety of the "juiciest meats" and a "fantastic selection" of "reasonably priced" wines "on display along the dining room walls"; "average Joes and culinary experts" alike appreciate the "sharp, informed" service and "relaxed atmosphere" – just arrive "hungry" and "don't tell your cardiologist where you're going"; P.S. a branch in Brickell opened post-Survey.

Hakkasan ● *Chinese* | 26 | 26 | 23 | $80 |

Miami Beach | Fontainebleau Miami Beach | 4441 Collins Ave. (41st St.) |
786-276-1388 | www.fontainebleau.com

"Just like the one in London, but with a much hotter crowd", this "contemporary" Cantonese by Britain's Alan Yau provides "top-of-the-charts" fare in a "beautifully designed" space in the Fontainebleau Miami Beach, distinguished by "private" niches with ornately carved screens; "no question, it's expensive", but a "well-trained" crew enhances the "unique, transporting" experience.

Hiro's Yakko San ● *Japanese* | 26 | 12 | 21 | $33 |

North Miami Beach | 17040-46 W. Dixie Hwy. (bet. 170th & 171st Sts.) |
305-947-0064 | www.yakko-san.com

"All the chefs go to eat" at this "late-night" "foodies' paradise" in North Miami Beach, where the "out-of-this-world" (yet "reasonably priced") Japanese small plates and "rare" sashimi selections reward an "open mind"; though there's "no real decor", it's staffed by "helpful" servers and "always jammin'" – so "be prepared to wait."

Hy-Vong Ⓜ *Vietnamese* | 27 | 8 | 15 | $28 |

Little Havana | 3458 SW Eighth St. (bet. 34th & 35th Aves.) |
305-446-3674 | www.hyvong.com

"Be prepared to wait . . . and wait" (alas, no reservations) at this "crowded" Little Havana "hole-in-the-wall" where the Vietnamese food "made with pure love" is "so good it takes your breath away"; "don't expect fast service or stellar decor", but if you "go with patience", "heaven on a dish rewards your efforts", and it's an "excellent value" at that.

Il Gabbiano ●Ⓢ *Italian* | 26 | 25 | 25 | $79 |

Downtown | One Miami Tower | 335 S. Biscayne Blvd. (SE 3rd St.) |
305-373-0063 | www.ilgabbianomia.com

A "slice of heaven" with "breathtaking" Biscayne Bay views, this "romantic" Downtowner from the owners of NYC's Il Mulino proffers "as good as it gets" Italian fare served in "giant portions" that "the smart will share"; waiters who "bend over backward" and a "superb" wine list help "make it the one place everyone's grateful to know about", and though budgeteers bemoan "outrageous" prices, most say "bring your appetite . . . and your wallet" and enjoy.

	FOOD	DECOR	SERVICE	COST

Joe's Stone Crab *Seafood*   27 | 20 | 24 | $65

South Beach | 11 Washington Ave. (bet. 1st St. & S. Pointe Dr.) |
Miami Beach | 305-673-0365 | www.joesstonecrab.com

"Everybody should experience" this SoBe "stone crab mecca" "at least
once" – and seemingly has, as it's voted Miami's Most Popular; the
"killer claws", "sinful Key lime pie" and "even the fried chicken" –
hauled through the "hectic" "cafeteria-type" space by "ruthlessly efficient" servers – "never disappoint", although the "top-dollar" tabs and
no-res policy ("prepare for the wait of your life") do; still, the consen-
sus is "go early, go late, but go", though "smart locals" get "takeout
and eat on the beach."

Matsuri Ⓜ *Japanese*   27 | 20 | 20 | $37

South Miami | 5759 Bird Rd. (bet. Red Rd. & SW 58th Ave.) |
305-663-1615

Yes, it's in a "nondescript strip mall", but this South Miami "institution" even has "sushi snobs" raving it's one of the "best Japanese" options in town; with a "sleek" makeover that's "improved the ambiance"
(if not the "spotty service") and "reasonably priced" fin fare so "fresh
it's still flapping", it's no wonder devotees demand you "put this one
on your A list."

Meat Market ❶ *Steak*   24 | 25 | 22 | $72

South Beach | 915 Lincoln Rd. (bet. Jefferson & Michigan Aves.) |
Miami Beach | 305-532-0088 | www.meatmarketmiami.com

"Sexy and chic", this "loungey" New American "meat heaven" catering to a "beautiful" South Beach clientele is "not your standard
steakhouse"; "excellent" beef (with "creative sauces"), "exquisite"
fish and an "incredible" wine selection served by a "delightful"
staff attract "big spenders" who keep the room "always busy" and
"noisy", so "get your lungs ready"; P.S. "Friday happy-hour specials
are an added bonus."

Michael's Genuine Food & Drink *American*   26 | 21 | 24 | $54

Design District | Atlas Plaza | 130 NE 40th St. (bet. NE 1st & 2nd Aves.) |
305-573-5550 | www.michaelsgenuine.com

"Everything rocks" at chef-owner Michael Schwartz's "justly popular"
New American, a "genuine delight" where fans "ooh and ahh" over the
"locally sourced and creatively cooked" concoctions from the "homey
open kitchen"; "attentive service without condescension", "pleasant"
if "understated" decor, "lovely patio" seating and "affordable prices"
add to the appeal, making this "Design District dining at its best."

Michy's Ⓜ *American/French*   27 | 20 | 25 | $62

Upper East Side | 6927 Biscayne Blvd. (bet. Biscayne Blvd. & 69th St.) |
305-759-2001 | michysmiami.com

Chef Michelle Bernstein "continues to reign over Miami's culinary
scene" at her "always innovative" Upper East Sider whose "constantly
changing menu" allows diners to order "full or half portions" of "melt-
in-your-mouth" New American–French "comfort food with Latin and
Southern twists"; service is predictably "attentive and knowledgeable", and while some dis "funky decor" and "high prices" for a neighborhood that's a "tad seedy", the majority proclaims this a "true gem
in a field of rocks."

Naoe Ⓜ *Japanese*

| - | - | - | M |

Sunny Isles Beach | 175 Sunny Isles Blvd. (bet. Collins Ave. & Intercoastal Waterways Bridge) | 305-947-6263 | www.naoemiami.com

Local piscivores are flipping over this omakase-only Japanese in Sunny Isles, a sleek and sublime jewelbox of a spot where chef Kevin Cory serves pristine fin fare at affordable prices; P.S. it shares the name of the brewery that provides the sake, which is also the chef's Japanese family name.

Nobu Miami Beach ❶ *Japanese*

| 27 | 22 | 22 | $85 |

South Beach | Shore Club | 1901 Collins Ave. (20th St.) | Miami Beach | 305-695-3232 | www.noburestaurants.com

"Fantastic, inventive, fresh, expensive": that pretty much sums up this "sizzling" SoBe spot from Nobu Matsuhisa that attracts the "biggest movers and shakers of Miami, NYC and Hollywood" for "exceptional" Japanese-Peruvian fare, including "imaginative" sushi of "unparalleled quality"; detractors dis "crowded, noisy" quarters and a "fashion mag"–ready staff that can be a bit "pretentious", but most say "rob a bank" and go – it's "an experience you'll never forget."

OLA *Pan-Latin*

| 27 | 22 | 24 | $64 |

South Beach | Sanctuary Hotel | 1745 James Ave. (bet. 17th & 18th Sts.) | Miami Beach | 305-695-9125 | www.olamiami.com

Even "locals feel like they're on vacation" at toque Douglas Rodriguez's "fantastic" "find" in South Beach's Sanctuary Hotel, where the "modern" mood mirrors the "innovative, playful Pan-Latin" fare (particularly the "spectacular ceviche"); "exceptional" servers "guide you through the many choices", and while the "small plates" can "add up", it's a small price to pay for a "gastronomic experience."

Ortanique on the Mile *Caribbean/New World*

| 26 | 22 | 23 | $54 |

Coral Gables | 278 Miracle Mile (Salzedo St.) | 305-446-7710 | www.cindyhutsoncuisine.com

There's a "fabulous" "island feel" in the air at this "creative" Coral Gables eatery, where "beautiful aromas" waft from the "flavorful" Caribbean-New World cuisine starring "fresh seafood" and the "cabanalike decor" evokes a "porch along the beach"; true, it's "pricey" and often "crowded", but servers "who love what they do" plus the "best mojitos in town" work their own magic.

Osteria del Teatro Ⓢ *Italian*

| 26 | 17 | 25 | $65 |

South Beach | 1443 Washington Ave. (Española Way) | Miami Beach | 305-538-7850 | www.osteriadelteatromiami.com

The "cooked-to-perfection" Northern Italian "food is the star" of this "small gem on South Beach" that offers "so many specials you'll need to take notes"; luckily, "super-friendly" servers who "really know the menu" are there to assist in the "loud, close quarters" (some suggest a "renovation" is in order), and if it's "not cheap", partisans remind you're paying for a "step above the rest."

Palm, The *Steak*

| 26 | 19 | 24 | $70 |

Bay Harbor Islands | 9650 E. Bay Harbor Dr. (96th St.) | 305-868-7256 | www.thepalm.com

"Old-school dining" is alive and well in Bay Harbor Islands at this "distinguished" chain carnivorium, born in NYC in 1926 and drawing "movers and shakers" ever since with its "enormous" steaks and lobsters plated in "distinguished" settings adorned with celebrity "caricatures"; sure, the tabs are reminiscent of "mortgage payments" and service can career from "top-notch" to "surly", but ultimately it's "consistently good."

Palme d'Or ⊠Ⓜ *French* | 28 | 28 | 28 | $80 |

Coral Gables | Biltmore Hotel | 1200 Anastasia Ave. (Columbus Blvd.) | 305-913-3201 | www.biltmorehotel.com

Rated No. 1 in the Miami Survey for Food, this "exquisite" New French is "as close to perfection as you can get", an "inviting, unintimidating" bastion of "old-world elegance" in Coral Gables' "magnificent" Biltmore Hotel; chef Philippe Ruiz's "innovative" small plates are "beautifully presented" "gastronomic delights" complemented by an "excellent wine list" and "tuxedoed servers" who "set the stage for an outstanding dining experience"; it's "pricey" for sure, but have no doubt: "you will be thrilled."

Pascal's on Ponce ⊠ *French* | 27 | 20 | 25 | $63 |

Coral Gables | 2611 Ponce de Leon Blvd. (bet. Almeria & Valencia Aves.) | 305-444-2024 | www.pascalmiami.com

"You can always expect creative dishes" from chef-owner Pascal Oudin, whose "intimate" Coral Gables bistro features "exquisitely prepared" New French fare paired with "gracious", "civilized" service; it can be "costly", "cramped" and "noisy", but *amis* aver this "little piece of Paris" is nonetheless *"très magnifique."*

Por Fin *Mediterranean/Spanish* | 22 | 23 | 21 | $51 |

Coral Gables | 2500 Ponce de Leon Blvd. (Andalusia Ave.) | 305-441-0107 | www.porfinrestaurant.com

"Catalan comes to Coral Gables" at this "happening" Spanish-Med "surprise" offering "unusual twists on traditional dishes" (with a "decadent" touch) by an alum of Spain's El Bulli; a few feel the kitchen is "overreaching" and the execution sometimes "falls short", but compensations include a "beautiful" setting amped up by a "sexy" upstairs bar scene and service that's "right on the mark."

Prime One Twelve ◐ *Seafood/Steak* | 26 | 23 | 23 | $85 |

South Beach | 112 Ocean Dr. (1st St.) | Miami Beach | 305-532-8112 | www.prime112.com

"Nothing exceeds like excess" at this "vibrant", even "frenzied" SoBe "steakhouse to end all steakhouses" serving up *"Flintstones"*-size portions of "extraordinary seafood and meat" amid an "eye candy"–crammed "scene" that lures "power brokers, celebs and pro athletes alike"; service ranges from "fast and friendly" to "rushed" and "rude" and "reservations are somewhat irrelevant", while even admirers admit the place is "too everything" ("too expensive, too crowded, too noisy"); in the end, though, it's "still the one to beat."

Red Light ◐Ⓜ *American* | 26 | 16 | 18 | $36 |

Upper East Side | Motel Blu | 7700 Biscayne Blvd. (77th St.) | 305-757-7773 | www.redlightmiami.com

You won't find "better food for prices like these" declare disciples of chef Kris Wessel, whose "oh-so-cool" Upper East Sider in a riverside "1950s hotel" turns out "local, seasonal, sustainable" New American fare with a "bit of New Orleans flavor" (the "BBQ shrimp alone is worth a visit"); that helps make up for "haphazard" service and a somewhat "dicey" location, though for some that's just "part of the charm."

Romeo's Cafe 🗷Ⓜ *Italian*　　　27 | 19 | 28 | $87

Coral Way | 2257 SW 22nd St./Coral Way (bet. 22nd & 23rd Aves.) | 305-859-2228 | www.romeoscafe.com

There's "no menu", "little" space and many "surprises" at this "foodie's dream" in Coral Way; chef-owner Romeo Majano "comes out to see what you like", then "takes you on a culinary journey" with "outstanding" multicourse Northern Italian meals "customized to each diner's preference"; it's "exquisite" and "expensive", with a staff "working like a precision timepiece" to ensure a "memorable experience" whether you're there to "celebrate, impress a date or propose."

Sardinia ❶ *Italian*　　　23 | 21 | 20 | $53

South Beach | 1801 Purdy Ave. (18th St.) | Miami Beach | 305-531-2228 | www.sardinia-ristorante.com

"Tucked away" on South Beach, this "out-of-the-ordinary" "gem" is "frequented mostly by locals" who appreciate its "inventive" Sardinian fare (including "fantastic wood-burning oven dishes") and "exceptional wine list" with choices that "won't cost you an arm and a leg"; the atmosphere is "chic" and "comfortable" with "cosmopolitan" service, and though a few detect a "pretentious" air, overall it's a "popular trysting place."

Scarpetta *Italian*　　　25 | 27 | 25 | $83

Miami Beach | Fontainebleau Miami Beach | 4441 Collins Ave. (41st St.) | 305-674-4660 | www.fontainebleau.com

Chef Scott Conant brings this NYC-bred Italian to the Fontainebleau Miami Beach, "impressing" guests with "unconventional", "incredible" dinners provided by a "spectacular" staff; the "intoxicatingly lovely" setting with a "seaside" ambiance enhances the "totally Miami vibe", and though the bill is a "shocker", fans affirm it's "100% worth it."

Spiga *Italian*　　　26 | 24 | 25 | $49

South Beach | 1228 Collins Ave. (bet. 12th & 13th Sts.) | Miami Beach | 305-534-0079 | www.spigarestaurant.com

For a "quiet retreat" in a "frenetic, youth-obsessed zip code", SoBe solace-seekers saunter "off the beaten path" (well, a "few blocks from the beach") to this "reliable", "romantic" Northern Italian; with "reasonable prices", "professional service" and "cozy" outdoor seating, no wonder it's "lasted a long time."

Sra. Martinez 🗷 *Spanish*　　　24 | 25 | 25 | $53

Design District | 4000 NE Second Ave. (40th St. & 2nd ave) | 305-573-5474 | www.sramartinez.com

Chef Michelle Bernstein (aka Señora Martinez) "has outdone herself" at this "happening" Design District Spaniard whose "insanely delicious" – and "adventurous" – "tapas with a twist" have diners "almost licking the plates"; "outstanding" service, "delicious cocktails" at the "upstairs bar" and "beautiful modern" decor (you'll forget you're in an "old post office") dull the pain of prices that "add up quickly", leaving the overall impression that "Miami could use more of this."

	FOOD	DECOR	SERVICE	COST

Sugarcane Raw Bar Grill ◐ *Eclectic*

| - | - | - | E |

Downtown | 3250 NE First Ave. (32nd St.) | 786-369-0353 |
www.sugarcanerawbargrill.com

The little sister of the ever-popular Sushi Samba, this sweet spot north of Downtown in Midtown offers a vast array of Pan-Asian tapas, including items from a raw bar, robata grill and sushi bar, as well as a few curveballs like buttery roast chicken and cheese and charcuterie plates; accommodating staffers and a funky industrial warehouse space with soaring ceilings and a vast outdoor patio complete the package, but beware: prices that seem cheap add up faster than you can say 'oh, sugar.'

Timo *Italian/Mediterranean*

| 25 | 21 | 23 | $51 |

Sunny Isles Beach | 17624 Collins Ave. (bet. 175th Terr. & 178th St.) |
305-936-1008 | www.timorestaurant.com

"You forget the strip-mall surroundings with the first bite" of "seasonal", "imaginative" Italian-Med fare (including "superb" wood-fired pizza) at this "sophisticated", "bustling and convivial" "favorite" by chef/co-owner Tim Andriola in "up-and-coming" Sunny Isles Beach; with its "excellent" service, "expertly mixed" drinks and "fair prices", guests agree it's "doing everything right."

Versailles ◐ *Cuban*

| 21 | 14 | 18 | $26 |

Little Havana | 3555 SW Eighth St. (SW 35th Ave.) | 305-444-0240
This "doyen of Cuban restaurants in Little Havana" offers the "ultimate Miami experience", with "large portions of tasty", "authentic" fare and a clientele dressed in everything from "flip-flips to furs" that includes "movie stars, politicians, even defeated dictators"; if the "tacky", "diner"-esque decor and "uneven" service elicit a few versighs, the "affordable" prices, "history" and "endless energy" lead most to "feel like they're in Cuba without the communism."

Milwaukee

		FOOD	DECOR	SERVICE	COST

TOP FOOD RANKING

	Restaurant	Cuisine
29	Roots	Californian
	Sanford	American
	Eddie Martini's	Steak
28	Lake Park Bistro	French
	Osteria del Mondo	Italian
	Ristorante Bartolotta	Italian
27	La Merenda	Eclectic
26	River Lane Inn	Seafood
	Coquette Cafe	French
	Hinterland Erie St.	American

OTHER NOTEWORTHY PLACES

Bacchus	American
Jake's Fine Dining	Steak
Karl Ratzch's	German
Le Rêve	Dessert/French
Mason St. Grill	American
Meritage	Eclectic
Pastiche	Eclectic
Sala da Pranzo	Italian
Smyth	American
Umami Moto	Asian

Bacchus 🅑 *American*　　　　　| 25 | 26 | 25 | $61 |

Downtown | Cudahy Tower | 925 E. Wells St. (Prospect Ave.) |
414-765-1166 | www.bacchusmke.com

With a "fabulous" Cudahy Tower setting (including a glassed-in conservatory with lake views) as a backdrop for chef Adam Siegel's "wonderful" American fare brought by a "marvelous staff", this Downtown sibling of Lake Park Bistro and Ristorante Bartolotta is built to "impress"; while some surveyors "save" it "for a special night out", power-lunchers and others "keep coming back" for an "experience" they deem "worth the price."

Coquette Cafe 🅑 *French*　　　　| 26 | 22 | 24 | $38 |

Third Ward | 316 N. Milwaukee St. (St. Paul Ave.) | 414-291-2655 |
www.coquettecafe.com

"Lovely" French bistro fare is "*la différence*" at this "Third Ward gem" of "real integrity" that draws Francophiles for "romantic dinners for two" and "lunch with clients" with its "superb steak frites" and "terrific" seasonal menus; the "cute" dining room festooned with an array of area rugs is like being "in Paris" (except for "no attitude" from the staff) with "reasonable prices" completing a package that patrons call "wonderful"; P.S. owner Sanford D'Amato passed the reins to two former protégés post-Survey, which is not reflected in the scores.

Eddie Martini's 🗷 *Steak*

29 | 26 | 28 | $65

Wauwatosa | 8612 W. Watertown Plank Rd. (86th St.) | 414-771-6680 |
www.eddiemartinis.com

"Forget the image of a smoke-filled supper club", this Wauwatosa "standout" is "elegant" say fans who call the clubby classic their "all-time favorite" for "huge steaks" and "wonderfully fresh, inventive" seafood; sure it's expensive but "you get what you pay for", and an "attentive", "knowledgeable staff" seals the deal for "a special night."

Hinterland Erie Street Gastropub 🗷 *American*

26 | 25 | 24 | $51

Third Ward | 222 E. Erie St. (Water St.) | 414-727-9300 |
www.hinterlandbeer.com

Admirers of this "creative" New American situated in a Third Ward storefront call its "expensive" seasonal menu emphasizing fish and local game "superbly crafted" and give service a thumbs-up too; the wood-filled modern quarters include a lounge that's an "excellent spot to grab a cocktail", and there's sidewalk dining in summer.

Jake's Fine Dining 🗷 *Steak*

- | - | - | E

Pewaukee | 21445 Gumina Rd. (Capital Dr.) | 262-781-7995 |
www.jakes-restaurant.com

"On a winter day", patrons procure a table near the "huge fireplace" at this 50-year-old Pewaukee "steak haunt" where the "classic comfort-food menu" (including the "much-imitated, never-surpassed onion rings") includes "selections for more modern tastes"; to "longtime fans", it feels "comfortably like the bar down the street."

Karl Ratzsch's 🗷 *German*

25 | 23 | 24 | $41

Downtown | 320 E. Mason St. (bet. B'way & Milwaukee St.) |
414-276-2720 | www.karlratzsch.com

For a "sauerbraten and spaetzle fix", this Downtown "classic" is a "destination of choice" dishing out "substantial" portions of "excellent", "hearty" "old-world" German "favorites" including "wonderful roast goose" in a Bavarian-inspired room that "oozes gemütlichkeit"; the ski-lodge decor is "a little over-the-top" ("where else can you dine under chandeliers made from antlers?") and some find prices a bit "high for comfort food", but good service helps make it "worth the trip."

Lake Park Bistro *French*

28 | 28 | 27 | $55

East Side | Lake Park Pavilion | 3133 E. Newberry Blvd. (Lake Dr.) |
414-962-6300 | www.lakeparkbistro.com

A "beautiful view of Lake Michigan" and the park from the historic Lake Park Pavilion provides the setting "for romance" at this East Side "French gem" where the "world-class" cuisine of chef Adam Siegel "matches any in Chicago or New York City" and is accompanied by "outstanding service" and an "attainable wine list"; fans of this "beauty" from restaurateur Joe Bartolotta feel transported "to the French countryside" whether seated "at the bar on a weeknight" or in the dining room during a "special evening out."

La Merenda 🗷 *Eclectic*

27 | 19 | 22 | $32

Walker's Point | 125 E. National Ave. (1st St.) | 414-389-0125 |
www.lamerenda125.com

"Not much on decor" but still "festive" and colorful, this "warm and comfortable" Walker's Point "little neighborhood gem" provides "outstanding", "well-presented" "international tapas" on an Eclectic menu of "creative" small plates; price points are "well within budget reach" "for larger groups", though it's also "perfect for a first date" or a "quick bite."

Le Rêve Patisserie & Café 🗷 *Dessert/French* ▽ 27 | 19 | 22 | $29

Wauwatosa | 7610 Harwood Ave. (Menomonee River Pkwy.) | 414-778-3333 | www.lerevecafe.com

Francophiles feel the "formidable" pull of this "perfect little French cafe" from the "luscious pastries in the counter display case" to the "freakishly high ceiling" and "European decor" that make "you think you're in Paris" (rather than a restored century-old Wauwatosa bank building); the "excellent", "reasonably priced" bistro bites (e.g. crêpes, quiche, steak frites) are made even better by the "brisk but friendly white-aproned service."

Mason Street Grill *American* 23 | 24 | 24 | $55

Downtown | Pfister Hotel | 425 E. Mason St. (bet. Jefferson & Milwaukee Sts.) | 414-298-3131 | www.masonstreetgrill.com

"Excellent steaks and chops" coupled with "good value" and "knowledgeable service" draw meat eaters to this American in Downtown's historic Pfister Hotel, where the "seafood is top-rate too", making for an all-around "solid stop"; patrons "grab a counter seat" facing the kitchen to "see how the food is prepared" or head for the "sleek", "upscale" dining room with light-brown leather and wood to spend a "pleasant" "evening lingering"; P.S. for the lounge lizards, there's live piano and vocals.

Meritage 🗷Ⓜ *Eclectic* - | - | - | E

West Side | 5921 W. Vliet St. (60th St.) | 414-479-0620 | www.meritage.us

Pilgrims who venture "off the beaten path" to the West Side proclaim this Washington Heights Eclectic a "delicious destination" for chef-owner Jan Kelly's dishes "using an abundance of local and organic ingredients" in a "creative menu" that blends "tastes from all over the world"; P.S. the "outdoor patio is a summertime must."

Osteria del Mondo 🗷 *Italian* 28 | 21 | 25 | $53

Downtown | Knickerbocker Hotel | 1028 E. Juneau Ave. (Astor St.) | 414-291-3770 | www.osteria.com

Chef/co-owner Marc Bianchini's Northern Italian "standards with flair" are "as close to authentic as you'll find in the Midwest" at this Downtown "favorite" that's been "consistent over the years" for "fine dining" in a "comfortable" Tuscan-themed setting; acolytes advise "trust the server" and say "sure it's expensive – especially for Milwaukee", but the "prix fixe menus are a great deal"; P.S. there's an outdoor patio and a cigar lounge too.

Pastiche 🗷 *French* - | - | - | M

Bay View | 3001 S. Kinnickinnic Ave. (Rusk Ave.) | 414-482-1446 | www.pastichebistro.com

Suffusing the sunny warmth of Provence into an unassuming corner storefront in Bay View, this casual newcomer with butter-colored walls and Gallic posters features chef-owner Michael Engel's French bistro cuisine; the neighborhood's rich stew of residents and workers from its eclectic businesses dig into hearty classics like cassoulet and escargots, all washed down with wines whose prices are as affordable as the fare.

Ristorante Bartolotta *Italian*   28 | 25 | 27 | $55

Wauwatosa | 7616 W. State St. (Harwood Ave.) | 414-771-7910 | www.bartolottaristorante.com

"Awesome" Italian flavors make it easy to "pretend you are in a small bistro in Rome" rather than "Downtown Wauwatosa" (in an old Pabst Brewery saloon, no less) at this "charming, noisy trattoria" that also offers an "extensive wine list" (all Italian labels) and "well-trained staff"; old family photos lining the walls provide a contrast with the "upscale sensibility" that surveyors expect from "the [Joe] Bartolotta empire" (which includes Lake Park Bistro and Bacchus).

River Lane Inn ☒ *Seafood*   26 | 18 | 26 | $42

North Shore | 4313 W. River Ln. (Brown Deer Rd.) | 414-354-1995

While the look of this longtime North Shore seafood specialist located inside a late 1800s building may be "dark and unchanged", its repertoire of moderately priced seafood items – many listed on the chalkboard roster of daily specials – is "fresh and creatively prepared"; fin fans say "you can't go wrong with anything on the menu", and further adding to its "steady-as-she-goes" status is the "experienced staff" and "friendly bartenders who pour an ample drink."

Roots Restaurant & Cellar *Californian*   29 | 27 | 22 | $38

Brewers Hill | 1818 N. Hubbard St. (Vine St.) | 414-374-8480 | www.rootsmilwaukee.com

You can "see the staff snipping herbs" at this green-minded Brewers Hill Californian – voted No. 1 for Food in the Milwaukee Survey – that's a "must-go" for chef John Raymond's "exceptional" midpriced menu using "local ingredients" (some "homegrown") in "adventurous", "seasonal" creations; the "cozy" yet "fabulous digs" include a two-level patio, gracious gardens and a "beautiful view of the Downtown skyline", and the "reliable wine list" is another "step up"; P.S. the lower-level Cellar offers casual options.

Sala da Pranzo *Italian*   - | - | - | M

East Side | 2613 E. Hampshire Ave. (Downer Ave.) | 414-964-2611 | www.sala-dapranzo.com

Locals and profs from the nearby university call this "family-owned and -operated" East Side trattoria a "real hidden gem" for saltimbocca, pastas and other midpriced Italian fare; eclectic artwork adorns the walls, and those who "wished" for it to be "open on Sundays" are likely glad to hear that brunch is now offered then.

Sanford ☒ *American*   29 | 27 | 29 | $74

East Side | 1547 N. Jackson St. (Pleasant St.) | 414-276-9608 | www.sanfordrestaurant.com

Co-owner and chef Sanford D'Amato's nationally recognized New American, residing in the East Side storefront home of his family's old grocery store, is "as impressive as any top New York restaurant" say surveyors who again vote it Most Popular in Milwaukee; "superb and imaginative", this "little neighborhood gem" pays "attention to every detail", from its "marvelous" cuisine – including a seven-course surprise tasting menu – to its "down-to-earth, professional" service to decor that mixes "modern" (a single chartreuse wall) and historical (old black-and-white family photos); while not cheap, it's a "great value considering what you get."

Smyth *American*

∇ 24 | 27 | 26 | $44

Walker's Point | Iron Horse Hotel | 500 W. Florida St. (6th St.) | 414-831-4615 | www.theironhorsehotel.com

Rustic 100-year-old warehouse decor including Cream City brick is the backdrop for "smitten" surveyors at this "stylish" Walker's Point New American "'in' place" inside the motorcycle-friendly Iron Horse Hotel, where the "energy is electrifying" and chef Tom Schultz shows a "great understanding of culinary trends and what Milwaukeeans want to eat" (e.g. veal osso buco and foie gras); while the cuisine is both "innovative and comforting", the "interesting wine list" and "knowledgeable staff" make the meal even "more special."

Umami Moto ⊠ *Asian*

∇ 24 | 25 | 19 | $50

Downtown | 718 N. Milwaukee St. (bet. Mason St. & Wisconsin Ave.) | 414-727-9333 | www.umamimoto.com

"Pretty people" populate this sleek Milwaukee Street place "to be seen" with an "amazing" interior design boasting wavelike walls, river-stone pillars and pale-green tile as a backdrop for executive chef Dominic Zumpano's "imaginative", "beautifully prepared" Asian fusion menu; though it's costly, the fare "hits all the high points for taste" ("love the sliders"), plus service is "friendly" and "helpful."

Minneapolis/St. Paul

	FOOD	DECOR	SERVICE	COST

TOP FOOD RANKING

	Restaurant	Cuisine
28	La Belle Vie	French/Mediterranean
	112 Eatery	Eclectic
27	Vincent	French
	Alma	American
	Bar La Grassa	Italian
	Meritage	American/French
	Lucia's	American
26	Manny's	Steak
	Heartland	American
	Oceanaire	Seafood

OTHER NOTEWORTHY PLACES

Café Levain	American
Cosmos	Eclectic
D'Amico Kitchen	Italian
Kincaid's	Seafood/Steak
FireLake	American
Modern Cafe	American
Punch	Pizza
Saffron	Mediterranean/Mideastern
Sea Change	Seafood
20.21	Asian

Alma *American*   27 | 22 | 26 | $54

Dinkytown | 528 University Ave. SE (6th Ave.) | Minneapolis | 612-379-4909 | www.restaurantalma.com

Chef Alexander Roberts' "ethereal", "frequently changing" New American menu, based on "high quality seasonal ingredients", is the draw at this "plain", "intimate" "bistro-like environment" in Dinkytown; "interesting wines by the glass" and a "knowledgeable staff" complete the "memorable experience", which is "a bit expensive, but worth it."

Bar La Grassa ◑ *Italian*   27 | 24 | 24 | $42

Warehouse | 800 N. Washington Ave. (8th Ave.) | Minneapolis | 612-333-3837 | www.barlagrassa.com

"Unquestionably the 'in' place" right now, this "vibrant", "urban" Warehouse District addition serves "amazing contemporary Italian" fare, featuring "wonderful homemade pastas" and "knockout small plates" with "unusual twists" ("have the lobster and egg bruschetta"); factor in a "pro" staff and "moderate prices", and no wonder it's "packed every night."

Café Levain Ⓜ *American*   24 | 19 | 22 | $38

South Minneapolis | 4762 Chicago Ave. (48th St.) | Minneapolis | 612-823-7111 | www.cafelevain.com

"Skillfully prepared", often "inspired" New American "bistro fare" comes via "attentive servers" at this "intimate" "neighborhood restaurant" in South Minneapolis; the "Sunday supper prix fixe is among the greatest bargains" around (and a real "treat" to boot), but dinner here is a "good value" any night of the week.

Cosmos *Eclectic*

| 24 | 26 | 24 | $54 |

Warehouse | Graves 601 Hotel | 601 First Ave. N. (bet. 6th & 7th Sts.) | Minneapolis | 612-312-1168 | www.cosmosrestaurant.com

"Groovy", "airy" contemporary decor that you'd expect to "see in NYC, not Minnie" puts this Eclectic in a "chic" Warehouse District hotel "in a league of its own"; complementing the setting is an "interesting menu" filled with "innovative" "twists" and matched by a "great wine list", and while tabs are generally "high", insiders say "the prix fixe menus are the way to go for a lovely sampling at an excellent price."

D'Amico Kitchen *Italian*

| 23 | 23 | 22 | $45 |

Downtown Mpls | Chambers Hotel | 901 Hennepin Ave. (Ninth St.) | Minneapolis | 612-767-6960 | www.damico-kitchen.com

"Contemporary", "airy" digs fashion a "hip atmosphere" for "interesting", "well-executed" Italian fare made with "top-tier ingredients" at this "'in' place" off the lobby of an "upscale boutique hotel" in the "heart" of Downtown Mpls; service that's "unobtrusive yet helpful" pleases, as do the prices, especially the "value" three-course prix fixes, offered at both lunch and dinner; BTW, there's a "patio that's great – when it's not 30 below."

FireLake *American*

| 22 | 20 | 22 | $30 |

Downtown Mpls | Radisson Hotel | 31 S. Seventh St. (bet. Hennepin & Nicollet Aves.) | Minneapolis | 612-216-3473 | www.firelakerestaurant.com

Devotees advise the "recommendations made by the staff" should be heeded at this "comfortable" maroon-and-earth-toned New American in a Downtown Mpls hotel, where the "solid" menu has a "great Minnesota" slant and the dishes arrive in "straightforward presentations"; businesspeople appreciate it as a "good place for a breakfast meeting", while theatergoers come for a reasonably priced "dinner before a play."

Heartland ☒ *American*

| 26 | 22 | 25 | $50 |

Downtown SP | 289 E. Fifth St. (bet. B'way & Wall Sts.) | St. Paul | 651-699-3536 | www.heartlandrestaurant.com

Get ready for a "gastronomic adventure" at this "somewhat pricey" "locavore restaurant" where "mad genius" chef Lenny Russo utilizes "organic, high-quality" ingredients plus "parts of animals you've never tried before" for his "splendid" daily changing Midwestern menu; post-Survey, it vacated its "unassuming" Groveland digs (outdating the Decor score) – and fans "hope the atmosphere is better" in its new Downtown St. Paul locale, while praying that everything else "stays the same."

Kincaid's *Seafood/Steak*

| 24 | 22 | 24 | $45 |

Bloomington | 8400 Normandale Lake Blvd. (84th St.) | 952-921-2255
Downtown SP | 380 St. Peter St. (6th St.) | St. Paul | 651-602-9000
www.kincaids.com

"Solid steaks", "outstanding fish", "huge portions and windows" and "wonderful service" top the list of reasons why "business diners" in Downtown St. Paul and Bloomington make this "attractive", "clubby" chain a "perennial favorite"; of course, it's "expensive", but the "prices can't be beat" during the "great twice-daily happy hour" at the bar, which houses a voluminous wine and beer selection.

La Belle Vie   *French/Mediterranean*   28 | 26 | 28 | $72

Loring Park | 510 Groveland Ave. (Hennepin Ave.) | Minneapolis | 612-874-6440 | www.labellevie.us

"Nothing else can hold a candle" to this "grand, elegant" "special-occasion place" in a "1920s apartment building" near Loring Park, whose "exquisite" Mediterranean–New French fare (from executive chef Tim McKee) garners the Twin Cities' No. 1 Food score (ask the "impeccable" staff about the "amazing tasting menus" with "well-paired wines"); make sure "your companions know CPR for when you get the bill", or patronize the "pretty", "romantic" lounge instead, which is "more casual and less expensive."

Lucia's   🅼   *American*   27 | 22 | 26 | $41

Uptown | 1432 W. 31st St. (Hennepin Ave.) | Minneapolis | 612-825-1572 | www.lucias.com

Chef-owner Lucia Watson is the "grande dame of local, seasonal ingredients", and she's been crafting "top-notch", "organic" (but "limited") New American menus at this "quaint" Uptown "legend" "for nearly 30 years"; there's "not much to look at" decorwise (excepting "a gorgeous floral arrangement"), yet it still "feels like a special-occasion spot" – on the other hand, you "could spend many an hour in the fabulous [attached] wine bar", and "the next-door cafe is the kind of place you could go to every morning for breakfast."

Manny's Steakhouse   *Steak*   26 | 22 | 26 | $65

Downtown Mpls | W Minneapolis, The Foshay | 821 Marquette Ave. (9th St.) | Minneapolis | 612-339-9900 | www.mannyssteakhouse.com

"The aura of power" and "testosterone" suffuses this "energetic" meat emporium, where "big eaters" pay "big prices" for "huge steaks" and "mega-sized sides" (everything's "scrumptious"); now that it's in Downtown Mpls' W Hotel, it's "much hipper", with "cowhides on the walls" and "sophisticated, urban" furnishings, while the staff is as "knowledgeable and friendly" as it ever was.

Meritage   🅼   *American/French*   27 | 24 | 25 | $46

Downtown SP | Hamm Building | 410 St. Peter St. (6th St.) | St. Paul | 651-222-5670 | www.meritage-stpaul.com

This "classy urban bistro" in Downtown St. Paul "captures the essence of French food", but in "well-executed, innovative" New American plates, which are listed on a "broad menu" and served in "always lively" (read: "crowded", "noisy") environs that seem "lifted right off the streets of Paris"; the "extensive wine list" entices oenophiles, "modest prices" please value-seekers, while "super service" gets ticket-holders to the nearby Ordway by curtain time; P.S. there's "charming sidewalk dining in summer."

Modern Cafe   🅼   *American*   24 | 17 | 21 | $25

Northeast | 337 13th Ave. NE (University Ave.) | Minneapolis | 612-378-9882 | www.moderncafeminneapolis.com

"Awesome", "lovingly presented" Traditional American "comfort food" fashioned from "locally grown products and livestock" is what's on the menu at this "longtime workhorse in the up-and-coming Northeast Minneapolis arts district"; the "retro" setting (once a soda fountain) is a bit "kitschy", but that's part of the fun, and the tabs "won't break the bank"; P.S. "try the pot roast" – "you'll never want anything else."

Oceanaire Seafood Room *Seafood*   26 | 23 | 25 | $57

Downtown Mpls | Hyatt Regency | 1300 Nicollet Mall (Grant St.) | Minneapolis | 612-333-2277 | www.theoceanaire.com

For "the freshest, most delicious seafood in flyover land" (including a "standout" raw bar), fin fans out for either "business or pleasure" head to this chain outpost in Downtown Minneapolis' Hyatt Regency, where the tabs are "pricey, but you get what you pay for"; "outstanding service" befits the "inviting", "elegant" 1940s-ocean-liner decor theme, for which nothing less than an "ice cold martini" will do.

112 Eatery ❶ *Eclectic*   28 | 22 | 25 | $43

Warehouse | 112 N. Third St. (1st Ave. N.) | Minneapolis | 612-343-7696 | www.112eatery.com

"Deliciously different, sometimes daring" Eclectic dishes, "absolutely fabulous service" and a "cool", "high-energy" yet "no-fuss environment" earn this Warehouse District "clubhouse for foodies" and "off-duty chefs" the Twin Cities' Most Popular restaurant ranking; it's "as hard to get into as heaven", but it's "worth the planning", especially since the fare's a relatively "excellent value" (the "artfully varied wine list" displays "lots of modest pricing" too).

Punch Neapolitan Pizza *Pizza*   26 | 16 | 20 | $17

Dinkytown | 802 Washington Ave. SE (Oak St.) | Minneapolis | 612-331-3122

Eden Prairie | 8353 Crystal View Rd. (Prairie Center Dr.) | 952-943-9557

Highland Park | 704 Cleveland Ave. S. (Highland Pkwy.) | St. Paul | 651-696-1066

Northeast | 210 E. Hennepin Ave. (University Ave.) | Minneapolis | 612-623-8114

South Minneapolis | Calhoun Vlg. Shopping Ctr. | 3226 W. Lake St. (Market Plaza) | Minneapolis | 612-929-0006

Summit Hill | 769 Grand Ave. (bet. Avon & Grotto Sts.) | St. Paul | 651-602-6068

Wayzata | 1313 Wayzata Blvd. E. (Hwy. 101) | 952-476-7991
www.punchpizza.com

"Best pizza we've had since Italy" cheer surveyors about this "laid-back", "inexpensive" local chain's "spectacular" thin-crust Neapolitan pies, which are "customizable" with "premium toppings", baked in a "scalding wood-fired oven" and offered along with "terrific", "crispy salads"; occasionally there are "lines out the door" to both "eat in or takeaway", but they "move fast" since once you place your order, it's only about "a 90-second wait" until you receive your food.

Saffron Restaurant & Lounge ⌧ *Mediterranean/Mideastern*   25 | 22 | 25 | $44

Warehouse | 123 N. Third St. (1st Ave.) | Minneapolis | 612-746-5533 | www.saffronmpls.com

From the "amazing small plates" to the "interesting entrees" and beyond, "everything on the menu works" at this value-minded Warehouse District Mediterranean–Middle Eastern, which also whips up "out-of-this-world specialty cocktails" "well suited to the food"; some survey-ors feel the "ambiance is lacking", but "friendly, professional" service elevates it to the "sophisticated" experience the "eager-to-please owners" intend it to be.

Sea Change ⬛ Seafood
25 | 25 | 24 | $54

Downtown Mpls | Guthrie Theater | 806 S. Second St. (Chicago Ave.) | Minneapolis | 612-225-6499 | www.seachangempls.com

The pre-show set calls this reconception of the Guthrie's flagship eat-ery a "change for the better", with "phenomenal" sustainable seafood served in "unique preparations", brought by "courteous" servers alongside "amazing wines" and "cool drinks"; another "wow factor" comes from the "theatrical", ocean-themed setting where you can "sit at the open-kitchen bar and watch the cooking" or, weather permit-ting, outdoors on the patio, all of which makes it "worth a visit even if you're not attending" a play.

20.21 ⬛⬛ Asian
25 | 24 | 22 | $49

Loring Park | Walker Art Ctr. | 1750 Hennepin Ave. (Lyndale Ave.) | Minneapolis | 612-253-3410 | www.wolfgangpuck.com

"You can't beat the view of Downtown Minneapolis" at this Asian fu-sion member of the Wolfgang Puck gang, whose "minimalist" "con-temporary ambiance" (some deem it "cold") befits its location in the "stunning" Walker Art Center; the "designed-for-sharing" dishes are as "superb" and "smart" as the art, and with generally "great service" thrown into the mix, most feel the "expensive" tabs are "worth every bite out of the wallet"; P.S. the three-course $20.21 happy-hour menu is "a steal."

Vincent ⬛ French
27 | 24 | 26 | $53

Downtown Mpls | 1100 Nicollet Mall (11th St.) | Minneapolis | 612-630-1189 | www.vincentarestaurant.com

"Whatever the occasion" – a "romantic dinner, a big business deal", "entertaining out-of-town guests" – chef-owner Vincent Francoual and his staff "rise to it" at this "gem" "in the heart of Downtown" Mpls, providing "splendid service" in the delivery of "exquisite" French bistro cuisine; though most deem the open, "white-linen setting" "beautiful" and "comfortable", a few surveyors find it "a bit stuffy" (and "expen-sive"), opting for the bar instead, where the "steal" of a happy hour stars one of the "greatest burgers" in the Twin Cities.

Naples, FL

TOP FOOD RANKING

	Restaurant	Cuisine
26	Truluck's	Seafood
	Chops City Grill	Seafood/Steak
	Ruth's Chris	Steak
	Bleu Provence	French
25	Roy's	Hawaiian
	Café & Bar Lurcat	American
	Escargot 41	French
23	Grouper & Chips	Seafood
	Campiello	Italian
	Pazzo!	Italian

OTHER NOTEWORTHY PLACES

Absinthe	Mediterranean/Seafood
Baleen	American/Seafood
Doc Ford	Floribbean/Seafood
I M Tapas	Spanish
Mira Mare	Italian
M Waterfront Grille	Continental
Naples Tomato	American/Italian
Sea Salt	Italian/Seafood
Strip House	Steak
Veranda	Southern

Absinthe *Mediterranean/Seafood*   - | - | - | E

Naples | Collection at Vanderbilt | 2355 Vanderbilt Beach Rd.
(Airport Pulling Rd.) | 239-254-0050 | www.absinthenaples.com
Ensconced in Naples' Collection at Vanderbilt, this nightclubby setting
intoxicates with luxurious white leather banquettes, gauzy curtains
and candlelight; stylishly composed, seafood-centric small and large
plates, sandwiches and sweets are grounded in Mediterranean tradition, while sassy signature cocktails keep tipplers in a dream state.

Baleen *American/Seafood*   22 | 26 | 21 | $61

Naples | LaPlaya Beach & Golf Resort | 9891 Gulf Shore Dr.
(Vanderbilt Beach Rd.) | 239-598-5707 | www.laplayaresort.com
A "gorgeous" "setting on the Gulf" boasting a "stepped terrace" "right
off" the "fantastic white beach" explains why surveyors "love the ambiance" at this American seafooder in Naples' LaPlaya Beach & Golf
Resort; detractors insist the "staff needs more polish" for this level
and price point, but most consider it a "special-occasion" "standout."

Bleu Provence Ⓜ *French*   26 | 22 | 24 | $60

Naples | 1234 Eighth St. S. (12th Ave.) | 239-261-8239 |
www.bleuprovencenaples.com
Francophiles find this "family-run restaurant" in Naples to be "a breath
of fresh air" with its "cozy Provençal decor", "20,000-bottle wine cellar" and "limited but well-chosen" menu of "pricey" yet "divine French

	FOOD	DECOR	SERVICE	COST

food"; "everything (including the accents) is authentic", and when the lapis blue dining room gets "a bit noisy in season", diners can "sit outside for a romantic, under-the-stars experience."

Café & Bar Lurcat   American   25 | 26 | 21 | $57

Naples | 494 Fifth Ave. S. (5th St.) | 239-213-3357 | www.cafelurcat.com
From the "owners of the ever-popular Campiello", this "sexy" spot includes a "trendy" "downstairs bar with sofas" and a small-plates menu and a "dramatic upstairs" room serving pricier, "more serious" New American cuisine with wine pairings; either way, expect dishes that are "edgier than typical Naples fare" and "save room" for "the hot mini-doughnuts" (which help make up for the "spotty service").

Campiello Ristorante   Italian   23 | 23 | 22 | $51

Naples | 1177 Third St. S. (Broad Ave.) | 239-435-1166 |
www.campiello.damico.com
"Creative Italian" fare matches the "upscale but not stuffy" ambiance at the Most Popular restaurant in the Naples area, this "place to be seen" where it's "all glass and light" inside and there's also a "wonderful patio overlooking Downtown's elegant shopping district"; there can be "long waits", but the "lively atmosphere" with an "indoor-outdoor" "bar scene" provides "great people-watching."

Chops City Grill   Seafood/Steak   26 | 23 | 24 | $54

Bonita Springs | Brooks Grand Plaza | 8200 Health Ctr. Blvd.
(bet. Coconut Rd. & US 41) | 239-992-4677
Naples | 837 Fifth Ave. S. (bet. 8th & 9th Sts. S) | 239-262-4677
www.chopscitygrill.com
"Everything is grilled to perfection" at these upscale surf 'n' turf specialists in Bonita Springs and Naples, where the "consistent quality" of the beef and seafood extends to the "nice sushi menu" and "fantastic wine flights"; "satisfying service", "minimalist decor" and a "lively bar scene" help explain why they're "always packed" with the local "who's who", making reservations "essential."

Doc Ford Fort Myers Beach   Floribbean/Seafood   21 | 19 | 21 | $28

Ft. Myers | 708 Fishermans Wharf (Old San Carlos Blvd.) | 239-765-9660 |
www.docfords.com

Doc Ford's Sanibel Rum Bar & Grille   Floribbean/Seafood

Sanibel | 975 Rabbit Rd. (Sanibel-Captiva Rd.) | 239-472-8311 |
www.docfordssanibel.com
"Innovative Floribbean seafood and cocktails" and a "kick-back" atmosphere are the draws at Sanibel's "funky" midpriced "classic island beach bar"; it and its Ft. Myers sibling are named for the hero of Randy Wayne White's novels, and fans insist "if you've ever read the books, you can imagine the bloke at the bar hauling in a 50-pound snook" as you "grab a cold beer, crack a shrimp" and watch the games on "multiple TVs."

Escargot 41   French   25 | 16 | 23 | $65

Naples | Park Shore Shopping Ctr. | 4339 N. Tamiami Trail (Morningside Dr.) |
239-793-5000 | www.escargot41.com
"Don't be put off" by its location "in the corner" of a "low-end shopping center", because this Naples "neighborhood favorite" turns out "exquisite", "expensive" classic French cuisine that includes "enormous" versions of the namesake "done several ways" to "buttery

goodness"; "the table is yours for the evening" and the staff "works hard to please", making the package "a true dining experience."

Grouper & Chips 🅰 *Seafood*

23 | 9 | 19 | \$22

Naples | 338 N. Tamiami Trail (3rd Ave.) | 239-643-4577 | www.grouperandchips.net

It may be "unbelievably small" with "no style", but groupies say "you don't come here for" the decor – "as the name implies", this Naples "favorite" is all about the "incredibly fresh, batter-fried grouper" and other seafood; a "cheery" staff and budget prices add to its appeal.

I M Tapas *Spanish*

- | - | - | M

Naples | 965 Fourth Ave. N. (bet. 9th & 10th Sts.) | 239-403-8272 | www.imtapas.com

Chef-owners Isabel Pozo Polo and Mary Shipman have garnered a broad following for their hip Spain-meets–Greenwich Village Naples tapas spot where the diverse small plates are paired with boutique Iberian wines; prices are moderate/expensive, while the simple space is cheek/jowl.

Mira Mare Ristorante *Italian*

- | - | - | M

Naples | Village on Venetian Bay | 4236 Gulf Shore Blvd. N. (Parkshore Dr.) | 239-430-6273 | www.miramarenaples.com

As the name implies, you'll be looking at the water at this Italian addition to Naples' Village on Venetian Bay, where both the sleek yet gracious contemporary Med interior and capacious patio boast breathtaking views; the menu lists a broad, mostly moderately priced selection of classics, featuring many housemade pastas, and the nightly live piano makes it an inviting place to linger over after-dinner cocktails.

M Waterfront Grille *Continental*

- | - | - | E

Naples | Village on Venetian Bay | 4300 Gulf Shore Blvd. N. (Park Shore Dr.) | 239-263-4421 | www.mwaterfrontgrille.com

This Village on Venetian Bay venue purveys gutsy reinterpretations of Continental classics by young yet pedigreed chef Brian A. Roland; tourist-friendly (and vacation-priced), the contemporary setting is bolstered by water views from nearly every seat in the dining room, lounge and covered veranda; P.S. reservations are a must in high season.

Naples Tomato *American/Italian*

21 | 19 | 19 | \$47

Naples | 14700 N. Tamiami Trail (Old 41) | 239-598-9800 | www.naplestomato.com

It "has it all" aver admirers of this American-Neapolitan in Naples that boasts everything from a pasta-making room and an on-site market to an "innovative" wine tasting lounge with "hard-to-find" vintages dispensed "by the ounce"; while a few find it "expensive" and "a bit out of the way", most call it "a real contender."

Pazzo! Cucina Italiana *Italian*

23 | 21 | 21 | \$51

Naples | 853 Fifth Ave. S. (9th St.) | 239-434-8494 | www.pazzoitaliancafe.com

"Right in the middle of all the action", this Naples Italian from the owners of Chops City Grill "feels like a big-city restaurant", serving "consistently" "solid" fare; though it's "a bit loud with a tight bar", its sidewalk tables provide "a nice break from a day of shopping" and it's "great for groups" – just "reserve early during the peak season."

	FOOD	DECOR	SERVICE	COST

Roy's *Hawaiian*
25 | 23 | 23 | $56

Bonita Springs | Promenade in Bonita Springs | 26831 S. Bay Dr. (S. Tamiami Trail) | 239-498-7697
Naples | 475 Bayfront Pl. (Goodlette-Frank Rd.) | 239-261-1416
www.roysrestaurant.com

Two "elegant" links in Roy Yamaguchi's national chain, these Bonita Springs and Naples restaurants offer a side of "aloha spirit" to go with the seafood-centric Hawaiian fusion cuisine that includes butterfish that's "as good as it gets" and a molten chocolate cake that's "a must"; it's "pricey but worth it for special occasions."

Ruth's Chris Steak House *Steak*
26 | 24 | 24 | $65

Estero | Coconut Point Mall | 23151 Village Shops Way (off S. Tamiami Trail) | 239-948-8888 | www.ruthschris.com

This steakhouse chain in Estero serves "sizzling sirloins, porterhouse for two" and "consistently buttery service"; although "expensive", it delivers "what's expected at this level", including the option to sup in a "pretty dining room", "eat casually at the bar" or dine alfresco on the patio.

Sea Salt *Italian/Seafood*
- | - | - | E

Naples | 1186 Third St. S. (12th Ave.) | 239-434-7258 | www.seasaltnaples.com

This Naples destination draws foodie throngs for Venice-born chef Fabrizio Aielli's constantly evolving menu of Italian-accented seafood, which utilizes wild-caught local fish and organic produce; the prices put it pretty much in the luxury category, but guests also get deluxe modern digs that include an intimate formal dining room, a long, casual bar that overlooks the open kitchen and a bustling sidewalk patio.

Strip House 🗷 *Steak*
22 | 22 | 20 | $75

Naples | Naples Grande Beach Resort | 475 Seagate Dr. (West Blvd.) | 239-598-9600 | www.striphouse.com

This "real Manhattan steakhouse" in the Naples Grande Beach Resort keeps beef-lovers primed with "expensive" but "huge" portions of well-marbled, "char-crusted meats"; the "catchy name" plays out in the signature NY strip steak and the "burlesque decor", which "feels like Vegas" with its "red drapes", "velvet walls" and photos of '20s-era strippers.

Truluck's *Seafood*
26 | 23 | 25 | $65

Naples | 698 Fourth Ave. S. (7th St.) | 239-530-3131 | www.trulucks.com

"It owns its own fishing fleet", so expect to find "superlative" "luxury seafood" at this Naples link in a Texas-based chain, where the "expensive" fare includes many kinds of "phenomenal crab" (with a Monday all-you-can-eat option), plus a variety of fish and steaks; a "classy operation", it boasts an "indoor-outdoor dining room" staffed by an "attentive" crew that exhibits a certain "Old Florida gentility and hospitality."

Veranda, The 🗷 *Southern*
23 | 24 | 25 | $58

Ft. Myers | 2122 Second St. (Monroe St.) | 239-332-2065 | www.verandarestaurant.com

Situated in a pair of "adjoining Victorian houses", this 32-year-old Ft. Myers "standby" serves "interesting" Southern fare with a touch of "elegant" "Old Florida charm", making it a local "favorite" for "special occasions" and "romantic dinners"; although it can be "expensive", "great service" and a "beautiful" garden courtyard add value.

New Jersey

(For Atlantic City, see page 24)

TOP FOOD RANKING

	Restaurant	Cuisine
28	Nicholas	American
	Lorena's	French
	Ajihei	Japanese
	Cafe Panache	Eclectic
	Saddle River Inn	American/French
	Serenade	French
27	Scalini Fedeli	Italian
	Washington Inn	American
	Whispers	American
	Bay Ave. Trattoria	American/Italian
	Sagami	Japanese
	CulinAriane	American
	André's	American
	Ebbitt Room	American
	DeLorenzo's Tomato Pies	Pizza
	Tre Figlio	Italian
	Cafe Matisse	Eclectic
	Blue Bottle Cafe	American
	Piccola Italia	Italian
26	Pluckemin Inn	American

OTHER NOTEWORTHY PLACES

Restaurant	Cuisine
Amanda's	American
Avenue	French
Cheesecake Factory	American
Cucharamama	South American
David Burke Fromagerie	American
elements	American
Fascino	Italian
410 Bank Street	Caribbean/Creole
Frog and the Peach	American
Liberty House	American
Mehndi	Indian
Ninety Acres	American
Nisi	Greek
Peacock Inn	American
Ram's Head Inn	American
Rat's	French
Restaurant Latour	American
River Palm	Steak
Ruth's Chris	Steak
Uproot	American

	FOOD	DECOR	SERVICE	COST

Ajihei ▣ *Japanese* | 28 | 12 | 17 | $34

Princeton | 11 Chambers St. (Nassau St.) | 609-252-1158

For "fish so fresh it swims to your table" step into this Japanese BYO in Princeton and let Koji Kitamura, "a real sushi master from Japan", make the selection for you; the "no-gimmicks" fare trumps the lack of ambiance and "spotty service" at this "tiny" spot that "won't let in groups larger than four."

Amanda's *American* | 25 | 24 | 24 | $49

Hoboken | 908 Washington St. (bet. 9th & 10th Sts.) | 201-798-0101 | www.amandasrestaurant.com

"Attention to detail is everywhere" at this "classy and elegant" New American in a "charming" 1895 Hoboken brownstone, where a "well-heeled clientele" enjoys "outstanding food that matches the wonderful ambiance" and "A+ service"; it's "pricey but worth it", particularly for the "best-value early-bird in NJ" and the "excellent Sunday brunch"; P.S. "a local garage comps patrons for up to three hours."

André's ▣▣ *American* | 27 | 21 | 24 | $53

Newton | 188 Spring St. (bet. Adams & Jefferson Sts.) | 973-300-4192 | www.andresrestaurant.com

It's "worth the trip" to this "romantic" storefront (with sidewalk cafe) in Newton for "super-talented" chef-owner Andre de Waal's "inventive" American cuisine, enhanced by a "wonderful" wine selection (there's also an on-site wine boutique open Wednesdays–Sundays) and "pleasant if not always polished" service; a less-pricey bistro menu is also available.

Avenue *French* | 20 | 26 | 18 | $57

Long Branch | 23 Ocean Ave. (Cooper Ave.) | 732-759-2900 | www.leclubavenue.com

"Step into St. Tropez" and "mingle with the beautiful people" at this "gorgeous" French brasserie in Long Branch with "breathtaking" ocean views and a "trendy" upstairs lounge – just "bring plenty of money or Daddy's AmEx"; some say service "could be better" but the food draws mostly good reviews, with special kudos for the "not-to-be-missed" raw bar and "superb" cocktails.

Bay Avenue Trattoria ▣ *American/Italian* | 27 | 12 | 22 | $41

Highlands | 122 Bay Ave. (Cornwell St.) | 732-872-9800 | www.bayavetrattoria.com

"No decor but who cares?" when Joe Romanowski "still puts out great" American-Italian fare and Maggie Lubcke is "out with the patrons being charming" at this "small" (40-seat), "low-key" BYO "gem" in Highlands; "tight tables" and "paper napkins" notwithstanding, reservations are "a must" being that it's a perennial high-scorer.

Blue Bottle Cafe ▣▣ *American* | 27 | 18 | 22 | $47

Hopewell | 101 E. Broad St. (Elm St.) | 609-333-1710 | www.thebluebottlecafe.com

"Reserve early and often" advise admirers of this "excellent" New American BYO in "charming" Hopewell, where "getting a table is half the battle"; husband-wife team Aaron and Rory Philipson make "delightfully delicious use of local ingredients", while "friendly" servers work three "tight" but "cute" dining rooms.

	FOOD	DECOR	SERVICE	COST

Cafe Matisse ⓜ *Eclectic* — 27 | 25 | 26 | $66

Rutherford | 167 Park Ave. (bet. Highland Cross & Park Pl.) | 201-935-2995 | www.cafematisse.com

A "wow in all aspects", this "transcendent", "romantic" Rutherford BYO "hidden" behind a wine shop (where you can purchase *le vin*) "dazzles and delights" with its seasonally inspired Eclectic cuisine offered in grazing portions (aka 'Matisse Plates') that come in three or four courses that are "worth the very expensive price tags"; a "consistently attentive" staff, "tastefully appointed" interior (with hand-blown Murano glass chandeliers) and "plush" outdoor dining complete the "outstanding" experience.

Cafe Panache ⓩ *Eclectic* — 28 | 23 | 25 | $58

Ramsey | 130 E. Main St. (Franklin Tpke.) | 201-934-0030 | www.cafepanachenj.com

Chef-owner Kevin Kohler's "sublime and imaginative" Eclectic fare "continues to impress" and service remains "superb" at this "pricey" Ramsey Eclectic, whose "beautiful redecoration" "makes it even more delightful"; just make sure you "reserve well in advance" to enjoy the "jewel of a space", which is "consistently one of the best BYOs in Bergen County"; P.S. jackets suggested.

Cheesecake Factory *American* — 19 | 18 | 18 | $30

Hackensack | Riverside Square Mall | 197 Riverside Sq. (Hackensack Ave.) | 201-488-0330 ◑

Wayne | Willowbrook Mall | 1700 Willowbrook Blvd. (Rte. 46) | 973-890-1400

Edison | Menlo Park Mall | 455 Menlo Park Dr. (Rte. 1) | 732-494-7000

Freehold | Freehold Raceway Mall | 3710 Rte. 9 S. (bet. Rtes. 33 & 537) | 732-462-2872

Cherry Hill | Marketplace at Garden State Park | 931 Haddonfield Rd. (bet. Graham & Severn Aves.) | 856-665-7550
www.thecheesecakefactory.com

Mall crawlers are among those who mob this "busy", "noisy" chain that doles out "ginormous portions" of Americana from a menu "the size of New Jersey"; predictably, there's "cheesecake to die for" and less predictably, salads earn raves too, and though service can be "slow", that doesn't detract from the "great value" - hence the "crazy long" waits for a table.

Cucharamama ⓜ *S American* — 25 | 23 | 21 | $44

Hoboken | 233 Clinton St. (3rd St.) | 201-420-1700 | www.cucharamama.com
This "top-tier ethnic restaurant" in Hoboken from celeb-chef (and food historian) Maricel Presilla is a "work of art", with "pricey", "inventive" South American meals (including "concoctions from a wood-burning oven") as vivid as the "vibrant oil paintings" by her father that are on view; a "sexy bar scene" serving "tremendous drinks" enhances the "unique experience."

CulinAriane ⓩⓜ *American* — 27 | 19 | 24 | $55

Montclair | 33 Walnut St. (Pine St.) | 973-744-0533 | www.culinariane.com
"Reliably amazing" is the word on the New American cuisine at this "off-the-beaten-path" BYO in Montclair, courtesy of husband-and-wife team Michael and Ariane Duarte (pastry chef and executive chef/*Top Chef* contender, respectively); "warm, friendly" service and

| | FOOD | DECOR | SERVICE | COST |

a "cozy" if "cramped" setting also attract; P.S. it's "very hard to get a reservation" as it's open for dinner only, Wednesdays–Saturdays, with seasonal outdoor dining.

David Burke Fromagerie ⓜ *American* | 25 | 24 | 23 | $71 |

Rumson | 26 Ridge Rd. (Ave. of Two Rivers) | 732-842-8088 | www.fromagerierestaurant.com

"Renowned" chef-owner David Burke brings his "top-of-the-line" "magic" to this "Rumson landmark", offering "expensive but divine" New American fare distinguished by "intriguing flavor profiles" and "artistic presentation", as evidenced in "signatures" like "angry lobster" and "cheesecake lollipops"; most applaud the "lighter and brighter" "pretty room", but some note "amateurish" hiccups in the generally "polite" service.

DeLorenzo's Tomato Pies ⓜ *Pizza* | 27 | 12 | 17 | $17 |

Robbinsville | Washington Town Ctr. | 2350 Rte. 33 (bet. Lake Dr. & Robbinsville Edinburg Rd.) | 609-341-8480
Trenton | 530 Hudson St. (bet. Hudson Ct. & Swan St.) | 609-695-9534 ⌂
www.delorenzostomatopies.com

"You haven't really eaten pizza" – make that "tomato pie" – until you've tasted "thin-crust, old-fashioned, piping-hot heaven" at this BYO "Central Jersey institution"; some say the original, cash-only Trenton row house ("no decor, no bathroom", "no antipasti") offers "the true experience", while others shout "hooray!" for the Robbinsville offshoot, which boasts appetizers and restrooms and takes credit cards; either way, expect "interminable" weekend waits; P.S. whole pies only.

Ebbitt Room *American* | 27 | 26 | 26 | $63 |

Cape May | Virginia Hotel | 25 Jackson St. (bet. Beach Ave. & Carpenter Ln.) | 609-884-5700 | www.virginiahotel.com

For "fine dining at its best" in Cape May, "allow yourself to be spoiled" at this "elegant" and "romantic" spot in the Virginia Hotel, a "jewel" that "charms"; expect "perfectly prepared" New American fare and "fantastic" wine "impeccably" served in a "beautiful dining room."

elements *American* | - | - | - | E |

Princeton | 163 Bayard Ln. (bet. Birch & Leigh Aves.) | 609-924-0078 | www.elementsprinceton.com

Chef-owner Scott Anderson sees food as a canvas, painting plates and exciting palates at this soothe-the-senses, fine-dining Princeton beauty; his New American take on worldwide cooking is making him the talk of the tony Princeton restaurant scene for those lucky enough to snag the chef's table for the nightly nine-course tasting menu.

Fascino ⓩ *Italian* | 26 | 22 | 24 | $57 |

Montclair | 331 Bloomfield Ave. (bet. Grove & Willow Sts.) | 973-233-0350 | www.fascinorestaurant.com

"Unbeatable", "soulful" *cucina* plus "gracious service" make this family-run Montclair BYO Italian storefront a "primo" place "for a special night out"; chef Ryan DePersio deftly blends "traditional" cooking with "modern updates" and mom Cynthia's desserts justify the caloric "splurge"; it's "expensive", "parking isn't easy" and "getting a reservation is a challenge", but it's ultimately "worth it."

	FOOD	DECOR	SERVICE	COST

410 Bank Street *Caribbean/Creole* | 26 | 21 | 24 | $52 |

Cape May | 410 Bank St. (bet. Broad & Lafayette Sts.) | 609-884-2127
"Chef Henry Sing Cheng's song is as beautiful as ever" at this veteran Cape May Caribbean-Creole in a circa-1880 Victorian, where the "consistently amazing" dinners are "so good you can take them to the bank"; "top-tier" service helps temper "long waits" and "special-occasion" prices; P.S. it serves NJ wines but you can also BYO.

Frog and the Peach *American* | 26 | 24 | 24 | $62 |

New Brunswick | 29 Dennis St. (Hiram Sq.) | 732-846-3216 | www.frogandpeach.com
Still "one of the tops" after almost 30 years, this "venerable" New Brunswick New American "keeps getting better" thanks to chef Bruce Lefebvre's "inventive and surprising" food that "looks and tastes like a dream"; "polished, friendly service", an "excellent" wine list and "gorgeous surroundings" add to its aura, and while it's "expensive", the lunch and dinner prix fixe options make it "more affordable."

Liberty House Restaurant M *American* | 20 | 23 | 19 | $52 |

Jersey City | Liberty State Park | 76 Audrey Zapp Dr. (Freedom Way) | 201-395-0300 | www.libertyhouserestaurant.com
With "unobstructed views" of Lady Liberty and lower Manhattan, this Jersey City Traditional American in Liberty State Park is a "great place to impress out-of-town visitors or a special date"; though the "pricey" food draws mixed reviews ("wonderful" vs. "hit-or-miss"), most agree on the "great Sunday brunch."

Lorena's M *French* | 28 | 22 | 27 | $57 |

Maplewood | 168 Maplewood Ave. (Highland Pl.) | 973-763-4460 | www.restaurantlorena.com
Set "in the heart" of Maplewood, this French BYO is "a real gem, albeit a small one"; "sublime" food from chef Humberto Campos Jr., a "warm welcome" from his partner – the "courteous and efficient" host Lorena Perez – and "impeccable" service "make up for the inconvenience" of the "cramped" but "perfectly appointed oasis."

Mehndi M *Indian* | 24 | 25 | 22 | $48 |

Morristown | 88 Headquarters Plaza | 3 Speedwell Ave. (Park Pl.) | 973-871-2323 | www.mehtanirestaurantgroup.com
There's "a fancy vibe" – and prices to match – at this "modern", "elegant" Morristown Indian from the Mehtani Restaurant Group, where the "creative", "gourmet" Mughlai and Punjab fare is complemented by "innovative cocktails", and "outstanding" service adds to the "fantastic experience" (as do the henna tattoos on Friday and Saturday nights); P.S. the lunch buffet is a locals' "cheap office favorite."

Nicholas M *American* | 28 | 27 | 29 | $86 |

Middletown | 160 Rte. 35 S. (bet. Navesink River Rd. & Pine St.) | 732-345-9977 | www.restaurantnicholas.com
"Still the gold standard", this New American on the Middletown–Red Bank border is again ranked NJ's Most Popular as well as No. 1 for Food; run by chef/co-owner Nicholas Harary and wife Melissa, it's "near perfect" all around, from the "stellar cuisine" and "deep", "well-researched" wine list to the "polished but not pretentious" service and "contemporary", "understated elegant ambiance", enhanced by the "brilliant ad-

dition" of a "more casual" bar for small-plates dining and a four-seat chef's table; yes it's "expensive", but the $59 three-course dinner (one of several prix fixe options) is "a great value"; P.S. jacket suggested.

Ninety Acres at Natirar ⓜ *American*

- | - | - | E

Peapack | Natirar Resort & Spa | 2 Main St. (bet. Old Dutch Rd. & Ramapo Way) | 908-901-9500 | www.ninetyacres.com

A "gem" set in a restored carriage house at Natirar, the sprawling Peapack estate once owned by the King of Morocco and now being turned into a Virgin Spa resort, this New American is earning kudos for "superb" fare from chef David Felton (ex Pluckemin Inn), who emphasizes "fresh local ingredients" including produce from the on-site farm; part of a culinary center that includes a cooking school and bar/lounge, it also boasts an 800-label wine list and "knowledgeable" staff – not surprisingly, the "good word is spreading fast."

Nisi Estiatorio *Greek*

- | - | - | E

Englewood | 90 Grand Ave. (bet. Englewood Ave. & Garret Pl.) | 201-567-4700 | www.nisirestaurant.com

Chef John Piliouras moors classic Aegean specialties to French techniques at this elegant Englewood Greek; evocative of Mediterranean grottoes, the nautically inspired interior complements his deft treatment of whole fish, which diners can select from an artistic display; P.S. dinner served daily, lunch Mondays–Saturdays.

Peacock Inn *American*

- | - | - | E

Princeton | 20 Bayard Ln. (bet. Boudinot & Stockton Sts.) | 609-924-1707 | www.peacockinn.com

This beautiful, historic Princeton landmark where Albert Einstein and F. Scott Fitzgerald frolicked has emerged proud as a you-know-what from its transformation into a modern boutique hotel; in the elegant, comfortable restaurant, executive chef Manuel Perez, an alumnus of NYC's Le Bernardin and NJ's No. 1 Food winner, Nicholas, instills his New American fare with global twists, possibly best sampled in the five-course tasting menu, a relative bargain considering the expensive à la carte prices.

Piccola Italia ⓜ *Italian*

27 | 23 | 24 | $48

Ocean Township | 837 W. Park Ave. (bet. Rtes. 18 & 35) | 732-493-3090 | www.piccolaitalianj.com

"Phenomenal", "decadent" Italian fine dining at the hands of "talented" chef-owner Brian Gualtieri affords "the cachet of NYC" to a "quiet suburban" strip mall in Ocean; the "exceptional quality" extends to the "unbeatable" service, "superb" wine list, "comfortable" atmosphere and "top-notch" bar – all at an affordable price.

Pluckemin Inn *American*

26 | 27 | 26 | $74

Bedminster | 359 Rte. 206 S. (Pluckemin Way) | 908-658-9292 | www.pluckemininn.com

Delivering an "awesome experience from start to finish", this "high-class" Bedminster New American is set in a "stunning" re-creation of a 19th-century farmhouse featuring a "unique" three-story wine tower (the "magical" sommelier can "please even the most esoteric tastes"); surveyors salute "splendid" fare and "impeccable" service – just "make sure your charge card has plenty of room on it", or try the at-

FOOD | DECOR | SERVICE | COST

tached, "more affordable" Plucky bar; P.S. the Food score may not reflect a post-Survey chef change.

Ram's Head Inn Ⓜ American
25 | 26 | 25 | $63

Galloway | 9 W. White Horse Pike (bet. Ash & Taylor Aves.) | 609-652-1700 | www.ramsheadinn.com

"Refinement and elegance live" at this "old-school" "special-occasion" Traditional American establishment in Galloway; "superb" fare, "polished" service and "beautiful" decor add up to an "awesome" place to "spend your Atlantic City winnings"; P.S. jacket suggested.

Rat's Ⓜ French
25 | 28 | 25 | $64

Hamilton | Grounds for Sculpture | 16 Fairgrounds Rd. (Sculptors Way) | 609-584-7800 | www.ratsrestaurant.org

Nestled inside Hamilton's "near mystical" Grounds for Sculpture park – inspired by Monet's fabled Giverny – is this New French "gastronomic feast" with an "enchanting", "magical" ambiance; be sure to walk the grounds before or after your "exquisite", "expensive-but-worth-it" meal because admission is included, as is "five-star" service; the equally "amazing" cafe/lounge offers casual dining at reasonable prices; P.S. post-Survey management and chef changes may outdate the Food and Service scores.

Restaurant Latour Ⓜ American
25 | 24 | 24 | $76

Hamburg | Crystal Springs Resort | 1 Wild Turkey Way (Crystal Springs Rd.) | 973-827-0548 | www.crystalgolfresort.com

This "small and special" contemporary American with "quiet elegance" in Hamburg's Crystal Springs Resort is an "exquisite find" for its "first-class" fare by chef Michael Weisshaupt, "unhurried", "white-glove" service and "awesome" wine list (4,700 labels); overall, it's "worth selling your firstborn for"; P.S. open Thursdays–Sundays.

River Palm Terrace Steak
24 | 19 | 22 | $63

Edgewater | 1416 River Rd. (Palisade Terrace) | 201-224-2013
Fair Lawn | 41-11 Rte. 4 W. (Saddle River Rd.) | 201-703-3500
Mahwah | 209 Ramapo Valley Rd. (Rte. 17) | 201-529-1111
www.riverpalm.com

"Well-aged beef given proper respect", "fish as good as the steaks" and other "reliable" selections served in "huge portions" keep these North Jersey chophouses so "packed" that a reservation merely "grants you the right to be on the waiting list"; "each location has its own personality and service varies", but "all are loud" and offer "extensive wine lists" (have a few glasses to numb the "sticker shock").

Ruth's Chris Steak House Steak
25 | 22 | 23 | $64

Weehawken | Lincoln Harbor | 1000 Harbor Blvd. (19th St.) | 201-863-5100
Parsippany | Hilton Hotel | 1 Hilton Ct. (Campus Dr.) | 973-889-1400
Princeton | Forrestal Village Shopping Ctr. | 2 Village Blvd. (College Rd.) | 609-452-0041
www.ruthschris.com

It "might be a chain", but the "sizzling" butter-topped steaks and "white-linen" service at these "classic" chophouses offer "pure bliss" to carnivores who also appreciate the "huge" sides – and say the similarly sized tabs are "worth the splurge"; P.S. decor is "polished, if standardized", but the window seats at the Weehawken location offer a "great" view of NYC.

Saddle River Inn ⛱ Ⓜ *American/French* 28 | 26 | 26 | $65

Saddle River | 2 Barnstable Ct. (bet. Allendale Ave. & Saddle River Rd.) | 201-825-4016 | www.saddleriverinn.com

"Phenomenal" French-American cuisine, "first-class" service and a "romantic", "casually elegant" setting in a restored 19th-century barn make this Saddle River BYO a "treasure"; though some think the menu could "vary a bit more" and complain that "if you aren't a regular, you're invisible", most agree this "charming" spot is "as close to heaven as it gets in NJ" – but like heaven, it's tough to get into ("good luck getting a reservation").

Sagami Ⓜ *Japanese* 27 | 15 | 21 | $36

Collingswood | 37 Crescent Blvd. (bet. Collingswood Circle & Haddon Ave.) | 856-854-9773

"Don't judge a book by its cover" admonish fans undeterred by the "'70s decor" and "tight parking" at this Collingswood Japanese BYO where there are "lines out the door" for some of the "best sushi this side of Tokyo" and "high-quality" cooked items, including "hot sukiyaki" that's just the thing on a "cold winter evening"; the staff is "nice" and the atmosphere "interesting", but "claustrophobics" caution that the low ceilings make it "best for the 5-foot-8-and-under crowd."

Scalini Fedeli ⛱ *Italian* 27 | 25 | 26 | $73

Chatham | 63 Main St. (bet. Parrott Mill Rd. & Tallmadge Ave.) | 973-701-9200 | www.scalinifedeli.com

"Prepare to be transported" to "gastronomy heaven" via Michael Cetrulo's "exceptional" Chatham Italian, offering a $54 four-course prix fixe at dinner with "loads of options" (lunch is à la carte); though a few claim "the chef is spread too thin" and find his flagship "overpriced" and "stuffy", given the "impeccable" cuisine, "elegant atmosphere" and "fantastic" staff, the faithful majority declares it a "first-class operation."

Serenade *French* 28 | 25 | 26 | $72

Chatham | 6 Roosevelt Ave. (Main St.) | 973-701-0303 | www.restaurantserenade.com

Paeans resound for James Laird and Nancy Sheridan Laird's "serene oasis" in Chatham, where the "exceptional" French cuisine with a locally grown bent is "smart and sexy" and the ambiance "refined" – though you may need "a chest of gold bullion to settle the bill"; some say the "excellent" staff's occasional "haughty" attitude can strike a flat note, but they're drowned out by the chorus of devotees singing "top shelf in every way"; P.S. jacket suggested.

Tre Figlio *Italian* 27 | 21 | 25 | $51

Egg Harbor | 500 W. White Horse Pike (Mannheim Ave.) | 609-965-3303 | www.trefiglio.com

"In all respects" this "special", "out-of-the-way gem" is "worth the drive" to Egg Harbor for a "stellar", "upscale" Italian "experience" that includes "the best" pasta, a "huge" wine list, a "lovely" setting and "superb" service, all courtesy of the Cordivari family, of which son James is the chef; P.S. there's live entertainment Wednesdays–Saturdays.

	FOOD	DECOR	SERVICE	COST

Uproot ☒ *American*
- - - E

Warren | 9 Mt. Bethel Rd. (Mountain Blvd.) | 908-834-8194 |
www.uprootrestaurant.com

At this upscale venue in Warren, chef Anthony Bucco utilizes farm-fresh ingredients in seasonal contemporary American fare, which can be paired with selections from a well-curated wine list; the ultramodern space with rustic accents is highlighted by a whimsical uprooted tree hanging overhead.

Washington Inn *American*
27 26 26 $62

Cape May | 801 Washington St. (Jefferson St.) | 609-884-5697 |
www.washingtoninn.com

Setting "the standard" for "fine dining" in Cape May is this "class act" voted "excellent in all respects", from the "top-tier" Traditional American fare and "wonderful", "deep" wine list to the "lovely" dining rooms set in a "beautiful" old plantation home; a "staff that goes the extra mile" helps make the predictably "high prices" easier to digest.

Whispers *American*
27 24 25 $58

Spring Lake | Hewitt Wellington Hotel | 200 Monmouth Ave. (2nd Ave.) |
732-974-9755 | www.whispersrestaurant.com

"Civility at the Shore" and "quiet elegance" can be found at this "intimate" Spring Lake BYO in a "lovely" Victorian inn; "always on top of its game", with "interesting" New American fare that "delivers big taste" and a "polished", "gracious" staff that "pays attention to the details", this "special-occasion mainstay" may be "a bit steep" but it's "worth it" for a "memorable" meal.

New Orleans

TOP FOOD RANKING

Restaurant	Cuisine
__28__ Bayona	American
Stella!	American
Brigtsen's	Contemp. Louisiana
__27__ Clancy's	Creole
Royal China	Chinese
August	Continental/French
Patois	American/French
Bistro Daisy	American/Southern
Herbsaint	American/French
Commander's Palace	Creole
Cochon Butcher	Cajun
Lilette	French
Cypress	Creole
La Boca*	Argentinean/Steak
Coquette	French
Galatoire's	Creole/French
Gautreau's	American/French
MiLa	Contemp. Louisiana
Mr. John's	Steak
Dakota	American/Contemp. Louisiana

OTHER NOTEWORTHY PLACES

Acme Oyster	Seafood
Boucherie	Southern
Cochon	Cajun
Emeril's	Contemp. Louisiana
GW Fins	Seafood
Iris	American
Jacques-Imo's	Creole/Soul Food
K-Paul's	Cajun
La Provence	Creole/French
Le Meritage	American
Martinique	French
Mesón 923	Contemp. Louisiana/Spanish
Mosca's	Italian
Mr. B's	Contemp. Louisiana
One Restaurant	American
Pelican Club	American
Ralph's on the Park	Contemp. Louisiana
RioMar	Seafood
Upperline	Contemp. Louisiana
Vizard's	Contemp. Louisiana

* Indicates a tie with restaurant above

	FOOD	DECOR	SERVICE	COST

Acme Oyster House *Seafood*
24 | 15 | 20 | $26

French Quarter | 724 Iberville St. (bet. Bourbon & Royal Sts.) | 504-522-5973
Metairie | 3000 Veterans Memorial Blvd. (N. Causeway Blvd.) | 504-309-4056
Covington | 1202 N. Hwy. 190 (bet. Crestwood Blvd. & 17th Ave.) | 985-246-6155
www.acmeoyster.com

"Sit at the bar, chat with the shuckers" and savor "bivalve bliss" at this French Quarter "legend" that's "famous" for "plump", "briny" raw oysters (as well as "awesome" char-grilled ones) and "fried anything else"; the "long lines" of "tourists" can be a drawback, but "even the locals love" its "clean, cold" beauts, "frosty brews" and lively "banter" amid a "casual but electric" atmosphere bursting with "joie de vivre"; P.S. the Covington and Metairie offshoots "lack the color" of the original, but are still a "wonderful value."

August *Continental/French*
27 | 27 | 27 | $72

Central Business Dist. | 301 Tchoupitoulas St. (Gravier St.) | 504-299-9777 | www.rest-august.com

"One of the best chefs in the country", John Besh "takes New Orleans cuisine into the future" while nurturing its "soul", turning "local ingredients" into "spectacular", "mind-blowing" Continental–New French dishes (with an "out-of-this-world" tasting menu option) at his flagship CBD "masterpiece"; "smart" service and "beautiful" surroundings with "tall brick walls and windows" complete the "stellar" meal, so while the tab is "hefty", it's "oh so worth it" – plus the weekday lunch lets you indulge for "a bit less cash."

Bayona 🅱 *American*
28 | 26 | 26 | $59

French Quarter | 430 Dauphine St. (bet. Conti & St. Louis Sts.) | 504-525-4455 | www.bayona.com

The "ever-amazing" Susan Spicer crafts "sublime" New American meals that "make your heart sing" at this "high-end" French Quarter "winner", voted No. 1 for Food in New Orleans – and "that's saying something" in a city where eating is a "way of life"; set inside a "lovely", "historic house" with an "understated" ambiance, it boasts a "gorgeous" "tropical" patio, "top-notch" service and lunch that's a "true bargain" (featuring a "famous" duck sandwich), making it the "perennial choice" for an "unparalleled dining experience."

Bistro Daisy 🅱🅼 *American/Southern*
27 | 23 | 26 | $52

Uptown | 5831 Magazine St. (bet. Eleonore St. & Nashville Ave.) | 504-899-6987 | www.bistrodaisy.com

"Exciting", "elevated" "regional cuisine" delights diners at this "diminutive" but "marvelous" New American–Southern by the "husband-and-wife team" of chef Anton and Diane Schulte; its "unassuming" setting in a "handsomely renovated Uptown house" is "comfortable", the wine list "reasonable" and the service "engaging" and "accommodating", so regulars always feel "warm, welcome and well fed."

Boucherie 🅱🅼 *Southern*
26 | 19 | 23 | $34

Carrollton | 8115 Jeannette St. (Carrollton Ave.) | 504-862-5514 | www.boucherie-nola.com

"Nathanial Zimet's creations always hit the mark" affirm fans "impressed" by the chef/co-owner's "showstopping", "incredibly flavor-

| | FOOD | DECOR | SERVICE | COST |

ful" contemporary Southern cooking (capped off with "bacon brownies and Krispy Kreme bread pudding") at this "surprising" "joint" housed in a "cute", purple-accented Carrollton cottage; staffed by a "fantastic", "informed" crew, including bartenders whose "powerful" drinks "stand up to the wizardry of the kitchen", it's "ridiculously cheap for the quality", delivering one of the city's best "fine-food bargains."

Brigtsen's ☒Ⓜ *Contemp. Louisiana* | 28 | 23 | 28 | $57 |
Riverbend | 723 Dante St. (Maple St.) | 504-861-7610 | www.brigtsens.com
"Sensational" Contemporary Louisiana cuisine by chef Frank Brigtsen and a "charming", "exemplary" staff overseen by wife and manager Marna keep this "converted shotgun house" in Riverbend "filled with locals"; the "homey" space is "a bit tight", but most consider it worth the squeeze, the price and the "ride on the streetcar" for the "splendid" dinners topped off with "unforgettable" pecan pie.

Clancy's ☒ *Creole* | 27 | 22 | 26 | $52 |
Uptown | 6100 Annunciation St. (Webster St.) | 504-895-1111
A "who's who of New Orleans" stirs up a "vibrant" scene at this "traditional", slightly "pricey" Uptown "power hangout", "running into friends" and "swooning" over "superb" Creole "classics" (like smoked soft-shell crab) complemented by "generous drinks" and an "exhaustive" wine list; "hidden among family homes", its "out-of-sight" locale and "professional", "old-style" staff enhance its status as a "locals' darling", but stick to the "packed" downstairs, rather than the quiet, somewhat "dreary" upstairs, for prime "people-watching."

Cochon ☒ *Cajun* | 26 | 22 | 23 | $43 |
Warehouse District | 930 Tchoupitoulas St. (bet. Andrew Higgins Dr. & S. Diamond St.) | 504-588-2123 | www.cochonrestaurant.com
Sample a "nonstop highlight reel" of "evolved" Cajun fare celebrating "everything piggy", plus the kinds of sides "our grandmothers cooked on Sunday", at this "compulsory stop" in the Warehouse District by chef-owners Donald Link (Herbsaint) and Stephen Stryjewski; the "noisy", "modern" space with "upscale picnic decor" attracts "large groups" of "knowledgeable locals" – some "in suits and others in blue jeans" – who end the night with "a piece of pie and a shot of moonshine."

Cochon Butcher *Cajun* | 27 | 18 | 21 | $19 |
Warehouse District | 930 Tchoupitoulas St. (Andrew Higgins Dr.) | 504-588-7675 | www.cochonbutcher.com
"OMG, just go!" exclaim "pork lovers" who "bring home the bacon", "load up on boudin" and even "go quackers" for the duck pastrami sliders, all prepared with the "highest integrity" and "Cajun flair", at this "temple of swine dining" by Donald Link – basically a "wine bar, meat counter and sandwich shop mashed together" under the same Warehouse District roof as Cochon; it's ideal for a "casual" lunch or "offbeat dinner" with "walk-up service", so "linger awhile" or simply "grab 'n' go" to indulge in a "primal" feast.

Commander's Palace *Creole* | 27 | 28 | 27 | $64 |
Garden District | 1403 Washington Ave. (Coliseum St.) | 504-899-8221 | www.commanderspalace.com
"Restored to her original splendor" (with "whimsical" touches in the "formal dining room"), this Garden District "grande dame" – once

again voted Most Popular in New Orleans – is "always a celebration", whether for a "special evening" or "not-to-be-missed" Sunday jazz brunch "with the swells"; "superlative" Creole cuisine, "outstanding" service and "quintessential" Crescent City ambiance make it a "treat for the senses", and while a few tut that it's "touristy" and "expensive", few find fault with the "weekday special" of "25-cent martinis at lunch"; P.S. no shorts; jackets suggested for dinner.

Coquette *French*

27 | 25 | 24 | $45

Garden District | 2800 Magazine St. (Washington Ave.) | 504-265-0421 | www.coquette-nola.com

"Thriving" in the Garden District, this "dynamite" newcomer enamors guests with its "beautiful", "brilliant", "seasonal" French bistro fare (including "terrific small plates") by "innovative" "up-and-coming" chef Michael Stoltzfus (ex August); "luscious cocktails" and a "stylish" setting that's "atmospheric in that wonderful old New Orleans way" add to the "charm", so even if the "engaged" service "could use a tad more polish", most feel it "does everything right."

Cypress ⊠M *Creole*

27 | 20 | 24 | $40

Metairie | 4426 Transcontinental Dr. (W. Esplanade Ave.) | 504-885-6885 | www.restaurantcypress.com

A "hidden treasure" in a strip mall, this "upscale yet relaxed" "Metairie gem" provides "top-notch" contemporary Creole cuisine that "could go up against any" in the city; the food's "much better than the decor", but with the owners, chef Stephen and manager Katherine Huth, pouring on the "warm neighborhood" charm, those in-the-know "can't stay away."

Dakota, The ⊠M *American/Contemp. Louisiana*

27 | 22 | 24 | $49

Covington | 629 N. Hwy. 190 (¼ mi. north of I-12) | 985-892-3712

"First-class" for "fine dining on the North Shore", this "spacious" spot graces Covington with a "terrific" New American–Contemporary Louisiana menu showcasing "glorious" dishes (the "crabmeat and Brie soup alone is worth any cab fare") matched with an "intelligently chosen" wine list and served by an "experienced" staff; high prices are part of the package, but it's still a "leading" reason to take "the trip across the lake."

Emeril's *Contemp. Louisiana*

26 | 25 | 25 | $64

Warehouse District | 800 Tchoupitoulas St. (Julia St.) | 504-528-9393 | www.emerils.com

"Home base" of "superstar chef" Emeril Lagasse's culinary "empire", this Warehouse District "institution" is "still going strong" as an "expert" staff sets down a "bam-a-licious" lineup of "dazzling" Contemporary Louisiana plates that "add inches to the waistline on-site" ("save room" for that banana cream pie); the "classy" industrial digs feature a "ringside" chef's bar that's "a show in itself", and even with "loud" acoustics and "top-dollar" tabs, everybody "needs to go at least once."

Galatoire's M *Creole/French*

27 | 26 | 27 | $61

French Quarter | 209 Bourbon St. (Iberville St.) | 504-525-2021 | www.galatoires.com

"Bravo for tradition!" declare devotees of this "old-line" "national treasure" in the French Quarter, where "Friday lunches live up to their raucous reputation" as "upper-crust, extravagantly dressed" guests dine on "superior" Creole-French fare (particularly the "fabulous" seafood) and often "drink their way right into dinner"; boasting "tuxedo-clad" waiters who "have been there for generations" and a "classic" main-floor dining room replete with "black-and-white-checkered-tile", it's the "real deal" that's "ultra-New Orleans in every way"; P.S. jackets required after 5 PM and all-day Sunday; reservations only accepted upstairs.

Gautreau's ☒ *American/French*   27 | 25 | 26 | $58

Uptown | 1728 Soniat St. (Danneel St.) | 504-899-7397 | www.gautreausrestaurant.com

"Consummate restaurateur" Patrick Singley and "talented" chef Sue Zemanick deliver a "masterful" meal of "outstanding" New American–New French dishes at this "elegant, simple" "local favorite" housed in a refurbished "old pharmacy" Uptown; service is "professional and accessible", and while the "hideaway" digs can be "hard to find", it's "well worth the hunt" and the "upmarket" tabs for the "impressive" repast.

GW Fins *Seafood*   26 | 25 | 25 | $53

French Quarter | D.H. Holmes Apartments | 808 Bienville St. (bet. Bourbon & Dauphine Sts.) | 504-581-3467 | www.gwfins.com

"Fin-omenal" "twists" on the "freshest" catch are a "fish lover's delight" at this "upscale" French Quarter seafooder that "draws as many locals as tourists" for its "mouthwatering" specialties, including "velvety" lobster dumplings and "addictive" housemade biscuits; service is likewise "top-notch", and if a few fret that the "modern" decor has a "chain feel", others "love the clean lines" and "awesome" bar.

Herbsaint ☒ *American/French*   27 | 22 | 25 | $51

Warehouse District | 701 St. Charles Ave. (Girod St.) | 504-524-4114 | www.herbsaint.com

Chef/co-owner Donald Link's "imaginative" yet "down-to-earth haute cuisine" "shines" at this "consistently pleasurable" (and "not incredibly expensive") Warehouse District destination known for "outstanding" New American–New French small plates and "terrific" Sazeracs, served by a "savvy" staff; though tables are a bit "tight", the "light-filled room" affords a view of the "St. Charles streetcars as they rumble past", adding to the "rewarding experience."

Iris ☒ *American*   26 | 23 | 23 | $49

French Quarter | Bienville House | 321 N. Peters St. (bet. Bienville & Conti Sts.) | 504-299-3944 | www.irisneworleans.com

At this "attractive" New American in the French Quarter's Bienville House, "creative" chef/co-owner Ian Schnoebelen spins "exceptional" seasonal ingredients into "delectable" "cosmopolitan" cuisine; it's "more laid-back than other fine-dining establishments" and something of an "unsung star", but with "personal service" and "fresh" cocktails by the bar's "magician" mixologist to "make it even better", it's "a must-try (and try and try)."

Jacques-Imo's Café ☒ *Creole/Soul Food*   26 | 21 | 22 | $38

Carrollton | 8324 Oak St. (bet. Cambronne & Dante Sts.) | 504-861-0886 | www.jacquesimoscafe.com

Reviewers relish the "only-in-New Orleans" atmosphere of this "colorful" Carrollton joint where "dynamo" chef-owner Jacques Leonardi – a "unique character" presiding in a chef's jacket and "funny shorts" –

whips up "diet-buster" portions of "crunchy" fried chicken and other Creole soul food ("alligator cheesecake, anyone?") that's "the stuff of dreams"; the "ultrafunky" digs are "mobbed" and "lively to say the least", so "have patience" for the "long, long wait"; P.S. reservations taken for five or more only.

K-Paul's Louisiana Kitchen 🗷 *Cajun*   26 | 21 | 24 | $52

French Quarter | 416 Chartres St. (between Conti & St. Louis Streets) | 877-553-3401 | www.chefpaul.com

"Prepare to be wowed" at gastronomic "master" Paul Prudhomme's "high-end" Cajun "mecca" in the French Quarter, which remains a "defining" Crescent City destination centered on "perfectly crafted" "taste sensations" from exec chef Paul Miller, served up by an "efficient" team in a "bistro-type setting"; "yes, the tourists flock here", but "even after all these years" it "earns its reputation" as a "knockout" for "locals too."

La Boca 🗷 *Argentinean/Steak*   27 | 20 | 23 | $46

Warehouse District | 857 Fulton St. (St. Joseph St.) | 504-525-8205 | www.labocasteaks.com

"Succulent", "unique cuts of meat", "incredible" fries and "sensual" gnocchi add up to "perfection" at this "authentic", upscale Argentinean steakhouse (a sib of RioMar) that inspires carnivorous "cravings"; a "reasonable wine list" and "huge" plates are a bonus, and while the Warehouse District space is "small", an "excellent" staff providing "personal" attention enhances the "wonderful meal."

La Provence 🅼 *Creole/French*   27 | 28 | 27 | $54

Lacombe | 25020 Hwy. 190 (bet. Bremermann & Raymond Rds.) | 985-626-7662 | www.laprovencerestaurant.com

"Since John Besh and company took over" this "romantic" "retreat" "across the lake in Lacombe", it's been "hitting its stride as it returns to its roots", providing "fresh", "excellent country French" cooking with a Creole accent, complemented by a "superb" wine list; "outstanding" service and an "enticing" setting in a house that "could be transported whole to Provence" further elevate the "pricey" meal, making for an "experience like no other" (and a "tough drive back to New Orleans").

Le Meritage 🗷🅼 *American*   25 | 25 | 25 | $56

French Quarter | Maison Dupuy Hotel | 1001 Toulouse St. (Burgundy St.) | 504-522-8800 | www.lemeriterestaurant.com

"They really know their wine" at this "winning" New American in the French Quarter's Maison Dupuy Hotel, an oenophile's "paradise" where each "inventive" selection on the "exceptional" menu is available as a "small or large plate" paired with "carefully selected" vinos "by the glass or half glass"; the "knowledgeable" staff and "beautiful", ivory-hued space round out a "refreshing" "departure from the typical" that merits the expense.

Lilette 🗷🅼 *French*   27 | 24 | 24 | $51

Uptown | 3637 Magazine St. (Antonine St.) | 504-895-1636 | www.liletterestaurant.com

Exactly "what a neighborhood restaurant should be", this "inviting" Uptown bistro "succeeds" thanks to chef-owner John Harris' "ambitious" French menu based on "stellar ingredients", served amid "chic" surroundings with "stamped tin panels on the ceiling"; "fantastic" drinks, "sumptuous" desserts and "knowledgeable" service round out the "delightful" (if "noisy") lunches and dinners, so most "love" joining in the "Paris-on-Magazine" scene.

Martinique Bistro ⓜ *French*

25	23	22	$43

Uptown | 5908 Magazine St. (Eleonore St.) | 504-891-8495 | www.martiniquebistro.com

Chef Eric LaBouchere creates a "shining" seasonal menu of "sophisticated" seafood and other "innovative", "expertly prepared" French bistro dishes that deliver "great value" for the "quality" at this "romantic" Uptown "secret"; the "cozy" quarters on tree-lined Magazine Street are tended by a "pleasant" staff, and "if the weather's right" the "beautiful" courtyard "is the way to go."

Mesón 923 🖿ⓜ *Contemp. Louisiana/Spanish*

▽	27	28	26	$53

Warehouse District | 923 S. Peters St. (N. Diamond St.) | 504-523-9200 | www.meson923.com

"Rising-star" chef Chris Lynch (ex Emeril's) "rocks" at this "excellent newcomer" to the Warehouse District, creating "fantastic", "artistic" contemporary New Orleans cuisine (with Spanish accents) in an "urbane" duplex born from a "tasteful" renovation of the 1840s-vintage Diamond Street Market building; the "beautiful" balconied second-story dining room, "outstanding" service and "handcrafted" cocktails help ensure its upmarket clientele is "rewarded with a terrific meal."

MiLa *Contemp. Louisiana*

27	26	25	$56

Central Business Dist. | Renaissance Pere Marquette | 817 Common St. (bet. Baronne & Carondelet Sts.) | 504-412-2580 | www.milaneworleans.com

"Adventuresome without losing sight of a New Orleans sensibility", this "modern", "upscale" destination in a CBD hotel offers "marvelously inventive, well-executed" Contemporary Louisiana fare, prepared by married chef-owners Allison Vines-Rushing and Slade Rushing and presented by a "knowledgeable" staff; with its "sleek" dining room, "hip bar" and "excellent, affordable" wine list, many consider it a "don't-miss", especially for the "bargain" prix fixe lunch.

Mosca's 🖿ⓜ⌷ *Italian*

26	12	20	$42

Avondale | 4137 Hwy. 90 W. (Live Oak Blvd.) | 504-436-9942 | www.moscasrestaurant.com

"A standard-setter for generations", this "unique" Avondale "outpost" is a circa-1946 "time warp" lodged in an "ancient roadhouse" and famed for family-style platters of "out-of-this-world" Italian-Creole cooking, all "homemade" with "no shortage of garlic"; "decor is an afterthought" and the "trek" "to Nowheresville" is "quite an adventure", but "the food justifies it" as long as you "wear loose-fitting clothes" and carry a "wad of cash" (they "don't take plastic").

Mr. B's Bistro *Contemp. Louisiana*

25	24	25	$47

French Quarter | 201 Royal St. (Iberville St.) | 504-523-2078 | www.mrbsbistro.com

The Brennan clan "gets an A+" for this "upbeat" French Quarter "star", an "all-time" "local favorite" known for the "consistently high quality" of its "delicious" Contemporary Louisiana fare, such as "fab" gumbo ya-ya and "finger-lickin'" BBQ shrimp that "can't be beat"; "gracious" servers oversee "upscale" surroundings where the "energetic" vibe is perfect for power-lunching, and it's a "price performer" to boot – "*cher,* it doesn't get much better than this."

Mr. John's Ristorante ☒Ⓜ *Steak*   27 | 20 | 24 | $48

Lower Garden Dist. | 2111 St. Charles Ave. (bet. Jackson Ave. & Josephine St.) | 504-679-7697 | www.mrjohnssteakhouse.com

Steaks "like butter" "rival the best anywhere" at this Lower Garden District meatery "right on St. Charles Avenue", an "old-fashioned" chophouse that bolsters its "excellent" beef with a lineup of "terrific" Italian dishes; the "intimate" "warmth" of the "tile-floor" setting is heightened by a "friendly staff", and while carnivores concede they'd "never call the place cutting-edge", they still "could eat here every night."

One Restaurant & Lounge ☒ *American*   26 | 20 | 23 | $40

Riverbend | 8132 Hampson St. (bet. Carrollton Ave. & Dublin St.) | 504-301-9061 | www.one-sl.com

"Inventive" chef/co-owner Scott Snodgrass (ex Clancy's) "keeps up with the changing times" at this "small", somewhat "hidden" Riverbend New American, where the open kitchen "delights" with "refreshing" seasonal cuisine and the "courteous" servers "know their stuff"; the "casual", stripped-down space that's "more NYC than NOLA" may "leave a little to be desired", but area admirers agree the "amazing quality" and "value" "save the day."

Patois Ⓜ *American/French*   27 | 23 | 23 | $51

Uptown | 6078 Laurel St. (Webster St.) | 504-895-9441 | www.patoisnola.com

"A top spot for serious foodies" (as well as "*Treme* fans"), this "popular" "Uptown gem" by "cutting-edge" chef/co-owner Aaron Burgau presents "inspired", "deftly" prepared French–New American dishes that make for "magnificent" meals with "semi-casual neighborhood appeal"; add in "pleasing" brasserie-style digs, "outstanding martinis" and a "hip" yet "solicitous" staff tending to the "noisy" "thirtysomething" crowd, and many feel it defines the "new New Orleans."

Pelican Club *American*   26 | 25 | 25 | $52

French Quarter | 312 Exchange Pl. (Bienville St.) | 504-523-1504 | www.pelicanclub.com

Away from the "hustle and bustle" of the rest of the Quarter, this "delicious" "find" from chef-owner Richard Hughes "aims high and hits the target" with "superior" New American fare that shows off an "imaginative" "edge" ("ever had a seafood martini?") in "subdued", appropriately "clublike" quarters bedecked with tony "art on the walls"; add an "accommodating" staff to make you "feel welcome", and it's an "elegant" "winner" "for all seasons."

Ralph's on the Park *Contemp. Louisiana*   25 | 27 | 26 | $48

Mid-City | 900 City Park Ave. (N. Alexander St.) | 504-488-1000 | www.ralphsonthepark.com

"What a lovely setting" sigh surveyors taking in "the scenery" at this "civilized" Mid-City haven where a "wonderful view" overlooking "the great oaks in City Park" complements "mighty fine" French-inflected Contemporary Louisiana cuisine and "equally impressive" service; sporting an "awesome balcony", the "beautifully designed" space is "delightful" for Sunday brunch or a "special occasion", rounding out "another stellar Brennan" entry that's well "worth the cash."

RioMar ☒ *Seafood* `25` `20` `23` `$43`

Warehouse District | 800 S. Peters St. (Julia St.) | 504-525-3474 | www.riomarseafood.com

"Seafood lovers" adore this "cool" Warehouse District Spaniard where "exceptional" ceviches head up a "rockin'" roster focusing on the "freshest" fish "prepared with a Latin touch", courtesy of "imaginative" chef/co-owner Adolfo Garcia; with its "attentive, smart" staff, "unfussy" brick-and-beam space and "lively" atmosphere right out of "Barcelona", it fills an "unusual" "niche" with "no folderol" – so "what's not to like?"

Royal China *Chinese* `27` `15` `21` `$25`

Metairie | 600 Veterans Memorial Blvd. (Aris Ave.) | 504-831-9633 | www.royalchinarest.com

"Fabulous dim sum" (served all day) and other "fresh", "incredible" dishes distinguish this affordable Metairie mainstay cooking up some of the "best Chinese in greater New Orleans"; "accommodating" owner Shirley Lee "knows everyone who comes in", so even though the plain old room "gets crowded", "warm, personal" service adds to the "remarkable value."

Stella! *American* `28` `26` `27` `$73`

French Quarter | Hotel Provincial | 1032 Chartres St. (bet. St. Philip & Ursuline Sts.) | 504-587-0091 | www.restaurantstella.com

"Star" chef-owner Scott Boswell takes "top-tier ingredients" and orchestrates a "culinary experience of epic proportions" with his "daring" New American dinners that "thrill", served with "expertise, style" and "white gloves" at this "foodie" "destination" on a "quiet stretch of the Quarter"; the "intimate" room was refurbished post-Survey with exposed brick and a more contemporary design, and while the check remains "regal", most feel it's justified by the "unforgettable" meal.

Upperline ☒ *Contemp. Louisiana* `26` `24` `26` `$49`

Uptown | 1413 Upperline St. (bet. Prytania St. & St. Charles Ave.) | 504-891-9822 | www.upperline.com

Its "devoted following" "will sure miss" chef Ken Smith (who departed mid-Survey), but this "one-of-a-kind" Uptowner carries on with its "sumptuous" Contemporary Louisiana cuisine that marries "traditional and creative" flavors under the aegis of "eccentric" owner and "hostess supreme" JoAnn Clevenger, who "defines the concept of hospitality"; occupying a "charmingly renovated" 1877 home "filled to the rafters" with "quirky" "native" artwork, it's a "memorable" "fixture" hereabouts, so "don't pass up the chance."

Vizard's ☒ *Contemp. Louisiana* `26` `21` `23` `$53`

Uptown | 5015 Magazine St. (Robert St.) | 504-895-2246 | www.vizards.net

"A real go-to" for "cutting-edge cuisine", "talented" chef-owner Kevin Vizard's "superb" Uptown namesake "consistently" hits "new heights" with "sophisticated but substantial" Contemporary Louisiana cooking that's a "rare treat"; with "attentive" servers providing "hospitality galore" in a "small" but "swanky" space lined with paintings by the chef's sister, it's typically "packed" and "swinging" with patrons who shrug off the "expensive" tabs.

New York City

TOP FOOD RANKING

	Restaurant	Cuisine
29	Le Bernardin	French/Seafood
28	Per Se	American/French
	Daniel	French
	Jean Georges	French
	Sushi Yasuda	Japanese
	La Grenouille	French
	Gramercy Tavern	American
	Eleven Madison Park	French
27	Bouley	French
	Blue Hill	American
	Gotham B&G	American
	Peter Luger	Steak
	Mas	American
	Degustation	French/Spanish
	Picholine	French/Mediterranean
	Marea	Italian/Seafood
	L'Atelier/Joël Robuchon	French
	Il Mulino	Italian
	Masa/Bar Masa	Japanese
	Babbo	Italian
	Café Boulud	French
	Di Fara	Pizza
	Momofuku Ko	American
	Tanoreen	Mediterranean
	Roberto	Italian

OTHER NOTEWORTHY PLACES

ABC Kitchen	American
Al Di La	Italian
Annisa	American
Aquagrill	Seafood
Balthazar	French
Buddakan	Asian
Del Posto	Italian
Dovetail	American
Gari/Sushi	Japanese
Grocery	American
Lincoln	Italian
Mark	American
Milos	Greek/Seafood
Modern	American/French
Nobu	Japanese
River Café	American
Sasabune	Japanese
Scalini Fedeli	Italian
SHO Shaun Hergatt	French

Sripraphai	Thai
Sugiyama	Japanese
Telepan	American
Trattoria L'incontro	Italian
Union Square Cafe	American
Wallsé	Austrian

ABC Kitchen *American*

24 | 23 | 23 | $55

Flatiron | ABC Carpet & Home | 35 E. 18th St. (bet. B'way & Park Ave. S.) | 212-475-5829 | www.abckitchennyc.com

The "locavore concept" gets a "smart take" via Jean-Georges Vongerichten at this Flatiron newcomer in ABC Carpet; it serves a "super-fresh", "haute green" seasonal menu of "farm-to-table" New American dishes, delivered by an "informed" team and set in a "white-washed", "country-chic" room; cheap no, worth it yes.

Al Di La *Italian*

27 | 19 | 23 | $47

Park Slope | 248 Fifth Ave. (Carroll St.) | Brooklyn | 718-783-4565 | www.aldilatrattoria.com

Al di "locals" laud this Park Slope, Brooklyn, trattoria where the "hearty, complex" Venetian specialties served by a "cordial" crew are a "huge treat" – "especially at these prices"; but while the cooking leaves most "blissed out", the "no-reservations policy" translates into "brutal waits", so regulars "get there early" or "go for lunch."

Annisa *American*

28 | 24 | 26 | $77

W Village | 13 Barrow St. (bet. 7th Ave. S. & W. 4th St.) | 212-741-6699 | www.annisarestaurant.com

Now fully "recovered" after a fire, this "intimate" West Villager show-cases the "exquisite" New American cooking of "masterful" chef Anita Lo; "stylish" new decor and "terrific service" round out a "first-class" experience with prices to match.

Aquagrill *Seafood*

26 | 19 | 23 | $60

SoHo | 210 Spring St. (6th Ave.) | 212-274-0505 | www.aquagrill.com

With its "wicked fresh" fish and "spectacular raw bar" stocked with "more oysters than Narragansett Bay", this "genial", 15-year-old SoHo enclave is "hard to beat" for "first-rate", "fairly priced" seafood; it's often "crazy busy" with finatics who've fallen for it "hook, line and sinker."

Babbo ❷ *Italian*

27 | 23 | 25 | $79

G Village | 110 Waverly Pl. (bet. MacDougal St. & 6th Ave.) | 212-777-0303 | www.babbonyc.com

"Still a wow", the Batali-Bastianich boys' "boffo" Village "linchpin" is "always on" with "transcendent" Italian cooking, "primo" wines and "well-informed service"; the handsome restored carriage house quarters are always "jammed" with "cacophonic" crowds, who say that the "hassle to get a table" and the check afterwards are "beyond worth it."

Balthazar ❷ *French*

23 | 23 | 20 | $56

SoHo | 80 Spring St. (bet. B'way & Crosby St.) | 212-965-1414 | www.balthazarny.com

"Unabashedly fabulous", Keith McNally's "grand pillar of SoHo" is a "like-Paris-used-to-be" brasserie whose "infectious allure" attracts everyone from "celebs" to "out-of-towners" with its "scrumptious"

| | FOOD | DECOR | SERVICE | COST |

Gallic eats and "big, bright, bustling" space; it's "always buzzing", even in the AM when regulars relish its "breakfast of champions."

Blue Hill *American*
27 | 23 | 27 | $82

G Village | 75 Washington Pl. (bet. MacDougal St. & 6th Ave.) | 212-539-1776 | www.bluehillfarm.com

The "farm-to-table" philosophy is in full bloom at Dan Barber's "civilized" Villager where uncommon "respect for ingredients" translates into "simply sublime" American cooking; its "earthy" ethos is echoed in the "warm" environs and "knowledgeable" service, and though undeniably "expensive", the biggest hurdle is scoring a reservation – especially since "Barack and Michelle" had dinner.

Bouley ● *French*
27 | 27 | 26 | $102

TriBeCa | 163 Duane St. (Hudson St.) | 212-964-2525 | www.davidbouley.com

On the rise again, David Bouley's "dazzling" TriBeCa flagship is "elegance personified", from its "impeccable" French country cooking to the "opulent", "no-expense-spared" setting and "seamless service"; those who "can't afford it in this economy" opt for the $36 prix fixe lunch, a "remarkable value" and perhaps the "best show in town."

Buddakan ● *Asian*
24 | 27 | 22 | $65

Chelsea | 75 Ninth Ave. (bet. 15th & 16th Sts.) | 212-989-6699 | www.buddakannyc.com

The decor's a "total knockout" at Stephen Starr's "dazzling" Chelsea "never-ending party", a "huge", "over-the-top" double-decker where "fashionable" "young" things toy with "expensive", "glammed-up" Asian dishes, "deftly" served by a "super" crew; but some find the "cacophonous" "bacchanal" "more theater than restaurant."

Café Boulud *French*
27 | 24 | 26 | $82

E 70s | Surrey Hotel | 20 E. 76th St. (bet. 5th & Madison Aves.) | 212-772-2600 | www.danielnyc.com

It's "first class all the way" at Daniel Boulud's "*extraordinaire*" Uptown annex where Gavin Kaysen's "heavenly" French cuisine, "spectacular" wines, "sophisticated" setting and "cosseting" service draw a "well-heeled" UES crowd; sure, the "prices are not 'cafe'", but the $35 prix fixe lunch is accessible to "mere mortals."

Daniel ☒ *French*
28 | 28 | 28 | $137

E 60s | 60 E. 65th St. (bet. Madison & Park Aves.) | 212-288-0033 | www.danielnyc.com

When it comes to "jacket-required", "special-occasion" dining, star chef Daniel Boulud's eponymous East Side flagship is the "gold standard" thanks to "perfection-on-a-plate" New French cooking, a "superb" wine list and "service with the precision of a symphony orchestra"; in short, such "seamless decadence" "should be on everyone's bucket list" as "you will leave your table richer – despite the bill"; P.S. the main room is prix fixe only, while the more casual lounge is à la carte.

Degustation *French/Spanish*
27 | 21 | 25 | $74

E Village | 239 E. Fifth St. (bet. 2nd & 3rd Aves.) | 212-979-1012 | www.degustationnyc.com

"Counter seating" gets a "foodie" spin at Jack and Grace Lamb's "stunning" East Village tasting bar where the "lucky few" experience "theater *and* a meal", as they watch the chef compose "sublime" Franco-Spanish small plates; "attention-to-detail" service rounds out the "one-of-a-kind" dining experience that leaves patrons "happy", despite the "expensive" denouement.

Del Posto *Italian*   26 | 26 | 25 | $94

Chelsea | 85 10th Ave. (bet. 15th & 16th Sts.) | 212-497-8090 | www.delposto.com

The "Batali-Bastianich dynasty" provides an experience that's "as much opera as restaurant" at this Way West Chelsea "luxe Italian" where the "divine", "complex" cooking meets its match in the "spectacular wine list"; "perfect" service and a "drop-dead", "marble-and-mahogany" setting (like the Excelsior in Rome) make fans "feel warm all over", even if it would be cheaper to fly there.

Di Fara Ⓜ🏴 *Pizza*   27 | 3 | 8 | $17

Midwood | 1424 Ave. J (15th St.) | Brooklyn | 718-258-1367 | www.difara.com

This Midwood, Brooklyn, "mecca" has pilgrims raving about "rockstar" Dom DeMarco's "work-of-art" pizzas and tolerating the circa-1964 "fluorescent"-and-"Formica" decor; waits are "eternal", but fans say it's worth it to sample "di-best."

Dovetail *American*   26 | 22 | 25 | $72

W 70s | 103 W. 77th St. (Columbus Ave.) | 212-362-3800 | www.dovetailnyc.com

The UWS takes a giant "culinary leap forward" via John Fraser's "world-class" New American duplex offering "incredibly tasty" food, "seamless" service and an "understated" setting; altogether, it's a "top-notch experience" that more than justifies the "East Side prices"; P.S. Sunday 'suppa' is a "fantastic bargain."

Eleven Madison Park 🅂 *French*   28 | 27 | 27 | $163

Flatiron | 11 Madison Ave. (24th St.) | 212-889-0905 | www.elevenmadisonpark.com

Everything an "upscale New York City restaurant should be", Danny Meyer's "knockout" New French off Madison Square Park in the Flatiron District is set in a "splendid" deco bank space that "makes a grand stage" for chef Daniel Humm's "world-class" work, shuttled by hospitable servers; though the prix fixe–only meals come with "soaring" price tags, there's agreement that such "pure elegance" is "worth every penny."

Gari *Japanese*   27 | 15 | 21 | $83

W 70s | 370 Columbus Ave. (bet. 77th & 78th Sts.) | 212-362-4816

Sushi of Gari ◑ *Japanese*
E 70s | 402 E. 78th St. (bet. 1st & York Aves.) | 212-517-5340

Sushi of Gari 46 ◑ *Japanese*
W 40s | 347 W. 46th St. (bet. 8th & 9th Aves.) | 212-957-0046
www.sushiofgari.com

The "gold-standard omakase" is the "way to go" at this "outstanding" Japanese trio where "master" chef Gari Sugio "astounds" sushi aficionados with "inventive", "pristine" morsels; despite "austere" quarters, the "revolutionary tastes" here are well "worth paying the arm and the leg."

Gotham Bar & Grill *American*

27 | 25 | 26 | $79

G Village | 12 E. 12th St. (bet. 5th Ave. & University Pl.) | 212-620-4020 | www.gothambarandgrill.com

"Still wowing" Gotham "after all these years", this "simply marvelous" Villager strikes all the "right chords", from "master chef" Alfred Portale's "glorious", "towering" New American dishes to the "soaring" setting and "exemplary" service; it's worth the "zillion-dollar tabs" for such a "thoroughly enjoyable", "first-class experience", though bargain-hunters tout its "amazing" $31 lunch.

Gramercy Tavern *American*

28 | 26 | 27 | $112

Flatiron | 42 E. 20th St. (bet. B'way & Park Ave. S.) | 212-477-0777 | www.gramercytavern.com

"Firmly established as one of the city's finest" (and again voted Most Popular), Danny Meyer's "perfecto" Flatiron "powerhouse" dazzles thanks to chef Michael Anthony's "dash-of-panache" New American cuisine, "tone-perfect" service and a "flower-festooned", "country-chic" setting that "oozes charm"; it's certainly worth the "steep prices" in the "stately", prix fixe-only main room, though the front bar is a "wonderful" alternative that "will save you some bucks."

Grocery, The 🗟 Ⓜ *American*

26 | 17 | 25 | $61

Carroll Gardens | 288 Smith St. (bet. Sackett & Union Sts.) | Brooklyn | 718-596-3335 | www.thegroceryrestaurant.com

"Consistently brilliant", "locavore"-leaning New Americana makes this Carroll Gardens, Brooklyn, spot a top "contender" in the "lively Smith Street scene"; a "beautiful garden" eases the squeeze in the minimalist, "matchbox"-esque dining room, while "personal attention" from a "gracious" staff renders the "splurge"-worthy tabs more palatable.

Il Mulino 🗟 *Italian*

27 | 19 | 24 | $87

G Village | 86 W. Third St. (bet. Sullivan & Thompson Sts.) | 212-673-3783 | www.ilmulino.com

"Voluminous", "voluptuous" dining is the calling card of this "one-of-a-kind" Village Italian where the "stunning" meals begin with a "bounty of freebies" served by a "marvelous staff" in black tie; despite soaring prices, it's always "jam-packed" and "ridiculously hard" to get into, so go at lunchtime when both access and prices are "easier."

Jean Georges 🗟 *French*

28 | 27 | 28 | $127

W 60s | Trump Int'l Hotel | 1 Central Park W. (bet. 60th & 61st Sts.) | 212-299-3900 | www.jean-georges.com

"Everything it's cracked up to be", Jean-Georges Vongerichten's "magical" Columbus Circle New French is a "pleasure all the way" from the "inventive", "wow-inducing" cuisine to the understatedly elegant "modernist" decor and service that "silently anticipates your wants"; all that "luxe" makes the "splurge"-worthy tabs easier to digest, while the $29 prix fixe lunch is quite probably NYC's best dining value.

La Grenouille 🗟 *French*

28 | 28 | 28 | $109

E 50s | 3 E. 52nd St. (bet. 5th & Madison Aves.) | 212-752-1495 | www.la-grenouille.com

NYC's "surviving grande dame" of "traditional haute French" cuisine, Charles Masson's Midtown "treasure" remains the "essence" of "luxe" with its "flawless" cooking, "splendid" setting bedecked with "flowers galore" and black-tie service fit for "Louis XIV"; it's "worth the big bucks" to be "swept away", though you can have the "bargain" $29 prix fixe lunch in the charming upstairs "artist's studio."

L'Atelier de Joël Robuchon *French*   27 | 25 | 27 | $128

E 50s | Four Seasons Hotel | 57 E. 57th St. (bet. Madison & Park Aves.) | 212-829-3844 | www.fourseasons.com

Most maintain a "front-row seat" at the counter "is the way to go" at "über-chef" Joël Robuchon's "opulent" "gastronomic experience", which "inspires and entertains" with its "ingenious", Japanese-accented French small plates and air of "true luxury"; it's designed to "knock your socks off", but given the "exorbitant price tag" ("bring your first-born"), a few say they "expected more."

Le Bernardin ⓩ *French/Seafood*   29 | 27 | 28 | $146

W 50s | 155 W. 51st St. (bet. 6th & 7th Aves.) | 212-554-1515 | www.le-bernardin.com

"You've reached the top of the line" at this Midtown "champ", once again voted NYC's No. 1 for Food, a "reserved", art-filled "temple" co-owned by the lovely Maguy LeCoze and "perfectionist" chef Eric Ripert, where diners "rejoice" over "unmatched" French seafood and "discreetly" "synchronized" service; prices are "heady" (prix fixe only dinner starts at $112), but you can "save a few bucks" by going at lunch; P.S. the "small" upstairs rooms are "nice for a private party."

Lincoln *Italian*   - | - | - | VE

W 60s | Lincoln Ctr. | 142 W. 65th St. (bet. Amsterdam Ave. & B'way) | 212-359-6500 | www.patinagroup.com

This striking, showstopping Modern Italian addition to Lincoln Center inhabits a freestanding glass wedge beside a reflecting pool, with a sloping, grass-planted roof that doubles as a picnic perch; the room - under a curved wood ceiling with windows on all sides - is centered around a glass-walled kitchen, whose daily changing, market-based menu from chef Jonathan Benno (ex Per Se) is served in the main area, lounge, bar or on the plaza.

Marea *Italian/Seafood*   27 | 26 | 25 | $96

W 50s | 240 Central Park S. (bet. B'way & 7th Ave.) | 212-582-5100 | www.marea-nyc.com

Co-owners Chris Cannon and chef Michael White turn "the wow factor" way up for "sophisticated diners" at this "sumptuous" CPS slice of "la dolce vita" offering "transcendent" seafood-focused Italian cuisine; "impeccable" service and "opulent" "modern" surroundings complete the "breathtaking" experience.

Mark, The ❶ *American*   24 | 24 | 22 | $73

E 70s | Mark Hotel | 25 E. 77th St. (bet. 5th & Madison Aves.) | 212-606-3030 | www.themarkrestaurantnyc.com

"The UES has met its match" in Jean-Georges Vongerichten's "upscale" newcomer to the Mark Hotel, which regales "chic" Park to Fifth sorts with a "plush" layout and a "top-notch" menu mixing gourmet pizza and burgers with a raw bar and "high-end" New American fare; it's "already a favorite" with a "buzzy" "bar scene" - just "be prepared for the bill."

	FOOD	DECOR	SERVICE	COST

Mas ❶ *American*

27 | 24 | 26 | $87

W Village | 39 Downing St. (bet. Bedford & Varick Sts.) | 212-255-1790 |
www.masfarmhouse.com

"One to remember", this "intimate", "understated" New American
"represents the best of the Village" with "innovative" chef Galen
Zamarra's "masterful" market-driven cuisine and "effortlessly" "courteous" service; though it's still something of a "secret gem", for those
willing to "run up a notable tab" it's an "incredible experience."

Masa ⊠ *Japanese*

27 | 24 | 26 | $520

W 60s | Time Warner Ctr. | 10 Columbus Circle, 4th fl. (60th St. at B'way) |
212-823-9800

Bar Masa ⊠ *Japanese*

W 60s | Time Warner Ctr. | 10 Columbus Circle, 4th fl. (60th St. at B'way) |
212-823-9800
www.masanyc.com

Yes, it's "masa-vely expensive", but "save up" because the TWC's
"reigning king" of "high-end Japanese" is an "inimitable" "church of
sushi" where renowned chef Masayoshi Takayama presents his "exquisite" prix fixes (starting at $400) in "luxurious", "Zen-like" surroundings;
while "still not cheap", the "sedate" next-door bar's à la carte menu
offers "a glimpse" of the same "exceptional" fare at a lower price.

Milos, Estiatorio ❶ *Greek/Seafood*

27 | 24 | 23 | $81

W 50s | 125 W. 55th St. (bet. 6th & 7th Aves.) | 212-245-7400 |
www.milos.ca

"If it swims, they have it" displayed on ice, ready to be "perfectly
grilled" at this "energetic" Midtown Greek "seafood-lover's dream";
add the "airy" "resortlike" space manned by a "knowledgeable" crew
and one might conclude "the gods of Olympus don't have it this good";
P.S. to control "way-high" by-the-pound pricing, consider making a
meal of the "fabulous appetizers."

Modern, The ⊠ *American/French*

26 | 27 | 25 | $114

W 50s | Museum of Modern Art | 9 W. 53rd St. (bet. 5th & 6th Aves.) |
212-333-1220 | www.themodernnyc.com

"Art on a plate" with art as a backdrop makes for a *très* sophisticated"
meal at Danny Meyer's MoMA "triumph", where "splendid" staffers
ferry Gabriel Kreuther's "refined", "luxury"-priced French–New
American cuisine to a "chic" crowd; the venue boasts two "gorgeous"
options: the "formal", prix fixe–only, jacket-required dining room overlooking the museum's sculpture garden or the "lively", comparatively
"less-expensive" front bar/cafe.

Momofuku Ko *American*

27 | 18 | 23 | $163

E Village | 163 First Ave. (bet. 10th & 11th Sts.) | 212-475-7899 |
www.momofuku.com

It's "heaven on a barstool" say the "fortunate" few who've snagged a
near-"impossible" online rez at David Chang's "austere" East Village
"crown jewel", where a "sublime", "super-inventive" multicourse parade of Asian-accented New Americana is "masterfully prepared" in
full view of the 12-capacity crowd; you "pay a price" for the privilege
($125, prix fixe–only), and the seating's "most uncomfortable", but
any "die-hard foodie" "must eat here."

	FOOD	DECOR	SERVICE	COST

Nobu *Japanese* | 26 | 23 | 23 | $81 |

TriBeCa | 105 Hudson St. (Franklin St.) | 212-219-0500

Nobu 57 ◐ *Japanese*

W 50s | 40 W. 57th St. (bet. 5th & 6th Aves.) | 212-757-3000

Nobu, Next Door *Japanese*

TriBeCa | 105 Hudson St. (bet. Franklin & N. Moore Sts.) | 212-334-4445
www.noburestaurants.com

Nobu Matsuhisa offers NYers three "upbeat", "celeb-peppered" venues in which to sample his Japanese-Peruvian culinary "ingenuity": the "still-fabulous", "tough-to-reserve" TriBeCa flagship, its "more relaxed", "cheaper" next-door adjunct and the "classy" newer Midtown outpost; it's "expensive", but "pro" service and "dazzling" decor ensure it's "worth every Benjamin."

Per Se *American/French* | 28 | 28 | 29 | $303 |

W 60s | Time Warner Ctr. | 10 Columbus Circle, 4th fl. (60th St. at B'way) | 212-823-9335 | www.perseny.com

"Words aren't adequate" to describe Thomas Keller's "food-lover's paradise" in the TWC, a "once-in-a-lifetime experience" hailed for its "utterly professional" service and $275 prix fixe-only "four-hour cavalcade" of "perfectly prepared", "divine" French–New American dishes presented in a "beautiful", "minimalist" room with views over Central Park; yes, the bill is "shocking" but "worth every penny" – especially "if you can't make it to Napa" to its sister, the French Laundry; P.S. à la carte small-plates dining is available in the salon.

Peter Luger Steak House ⊄ *Steak* | 27 | 15 | 20 | $78 |

Williamsburg | 178 Broadway (Driggs Ave.) | Brooklyn | 718-387-7400 | www.peterluger.com

"The Godfather of steakhouses", this "essential" Williamsburg, Brooklyn, "institution" is as "aged to perfection" as its slabs of "sizzling porterhouse" sliced by "sarcastic" waiters who contribute to its "old-school" brauhaus "charm"; "nightmare"-to-nab reservations and a "cash-only" policy vex, but "if you're a beef-lover", it's a "must-go."

Picholine ⊠ *French/Mediterranean* | 27 | 26 | 26 | $120 |

W 60s | 35 W. 64th St. (bet. B'way & CPW) | 212-724-8585 | www.picholinenyc.com

"Off-the-charts" French-Med cuisine, including the city's "best cheese course", is served in "exquisite" formal surroundings at Terrance Brennan's prix fixe-only "crown jewel", where "everything is performed well – just like at nearby Lincoln Center"; sure, it can strain your budget, but it's bound to be a "memorable" experience – and now there's a $28 lunch deal too; P.S. "try its marvelous wines" and fromages at the "pleasant" non-reserving front bar, or go for a party-perfect private room.

River Café *American* | 26 | 28 | 26 | $127 |

Dumbo | 1 Water St. (bet. Furman & Old Fulton Sts.) | Brooklyn | 718-522-5200 | www.rivercafe.com

"Nestled beneath the Brooklyn Bridge", Buzzy O'Keeffe's "impeccable", jackets-required Dumbo, Brooklyn, doyenne is an all-around "divine" experience, from the "inventive" New American cuisine proffered by "attentive" servers to the "mesmerizing" views of Lower Manhattan and the Harbor; the "over-the-top" milieu is matched with "splurge-worthy" tabs (prix fixe–only dinner is $98), but to most it's "worth every penny" for such a "magical event."

Roberto ⓈItalian

27 | 18 | 22 | $54

Bronx | 603 Crescent Ave. (Hughes Ave.) | 718-733-9503 | www.roberto089.com

"Sensational" Salerno specialties prepared "under the watchful eye" of chef Roberto Paciullo will make you "swear you're in Italy" rather than the Bronx at this Arthur Avenue perennial "star"; the prices are "reasonable" given the "enormous portions" and the "pro" service is "pleasant" – now "if only they'd take reservations."

Sasabune Ⓢ Ⓜ Japanese

29 | 11 | 21 | $102

E 70s | 401 E. 73rd St. (bet. 1st & York Aves.) | 212-249-8583

"You have no choice" but to "trust the master" at Kenji Takahashi's omakase-only UES Japanese, a "close-to-Tokyo" "must" where the chef doles out "NYC's finest sushi"; the only drawbacks are the "small", "not-fancy" venue and "extremely expensive" check.

Scalini Fedeli Ⓢ Italian

27 | 24 | 25 | $86

TriBeCa | 165 Duane St. (bet. Greenwich & Hudson Sts.) | 212-528-0400 | www.scalinifedeli.com

"Exquisite" Northern Italian cooking in a "romantic", "high"-vaulted-ceilinged setting that recalls "Tuscany", matched with an "impressive wine list" and "first-class" service, make Michael Cetrulo's TriBeCan a favored "special-occasion" destination; it's far from cheap (prix fixe–only dinner is $65), but the "memorable evening" is "worth every penny."

SHO Shaun Hergatt Ⓢ French

26 | 27 | 26 | $91

Financial District | 40 Broad St., 2nd fl. (Exchange Pl.) | 212-809-3993 | www.shoshaunhergatt.com

There "aren't enough oohs and aahs" to describe the "top-shelf-all-the-way" experience at Shaun Hergatt's "glamorously modern" Financial District stunner, where the "seriously inventive and skilled" Asian-inflected French cuisine takes "taste buds to nirvana" and the kitchen provides a "show" via its glass wall; naturally it's "expensive" (prix fixe–only dinner starts at $69), but non-"overpaid bankers" can eat à la carte at lunch, or dine in the Pearl Room bar.

Sripraphai Ⓩ Thai

26 | 13 | 16 | $27

Woodside | 64-13 39th Ave. (bet. 64th & 65th Sts.) | Queens | 718-899-9599 | www.sripraphairestaurant.com

"No gimmicks", just "Thai-no-mite" cooking is the deal at this "cheap", cash-only Woodside, Queens, "hot spot", where the "authentic", "divine" flavors are "unwavering"; it may be "the best reason to discover the 7 train", but "go early" or plan to "take a number and wait."

Sugiyama ●⒮Ⓜ Japanese

26 | 19 | 24 | $96

W 50s | 251 W. 55th St. (bet. B'way & 8th Ave.) | 212-956-0670 | www.sugiyama-nyc.com

"Stunning" kaiseki repasts rank up there with "Tokyo's best" at this Midtown Japanese, where "charming" chef-owner Nao Sugiyama "never steers you wrong" with his "seasonal" extravaganzas; it'll cost you (prix fixe–only options start at $51), and as for the "unimpressive" decor, that just "keeps it from being snooty."

Sushi Yasuda ⊠ *Japanese*   28 | 21 | 24 | $84

E 40s | 204 E. 43rd St. (bet. 2nd & 3rd Aves.) | 212-972-1001 | www.sushiyasuda.com

"Reservations are mandatory" at this "minimalist" sushi "standard-bearer" near Grand Central, where "Yasuda-san" rewards "adventurousness" at the bar with "masterful delivery" of "flawless" fish, including "unusual varieties"; this "level of bliss" costs "bucks", but it's "cheaper than a flight to Tokyo", and the $23 dinner prix fixe is a super "bargain."

Tanoreen Ⓜ *Mediterranean/Mideastern*   27 | 18 | 22 | $36

Bay Ridge | 7523 Third Ave. (76th St.) | Brooklyn | 718-748-5600 | www.tanoreen.com

"There aren't enough superlatives" to describe the "fabulous" Med-Mideastern fare at this "lively" Bay Ridge, Brooklyn, "must-try" boasting an "eager-to-please" staff; "spacious, attractive" new digs mean "no more banging elbows", while "low prices" keep the far-flung convinced it's "worth the drive."

Telepan *American*   26 | 21 | 25 | $71

W 60s | 72 W. 69th St. (bet. Columbus Ave. & CPW) | 212-580-4300 | www.telepan-ny.com

To experience the "glories of fresh, locally grown food" "artfully prepared", hit "farm-to-table pioneer" Bill Telepan's "brilliant" UWS New American; its "thoughtful" "prix fixe options" suit "varied budgets", the "refined", "monotone" decor strikes most as "calming" and service is "prompt and helpful", making it an all-around "favorite."

Trattoria L'incontro Ⓜ *Italian*   27 | 19 | 25 | $56

Astoria | 21-76 31st St. (Ditmars Blvd.) | Queens | 718-721-3532 | www.trattorialincontro.com

There's "always something new" and "off-the-charts delicious" at this "buzzy" Astoria, Queens, Italian, where the servers reciting the "mile-long list of specials" are a "floor show", and chef-owner Rocco Sacramone "makes time to greet customers" too; borough boosters stack it against "anything Manhattan has to offer"; P.S. the next-door wine bar is "a must while waiting for your table."

Union Square Cafe *American*   26 | 23 | 26 | $70

Union Sq | 21 E. 16th St. (bet. 5th Ave. & Union Sq. W.) | 212-243-4020 | www.unionsquarecafe.com

"Year in, year out", Danny Meyer's "ultrapopular" Union Square "paragon" "lives up to its top-notch reputation" for "superior" New American cooking based on "fresh produce from the Greenmarket", delivered by a "polished", "never-snooty" staff in "civilized", "understated" digs; prices are "high-end", but considering that it's a "class act from start to finish", you'll leave thinking it's "worth every cent."

Wallsé *Austrian*   26 | 22 | 24 | $72

W Village | 344 W. 11th St. (Washington St.) | 212-352-2300 | www.kg-ny.com

"Austrian haute cuisine" is no "oxymoron" at Kurt Gutenbrunner's "elegant" West Village "jewel", where he "reinvents" schnitzel and other "favorites" as "superb" "delicacies"; "pristine" service and a "tranquil" setting with artwork by Julian Schnabel add to the "transcending" experience – for those who "can afford it."

Orange County, CA

TOP FOOD RANKING

	Restaurant	Cuisine
28	Marché Moderne	French
	Basilic	French/Swiss
	Tradition by Pascal	French
	Hobbit	Continental/French
27	Studio	Californian/French
	Napa Rose	Californian
	Bluefin	Japanese
26	Tabu Grill	Seafood/Steak
	Mastro's	Steak
	Park Ave	American

OTHER NOTEWORTHY PLACES

Charlie Palmer	American
Five Crowns	Continental
Gabbi's	Mexican
Il Barone	Italian
In-N-Out	Burgers
Mastro's Ocean Club	Seafood/Steak
Old Vine	Eclectic
Pizzeria Ortica	Pizza
Ramos	American
Wildfish	American/Seafood

Basilic 🗷 Ⓜ *French/Swiss*   28 | 20 | 26 | $59

Newport Beach | 217 Marine Ave. (Park Ave.) | 949-673-0570 | www.basilicrestaurant.com

Chef Bernard Althaus "continues to amaze" at this enduring, "enchanting" "hideaway" on Balboa Island, where the "delicious" French-Swiss specialties, "spot-on service" and "old-world charm" evoke "the best bistros in Europe"; prices are on the high side, but the experience is "always a treat"; P.S. "reserve well ahead", since this "quaint" nook only seats 24.

Bluefin *Japanese*   27 | 21 | 22 | $60

Newport Coast | Crystal Cove Promenade | 7952 E. PCH (Crystal Heights Dr.) | 949-715-7373 | www.bluefinbyabe.com

"Blue-finatics" urge you to just "open your wallet" for the "delectable experience" of chef-owner Takashi Abe's "art gallery"–worthy sushi and "adventurous" "fusions" at this sparse Newport Coast Japanese eatery; sure, the staff can be "cool" and the dining room is so "small" that "eavesdropping is part of the experience", but "lunch is a deal."

Charlie Palmer at Bloomingdale's   22 | 25 | 23 | $62
South Coast Plaza *American*

Costa Mesa | South Coast Plaza | 3333 S. Bristol St. (Anton Blvd.) | 714-352-2525 | www.charliepalmer.com

"Quiet and sophisticated without being stuffy", chef Charlie Palmer's "contemporary" New American eatery in South Coast Plaza offers "shopping-mall" dining that "can't be beat" with its "spacious" room, "sleek" leather seating and "faultless" service; expect "high-style temptation" (with prices to match) in the form of "small portions" and the "freshest ingredients."

Five Crowns *Continental*   24 | 23 | 25 | $50

Corona del Mar | 3801 E. Coast Hwy. (Poppy Ave.) | 949-760-0331 | www.lawrysonline.com

Offering a "trip across the pond without a passport", this Corona del Mar "standby" caters to the "old-school Newport crowd" with Continental plates – including the "best dang" Lawry's prime rib and Yorkshire pudding around; though the "tired" English-inn decor draws some yawns, fans appreciate this "step back in time" aided by a "been-here-for-years" staff, and the Sunday brunch on the patio is "fabulous."

Gabbi's Mexican Kitchen *Mexican*   26 | 21 | 22 | $32

Orange | 141 S. Glassell St. (Chapman Ave.) | 714-633-3038 | www.gabbipatrick.com

"It's not your typical tacos-and-beans place" aver admirers of this "upscale" Mexican eatery in "funky" Old Town Orange, where "creative twists" and "better ingredients" equal "spectacular gastronomic experiences"; agreeable service amid hacienda-style decor and a dimly lit dining room make for a "worthwhile date" spot, but when driving by, "don't look for signage" because there is none.

Hobbit, The Ⓜ *Continental/French*   28 | 23 | 28 | $84

Orange | 2932 E. Chapman Ave. (Malena St.) | 714-997-1972 | www.hobbitrestaurant.com

"Epicures and oenophiles alike" "treat their palates" at chef-owner Michael Philippi's Orange standout offering a seven-course French-Continental "adventure" served by an "elegant" staff; though prices are equally "extravagant", the "charming" converted Spanish-style dwelling adds to a "unique experience" that unfolds "like a play", beginning with champagne and hors d'oeuvres "in the wine cellar" and spanning "several hours of heaven"; P.S. "reservations are necessary", as there's only one seating a night (Wednesday–Sunday).

Il Barone Ristorante Ⓩ *Italian*   - | - | - | M

Newport Beach | 4251 Martingale Way (bet. Birch St. & MacArthur Blvd.) | 949-955-2755 | www.ilbaroneristorante.com

Franco and Donatella Barone, chef and GM, respectively, present this stylish Italian near John Wayne airport in Newport Beach; the menu's packed with classics and fresh pastas, plus seafood and game dishes with Northern twists, and housemade desserts are a special treat.

In-N-Out Burger ◗ *Burgers*   24 | 11 | 20 | $9

Costa Mesa | 594 W. 19th St. (bet. Anaheim & Maple Aves.)
Huntington Beach | 18062 Beach Blvd. (Talbert Ave.)
Irvine | 4115 Campus Dr. (Bridge Rd.)
Laguna Niguel | 27380 La Paz Rd. (Avila Rd.)
Tustin | Tustin Mktpl. | 3020 El Camino Real (Jamboree Rd.)
800-786-1000 | www.in-n-out.com
Additional locations throughout the Orange County area

This "legendary" West Coast bang-for-the-buck hamburger chain inspires a widespread "cult following", with converts to the "church of

In-N-Out" swearing that the "cooked-to-order" "never-frozen" patties, "freshly cut french fries" ("order them crispy") and "off-menu" "customizing" options are so "phenomenal" they must have been "created on the eighth day"; yes, they're always "mobbed" and drive-thru "lines are interminable", but "it's the food of the gods."

Marché Moderne *French*   28 | 24 | 26 | $58

Costa Mesa | South Coast Plaza | 3333 Bristol St. (Anton Blvd.) | 714-434-7900 | www.marchemoderne.net

"Yes, it's in a mall", but "get over it" say the many fans of this "joyous discovery", a "sophisticated" South Coast Plaza bistro where chef-owners Florent and Amelia Marneau turn out "unforgettable" French fare – from "comforting" classics to "adventurous" small plates – ranked No. 1 for Food and Most Popular in Orange County; it's not cheap, but it pays off with an "elegant" setting complete with "romantic" cabanas on the patio and service that makes you feel "well taken care of"; P.S. the "prix fixe lunch" is one of the "best deals" around.

Mastro's Ocean Club *Seafood/Steak*   25 | 26 | 25 | $76

Newport Coast | Crystal Cove Promenade | 8112 E. PCH (Reef Point Dr.) | 949-376-6990 | www.mastrosrestaurants.com

A glittery crowd tucks into "fantastic" *Flintstones*-size" steaks, seafood towers and "decadent" sides at this "outrageously expensive" Crystal Cove chophouse set in luxe ocean liner–inspired digs with "stunning views" of the Pacific; it's a tad "pretentious" to some, but "first-class" service makes it "the place to go celebrate something special", and you just can't beat the "people-watching" either ("yow, the cleavage!").

Mastro's Steakhouse *Steak*   26 | 23 | 25 | $73

Costa Mesa | 633 Anton Blvd. (Park Center Dr.) | 714-546-7405 | www.mastrosrestaurants.com

"Still the king" of carnivorous consumption, this "über-steakhouse" chain hosts "wheeler dealer" types "paying a fortune" for "generous" cuts of "mouthwatering" "prime meat", "extravagant" seafood towers and "sinful" sides, all matched with "world-class" service; the setting is quite "showy."

Napa Rose *Californian*   27 | 26 | 26 | $65

Anaheim | Disney's Grand Californian Hotel & Spa | 1600 S. Disneyland Dr. (Katella Ave.) | 714-300-7170 | www.disneyland.com

"There's not a mouse in sight" at this "first-class", "grown-up" "oasis of calm" within the Disneyland theme park showcasing "brilliant" seasonal Californian fare by chef Andrew Sutton and an "epic" wine list; the Craftsman-style setting boasts "engaging, knowledgeable" servers and a "surprisingly kid-friendly" vibe, though a few find the experience marred by "high" prices and an abundance of diners "dragging in from the park" in "sweatshirts and tennis sneakers" ("wish they had a dress-up only room!").

Old Vine Café *Eclectic*   25 | 17 | 22 | $32

Costa Mesa | The Camp | 2937 Bristol St. (Baker St.) | 714-545-1411 | www.oldvinecafe.com

For wine tasting without the "snob" factor, a "young" crowd favors this rustic little cafe in Costa Mesa's retail venue The Camp, where "refined" Eclectic small plates meet up with an "excellent" array of bottles; prices are modest, and the "fresh" fare's also a "favorite" for breakfast and brunch.

Park Ave ⓜ *American*   26 | 23 | 24 | $40

Stanton | 11200 Beach Blvd. (bet. Katella & Ruthann Aves.) | 714-901-4400 | www.parkavedining.com

"Yes Virginia, there is a reason to drive to Stanton" brag boosters of this "unlikely" "find" where "hands-on" chef-partner David Slay presents "exceptional" American "comfort food" crafted with "fresh" "veggies picked from their own garden"; refreshingly "reasonable" prices, "personable" service and a delightfully "retro" setting in a "beautifully maintained midcentury Googie masterpiece" make it "worth a visit"; P.S. "don't miss the special brined fried chicken" on Sunday nights.

Pizzeria Ortica ⓩ *Pizza*   24 | 17 | 20 | $38

Costa Mesa | 650 Anton Blvd. (bet. Bristol St. & Park Center Dr.) | 714-445-4900 | www.pizzeriaortica.com

"OC's answer to Pizzeria Mozza" is this Costa Mesa Italian and instant "favorite" from David Myers purveying "amazing, thin-crust" Neapolitan pies and "perfectly al dente" pastas in a stripped-down space with an open kitchen; "quick" service and accessible pricing help mitigate oft-"crowded" conditions and a setting so "loud" that "sign language" is almost a necessity.

Ramos House Café ⓜ *American*   25 | 18 | 22 | $35

San Juan Capistrano | 31752 Los Rios St. (Ramos St.) | 949-443-1342 | www.ramoshouse.com

Set in an "adorable", little cottage "right on the train tracks" in "historic" Old San Juan Capistrano, this "delightful" New American showcases chef-owner John Q. Humphreys' "incredible" Southern-inflected daytime fare backed by an "overstuffed Bloody Mary" that's a meal in itself; the seating outside on a "rustic", tree-shaded patio is sure to "melt your stress away" providing you can overlook the "rather pricey" bills.

Studio ⓜ *Californian/French*   27 | 29 | 27 | $102

Laguna Beach | Montage Laguna Bch. | 30801 S. Coast Hwy. (Montage Dr.) | 949-715-6420 | www.studiolagunabeach.com

A "picture-perfect" clifftop locale affords "sublime" sunset views over the Pacific at this "fine-dining" venue in the Montage Laguna Beach resort; equally "wow"-worthy is chef Craig Strong's "imaginative" Cal-New French menu and "flawless" service, so "what more can you ask for" aside from "a loan to pay for it" all?

Tabu Grill *Seafood/Steak*   26 | 20 | 24 | $63

Laguna Beach | 2892 S. PCH (bet. Hinkle & Nyes Pls.) | 949-494-7743 | www.tabugrill.com

Now flaunting a newly expanded dining room, this "dark", "sophisticated" Laguna Beach "gem" continues to "delight" with chef Kevin Jerrold-Jones' "beautifully presented" surf 'n' turf fare prepared with Pacific Rim influences and presented by an effortlessly "hip" staff; prices are "expensive" and a few note a "dip in quality" since the revamp (indeed, the Food score's down three points), though it's still "crowded" most nights, so make a "reservation."

	FOOD	DECOR	SERVICE	COST

Tradition by Pascal *French*

`28` `22` `26` `$62`

Newport Beach | 1000 N. Bristol St. (Jamboree Rd.) | 949-263-9400 |
www.pascalnewportbeach.com

"Simply terrific" declare devotees of this "little bit of France" tucked in
a ho-hum Newport Beach strip mall, where chef-owner Pascal Olhats
himself turns out "top-notch" Gallic cuisine and his crew offers tableside finishes on Thursday evenings; a "quiet", "elegant" setting and
"attentive" service that "isn't snooty" all make it "easy to drop a bundle" here; P.S. Sunday's prix fixe is a "good deal."

Wildfish Seafood Grille *American/Seafood*

`24` `22` `21` `$54`

Newport Beach | The Bluffs | 1370 Bison Ave. (Macarthur Blvd.) |
949-720-9925 | www.wildfishseafoodgrille.com

"Exceptional" seafood plus a "lively" bar with some of the best "people-
watching" around keep this handsome Newport Beach American
"buzzing" with a "typical OC" crowd (think *Real Housewives*); regulars note the bills "add up quickly" although the "fantastic" happy hour
every night offers some relief.

Orlando

TOP FOOD RANKING

	Restaurant	Cuisine
28	Victoria & Albert's	American
	Le Coq au Vin	French
27	Primo	Italian/Mediterranean
	Chatham's Place	Continental
	Enzo's	Italian
	California Grill	Californian
	Del Frisco's	Steak
26	Jiko	African
	Artist Point	Pacific NW
	K Restaurant	Eclectic
	Palm	Steak
	Morton's	Steak
	Christini's	Italian
	Ruth's Chris	Steak
	Yachtsman	Steak
	Norman's	New World
25	Le Cellier	Canadian/Steak
	Oceanaire	Seafood
	Todd English's Bluezoo	Seafood
	Cítricos	Mediterranean

OTHER NOTEWORTHY PLACES

Antonio's	Italian
Boma	African
Bosphorous	Turkish
Capital Grille	Steak
Columbia	Cuban/Spanish
Emeril's Orlando	Creole
Emeril's Tchoup Chop	Asian/Hawaiian
Four Rivers	BBQ
Hue	American
La Luce	Italian
La Nuovo	Italian
Luma on Park	American
Ocean Prime	Seafood/Steak
Raglan Road	Irish
Ravenous Pig	American
Roy's	Hawaiian
Sanaa	African/Indian
Seasons 52	American
Vines Grille	Steak
WA Restaurant	Japanese

Menus, photos, voting and more – free at ZAGAT.com

	FOOD	DECOR	SERVICE	COST

Antonio's La Fiamma Ristorante ⓧ *Italian* | 24 | 21 | 24 | $36 |

Maitland | 611 S. Orlando Ave., 2nd fl. (Maitland Ave.) | 407-645-1035

Antonio's Cafe & Deli *Italian*

Maitland | 611 S. Orlando Ave. (Maitland Ave.) | 407-645-1039

Antonio's Sand Lake ⓧ *Italian*

Bay Hill/Dr. Phillips | Fountains Plaza | 7559 W. Sand Lake Rd.
(bet. Dr. Phillips Blvd. & Turkey Lake Rd.) | 407-363-9191
www.antoniosonline.com

Whether you're celebrating "a special occasion" in the "sophisticated" upstairs dining room or simply enjoying "a relaxing evening" in the "casual" first-floor cafe, deli and wine shop, this Maitland duo is almost like "being in Italy"; the Sand Lake Road offshoot is equally "divine", dishing up the same "traditional" fare "with flair" ("fresh ingredients, creativity and attention") served by "professional" staffs that are "friendly", "efficient" and "way above average."

Artist Point *Pacific NW* | 26 | 26 | 25 | $50 |

Magic Kingdom Area | Disney's Wilderness Lodge | 901 Timberline Dr.
(Wilderness Rd.) | Lake Buena Vista | 407-939-3463 | www.disneyworld.com

"The Northwest meets the Southeast" at this Disney darling delivering "Oregon-chic food" in an "amazing" Wilderness Lodge setting that "feels like a genuine Frank Lloyd Wright retreat" with its "inviting views" and "gorgeous ceiling murals"; whether you opt for the "best salmon ever" cooked on a cedar plank or try one of the "unusual game specials", be sure to pair it with an "interesting Pacific NW wine" and then "walk around the resort after dinner."

Boma – Flavors of Africa *African* | 24 | 25 | 23 | $35 |

Animal Kingdom Area | Disney's Animal Kingdom Lodge |
2901 Osceola Pkwy. (Sherberth Rd. off Hwy. 192) | Lake Buena Vista |
407-939-3463 | www.disneyworld.com

Set "in Disney's stunning Animal Kingdom Lodge", this buffet will "make you feel as if you're visiting Africa" as you pick from the "dazzling" "array of choices", including "unusual, authentic foods" for "epicurean thrill-seekers" ("don't miss the Durban-spiced chicken") plus "well-prepared staples" for "the picky eater"; "sure, there are screaming kids running around", but overall it's a "fun", "safari-casual" "must-do" – "all that's missing is the meat on a spear!"

Bosphorous Turkish Cuisine *Turkish* | 23 | 19 | 20 | $33 |

Winter Park | 108 S. Park Ave. (W. Morse Blvd.) | 407-644-8609 |
www.bosphorousrestaurant.com

Be "transported back to Istanbul" at this "wonderful change of pace" on "tony Park Avenue", where the "rich stews, zesty kebabs" and other "delicious", "interesting" Turkish food "provide plenty of flavor" for Winter Park palates; the "attention to detail" extends to the "gracious service", "eclectic decor" and "great outdoor seating."

California Grill *Californian* | 27 | 25 | 24 | $55 |

Magic Kingdom Area | Disney's Contemporary Resort, 15th fl. |
4600 N. World Dr. | Lake Buena Vista | 407-939-3463 |
www.disneyworld.com

The "holy grail of restaurants" in the Disney domain (it's the Most Popular spot in the Orlando area), this Californian "favorite" offers an "enchanting" combination of "creative, seasonal" fare, "solicitous" service and "one of the most extensive wine lists east of Napa"; it also boasts a "fabulous location" on the 15th floor of the Contemporary Resort, so be sure to "time your reservation" to take advantage of the "killer view of the fireworks" over Cinderella's Castle.

Capital Grille *Steak*

25 | 23 | 23 | $62

International Drive | Pointe Orlando | 9101 International Dr. (Pointe Plaza Ave.) | 407-370-4392 | www.thecapitalgrille.com
An "enjoyable experience" "in all regards", this I-Drive link in an "up-scale" national chain pairs what some call "the best steak in Orlando, bar none", with a "good wine selection" and a "highly trained staff" that provides "professional service" "from the moment you walk in the door to when you leave"; the "serious" setting is capital "for business dinners and martini lunches", which would explain all the "convention-goers wearing khaki pants and lanyards."

Chatham's Place ⊠ *Continental*

27 | 20 | 28 | $64

Bay Hill/Dr. Phillips | 7575 Dr. Phillips Blvd. (Sand Lake Rd.) | 407-345-2992 | www.chathamsplace.com
In a "hard-to-find" spot just "steps from Restaurant Row", this "cozy, comfortable" Dr. Phillips "charmer" is "where the locals eat", in part because they "always feel welcome" while indulging in "divine" Continental cuisine (the "flavors are bold yet well-balanced") accompanied by a "wonderful wine selection"; it's "pricey", but the "impeccable service" and occasional guitar "serenading" will have you feeling like you're eating at "your personal restaurant."

Christini's Ristorante Italiano *Italian*

26 | 22 | 25 | $64

Bay Hill/Dr. Phillips | The Marketplace | 7600 Dr. Phillips Blvd. (Sand Lake Rd.) | 407-345-8770 | www.christinis.com
Be "blown away" by a meal at this "elegant" Dr. Phillips Italian where the "exceptional experience" includes "fabulous" old-world cuisine made with "the finest and freshest ingredients", a "gracious", "attentive" staff and a selection of "hard-to-find wines" (let the "knowledge-able sommelier" help you choose); female patrons "get a rose" at the end of their meal, but given the "high prices", some suggest "it turns out to be a very expensive rose."

Cítricos Ⓜ *Mediterranean*

25 | 23 | 23 | $53

Magic Kingdom Area | Disney's Grand Floridian Resort & Spa | 4401 Grand Floridian Way (bet. Maple Rd. & W. Seven Seas Dr.) | Lake Buena Vista | 407-939-3463 | www.disneyworld.com
"Pure poetry" profess patrons who say this "hidden gem" in Disney's Grand Floridian Resort "rivals its neighbor", the posh Victoria & Albert's, thanks to "innovative" Med–New American "magic on a plate" plus an "attentive" staff that "goes out of its way" to please; factor in an "awesome" wine list and "spectacular" views (from some tables), and this "favorite" is "worth it for a special occasion" or a "vacation date night."

Columbia *Cuban/Spanish*

22 | 22 | 20 | $36

Celebration | 649 Front St. (Sycamore St.) | 407-566-1505 | www.columbiarestaurant.com
At this "wonderful" offshoot of a Tampa-area chain, the "old-world" ambiance will "transport you" from Celebration "to a villa on the

Mediterranean Sea" - think wrought iron and arched windows - while the menu sates your appetite for "authentic, delicious" Cuban-Spanish cuisine (the "1905 salad rules!"); a few fret about "slow service" and "Disney character", but that's easy to overlook as you "sit and relax" on the "quiet patio" with a glass of "excellent" sangria.

Del Frisco's Prime Steak & Lobster 🗷 *Steak*   27 | 17 | 23 | $65

Winter Park | 729 Lee Rd. (Alloway St.) | 407-645-4443 | www.delfriscosorlando.com

For some of "the best steaks in O-Town", head to this "clubby" Winter Park staple serving "sinfully delicious" beef that's "still sizzling when it hits the table", plus "perfectly cooked" lobster, a "killer wine list" and all "the requisite sides"; a few folks suggest the "dark, bordello-style" decor is a bit "dated", but a staff that "goes the extra mile" is yet another reason your "business dinner" will be "worth every penny."

Emeril's Orlando *Creole*   24 | 21 | 23 | $57

Universal Orlando | Universal Studios CityWalk | 6000 Universal Blvd. (Hollywood Way) | 407-224-2424 | www.emerils.com

"A welcome respite", this Creole "classic" from celebrity chef Emeril Lagasse "whisks you away" from the "Universal Studios hustle and bustle" with "imaginative" fare that's "beautifully prepared" and complemented by "premier presentation" and "friendly service"; it's "worth the price for a true foodie", although the "loud", "busy" ambiance has mellow types murmuring "the food is terrific, the tourists are annoying"; P.S. "if you can't get a seat, eat at the bar."

Emeril's Tchoup Chop *Asian/Hawaiian*   24 | 26 | 24 | $54

Universal Orlando | Loews Royal Pacific Resort | 6300 Hollywood Way (Universal Blvd.) | 407-503-2467 | www.emerils.com

"Emeril does Roy Yamaguchi" at this Hawaiian–Asian fusion "favorite" in the Loews Royal Pacific Resort, where guests feast on a "fabulous" array of "innovative" dishes in a "gorgeously exotic" "Pacific island-meets-theme park" setting that's perhaps even "more delicious than the food"; whether you sit at a table or "watch the kitchen ballet" at the chef's bar, "superb service on every visit" ensures it's among "the best at Universal" and "well worth the wait on weekends."

Enzo's Restaurant on the Lake 🗷🅼 *Italian*   27 | 23 | 24 | $51

Longwood | 1130 S. Hwy. 17-92 (½ mile south of Rte. 434) | 407-834-9872 | www.enzos.com

As "reliable as a good Tuscan wine", this Longwood "gem" remains an "institution for special occasions" thanks to its "outstanding", "high-end" Italian cuisine and a "romantic atmosphere" that includes "beautiful" "lakeside dining"; it's equally "a pleasure" for "socializing with business colleagues", and the family of late founder Enzo Perlini continues in the tradition of "cordial, welcoming" service; P.S. be sure to try plenty of the "wonderful antipasti."

Four Rivers Smokehouse 🗷 *BBQ*   - | - | - | I

Winter Park | 2103 W. Fairbanks Ave. (Formosa Ave.) | 407-474-8377 | www.4rsmokehouse.com

Tender brisket smoked Texas-style for 18 hours over hickory wood is the calling card at this affordable Winter Park yearling where the lines are long and seating is limited to a covered patio; still, BBQ fans are

	FOOD	DECOR	SERVICE	COST

happily joining the queue to load up on the tiny eatery's signature beef, plus pulled pork, burnt-end sandwiches, a sea of sides (e.g. collards, fried okra) and unusual items like bacon-wrapped jalapeños; P.S. parking can be a challenge.

Hue *American*
23 | 23 | 21 | $44

Thornton Park | 629 E. Central Blvd. (bet. Eola Dr. & Summerlin Ave.) | 407-849-1800 | www.huerestaurant.com

The "cool factor" looms large at Thornton Park's "oasis of sophistication", a "see-and-be-seen" magnet for Downtown Orlando's "beautiful people", who congregrate over "consistently creative" New American cuisine served by a "helpful, friendly" staff; those who find it "noisy inside" can opt for a seat on the "A+ patio", but regulars recommend "putting your stuffed shirt away" to enjoy the monthly disco brunch, "a fun way to spend a Sunday afternoon."

Jiko – The Cooking Place *African*
26 | 27 | 26 | $47

Animal Kingdom Area | Disney's Animal Kingdom Lodge | 2901 Osceola Pkwy. (Sherberth Rd. off Hwy. 192) | Lake Buena Vista | 407-938-4733 | www.disneyworld.com

Experience a "taste of Africa without the exorbitant airfare" at this "welcome departure" in Disney's Animal Kingdom Lodge, where the "unexpected flavors" – think comfort foods prepared with "exotic" sub-Saharan spices – "don't fail to exceed expectations"; the "wonderful experience" includes a "sleek, tranquil" setting, "impeccable" service and an "awesome" South African wine list that will make oenophiles "weep with excitement."

K Restaurant 🗷 *Eclectic*
26 | 21 | 23 | $42

College Park | 1710 Edgewater Dr. (bet. New Hapshire Dr. & Yates St.) | 407-872-2332 | www.kwinebar.com

"You can't go wrong" at this College Park "stalwart" that's "built a solid reputation for innovative" Eclectic fare that's "always fresh and always delicious"; post-Survey, it moved to the cozy 1920s home that housed the erstwhile Nonna's (also adopting some of Nonna's signature dishes), but it still benefits from "artwork on the wall", "great outdoor seating" and servers who "remember guests from past visits."

La Luce *Italian*
- | - | - | M

Kissimmee | Hilton Orlando Bonnet Creek | 14100 Bonnet Creek Resort Ln. (Chelonia Pkwy.) | 407-597-3600 | www.laluceorlando.com

Chef-restaurateur Donna Scala brings her no-nonsense Napa Valley culinary sensibilities to the Disney area at this contemporary Italian restaurant in the new Hilton Bonnet Creek; the sleek decor – including chalk murals that are created anew quarterly and an exposition kitchen – is the backdrop for creative and traditional takes on mid-priced Italian fare fashioned from farm-fresh ingredients, especially housemade pastas and house-stuffed sausages.

La Nuovo Cucina *Italian*
- | - | - | M

Bay Hill/Dr. Phillips | 7724 W. Sand Lake Rd. (Dr. Phillips Blvd.) | 407-354-4909 | www.lanuovacucina.com

There's pampering aplenty at this intimate brick-walled newcomer on Dr. Phillips' Restaurant Row, particularly when one considers that chef-owner Paulo Baroni provides guests with an amuse-bouche before every course (even dessert); while all those little extras result in a relative value, they don't take away from the menu's New World takes on Italian flavors, like the curry-pumpkin soup, cheese-and-pear-stuffed fagottini and a caramel-crusted chocolate pudding.

Le Cellier Steakhouse *Canadian/Steak* 25 | 22 | 24 | $43

Epcot, World Showcase | Canada Pavilion | Walt Disney World Resort (W. Seven Seas Dr.) | Lake Buena Vista | 407-939-3463 | www.disneyworld.com

Visitors "will want to sing 'Oh Canada' after trying the steak" at this "lively" option in Epcot's Canada Pavilion, where the filet is "so tender you could cut it with a plastic spoon" and the "hearty" cheddar cheese soup and "soft, warm" pretzel breadsticks will make you "swear you're in our 51st state"; plus, as you "eat underground in an old wine cellar" attended to by "friendly" "Canadian college students", you'll be apt to "forget you're in Disney World"; P.S. "reservations are a must!"

Le Coq au Vin Ⓜ *French* 28 | 19 | 25 | $48

South Orlando | 4800 S. Orange Ave. (Gatlin Ave.) | 407-851-6980 | www.lecoqauvinrestaurant.com

"Where locals go to get away from the tourists", this "hidden delight" in South Orlando demonstrates its "commitment to quality and consistency" via a "spectacular" lineup of French cuisine "not to die for, but to live for!"; a few suggest it "can be noisy", but its "perfectly paired wines", "country ambiance", "warm service" and "moderate prices" are all reasons it's been a "perennial favorite" for over 30 years; P.S. Sandy Pitz and chef Reimund Pitz took over from longtime chef-owner Louis Perrotte post-Survey, adding Floridian dishes to the menu.

Luma on Park *American* 24 | 27 | 23 | $49

Winter Park | 290 S. Park Ave. (bet. W. Lyman & W. New England Aves.) | 407-599-4111 | www.lumaonpark.com

Discover "New York in Winter Park" at this "hot spot" on Park Avenue, where "chic, modern" decor (even "the washrooms look like something out of *Star Trek*") sets the stage for Brandon McGlamery's "superb work": an array of "cutting-edge", "inventive" seasonal New American dishes; a "helpful, knowledgeable" staff and an "extensive wine list" are two more reasons surveyors call it "fabulous in all respects."

Morton's The Steakhouse *Steak* 26 | 22 | 25 | $71

Bay Hill/Dr. Phillips | The Marketplace | 7600 Dr. Phillips Blvd. (Sand Lake Rd.) | 407-248-3485 | www.mortons.com

"The poster boy of steakhouses", this "classic" on Dr. Phillips' Restaurant Row caters to carnivores with "gigantic" "steaks the way you would expect" accompanied by "flavorful" side dishes "the size of entrees"; "impeccable service" and a "manly club atmosphere" add to the "wonderful experience", and though it's "expensive", rest assured "you get what you pay for!"

Norman's *New World* 26 | 28 | 25 | $83

South Orlando | Ritz-Carlton Orlando, Grande Lakes | 4012 Central Florida Pkwy. (John Young Pkwy.) | 407-393-4333 | www.normans.com

At this "decadent" Ritz-Carlton Grande Lakes dining room, the "high-end" ambiance is "exquisite" "from top to bottom", while "sophisticated

	FOOD	DECOR	SERVICE	COST

palates" can expect a similar degree of "excellence" from the "pricey" but "delicious" New World cuisine; "attentive" "but not overbearing" service seals the deal, making this a "special-occasion" destination that's "not to be missed", especially "when someone else is buying."

Oceanaire Seafood Room *Seafood*   25 | 23 | 24 | $60

International Drive | 9101 International Dr. (Pointe Plaza Ave.) | 407-363-4801 | www.theoceanaire.com

"A cut above the other seafood chains", this "absolutely wonderful" option near the convention center delivers "swimmingly good" "fresh-off-the-boat fish" and other ocean fare in a room awash with the "retro elegance" of an "old cruise ship"; the "professional" service also "couldn't be of a higher quality", and while it's "ultra-expensive", most say it's "worth the money" for that "business dinner or special occasion."

Ocean Prime *Seafood/Steak*   - | - | - | E

Bay Hill/Dr. Phillips | Rialto | 7339 W. Sand Lake Rd. (bet. Dr. Phillips Blvd. & Turkey Lake Rd.) | 407-781-4880 | www.ocean-prime.com

Surf 'n' turf is served along with a healthy dose of drama at this mini-chain link on Dr. Phillips' Restaurant Row, where backlit bars, amber lighting, piano music and dry-ice-cooled martinis abound; fish and chop preparations both classic and creative fetch prices that are fittingly expensive for such a swanky, clubby experience.

Palm, The *Steak*   26 | 21 | 24 | $60

Universal Orlando | Hard Rock Hotel | 5800 Universal Blvd. (Major Blvd.) | 407-503-7256 | www.thepalm.com

"Lipitor should be the corporate sponsor" of this "top-of-the-line" chain chophouse that lures "unabashed carnivores" to Universal's Hard Rock Hotel with its "perfectly done" steaks, "huge, wonderful lobsters" and "luscious martinis – what else do you need?"; a few find the "noisy", "caricature-filled" room to be "nothing special", but others suggest it's just like the original in NYC "but without the snob appeal and service attitude."

Primo *Italian/Mediterranean*   27 | 25 | 26 | $67

South Orlando | JW Marriott Orlando, Grande Lakes | 4040 Central Florida Pkwy. (John Young Pkwy.) | 407-393-4444 | www.grandelakes.com

"Worth the extra drive" to South Orlando's JW Marriott Grande Lakes, this "elegant" option is "in a class of its own" thanks to "master" chef Melissa Kelly and her "unbelievable", "imaginative" Italian-Med cuisine that "transports you to food heaven" with its "freshness and taste" (much of the produce is organic, and grown on-site to boot); plus, it's set in a "beautiful" space that "makes you forget you're in a hotel."

Raglan Road Irish Pub & Restaurant ● *Irish*   21 | 24 | 21 | $33

Downtown Disney Area | 1640 E. Buena Vista Dr. (bet. Epcot Center Dr. & Sycamore Loop) | Lake Buena Vista | 407-938-0300 | www.raglanroadirishpub.com

"There's a pot of unexpected gold" at Irish über-chef Kevin Dundon's pub import, "a little piece of Ireland" in Downtown Disney that serves "fantastic" Gaelic eats that are "a full step above typical pub grub"; "properly prepared pints" and "authentic Irish music" ensure it's an "insanely crowded" gathering spot that's also a "rowdy good time."

	FOOD	DECOR	SERVICE	COST

Ravenous Pig, The 🗷Ⓜ *American* — 25 | 20 | 23 | $45

Winter Park | 1234 N. Orange Ave. (bet. Denning & Orlando Sts.) |
407-628-2333 | www.theravenouspig.com

"A favorite of the Winter Park crowd", this "fantastic" gastropub with a
somewhat "strange name" just "keeps getting better" thanks to chef-
owners James and Julie Petrakis, who turn out a "daring and delicious"
menu of local, seasonal, "gourmet American" cuisine; "well-thought-
out" beer and wine lists and "knowledgeable" staff add to its appeal.

Roy's *Hawaiian* — 25 | 22 | 22 | $53

Bay Hill/Dr. Phillips | Plaza Venezia | 7760 W. Sand Lake Rd. (bet. Della Dr. &
Dr. Phillips Blvd.) | 407-352-4844 | www.roysrestaurant.com

"Those who miss the real thing" can experience "Hawaii in Orlando"
at this link in celebrity chef Roy Yamaguchi's "consistent" national
chain on Dr. Phillips' Restaurant Row, where "gorgeous" presentations
of the "freshest seafood" are served in a "classy", "minimalist" space;
the staff is "friendly and its enthusiasm is contagious", so while it can
be "a bit noisy", it remains a "favorite" for "a special-occasion meal."

Ruth's Chris Steak House *Steak* — 26 | 23 | 24 | $63

Bay Hill/Dr. Phillips | 7501 W. Sand Lake Rd. (bet. Dr. Phillips Blvd. &
Turkey Lake Rd.) | 407-226-3900
Lake Mary | 80 Colonial Center Pkwy. (County Rd. 46A) | 407-804-8220
Winter Park | Winter Park Village | 610 N. Orlando Ave. (Webster Ave.) |
407-622-2444
www.ruthschris.com

"Steak doesn't get any better than Ruth's, baby" chime champions of
these Central Florida outlets of the "upscale" chophouse chain revered for "sizzling, buttery" beef and "terrific sides" served in "exceptionally plush" dining rooms manned by "high-quality servers";
P.S. "you'll have to leave your car there to cover the bill."

Sanaa *African/Indian* — - | - | - | M

Disney World | Disney's Animal Kingdom Villas | 2901 Osceola Pkwy.
(I-4) | Lake Buena Vista | 407-939-3463 | www.disneyworld.com

This midpriced Disney offering presents bold subcontinental flavors
alongside intriguing preparations from Madagascar, Seychelles,
Zanzibar and other Indian Ocean island nations, pairing them with
wines from both worlds and beyond; the exotic setting features columns made from large, colorful beads and views of zebras, giraffes
and more African fauna through the windows.

Seasons 52 *American* — 25 | 26 | 24 | $41

Altamonte Springs | 463 E. Altamonte Dr. (Palm Springs Dr.) | 407-767-1252
Bay Hill/Dr. Phillips | Plaza Venezia | 7700 W. Sand Lake Rd.
(bet. Della Dr. & Dr. Phillips Blvd.) | 407-354-5212
www.seasons52.com

"Sheer genius" say smitten surveyors of these Altamonte Springs and
Dr. Phillips links in a local chain, whose "wonderful" New American
menu offers "decadent food without the guilt": each "seasonally ad-
justed" savory is "under 475 calories" and "tempting, rational" "mini-
desserts are served in shot glasses"; they're "on the pricey side", but
the "stunning" "modern" settings ("Frank Lloyd Wright–inspired")
abet the feeling they're "well worth every penny"; P.S. "without reservations, there can be significant waits."

	FOOD	DECOR	SERVICE	COST

Todd English's Bluezoo *Seafood*

25 | 25 | 23 | $63

Epcot Area | Walt Disney World Dolphin | 1500 Epcot Resort Blvd.
(E. Buena Vista Dr.) | Lake Buena Vista | 407-934-1111 |
www.thebluezoo.com

"Tantalize your taste buds" at celeb chef Todd English's "innovative", "trendy" seafooder "for adults" at Epcot's Dolphin, where "simple fish meets a complexity of flavors" thanks to "creative" (if "pricey") preparations and sauces; the "visually stunning" design makes you feel like you're "dining underwater" but, despite the name, "the only animals at this zoo are the party animals who crowd the bar."

Victoria & Albert's *American*

28 | 27 | 28 | $163

Magic Kingdom Area | Disney's Grand Floridian Resort & Spa |
4401 Grand Floridian Way (bet. Maple Rd. & W. Seven Seas Dr.) |
Lake Buena Vista | 407-939-3463 | www.victoria-alberts.com

"Want to know what dinner would be like in heaven?" – then "dress up" and tow "a boatful of money" to this "fantasy" in Disney's Grand Floridian Resort, where "meticulous" servers present "genius" chef Scott Hunnel's "inventive", "decadent" six-course, prix fixe–only New American menu that earns the No. 1 Food rating in the Orlando area; "thankfully, no children [under 10] are allowed" in the "sophisticated" room, making it "wonderful for romance"; P.S. "book well in advance" and try for the "coveted chef's table."

Vines Grille & Wine Bar *Steak*

- | - | - | E

Bay Hill/Dr. Phillips | The Fountains | 7533 W. Sand Lake Rd.
(Dr. Phillips Blvd.) | 407-351-1227 | www.vinesgrille.com

Dramatic water features, towering wine racks, private nooks and other snazzy accoutrements are the hallmarks of this steakhouse planted on Dr. Phillips' Restaurant Row; the bill of fare is thick with influences from around the world, just as the densely packed wine list features abundant global varieties, while the prices for everything climb toward the sky; P.S. hit the swish bar for live jazz nightly.

WA Restaurant ⊠ *Japanese*

- | - | - | M

Universal Orlando | 5911 Turkey Lake Rd. (bet. Production Plaza & Vineland St.) | 407-226-0234 | www.warestaurant.com

Outside Universal Orlando in a nearly empty office complex, this sleek, attention-getting Japanese features dramatic high-back booths, cool woods, recessed lighting and moderate prices; in addition to sushi and Asian classics, the fusion fare includes seemingly incompatible Pacific, American and European flavors like raw fish, pork belly, truffle oil, ponzu sauce, blue cheese and shiso leaves, all melded magically and plated artistically.

Yachtsman Steakhouse *Steak*

26 | 22 | 25 | $59

Epcot Area | Disney's Yacht Club Resort | 1700 Epcot Resort Blvd.
(E. Buena Vista Dr.) | Lake Buena Vista | 407-939-3463 |
www.disneyworld.com

"Everything a top-notch steakhouse should be" rave Epcot epicureans of this "classy" "treat" in Disney's Yacht Club Resort, where the "amazing" cuts "melt in your mouth" and the occasionally "snooty" staff "knows how to pair wines" from the "awesome list"; in short, for a "special evening", it's "worth the cost."

Palm Beach

				FOOD	DECOR	SERVICE	COST

TOP FOOD RANKING

	Restaurant	Cuisine
28	11 Maple St.	American
27	Marcello's La Sirena	Italian
	Chez Jean-Pierre	French
	Café Boulud	French
	Casa D'Angelo	Italian
26	Chops Lobster Bar	Seafood/Steak
	32 East	American
	Four Seasons	Seafood
	Little Moir's	Seafood
	L'Escalier	French

OTHER NOTEWORTHY PLACES

Abe & Louie's	Steak
Bonefish Grill	Seafood
Café Chardonnay	American
Café L'Europe	Continental
Captain Charlie's	Seafood
Dolce de Palma	Italian
Forté	Italian
Kee Grill	Seafood/Steak
New York Prime	Steak
Truluck's	Seafood

Abe & Louie's *Steak*   `26` `24` `25` `$64`

Boca Raton | 2200 W. Glades Rd. (NW Sheraton Way) | 561-447-0024 | www.abeandlouies.com

Carnivores converge on this Boston-based "real men's steakhouse" – a Boca Raton "classic" voted the Palm Beach area's Most Popular – where diners gush over "amazing" "bone-in filets", "wonderful seafood" and "quality sides" that can be "shared"; though some grumble about "noise levels that'll give you nightmares" and "expensive" tabs, an "ultraprofessional" staff with "deep knowledge" of the "diverse, fairly priced wine list" and "elegant, clubby surroundings" help make it a "winner."

Bonefish Grill *Seafood*   `22` `20` `21` `$35`

Stuart | Stuart Ctr. | 2283 S. Federal Hwy. (SE Monterey Rd.) | 772-288-4388
Palm Beach Gardens | 11658 Hwy. 1 (PGA Blvd.) | 561-799-2965
Boca Raton | Shops at Boca Grove | 21069 Powerline Rd. (Boca Grove Blvd.) | 561-483-4949
Boynton Beach | 1880 N. Congress Ave. (Gateway Blvd.) | 561-732-1310
www.bonefishgrill.com

You can almost "feel the sea breeze" at these "upscale yet casual" chain seafooders whose "broad selection" of "consistently delicious", "always-fresh" fish ("if it swims, they have it") has habitués "hooked"; "fair prices" and "courteous", "well-trained" servers help explain why they're usually "jam-packed" with a "loud" crowd, so "be prepared to wait"; P.S. "the bang-bang shrimp is to die-die for."

Café Boulud *French*   27 | 27 | 26 | $76

Palm Beach | Brazilian Court Hotel | 301 Australian Ave. (Hibiscus Ave.) | 561-655-6060 | www.danielnyc.com

"A little slice of New York heaven", this "magical" Daniel Boulud outpost in the Brazilian Court Hotel is "*the* big deal in Palm Beach", where the "beautiful people" say *oui* to "fab chef" Zach Bell's "sublime" "French cuisine without the French attitude" and an "exemplary" wine list overseen by "class-act" sommeliers; you'll need to "open your pocketbook" and hand over the "black card", but after being pampered by a "superior" staff in a "gorgeous tropical setting", many sigh "it doesn't get better than this."

Café Chardonnay *American*   25 | 22 | 24 | $56

Palm Beach Gardens | Garden Square Shoppes | 4533 PGA Blvd. (Military Trail) | 561-627-2662 | www.cafechardonnay.com

"It may not look like much from the outside", but this "inventive" New American in a Palm Beach Gardens "strip mall" ("*so* Florida") is "still living up to its fabulous reputation" after "more than 20 years"; "well-educated" waiters help diners decipher an "outstanding" selection of "wines by the glass" and bottle, and if a few fret it's all too "pricey", devotees decree "it's the best thing" for a "special occasion" "next to child care."

Café L'Europe ☒ *Continental*   25 | 26 | 25 | $72

Palm Beach | 331 S. County Rd. (Brazilian Ave.) | 561-655-4020 | www.cafeleurope.com

You'll "feel like you've made it" at this "exquisite", "flower-filled" "landmark" whose owners "stay on top of all details", from the "extraordinary" Continental cuisine and "comprehensive" wine list to the "impeccable" service; while a few tsk "the grande dame is getting old" and rip into "expensive" tabs, the majority maintains it's "Palm Beach with a capital P" – so "wear your good jewelry" and "see how the other half lives"; P.S. recessionistas should consider the three-course lunch and dinner specials.

Captain Charlie's Reef Grill *Seafood*   26 | 12 | 22 | $36

Juno Beach | Beach Plaza | 12846 U.S. 1 (bet. Juno Isles Blvd. & Olympus Dr.) | 561-624-9924

"The freshest fish" is served in "imaginative, delicious" preparations – or "however you want it" – at this "informal" Juno Beach strip-mall seafooder whose "incomparable value" extends to the "awesome wine list" (possibly the "lowest markups" around); just "don't be put off" by the "dumpy" "Old Florida" "bar setting", the "noise" or a no-reservations policy that leads to "long waits in season."

Casa D'Angelo *Italian*   27 | 22 | 25 | $59

Boca Raton | 171 E. Palmetto Park Rd. (bet. Federal Hwy. & Mizner Blvd.) | 561-996-1234 | www.casa-d-angelo.com

"*Magnifico*" rave regulars who say "master chef" Angelo Elia turns out some of the "best" and most "authentic" Italian cuisine at this "more stylish" and "quieter" Boca sib of the "expensive" Ft. Lauderdale original; "generous servings" of "homemade pasta" star in "dishes so out

| | FOOD | DECOR | SERVICE | COST |

of this world it's hard to choose", all paired with a "world-class" wine list and "ready-to-please" service.

Chez Jean-Pierre Bistro 🅱 *French* | 27 | 23 | 26 | $73 |

Palm Beach | 132 N. County Rd. (bet. Sunrise & Sunset Aves.) | 561-833-1171
"Observe the social rituals of the Palm Beach elite" while indulging in chef-owner Jean-Pierre Leverrier's "fantastic" French fare ("makes you feel like you can fly") at this "sparkling" bistro that's "always packed"; "perfect" Dover sole and "knowledgeable" staffers wow a crowd that includes some regulars "older than the vintage wines", while aesthetes appreciate the "funky, Magritte-like art"; if a few *non*-sayers sniff it's "not all that", for most it's a "breath of fresh country air."

Chops Lobster Bar *Seafood/Steak* | 26 | 25 | 25 | $71 |

Boca Raton | Royal Palm Pl. | 101 Plaza Real S. (1st St.) | 561-395-2675 | www.chopslobsterbar.com
While claw-noisseurs commend the "flash-fried lobster" ("so much better than it sounds"), it's the "fantastic steaks" and "delicious sides" that have turned this "high-quality" "Atlanta import" into a "major Boca scene"; add in "gorgeous" surroundings with an open kitchen, a "happening" bar with live entertainment and "telepathic" staffers, and you've got "dining bliss" – which explains the "long waits" even "with a reservation"; of course, it's "expensive" "unless you own (not lease) a Bentley", but a "satisfying" "splurge" nonetheless.

Dolce de Palma 🅱 *Italian* | 26 | 15 | 22 | $43 |

West Palm Beach | 1000 Okeechobee Rd. (Parker Ave.) | 561-833-6460 | www.dolcedepalma.com
"Amazing food comes out of the tiny kitchen" at this "pricey" West Palm place that's praised for its "sense, style and substance", as well as its "well-presented" Italian fare that's "interesting without scaring off the retirees"; though there's "no decor" and it's "next to railroad tracks", "reservations may be hard to come by", leaving loyalists lamenting "too bad it's no longer a secret."

11 Maple Street Ⓜ *American* | 28 | 23 | 26 | $60 |

Jensen Beach | 3224 NE Maple Ave. (NE Jensen Beach Blvd.) | 772-334-7714 | www.11maplestreet.net
Admittedly, you'll drive a "bit far" to get to this "fantasy house" in Jensen Beach, but it's "worth it" once chef-owner Mike Perrin's "outstanding" New American fare – and its rating as PB's No. 1 for Food – is put to the test; "farm-raised meats and veggies many can't pronounce" are "superbly" presented and paired with a "unique wine list", while "friendly yet professional" staffers and "quaint" decor seal its rep as a "charming" "gem"; P.S. also closed Tuesdays.

Forté *Italian* | ▽ 26 | 25 | 24 | $57 |

West Palm Beach | 225 Clematis St. (Olive Ave.) | 561-833-3330 | www.fortepalmbeach.com
The "team knows what it's doing" at this Downtown West Palm Italian proffering "consistently wonderful" fare, "attentive" service and an "extensive, interesting" wine list amid the "Clematis Street bar scene"; the "super-modern decor" (neon lighting, gauzy curtains, etc.) "may be a bit much" for the less adventurous, but overall expect "an enjoyable evening."

	FOOD	DECOR	SERVICE	COST

Four Seasons – The Restaurant *Seafood* 26 | 27 | 26 | $76

Palm Beach | Four Seasons Resort | 2800 S. Ocean Blvd. (Lake Ave.) | 561-533-3750 | www.fourseasons.com

"Quietly elegant in every way", this "special place for a special night" offers just "what you'd expect from the Four Seasons", including "near perfect service" that complements the "spectacular setting" and "gorgeous ocean views"; chef Darryl Moiles' "flavorful" seafood is "a good as it gets", and while you may need a "second mortgage" to cover the tab, it's a "small price to pay" for an "unforgettable experience."

Kee Grill *Seafood/Steak* 24 | 21 | 22 | $47

Juno Beach | 14020 US Hwy. 1 (Donald Ross Rd.) | 561-776-1167
Boca Raton | 17940 N. Military Trail (Clint Moore Rd.) | 561-995-504

The "early bird" gets the "bargain" at these midpriced, "tropical" themed Boca and Juno Beach "seafood shrines" (there's also "flavorfu meat") that are "packed" with devotees digging into the "fabulously fresh" fin fare and the "scrumptious" spinach side; while it's "good news" they "now take reservations", "unending waits" persist, and "rushed service" in a "noisy" setting rankle some; still, for most they're "always a treat."

L'Escalier 🗷🅼 *French* 26 | 27 | 26 | $101

Palm Beach | The Breakers | 1 S. County Rd. (Breakers Row) | 561-655-6611 | www.thebreakers.com

"Does it get much better than this?" ponder partisans of this "elegant" French in Palm Beach's "historic" Breakers resort that whispers "class all the way"; post-Survey, a new chef has instituted forays into molecular gastronomy and the "beautiful decor" has been given a softer less-stuffy update with whimsical mushroom-shaped light sculptures (outdating both the Food and Decor scores), but what hasn't changed is the "world-class service" and tabs for which you should "be prepared to spend and spend."

Little Moir's Food Shack 🗷 *Seafood* 26 | 14 | 21 | $34

Jupiter | Jupiter Sq. | 103 S. Hwy. 1 (E. Indiantown Rd.) | 561-741-3626
Little Moir's Leftovers Café 🗷 *Seafood*
Jupiter | Abacoa Bermudiana | 451 University Blvd. (Military Trail) | 561-627-6030
www.littlemoirsfoodshack.com

There's "always a line" at this "crowded" Jupiter seafooder that's so "casual" "if you're wearing something other than flip-flops you're over-dressed"; sure, "it looks like a dive" (thanks to its "shopping-center" locale) and the "surf shop atmosphere isn't for everyone", but few can resist its "fabulous fresh fish" with "mix-and-match toppings, salads and sauces" – and it's "a bargain" at that; P.S. the Abacoa venture is in "nicer digs" with "less waiting" and the "same food."

Marcello's La Sirena 🗷 *Italian* 27 | 21 | 26 | $63

West Palm Beach | 6316 S. Dixie Hwy. (bet. Franklin & Nathan Hale Rds.) | 561-585-3128 | www.lasirenaonline.com

"Palm Beachers cross the bridge" for the "unbelievable" (if "expensive") Italian food at this "impress-a-date" West Palm "classic" complete with an "outstanding wine cellar", "professional service" (the "black-tie maitre d' treats each guest like royalty") and an "old-fashioned" dining room that got a boost with a remodel; no wonder regulars "go through withdrawal" when it "closes for the summer."

New York Prime *Steak*

25	21	21	$75

Boca Raton | 2350 Executive Center Dr. NW (Glades Rd.) | 561-998-3881 | www.newyorkprime.com

You'll need a "line of credit" to chow at this "noisy" but "elegant" meatery where "Boca's brattiest" come for "awesome cuts" of "prime cow" that would sate "Fred Flintstone"; natterers note an "NYC edge" (read: "lots of attitude") and an "unreliable" reservations policy, but it maintains "favorite" status for many.

32 East *American*

26	21	23	$53

Delray Beach | 32 E. Atlantic Ave. (bet. 1st & Swinton Aves.) | 561-276-7868 | www.32east.com

"On the Avenue and on the ball", this "hopping" Delray Beach New American "remains a class act" thanks to "passionate chef" Nick Morfogen, who creates a "nightly changing menu" with "deliciously different twists" on "market-fresh" cuisine; expect to find a "hip crowd" alternately "people-watching", quaffing "tempting libations" and making lots of "noise" (ask the "accommodating servers" for a "quieter" table upstairs); P.S. diners deem the "half-portion" options "palatable for the pocketbook."

Truluck's *Seafood*

24	24	23	$64

Boca Raton | Mizner Park | 351 Plaza Real (bet. E. Palmetto Park & Glades Rds.) | 561-391-0755 | www.trulucks.com

Fin-atics gush that this "upscale" Mizner Park boîte is "how Boca does seafood": with a "wide variety" of "fresh" fare that's "consistently good", especially on "all-you-can-eat crab Monday nights"; the "classy, supper-club atmosphere" with "live piano player" makes it "worth lingering" ("you won't believe it's a chain"), and the "well-trained staff" is a plus; just "bring your banker" to "cosign a loan", because this "tru winner" is truly "expensive."

Philadelphia

TOP FOOD RANKING

	Restaurant	Cuisine
28	Vetri	Italian
	Fountain	Continental/French
	Birchrunville Store	French/Italian
	Amada	Spanish
	Gilmore's	French
	Bluefin	Japanese
	Morimoto	Japanese
27	Talula's Table	European
	Bibou	French
	John's Roast Pork	Sandwiches
	Le Bec-Fin	French
	Lacroix	Eclectic
	Sovana Bistro	French/Mediterranean
	Horizons	Vegan
	Savona	Italian
	Prime Rib	Steak
	Le Bar Lyonnais	French
	Fond	American
	Matyson	American
	Restaurant Alba	American

OTHER NOTEWORTHY PLACES

Restaurant	Cuisine
Barclay Prime	Steak
Bistrot La Minette	French
Blue Sage	Vegetarian
Buddakan	Asian
Caffe Casta Diva	Italian
Capital Grille	Steak
Dmitri's	Greek
fish	Seafood
James	American
L'Angolo	Italian
Le Virtù	Italian
Lolita	Mexican
Modo Mio	Italian
Osteria	Italian
Pumpkin	American
Sola	American
Swann Lounge	American/French
Tiffin	Indian
Tinto	Spanish
Zahav	Israeli

	FOOD	DECOR	SERVICE	COST

Amada *Spanish*

28 | **24** | **25** | **$53**

Old City | 217 Chestnut St. (bet. 2nd & 3rd Sts.) | 215-625-2450 |
www.amadarestaurant.com

"Ama-zing!" is how amigos describe Jose Garces' "contemporary" Spaniard, voted Philly's Most Popular restaurant thanks to "magnificent", "elegantly presented" tapas that "make your taste buds swoon", and while the tabs can add up, many agree the "tasting menu is the best deal in Old City"; "knowledgeable", "gracious" service and a "beautiful" ("perhaps too dark") space add to the "incredible experience" you can share with a "hot date" or "several friends" – just be sure to book "months in advance."

Barclay Prime *Steak*

27 | **26** | **26** | **$76**

Rittenhouse | The Barclay | 237 S. 18th St. (Locust St.) | 215-732-7560 |
www.barclayprime.com

Carnivores feel as if they "died and went to steak heaven" at this "celeb"-heavy meatery in the Barclay Hotel, where signature "Kobe sliders" and "melt-in-your-mouth" beef are proffered with "a selection of spectacular, but quite unnecessary, steak knives" ("I could have cut the filet with a butter knife") in "retro library" digs with all the "Stephen Starr trimmings" (alas, "unisex bathrooms"); though it "can make your accountant cry", this "splurge" is "why the Lord created expense accounts."

Bibou ☒⇌ *French*

27 | **18** | **26** | **$50**

South Philly | 1009 S. Eighth St. (Kimball St.) | 215-965-8290 |
www.biboubyob.com

The "only thing missing is the Seine" at this cash-only BYO "jewel box" in South Philly from Le Bec-Fin alum Pierre Calmels, who creates "beautifully rendered" French "masterpieces", and his "charming" wife, Charlotte, who oversees "efficient" though "leisurely" service in an "informal" setting; the "snug" space seats only 32, so before you "dust off a great bottle of wine", keep in mind it's "hard to get a reservation" – especially for the $45 Sunday tasting dinners – now that the secret is out.

Birchrunville Store Cafe ☒☒⇌ *French/Italian*

28 | **24** | **27** | **$54**

Birchrunville | 1403 Hollow Rd. (School House Ln.) | 610-827-9002 |
www.birchrunvillestorecafe.com

Francis Trzeciak's "quaint" Franco-Italian BYO "hideaway" in a circa-1892 Chester County store wows city folk and others with "magical" cuisine that yields an "ah-hah with every bite", served in a "relaxed" setting that exudes a "hands-on family-ownership feel"; it's a "little piece of heaven" all right – and some quip "you will think you drove that far" to get there (even the restroom is a "schlep") – but nearly all agree it's "more than worth" the trip (as long as you bring cash; no plastic).

Bistrot La Minette *French*

25 | **23** | **24** | **$49**

Queen Village | 623 S. Sixth St. (Bainbridge St.) | 215-925-8000 |
www.bistrotlaminette.com

"Cheaper than a trip to Paris", this "sweet" Queen Village bistro is a "must-go" for its "sumptuous" Gallic "country" fare, served in "simple" yet "elegant" surroundings "without pretense" or "attitude" – "it's just like home, if mom was French and could cook like a chef"; "handmade" chocolates provide a sweet coda to the meal.

	FOOD	DECOR	SERVICE	COST

Bluefin ☒ *Japanese* — 28 | 14 | 21 | $39

Plymouth Meeting | 1017 Germantown Pike (Virginia Rd.) | 610-277-3917

"Don't just show up and hope for a table, it's not going to happen" at this "quality" Japanese BYO in a "dumpy" Plymouth Meeting strip mall, where suburban sushi "snobs" "fill themselves to the gills" with "spicy tuna sundaes" and other "phenomenal" offerings, served by an "over-the-top friendly" staff; most agree it's one of the "best around", and some lament "maybe if we hadn't told so many people, it would be easier to get a reservation."

Blue Sage Vegetarian Grille ☒ Ⓜ *Vegetarian* — 26 | 16 | 23 | $28

Southampton | 772 Second St. Pike (Rte. 132/Street Rd.) | 215-942-8888 | www.bluesagegrille.com

"Even guy's guys" are down with this affordable, "unpretentious" BYO "veg with an edge" located in a Bucks "strip mall", where Mike Jackson's kitchen "extracts amazing flavors out of vegetables, beans and grains" ("no tofu or mock meats") and turns them into "rich" creations, which come in "generous portions"; the "professional" waiters help you "forget any preconceptions" about meatless eats, and the "only downsides" reported are the "noise level" and "crowds."

Buddakan *Asian* — 26 | 27 | 24 | $56

Old City | 325 Chestnut St. (bet. 3rd & 4th Sts.) | 215-574-9440 | www.buddakan.com

The "beautiful, cool people" expect a "sublime" experience and "get it every time" at Stephen Starr's "tried-and-true", "loud, loud, loud" Pan-Asian "winner" in Old City, where the "amazing" fare can "send you into a food coma", served by a "top-notch" staff in a "handsome", "trendy" setting; a few suggest "Buddha would be offended", for "there is nothing in moderation" here – including the prices, though most agree "taste trumps budget" at this "awesome" "wonder."

Caffe Casta Diva ☒ Ⓜ ⇶ *Italian* . — 26 | 20 | 24 | $41

Rittenhouse | 227 S. 20th St. (Locust St.) | 215-496-9677

Rock-solid ratings reflect how Stephen Vassalluzzo "puts a lot of effort" into his "unsung", midpriced Italian BYO near Rittenhouse Square, where diners feel "transported" to "an apartment somewhere in Rome" over the "veal chop" and other "outstanding" options (the "desserts are off the charts"), served "graciously" in a "simple" room exuding a "soupçon of elegance"; the only quibbles are over the "cash-only" policy and the challenge of making "reservations on weekends."

Capital Grille *Steak* — 26 | 24 | 25 | $66

Avenue of the Arts | 1338 Chestnut St. (Broad St.) | 215-545-9588 | www.thecapitalgrille.com

"Although it's a chain", when it comes to "entertaining business clients" who "want to be seen" – or enjoying a night out with your "rich uncle" – it's tough to beat this "man-cave" hailed by "carnivores on expense accounts" as the "mac daddy" of "top-notch" steaks, which are complemented by killer "Stoli dolis", near-"flawless" service and a "clubby", "contemporary" Avenue of the Arts setting; while some gripe that "if you're not A-list here, you're invisible", the majority sees "Capital Thrill" as the steakhouse "gold standard."

	FOOD	DECOR	SERVICE	COST

Dmitri's *Greek*

| | 24 | 13 | 19 | $33 |

Northern Liberties | 944 N. Second St. (Laurel St.) | 215-592-4550 ⊄
Queen Village | 795 S. Third St. (Catharine St.) | 215-625-0556 ⊄
Rittenhouse | 2227 Pine St. (23rd St.) | 215-985-3680

Dmitri Chimes' "unpretentious" and "affordable" Hellenic tavernas are in a "league of their own", serving "simply prepared" "grilled seafood" and "Greek salads that would make Greece jealous"; claustrophobes quip that the "attentive" servers must be "size five or less" to navigate the "tight tables", and some grouse about "noise" that "reaches airport runway levels", but the "consistently fresh" fare "keeps 'em coming back for more"; the Northern Liberties branch and Queen Village flagship are cash-only BYOs, while Fitler Square takes credit cards and serves wine and beer.

fish *Seafood*

| | 25 | 19 | 22 | $50 |

Graduate Hospital | 1708 Lombard St. (17th St.) | 215-545-9600 | www.fishphilly.com

Mike Stollenwerk's "creative" preparations of fin fare are "beyond compare" at his "adorable" "boutique" seafooder in a Graduate Hospital storefront; in addition to offering some of the "best-tasting fish in the city", he reels in afishionados with "reasonable wines by the glass", "knowledgeable" service and a "relaxed" vibe in the "sparsely decorated", "candlelit" setting.

Fond 🅂🅜 *American*

| | 27 | 18 | 26 | $44 |

South Philly | 1617 E. Passyunk Ave. (Tasker St.) | 215-551-5000 | www.fondphilly.com

Virtually all agree this "bright" BYO "star" in a "high-end storefront" on South Philly's "ever-growing East Passyunk strip" is a "can't-miss experience", thanks to Le Bec-Fin alum Lee Styer's "creative", "excellent" New American cuisine and Jessie Prawlucki's breads and desserts, for which "your mouth will keep thanking you"; "superb" service helps make up for the "noise", but "space is limited", so be sure to snag a reservation.

Fountain Restaurant *Continental/French*

| | 28 | 28 | 28 | $89 |

Logan Square | Four Seasons Hotel | 1 Logan Sq. (Benjamin Franklin Pkwy.) | 215-963-1500 | www.fourseasons.com

"When you want to impress" someone, the Four Seasons' "swish" main room is the "gold standard" for "luxurious" "power" dining, where Rafael Gonzalez's Continental-French cuisine will "blow you away", as will the "unparalleled" service "fit for a king and queen"; jackets are required and it'll "cost you more than three coins" in Logan Square's fountain outside, but most agree it's "worth every penny" and "calorie."

Gilmore's 🅂🅜 *French*

| | 28 | 24 | 27 | $56 |

West Chester | 133 E. Gay St. (bet. Matlack & Walnut Sts.) | 610-431-2800 | www.gilmoresrestaurant.com

You "always feel well cared for and well fed" at Peter Gilmore's "plush" French BYO "destination" in West Chester, where his "exquisite" "epicurean delights" and "solicitous" service from a "professional" staff "add up to a first-rate" experience that transports you to "France" and "that little place in the valley that everyone whispers about"; it takes "three to

FOOD | DECOR | SERVICE | COST

four weeks' advance notice" to book a table in the "compact" townhouse space, but almost all agree it's "well worth the wait"; P.S. the $35, four-course feast served Tuesday–Thursdays is a "genuine bargain."

Horizons ⑤Ⓜ *Vegan* — 27 | 23 | 26 | $40

South St. | 611 S. Seventh St. (Kater St.) | 215-923-6117 | www.horizonsphiladelphia.com

Rich Landau and Kate Jacoby "delete the meat" from the "complex" "haute" vegan cuisine at their "unpretentious" bistro off South Street, proving that "you don't need to kill your food to have a killer menu"; "fabulous" "margatinis" and an "interesting", all-vegan wine list complement the "incredible" fare, served by a "fantastic" staff in "serene", "romantic" surroundings – in sum, it's a "superb dining experience" for "vegetarians" and "carnivores" alike.

James Ⓜ *American* — 27 | 24 | 25 | $59

South Philly | 824 S. Eighth St. (bet. Catharine & Christian Sts.) | 215-629-4980 | www.jameson8th.com

"Long live King James" – aka Jim Burke, who gives a "lesson" in "daring", "imaginative" food featuring "sustainably sourced ingredients" at his "fab, fab, fab" New American in South Philly, which exudes a "touch of class" at every turn thanks to wife Christina, who "runs a very tight ship"; the "hip", yet "intimate" setting "puts you at ease" (though some find it "too dark") and is one of the "best places for a romantic evening" in town, albeit an "expensive" one.

John's Roast Pork ⑤⊄ *Sandwiches* — 27 | 7 | 17 | $11

South Philly | 14 E. Snyder Ave. (Weccacoe Ave.) | 215-463-1951 | www.johnsroastpork.com

This highly rated sandwich shop occupies a "cramped", "nondescript" shack hidden behind a South Philly Lowe's, where groupies solve the "impossible decision" between the "best cheesesteak in town" and "equally outstanding" roast pork "with greens and provolone" by "getting both"; "surly service adds to the experience", and the only drawbacks are the "long lines" and "short hours" (until 3 PM or whenever the "bread runs out").

Lacroix at The Rittenhouse *Eclectic* — 27 | 27 | 27 | $76

Rittenhouse | Rittenhouse Hotel | 210 W. Rittenhouse Sq. (bet. Locust & Walnut Sts.) | 215-790-2533 | www.lacroixrestaurant.com

"Classy with a capital C", this "magnificent" Rittenhouse Hotel establishment is a "luxurious", "über-modern" showcase for chef Jason Cichonski's "inventive", "awesome" Eclectic tasting menus, which are "matched with amazing views" of the square and "attentive" service from a staff that's "sometimes a little too eager to please"; the "$59 Sunday brunch" buffet, $24 lunch and $35 dinner prix fixes, and the "new bar" are budget-friendlier slices of "foodie heaven."

L'Angolo Ⓜ *Italian* — 26 | 14 | 22 | $38

South Philly | 1415 W. Porter St. (Broad St.) | 215-389-4252 | www.salentorestaurant.com

You "walk through the kitchen" to get to the "sardine can" of a "dining room at this "inviting" South Philly BYO where "stellar", "authentic" Italian dishes are served by "tip-top" waiters who "make each trip seem like a visit to Italy", while the kitchen "graciously accommodates

FOOD | DECOR | SERVICE | COST

special requests"; "reasonable" prices are another reason many recommend it "for your to-go list" – just be sure to "make a reservation."

Le Bar Lyonnais ⧄ French
27 | 23 | 25 | $55

Rittenhouse | 1523 Walnut St. (bet. 15th & 16th Sts.) | 215-567-1000 | www.lebecfin.com

At Le Bec-Fin's subterranean spin-off in Rittenhouse, you can enjoy "true French cooking" and "excellent", "but not obtrusive" service in "intimate, sophisticated" environs, with Georges Perrier "always around to schmooze"; it's "half the price" of dining upstairs, and while it comes "without the elegance and drama" of the mother ship, "after two glasses of wine, you won't be able to tell the difference."

Le Bec-Fin ⧄ French
27 | 27 | 27 | $98

Rittenhouse | 1523 Walnut St. (bet. 15th & 16th Sts.) | 215-567-1000 | www.lebecfin.com

"Save your calories for days" before heading to Georges Perrier's "gorgeous", "sense-seducing" Rittenhouse "institution", where the dress code may have been "relaxed" but not the kitchen's standards: expect "sublime" French cuisine "prepared to perfection" and enhanced by an "amazing dessert cart" and "impeccable" service; if a few think "time has passed" this "legend" by and quip that you have to "sell your kids" to pay the bill, "everyone should experience at least once."

Le Virtù Italian
26 | 20 | 22 | $47

South Philly | 1927 E. Passyunk Ave. (bet. McKean & Mifflin Sts.) | 215-271-5626 | www.levirtu.com

Even though chef Luciana Spurio "does not seek to dazzle", her "hands of gold" still create "beautiful", "homemade" dishes that exemplify "the special charm of the Abruzzese table" at this "spectacular" Italian that "rises above South Philly expectations"; the service is "friendly", and though the "unassuming" decor "lets you know you're in the neighborhood", the patio is "wonderful" in "warm weather."

Lolita ⧄ Mexican
26 | 19 | 21 | $36

Washington Square West | 106 S. 13th St. (bet. Chestnut & Sansom Sts.) | 215-546-7100 | www.lolitabyob.com

There are "long waits" "for a reason" at this "haute", "trendy" cash-only "BYOT(equila)" in Wash West, which takes "Mexican to a new level" with "original flavors and combinations" and not "a chimichanga in sight", while "fantastic" "margarita mixers" will "change your perception of the drink"; though the "open kitchen" and "lively" scene cause a few to grouse that "some soundproofing would go a long way", "friendly, efficient" service helps smooth things over.

Matyson ⧄ American
27 | 19 | 24 | $45

Rittenhouse | 37 S. 19th St. (bet. Chestnut & Ludlow Sts.) | 215-564-2925 | www.matyson.com

"Foodies" call this "classy" New American near Rittenhouse Square the "best BYO in the city", thanks to the "wonderful, creative" and "always changing" menu from Brian Lofink and Ben Puchowitz that is at once "consistent" and "refreshing"; the staff "feels like family", and while some chafe at the "forced intimacy" of the "small storefront" space and "noise" that'll have you "communicating in sign language", the majority deems it a "cut above the rest."

Modo Mio ⓂＢＹＯ Italian
26 | 16 | 21 | $39

Northern Liberties | 161 W. Girard Ave. (Hancock St.) | 215-203-8707 | www.modomiorestaurant.com

Foodies "swoon" over Peter McAndrews' "lusty", "spot-on" Italian cuisine (including "some of the best bread in town") at his "inviting" trattoria on the edge of Northern Liberties, which fans proclaim one of the city's "best" BYOs, "hands-down"; the cash-only $33 prix fixe 'turista' menu offers "Vetri quality at McDonald's prices", while staffers "care that you have a good meal", so "run, don't walk" (and "bring earplugs") for a "special experience."

Morimoto Japanese
28 | 26 | 25 | $76

Washington Square West | 723 Chestnut St. (bet. 7th & 8th Sts.) | 215-413-9070 | www.morimotorestaurant.com

"Amazing", "pristine sushi", a "fascinating array" of cooked dishes and "top-notch" service all "dazzle" at this Japanese from Stephen Starr and *Iron Chef* Masaharu Morimoto, set in a "luminescent", "postmodern whale's belly of a space" in Wash West; besides maybe the "trippy" "phallic lamps" on the tables, the "only hindrance comes at the end" "on a little piece of paper" quip sticker-shocked surveyors, but "rest assured" it's worth it – especially if you "jump off the deep end" and try the "sublime" omakase tasting menu.

Osteria Italian
27 | 24 | 24 | $56

North Philly | 640 N. Broad St. (Wallace St.) | 215-763-0920 | www.osteriaphilly.com

"Let your inhibitions go" at the Vetri gang's "industrial"-meets-"rustic" Italian in a "pioneering" North Philly location; it's "perfect" for a "date" or "celebratory night out" thanks to chef Jeff Michaud's "swoon-worthy" pizzas, charcuterie and pastas, which are backed by an "expansive" wine list and served by a staff that makes you feel "snuggled up in a warm, doughy embrace" in a room that's "full of energy"; while it's "not cheap", "easy street parking" (albeit in a "questionable" area) will save you some $$$.

Prime Rib Steak
27 | 26 | 26 | $63

Rittenhouse | Radisson Plaza-Warwick Hotel | 1701 Locust St. (17th St.) | 215-772-1701 | www.theprimerib.com

You "feel like you're in a movie" at this "special-occasion" steakhouse in the Warwick, where a "fancy-shmancy", "'40s nightclub" tableaux sets the stage for "caveman cuts" of "primo" beef, "large cocktails" and "tuxedo-clad" waiters who are "true professionals" (even when serving the "bargain" $35 prix fixe special); add "unobtrusive", "romantic" live piano music to the mix, and fans insist it's "all you need to feel that things will get better" in "tough economic times."

Pumpkin Ⓜ ＢＹＯ American
26 | 18 | 23 | $41

Graduate Hospital | 1713 South St. (17th St.) | 215-545-4448 | www.pumpkinphilly.com

Ian Moroney's "knockout" New American "combinations" star at his "intimate" cash-only BYO in Graduate Hospital, where the staff is "friendly and knowledgeable" and the $35 five-course Sunday night prix fixe is "especially enticing"; the "matchbox-size" room is "not the most comfortable", but hey, "you can't eat decor."

	FOOD	DECOR	SERVICE	COST

Restaurant Alba ⊠ⓜ *American* — 27 | 22 | 24 | $52

Malvern | 7 W. King St. (Warren Ave.) | 610-644-4009 |
www.restaurantalba.com

A "mecca for seasonal locavores", Sean Weinberg's "open kitchen" in
Malvern creates "amazingly creative" "Euro-style" New American
"grill" dishes in a "micro"-sized, "rustic" setting; "you can't go wrong"
with the "new" Italian wine list from "small producers", but some who
find it "pricey" in general lament that it "now charges $10 corkage."

Savona *Italian* — 27 | 26 | 26 | $66

Gulph Mills | 100 Old Gulph Rd. (Rte. 320) | 610-520-1200 |
www.savonarestaurant.com

While Evan Lambert has freshened his "elegant" Italian "mainstay" in
Gulph Mills, shrinking the "special-occasion" dining room, boosting
the outside patio and expanding the bar, Main Liners still come for
chef Andrew Masciangelo's "Rolls-Royce" cuisine "at Kia pricing"; the
"informative" staff provides "superb", "consistent" service, while
master sommelier Melissa Monosoff oversees a 1,000-bottle list
housed in a "really cool wine cellar."

Sola ⊠ⓜ *American* — 27 | 19 | 24 | $53

Bryn Mawr | 614 W. Lancaster Ave. (Penn St.) | 610-526-0123 |
www.solabyob.com

"It can be hard to snag a seat" at Dave Clouser's New American BYO
"treasure" in Bryn Mawr, thanks to his "excellent", "elegant" dishes
"presented superbly" by an "attentive" staff (which, some fret, seems
a "smidge overworked"), and $40 weekly prix fixes worthy of "that
special bottle", served in Schott Zwiesel stemware ($2 corkage); the
only downside is the "tight space", but if you "run out of conversation", "you'll be able to listen in on your neighbor."

Sovana Bistro ⓜ *French/Mediterranean* — 27 | 22 | 24 | $48

Kennett Square | 696 Unionville Rd. (Rte. 926) | 610-444-5600 |
www.sovanabistro.com

"Competition for tables can be fierce" at Nicholas Farrell's French-
Med bistro "gem" that's "worth the drive" to "horse country" outside
Kennett Square, where he "knocks" the "socks off" "locavores" with
"terrific" "presentations" of "amazing" dishes ("heavenly cheese
plates", "gourmet pizzas") from his "100-mile menu"; the "warm"
front-of-the-house provides "impeccable" service, while the servers
are "knowledgeable", and even though it offers a "nice wine list", BYO
is permitted with an $8 corkage.

Swann Lounge ❂ *American/French* — 26 | 26 | 27 | $59

Logan Square | Four Seasons Hotel | 1 Logan Sq.
(bet. Benjamin Franklin Pkwy. & 18th St.) | 215-963-1500 |
www.fourseasons.com

"The Four Seasons still is, well, the Four Seasons" on Logan Square, and
though some say this lounge plays "second fiddle" to the "famous Fountain", fans insist it more than "holds its own" "for an elegant but casual
meal or drink", afternoon tea or Sunday brunch buffet, with "impeccable" service, "outstanding" New American and French fare, and a "civilized", "less formal" setting; many call it the city's "best place for
after-work drinks" in town – "particularly if you have a trust account."

	FOOD	DECOR	SERVICE	COST

Talula's Table *European* | 27 | 20 | 26 | $125

Kennett Square | 102 W. State St. (Union St.) | 610-444-8255 |
www.talulastable.com

"Sure, you gotta wait a year" for a reservation (and show up at 7 PM sharp) at this "foodie's paradise" in the back of a Kennett Square market-cum-takeaway, but fans insist it's "worth it" for the eight-course, $125-a-head Euro-style "farmhouse-table dinners" for groups of five to 14 people that are like "a wonderful homey dinner party" – except with "knowledgeable" servers; it's a "culinary adventure" that'll make even hard-core gourmands "cry uncle."

Tiffin *Indian* | 25 | 12 | 18 | $22

Northern Liberties | 710 W. Girard Ave. (Franklin St.) | 215-922-1297
Mount Airy | 7105 Emlen St. (W. Mt. Pleasant Ave.) | 215-242-3656
Wynnewood | 50 E. Wynnewood Rd. (Williams Rd.) | 610-642-3344
Elkins Park | Elkins Park Sq. | 8080 Old York Rd. (Church Rd.) | 215-635-9205
www.tiffin.com

"Dependable", "affordable", "delicious" are just a few of the superlatives that flow over this fast-growing, "no-frills" Indian BYO mini-chain rooted in a Girard Avenue storefront; supporters have "fun" working their "way through the menu", whether it's delivery by "nattily" dressed drivers, eat-in or "beautifully packaged" takeout ("my stovetop may start collecting dust").

Tinto *Spanish* | 27 | 23 | 23 | $54

Rittenhouse | 114 S. 20th St. (Sansom St.) | 215-665-9150 |
www.tintorestaurant.com

"Basque in the glow" of Jose Garces' *Iron Chef*-ness" at his "sexy", "go-to" small-plates "standard" near Rittenhouse Square ("complementing" Amada crosstown), where the pintxos' "unusual flavors and combinations" make for "exhilarating" meals, orchestrated by a "knowledgeable" staff that also helps you navigate an "awesome wine list"; insiders suggest the "tasting menu is the way to go", unless you're willing to "throw all caution of a budget to the wind."

Vetri ⧉ *Italian* | 28 | 23 | 27 | $97

Washington Square West | 1312 Spruce St. (bet. Broad & 13th Sts.) |
215-732-3478 | www.vetriristorante.com

A "religious experience" is how devotees describe Marc Vetri's "splendid" Italian "splurge", rated No. 1 for Food in the Philadelphia Survey and deemed a sure way to "impress your date" thanks to its "quaint" Wash West brownstone setting, "polished" service, "wonderful" wine pairings and "sublime" tasting menus; though most agree it's "worth every penny", you may want "a stiff drink just before the check arrives."

Zahav *Israeli* | 25 | 23 | 24 | $48

Society Hill | 237 St. James Pl. (2nd St.) | 215-625-8800 |
www.zahavrestaurant.com

A "revelation" to many, Michael Solomonov's "upper-crust" nouveau Israeli "fires on all 18 cylinders" in "spare", "modern" digs in Society Hill Towers, where the *mazel tovs* flow for its "addictive" hummus, "homemade breads", "coal-grilled meats and fish" and "enough adventurous things" to "scare your entire family" ("duck hearts, anyone?"); "let the staff guide you" as you "drop your paycheck."

Phoenix/Scottsdale

TOP FOOD RANKING

	Restaurant	Cuisine
28	Kai	Eclectic
	Binkley's	American
27	Pizzeria Bianco	Pizza
26	Atlas	Eclectic
	T. Cook's	Mediterranean
	Vincent's	French/Southwestern
	Rancho Pinot	American
	Cyclo	Vietnamese
	Barrio	Mexican
	Mastro's City Hall	Steak

OTHER NOTEWORTHY PLACES

Cafe Bink	American
Eddie V's	Seafood/Steak
FnB	American
Lon's	American
Mastro's Ocean Club	Seafood
Mission	Nuevo Latino
Noca	American
P.F. Chang's	Chinese
Quiessence	American
Tarbell's	American

Atlas Bistro ☒Ⓜ *Eclectic*   26 | 14 | 24 | $46

South Scottsdale | Wilshire Plaza | 2515 N. Scottsdale Rd. (E. Wilshire Dr.) | Scottsdale | 480-990-2433 | www.atlasbistrobyob.com

"Heaven for foodies", this South Scottsdale BYOB serves "imaginative" Eclectic fare with a Southwestern "kick" that "never disappoints" (unlike the "funky" and admittedly "cramped" digs, but "you'll forget" about all that "once you take a bite"); it's also "paradise" for oenophiles, as guests "select the perfect bottle to accompany a memorable meal" at the attached "discount wine store" and then "save a bundle" thanks to waived corkage fees (if you bring it from elsewhere, it's only $10).

Barrio Cafe Ⓜ *Mexican*   26 | 17 | 21 | $33

Phoenix | 2814 N. 16th St. (Thomas Rd.) | 602-636-0240 | www.barriocafe.com

"No Tex-Mex found here" declare devotees who suffer a "lousy" Phoenix location with "difficult parking", a "no-reservations policy" and "long waits" for Silvana Salcido Esparza's "out-of-the-ordinary", "crave-able" Southern Mexican fare featuring "fascinating blends" of lighter, less-spicy flavors (start off with the "outstanding" "tableside-prepped guacamole"); a "unique selection of wines", hundreds of tequilas and margaritas that "knock you on your *culo*" fuel the "noisy", "fun-filled" atmosphere.

| | FOOD | DECOR | SERVICE | COST |

Binkley's Restaurant 🏵Ⓜ American — 28 | 20 | 26 | $76

Cave Creek | 6920 E. Cave Creek Rd. (Tom Darlington Dr.) | 480-437-1072 | www.binkleysrestaurant.com

"Napa Valley meets funky Cave Creek" at this "small" "foodie oasis" from "super-talented" French Laundry alum Kevin Binkley, whose "adventurous" French-influenced New American fare comes with "fresh local ingredients" and "molecular-gastronomy flourishes" that yield "magical flavor combinations"; "whether you order the [four-to-six-course] tasting menu or not", you'll "be blown away" by the "variety of amuse-bouches" "sprinkled" throughout the meal by "bend-over-backwards" servers, not to mention the "expensive" tabs.

Cafe Bink Ⓜ American — - | - | - | M

Carefree | 36899 N. Tom Darlington Dr. (Cave Creek Rd.) | 480-488-9796 | www.cafebink.com

Bright, modern artwork, a handsome bar, banquettes and a patio with nice views are some of the components of this casual New American bistro in Carefree; it's a whole lot cheaper than its sibling, the legendary Binkley's in nearby Cave Creek.

Cyclo 🏵Ⓜ Vietnamese — 26 | 13 | 21 | $20

Chandler | 1919 W. Chandler Blvd. (Dobson Rd.) | 480-963-4490 | www.cycloaz.com

She may be the "hottest restaurant owner" in Chandler, but "sassy" Justina Duong delivers far more than "wisecracking" "personality" and "eye candy" at this Vietnamese BYOB; the "authentic" fare "with gourmet flair" – "always fresh" and "inexpensive" – also makes it "worth the trip", despite the "unamusing strip-mall setting" and "depressing decor" (a post-Survey modernization should cheer things up).

Eddie V's Prime Seafood Seafood/Steak — 25 | 23 | 23 | $60

North Scottsdale | 20715 N. Pima Rd. (E. Thompson Peak Pkwy.) | Scottsdale | 480-538-8468 | www.eddiev.com

"The freshest fish you'll find in the desert", "outstanding steaks" and "hearty sides" are "well presented" in "exciting" preparations at this "clubby", "bustling" North Scottsdale surf 'n' turfer; sure, there's "lots of money" on display, but the "nice crowd" is not above a bargain, sometimes preferring to "make a great meal" out of the "yummy" half-price happy-hour appetizers in the "jazz bar."

FnB Restaurant Ⓜ American — - | - | - | M

Old Town | 7133 E. Stetson Dr. (Scottsdale Rd.) | Scottsdale | 480-425-9463 | www.fnbrestaurant.com

Charleen Badman preps the comforting New American fare in the open kitchen, while co-owning partner Pavle Milic heads the front of house at this tiny, lively Old Town bistro with black-and-white, latter-day-diner decor; local pride is evident in many farm-to-table ingredients and the Arizona-only wine list, and everything's affordably priced.

Kai 🏵Ⓜ Eclectic — 28 | 26 | 27 | $71

Chandler | Sheraton Wild Horse Pass Resort & Spa | 5594 W. Wild Horse Pass Blvd. (Loop Rd.) | 602-225-0100 | www.wildhorsepassresort.com

Situated on tribal land in Chandler, this "consistently phenomenal" resort restaurant earns Phoenix-Scottsdale's No. 1 Food rating with an "innovative", "exquisite" "blending of Native American" and Eclectic fare that utilizes "modern techniques" to turn "locally sourced ingredients from the reservation and nearby communities" into edible "artwork"; the "polished service" adds another "first-class" layer to the "worth-every-penny" experience, available in an "understated" contemporary interior and on a "quiet, romantic patio" exhibiting "spectacular sunset views."

Lon's at the Hermosa *American*

| 25 | 26 | 25 | $58 |

Paradise Valley | Hermosa Inn | 5532 N. Palo Cristi Rd. (E. Stanford Dr.) | 602-955-7878 | www.lons.com

For "old time Arizona at its best", settle into this "romantic" New American in a "gorgeous" Paradise Valley hacienda that once "belonged to famous cowboy artist" Lon Megargee; the "exquisitely prepared" fare exhibits "innovative Southwestern" "flair", and though it's "pricey", "you get what you pay for", especially when you procure a table on the "magical" patio, which is "warmed by juniper-fueled" fireplaces and backed by "stunning views" of Camelback Mountain.

Mastro's City Hall Steakhouse *Steak*

| 26 | 24 | 25 | $71 |

Scottsdale | 6991 E. Camelback Rd. (Goldwater Blvd.) | 480-941-4700 | www.mastrosoceanclub.com

Primo for "people-watching", this steakhouse in a "trendy area of Scottsdale" "impresses" with a "dynamic setting", dim lighting, "bar action" and "enjoyable entertainment"; more important, the "juicy, buttery" beef is joined by a "nice selection of other entrees and sides", plus "stiff cocktails" brought to table by "stellar" servers; in short, if "money's not a problem, this is the place for you."

Mastro's Ocean Club *Seafood*

| 25 | 25 | 24 | $68 |

North Scottsdale | Kierland Commons | 15045 N. Kierland Blvd. (E. Greenway Pkwy.) | Scottsdale | 480-443-8555 | www.mastrosoceanclub.com

"Bring lots of plastic" to this "glitzy" eatery in North Scottsdale to fully enjoy the "abundant choice" of "beautifully prepared" fish and "delicious sides" served in "lavish portions" by "professional staffers"; "even though it's a seafood restaurant", there's "a reliable meat market at the bar" from "happy hour into the evening", so "bring your earplugs" too or risk going "deaf" from the roar of the "cougars."

Mission, The *Nuevo Latino*

| – | – | – | M |

Old Town | 3815 N. Brown Ave. (bet. 1st & 2nd Sts.) | Scottsdale | 480-636-5005 | www.themissionaz.com

This moderately priced Old Town spot serves Nuevo Latino cuisine amid a mission decor theme sexed up with candlelight and a glowing wall of Himalayan salt blocks; there's fireside seating on the patio, plus a separate bar/lounge where exotic margaritas and over 50 premium tequilas can be sampled at a communal table.

Noca ☒ *American*

| – | – | – | E |

Camelback Corridor | 3118 E. Camelback Rd. (32nd St.) | Phoenix | 602-956-6622 | www.restaurantnoca.com

Notable chef Chris Curtiss creates sophisticated, ingredient-driven New American cuisine with French methodology at this sleek yet relaxed spot with an open kitchen and a name that's an acronym for North of

Camelback; the prices are slightly steep, but the multicourse Sunday Simple Supper, with a weekly changing theme, is a bargain at $35.

P.F. Chang's China Bistro *Chinese*　　20 | 20 | 19 | $30

Chandler | Chandler Fashion Ctr. | 3255 W. Chandler Blvd. (bet. Chandler Village Dr. & Rte. 101) | 480-899-0472
Fashion Square | The Waterfront | 7135 E. Camelback Rd. (N. Scottsdale Rd.) | Scottsdale | 480-949-2610
Mesa | 6610 E. Superstition Springs Blvd. (Power Rd.) | 480-218-4900
North Scottsdale | Kierland Commons | 7132 E. Greenway Pkwy. (N. Scottsdale Rd.) | Scottsdale | 480-367-2999
Tempe | 740 S. Mill Ave. (bet. E. 7th St. & E. University Dr.) | 480-731-4600
www.pfchangs.com

While "not for purists", the "Americanized" Chinese fare offered at these outposts of the "midpriced" chain is "remarkably consistent" and "delicious", so surveyors cut them "some slack"; besides, the "fun atmosphere" "beats takeout" any day, even though they're "noisy" and often "hard to get into."

Pizzeria Bianco ⊠Ⓜ *Pizza*　　27 | 19 | 20 | $27

Downtown Phoenix | Heritage Sq. | 623 E. Adams St. (N. 7th St.) | Phoenix | 602-258-8300 | www.pizzeriabianco.com

Featuring "only the best fresh ingredients", "brilliant" Chris Bianco's "glorious" wood-fired Neapolitan-style pizzas are deemed the "best in the known world" by Phoenix "locals and traveling foodies alike"; get in line "before they open" at 5 PM and you may get seated within "40 minutes" – as opposed to "horrendous"-"beyond-belief" "three-to-four-hour" waits ("raise your spirits" at the "wine bar next door").

Quiessence Restaurant &　　▽ 27 | 25 | 25 | $59
Wine Bar ⊠Ⓜ *American*

South Phoenix | Farm at South Mountain | 6106 S. 32nd St. (Southern Ave.) | Phoenix | 602-276-0601 | www.quiessencerestaurant.com

"Tucked away in a pecan grove" on the Farm at South Mountain, this "cozy gem" features the "simple gourmet" New American fare of chef Greg LaPrad, who "walks the walk" by using "local, seasonal and organic ingredients" (special kudos are reserved for the "awesome" "in-house charcuterie and handmade pastas"); "it's pricey", but the "rustic", "romantic" setting makes for a "special night" that's "worth every penny."

Rancho Pinot ⊠ *American*　　26 | 20 | 24 | $52

Scottsdale | Lincoln Vill. | 6208 N. Scottsdale Rd. (bet. Lincoln & McDonald Drs.) | 480-367-8030 | www.ranchopinot.com

Although it's "hidden away" in a Scottsdale strip mall, this "neighborhood" "jewel" with "cowboy-chic" decor is a "real find" thanks to chef Chrysa Robertson (a "huge talent"), who lends an "Arizona accent" to her "sophisticated" New American "comfort food" by using "seasonal and locally grown" ingredients; praise also goes to her "gracious", "funny" partner, Tom Kaufman, who oversees the "superb wine program" and the "charming", "well-informed" staff.

Tarbell's *American*　　26 | 20 | 25 | $53

Camelback Corridor | Camelback East Shops | 3213 E. Camelback Rd. (N. 32nd St.) | Phoenix | 602-955-8100 | www.tarbells.com

"This is the way to run a neighborhood restaurant" cheer boosters of this "comfortable", "cosmopolitan" Camelback Corridor American bistro beloved for its "upbeat" atmosphere and "consistently delicious", "seasonally current" "classic" dishes; Mark Tarbell (the "consummate host") manages a "brilliant wine list" as well as schmoozes "beautiful locals" who wish they "could eat here every night" (it's a bit "expensive" for that).

T. Cook's *Mediterranean*   26 | 28 | 26 | $65

Phoenix | Royal Palms Resort & Spa | 5200 E. Camelback Rd.
(bet. N. Arcadia Dr. & 56th St.) | 602-808-0766 | www.royalpalmshotel.com
"Dripping with romance", this "gorgeous-in-all-seasons" "date-night" and "special-occasion" staple (voted Most Popular in Phoenix-Scottsdale) features "elegant", "enchanting" "Southwestern-style decor" and the Royal Palms' "beautiful grounds"; the "freshest ingredients are always the star" of the "far-from-ordinary", "gourmet" Mediterranean cuisine, which is "beautifully presented" by staffers who "know what professional service means"; P.S. while dinner is "expensive" (and "worth it"), lunch and Sunday brunch are relative "steals."

Vincent's on Camelback ⊠ *French/Southwestern*   26 | 22 | 24 | $60

Camelback Corridor | 3930 E. Camelback Rd. (40th St.) | Phoenix |
602-224-0225 | www.vincentsoncamelback.com
"Phoenix food legend" Vincent Guerithault crafts a "magnificent fusion" of French and Southwestern (the "menu's divided into classic and nouveau") at this "quaint" Camelback Corridor "oldie but goodie" also known for a "super array of wines", "out-of-this-world service" and "expensive" checks; while carpers contend that the whole endeavor "needs a creative kick in the pants" (particularly "tiresome" decor), the majority opines "it's hard to improve on perfection."

TOP FOOD RANKING

	Restaurant	Cuisine
28	Painted Lady	Pacific NW
27	Apizza Scholls	Pizza
	Beast	French/Pacific NW
	Toro Bravo	Spanish
	Nuestra Cocina	Mexican
	Paley's Place	Pacific NW
	Andina	Peruvian
	Higgins	Pacific NW
26	Castagna/Café Castagna	European
	Joel Palmer House	Pacific NW

OTHER NOTEWORTHY PLACES

Alba Osteria	Italian
Clyde Common	American/Eclectic
Genoa/Accanto	Italian
Heathman	French/Pacific NW
Jake's	Seafood
Ken's	Pizza
Laurelhurst Market	Steak
Le Pigeon	French
Park Kitchen	American/Pacific NW
Pok Pok	SE Asian/Thai

Alba Osteria & Enoteca 🗷🅼 *Italian*   26 | 20 | 24 | $41

Southwest Portland | 6440 SW Capitol Hwy. (Bertha Blvd.) | 503-977-3045 |
www.albaosteria.com

This "rustic" "hidden gem" in suburban SW Portland is the "real deal" for
"interesting, well-prepared" Piedmontese cuisine ("unique" to the area),
highlighted by "heavenly" homemade pastas and served alongside
"superb" Northern Italian wines with "decent price ranges"; "attentive" staffers are another reason it's "worth the drive for Downtowners."

Andina *Peruvian*   27 | 24 | 24 | $42

Pearl District | Pennington Bldg. | 1314 NW Glisan St. (bet. 13th &
14th Aves.) | 503-228-9535 | www.andinarestaurant.com

Prepare for a "dining adventure" at this "festive yet classy" Pearl District
"hot spot", because the modern Peruvian fare is "unusual and spectacular", plus you can "experiment freely" thanks to "tasty" tapas that
come in "three different sizes"; some opine the "fruity, spicy" "cocktails are the main attraction" (try the one whose name "sounds like
'sexy woman'"), while "great" live music adds to the overall appeal.

Apizza Scholls *Pizza*   27 | 13 | 18 | $22

Hawthorne | 4741 SE Hawthorne Blvd. (48th Ave.) | 503-233-1286 |
www.apizzascholls.com

"Euphoric" surveyors say it's like they've "died and gone to Brooklyn"
at this SE Hawthorne pizzeria where "heavenly", "charred" thin-crust

FOOD | DECOR | SERVICE | COST

pies are served by "stressed" staffers amid "no ambiance"; "arrive 30 minutes before opening" and you'll still "find a line down the street", and once inside, you must "adhere to the rules" ("no takeout" Thursdays–Sundays, "no single slices", no "special requests" regarding the "minimal toppings", etc.), but the pizza's "well worth the hassle."

Beast ☒ French/Pacific NW
27 | 20 | 25 | $98

Northeast Portland | 5425 NE 30th Ave. (Killingsworth St.) | 503-841-6968 | www.beastpdx.com

"Creative dictator" Naomi Pomeroy grants "no substitutions" on the pricey prix fixes she whips up twice nightly (Wednesday–Saturday, augmented by two Sunday brunch seatings) at her "minimal" NE Portland eatery, but that's no issue for fans of "rich", "fabulous" French-Pacific NW fare, which is "well presented" by a "professional" staff and paired with "inspired wines"; the two communal tables are "a little too communal" for some, but "if you're comfortable" "with strangers", you'll have an "entertaining experience" – "unless you're a vegetarian" (think about the name).

Castagna ☒☒ European
26 | 22 | 24 | $40

Hawthorne | 1752 SE Hawthorne Blvd. (18th Ave.) | 503-231-7373

Café Castagna European
Hawthorne | 1758 SE Hawthorne Blvd. (bet. 17th & 18th Aves.) | 503-231-9959
www.castagnarestaurant.com

Post-Survey, SE Hawthorne's "sophisticated, expensive" Castagna, known for its "wonderful service" and "smart" wines, premiered a new Modern European menu while sprucing up its "modern" environs, outdating the Food and Decor scores; the "lively", "casual" cafe next door "offers a similar experience at a more budget-minded level", plus one of Portland's most "excellent burgers."

Clyde Common American/Eclectic
24 | 20 | 20 | $36

Downtown | 1014 SW Stark St. (bet. 10th & 11th Aves.) | 503-228-3333 | www.clydecommon.com

"One of the most interesting kitchens in Portland" churns out "whimsical", "delicious" New American–Eclectic fare that's "priced fairly" and made with "fresh, local" ingredients at this Downtowner; the "loud", "hip", "industrial"-inflected digs come "stocked with communal tables", a "bustling bar" where "amazing drinks" are mixed, a somewhat "secluded" balcony and a "quirky staff."

Genoa ☒ Italian
- | - | - | VE

NE/SE 28th | 2832 SE Belmont St. (bet. 28th & 29th Aves.) | 503-238-1464 | www.genoarestaurant.com

Accanto ● Italian
NE/SE 28th | 2838 SE Belmont St. (29th Ave.) | 503-235-4900 | www.accantopdx.com

One of Portland's long-standing fine-dining destinations, this Northern Italian on Belmont shuttered in 2008 and recently reopened with new ownership and a lush new look, with a fireplace, earth-toned banquettes and glimmering chandeliers; true to tradition, the kitchen turns out a prix fixe-only menu (five courses for $55) of rotating regional specialties, all complemented by an extensive wine list; P.S. its attached cafe, Accanto, features small plates at modest tabs.

	FOOD	DECOR	SERVICE	COST

Heathman Restaurant, The *French/Pacific NW* | 26 | 24 | 25 | $50 |

Downtown | Heathman Hotel | 1001 SW Broadway (Salmon St.) |
503-790-7752 | www.heathmanrestaurantandbar.com

"All class, all the time" is evident at this Downtown "sophisticate" in
the "lovely" Heathman Hotel, where "creative" "Gallic inspiration"
and "fresh", "seasonal produce" are the hallmarks of the Pacific NW
fare; "gracious", "old-school service", "elegant" yet "subtle" surroundings and "wonderful wines" complete the "high-end" experience, which includes a "pleasurable breakfast" ("try the salmon
hash"), "memorable" high tea and "excellent happy hour."

Higgins Restaurant & Bar *Pacific NW* | 27 | 22 | 26 | $48 |

Downtown | 1239 SW Broadway (Jefferson St.) | 503-222-9070

"One of the originals" to make a "commitment to local, sustainable ag-
riculture", chef Greg Higgins still delivers an "endlessly interesting",
"incredibly prepared" Pacific NW menu that's "pricey" but "well worth
the money" at his Downtown "benchmark"; "exceptional" Oregon
wines and an "awesome beer list" also impress, as does the "professional service"; P.S. "reservations are important" in the "homey" main
room, while it's "easier" to get into the less-expensive bar/bistro area.

Jake's Famous Crawfish *Seafood* | 23 | 21 | 23 | $41 |

Downtown | 401 SW 12th Ave. (Stark St.) | 503-226-1419 |
www.jakesfamouscrawfish.com

Voted Portland's Most Popular restaurant, this Downtown "icon" with
a "convivial" "old-school boy's-club feel" has been proffering a "comprehensive menu" of "always fresh", "well-prepared", "fair-priced"
seafood since the late 19th century; it's "sometimes considered a
tourist joint, but in reality" "locals can't keep away either", especially
during the "lively" happy hour when "outstanding bargains" abound.

Joel Palmer House 🛇Ⓜ *Pacific NW* | 26 | 23 | 25 | $54 |

Dayton | 600 Ferry St. (6th St.) | 503-864-2995 | www.joelpalmerhouse.com

"The wild mushroom is king" at this "isolated", "historic house" "with
furnishings to match" in "bucolic" Dayton, where the "genius" chef
hunts for seasonal fungi that "invade almost every course" of the
"unique", "memorable" Pacific NW menu (there's a healthy sprinkling
of truffles too); an "extensive" selection of Oregon wines adds to its
reputation as a "special-occasion" place, as do the prices.

Ken's Artisan Pizza Ⓜ *Pizza* | 26 | 19 | 19 | $23 |

NE/SE 28th | 304 SE 28th Ave. (Pine St.) | 503-517-9951 |
www.kensartisan.com

"Superb toppings", "zesty sauce" and "thin, crispy" crust are the components of the "terrific wood-fired pizza" served up at this "lively", "modern" joint on SE 28th; "amazing salads" are "exquisite accompaniments",
and when it comes to the check, you get "fine value for your dough" – so
it should come as no surprise that there's "a full house every night"
and the wait for a table usually takes "forever" (no reservations).

Laurelhurst Market *Steak* | – | – | – | E |

E. Burnside | 3155 E. Burnside St. (32nd Ave.) | 503-206-3097 |
www.laurelhurstmarket.com

A casually minimalistic space with exposed rafters, an open kitchen
and a case crammed with artisan meats and charcuterie greets pa-

trons at this buzzing (and pricey) East Burnside steakhouse-cum-butcher shop housed inside a former convenience store; uncommon cuts – brisket, skirt, etc. – are plated with local produce, and strong cocktails come from the bar, where patrons can cool their heels while waiting for seats.

Le Pigeon *French*   26 | 18 | 22 | $48

E. Burnside | 738 E. Burnside St. (8th Ave.) | 503-546-8796 | www.lepigeon.com

"Adventurous" foodies squeeze into this "postage stamp"–size eatery on gritty East Burnside for seats at communal tables or "at the counter to watch" "artist" chef Gabriel Rucker "work his magic" on "brilliant", "creative", "occasionally challenging" French cuisine; some feel it's "a little pricey" for "funky" digs and "mismatched silverware" and china, but the majority calls it a "transcendental" experience that's "absolutely worth it."

Nuestra Cocina 🖾 🅼 *Mexican*   27 | 20 | 22 | $31

Southeast Portland | 2135 SE Division St. (22nd Ave.) | 503-232-2135

"Authentic" regional Mexican preparations sauced with "ever-changing moles" are whipped up by cooks in an open kitchen at this "friendly", cozy, somewhat "upscale" SE Portland spot with an "inviting" tiled dining room; the fare is "yummy" and "everyone knows it", so "get there early or be prepared to wait" (you can pass the time with a "fabulous" spicy margarita at the "outstanding bar" – it'll "leave you breathless!").

Painted Lady 🅼 *Pacific NW*   28 | 26 | 27 | $78

Newberg | 201 S. College St. (2nd St.) | 503-538-3850 | www.thepaintedladyrestaurant.com

For the "best dining experience in Oregon wine country" (complete with the Portland area's No. 1-rated Food), seek out this "hidden pearl" in Newberg, a "charming", "intimate", "gloriously restored" Victorian where the "superb", seasonal Pacific NW fare, offered in "wonderful tasting menus" only, boasts "unique blends of flavors"; the "divine" wines include "enough hard-to-find" local labels "to give other restaurants Pinot envy."

Paley's Place Bistro & Bar *Pacific NW*   27 | 23 | 26 | $55

Northwest Portland | 1204 NW 21st Ave. (Northrup St.) | 503-243-2403 | www.paleysplace.net

It's "worth planning ahead to snag one of the few tables" in this "old house" in NW Portland, where "gifted chef" Vitaly Paley prepares "creative, intelligent", "sublime" Pacific NW fare featuring "beauti-fully selected" local provender and Southern French–Northern Italian influences; in the "charming" dining room, his wife, Kimberly, displays "warmth as a hostess and acumen as a sommelier" as she oversees servers who are "professional in every aspect"; P.S. "outdoor seating is a plus."

Park Kitchen 🖾 *American/Pacific NW*   25 | 20 | 23 | $42

Pearl District | 422 NW Eighth Ave. (bet. Flanders & Glisan Sts.) | 503-223-7275 | www.parkkitchen.com

Some of Portland's most "innovative", "unexpected" New American fare – made with "unusual combinations" of "seasonal NW ingredients" – is served up in "superb" fashion by "knowledgeable"

FOOD | DECOR | SERVICE | COST

staffers at this "intimate" Pearl District neighborhood spot; take a seat in the rear to watch the "fun" in the open kitchen, or choose a table up front where it's "usually quieter" and there's a "nice view of the Park Blocks."

Pok Pok *SE Asian/Thai*

25 | 17 | 20 | $29

Southeast Portland | 3226 SE Division St. (32nd Ave.) | 503-232-1387 | www.pokpokpdx.com

"Standing out from the masses" of pad joints, this SE Portland "destination" in a "redone house" "elevates Thai street food to sublime new heights" while offering "authentic", "high-powered" "specialty dishes from all over" Southeast Asia; "innovative drinks", many of which are made with "excellent whiskeys", keep the "wacky", "exotic" dining room, basement lounge and patio "boisterous"; P.S. reservations taken only for groups of five or more, otherwise there's "often a long wait."

Toro Bravo *Spanish*

27 | 21 | 23 | $37

Northeast Portland | 120 NE Russell St. (bet. Martin Luther King Jr. Blvd. & Rodney Ave.) | 503-281-4464 | www.torobravopdx.com

"Bravo indeed!" – this "hot spot" for tapas in NE Portland specializes in "morsels of intense, moan-inducing flavor" "made with locally sourced ingredients" in "warm", "friendly", Spanish-style digs; "go early or late to avoid" the "long lines" (it "takes reservations only for large parties", except on Fridays and Saturdays when there are no bookings), or just "chillax at the bar" over a glass of "reasonably priced" wine.

Sacramento

TOP FOOD RANKING

	Restaurant	Cuisine
29	La Bonne Soupe	French
28	Kitchen	American
	Waterboy	Californian
27	Mulvaney's	American
	Biba	Italian
	Ella	American
	Hawks	American
	Tuli	Eclectic
26	Mikuni	Japanese
	Kru	Japanese

OTHER NOTEWORTHY PLACES

Bidwell St. Bistro	Californian/French
Boulevard Bistro	American
Buckhorn	Steak
Firehouse	Continental
Frank Fat's	Chinese
Grange	Californian
Lemon Grass	Thai/Vietnamese
OneSpeed	Pizza
Paragary's	French/Italian
Tower Café	Eclectic

Biba 🅱 *Italian* `27` `23` `26` `$51`

Midtown | 2801 Capitol Ave. (28th St.) | 916-455-2422 |
www.biba-restaurant.com

"Viva Biba!" exclaim devotees of this "venerable" Midtown "winner"
owned by celebrated chef Biba Caggiano, who "wrote the book" (eight
of them, in fact) on Italian cooking and "continues to amaze" with seasonal dishes that make "taste buds tingle"; though some find the white
walls, "brass and mirrors galore" design "stuck in 1985", most consider
it sufficiently "sophisticated" for such an "expensive" experience.

Bidwell Street Bistro 🅱 *Californian/French* `25` `19` `24` `$39`

Folsom | 1004 E. Bidwell St. (Blue Ravine Rd.) | 916-984-7500 |
www.bidwellstreetbistro.com

"*Magnifique!*" praise patrons of this "intimate", "reasonably priced"
bistro in a Folsom strip mall, "an oasis" serving "exceptional", "attrac-
tively plated" Gallic fare whose "fresh" Cal influences are evident in the
lack of "heavy sauces normally associated with French fare"; the "outstanding wine list" also wins raves – ditto the "service par excellence."

Boulevard Bistro 🅜 *American* ∇ `25` `22` `23` `$42`

Elk Grove | 8941 Elk Grove Blvd. (3rd Ave.) | 916-685-2220 |
www.blvdbistro.com

"It may look like grandma's house outside, but she never cooked like
this!" gush admirers of this "quaint" New American in Elk Grove, an

	FOOD	DECOR	SERVICE	COST

"intimate", 30-seat bungalow where "true artist" Bret Bohlmann "magically transforms the familiar" via his "innovative seasonal" dishes; add "attentive" service and a "wonderful wine selection", and this is "as good as it gets" in the 'burbs.

Buckhorn Steak & Roadhouse *Steak*

| 25 | 18 | 22 | $35 |

Winters | 2 Main St. (Railroad Ave.) | 530-795-4503 | www.buckhornsteakhouse.com

Buccaneers say it's "well worth a ride" to tiny Winters for the "dazzling", "succulent" sirloins at this veteran "rural steakhouse" where "attentive service" complements the "generous" cuts; the "Old West" quarters adorned with "mounted trophy heads" "could be updated a bit", but "for a meatasaurus", this one's "hard to beat."

Ella Dining Room & Bar 🗷 *American*

| 27 | 28 | 26 | $54 |

Downtown | The Cathedral Building | 1131 K St. (12th St.) | 916-443-3772 | www.elladiningroomandbar.com

Randall Selland, "one of the town's leading chefs", "hits it out of the park" with this "memorable" "place to be seen" Downtown, hailed as much for its "breathtaking" decor – bedecked with hundreds of "beautiful", "well-worn" shutters – as for its "impeccable" New American cuisine, "a symphony of fresh, fabulous ingredients"; the "interesting small plates" make it "easy to rack up a big bill", but pluses like a "heavenly wine list" and "solicitous service" make this "foodie find" "worth it."

Firehouse *Continental*

| 25 | 26 | 26 | $54 |

Old Sacramento | 1112 Second St. (bet. K & L Sts.) | 916-442-4772 | www.firehouseoldsac.com

If you're looking for an "ornate, lavish" "special-occasion" place with "world-class service", this "grande dame" of Old Sacramento in a "nostalgic old firehouse" fits the bill with an "elegant", Victorian artwork–festooned interior and a "beautiful patio"; it's also a "go-to" for "inventive Continental cuisine" that "sparkles" with paired wines from an "incredible" list "roughly the size of a small-town phone book" – just "bring two credit cards" to cover the bill (it's "well worth" it).

Frank Fat's *Chinese*

| 23 | 22 | 22 | $32 |

Downtown | 806 L St. (8th St.) | 916-442-7092 | www.fatsrestaurants.com

The oldest continuously running restaurant in Sacramento, this "beautiful" over-70-year-old is a Downtown Chinese "institution" where "ghosts of legendary legislators linger" and "you're likely to bump into state politicians" "doing their deals" while being "served whip-crack fast"; the "upscale" menu (which includes some "tasty" American dishes too) contains "so many standouts, it's hard to choose", but "everyone goes for" the "dreamy" honey walnut prawns and "famous banana cream pie."

Grange *Californian*

| - | - | - | E |

Downtown | Citizen Hotel | 926 J St. (bet. 9th & 10th Sts.) | 916-492-4450 | www.grangesacramento.com

Chef Michael Tuohy works closely with area farmers to imbue his Californian breakfasts, lunches and dinners with seasonal flavor at this somewhat pricey Downtowner attached to the stylish Citizen Hotel; the two-story space, with views of the street through high windows, displays a modern-rustic aesthetic, as evidenced in historic photographs on the walls, exposed beams, concrete columns and a dramatic cantilevered private loft.

Hawks Ⓜ American

27 | 28 | 26 | $54

Granite Bay | Quarry Ponds Town Ctr. | 5530 Douglas Blvd. (bet. Barton Rd. & Berg St.) | 916-791-6200 | www.hawksrestaurant.com

"Exceeding expectations" "in every respect", this "fantastic" Granite Bay New American exudes "understated elegance" with its "gorgeous" contemporary decor, a fitting backdrop for "exquisite", "beautifully presented" cuisine made with "seasonal awareness" from mostly local ingredients and ferried by "impeccable" servers; the fare and "interesting wines" "will set you back dollarwise", but for such "truly fine" dining, it's "worth it."

Kitchen, The Ⓜ American

28 | 24 | 28 | $163

Arden-Arcade | 2225 Hurley Way (Howe Ave.) | 916-568-7171 | www.thekitchenrestaurant.com

"Book months in advance" for this Arden-Arcade "Super Bowl of fine dining", a one-seating-only, "buckets-of-fun" "four-plus-hour event" in which either owner Randall Selland or chef Noah Zonca performs an "entertaining", "humorous" New American cooking demo emphasizing "locally grown, organic fare" while providing "engaging commentary"; true, its $125 price tag (without "amazing wine" pairings) is "crazy expensive", but if you want more of the "heavenly" dishes, the "superb servers" will "bring you seconds."

Kru Japanese

26 | 20 | 21 | $31

Midtown | 2516 J St. (bet. 25th & 26th Sts.) | 916-551-1559 | www.krurestaurant.com

"Try something new" at this "sleek, casual" Midtown Japanese, which provides a "needed break from the mayonnaise-based, sauce-covered rolls" doled out at some other sushi spots with its "fascinating" combos praised for their "sublime presentation" and "unique flavors that pack a punch"; sit at the bar, start off with some of the "always-changing, inventive sashimi tapas" and prepare "for a great show and scraps" given by "artist" chef-owner Billy Ngo and his crew.

La Bonne Soupe Café Ⓢ French

29 | 11 | 20 | $11

Downtown | 920 Eighth St. (bet. I & J Sts.) | 916-492-9506

"Don't miss" this "totally unique" Downtown lunch "treasure", the winner of Sacramento's No. 1 Food rating, where "sweet" French chef-owner Daniel Pont serves "love between two pieces of bread" and what's possibly "the best onion soup in the universe", all "artistically made" to order; "monsieur is the sole staff" in this "shoebox"-size storefront, causing the "slow moving" lines to stretch "down the block", but it's probably the "only place you'll ever wait 40 minutes for a sandwich and not mind"; P.S. "if you come late, plan to sit in the park."

Lemon Grass Ⓢ Thai/Vietnamese

26 | 19 | 23 | $33

Arden-Arcade | 601 Munroe St. (Fair Oaks Blvd.) | 916-486-4891 | www.lemongrassrestaurant.com

"Pay no mind to its "odd" "former A&W" restaurant setting – this "white-tablecloth" "classic" features a "pretty", "airy" interior where fabulous chef Mai Pham whips up "inventive", "consistently terrific", "beautifully presented" Thai-Vietnamese dishes (fused with "a little Californian"); its Arden-Arcade location may be a bit "hard to find", but it's "worth the hunt", especially when factoring in the "attentive", "knowledgeable servers" and "consumer-friendly" tabs.

Mikuni *Japanese*

26 | 20 | 21 | $32

Elk Grove | 8525 Bond Rd. (bet. E. Stockton Blvd. & Elk Crest Dr.) | 916-714-2112
Fair Oaks | 4323 Hazel Ave. (Winding Way) | 916-961-2112
Midtown | 1530 J St. (bet. 15th & 16th Sts.) | 916-447-2112
Roseville | 1565 Eureka Rd. (bet. Lead Hill Blvd. & Rocky Ridge Dr.) | 916-797-2112
www.mikunisushi.com

"There's a reason these places are always crowded": they're Sacramento's Most Popular "institutions", beloved by a "faithful", "trendy" clientele that knows the "artfully prepared", "ultrafresh" sushi, "flavorful tempura", "generous bento boxes" and other Japanese fare printed on a "menu the size of a small novel" are "guaranteed delicious"; Midtown is the chain's "crazy" "rock 'n' roll" iteration, but all locations are "noisy and clublike" to some extent.

Mulvaney's B&L 🏠Ⓜ *American*

27 | 24 | 26 | $45

Midtown | 1215 19th St. (bet. Capitol Ave. & L St.) | 916-441-6022 | www.mulvaneysbl.com

It's no wonder this Midtown "foodie restaurant" is so "hot": not only is it set in a former firehouse, but fans "can't eat here enough" given chef/"consummate host" Patrick Mulvaney's "simple but not simplistic", "creative" and downright "spectacular" "farm-to-table" New American fare that "changes daily"; the "lovely patio" is "tempting", but many are drawn to the "rustic, whimsical" interior (despite there being no pole) with its "cozy feel and wonderful display kitchen."

OneSpeed Ⓜ *Pizza*

- | - | - | I

East Sacramento | 4818 Folsom Blvd. (48th St.) | 916-706-1748 | www.onespeedpizza.com

This East Sacramento joint from chef-owner Rick Mahan – a local culinary celeb thanks to his long tenure at The Waterboy – may look like a cheap-and-casual pizzeria, but its blister-crusted pies exhibit gourmet aspirations with creative topping combinations of traditional Italian ingredients; also on offer are antipasti, hand-rolled gnocchi and salads.

Paragary's Bar & Oven *French/Italian*

22 | 21 | 22 | $35

Midtown | 1401 28th St. (N St.) | 916-457-5737 | www.paragarys.com

You "can't beat the original" assure admirers of this "classic" Midtowner, the oldest in local restaurateur Randy Paragary's empire, serving a "varied" menu of "lighter, Californian-style" French-Italian fare; revered for its "creative", "upscale pizzas" baked in a wood-burning oven, it's also well known for "top-notch" service and an "inviting", "relaxing" back patio featuring olive trees and waterfalls ("like being in a Tuscan courtyard!").

Tower Café *Eclectic*

22 | 21 | 18 | $21

Downtown | 1518 Broadway (bet. 15th & 16th Sts.) | 916-441-0222 | www.towercafe.com

"Fun, funky and cheap", this "landmark" all-day cafe beside the art deco Tower Theater Downtown boasts "eccentric", "rather bohemian" "global decor" matched with "creative" Eclectic eats served in "large portions" (highlights include "spectacular custard-soaked French toast", "beautiful, tasty desserts" and a "huge selection of micro-brews"); there's usually "a wait to get in", especially for the "cele-brated" garden patio, a bastion of "lush plants, fountains" and "quirky" "people-watching."

Tuli Bistro *Eclectic*

27 | 21 | 22 | $31

Midtown | 2031 S St. (21st St.) | 916-451-8854 | www.tulibistro.com

This "charming", "spunky" Midtown Eclectic "never fails" in its prepa-ration of "exquisite wood-oven pizzas", "playful" small plates and other "innovative", "delicious cuisine" that's "fairly priced" and changes daily – and there's a "nice wine and beer selection too"; the "teeny-tiny" interior has only "a couple of cocktail tables" and an open-kitchen counter where you can "watch the process", and while there's a "large" patio outside, you can "expect to wait" for it too ("wish it took reservations").

Waterboy *Californian*

28 | 22 | 26 | $46

Midtown | 2000 Capitol Ave. (20th St.) | 916-498-9891 | www.waterboyrestaurant.com

"Fawning fans" of this "upscale" "Midtown mainstay" run the gamut from "Sacramento's top chefs" to "Bay Area foodies" – that's how "eyes-rolling-to-the-back-of-your-head good" "genius" chef Rick Mahan's "edgy", "passionately prepared" Southern French/Northern Italian–inspired seasonal Californian fare is; the "beautiful", "airy" hard-wood-and-tile interior "says relax, enjoy and stay as long as you want" – and the "wonderful" servers certainly won't rush you.

Salt Lake City & Mountain Resorts

TOP FOOD RANKING

	Restaurant	Cuisine
__28__	Mariposa	American
	Forage	American
__27__	Takashi	Japanese
	Mandarin	Chinese
	Tree Room	American
	Spruce	American
	Hell's Backbone	American
	Seafood Buffet	Seafood
	Red Iguana	Mexican
__26__	Pizzeria 712	Pizza

OTHER NOTEWORTHY PLACES

Restaurant	Cuisine
Bambara	American
Caffe Molise	Italian
Copper Onion	American
Cucina Toscana	Italian
High West Distillery	American
Log Haven	American
Market Street	Seafood
Martine	European/Mediterranean
Mazza	Mideastern
Pago	American

Bambara *American*   25 | 25 | 24 | $45

Downtown | Hotel Monaco | 202 S. Main St. (200 South) | Salt Lake City | 801-363-5454 | www.bambara-slc.com

"Modern, eclectic decor" and a "cool open kitchen" in an "old, marble-walled bank lobby" sets a "swanky" stage for chef Nathan Powers' "delightful", "creative" cuisine at this "chic" Downtown New American in the Hotel Monaco, where the atmosphere is at once "romantic" and "energetic"; "exceptional service" and "fair prices" for the quality make it a "special-occasion" destination.

Caffè Molise *Italian*   22 | 20 | 21 | $33

Downtown | 55 W. 100 South (bet. Main & SW Temple) | Salt Lake City | 801-364-8833 | www.caffemolise.com

At this Downtowner, the "casual" interior is filled with art and the "beautiful patio" is "seductive", but the "dependable", moderately priced Northern Italian fare is "what attracts"; fans give a nod to the "extremely friendly, attentive staff", and if some quibble about the somewhat "limited menu", most opine it's "well worth a visit."

Copper Onion, The *American*   26 | 19 | 22 | $32

Downtown | 111 E. 300 South (State St.) | Salt Lake City | 801-355-3282 | www.thecopperonion.com

With "delicious" "twists" on regional "comfort foods" that are as "unique as its name", this New American is a "refreshing addition to the Downtown dining scene"; it's "a great place to grab a bite before a flick at the Broadway" next door, not least of all because the atmosphere is "unpretentious", the "staff is knowledgeable and friendly" and the "prices are really good."

Cucina Toscana ☒ Italian   26 | 23 | 24 | $49

Downtown | 307 W. Pierpont Ave. (S. 300 West) | Salt Lake City | 801-328-3463 | www.cucina-toscana.com

Chef-host Valter Nassi "hugs, kisses" and "fusses" over guests "like they are all old friends" while plying them with "luxurious" Northern Italian fare (the "expansive menu" includes "amazing housemade pastas", accompanied by an "abundant wine list") at this "attractive" Downtown "gem"; there are a few grievances – tables are "close together", there may be "a long wait even with reservations" and it's "spendy" – but since each meal here is "an event", acolytes aver the hassles are "well worth it."

Forage ☒Ⓜ American   28 | 22 | 26 | $69

Eastside | 370 E. 900 South (S. 400 East) | Salt Lake City | 801-708-7834 | www.foragerestaurant.com

"Edgy, exciting" combinations of "seasonal produce" "will shock and awe your palate" at this "unique" New American, whose "superbly crafted", "artistically presented" prix fixes come from two "passionate" chef-owners; "imaginative wine pairings" bolster the "cosmopolitan experience", and if some find the intimate, "minimally decorated" space "too stark", at least the staff is "warm" ("efficient" too); BTW, "it's dinner or the mortgage, not both."

Hell's Backbone Grill American   27 | 24 | 26 | $40

Boulder | Boulder Mountain Lodge | 20 N. Hwy. 12 (Burr Trail) | 435-335-7464 | www.hellsbackbonegrill.com

At this "remote jewel" at the "wonderful Boulder Mountain Lodge" in Southern Utah's Red Rock desert, the "inventive", "outstanding" American menu is "prepared with love" using "fresh veggies and spices" from its "own farm" plus "locally raised" meats; everything's "served with honest pleasure" by the "professional staff" in the "funky, fun" setting, which is "casual" enough for "families" but sufficiently "romantic" for couples; P.S. open March 15–Thanksgiving.

High West Distillery American   23 | 25 | 21 | $42

Park City | 703 Park Ave. (7th St.) | 435-649-8300 | www.highwest.com

Saddle up for some "fine" Western-inspired American grub "with fresh local ingredients" at this "cool", "ski-in" Park City "saloon", "Utah's first distillery since the 1800s", offering "intimate", "comfortable" dining rooms" that exhibit "awesome" "attention to detail"; downstairs, there's a "friendly bar area" where "whiskey is what it's about" – straight-up, in flights or mixed into "inventive, delicious drinks."

Log Haven American   24 | 28 | 25 | $48

Eastside | 6451 E. Millcreek Canyon Rd. (Wasatch Blvd.) | Salt Lake City | 801-272-8255 | www.log-haven.com

"Escape to a haven in the woods" at this "romantic" Eastside "log cabin nestled on a hillside" with "amazing views" of Millcreek Canyon's "stunning natural scenery" ("complete with a waterfall in the outdoor dining area"); the "marvelous" New American fare boasts "imaginative" "twists on old favorites", and the "staff is attentive" and "friendly", all of which warrants prices that veer toward "splurge."

Mandarin, The 🖪 *Chinese*
27 | 22 | 25 | $25

Bountiful | 348 E. 900 North (400 East) | 801-298-2406 | www.mandarinutah.com

"Extraordinary", "gourmet Chinese" offered in "abundant" servings, at "reasonable" prices and with "to-die-for Western desserts", make this Bountiful "staple" "worth the drive" from SLC – or even "from Idaho"; the "classic" setting with "lovely" "carved screens and ornamented ceilings" makes for an "entertaining" atmosphere, but be prepared for "long waits" to be seated – the "locals are very aware how special this place is."

Mariposa, The 🖩 *American*
28 | 26 | 26 | $72

Deer Valley | Silver Lake Lodge, Deer Valley Resort | 7600 Royal St. (Rte. 224) | 435-645-6715 | www.deervalley.com

"Amazing" New American cuisine – earning the No. 1 Food score in the Salt Lake City/Mountain Resorts Survey – and an "excellent wine list" make this "beautiful", "romantic", winter-only Alpine lodge a "Deer Valley must" for a "special occasion"; tabs are unsurprisingly "expensive, but you get what you pay for", including "knowledgeable", "ingratiating" service.

Market Street Grill *Seafood*
23 | 22 | 22 | $37

Cottonwood | 2985 E. Cottonwood Pkwy. (S. 3000 East) | Salt Lake City | 801-942-8860
Downtown | 48 W. Market St. (Main St.) | Salt Lake City | 801-322-4668
South Jordan | 10702 S. River Front Pkwy. (S. 700 West) | 801-302-2262
www.gastronomyinc.com

"You couldn't ask for fresher seafood" (not to mention "to-die-for clam chowder") at these "tried-and-true", "bang-for-your-buck" "icons", once again voted Salt Lake City's Most Popular restaurants, all with attached oyster bars shucking a "great selection" of "slimy joy"; service is usually "fine", while the settings vary from "beautiful" with "great mountain views" (Cottonwood) to "swanky" (South Jordan) to "cool" but "showing its age" (Downtown, also a "great power-breakfast location").

Martine 🖪 *European/Mediterranean*
26 | 23 | 25 | $39

Downtown | 22 E. 100 South (bet. Main & State Sts.) | Salt Lake City | 801-363-9328 | www.martinecafe.com

"Quaint", "quiet", "sexy and sophisticated", this Downtown brownstone pleases with "terrific", "beautifully presented" Mediterranean-Modern Euro dishes starring "inventive" tapas that "never bore"; factor in the "professional service", "excellent wine list" (possibly the "best priced in town") and "romantic" atmosphere, and it's no wonder acolytes ask "what more do you need (aside from a room afterward)?" P.S. basic pub fare is served for lunch.

Mazza 🖪 *Mideastern*
25 | 19 | 21 | $27

Downtown | 912 E. 900 South (S. 900 East) | Salt Lake City | 801-521-4572
Eastside | 1515 S. 1500 East (bet. Emerson & Kensington Aves.) | Salt Lake City | 801-484-9259
www.mazzacafe.com

Hit the "dining jackpot" at these "consistent" Mideasterners where not only is the fare "visually pleasing and delicious" (the baba ghanoush is particularly "dreamy"), but it's an "incredible value" to boot; the "tight" Eastside original is "grittier" than its bigger, "tasteful" Downtown off-spring, but expect "helpful staffs" at both, as well as lots of "laughter" and "clinking glasses" filled with "excellent" Lebanese wines.

Pago 🅼 *American*

| 24 | 22 | 23 | $40 |

Eastside | 878 S. 900 East (900 South) | Salt Lake City | 801-532-0777 | www.pagoslc.com

"A breath of fresh air" in the Eastside's "bohemian 9th and 9th" neigh-borhood, this New American whips "locally grown food" into "fabu-lous" seasonal dishes whose prices equal "tremendous value for the quality", and all are brought by "friendly" servers who are also "well in-formed" about the "wonderful wines"; remember that "reservations are a must" because the green-built space with exposed brick, re-claimed wood and open kitchen is "tiny" – and "noisy" to boot.

Pizzeria 712 🆉 *Pizza*

| 26 | 23 | 24 | $22 |

Orem | 320 S. State St., Ste. 147 (Center St.) | 801-623-6712 | www.pizzeria712.com

This "fashionable, hip place" in "bland-national-chain-addicted" Orem specializes in "innovative", "fantastically delicious" wood-fired pizzas based on seasonal ingredients and paired with "tasty starters" plus "wonderful wines"; it's "ridiculously cheap" for being relatively "classy", and contrary to its locale in a "giant" office complex, it boasts an "intimate" feel.

Red Iguana *Mexican*

| 27 | 16 | 21 | $20 |

Downtown | 736 W. North Temple St. (800 West) | Salt Lake City | 801-322-1489

Red Iguana 2 *Mexican*

Downtown | 866 W. South Temple (900 W.) | Salt Lake City | 801-214-6050 www.rediguana.com

"In the mood for mole?" – Downtowners declare "this is the place", as the "fantastic selection" of the aforementioned sauce is the star of the "outstanding", "authentic, cheap" Mexican menu; "charming" staffers are "pretty quick for being so busy" – still, expect "lines winding out the door" for both the "funky", "cramped, always bustling" original and the new sequel, with "bright, cheerful colors", "chrome accents" and a small patio.

Seafood Buffet 🆉 *Seafood*

| 27 | 18 | 23 | $65 |

Deer Valley | Snow Park Lodge | 2250 Deer Valley Dr. (Mellow Mountain Rd.) | 435-645-6632 | www.deervalley.com

For a "seafood fantasy come true", dig into the "amazing" variety of fish "you wouldn't know came from a buffet" (plus "plenty of prime rib" and "yummy" desserts) at this "rustic" retreat in Deer Valley's Snow Park Lodge; it's "expensive", but given the "extravagant amount of food", it could be "the best deal in town" if you're "really, really hun-gry"; "alas, only in ski season" is it open.

Spruce *American*

| 27 | 28 | 25 | $68 |

Park City | Waldorf Astoria | 2100 Frostwood Dr. (Cooper Ln.) | 435-647-5566 | www.sprucepc.com

"One of San Francisco's best restaurants" presents its "sublime", "so-phisticated" New American cuisine at this offshoot in Park City's

Waldorf Astoria; the "stellar experience" is complete with "knock 'em-dead gorgeous" "modern" decor, "impeccable service" and an "incredible wine list" (caveat: "the markup is steep", which matches the elevated food prices); FYI, there's outdoor deck dining too.

Takashi ☒ *Japanese* | 27 | 22 | 23 | $40 |

Downtown | 18 W. Market St. (W. Temple St., bet. 300 South & 400 South) | Salt Lake City | 801-519-9595 | www.takashisushi.com

"Who needs to go to NY or LA for great sushi" when "master crafts-man" Takashi Gibo whips up "an exceptional selection" of "creative", "super-fresh fish" with "Peruvian tangents" right at this Downtown "hot spot"?; the "cool green room with splashes of bright artwork" plus the "extensive sake selection" befit the "hipsters, stars-in-town" and other "trendy clientele", and all things considered, everything comes "at a good price."

Tree Room ☒ Ⓜ *American* | 27 | 29 | 27 | $54 |

Sundance | Sundance Resort | 9521 Alpine Loop Rd. (Hwy. 189) | 801-223-4200 | www.sundanceresort.com

"The room exudes warmth while the food and service say opulence" at this "lovely place for a splurge" at Sundance, where owner "Robert Redford's American Indian artifacts" fill a "rustic, elegant" room that "surrounds a tree" and is "surrounded by breathtakingly beautiful mountains"; well known for its "impeccable game" dishes, the Regional U.S. menu boasts a "sustainable, local" pedigree and is matched by a "worthwhile wine list."

San Antonio

TOP FOOD RANKING

	Restaurant	Cuisine
28	Dough	Pizza
27	Il Sogno	Italian
	Bohanan's	Seafood/Steak
	Frederick's	Asian/French
	Bistro Vatel	French
	Lodge*	American
	Magnolia*	American
26	Biga	American
	La Frite	Belgian
	Sandbar*	Seafood

OTHER NOTEWORTHY PLACES

Restaurant	Cuisine
Auden's Kitchen	American
Boudro's	Seafood/Steak
Citrus	American
Grill at Leon Springs	Eclectic
La Gloria	Mexican
Le Midi	French
Paesanos	Italian
Restaurant Insignia	American
Rudy's	BBQ
Silo	American

Auden's Kitchen *American*

`- | - | - | M`

Stone Oak | Plaza at Concord Park | 700 E. Sonterra Blvd. (Sigma Rd.) | 210-494-0070 | www.audenskitchen.com

Lauded chef Bruce Auden (Biga on the Banks) expands his New American comfort food reach to Stone Oak, merging childhood memories with solid gourmet skills in an affordable menu that romps through gastronomic styles, from fried chicken to sticky toffee pudding; the casual space sports a chef's counter and a perimeter lined with shelving units holding wine, plates and kitchen bric-a-brac, while the crowd includes everyone from parents with kids in tow to couples on dates to business folk.

Biga on the Banks *American*

`26 | 24 | 25 | $50`

River Walk | 203 S. St. Mary's St. (Market St.) | 210-225-0722 | www.biga.com

An "elegant" respite from the "tourist traps" downriver, this "premier" restaurant from "legendary" chef-owner Bruce Auden lures "business" types and "out-of-towners" with "artistic" New American plates and "pitch-perfect" service; surveyors say "you'll spend a little more" than you might elsewhere, but in return you can expect a "memorable" meal.

---

* Indicates a tie with restaurant above

Bistro Vatel ⓜ *French*

27 | 19 | 25 | $50

Olmos Park | 218 E. Olmos Dr. (McCullough Ave.) | 210-828-3141 | www.bistrovatel.com

"Still one of the best in town" swoon fans of this "top-notch" longtimer "tucked away" in an Olmos Park strip mall, where chef-owner Damien Watel sends out "sophisticated" French dishes in a "cozy" setting; it's not inexpensive, but the "wonderful" food combined with "relaxed" atmosphere and "attentive" service makes it well "worth a visit."

Bohanan's Prime Steaks & Seafood *Seafood/Steak*

27 | 27 | 26 | $73

Downtown | 219 E. Houston St. (bet. Navarro & St. Mary's Sts.) | 210-472-2600 | www.bohanans.com

For "elegant dining", surveyors sing the praises of this upscale chophouse "in the heart of Downtown" laying out "cooked-to-perfection" steaks, seafood and tableside desserts in "intimate" Victorian-style surroundings; yet while the staff "treats you like royalty", prices strike some as "much too expensive" for commoners.

Boudro's on the Riverwalk *Seafood/Steak*

25 | 21 | 22 | $40

River Walk | 421 E. Commerce St. (bet. Losoya & Presa Sts.) | 210-224-8484 | www.boudros.com

Full of "Texas spirit" (and "tourists"), this time-honored "favorite" on the River Walk – San Antonio's Most Popular restaurant – doles out "fabulous" steaks and seafood along with "innovative" "regional dishes" matched by some "amazing" prickly pear 'ritas; "tight and noisy" digs and upper-end pricing aside, many consider it "the only place to eat" along the water; P.S. "ask for a table outside."

Citrus *American*

25 | 24 | 24 | $45

Downtown | Hotel Valencia | 150 E. Houston St. (St. Mary's St.) | 210-230-8412 | www.hotelvalencia.com

"Better than the typical hotel restaurant", this chic Downtown enclave showcases chef Jeffery Balfour's Eclectic–New American creations; "excellent" service and a posh setting make it fit for "power lunches", while the River Walk views from the upper deck suit "visitors" as well.

Dough ⓩⓜ *Pizza*

28 | 19 | 23 | $26

North Central | Blanco Junction Shopping Ctr. | 6989 Blanco Rd. (Loop 410) | 210-979-6565 | www.doughpizzeria.com

"Show up early" and "wait as long as it takes" instruct acolytes of this ultrapopular North Central pizzeria – rated No. 1 for Food in San Antonio – turning out "mouthwatering", "authentic" wood-fired Neapolitan pies complemented by "inventive" salads, "plate-licking" desserts and an all-Italian wine list; "bad acoustics" and a strip-mall setting aside, you really "can't miss" here – "go!"

Frederick's ⓩ *Asian/French*

27 | 18 | 24 | $46

Alamo Heights | 7701 Broadway St. (Nottingham Pl.) | 210-828-9050 | www.frederickssa.com

Frederick's Bistro *Asian/French*

North Central | 14439 NW Military Hwy. (Huebner Rd.) | 210-888-1500 | www.fredericksbistro.com

"Gentlemanly" owner Frederick Costa makes you "feel welcome" at these white-linen bistros in Alamo Heights and North Central rolling out "exquisite" French-Asian cuisine; expect food and service that "rarely get better" elsewhere, but note that prices are "expensive" and style-mavens find the strip-center locales detract from an otherwise "elegant" experience.

Grill at Leon Springs *Eclectic*

21	20	21	$34

Leon Springs | 24116 I-10 W. (Boerne Stage Rd.) | 210-698-8797 | www.leonspringsgrill.com

"Casually dressed Texans" sup on seasonal Eclectic fare at this well-priced grill in Leon Springs; although the "creative" menu earns kudos, it's the "lovely" "old stone building" and "lively" outdoor scene (with music Thursdays–Saturdays) that make this out-of-towner truly "worth the drive."

Il Sogno ⓜ *Italian*

27	26	27	$47

Near North | Pearl Brewery | 200 E. Grayson St. (Karnes St.) | 210-223-3900

A "warm, knowledgeable" staff presides over this "superb" Italian from chef Andrew Weissman who sends out "refined" dishes from an open kitchen set in "industrial-chic" digs in the historic Pearl Brewery; tabs can feel "a bit pricey", but it pays off with an experience that's as "authentic as you'll get in San Antonio."

La Frite ⓈⓂ *Belgian*

26	20	21	$33

Southtown | 728 S. Alamo St. (Presa St.) | 210-224-7555 | www.lafritesa.com

Southtown habitués hail this "charming" little cafe in the arts district known for its lineup of "real Belgian" "treats", starring some of the "best moules frites in town"; inside, the bistro-like space feels like "Europe", while the outside tables are ideal for people-watching; P.S. scores do not reflect a post-Survey ownership change.

La Gloria Ice House *Mexican*

-	-	-	I

Near North | Pearl Brewery | 100 E. Grayson St. (bet. Elmira & Isleta Sts.) | 210-267-9040 | www.lagloriaicehouse.com

Richly flavored street food from the interior of Mexico, including earthy vegetarian options, comes to Near North courtesy of chef-owner Johnny Hernandez, who pairs authentic regional techniques with locally sourced ingredients; the garage-chic structure, outfitted with funky folkloric metal sculptures, sets a chill atmosphere befitting the inexpensive price points.

Le Midi Ⓢ *French*

-	-	-	E

Downtown | 301 E. Houston St. (Navarro St.) | 210-858-7388 | www.lemidirestaurant.com

South Texas meets Southern France at this venue exuding a relaxed elegance on Downtown's bustling main drag; the richly hued bistro-style setting matches the kitchen's lusty Lyon roots, evident from pricey items like pâté and escargots to tarte Tatin; the cozy bar is also a popular pre- and post-theater hot spot.

Lodge Restaurant of Castle Hills, The ⓈⓂ *American*

27	25	26	$61

Castle Hills | 1746 Lockhill Selma Rd. (West Ave.) | 210-349-8466 | www.thelodgerestaurant.com

Prepare to be "blown away" by this "outstanding" New American tucked inside a "lovely, old" "mansion" in Castle Hills where chef

Jason Dady rolls out "exceptional" cuisine, available à la carte or in an "adventurous" eight-course tasting menu; factor in "impeccable service" from a staff that "really knows its stuff", and in all it's a "first-class" experience, and priced like one too.

Magnolia Pancake Haus *American*　　27　17　23　$15

North Central | 606 Embassy Oaks (West Ave.) | 210-496-0828 | www.magnoliapancakehaus.com

It's "worth waking up" early for this North Central "country kitchen", an all-time "favorite" for "light and fluffy" pancakes plus other "wonderful" breakfast and lunchtime chow; yes, you'll "wait", but service is "fast" once you're seated, and it's a good value since one meal "will hold you over until dinner."

Paesanos *Italian*　　23　22　21　$35

Quarry | 555 E. Basse Rd. (Treeline Pk.) | 210-828-5191
Paesanos Riverwalk *Italian*
River Walk | 111 W. Crockett St. (Presa St.) | 210-227-2782
Paesanos 1604 *Italian*
Loop 1604 | 3622 Paesanos Pkwy. (N. Loop 1604 W.) | 210-493-1604
www.joesfood.com

"The shrimp Paesano is legendary" at this "popular", decades-old Quarry Italian pumping out "dependable" dishes in "comfy" if "noisy" quarters that "work well with big parties"; despite the same "wonderful" menu and "accommodating" service at both the 1604 and River Walk spin-offs, loyalist sniff they're "not nearly as good" as the original.

Restaurant Insignia *American*　　-　-　-　M

Downtown | Fairmount Hotel | 401 S. Alamo St. (E. Nueva St.) | 210-223-0401 | www.restaurantinsignia.com

Chef Jason Dady strikes a casual note with this New American spot that adds Texas twang to a reasonably priced roster of pizzas, burgers and more substantial mains; it's all set in the storefront space of the historic Fairmount Hotel Downtown, with a wood-burning oven as the centerpiece; P.S. valet parking is free for diners.

Rudy's Country Store and Bar-B-Q *BBQ*　　25　14　18　$16

Northeast | 15560 I-35 N. (S. Laredo St.) | 210-653-7839
Northwest | 10623 Westover Hills (Hwy. 151) | 210-520-5552
Leon Springs | 24158 W. IH 10 (Boerne Stage Rd.) | 210-698-2141
www.rudys.com

You can smell the smoke from "a mile away" at these "solid-as-a-rock" Central Texas pit stops doling out "tender" BBQ brisket ("go for the extra moist") and "mouthwatering ribs" sided with "amazing" "signature creamed corn"; most are set in refurbished gas stations, so you can line up "cafeteria-style", "order by the pound" and fill up your tank on the way out – talk about "true fast food."

Sandbar Fish House & Market 🅢 🅜 *Seafood*　　26　-　21　$49

Near North | Pearl Brewery | 200 E. Grayson St. (Karnes St.) | 210-222-2426

Diners devour "divine" lobster bisque, "fresh" oysters and other "excellent" seafood items at this Near North eatery from Andrew Weissman (Il Sogno), who also spotlights a smattering of dishes from

	FOOD	DECOR	SERVICE	COST

his departed Le Rêve; occasionally "slow" service aside, most find it entirely "worth the cost"; P.S. a move to industrial-style digs in the Pearl Brewery complex has outdated the Decor score.

Silo *American* | 26 | 24 | 25 | $41 |

Terrell Heights | 1133 Austin Hwy. (Mt. Calvary Dr.) | 210-824-8686

Silo 1604 *American*

Loop 1604 | Ventura Plaza | 434 N. Loop 1604 W. (off Access Rd. 1604) | 210-483-8989

www.siloelevatedcuisine.com

Admirers attest it's "impossible to go wrong" at this Terrell Heights bistro or its Loop 1604 spin-off serving up "surprising" New American fare in "chic" digs blessed with "cool" bar scenes; tabs are "pricey, but not outrageous" – no wonder both are so "popular."

San Diego

| | | | FOOD | DECOR | SERVICE | COST |

TOP FOOD RANKING

	Restaurant	Cuisine
28	Sushi Ota	Japanese
	WineSellar	French
27	El Bizcocho	French
	Karen Krasne's	French/Italian
	Pamplemousse	American/French
	Market	American
	Tapenade	French
	A.R. Valentien	Californian
26	Primavera	Italian
	Morton's	Steak

OTHER NOTEWORTHY PLACES

Bankers Hill	American
Bencotto	Italian
Donovan's	Steak
George's California Modern	Californian
George's Ocean Terrace	Californian
Mille Fleurs	French
Prado	Californian
Roppongi	Asian
Sammy's	Pizza
Sapori	Italian

A.R. Valentien *Californian*   27 | 27 | 26 | $65

La Jolla | The Lodge at Torrey Pines | 11480 N. Torrey Pines Rd. (Callan Rd.) | 858-777-6635 | www.arvalentien.com

"Exquisite Craftsman-style architecture", a study in gleaming woods and stained-glass light fixtures amid the "ethereal surroundings" of the Torrey Pines golf course, "amazes" the "high rollers" who habituate this "fantastical dining experience" in La Jolla; just as "unforgettable" is chef Jeff Jackson's "amazing", "innovative" Californian cuisine, which utilizes "farm-fresh local produce" and is served by an "impeccable" staff.

Bankers Hill *American*   - | - | - | M

Bankers Hill | 2202 Fourth Ave. (bet. India & Ivy Sts.) | 619-231-0222 | www.bankershillsd.com

Taking the same name as its Bankers Hill setting, this sizable, airy newcomer clad in rustic woods showcases accomplished chef Carl Schroeder's (Market Restaurant & Bar) New American cuisine; a casual, hipster-heavy crowd rattles the rafters, while the cool young staff ferries the moderately priced fare (all entrees are priced under $20).

Bencotto Ⓜ *Italian*   - | - | - | M

Little Italy | 750 W. Fir St. (Kettner Blvd.) | 619-450-4786 | www.lovebencotto.com

Housed in Little Italy's chic Q building, this new Italian offers shareable plates, handcrafted pastas, steaks, seafood and more at affordable rates; the concrete, steel and glass space reverberates with the voices of designer-denim-clad throngs, and though it's spacious and spread over two floors, its instant popularity means there's often a line to get in on weekends.

Donovan's Steak & Chop House *Steak* 26 | 23 | 25 | $61

Gaslamp Quarter | 570 K St. (6th Ave.) | 619-237-9700
Golden Triangle | 4340 La Jolla Village Dr. (Genesee Ave.) | 858-450-6666 🗷
www.donovanssteakhouse.com

"You simply can't go wrong" with any "hunk of mouthwatering beef" you order at this Golden Triangle "steakhouse extraordinaire", be it an "outstanding bone-in rib-eye" or an "off-the-charts New York strip", all of which come with "luscious sides" ("unlike at others" of this ilk); in a manner befitting the "refined, wood-paneled" "gentleman's club"-like" environs, the "superb" servers remain "unruffled" even when the "rather large" tabs (especially from the "overpriced wine list") draw protests; P.S. the Gaslamp locale debuted post-Survey.

El Bizcocho Ⓜ *French* 27 | 26 | 27 | $71

Rancho Bernardo | Rancho Bernardo Inn | 17550 Bernardo Oaks Dr. (Francisco Dr.) | 858-675-8550 | www.ranchobernardoinn.com

This Rancho Bernardo Inn "delight" creates "spectacular" French cuisine worthy of the "beyond-description" 1,600-label wine cellar; "discreet" yet "responsive" servers and an "elegant" setting add to the "special-occasion" feel, so "bring the diamond ring to propose to your sweetie" (or hock it beforehand to pay for it all); P.S. a new chef redid the menu post-Survey, outdating the Food score.

George's California Modern *Californian* 26 | 25 | 25 | $58

La Jolla | 1250 Prospect St. (bet. Cave St. & Ivanhoe Ave.) | 858-454-4244 |
www.georgesatthecove.com

"By George, it's still superb!" – this La Jolla "classic" features chef Trey Foshee's "brilliant", "edgy", "light", "delectable Californian" cuisine, boasting "the freshest ingredients" and "elegant flavor pairings" (even before the first bite, "the dishes come alive" as the "warm" servers explain them); the "contemporary" decor (an "abundance of glass and steel") "ranks high" but will always place second to the "spectacular sunsets" "over the ocean" – and though "you pay for the privilege", it's "worth the pretty penny."

George's Ocean Terrace *Californian* 24 | 24 | 23 | $42

La Jolla | 1250 Prospect St. (bet. Cave St. & Ivanhoe Ave.) | 858-454-4244 |
www.georgesatthecove.com

Feel like you're "sitting on top of the world" as you take in "wine, sunshine" and "incomparable ocean views" at this rooftop "tradition" "overlooking La Jolla Cove", the "perennial favorite for tourists and locals alike", voted San Diego's Most Popular restaurant; a "more casual", "less expensive version of George's California Modern downstairs", it offers the "same great quality", "inventive", "artistic" Californian fare for "languid lunches" or dinners; P.S. a post-Survey refresh that added a 12-seat ocean-view bar adds to the "wow" factor.

Karen Krasne's Little Italy *French/Italian* 27 | 21 | 17 | $19

Little Italy | 1430 Union St. (bet. W. Ash & W. Beech Sts.) | 619-294-7001
(continued)

(continued)

Karen Krasne's Extraordinary Desserts *Dessert*

Bankers Hill | 2929 Fifth Ave. (bet. Palm & Quince Sts.) | 619-294-2132
www.extraordinarydesserts.com

"You'll moan in ecstasy" when tasting the "decadent" "über-desserts" at this "cozy cottage" in Bankers Hill and its Little Italy offshoot, which also offers a "savory menu" of "light" French and Italian "small plates", a "wide selection of wines" and a "techno-modern" design that's of definite "architectural interest"; everything at both is so "artfully crafted", you may forgive counter help that can be "lackadaisical" and somewhat "snobby" – that is, if they don't "ignore you."

Market Restaurant & Bar *American*   27 | 21 | 23 | $56

Del Mar | 3702 Via de la Valle (El Camino Real) | 858-523-0007 |
www.marketdelmar.com

"Creative" "genius" Carl Schroeder "raises the bar" at this Del Mar "star" with his "daily changing menu" of New American dishes "so fresh and carefully thought out", they yield an "absolutely mouthwatering" "mix of flavors and textures"; persimmon walls and chocolate leather banquettes figure heavily into decor that's "hip but not tragically so", and the staff is "well trained"; P.S. there's also a sushi bar.

Mille Fleurs *French*   26 | 25 | 26 | $72

Rancho Santa Fe | Country Squire Courtyard | 6009 Paseo Delicias (Avenida de Acacias) | 858-756-3085 | www.millefleurs.com

You can just "smell the money around you" at this "world-class" exercise in "investment dining" where the "glitterati of Rancho Santa Fe" revel in chef Martin Woesle's "sublime" New French fare that's "fresh and exciting without being too off-the-wall"; the "impeccably presented" dishes are then conveyed by "utterly professional" servers through the "lovely", "formal" space, which was augmented by a casual bar area offering lunches, tapas and bistro fare post-Survey.

Morton's The Steakhouse *Steak*   26 | 22 | 24 | $62

Downtown | 285 J St. (bet. 2nd & 3rd Aves.) | 619-696-3369 |
www.mortons.com

"A guy's steakhouse that women love" too, this Downtown spot may be a "typical" representation of the chain, but it's "nonetheless great" for "piping-hot, juicy and tender" beef paired with "fine trimmings", served in "wow" sizes and "outrageously priced" (don't forget about the lobster, it "will thrill you as well"); though many diners deem the "waiters bringing the trays" of raw meat "out for you to admire" "just plain idiotic", said servers are "fun and nice."

Pamplemousse Grille *American/French*   27 | 22 | 25 | $65

Solana Beach | 514 Via de la Valle (I-5) | 858-792-9090 | www.pgrille.com

"If you win big at the racetrack" "across the street", "blow it" at this "elegant" Solana Beach "special-occasion" "splurge" where chef Jeffrey Strauss provides "dinner and a show" by first whipping up "amazing" American-French fare that displays "a great flair for the unusual", then "floating through the dining room" to "entertain guests" with his "amusing", "schmoozing" ways; P.S. lunch is served Friday only, while a weekday happy hour, beginning at 4:30 PM and offering discounted food and drink, was instituted post-Survey.

	FOOD	DECOR	SERVICE	COST

Prado at Balboa Park *Californian*

22 | 26 | 22 | $39

Balboa Park | House of Hospitality | 1549 El Prado (Plaza de Panama) | 619-557-9441 | www.pradobalboa.com

"Top off a day" in "famously gorgeous" Balboa Park with this "special treat": "gracious" Californian dining in a "magical" "paradise", a vision of "pure loveliness" embodied by a "beautiful garden" and a "cool" "blown glass"–bedecked interior; the "divine dishes" "dazzle the eye and palate", while "silky smooth service" makes it a "great place to bring out-of-town guests" or the object of your affection.

Primavera Ristorante *Italian*

26 | 21 | 25 | $50

Coronado | 932 Orange Ave. (bet. 9th & 10th Sts.) | 619-435-0454 | www.primavera1st.com

It may be "under the radar", but this "tiny jewel" "in the heart of Coronado" "flies high", as "mouthwatering" Northern Italian cuisine "for the discerning palate" is conveyed by "superb" servers; also "top-notch" is a wine list that's sufficiently "proper" for such an "intimate", "old-fashioned" "high-class" setting.

Roppongi *Asian*

25 | 22 | 21 | $45

La Jolla | 875 Prospect St. (Fay Ave.) | 858-551-5252 | www.roppongiusa.com

"Amazing Asian-fusion" small plates are "creatively crafted" at this La Jolla "winner"; it's "elegant without being stuffy" inside, while the "beautiful outdoor fire-pit seating" gets the "stylish crowd" to engage in "excessive frivolity"; P.S. your "best bets" are the "half-price tapas and sushi 3–6 PM daily", so "order up a storm and share with friends."

Sammy's Woodfired Pizza *Pizza*

21 | 15 | 18 | $22

Del Mar | Del Mar Highlands | 12925 El Camino Real (Del Mar Heights Rd.) | 858-259-6600

Downtown | 770 Fourth Ave. (F St.) | 619-230-8888

Golden Triangle | Costa Verde Ctr. | 8650 Genesee Ave. (La Jolla Vill.) | 858-404-9898

La Jolla | 702 Pearl St. (Draper Ave.) | 858-456-5222

Mission Valley | Mission Valley Mall | 1620 Camino de la Reina (Mission Center Rd.) | 619-298-8222

Carlsbad | 5970 Avenida Encinas (Palomar Airport Rd.) | 760-438-1212

Point Loma | Liberty Station | 2401 Truxtun Rd. (Womble Rd.) | 619-222-3111

San Marcos | 121 S. Las Posas Rd. (Ronald Packard Pkwy.) | 760-591-4222

Scripps Ranch | 10785 Scripps Poway Pkwy. (Spring Canyon Rd.) | 858-695-0900

www.sammyspizza.com

"Savvy restaurateur" Sami Ladeki's homegrown chain is a "San Diego favorite" for "fresh and tasty" "West Coast pizza" with "innovative toppings" ("arugula and pear is a true wonder"), "massive", "addictive salads" and "yummy messy sundaes" for dessert ("be sure to scrape the glass, that's where all the caramel is!"); the staff of "surfers" sometimes "moves at a snail's pace", and with "a lot of kids" eating, they're "a bit on the noisy side", but the pies "never disappoint."

Sapori *Italian*

− | − | − | E

Coronado | 120 Orange Ave. (bet. 1st & 2nd Sts.) | 619-319-5696 | www.saporicoronado.com

Charming Coronado is the setting of this easygoing Italian that pairs pricey antipasti, pastas, mains and desserts with old-world service;

though there's one campy design touch – wallpaper sporting sexy red lips sucking up spaghetti – the interior is on the whole handsome, and the patio, though a block away from the waterfront, exhibits fine views of San Diego Bay.

Sushi Ota *Japanese*
28 | 12 | 19 | $41

Pacific Beach | 4529 Mission Bay Dr. (Bunker Hill St.) | 858-270-5670 | www.sushi-ota.com

As "amazing" "as any place on the planet", this "pearl in a trashcan" conjures not only the "absolute best Japanese" in Pacific Beach but the No. 1 Food in San Diego courtesy of "genius" chef Yukito Ota and his "expert panel of sushi doctors" who assemble "silky" "treats" "so fresh, they almost evaporate on your tongue" ("sit at the bar" and let them "guide you"); its "oddball" setting in a strip mall is "lame", and you "need to book way too far in advance", so just "ignore everything but the taste" and "you'll have an experience you'll never forget."

Tapenade *French*
27 | 21 | 25 | $59

La Jolla | 7612 Fay Ave. (bet. Kline & Pearl Sts.) | 858-551-7500 | www.tapenaderestaurant.com

"You're in for a great experience" when you venture "off the beaten" La Jolla path to this "close-to-ideal" New French "destination" where diners "trust" chef Jean-Michel Diot's "obvious commitment to quality ingredients" in creating "inventive" dishes that display "harmonious flavors and a counterplay of textures" (they're "well matched" by "extraordinary wines" too); it may be "a little stark" for being so "expensive", but it's "quiet and intimate", and "cordial" servers make sure everyone "goes home happy"; P.S. there's also a happy-hour bites menu.

WineSellar & Brasserie ⑤Ⓜ *French*
28 | 20 | 27 | $61

Golden Triangle | 9550 Waples St. (off Mira Mesa Blvd.) | 858-450-9557 | www.winesellar.com

It's "hard to find" in a "random" Golden Triangle "industrial zone", but this "tiny" "dream restaurant" is "well worth the hunt" for "imaginatively prepared", "beautifully presented" French fare; the "staggering" selection from the *vin* "warehouse" below is available upstairs at "minimal markups", the corkage fees are "nominal" and the "phenomenal", top-rated servers "recommend delicious pairings", all of which makes it "a must" for "wine dummies" and "oenophiles" alike.

San Francisco Bay Area

TOP FOOD RANKING

	Restaurant	Cuisine
29	Gary Danko	American
	French Laundry	American/French
28	Cyrus	French
	Sierra Mar	Californian/Eclectic
	Acquerello	Italian
	La Folie	French
	Erna's Elderberry	Californian/French
	Hana	Japanese
	Chez Panisse	Californian/Mediterranean
27	Kaygetsu	Japanese
	La Toque	French
	Marinus	French
	Sushi Zone	Japanese
	Canteen	Californian
	Chez Panisse Café	Californian/Mediterranean
	Masa's	French
	Ritz-Carlton Dining Room	French
	Boulevard	American
	Sushi Ran	Japanese
	Manresa	American

OTHER NOTEWORTHY PLACES

Restaurant	Cuisine
Ad Hoc	American
Ame	American
A16	Italian
Benu	American
Bouchon	French
Delfina	Italian
Frances	Californian
Jardinière	Californian/French
Kokkari Estiatorio	Greek
Morimoto Napa	Japanese
Nopa	Californian
Perbacco	Italian
Prospect	American
Quince	French/Italian
RN74	French
Slanted Door	Vietnamese
Spruce	American
Waterbar	Seafood
Wayfare	American
Zuni Café	Mediterranean

Acquerello ☒Ⓜ *Italian*

28 | 25 | 28 | $84

Polk Gulch | 1722 Sacramento St. (bet. Polk St. & Van Ness Ave.) | San Francisco | 415-567-5432 | www.acquerello.com

Ever "elegant", this "enchanting" Italian in a "tranquil" converted chapel off Polk presents "glorious", "masterfully prepared" prix fixe dinners complemented by a "daunting" but "extraordinary" wine list; "impeccable maitre d' oversight" and "outstanding" "choreographed service" complete the picture, so even if it feels a bit "stodgy" to some – and "only the Medicis can afford" the bill – it offers an "exquisite" dining experience that remains "unequaled in the city"; P.S. jacket suggested.

Ad Hoc *American*

27 | 21 | 25 | $58

Yountville | 6476 Washington St. (bet. Mission St. & Oak Circle) | 707-944-2487 | www.adhocrestaurant.com

Grandma's cookin' "amped up" with "French Laundry–quality ingredients" and "technique" is "what's for dinner" at Thomas Keller's "foodie" "boarding house" in Yountville where "omnivores" "roll the dice" and always win with "positively brilliant" "family-style" set-menu suppers (and Sunday brunch) served by "jean-clad" waiters; those few who cluck about "expensive" tabs for "homey" meals (including the "incredible" fried chicken served "every other Monday") have the option of dining "à la carte at the bar"; P.S. closed Tuesdays and Wednesdays.

Ame *American*

26 | 25 | 25 | $74

SoMa | St. Regis | 689 Mission St. (3rd St.) | San Francisco | 415-284-4040 | www.amerestaurant.com

"Brilliant" New American cooking (with a "haute Japanese" streak) in the St. Regis offers a "delicious coda to a day of sightseeing", or simply an "ame-zing", "adventurous" "date-night" dinner, at Hiro Sone and Lissa Doumani's "swanky" SoMa spot; replete with "Eastern"-style, "polished" service in the "immaculately designed" main room and "choreographed action" behind the sushi bar, it's a "steep" but "memorable" "Zen gourmet dining experience."

A16 *Italian*

25 | 20 | 21 | $45

Marina | 2355 Chestnut St. (bet. Divisadero & Scott Sts.) | San Francisco | 415-771-2216 | www.a16sf.com

"If you can make it through" the "racy" bar crowd and "crushing" "noise that reminds you of an Italian speedway" at this "hot" Marina trattoria, you're in for a "sublime" time "nibbling on the house-cured meats", "stellar" pastas and "incredible", "wood-fired" Neapolitan pies while watching the "pizza chefs" at work; the "hip, knowledgeable" staff can get "overwhelmed" but ultimately offers "lots of help" navigating the "obscure" but "outstanding" wine list; P.S. lunch is available Wednesday–Friday.

Benu ☒Ⓜ *American*

- | - | - | E

SoMa | 22 Hawthorne St. (bet. Folsom & Howard Sts.) | San Francisco | 415-685-4860 | www.benusf.com

Rising from the ashes where the now-shuttered Two and Hawthorne Lane stood in SoMa, this contemporary American arrival named after the Egyptian version of the mythical phoenix showcases the cuisine of French Laundry protégé Corey Lee, who crafts elaborate multicourse tasting menus as well as more accessible à la carte dishes; the small but sleek dining room keeps the focus on the food, which is served on custom-made porcelain plates and reclaimed-wood petit-four boxes, while the secluded courtyard provides a peaceful perch for apéritifs.

Bouchon French
26 | 23 | 23 | $56

Yountville | 6534 Washington St. (Yount St.) | 707-944-8037 | www.bouchonbistro.com

Thomas Keller "can do no wrong" swear supporters of his "quintessential French bistro" in Yountville, "your next best bet" (and a "wallet-friendly" alternative) when "you can't secure a reservation at the French Laundry"; "casual perfection is the watchword here", from the "inspired", "superb" dishes to the "crisp" service to the "upbeat" "Paris-in-Napa" setting, so no wonder "there's always a crowd" filling the "close" tables that force you to "get to know your neighbor."

Boulevard American
27 | 25 | 26 | $69

Embarcadero | Audiffred Bldg. | 1 Mission St. (Steuart St.) | San Francisco | 415-543-6084 | www.boulevardrestaurant.com

"One of the few 'sure thing' restaurants" (for "business or pleasure"), Nancy Oakes' "pricey" yet "recession-proof" "belle epoque"–meets–"Barbary Coast" "institution" boasting "knockout views" of the Embarcadero delivers the "total package", with her "phenomenal", "delectable" New American dishes, a "wine list from Bacchus" and "gorgeous design"; the "high-energy crowd" never quits, so it's "tough to land a table", but once you're inside the "staff lives to please."

Canteen Ⓜ Californian
27 | 14 | 23 | $47

Tenderloin | Commodore Hotel | 817 Sutter St. (Jones St.) | San Francisco | 415-928-8870 | www.sfcanteen.com

How "magician" Dennis Leary continuously conjures such "bad-ass" Californian dinners (and weekend brunch) with "incredibly intricate" flavors at this "tiny" "Tenderloin star" "is a mystery, but one to be appreciated often" assure fans who angle to "snag" one of the "swift" nightly seatings; the "glorified" lunch-counter setting is part of the "charm", as it lets "serious foodies" watch the chef "go crazy" crafting "miracles out of a minute kitchen"; P.S. the Tuesday night prix fixe is a "deal."

Chez Panisse Ⓢ Californian/Mediterranean
28 | 23 | 26 | $83

Berkeley | 1517 Shattuck Ave. (bet. Cedar & Vine Sts.) | 510-548-5525 | www.chezpanisse.com

"Alice may not live here as much anymore", but her "landmark" kitchen still "works wonders", crafting the "freshest organic" ingredients into "simple" yet "outstanding" Cal-Med prix fixes, served by a "courteous" staff to patrons on a "pilgrimage" to this "gastronomic sanctuary"; it's "very Berkeley", down to the Arts and Crafts decor, and while some find the ambiance "a little too holy", most effuse it's "everything it's cracked up to be" – "well worth the cost" and the "tough reservation."

Chez Panisse Café Ⓢ Californian/Mediterranean
27 | 23 | 25 | $52

Berkeley | 1517 Shattuck Ave. (bet. Cedar & Vine Sts.) | 510-548-5049 | www.chezpanisse.com

"Never has walking up a few steps resulted in reaching foodie heaven at such a savings" "gloat" Berkeleyites who "skip the religious experience downstairs" and grab an à la carte lunch or dinner at Alice Waters' "reliable-as-the-sunrise", "Craftsman-style" cafe; the "shockingly

FOOD DECOR SERVICE COST

simple" yet "sublime" Cal-Med dishes (including pizzas with "pristine" toppings) and "exemplary" service are "every bit as good" as the original, plus you can "go in jeans" and still "tour the joint."

Cyrus *French*   28 | 28 | 28 | $130

Healdsburg | 29 North St. (Foss St.) | 707-433-3311 |
www.cyrusrestaurant.com

"Traveling foodies" know they're in for a night of "sheer indulgence" when the servers begin by "measuring the caviar against a gold coin" at this "beautiful", "incomparable" "temple of high cuisine" in Healdsburg that "puts the fine in dining"; sure, you can eat "à la carte at the bar", but most "go for broke" (literally) over chef-owner Douglas Keane's "mind-blowing" New French tasting menus embellished by "abounding carts", and while it's a bit "overwrought" for "sleepy Sonoma", the "outstanding" service makes for "memorable" "dinner theater"; P.S. dinner Thursday–Monday, plus Saturday lunch.

Delfina *Italian*   26 | 19 | 22 | $47

Mission | 3621 18th St. (bet. Dolores & Guerrero Sts.) | San Francisco | 415-552-4055 | www.delfinasf.com

Chef/co-owner Craig Stoll "hits every note right" at this Mission "must", preparing "simple, soulful", "swoon-worthy" Northern Italian food, matched by a "well-curated" wine list, that's worth the "hoops required to get a reservation"; the "young" staff is "terrific" and prices are "decent", so while the "New York-y" atmosphere can be a "madhouse", most agree it "never ceases to impress."

Erna's Elderberry House *Californian/French*   28 | 27 | 27 | $88

Oakhurst | Château du Sureau | 48688 Victoria Ln. (Hwy. 41) |
559-683-6800 | www.elderberryhouse.com

Experience "complex" French-Californian cuisine and "European sophistication" at this "fanciful baroque" "foodie paradise" in a "fantastic" B&B that's "worth a special trip" to "unlikely" Oakhurst in the Sierra foothills; what with "mind-blowing" (if "high-priced") prix fixe menus, "not-to-be-missed Sunday brunch" and "visits" from Erna herself, you'll be "treated royally", making it "one of the greatest lodging/dining" "jewels" – especially "if you want to see Yosemite without roughing it."

Frances Ⓜ *Californian*   27 | 20 | 25 | $51

Castro | 3870 17th St. (Pond St.) | San Francisco | 415-621-3870 |
www.frances-sf.com

The "euphoria" is mounting at this "boiling-hot" Castro newcomer where chef-owner and "master at her craft" Melissa Perello is "blowing away" the competition, delighting "elbow-to-elbow" "foodies" with a "limited", changing roster of "locally sourced" Californian fare that's "comforting and brilliant at the same time"; "welcoming" service and "delicious house wine by the ounce" add to the "charm", but "reservations are just about impossible" – fortunately, "squeezing" in at the "walk-in" bar is "as good as gold."

French Laundry, The *American/French*   29 | 27 | 28 | $275

Yountville | 6640 Washington St. (Creek St.) | 707-944-2380 |
www.frenchlaundry.com

"This one goes to 11!" exclaim reviewers who run out of "superlatives" to describe Thomas Keller's "glorious" stone lair in Yountville, where they "melt away" the afternoon (Friday–Sunday) or evening with an "unforgettable" New American–French tasting "extravaganza" that's "so far out of the box, you can't compare it to any other restaurant"; the "exceptional" staff "puffs out its chest a bit", but the wine pairings "take the meal from fabulous to magical", and "what's another few $100" for an experience this tough to "afford" (or "snag") more than "once in a lifetime"?

Gary Danko *American* | 29 | 27 | 28 | $109 |

Fisherman's Wharf | 800 N. Point St. (Hyde St.) | San Francisco | 415-749-2060 | www.garydanko.com

"Who needs a special occasion?" when simply "going to Gary Danko's" Wharf wonder – once again voted No. 1 for Food as well as Most Popular – "*is* the occasion" swoon diners who "save up" and "dress up" (and if need be, drop in at the bar) for a "feast de resistance" starring "magnificent" New American tasting menus with "choices galore" and an "epic wine list"; the "sexy" interior is almost "superfluous" given the "drop-dead gorgeous" plates, purveyed by "ninja" waiters (invisible, yet there "when you need them"), and it all culminates with a "showstopping" cheese cart and "pastry parting gifts."

Hana Japanese Restaurant *Japanese* | 28 | 17 | 22 | $45 |

Rohnert Park | 101 Golf Course Dr. (Roberts Lake Rd.) | 707-586-0270 | www.hanajapanese.com

Offering an "exceptional selection of raw fish", "traditional" dishes and "exquisitely crafted" Sonoma-inspired specials, chef-owner Ken Tominaga strives for "perfection" at this "must-stop" "sushi spot" that's definitely "one of the best Japanese restaurants in the area"; a "sake sommelier" only enhances the "great dining experience", making it even harder to "believe it's in a Rohnert Park" strip mall.

Jardinière *Californian/French* | 26 | 26 | 25 | $71 |

Civic Center | 300 Grove St. (Franklin St.) | San Francisco | 415-861-5555 | www.jardiniere.com

A "stylish" "splurge" near the Civic Center, Traci Des Jardins' "deco beauty has it all" – "fabulous", "sumptuous" (and sustainable) Cal-French food, "resplendent" decor and "first-class" servers who "bust their butts" to ensure the "ritzy" showgoer crowds make "curtain time"; the "center"-stage cocktail bar "offers modest monetary relief" and last-minute seating "for oysters" and champers, but rather than "rush the pleasure by double-booking", many say skip the theater and "let dining be the event of the evening."

Kaygetsu Ⓜ *Japanese* | 27 | 20 | 26 | $84 |

Menlo Park | Sharon Heights Shopping Ctr. | 325 Sharon Park Dr. (Sand Hill Rd.) | 650-234-1084 | www.kaygetsu.com

"Close your eyes and you could be in Tokyo" at this "labor of love" tucked into a Menlo Park "shopping plaza", where the "exquisite" kai-seki dinners – matched with "rare" sakes – have "no peer outside of Japan"; it costs a "fortune" (though à la carte options and the prix fixe lunch are "cheaper") and the atmosphere is "more traditional" than a "Nobu-type" joint, but a "server-to-diner ratio that seems to be 1:1" and the parade of "textures and tastes" "almost too lovely to eat" add up to an "unforgettable culinary experience."

	FOOD	DECOR	SERVICE	COST

Kokkari Estiatorio *Greek*   27 | 26 | 25 | $54

Downtown | 200 Jackson St. (bet. Battery & Front Sts.) | San Francisco |
415-981-0983 | www.kokkari.com

"Exquisite" Greek "delicacies" delight Downtown devotees of this
"cosmopolitan" "Hellenic heaven" that boasts a "gorgeous", "romantic"
main room where "spit-roasted meat" turns above a "blazing" fire; since
the "superb" staff ensures a "feel-good" experience, it's "packed every
night" with a savvy, "eclectic" crowd – including "politicos" and lovebirds
"splurging" on a "special occasion" – so "reservations are a must."

La Folie ⓩ *French*   28 | 25 | 26 | $95

Russian Hill | 2316 Polk St. (bet. Green & Union Sts.) | San Francisco |
415-776-5577 | www.lafolie.com

"After all these years", chef-owner Roland Passot "still wows" at his
"cathedral of French cuisine" on Russian Hill, "personally greeting
guests" and crafting "rich", "*magnifique*" tasting menus, "perfectly
coupled" with "brother George's fabulous wine program"; the "fussy
presentations, fussier service" and "intimate", "elegantly" remodeled
digs are tailor-made for "special evenings" and well worth the "considerable investment"; P.S. "for everyday dining, try the lounge next door."

La Toque *French*   27 | 25 | 27 | $103

Napa | Westin Verasa | 1314 McKinstry St. (Soscol Ave.) | 707-257-5157 |
www.latoque.com

"Hats off" to chef Ken Frank whose "move down to Napa only improved" what's "frankly one of the best restaurants" in the Valley,
proffering "pricey" but "extraordinary" New French tasting menus (including "awesome annual truffle" dinners) with "exceptional" wine
pairings; the "beautiful" albeit hotellike digs and "wonderful" service
make you feel "pampered" for a "special" evening, while his adjacent
Bank Café allows for more "casual" dining.

Manresa Ⓜ *American*   27 | 25 | 27 | $128

Los Gatos | 320 Village Ln. (bet. N. Santa Cruz & University Aves.) |
408-354-4330 | www.manresarestaurant.com

"Mad scientist" chef-owner David Kinch creates "visionary", "knockout" prix fixe meals in his "movie-set kitchen" at this New American
"food paradise" in Los Gatos, using his own biodynamic produce and
tying everything together with "fantastic" wines; "the expense is deep,
but the experience" – from the "slightly bent presentations" to the "incredible" service – is "like going to the opera", delivering a command
"performance" "you'll remember for a lifetime"; P.S. plans to add a
front lounge with a small-bites menu are slated to begin in fall 2010.

Marinus *French*   27 | 27 | 27 | $96

Carmel Valley | Bernardus Lodge | 415 Carmel Valley Rd. (Laureles Grade Rd.) |
831-658-3500 | www.bernardus.com

For some of the finest dining "in Monterey County by a mile", foodies
make the "wonderful" (albeit "far") drive through Carmel Valley and
"splurge" at this "beautifully landscaped resort" where Cal Stamenov
prepares "stellar" Cal-French tasting menus and the sommelier provides "inspired suggestions"; whether you sit at the chef's table or by
the grand fireplace that "could melt even the coldest critic", it's the
"meal of a lifetime" – even "nicer" if you "stay at the lodge."

	FOOD	DECOR	SERVICE	COST

Masa's 🗷Ⓜ French | 27 | 24 | 27 | $114 |

Downtown | Hotel Vintage Ct. | 648 Bush St. (bet. Powell & Stockton Sts.) |
San Francisco | 415-989-7154 | www.masasrestaurant.com

"Throughout its varying incarnations", this "sublime" Downtown destination "still wows" with its "marvelous", "superbly executed" New French cuisine by Gregory Short, matched with "superior" wines and served by a "top-notch" staff in a "serene jewel-box" setting; a post-Survey move to jettison its elaborate degustation menus for more recession-friendly four- and seven-course prix fixes makes the "pricey", somewhat "formal" meal a touch more accessible, but you still won't spot anyone here "wearing jeans and a baseball cap"; P.S. a three-course prix fixe is available by request.

Morimoto Napa Japanese | - | - | - | VE |

Napa | 610 Main St. (5th St.) | 707-252-1600 | www.morimotonapa.com

The first West Coast branch of Masaharu Morimoto's empire arrives on Downtown Napa's revitalized Riverfront, where the dramatic, traditional-meets-modern digs include a dining room, sushi bar and waterfront patio, and the pricey menu pairs fish flown in from Tokyo with Californian ingredients; the offerings are rounded out by soups, noodles and rice dishes and complemented by NorCal wines, imported sakes, artisanal cocktails and a selection of beers, including the chef's own line of Rogue Brewery suds.

Nopa ◗ Californian | 25 | 21 | 22 | $46 |

Western Addition | 560 Divisadero St. (Hayes St.) | San Francisco |
415-864-8643 | www.nopasf.com

Denizens of this "late-night" "darling of the foodies" in "the once-unfashionable" Western Addition "sit upstairs and watch the show" or "downstairs in the thick of it" with the "hipster masses" getting "stoked on" "inventive" spirits at the "hopping bar" and "fantastic" "as-California-as-you-get" "farm-fresh" fare for "down-to-earth prices"; despite the "mind-numbing noise", "forever waits" and the reality that "nopa is short for no parking", everyone, including "the waiters, still manages a smile."

Perbacco 🗷 Italian | 25 | 22 | 23 | $54 |

Downtown | 230 California St. (bet. Battery & Front Sts.) | San Francisco |
415-955-0663 | www.perbaccosf.com

Still the "Downtown favorite" (second only to new spin-off Barbacco "next door") for "power lunches galore", "after-work drinks" or a "night out", this "energetic", expensive "hot spot" draws torrents of "FiDi foodies" who fall for the "handmade pastas", salumi and other "first-rate" Piedmontese specialties; "chic" decor, "professional" service and a "superlative Italian wine list" seal the deal, "but mamma mia, it's noisy", so gray hairs tend to "head upstairs to escape the din" while "gray suits" party on at the bar.

Prospect American | - | - | - | E |

SoMa | Infiniti Towers | 300 Spear St. (Folsom St.) | San Francisco |
415-247-7770 | www.prospectsf.com

In SoMa's Infiniti Towers, this breezier younger sister to Boulevard aims to lure in a new breed of diners with a less expensive (but still high-end), more contemporary New American menu that's geared toward casual grazing; the handsome yet understated dining room features floor-to-ceiling windows and plush banquettes, but much of the activity revolves around the square-shaped bar dispensing innovative cocktails.

Quince   *French/Italian*   26 | 26 | 26 | $85

Downtown | 470 Pacific Ave. (bet. Montgomery St. & Osgood Pl.) | San Francisco | 415-775-8500 | www.quincerestaurant.com

Michael and Lindsay Tusk have taken their former Pacific Heights "neighborhood charmer" "to even greater heights" at this "sensational" new Downtown locale, where the "posh", "spacious" digs reflect the caliber of the nightly changing "knock-your-socks-off" French-Italian fare (particularly the "fabulous pastas") and "beyond impeccable service"; "yes, the portions are small" and there's a "heavy sticker price", but even nostalgists who miss the "quaintness" aver it's "still a special place" to create "restaurant memories."

Ritz-Carlton Dining Room   🗷 Ⓜ *French*   27 | 27 | 27 | $104

Nob Hill | Ritz-Carlton | 600 Stockton St. (Bet. California & Pine Sts.) | San Francisco | 415-773-6198 | www.ritzcarltondiningroom.com

"A throwback to another era", this "calm, romantic" Nob Hill "grande dame" remains "one of the few places where you can dress up and feel like you're going out for a special evening", especially once you sample chef Ron Siegel's "exquisite", often "adventurous" New French prix fixes with "Japanese influences"; you'll "need to pay up", of course, but add in a "decadent dessert cart", "one of the best wine cellars" in town and "pampering" service and you've got a "delight from start to finish."

RN74   *French*   22 | 24 | 22 | $62

SoMa | Millennium Tower | 301 Mission St. (Beale St.) | San Francisco | 415-543-7474 | www.rn74.com

Oenophiles are "happy to get on board" Michael Mina's "casually elegant" SoMa newcomer, whose "eye-catching" decor – a "modern interpretation of a Euro train station", complete with an "old-style railroad departure board" announcing "wine specials" – vies for attention with "inventive" (and "pricey") New French large and small plates; "jammed" with "young business types" and "wealthy Millennium Tower tenants" sampling the "incredible" vino selection, it's a real "scene", and if some "don't get the hype", the majority deems it a "worthy" arrival.

Sierra Mar   *Californian/Eclectic*   28 | 29 | 27 | $89

Big Sur | Post Ranch Inn | Hwy. 1 (30 mi. south of Carmel) | 831-667-2800 | www.postranchinn.com

"Relax" "on a bluff above the Pacific" and "feel at one with nature" as you take in the "unsurpassed" "view extraordinaire" from this "stunning" glass-enclosed aerie at the Post Ranch Inn; "irrespective of location", the "unique, flavorful" Cal-Eclectic fare, "encyclopedia-sized wine list" and servers who "spoil you" will "please any gourmand", but since the "tab is as close to the clouds as you are", consider going for "lunch out on the deck."

Slanted Door, The   *Vietnamese*   26 | 22 | 22 | $50

Embarcadero | 1 Ferry Bldg. (Market St.) | San Francisco | 415-861-8032 | www.slanteddoor.com

Diners experience an "epiphany" "by the Bay" at Charles Phan's "high-end" Vietnamese where "knockout views" enhance the "stupendous" food ("shaking beef, 'nuff said") and "unfamiliar" wines, while "educated" servers hustle in the "industrial-cool" glassed-in Ferry Building digs; true, it's "l-o-u-d", "jammed" and "impossibly" "hard to get in the door, slanted or not", now that everyone from "presidents and locals" to "tourists" "has it on their 'bucket list'", so some savvy types simply "duck into the bar as soon as it opens."

Spruce *American*

26 | 26 | 24 | $70

Presidio Heights | 3640 Sacramento St. (bet. Locust & Spruce Sts.) | San Francisco | 415-931-5100 | www.sprucesf.com

"The Upper East Side comes" to Presidio Heights at this "lively", "alluring" boîte, a "power scene" boasting "posh" looks and "pampering" service to suit "ladies who lunch", "debutantes and the parents who pay"; the kitchen "dazzles" with "exquisite", "farm"-fresh New American fare matched by a "world-class" wine list, but those "not up for the full press" (and tab) join the "spruced-up" walk-ins for a "burger at the bar."

Sushi Ran *Japanese*

27 | 20 | 23 | $56

Sausalito | 107 Caledonia St. (bet. Pine & Turney Sts.) | 415-332-3620 | www.sushiran.com

"If God opened a sushi bar", it might resemble this "posh" Sausalito spot that's "worth the trip over the bridge", since it proffers "top-notch" fish "flown in from Japan" and "wonderful cooked dishes" in "tranquil" digs; "Marin attitude and crowds can be a drag" and it's "no bargain", but savvy surveyors who sample it during the "busy lunch hour" snag delicious "deals", while sake-seekers who "enhance the experience" with the "insane" selection at the next-door "wine bar" "almost never wait."

Sushi Zone ⊠⌖ *Japanese*

27 | 11 | 15 | $33

Castro | 1815 Market St. (Pearl St.) | San Francisco | 415-621-1114

Talk about getting into the Zone: the "brutal waits" at this "tiny" sushi "gem" in the Castro "will melt the life out of you" ("even if you arrive before opening"), and once seated, the "chef is slower than an elderly gent behind the wheel of a Buick"; nevertheless, devotees declare "it's worth it" for the "glorious", "California-ized" rolls (i.e. "full of mangos and macadamias"), and it's one of the "best values" in town to boot.

Waterbar *Seafood*

20 | 26 | 20 | $58

Embarcadero | 399 The Embarcadero (Folsom St.) | San Francisco | 415-284-9922 | www.waterbarsf.com

"Watch the antics of the sea life" in the "floor-to-ceiling" "aquarium columns" (sure to "wow the out-of-towners"), the "beautiful-people" "action at the bar" or just drink in the "spectacular" "Bay Bridge outside" at Pat Kuleto's "water-themed" Embarcadero fish house; finatics find the seafood "rock solid", adding you "can't beat" the "$1 oyster specials" for "happy hour", but sharkier sorts snap "unfortunately" the "pricey" "food does not measure up" to the "killer view."

Wayfare Tavern *American*

- | - | - | E

Downtown | 558 Sacramento St. (bet. Montgomery & Sansome Sts.) | San Francisco | 415-772-9060 | www.wayfaretavern.com

Celebrity chef Tyler Florence's ode to the Barbary Coast lures power-lunchers and Downtown diners with upscale Traditional American fare, like organic fried chicken and steak and eggs, proffered in a stunning turn-of-the-century building tricked out with Victorian hunting bric-a-brac and dark leather booths; the tri-level setting includes a gentlemen's club-esque billiards room upstairs, plus two bars mixing retro cocktails (courtesy of the Bon Vivants) and pouring Golden State wines.

Zuni Café Ⓜ *Mediterranean*   25 21 22 $52

Hayes Valley | 1658 Market St. (bet. Franklin & Gough Sts.) | San Francisco | 415-552-2522 | www.zunicafe.com

"Like an old girlfriend who never seems to age", Judy Rodgers' Hayes Valley "treasure" "filled with light and laughter" still "holds onto the hearts" of "locavores" with its "simple but amazing" Med fare; "noon or night", it's "always buzzing", with everyone from "politicians" to "drag queens" devouring the "perfect" "wood-fired chicken" for two, "legendary Caesar salad" and the "best burgers" (at lunch and after 10 PM) or indulging in "super Bloodys" and oysters at the "cool zinc bar", so most don't mind the occasional "attitude."

Seattle

TOP FOOD RANKING

	Restaurant	Cuisine
28	Cafe Juanita	Italian
	Paseo	Caribbean
	Mashiko	Japanese
	Spinasse	Italian
	Herbfarm	Pacific NW
	Rover's	French
	Corson Building	Eclectic
	Tilth	American
27	Nishino	Japanese
	Kisaku Sushi	Japanese
	Lark	American
	Shiro's Sushi*	Japanese
	La Carta de Oaxaca	Mexican
	Harvest Vine	Spanish
	Il Terrazzo Carmine	Italian
	Cantinetta	Italian
	Boat St. Cafe	French
	Salumi	Italian/Sandwiches
	Restaurant Zoë	American
	Nell's	American

OTHER NOTEWORTHY PLACES

Restaurant	Cuisine
Anchovies & Olives	Italian/Seafood
Bisato	Italian
Campagne	French
Canlis	Pacific NW
Carmelita	Mediterranean
Chez Shea	French/Pacific NW
Crush	American
Dahlia Lounge	Pacific NW
Delancey	Pizza
Green Leaf	Vietnamese
Joule	Eclectic
Le Gourmand	French
Metropolitan Grill	Steak
Mistral Kitchen	American
Serious Pie	Pizza
Sitka & Spruce	Eclectic
Spring Hill	Pacific NW
Staple & Fancy	Italian
Tosoni's	Continental
Wild Ginger	Pacific Rim

* Indicates a tie with restaurant above

	FOOD	DECOR	SERVICE	COST

Anchovies & Olives ◑ *Italian/Seafood*   25 | 20 | 21 | $43

Capitol Hill | 1550 15th Ave. (Pine St.) | 206-838-8080 |
www.anchoviesandolives.com
Ethan Stowell's Italian seafooder in Capitol Hill gets kudos for "amazing-quality fish, expertly prepared", including "raw small plates" and "oysters at their finest"; the "industrial-hip" digs are navigated by a "relaxed" staff, and if the budget brigade finds it "a little expensive", some swear they'd go "even if all they served was anchovies and olives."

Bisato Ⓜ *Italian*   25 | 21 | 25 | $46

Belltown | 2400 First Ave. (Battery St.) | 206-443-3301 | www.bisato.com
Chef-owner Scott Carsberg's "revamping" of his shuttered Lampreia is this Venetian cicchetti–small plates "winner" in Belltown that's "down-scaled" from its predecessor, serving "outstanding" Italian fare for more "affordable prices"; a sophisticated setting offers a combination of counter and table seating, and the staff "takes care of everyone."

Boat Street Cafe *French*   27 | 22 | 24 | $39

Queen Anne | 3131 Western Ave. (Denny Way) | 206-632-4602 |
www.boatstreetcafe.com
Bon vivants feel like they're "escaping to France" at chef Renee Erickson's "unpretentious" lower Queen Anne bistro where the "fabulous" mid-priced fare – including "killer housemade pickles" and charcuterie – is served by a "brilliant" staff; antique posters of Babar the Elephant add to the "delightful" dinner setting complete with slate tables and candlelight, while the more "sparse" adjacent area called the Kitchen serves lunch and weekend brunch.

Cafe Juanita Ⓜ *Italian*   28 | 24 | 27 | $62

Kirkland | 9702 NE 120th Pl. (97th St.) | 425-823-1505 |
www.cafejuanita.com
"Dazzled" fans "can't say enough" about the "superbly prepared" "creative" dishes chef-owner Holly Smith turns out at her "charming" Northern Italian "hidden" in Kirkland and rated No. 1 for Food in Seattle; set in a midcentury house with a "cozy fireplace", the simple dining room has a "warm", "romantic" feel and the "top-notch" staff is "congenial" and "knowledgeable", making for an experience that's "expensive" but "all-around outstanding."

Campagne Ⓜ *French*   26 | 23 | 25 | $57

Pike Place Market | Inn at the Market | 86 Pine St. (1st Ave.) |
206-728-2800 | www.campagnerestaurant.com
A "quiet oasis" in the Pike Place Market, this "classy", "entirely comfortable" dinner-only French perennial under the eye of chef Daisley Gordon manages to set out "amazing", "pricey" haute fare without feeling "stuffy or pretentious"; the "flawless" service and bistro setting with "wonderful views" of the market "go a long way" to making it suitable for a "romantic" "night to remember"; P.S. the less-expensive Cafe Campagne is open all day.

Canlis Ⓩ *Pacific NW*   27 | 28 | 27 | $80

Lake Union | 2576 Aurora Ave. N. (Westlake Ave.) | 206-283-3313 |
www.canlis.com
"Opulent" cuisine and "exceptionally polished" service with a backdrop of "stunning Lake Union views" have put this "longtime favorite"

	FOOD	DECOR	SERVICE	COST

of Seattle's "who's who" in a "class of one" since it opened in 1950 – only now chef Jason Franey adds his "own spin" to a "very contemporary" Pacific NW menu; the overall package of "civilized fine dining" and "wonderful ambiance" in a "perfect midcentury modern room" means "you'll pay dearly", but "they do it so well."

Cantinetta Ⓜ Italian

| 27 | 22 | 23 | $39 |

Wallingford | 3650 Wallingford Ave. N. (bet. 36th & 37th Sts.) | 206-632-1000
Bellevue | 10038 Main St. (bet. 100th Ave. SE and 101st Ave. SE) | 425-233-6040
www.cantinettaseattle.com

Handmade pasta that "melts in your mouth" is a highlight of the "fabulous" Italian menu drawing Wallingford locals to this pricey yet "unassuming" Tuscan-themed "gem"; the "lively crowd" keeps the "cozy" room "packed" and "noisy", but a "pleasant staff that tries hard" "lets you forgive a little"; P.S. a mid-Survey chef change is not reflected in the Food score, and the Bellevue branch opened post-Survey.

Carmelita Ⓜ Mediterranean

| 25 | 22 | 23 | $35 |

Greenwood | 7314 Greenwood Ave. N. (bet. 73rd & 74th Sts.) | 206-706-7703 | www.carmelita.net

"Gourmet" fare with a "creative" "melding of flavors" has long been luring herbivores to this "upscale" Greenwood Mediterranean that's one of the few "totally vegetarian" places in Seattle; a "warm, inviting setting" including a garden patio and "amazing cocktails" ferried by a "helpful staff" add to the "pleasant surprise."

Chez Shea Ⓜ French/Pacific NW

| 26 | 22 | 24 | $55 |

Pike Place Market | Pike Place Mkt. | 94 Pike St. (1st Ave.) | 206-467-9990 | www.chezshea.com

"Innovative" but not "over-the-top" cuisine makes for "romantic" candlelit dinners at this Pacific NW–French "hidden" in Pike Place Market, where arched windows open for summer breezes while looking out on Elliott Bay and "caring" service completes an "unforgettable experience"; P.S. those seeking something "considerably less expensive" head for snacks at the adjacent Shea's Lounge.

Corson Building Ⓜ Eclectic

| 28 | 23 | 26 | $87 |

Georgetown | 5609 Corson Ave. S. (Airport Way) | 206-762-3330 | www.thecorsonbuilding.com

"Incredible" locavore prix fixe meals served "family-style" at "communal tables" draw "in-the-know diners" to Matt Dillon's Georgetown Eclectic "local food mecca", where a kitchen garden (with chickens) and a "cool" old Spanish house conjure up the feeling of a "provincial home"; courses start with an "unpretentious introduction" from the chef and proceed with "extremely professional" service, so acolytes assess it "worth every pretty penny."

Crush Ⓜ American

| 25 | 22 | 24 | $64 |

Madison Valley | 2319 E. Madison St. (23rd Ave.) | 206-302-7874 | www.crushonmadison.com

Fans find chef Jason Wilson's New American in Madison Valley "awesome in every way", from the "inventive" menus to the 100-year-old farmhouse exterior to the "elegant" white "mod" decor inside; an "outstanding staff" "happily guides you" through the "feast", adding up to a "class act" with a bill to match.

Dahlia Lounge *Pacific NW*   26 | 24 | 25 | $48

Downtown | 2001 Fourth Ave. (Virginia St.) | 206-682-4142 |
www.tomdouglas.com

Local flavor wiz Tom Douglas' founding Downtown restaurant is "still buzz-worthy" after 22 years, dishing out Pacific Northwest fare including "fabulous crab cakes" and "beyond heavenly" coconut cream pie; the "sultry" red dining room has "arty" touches like papier-mâché fish lamps and the staff is "first-class", so it's understandably "busy" – be sure to "reserve a table."

Delancey Ⓜ *Pizza*   26 | 18 | 20 | $28

Ballard | 1415 NW 70th St. (bet. Alonzo & Mary Aves.) | 206-838-1960 |
www.delanceyseattle.com

At this midpriced "hip pizzeria" in Ballard, Brandon Pettit and Molly Wizenberg offer wood-fired pies with "perfectly cooked, slightly charred" crusts and "well-thought-out" artisanal toppings like housemade sausage; service with "attitude" goes with the terrain, and since the simple setting is small, it's "crowded" with sometimes "long waits."

Green Leaf *Vietnamese*   27 | 13 | 19 | $20

International District | 418 Eighth Ave S. (Jackson St.) | 206-340-1388 |
www.greenleaftaste.com

At this "always busy" spot in the ID, "servers rush through the tight spaces" bearing "delicious" Vietnamese dishes filled with flavors "that are always balanced perfectly"; the opening of a second dining level added more seats, so there's "lots to like for the money."

Harvest Vine *Spanish*   27 | 21 | 23 | $49

Madison Valley | 2701 E. Madison St. (27th Ave.) | 206-320-9771 |
www.harvestvine.com

Cognoscenti congregate at the copper bar to "watch the magic" as chefs prepare "fabulous" Basque tapas to "mix and match" with a "broad selection of Spanish wines" at this "romantic" Madison Valley casa; service is "knowledgeable" and the place is "always packed" (thankfully it now takes reservations) – just "watch what you're ordering because those small plates can add up."

Herbfarm Ⓜ *Pacific NW*   28 | 26 | 28 | $215

Woodinville | 14590 NE 145th St. (Woodinville-Redmond Rd.) |
425-485-5300 | www.theherbfarm.com

"Atop the bucket list" of sybaritic surveyors is the "amazing" evening of "serious dining" at this Woodinville wine country "destination" where "you're never sure what will come next" during the nine-course Pacific NW "extravaganza" of "pure perfection" complete with wines and "unparalleled service"; it all begins with a tour of the garden and afterward some "stay the night" in the suites, but be aware that you might need to "get a second job" to foot the bill.

Il Terrazzo Carmine Ⓩ *Italian*   27 | 25 | 26 | $51

Pioneer Square | 411 First Ave. S. (bet. Jackson & King Sts.) |
206-467-7797 | www.ilterrazzocarmine.com

Carmine Smeraldo makes everyone "feel like a regular" at his "suave" Pioneer Square Italian where the "stellar" fare is "sinfully delicious" and the "exceptional" staff is "warm and friendly"; the Florentine country setting "breathes power and elegance" and it's always full of "movers and shakers", so just remember to "bring the moolah" and "you will be happy."

Joule 🅼 *Eclectic*

26 | 20 | 23 | $41

Wallingford | 1913 N. 45th St. (Burke Ave.) | 206-632-1913 | www.joulerestaurant.com

"Wonderfully thought-out" combinations of ingredients define the 'super-creative" offerings with French, Korean and American influences at this "intriguing" Wallingford Eclectic from chefs Rachel Yang and Seif Chirchi; the modern room in a vintage mercantile building tends to be "crowded" and "a little too loud", but service is "pleasant" and fans agree it "can't be beat for the price."

Kisaku Sushi *Japanese*

27 | 20 | 23 | $37

Green Lake | 2101 N. 55th St. (Meridian Ave.) | 206-545-9050 | www.kisaku.com

At this "go-to" Japanese sushi spot in Green Lake, chef-owner Ryuichi Nakano transforms a "wide variety" of the "freshest seafood" into "classic and innovative" rolls and much-lauded omakase dinners; it's "always busy", so generally "attentive" service can get a bit "rushed", but prices are "reasonable" and it's "kid-friendly" – a welcome touch in this family-centric neighborhood; P.S. closed Tuesday.

La Carta de Oaxaca 🅢 *Mexican*

27 | 17 | 19 | $23

Ballard | 5431 Ballard Ave. NW (22nd Ave.) | 206-782-8722 | www.lacartadeoaxaca.com

"It tastes like Mexico" say fans of the "spectacular" "authentic Oaxacan cuisine" at this "buzzing" Ballard cantina where the "affordable" "full-bodied" fare features "wow"-inducing mole and "even the salsa and chips are out-of-the-ordinary"; though the "space can get a little cramped" with "long lines", a "friendly", "bustling staff" and margaritas that "hit the spot" ease "waits."

Lark 🅼 *American*

27 | 22 | 25 | $51

Capitol Hill | 926 12th Ave. (bet. Marion & Spring Sts.) | 206-323-5275 | www.larkseattle.com

The "exceptional" menu "takes small plates to a new level" with "local, seasonal ingredients" at John Sundstrom's "rustic" New American on Capitol Hill's up-and-coming 12th Avenue; the wood-beamed room is "tasteful" and "intimate", and though some say it seems "expensive" because "you can't help" over-ordering, it's agreed "every bite's a winner"; P.S. though primarily a walk-in spot, it accepts same-day reservations.

Le Gourmand 🅢🅼 *French*

26 | 22 | 25 | $68

Ballard | 425 NW Market St. (6th Ave.) | 206-784-3463 | www.legourmandrestaurant.com

Chef Bruce Naftaly was a "locavore before it was trendy" remind regulars who call him a "master at blending" the "freshest" organic and sustainable ingredients (some from his own garden) into "superb" dinners at his and Sara Naftaly's "long-standing" French in Ballard; the 'lovely" white modern dining room is "quiet" and service is "unobtrusive", all lending to its "romantic" appeal as an "expensive special-occasion" choice; P.S. open Wednesday–Saturday.

	FOOD	DECOR	SERVICE	COST

Mashiko *Japanese*

28 | **19** | **22** | **$39**

West Seattle | 4725 California Ave. SW (bet. Alaska & Edmunds Sts.) | 206-935-4339 | www.sushiwhore.com

An "amazing assortment" of sustainable seafood "not to be had elsewhere" plus moderate prices equal lines and "a decent wait" at this "edgy", "inventive" West Seattle Japanese "joint"; afishionados sit at the sushi bar and order chef-owner Hajime Sato's "omakase to die for", and though the decor might be a mite "dated", scores have improved across the board.

Metropolitan Grill *Steak*

26 | **24** | **25** | **$63**

Downtown | 820 Second Ave. (Marion St.) | 206-624-3287 | www.themetropolitangrill.com

"Bring it on" cheer meat mavens at this Downtown "steakhouse par excellence" where beef rules but "anything on the menu is good" and comes in "huge portions"; the "friendly" staff makes everyone "feel comfortable" in the "old-style", "clubby" environs, leaving the big-spenders who dine here chuckling "healthy, schmealthy."

Mistral Kitchen *American*

26 | **24** | **24** | **$62**

Lake Union | 2020 Westlake Ave. (8th Ave.) | 206-623-1922 | www.mistral-kitchen.com

Chef-owner William Belickis (the shuttered Mistral) walks a "no-net culinary tightrope" at his "stunning", "ambitious" Lake Union New American proffering multiple "creative" menus and "dazzling cocktails" in a variety of settings; the modern dining room is casual and less costly than the "beautiful" Jewel Box room and "marvelous" chef's table where tasting menus are served, and there are lounge bites too.

Nell's *American*

27 | **22** | **25** | **$48**

Green Lake | 6804 E. Green Lake Way N. (1st Ave NE) | 206-524-4044 | www.nellsrestaurant.com

From a "superb", "innovative" menu featuring the likes of veal sweetbreads and grilled Mangalitsa pork, chef-owner Philip Mihalski cooks up "consistently first-rate" fare at his "beautiful" and expensive Green Lake New American; the "quiet setting" is conducive to conversation (some say "boring") and service is "elegant", so acolytes attest it's an experience "you can count on" all-around.

Nishino *Japanese*

27 | **23** | **25** | **$52**

Madison Park | 3130 E. Madison St. (Lake Washington Blvd.) | 206-322-5800 | www.nishinorestaurant.com

"Supreme sushi" "sparkling with creativity" pleases the well-heeled patrons of this "mellow" Madison Park Japanese, where "beautiful" fish is fashioned into "traditional" and "contemporary" fare by Nobu-trained co-owner Tatsu Nishino; insiders "go omakase" and let the masters "do their work" in the "lovely", stylish room that's comfortable whether you're in "jeans or a suit", and don't mind a bill that's a "splurge."

Paseo 🖪 Ⓜ ⇆ *Caribbean*

28 | **9** | **16** | **$13**

Ballard | 6226 Seaview Ave. NW (62nd St.) | 206-789-3100
Fremont | 4225 Fremont Ave. N. (bet. 42nd & 43rd Sts.) | 206-545-7440 | www.paseoseattle.com

"Magnificent" and "messy" Cuban sandwiches stuffed with "pork that melts in your mouth" practically "inspire poetry" at this "busy", wallet-friendly Caribbean duo; it may "run out of bread" and is "cash-only", but that doesn't stop fans from forming "lines out the door", especially at the "wee" Fremont original, though the newer Ballard branch has "shorter" waits.

Restaurant Zoë *American*

27 | 22 | 25 | $50

Belltown | 2137 Second Ave. (Blanchard St.) | 206-256-2060 | www.restaurantzoe.com

"Through-the-roof" New American fare from chef-owner Scott Staples feels the "love" from "adventurous eaters" at this pricey Belltowner offering local, "seasonal" fare such as wild boar Bolognese; the contemporary bistro setting is "hopping" with a "hip" crowd, but the staff stays "attentive and flexible", so add in "specialty cocktails" and it's a "must-do."

Rover's ◪ *French*

28 | 25 | 27 | $94

Madison Valley | 2808 E. Madison St. (28th Ave.) | 206-325-7442 | www.thechefinthehat.com

"Charming" and "talented chef-owner" Thierry Rautureau "reinterprets" French cuisine in "gorgeous", "imaginative" dishes fashioned from the "finest Pacific Northwest ingredients" at his genteel Madison Valley farmhouse enhanced by "flowers, linens" and a "phenomenal staff" that exhibits the "right combination of proper and friendly"; while it's not cheap, degustation menus start at $59 and Friday lunches are a local favorite.

Salumi ◪◪ *Italian/Sandwiches*

27 | 11 | 18 | $16

Pioneer Square | 309 Third Ave. S. (bet. Jackson & Main Sts.) | 206-621-8772 | www.salumicuredmeats.com

Hot porchetta sandwiches and Italian salami from Gina Batali (Mario's sister) induce "OMGs" from surveyors who bow to this affordable Pioneer Square "cured piggy product" shrine started by papa Armandino; though lines aren't quite as long as they once were at Seattle's "worst-kept secret", there's still a "wait" – but plan ahead and you can book a lunch party in the private back room.

Serious Pie *Pizza*

26 | 18 | 21 | $26

Downtown | 316 Virginia St. (bet. 3rd & 4th Aves.) | 206-838-7388 | www.tomdouglas.com

"Seriously good pizza" for "not-too-serious people" makes this relatively "spendy" Downtowner "not your typical" pie joint, turning out "addictive" "thin wood-fired crusts" with "sophisticated toppings" like "truffled cheese and chanterelles"; true, "you're crammed in like anchovies", but the "communal tables spark conversation" and the "staff is courteous" – all in all, "deservedly a crowd-pleaser."

Shiro's Sushi *Japanese*

27 | 15 | 23 | $48

Belltown | 2401 Second Ave. (Battery St.) | 206-443-9844 | www.shiros.com

"Master" Shiro Kashiba's Pacific Northwest–inspired Japanese Belltowner is "pitch-perfect" and poised to "expand your sushi comfort-zone" declare devotees who call the omakase at the 11-seat sushi bar a "life-altering experience"; a "knowledgeable staff" helps explain "traditional delicacies", and though it's "pricey", there's "no attempt whatsoever to be cool or trendy" – but "if you're lucky", you'll spot a celebrity.

	FOOD	DECOR	SERVICE	COST

Sitka & Spruce ⓩ *Eclectic* | 26 | 19 | 22 | $46

Capitol Hill | 1531 Melrose Ave. E. (bet. Pike & Pine Sts.) | 206-324-0662 |
www.sitkaandspruce.com

Relocated to Capitol Hill's Melrose Building, this locally focused Eclectic-Mediterranean from chef-owner Matthew Dillon (the Corson Building) continues to turn out a "thoughtful", seasonal menu that's "creative without being strange" and "reasonably priced for the quality"; service is "efficient" in "relaxed" quarters filled with warehouselike "character", and Bar Ferd'nand is right next door; P.S. weekday lunch and weekend brunch are also served.

Spinasse *Italian* | 28 | 22 | 23 | $48

Capitol Hill | 1531 14th Ave. (bet. Pike & Pine Sts.) | 206-251-7673 |
www.spinasse.com

"Fabulous" Piedmont cuisine and "light-as-a-feather" handmade pasta are the "real deal", channeling "little joints in Italy" for patrons of this Capitol Hill Italian "gem"; toque Jason Stratton keeps the rustic quarters "buzzing with energy", including the seats at the chef's counter offering a "wonderful kitchen view" and their own 10-course menu Friday–Saturday, and it's all deemed "well worth the cost."

Spring Hill *Pacific NW* | 25 | 20 | 22 | $49

West Seattle | 4437 California Ave. SW (Genessee St.) | 206-935-1075 |
www.springhillnorthwest.com

Surveyors "expect good things" from Mark Fuller's "clever menu" featuring "fabulous" seasonal food and the "holy grail of hamburgers" at this "high-style" West Seattle Pacific Northwester; the "pro" staff is "friendly", and though tabs might be "a bit expensive", the "cool" industrial-chic room is "always crowded."

Staple & Fancy Mercantile *Italian* | - | - | - | M

Ballard | 4739 Ballard Ave. (bet. NW Ballard Way & Dock Pl.) |
206-789-1200 | www.ethanstowellrestaurants.com

Busy chef Ethan Stowell's latest is this Ballard Italian offering midpriced à la carte dishes or an adventurous $45 four-course menu; the historic brick space in the Kolstrand Building was once a grocery store (hence the name), and some of the original wood and metal has been recycled into the decor.

Tilth *American* | 28 | 21 | 25 | $53

Wallingford | 1411 N. 45th St. (International Ave.) | 206-633-0801 |
www.tilthrestaurant.com

Eco-savvy chef Maria Hines dishes out "wonderful, inventive" locavore fare in "surprising preparations" tailored to both "vegans and carnivores" at her organic-certified Wallingford New American; a "welcoming", "knowledgeable" staff and a "cheerfully informal" Craftsman bungalow are more reasons fans "would eat here every day if we could afford it", plus weekend brunch is a "delight."

Tosoni's ⓩⓜ *Continental* | 26 | 18 | 24 | $55

Bellevue | 14320 NE 20th St. (bet. 140th & 148th Aves.) |
425-644-1668

Bellevue's "best-kept secret" "never disappoints" with its "fantastic", pricey Continental cuisine and "excellent wine list" served in a "homey", "intimate" setting that's surprisingly "hidden in a strip mall"; chef

	FOOD	DECOR	SERVICE	COST

Walter Walcher "wears a tall toque" and when not preparing the likes of veal tenderloin with chanterelle sauce "will usually come out to greet you", enhancing "special nights out and celebrations."

Wild Ginger *Pacific Rim* | 25 | 23 | 22 | $42 |

Downtown | Mann Building | 1401 Third Ave. (Union St.) | 206-623-4450
Bellevue | The Bravern | 11020 NE Sixth St. (110th Ave.) | 425-495-8889
www.wildginger.net

Once again Seattle's Most Popular, this "classy" Downtown and Bellevue duo proffers "pricey" "one-of-a-kind" Pacific Rim fare including "imaginative" dishes with housemade sauces and a specialty of "fragrant roasted duck on cloudlike buns"; weekend dim sum brunches add to the attraction, and though the bustling, "sleek" dining rooms hold hundreds of diners, "reservations are a must."

St. Louis

TOP FOOD RANKING

	Restaurant	Cuisine
28	Niche	American
27	Stellina	American/Italian
	Sidney St. Cafe	American
	Trattoria Marcella	Italian
	Tony's	Italian
	Paul Manno's	Italian
26	Dominic's	Italian
	Pappy's	BBQ
	Annie Gunn's	American
	Atlas	French/Italian

OTHER NOTEWORTHY PLACES

Brasserie by Niche	French
Cardwell's	American
Crossing	American
1111 Mississippi	Californian/Italian
Farmhaus	American
Gian-Tony's	Italian
Harvest	American
Oceano	Seafood
O'Connell's	Pub Food
Pomme	American/French

Annie Gunn's Ⓜ *American*   26 | 21 | 24 | $51

Chesterfield | 16806 Chesterfield Airport Rd. (Baxter Rd.) | 636-532-7684 | www.anniegunns.com

"Never misfiring", this "loud", "crowded" and "dark" far West County "slice of heaven" matches "excellent" chef Lou Rook's "creative side dishes" with his "delectable", "just-a-little-left-of-familiar" American mains ("fabulous meats" are the specialty, as the restaurant was "birthed from the adjacent Smoke House Market"); just know that it's not cheap, you "definitely need reservations on weekends" and if you're "leery of smoke" (from the "lively bar"), you should ask for the year-round enclosed sun room.

Atlas Restaurant ⓈⓂ *French/Italian*   26 | 20 | 26 | $39

Forest Park | 5513 Pershing Ave. (bet. De Baliviere Ave. & Union Blvd.) | 314-367-6800 | www.atlasrestaurantstl.com

Aim your compass north of Forest Park for this "quaint", "charming bistro" where the "tantalizing" dishes – a combination of traditional French and Italian cuisines – are "consistently superb" and filled with "seasonal treats" (don't "shrug off" dessert – the "butterscotch pudding is a masterpiece"); "friendly owners who act as chef and maitre d'" "see that everything runs smoothly" as they provide the "loyal clientele" with "excellent value"; P.S. ratings don't reflect a post-Survey change of ownership and chef.

	FOOD	DECOR	SERVICE	COST

Brasserie by Niche ⓜ *French*
| | - | - | - | M |

Central West End | 4580 Laclede Ave. (Euclid Ave.) | 314-454-0600 | www.brasseriebyniche.com

Gerard Craft, of the Benton Park area's highly rated Niche, brings his own riff on a traditional French brasserie to the food-conscious Central West End; pressed-tin ceilings, red-checkered tablecloths and classic illustrated posters create a bright, cheerful atmosphere that's boosted by modest prices, which extend to the well-rounded wine list.

Cardwell's at the Plaza *American*
| | 24 | 22 | 22 | $40 |

Frontenac | 94 Plaza Frontenac (Clayton Rd. & Lindbergh Blvd.) | 314-997-8885 | www.cardwellsattheplaza.com

"Dress up" and "meet your wealthy friends" for a "ladies' lunch" - or court clients over an "upscale" "business" dinner - at this "sleek, stylish" Plaza Frontenac New American, so "much more than a mall restaurant" thanks to "inventive chef Bill Cardwell's" "fantastic", "always-evolving", "something-for-everyone menu"; if you're "hungry for love", hit the "large", "noisy" bar, which is usually "crowded with hip singles."

Crossing, The ⓢ *American*
| | 26 | 20 | 24 | $49 |

Clayton | 7823 Forsyth Blvd. (Central Ave.) | 314-721-7375 | www.fialafood.com

"Flexible and appealing multicourse tasting menus" - available with "expertly matched" pours from an "intelligent wine list" - make "ambitious" chef-owner Jim Fiala's "intimate" Clayton New American (with "inventive" seasonal French and Italian influences) "more affordable"; the "fine-dining" experience is abetted by "attentive service", but belied by digs with "no pizzazz."

Dominic's ⓢ *Italian*
| | 26 | 23 | 27 | $53 |

The Hill | 5101 Wilson Ave. (Hereford St.) | 314-771-1632
Dominic's Trattoria ⓢ *Italian*
Clayton | 200 S. Brentwood Blvd. (Bonhomme Blvd.) | 314-863-4567
www.dominicsrestaurant.com

"Exquisite service" is the hallmark of this "fine Italian eatery on The Hill", where tuxedo-clad staffers ferry "fantastic", "pricey" fare amid "lovely", "formal" surroundings; a modernist minority deems the whole experience "dated", but most folks appreciate it as a "tradition" for "special occasions" or just dinner with friends - and "leave wanting more"; P.S. the Clayton branch was not surveyed.

1111 Mississippi ⓢ *Californian/Italian*
| | 24 | 24 | 23 | $38 |

Lafayette Square | 1111 Mississippi Ave. (Chouteau Ave.) | 314-241-9999 | www.1111-m.com

"Challenge your palate" at this "gastronomic adventure" in Lafayette Square, where "flavor combinations you would never imagine come together flawlessly" on a "reasonably priced" Italian menu boasting "fresh local ingredients" and "Californian influences"; the multi-tiered setting in a "restored brick" warehouse manages to be "chic but not stuffy" (ditto the "charming", "capable" staff), and while it's often "crowded" and "noisy", the patio is always "delightful."

| | FOOD | DECOR | SERVICE | COST |

Farmhaus 🖪 *American*

- | - | - | M

South City | 3257 Ivanhoe Ave. (Bradley Ave.) | 314-647-3800 |
www.farmhausrestaurant.com

Notable chef Kevin Willmann takes his local, sustainable and organic
act from Erato in Edwardsville, IL, to South St. Louis at this first solo
venture where he presents fresh twists on frequently changing American
classics; prices are for the most part affordable, which befits the
small, informal, often lively setting.

Gian-Tony's *Italian*

25 | 18 | 24 | $34

The Hill | 5356 Daggett Ave. (Macklind Ave.) | 314-772-4893 |
www.gian-tonys.com

"A cheaper alternative on The Hill that is in no way inferior to its
more posh competitors", this bit of "Palermo in St. Louis" is "dependable" for "everyday Italian", especially "divine pasta dishes";
sufficiently "quaint" for a "romantic dinner", it's also "homey"
enough to be "family-friendly", with "polished service" helping to
make all feel welcome.

Harvest 🅼 *American*

26 | 21 | 25 | $43

Richmond Heights | 1059 S. Big Bend Blvd. (Clayton Rd.) | 314-645-3522 |
www.harveststlouis.com

"As its name implies", this Richmond Heights New American utilizes
"creative ingredients" from "local purveyors" in its "exceptional", "always evolving" cuisine (there's also a "delicious" spa menu); "gracious service", "great midweek deals" (it can be "a bit pricey" at other
times) and "amazing bread pudding" yield bushels of praise, but the
"update"-ready "1993 Santa Fe" decor reaps little acclaim.

Niche 🅼 *American*

28 | 24 | 26 | $49

Benton Park | 1831 Sidney St. (I-55) | 314-773-7755 |
www.nichestlouis.com

At this "trailblazer" in "historic Benton Park", "gifted" chef Gerard
Craft's "adventurous", "exquisite" New American cuisine - voted No. 1
in St. Louis - "tantalizes" with "inspired combinations" of "local ingredients"; you'll "feel sophisticated" just stepping into the "cosmopolitan",
"minimalist" digs, but don't come without a reservation, because
"space is at a premium" (the fee, conversely, "isn't all that expensive");
P.S. ask a "savvy" server to recommend a "triumphant" dessert.

Oceano Bistro *Seafood*

24 | 22 | 22 | $42

Clayton | 44 N. Brentwood Blvd. (Maryland Ave.) | 314-721-9400 |
www.oceanobistro.com

"Unique preparations" of what may be "the freshest seafood in St.
Louis" lure afishionados to this Clayton "find" exhibiting "value" in
"lots of price ranges"; the "lovely", "modern space" is just "one big
open room" with arched ceilings, making it often "too noisy" - but that
"befits" such a "happening place" (ask for the enclosed porch for a
"more intimate" meal).

O'Connell's Pub ● *Pub Food*

23 | 17 | 18 | $18

South City | 4652 Shaw Ave. (Kingshighway Blvd.) | 314-773-6600

"Generally recognized" as still serving "the best burger in town", this
"classic" South City "wood-paneled Irish pub" is also "wildly popular"
for its "fabulous roast-beef sandwiches", "fantastic Reubens" and

other "hearty", "super-cheap" grub; sure, the staff can be "grumpy" and you "come out smelling like you rolled around in an ashtray", but for its legions of fans, many of whom have been coming "since childhood", it's "like going home."

Pappy's Smokehouse *BBQ*

26 | 16 | 21 | $17

Midtown | 3106 Olive St. (Cardinal Ave.) | 314-535-4340 |
www.pappyssmokehouse.com

"Unbelievably succulent" BBQ, sides that are "not an afterthought" and "reasonable prices" draw pit fans to this Memphis-style Midtowner (never mind the "sparse decor"); on "most days", the line "winds throughout the entire restaurant", but "quick", "friendly" staffers "keep things moving" – just "be sure to arrive early", 'cause "when the smoker empties", the place closes.

Paul Manno's ⓩ *Italian*

27 | 18 | 25 | $45

Chesterfield | 75 Forum Shopping Ctr. (Woods Mill Rd.) |
314-878-1274

It's "tucked away in an unassuming strip mall", but "man oh man", the Italian "food far outshines" the location at this "spectacular little place" with "Rat Pack–era" decor in Chesterfield; even though it's "always crowded", "noisy" and the "tables are close together", "excellent host" Paul and his "incredible" staff make everyone feel at ease.

Pomme *American/French*

26 | 23 | 25 | $45

Clayton | 40 N. Central Ave. (bet. Forsyth Blvd. & Maryland Ave.) |
314-727-4141 | www.pommerestaurant.com

"For a romantic dinner" in Clayton, lovebirds glide into this "intimate", "quiet, sophisticated bistro" with "dark lighting, brick walls and dramatic artwork", where chef-owner Bryan Carr whips up "ever-changing" New French–New American plates that "taste like they were sent from heaven"; the portions may be a "bit skimpy for the price", but "fair" fees can be found on the "great" *carte du vin*; P.S. "for a more casual night", "try the Pomme Cafe and Wine Bar" two doors down.

Sidney Street Cafe ⓩ Ⓜ *American*

27 | 24 | 26 | $49

Benton Park | 2000 Sidney St. (Salena St.) | 314-771-5777 |
www.sidneystreetcafe.com

The "cozy", brick-lined setting is just as "perfect for romance" or a "special occasion" as it is for "casual" dining at this New American "jewel" in Benton Park, voted St. Louis' Most Popular restaurant; "talented" chef Kevin Nashan's "knock-your-socks-off" fare (a bit "expensive" but prices are "fair" for the quality) is "written on tabletop chalkboards" and "described with wit and accuracy by the able staff" – just "make reservations well in advance" to experience it.

Stellina Pasta Cafe ⓩ Ⓜ *American/Italian*

27 | 18 | 21 | $23

South City | 3342 Watson Rd. (bet. Arthur & Hancock Aves.) |
314-256-1600 | www.stellinapasta.com

There's "always something new" to try at this South City American-Italian, which gets high marks thanks to "fabulous homemade pastas" featuring "seasonal, local ingredients", plus "marvelous sandwiches, salads" and "decadent desserts", all at "fair prices"; surveyors also say the "service is impressive"; P.S. a post-Survey expansion nearly doubled the seating and added a bar, outdating the Decor score.

	FOOD	DECOR	SERVICE	COST

Tony's ⑤ *Italian* | 27 | 25 | 28 | $69

Downtown | 410 Market St. (B'way) | 314-231-7007 | www.tonysstlouis.com

There's "none other like this" "venerable" Downtown "gem" that manages to "hit new highs, year after glorious year", with "service as if for nobility" and "outstanding" "gourmet Italian cuisine"; some say the "fancy" setting's frozen in "1985", yet it remains a "go-to for special occasions"; P.S. don't forget to "bring your trust fund."

Trattoria Marcella ⑤ Ⓜ *Italian* | 27 | 20 | 24 | $38

South City | 3600 Watson Rd. (Pernod Ave.) | 314-352-7706 | www.trattoriamarcella.com

"Trot to the Trat as fast as you can" for "to-die-for lobster risotto" (a daily "off-menu special") and other "spectacular" Italian fare – but "make a reservation" first, because the "comfortable", "casual" South City setting is "packed every night" with a "loyal following"; the "knowledgeable staff" garners its share of praise, but prices that are an "absolute steal" "for the quality" get the heartiest applause.

Tampa/Sarasota

TOP FOOD RANKING

	Restaurant	Cuisine
28	Cafe Ponte	American
	Beach Bistro	Floridian
27	Mise en Place	American
26	Bern's	Steak
	Pane Rustica	Eclectic
	Euphemia Haye	Eclectic
	Vernona	Mediterranean
	Roy's	Hawaiian
25	Capital Grille	Steak
	Donatello	Italian

OTHER NOTEWORTHY PLACES

Armani's	Italian
Bonefish Grill	Seafood
Columbia	Cuban/Spanish
Libby's	Floridian
Mozaic	American/Mediterranean
Ocean Prime	Seafood/Steak
Owen's Fish Camp	Seafood
Pelagia	Mediterranean
Salt Rock	Seafood/Steak
SideBern's	Mediterranean

Armani's ☒Ⓜ *Italian* — 25 | 26 | 26 | $67

Tampa | Grand Hyatt Tampa Bay | 2900 Bayport Dr., 14th fl. (Hwy. 60) | 813-207-6800 | www.grandtampabay.hyatt.com

Watch the "sun set over Tampa Bay" at this "high-in-the-sky" Northern Italian on the 14th floor of the Grand Hyatt that's a "heavenly" "spot to celebrate" "special occasions"; it's equally "high on service, romantic atmosphere and price"; P.S. a contempo remodel of the space and the advent of a new chef (who streamlined the menu) post-Survey outdates the Decor and Food scores.

Beach Bistro *Floridian* — 28 | 24 | 27 | $73

Holmes Beach | 6600 Gulf Dr. (66th St.) | 941-778-6444 | www.beachbistro.com

"Imaginative, gourmet" Floridian cuisine backed by a "stunning view" lures loyalists to owner Sean Murphy's "expensive", "casual-chic" tour de force that's "somewhat out of the way" on Anna Maria Island; while "noisy" and "tight", it nonetheless has a "romantic ambiance" thanks to a "spectacular" "beach setting."

Bern's Steak House *Steak* — 26 | 20 | 27 | $66

Tampa | 1208 S. Howard Ave. (bet. W. Marjory & W. Watrous Aves.) | 813-251-2421 | www.bernssteakhouse.com

Carnivores insist the steakhouse "chains just can't compete" with this nearly 55-year-old Tampa "icon" (voted Most Popular in the Tampa/

Sarasota area) where "everything is fabulous" – right down to the "old school" "charm" and the "veggies they grow themselves"; "if you can get past the bordello appearance" and the big check, fans extol the "flawless" service, "encyclopedic" vino list, "outstanding kitchen and wine-cellar tour" and "fabled" upstairs dessert room, dubbing it an overall "incredible experience"; P.S. jackets are encouraged.

Bonefish Grill *Seafood*
21 | 19 | 20 | $37

Bradenton | 7456 W. Cortez Rd. (75th St.) | 941-795-8020
Sarasota | 3971 S. Tamiami Trail (Bee Ridge Rd.) | 941-924-9090
Sarasota | 8101 Cooper Creek Blvd. (University Pkwy.) | 941-360-3171
Bellaire Bluffs | 2939 West Bay Dr. (Indian Rocks Rd.) | 727-518-1230
Clearwater | Kash 'N Karry Plaza | 2519 McMullen Booth Rd. (Enterprise St.) | 727-726-1315
St. Petersburg | Harmon Meadow Plaza | 2408 Tyrone Blvd. (66th St.) | 727-344-8600
St. Petersburg | 5062 Fourth St. N. (bet. 38th & 64nd Aves.) | 727-521-3434
Brandon | 1015 Providence Rd. (Lumdsen St.) | 813-571-5553
Tampa | 13262 N. Dale Mabry Hwy. (Fletcher Ave.) | 813-969-1619
Tampa | 3665 Henderson Blvd. (Sterling St.) | 813-876-3535
www.bonefishgrill.com
Additional locations throughout the Tampa/Sarasota area

"Consistent, kid-friendly and delicious", this seafood franchise has an "independent-restaurant feel", which may explain why "there's always a wait" ("the lively bar is a plus on crowded weekends"); "über-friendly" staffers deliver the "tasty" fin fare paired with "innovative" sauce choices, but note that the rooms "can get noisy", perhaps from the sounds of "Bang Bang Shrimp appetizers that will shoot you into orbit."

Cafe Ponte ⊠ *American*
28 | 23 | 25 | $48

Clearwater | Icot Ctr. | 13505 Icot Blvd. (Ulmerton Rd.) | 727-538-5768
www.cafeponte.com

"Talented" executive chef–owner Christopher Ponte's "creative dishes" and thoughtful variations on the expected" help this New American "gem" located in a Clearwater strip mall to "rise above its peers" as No. 1 for Food in the Tampa/Sarasota area; plus, "sparse but refined" decor and "friendly, knowledgeable service" help make it equally "perfect for that quiet romantic dinner or important business lunch"; P.S. there's a live pianist every other weekend, except in summer.

Capital Grille *Steak*
25 | 24 | 25 | $62

Tampa | International Plaza | 2223 N. West Shore Blvd. (Spruce St.) | 813-830-9433 | www.thecapitalgrille.com

With a "clubby" "big-city atmosphere", this "classic" Tampa link in a national chophouse chain is perfect "for closing a deal" thanks to "consistently excellent steaks and sides" plus "the most sophisticated burger anywhere" and "a wine list with plenty of appealing choices"; although "a bit pricey", it boasts "smooth service" and there's also "outdoor seating with people-watching" and a "fun bar" area with a "kazillion TV screens."

Columbia *Cuban/Spanish*
21 | 21 | 20 | $37

Sarasota | 411 St. Armands Circle (Blvd. of Presidents) | 941-388-3987
Clearwater | 1241 Gulf Blvd. (½ mi. south of Sand Key Bridge) | 727-596-8400

(continued)

Columbia

St. Petersburg | St. Petersburg Pier | 800 Second Ave. NE (Beach Dr.) |
727-822-8000
Ybor City | 2117 E. Seventh Ave. (bet. 21st & 22nd Sts.) | 813-248-4961

Columbia Café *Cuban/Spanish*

Tampa | Tampa Bay History Center | 801 Old Water St. (Channelside Dr.) |
813-229-5511
www.columbiarestaurant.com

"Awash in history", this midpriced Florida chain's more-than-a-century-
old original in Ybor City is known for its Cuban-Spanish cuisine (including a "1905 salad that never fails to delight"), "excellent sangria",
"Iberian decor" and "noisy", "vibrant" flamenco show; though some say
it's "a bit past its prime", they're outnumbered by fans who find the
dining experience at all of them "most memorable", especially at the
Sarasota branch, where you can "watch the world from a sidewalk table" on St. Armands Circle; P.S. the Tampa cafe serves a limited menu.

Donatello *Italian*   25 | 20 | 26 | $67

Tampa | 232 N. Dale Mabry Hwy. (1 block north of JFK Blvd.) |
813-875-6660 | www.donatellorestaurant.com

Proprietors "Guido and Gino Tiozzo set the standard for tip-top service" at this "old-school" "institution" in Tampa that "dazzles" diners
with "sensational" Northern Italian cuisine, "much of it prepared tableside" by a "superb" staff; while a few suggest it's "past its prime",
most insist the "low lighting", "romantic" ambiance and "fresh roses
on every table" make for an experience that's "ideal for a special occasion" – so "rob a bank and then indulge."

Euphemia Haye *Eclectic*   26 | 23 | 24 | $62

Longboat Key | 5540 Gulf of Mexico Dr. (Gulfbay Rd.) | 941-383-3633 |
www.euphemiahaye.com

It's "worth it" to visit this 30-year-old "Longboat Key tradition" where
an "attentive" staff serves Eclectic cuisine – including signature roast
duckling with seasonal sauces – in a "beachy spot" that's "one of the
prettiest settings on the Gulf"; full of "Old Florida" "charm" and "romantic" ambiance, it's especially suited "for a special night"; P.S. "after
dinner, go upstairs" for jazz and "dessert heaven."

Libby's *Floridian*   - | - | - | M

Sarasota | 1917 S. Osprey Ave. (Hillview St.) | 941-487-7300 |
www.libbyscafebar.com

In Sarasota's charming Southside Village, this bustling, elegant-casual,
indoor-outdoor venue focuses on moderately priced burgers and sandwiches at lunchtime, and a vast array of shareable, seasonal Floridian
plates, sophisticated grilled fish and steak and whimsical desserts during dinner; the large wine list displays an array of price points, and early-
bird, happy-hour and late-night menus are offered in two bar areas.

Mise en Place 🍴Ⓜ *American*   27 | 23 | 24 | $54

Tampa | 442 W. Kennedy Blvd. (Hyde Park Ave.) | 813-254-5373 |
www.miseonline.com

Located "across from the University of Tampa", this casually "elegant"
"stalwart" "keeps its clientele coming back for more" of chef/co-
owner Marty Blitz's "creative" New American food that "remains cur-

rent and fresh" via "seasonal" à la carte and "chef's tasting menus"; a sophisticated cheese selection and a "witty staff" with "wine smarts" are two more reasons it's "still going strong."

Mozaic *American/Mediterranean*
`-` `-` `-` `M`

Sarasota | 1377 Main St. (bet. Palm & Pineapple Aves.) | 941-951-6272 | www.mozaicsarasota.com

Moroccan chef Dylan Elhajoui creates a colorful mosaic of moderate-to-pricey Mediterranean-inflected New American fare that's plated with an eye for luxury at this Sarasota date-night destination, which also offers short- or regular-sized pours from an eclectic wine list; though spread out over two floors, the space feels intimate, and while the decor scheme is spare, there's ocular stimulation to be found in artwork specially created for the restaurant by a local artist.

Ocean Prime *Seafood/Steak*
`-` `-` `-` `E`

Westshore Business District | International Plaza | 2205 N. West Shore Blvd. (Spruce St.) | Tampa | 813-490-5288 | www.ocean-prime.com

This expensive mini-chain link at International Plaza in the Westshore Business District looks like the dining room of a stately cruise ship (gleaming wood panels, giant lanterns) where white-jacketed servers ferry plates of simply prepared à la carte prime meats and seafood, plus a raft of sides; at the clubby bar, the creative martinis are cooled with dry ice while live piano or guitar music floats in the background.

Owen's Fish Camp *Seafood*
`-` `-` `-` `M`

Sarasota | 516 Burns Ct. (Selby Ln.) | 941-951-6936 | www.owensfishcamp.com

In a charming cottage beneath a gargantuan banyan tree, this Sarasota newcomer re-creates an Old Florida–style fish camp from the 1920s; the moderately priced likes of fried fish baskets, oyster shooters, peel 'n' eat shrimp, smoked mullet spread and boiled peanuts are served in a setting festooned with period fishing gear and historic photos of anglers with their catch; P.S. the Burns Court Cinema is nearby, making it a natural for a pre-flick dinner.

Pane Rustica Ⓜ *Eclectic*
`26` `17` `19` `$29`

Tampa | 3225 S. MacDill Ave. (Bay to Bay Blvd.) | 813-902-8828 | www.panerusticabakery.com

Known for its "artisan breads, wood-fired pizzas" and "magnificent cookies", this "order-at-the-counter lunch" spot in "so-chic South Tampa" turns into "a romantic bistro at night" (Wednesday–Saturday), serving "delicious" Eclectic fare; it's "one of the best values" around, so expect it to be "crowded" with a staff that can seem "harried"; P.S. some communal seating "means you may share a table with strangers."

Pelagia Trattoria *Mediterranean*
`22` `22` `21` `$51`

Tampa | Renaissance Tampa Hotel Intl. Plaza | 4200 Jim Walter Blvd. (Bay St.) | 813-313-3235 | www.pelagiatrattoria.com

Still somewhat "undiscovered", this swank trattoria in the Renaissance Tampa Hotel features punchy jewel tones in a Milan-hip interior that's an "attractive" backdrop for an "inventive" yet "not overly ambitious" Med menu with "an emphasis on olives and fish"; factor in service that's "accommodating" and surveyors say the "overall experience leaves you feeling a little spoiled."

Roy's *Hawaiian*

26 | 23 | 24 | $53

Sarasota | 2001 Siesta Dr., Ste. 100 (S. Tamiami Trail) | 941-952-0109
Tampa | 4342 W. Boy Scout Blvd. (bet. N. Lois & N. Manhattan Aves.) |
813-873-7697
www.roysrestaurant.com

Celebrity chef Roy Yamaguchi's national chain (with links in Sarasota
and Tampa) remains "a favorite for special occasions" courtesy of a
"lively, loud" ambiance, "service with an aloha spirit" and "signature
Hawaiian fusion cuisine" that includes macadamia-crusted fish and
"out-of-this-world" chocolate lava soufflé; while the à la carte menu is
"pricey", regulars attest "the prix fixe dinner is a real bargain."

Salt Rock Grill *Seafood/Steak*

25 | 23 | 21 | $50

Indian Shores | 19325 Gulf Blvd. (Park Blvd.) | 727-593-7625 |
www.saltrockgrill.com

Indian Shores' most seasoned critics say "Salt rocks" thanks to "outstanding" seafood and "well-prepared" steaks backed by "gorgeous
views" of both the Intracoastal Waterway and the "see-and-be-seen"
clientele; it's an "escapist" spot that's "always jumping" (read:
"noisy") inside and on the "beautiful deck", but critics cite "hit-or-
miss" service, "pricey" tabs and "long waits", especially for the ultrapopular $20.10 three-course early-bird special.

SideBern's ⊠ *Mediterranean*

25 | 23 | 22 | $59

Tampa | 2208 W. Morrison Ave. (S. Howard Ave.) | 813-258-2233 |
www.sideberns.com

At "Bern's unique sister restaurant" in Tampa, chef Chad Johnson
whips up "creative" fare that patrons profess is "expensive but worth
it"; the "upscale crowd" overlooks occasionally "sluggish service", focusing instead on the "to-die-for" martinis and "lovely bar area"
boasting a "big singles scene"; P.S. post-Survey, the Med-influenced
New American menu was jiggered into full-on Modern Mediterranean
(charcuterie and other house-cured meats being highlights), and the
space was remodeled to reflect it, outdating the Food and Decor scores.

Vernona *Mediterranean*

26 | 28 | 28 | $79

Sarasota | Ritz-Carlton Sarasota | 1111 Ritz-Carlton Dr. (Tamiami Trail) |
941-309-2008 | www.ritzcarlton.com

Surveyors "hope heaven" resembles this "top-of-the-list"
Mediterranean in the Ritz-Carlton Sarasota, especially its "classy"
villa setting and "fabulous service"; the organic "menu changes de-
pending" on what the chef "can get locally", and while the "phenomenal experience" may be "expensive", it's far "too good to save only for
a special occasion"; P.S. the "Sunday brunch is incredible."

Tucson

TOP FOOD RANKING

	Restaurant	Cuisine
27	Vivace	Italian
	Cafe Poca Cosa	Mexican
	Janos	Southwestern
26	Le Rendez-Vous	French
	Feast	Eclectic
	Grill at Hacienda del Sol	American
25	Acacia	American
	Dish	American
	Tavolino	Italian
24	Mi Nidito	Mexican

OTHER NOTEWORTHY PLACES

Restaurant	Cuisine
Arizona Inn	Continental
Bluefin	Seafood
Casa Vicente	Spanish
El Charro	Mexican
Flying V	Southwestern
Jax	American/European
J BAR	Nuevo Latino
Maynards	American
Pastiche	American
Primo	Mediterranean

Acacia *American* 25 | 23 | 22 | $49

Midtown | St. Philip's Plaza | 4340 N. Campbell Ave. (E. River Rd.) | 520-232-0101 | www.acaciatucson.com

At this "pricey" Midtown New American, chef-owner "Albert Hall knows how to please" his customers with "outstanding food quality", plus "creative" presentations and "terrific wines"; just as "superb" is an atmosphere that manages to achieve "the perfect balance of elegance and comfort" with "sleekly modern decor" and a "peaceful" patio ideal for "hiding from your boss at lunchtime amid the trees" or watching "the twinkling stars and lights" in the evening; P.S. the attached Marketplace, offering retail specialties and casual breakfasts and lunches for takeaway, opened post-Survey.

Arizona Inn *Continental* 21 | 26 | 25 | $47

Midtown | Arizona Inn | 2200 E. Elm St. (bet. N. Campbell Ave. & N. Tucson Blvd.) | 520-325-1541 | www.arizonainn.com

Exuding "tasteful" "elegance", this Continental in a "world-class" "luxury" inn (which was "once frequented by the likes of Eleanor Roosevelt") located in a "beautiful and historic" section of Midtown is "where to go for all those classic European dishes", which are matched with an "extensive" wine list, "nice live piano music" in the bar and "impeccable" service (there are "even finger bowls!"); it's "pricey", but that's to be expected for a place so filled with "old money."

	FOOD	DECOR	SERVICE	COST

Bluefin *Seafood*
23 | 21 | 21 | $39

Northwest | Casas Adobes Plaza | 7053 N. Oracle Rd.
(bet. W. Giaconda Way & W. Ina Rd.) | 520-531-8500 |
www.bluefintucson.com

For "fresh seafood in the middle of the desert", head to Northwest's "charming" Casas Adobes Plaza where this fish house offers an "interesting menu" featuring everything from "great oysters on the half shell" to "nicely grilled" fillets at "fair" (if "a little high") prices; the "cozy" "red-brick-and-wood" dining rooms, "friendly, attentive service" and "lovely", "not-overpowering" live jazz in the "great indoor/outdoor bar" all conspire to create "perfect romantic dinners."

Cafe Poca Cosa 🅢🅜 *Mexican*
27 | 21 | 23 | $34

Downtown | 110 E. Pennington St. (Scott Ave.) | 520-622-6400 |
www.cafepocacosatucson.com

Boasting a "well-deserved reputation", this Downtown Mexican stars Suzana Davila's "gourmet", "heavenly" cuisine and its "emphasis on freshness" and "innovation" (the "menu changes daily", but the "best bet is always the sampler plate, which includes three items of the chef's choosing"); the "swanky, spacious" new-ish digs feel like "a hip NYC restaurant", and if "many old-school Tucsonans complain" it "lacks the same charm as the old one", still, they "would follow it anywhere."

Casa Vicente 🅢🅜 *Spanish*
21 | 15 | 18 | $28

Downtown | 375 S. Stone Ave. (14th St.) | 520-884-5253 |
www.casavicente.com

"Every city should have a Spanish hideaway", and this Downtowner with a "seemingly endless" menu of "intriguing tapas" and "out-of-this-world paella" ("worth calling ahead to order") is "the real deal" as well as a "value"; "not-to-be-missed" entertainment like live guitar, tango and flamenco dancing and "great sangria" make it especially "fun with a big group."

Dish, The 🅢🅜 *American*
25 | 16 | 22 | $43

Midtown | 3131 E. First St. (N. Country Club Rd.) | 520-326-1714 |
www.dishbistro.com

At this somewhat "pricey" Midtown New American, "every dish is 'the dish'", as they're all "succulent" and proffered in "superb presentations" by "skilled servers"; set within a wine store (whether you find "an evening among bottles" "weird" or "creative", "an endless list is the result"), it's small, so make a reservation – but "come early" or possibly brave a "long wait."

El Charro Café *Mexican*
21 | 19 | 19 | $25

Downtown | 311 N. Court Ave. (W. Council St.) | 520-622-1922
Foothills | 6910 E. Sunrise Dr. (N. Kolb Rd.) | 520-514-1922
Midtown | El Mercado | 6310 E. Broadway Blvd. (N. Wilmot Rd.) |
520-573-8222
Northwest | 7725 N. Oracle Rd. (Orange Grove Rd.) |
520-229-1922
Sahuarita | 15920 S. Rancho Sahuarita Blvd. (Helmet Peak Rd.) |
520-325-1922
www.elcharrocafe.com

A "true Tucson classic", the "always packed" 1922 Downtown original of this "reasonably priced" local Mexican chainlet is a "must-stop" "landmark" for its "authentic atmosphere" – but all locations are "very popular" for "extremely tasty" "Sonoran-style" faves such as the "fantastic carne seca" ("get it in a chimichanga", which is "claimed to have been invented here"); though service can be "inconsistent", it's "well worth it" for the "fun" and "history."

Feast ☑ Eclectic   26 | 16 | 22 | $28
Midtown | 4122 E. Speedway Blvd. (bet. Alvernon Way & N. Columbus Blvd.) | 520-326-9363 | www.eatatfeast.com
Doug Levy, owner/"splendid host" of this "affordable", "no-reservations" Midtown Eclectic, may be "Tucson's most imaginative chef", and his "delicious", "well-prepared food" on "monthly changing menus" is matched by a "terrific" "value wine list", including many "unusual" varieties and half bottles; the "simply decorated" space "can get loud", but "personalized service" helps offset any "auditory discomfort."

Flying V Southwestern   21 | 24 | 22 | $43
Foothills | Loews Ventana Canyon Resort | 7000 N. Resort Dr. (N. Kolb Rd.) | 520-615-5495 | www.flyingvbarandgrill.com
"Gorgeous views" of the Santa Catalina mountains from the "fabulous patio" of this "casual" Foothills Southwestern make it a "romantic spot" "to sit outside on a warm night" while enjoying the "fragrance of mesquite wood" and "sunset views"; surveyors say the "creative menu" of "tasty" fare is also reason to come (the "tableside guacamole" will "fly you to the moon"), as are "great margaritas" and "warm service."

Grill at Hacienda del Sol American   26 | 27 | 25 | $56
Foothills | Hacienda del Sol | 5601 N. Hacienda del Sol (bet. E. Sunrise Dr. & River Rd.) | 520-529-3500 | www.haciendadelsol.com
"Wow out-of-towners" at Tucson's Most Popular restaurant, which proffers "superb", "expensive but worth-every-penny" New American fare "with Southwestern flair" in an "elegant", "historic" Foothills resort whose previous incarnations were a "1930s girls' school" and Hollywood A-list guest ranch ("Hepburn and Tracy linger around every gorgeous corner"); "a terrific wine list", "professional service", "marvelous views" and "romantic sunsets" add to the "unique, memorable destination-dining experience."

Janos ☒ Southwestern   27 | 25 | 26 | $68
Foothills | Westin La Paloma | 3770 E. Sunrise Dr. (bet. N. Campbell Ave. & N. Swan Rd.) | 520-615-6100 | www.janos.com
"Genius" chef-owner Janos Wilder "lights up" this Foothills Southwestern not only by demonstrating in his "outside-the-box" cuisine "just how much better fresh, seasonal ingredients can make a dish" (they're "pricey but worth it"), but by frequently "circulating among guests"; not to be outdone, his staff "bends over backwards" in the "elegant", "romantic" space.

Jax Kitchen ☑ American/European   - | - | - | M
Northwest | 7286 N. Oracle Rd. (Ina Rd.) | 520-219-1235 | www.jaxkitchen.com
Comfort food is raised to an art form at this Northwest European-New American, which combines simplicity with good taste at reasonable

prices; the intimate environs with muted peach-and-cream hues manage to be both romantic and lively, which helps attract intimacy-seeking couples and neighborhood foodies out for a casual meal accompanied by a lime rickey and other retro cocktails.

J BAR 🖾 *Nuevo Latino*　　23 | 21 | 22 | $35

Foothills | Westin La Paloma | 3770 E. Sunrise Dr. (bet. N. Campbell Ave. & N. Swan Rd.) | 520-615-6100 | www.janos.com

The "casual neighbor of gourmet Janos", this "hip" Foothills Nuevo Latino presents chef Janos Wilder's "creative" "excellence" on a "top-notch" menu whose tabs are "half the price" of its sibling; the interior boasts "a relaxing atmosphere", while on the "sumptuous terrace", "incomparable views" form the backdrop for "fun-filled evenings" abetted by "fantastic cocktails."

Le Rendez-Vous 🖾 *French*　　26 | 20 | 23 | $49

Midtown | 3844 Fort Lowell Rd. (Alvernon Way) | 520-323-7373 | www.lerendez-vous.com

Salivating surveyors "would walk a mile in 120-degree heat just for the pâté" at this "traditional" French bistro in Midtown, where everything on the menu is "wonderful" and "worth every penny" (save room for the "phenom desserts"); "wonderful lunches" are offered, but for a "picture-perfect romantic date", come post-sunset when "softer lighting obscures" the somewhat "dated decor."

Maynards Market & Kitchen *American*　　- | - | - | M

Downtown | Historic Train Depot | 400 N. Toole Ave. (Congress St.) | 520-545-0577 | www.maynardsmarkettucson.com

Young hipsters have made this retro-chic New American in Downtown's historic railroad depot such a hit, they often overflow from the intimate dining room onto the large patio; midrange prices for creative pastas, designer pizzas and other comfort foods are appreciated, and if nothing on the large vino list floats your boat, the relatively small corkage fee makes it easy to pop over to the affiliated wine store and find one that does.

Mi Nidito 🖾 *Mexican*　　24 | 15 | 19 | $20

South Tucson | 1813 S. Fourth Ave. (bet. 28th & 29th Sts.) | 520-622-5081 | www.minidito.net

"Real-deal", "outstanding" "Sonoran-style Mexican food" offered in "huge portions" and "without high price tags" has made this nearly 60-year-old spot an "institution" in South Tucson; "you don't go here for the decor" ("the silverware and plates don't match"), but you do come for the "famous", "fabulous" frozen margaritas, which help to pass the "long waits to be seated" – even President Clinton, who "loved it", "was forced to stand in line."

Pastiche Modern Eatery ●🖾 *American*　　22 | 19 | 20 | $34

Midtown | Campbell Vill. | 3025 N. Campbell Ave. (Blacklidge Dr.) | 520-325-3333 | www.pasticheme.com

"Fresh and delicious", internationally influenced, "affordable" American fare that "never disappoints" keeps diners "returning" to this Midtown venue; other reasons include "attentive but not intrusive service", an "outstanding wine list" and a "quiet", "dimly lit" room "in which one can converse at normal volume."

	FOOD	DECOR	SERVICE	COST

Primo ☒ Mediterranean

	24	26	25	$54

Westside | JW Marriott Starr Pass Resort & Spa | 3800 W. Starr Pass Blvd. (bet. Deer Bend Ct. & Players Club Dr.) | 520-791-6071 | www.primotucson.com

At this "romantic" and "sophisticated" Mediterranean in a Westside resort, ingredients are culled from an on-site garden to create chef Melissa Kelly's "thoughtfully edited menu" of "innovative", "healthful" dishes; the serving skills of the "friendly staff" are just as "spotless" as the "gorgeous grounds", which boast "superb" views of the city and the surrounding mountains – just "don't even look at the check when it comes" if you want that "relaxing" feeling to linger.

Tavolino ☒ Italian

	25	17	22	$38

Foothills | 2890 E. Skyline Dr. (Ina Rd.) | 520-531-1913 | www.tavolinoristorante.com

This "fairly priced" place "where the staff remembers you" is a "genuine" "piece of Italy in Tucson", with "succulent meats, poultry" and homemade pastas that "serenade your taste buds"; surveyors said that, because of its "popularity", it was "impossible to get in at the spur of the moment" – but that may no longer be true now that its completed its post-Survey move to much larger digs in the Foothills, outdating the Decor score.

Vivace ☒ Italian

	27	22	24	$42

Foothills | St. Philip's Plaza | 4310 N. Campbell Ave. (E. River Rd.) | 520-795-7221 | www.vivacetucson.com

Rated No. 1 for Food in Tucson, this Foothills trattoria provides "marvelous" Northern Italian fare "prepared thoughtfully with excellent ingredients", prompting fans to "rave like a lunatic" over its virtues; prices that are "reasonable" for the quality, both for the victuals and "worldly wine list", plus "accommodating service" help ensure that it's "packed even in low season", so "make reservations" early; P.S. the "warm Tuscan decor" inside is "relaxing", but for many, the "lovely" "patio beckons."

Washington, DC

TOP FOOD RANKING

	Restaurant	Cuisine
29	Marcel's	Belgian/French
	Inn at Little Washington	American
	Komi	American/Mediterranean
28	CityZen	American
	Rasika	Indian
	Makoto	Japanese
	Eve	American
	Citronelle	French
	Palena	American
27	L'Auberge Provençale	French
	Prime Rib	Steak
	Obelisk	Italian
	Tosca	Italian
	Corduroy	American
	L'Auberge Chez François	French
26	2941 Restaurant	American
	Blue Duck Tavern	American
	Honey Pig	Korean
	Café Atlántico/Minibar	Nuevo Latino
	Central Michel Richard	American/French

OTHER NOTEWORTHY PLACES

Restaurant	Cuisine
Adour	American/French
Birch & Barley/Churchkey	American
BlackSalt	American/Seafood
Bourbon Steak	Steak
Bread Line	Bakery/Sandwiches
Café du Parc	French
Cork	American
DC Coast	American
Equinox	American
J&G Steakhouse	American/Steak
Johnny's Half Shell	American/Seafood
Pizzeria Paradiso	Pizza
Ray's Hell Burger	Burgers
RIS	American
1789	American
Source	American
2 Amys	Pizza
Vidalia	American
Westend	American
Zaytinya	Mediterranean/Mideastern

	FOOD	DECOR	SERVICE	COST

Adour at the St. Regis *American/French* | 24 | 26 | 24 | $82 |

Downtown | St. Regis | 923 K St. NW (16th St.) | 202-509-8000 | www.adour-washingtondc.com

"Superb" contemporary French-American fare and "elegant service" define Alain Ducasse's "tucked-away" venue in Downtown's stately St. Regis Hotel, where white-leather appointments, "stunning chandeliers and glass wine displays" overseen by a "genius sommelier" set the stage for an "extravagant" meal; penny-pinchers pale at the "New York prices", but from the "terrific" amuse-bouche and "beautiful" plating ("hot dogs would be presented lavishly" here) to the "divine" macarons, most agree it's "worth it."

Birch & Barley/Churchkey Ⓜ *American* | 22 | 25 | 23 | $36 |

Farragut | 1337 14th St. NW (bet. P St. & Rhode Island Ave.) | 202-567-2576 | www.birchandbarley.com

Something "big" is brewing at this hopshead "paradise" above Logan Circle – just ask the "youthful crowd" packing the "gorgeous" upstairs bar/lounge (Churchkey) that pairs "great" New American small plates with a 550-count "beer list that'll make your head spin, literally and figuratively"; below, Birch & Barley's "beautiful" dining room (flickering oil lamps, brick walls) sets the scene for "seasonal, creative" fare delivered by a "knowledgeable" crew – and best of all, it's "decently priced"; P.S. oenophiles salute a "wonderful" wine list.

BlackSalt *American/Seafood* | 26 | 19 | 22 | $53 |

Palisades | 4883 MacArthur Blvd. NW (U St.) | 202-342-9101 | www.blacksaltrestaurant.com

They "shore" please at this Palisades New American, "another winner" in the Blacks' "empire" whose "wake-up-your-mouth" fin fare is "simply but expertly prepared" and "graciously" served by staffers who "make every person feel special"; choose among the "classy" raw bar, "elegant tasting room" or "minimalist" dining area where you may be seated next to "some high-powered Washingtonian", or just "pick up fresh seafood" from the "first-rate" market up front ("a cheaper option") and "grill it at home."

Blue Duck Tavern *American* | 26 | 24 | 25 | $62 |

West End | Park Hyatt | 1201 24th St. NW (bet. M & 24th Sts.) | 202-419-6755 | www.blueducktavern.com

"Lucky ducks" are "cosseted" by a "marvelous" staff at this "outstanding" West End New American, a "farm-to-table" "delight" spotlighting chef Brian McBride's "innovative" "comfort cuisine" – including "perfect french fries" and "wickedly scrumptious" apple pie; add in "atmospheric" decor both "inside and out" and prices that are "reasonable for the quality", and, yes, it's "all it's quacked up to be."

Bourbon Steak *Steak* | 23 | 24 | 24 | $76 |

Georgetown | Four Seasons Hotel | 2800 Pennsylvania Ave. NW (28th St.) | 202-944-2026 | www.michaelmina.net

The "delightful" New American cuisine can be "as thrilling as the frequent celebrity sightings" at this Georgetown "power place" from Michael Mina, who "scores a home run" at the Four Seasons Hotel with "designer steaks", "terrific" seafood and "arguably the best burger" in town; predictably "professional" service, a "buzzy bar" and "eye-catching" decor ("warm" hues, polished wood, black marble) also entice, and while a few nostalgists "miss the Garden Terrace" and fret over "noise" and "whopping" tabs, most deem it "worth the splurge."

Bread Line ⓈBakery/Sandwiches — 22 | 9 | 14 | $14

World Bank | 1751 Pennsylvania Ave. NW (bet. 17th & 18th Sts.) | 202-822-8900 | www.breadline.com

At this "one-of-a-kind" weekday bakery/cafe near the White House and World Bank, expect "creative" "world cuisine on paper plates", including "superior sandwiches and soups", "marvelous bread" and "hand-cut" fries; it's a "bit pricey" but "well worth it", and given the "crowds" packing its "sterile" industrial space, there's "surprisingly quick service" and seating (indoor and out) that's "less impossible than it looks."

Café Atlántico/Minibar Ⓜ Nuevo Latino — 26 | 21 | 24 | $64

Penn Quarter | 405 Eighth St. NW (bet. D & E Sts.) | 202-393-0812 | www.cafeatlantico.com

"Expect the unexpected" from "magician" José Andrés and his "engaging" team at this "colorful" Penn Quarter Nuevo Latino, from the "cotton-candy mojitos" and "tableside guacamole" to the "incredible fish" and other "innovative though not intimidating" cuisine; for a real blowout, "do whatever it takes to score" a seat at the $120-per-person Minibar, an "incredible" 30-bite "science class and chef's tasting" that may be "America's closest approximation" to an "el Bulli experience" of "molecular gastronomy"; P.S. the "Latin dim sum brunch" is a "deal."

Café du Parc French — 22 | 20 | 21 | $48

Downtown | Willard InterContinental Washington | 1401 Pennsylvania Ave. NW (bet. 14th & 15th Sts.) | 202-942-7000 | www.cafeduparc.com

You almost "expect to see Edith Piaf singing in the corner" at the Willard InterContinental's "bustling" French brasserie, where dreamers who think they're "back in Paris" partake of "deliciously rich" fare like "melt-in-your-mouth" pork belly and enjoy "professional" care; even those few who find meals "not all that special" for the price and deem its "airy" interior "bland" find it hard to resist its "lovely terrace" – a "perfect place" to "people-watch on a gorgeous day."

Central Michel Richard American/French — 26 | 21 | 23 | $54

Penn Quarter | 1001 Pennsylvania Ave. NW (11th St.) | 202-626-0015 | www.centralmichelrichard.com

"Stylish, great food, fun, exciting, chic" – chef Michel Richard's "genius" makes it all come together at this Penn Quarter "gem", a "bustling" New American–French brasserie where "comfort food gone way beyond your imagination" comes with "polished" service in an "airy California atmosphere"; yes, the "hopping bar scene" and "high-energy" dining room can be "noisy" ("sit in back" by the open kitchen), but "amazing" meals for "prices you can afford" quiet most skeptics.

Citronelle ⓈⓂ French — 28 | 25 | 26 | $106
(aka Michel Richard Citronelle)

Georgetown | Latham Hotel | 3000 M St. NW (30th St.) | 202-625-2150 | www.citronelledc.com

"If heaven had its own dining room", it might look a lot like Michel Richard's "exquisite" Georgetown New French, where the "master chef's" "joie de vivre" still inspires each plate, and a "stunning" wine list and servers who "make you feel special" add to the "unforgettable memories"; naturally, tabs are "up there", but that's the price of "culinary nirvana" (the lounge menu is a bit "more limited" and a bit easier on the wallet); P.S. for a "special splurge, eat at the chef's table."

CityZen 🅩 Ⓜ American   28 | 27 | 28 | $105

SW | Mandarin Oriental | 1330 Maryland Ave. SW (12th St.) | 202-787-6006 | www.mandarinoriental.com

Scoring a "trifecta" of near "perfection on all fronts", this "first-class" New American in the Mandarin Oriental showcases chef Eric Ziebold's "creative brilliance" in a "sleek and sensual" setting with "top-tier" servers and a "fantastic" sommelier; from the "intriguing" six-course tasting menu to the "heavenly mini-Parker House rolls", it's a "transformational experience" that's "worth every penny"; P.S. "smaller" three-course prix fixes in the more casual bar ($50) and dining room ($80) are likewise rife with "delectable delights."

Corduroy 🅩 American   27 | 24 | 25 | $63

Mt. Vernon Square/Convention Center | 1122 Ninth St. NW (bet. L & M Sts.) | 202-589-0699 | www.corduroydc.com

Chef Tom Powers' "remarkably sophisticated" New American cuisine has finally found its "niche" – and it's virtually "outside the Convention Center door" in a townhouse that provides an "elegant", "conversation-conducive" setting for his "creativity"; a "well-priced wine list" that's "thorough without being overwhelming" and a "professional" staff complement the "powerful" cooking, while an "underutilized" upstairs bar provides a "perfect retreat", along with a three-course prix fixe.

Cork Ⓜ American   23 | 20 | 20 | $41

Logan Circle | 1720 14th St. NW (bet. R & S Sts.) | 202-265-2675 | www.corkdc.com

At this "insanely popular" Logan Circle destination, a "top-notch" selection of "affordable" European wines, "deceptively simple but flavorful" New American small plates and "superb" pairing recommendations from "educated" servers "make for a wonderful night out"; snagging a table in its "dark", "exposed-brick" quarters ("are we in Paris?") can be a "challenge", so try its "call-ahead" system, make an early reservation or "just hang by the bar" – it's "worth a wait."

DC Coast American   23 | 22 | 22 | $53

Downtown | Tower Bldg. | 1401 K St. NW (14th St.) | 202-216-5988 | www.dccoast.com

Out-of-towners can see firsthand "what the K Street scene is all about" at this "top-flight" "power-lunch" locus awash in "swanky", "art deco-style" trappings and "imaginative", predictably "pricey" New American fare with a seafood hook; choose between the "high-energy", sometimes "frantic" dining room and the "intimate" balcony (both "professionally" tended by "spot-on" servers), or grab a seat at the "hopping bar" and start "eavesdropping" – "you may learn something important."

Equinox American   25 | - | 23 | $64

Golden Triangle | 818 Connecticut Ave. NW (bet. H & I Sts.) | 202-331-8118 | www.equinoxrestaurant.com

Emerging lighter, brighter and more modern-looking "post kitchen fire", this New American "oasis of grace and charm" – conveniently set in the Obamas' neighborhood and long favored for "special nights out" - is "still special", showcasing as it does chef/co-owner Todd Gray's "classically elegant approach" to the "freshest, finest local ingredients" (hence, there's "always something interesting and different on the menu"); "professional service" adds to the appeal, making it a relatively "good value at the high end."

Eve, Restaurant 🛇 *American*

28 | 25 | 27 | $84

Old Town | 110 S. Pitt St. (bet. King & Prince Sts.) | Alexandria, VA | 703-706-0450 | www.restauranteve.com

"Hitting on all cylinders", this "magical" Old Town New American proffers a choice of "unforgettable" experiences: an "ambrosial" nine-course romp in the "serene" tasting room, or a "gastronomic extravaganza on a smaller scale" in the "hip" bistro and lounge; chef/co-owner Cathal Armstrong "coaxes the best" from his "superb ingredients" (including "vegetables from the garden in back") and "impeccable" staff - from the "mesmerizing mixologist" to the "knowledgeable" sommelier - so naturally devotees deem it well "worth the splurge"; P.S. the $13.50 "daily bar lunch is a steal."

Honey Pig
Gooldaegee Korean Grill ◐ *Korean*
(aka Seoul Gool Dae Gee)

26 | 12 | 17 | $24

Annandale | 7220-C Columbia Pike (Maple Pl.), VA | 703-256-5229

"Gastronomic delights" and a "crazy atmosphere collide" in Annandale at this Korean BBQ "joint", a "24/7" "hoot" whose "cheap, tasty" fare - including "fantastic" grilled meats and deep-fried dishes - takes your mind off the "blaringly loud music" and "funky" decor ("advertising posters" and "sparse tables" in a "warehouse" setting); even if "efficient" servers seem "gruff" to sensitive sorts, most everyone's "gotta go back to see the Pig!"

Inn at Little Washington *American*

29 | 28 | 29 | $145

Washington | Inn at Little Washington | 309 Middle St. (Main St.), VA | 540-675-3800 | www.theinnatlittlewashington.com

From the "truffle popcorn to the last lick of the sorbet sampler", there's "brilliance in every bite" at Patrick O'Connell's "magical" New American in the Virginia countryside; with a "drop-dead gorgeous" setting and "irreproachable" staffers who strive for "perfection in every detail", it's no surprise that fans happily dip into their "life's savings" to "savor" the "exquisite experience"; P.S. "stay the night to keep the fairy tale going."

J&G Steakhouse *American/Steak*

25 | 25 | 23 | $67

Downtown | W Hotel | 515 15th St. NW (bet. F St. & Pennsylvania Ave.) | 202-661-2440 | www.jgsteakhousewashingtondc.com

Steps from the White House, Jean-Georges Vongerichten's "bright star" in the W Hotel is anything but a "stodgy Washington steakhouse" (despite its name); indeed, its "fantastic" seafood and "creative" New American options are the real "reasons to go" to this "sophisticated" space blending "old architectural elements" with "modern" cool and "attentive" hospitality - and, happily, most feel it's "worthy" of the "pricey" tabs; P.S. "go upstairs" to the POV bar for cocktails and amazing vistas.

	FOOD	DECOR	SERVICE	COST

Johnny's Half Shell ⓈⒶ American/Seafood   20 | 17 | 19 | $44

Capitol Hill | 400 N. Capitol St. NW (Louisiana Ave.) | 202-737-0400 | www.johnnyshalfshell.net

Capitol Hill "politicos" and their acolytes set sail for Ann Cashion's "hip", "high-end" New American seafooder, where "delicious" po' boys, bivalves and other "fresh" fin fare vie for attention with a "hopping" wood-and-marble bar and "live music" on the terrace; notwithstanding nostalgia for its former "intimate" Dupont Circle digs, many agree it's "worth a visit."

Komi ⓈⓂ American/Mediterranean   29 | 22 | 28 | $123

Dupont Circle | 1509 17th St. NW (P St.) | 202-332-9200 | www.komirestaurant.com

"Way out of the box and over the top" describes the "dazzling" "food adventure" at chef-owner Johnny Monis' "intimate" Dupont Circle "star", where a *degustazione* "marathon" of "intricate" Med-American courses – from "delectable bite-sized morsels" to "gourmet goat" – is matched "beautifully" with "esoteric wines"; "unpretentious" servers provide a "seamless experience from the front end to the kitchen", and if the "price is high and choices minimal", few dispute it "delivers on the 'wow' scale."

L'Auberge Chez François Ⓜ French   27 | 26 | 27 | $81

Great Falls | 332 Springvale Rd. (Beach Mill Rd.), VA | 703-759-3800 | www.laubergechezfrancois.com

A "five-star" drive down "winding country roads" to Great Falls, VA, sets the mood for an "exceptional experience" at this "French classic" nestled in "gorgeous" surroundings; it's "not as glitzy" as some, but after "professional, caring" servers deliver multiple courses of "rich" Alsatian fare and wine from a "list that'll blow you away", most are won over by its "old-timey elegance" that harks back to a "more relaxed era" – and at a price that makes it a "bargain compared with Downtown" restaurants lacking its enduring "charm."

L'Auberge Provençale French   27 | 25 | 25 | $78

Boyce | L'Auberge Provençale | 13630 Lord Fairfax Hwy. (Rte. 50), VA | 540-837-1375 | www.laubergeprovencale.com

"An hour or so outside the city but a world away", this "beautiful" Boyce "getaway" is a "romantic" (and "expensive") fireplace-filled retreat for "lovers of fine food" and the "great outdoors"; "delectable" French tasting menus, an "extensive" wine list and "divine" service make it a "treasure" for a "special" meal, but for a truly "amazing" experience, "stay the night" and have breakfast too.

Makoto Ⓜ Japanese   28 | 20 | 25 | $84

Palisades | 4822 MacArthur Blvd. NW (U St.) | 202-298-6866

"As authentically Japanese as you can get", this "intimate" Palisades kaiseki specialist reaches the "pinnacle of quality" with an "adventurous" chef's menu showcasing eight to 10 courses of "exquisite" "works of art" accompanied by "geishalike service"; "delicate" sushi also figures in a "fabulous experience" that's "like leaving the country for the night" (you'll even trade your shoes for "slippers" on entry), so despite "limited room" and seating on hard "wooden boxes" it's "totally worth" the premium price.

	FOOD	DECOR	SERVICE	COST

Marcel's *Belgian/French*

29 | 26 | 28 | $88

West End | 2401 Pennsylvania Ave. NW (24th St.) | 202-296-1166 | www.marcelsdc.com

"Master" chef Robert Wiedmaier "orchestrates" culinary "miracles" at this West End Belgian-French "class act", where the "superlative" cuisine (e.g. the "famous", foie gras–enriched boudin blanc) earns the No. 1 Food rating in the DC Survey; "stellar service" and a "romantic" Provençal setting enhance an "exceptional" performance that justifies "dropping serious cash"; P.S. the pre-theater deal includes "complimentary limo service to the Kennedy Center."

Obelisk ⊠Ⓜ *Italian*

27 | 20 | 27 | $87

Dupont Circle | 2029 P St. NW (bet. 20th & 21st Sts.) | 202-872-1180

"Balanced perfection" is the keystone of this "tiny" Italian prix fixe "treasure" off Dupont Circle, where "well-chosen wines" complement a "never-ending feast" of "inventive" fare that "changes daily" and is "special without being showy"; it comes at a "surprisingly reasonable cost" given the "quality" and the "high level of service", so "bring a special friend for a fine, long evening" – just be sure to "make reservations."

Palena ⊠ *American*

28 | 21 | 24 | $63

Cleveland Park | 3529 Connecticut Ave. NW (bet. Ordway & Porter Sts.) | 202-537-9250 | www.palenarestaurant.com

"Exemplary" chef-owner Frank Ruta conjures "meals that fire on all cylinders" at his Cleveland Park New American, where diners "savor every morsel" of "wonderful and imaginative" French-Italian–inspired prix fixe selections in an "old-world" dining room manned by "cordial, attentive" servers; up front, the "casual" cafe is an "absolute steal", offering what may be the "city's top burger" and earning "high-fives for the battered lemon slices" that come with the fries (but "get there early or late" to "snag a seat").

Pizzeria Paradiso *Pizza*

22 | 16 | 18 | $26

Dupont Circle | 2003 P St. NW (bet. Hopkins & 20th Sts.) | 202-223-1245
Georgetown | 3282 M St. NW (bet. Potomac & 33rd Sts.) | 202-337-1245
www.eatyourpizza.com

Find "paradise on a pizza pie crust" at these "friendly" "must-stops" where "fresh dough and fresher ingredients" add up to "some of the best" 'za for "miles around", though the "awesome beer menus" (including "hard-to-find drafts") may be the "real prize"; the Georgetown venue boasts a "cozy cellar complete with fireplace" and Dupont's "homey" new digs are "larger and brighter", but no matter: "there's still a wait" at both "during prime dining hours."

Prime Rib ⊠ *Steak*

27 | 25 | 27 | $68

Golden Triangle | 2020 K St. NW (bet. 20th & 21st Sts.) | 202-466-8811 | www.theprimerib.com

In DC's Golden Triangle, the "godfather of steakhouses" mixes "old-world elegance" with "just the right touch of film-noir decadence", live music and "dynamite food" – the "best slab-o-meat in town", "first-rate" crab and "huge" sides – to make each "expensive" meal an "event"; the "retro-classy" digs are attended by "tuxedoed waiters" (there's a "dress code" for customers too), while the "bar scene will hurt your eyes if you're married."

	FOOD	DECOR	SERVICE	COST

Rasika ⓈⒹ Indian
28 | 25 | 25 | $50

Penn Quarter | 633 D St. NW (bet. 6th & 7th Sts.) | 202-637-1222 |
www.rasikarestaurant.com

"Does anyone really not rave about the food?" at this Penn Quarter "winner", where "intensely flavorful" Indian dishes take palates on "wondrous culinary journeys" that have dreamers wishing for an "extra stomach" (for the likes of "crispy" fried spinach that "Popeye would kill for"); "deft" servers who "appear to enjoy" their jobs and a "glittering" (if "noisy") atmosphere bolster its status as one of DC's "best restaurants – without 'best restaurant' price tags."

Ray's Hell Burger ⊘ Burgers
26 | 8 | 14 | $15
(aka Ray's Butcher Burgers)

Courthouse | Colonial Vill. | 1725 Wilson Blvd. (bet. Quinn & Rhodes Sts.) |
Arlington, VA | 703-841-0001

Ray's Hell Burger Too ⊘ Burgers

Courthouse | 1713 Wilson Blvd. (bet Quinn & Rhodes Sts.) | Arlington, VA |
703-841-0001

"Just ask Prez Obama" – even "he stood in line" for one of the "heavenly" headliners at Michael 'Ray' Landrum's "burger nirvana"; it's "absolute mayhem" within the original Courthouse-area "bare-bones" storefront (the nearby 'Too' spin-off, with table service, opened post-Survey), but "none of that matters" since the "juicy", "fresh-made" patties of "unsurpassed quality" and "high-end" toppings like foie gras are what "it's all about"; "draft root beer", "limited sides" ("finally added fries") and "decent prices" round out the cash-only experience.

RIS American
23 | 23 | 23 | $49

West End | 2275 L St. NW (23rd St.) | 202-730-2500 | www.risdc.com
Chef Ris Lacoste's "welcome return" to the DC dining scene brings the newly "hip West End" a "comfortable" yet "sophisticated" bistro serving "upscale" New American "comfort food", including "not-to-be-missed" lamb shank; "multiple room designs" ("tablecloth" and informal), a sweeping patio and "one of the best bars in town" ensure there's a space for every taste, and while some say a few "kinks" remain, it's generally "excellent from the moment you walk in."

1789 American
25 | 25 | 25 | $65

Georgetown | 1226 36th St. NW (Prospect St.) | 202-965-1789 |
www.1789restaurant.com

Hark back to a "time when elegance mattered" at this "gorgeous" Georgetown townhouse, where the seasonal New American fare "always delivers", "welcoming" staffers "attend to you as if they've known you for decades" and romance blossoms amid "intimate tables", fireplaces and "classic" decor ("sit downstairs"); expect to find the neighborhood "hoi polloi", "witty pols" and "visiting parents" taking advantage of that rarity: a "pricey place that isn't overpriced", thanks in part to a $35 three-course prix fixe.

Source, The ⓈⒹ American
25 | 25 | 23 | $67

Penn Quarter | Newseum | 575 Pennsylvania Ave. NW (6th St.) |
202-637-6100 | www.wolfgangpuck.com

"Newsworthy" "Modern American–meets-Asian" fare headlines Wolfgang Puck's "dazzling" outpost next to the Penn Quarter's Newseum, where a "stunning" yet "stark" second-story dining room provides a "serene" milieu for "high-end" meals melding "wonderful flavors"; other pluses include a "cordial, responsive" staff and "lively" happy hour, when its downstairs lounge fills with "hip DCers" digging in to "recognizable faves" and Far Eastern izakaya (small plates) in an atmosphere akin to "Vegas, LA or New York."

Tosca ☒ *Italian* | 27 | 23 | 26 | $66 |

Penn Quarter | 1112 F St. NW (bet. 11th & 12th Sts.) | 202-367-1990 | www.toscadc.com

Celebrated for its "quiet elegance" and "divine" Italian cuisine paired with wines to "match every dish and taste", this Penn Quarter "standout" is lined with "power players" at lunch and "romantic" sorts at night – because "no matter whom you bring here", its "seasoned" pros make the "experience special"; "understated" decor (some say "boring") completes the package, one with "pricey" tabs tempered by a "bargain" $35 prix fixe deal; P.S. "try the chef's table in the kitchen."

2941 Restaurant ☒ *American* | 26 | 27 | 26 | $73 |

Falls Church | 2941 Fairview Park Dr. (I-495), VA | 703-270-1500 | www.2941.com

Enter past a "shimmering" koi pond and you'll discover "lush views" of a "tranquil" garden and lake from this "top-flight" New American's "impressive" dining rooms, whose "floor-to-ceiling windows", "artisan lighting and huge mirrors" belie its Falls Church office park locale ("who knew?"); the "exquisite" French-accented fare from chef Bertrand Chemel is presented with "polished" professionalism, making it a "special-occasion favorite", and while "being treated this well" is "not inexpensive", there are "good deals" at the bar and a "bargain" three-course lunch ($20.10).

2 Amys *Pizza* | 25 | 16 | 19 | $25 |

Cleveland Park | 3715 Macomb St. NW (Wisconsin Ave.) | 202-885-5700 | www.2amyspizza.com

Making "pizza like God intended" (or at least with the Naples pizza association's "blessing"), this "always crowded" Cleveland Parker proffers "sublime" "wood-fired, heat-blistered" pies that vie with its "fantastic charcuterie" as reasons to "battle hungry stroller-wielding" families for space in its "hectic" white-tiled premises; since grown-ups can seek refuge on the "lovely patio" or in the "well-stocked" wine bar and "quieter" upstairs dining room, the vast majority agree that "although wait times are 2 often 2 long", the place is "not 2 be missed."

Vidalia *American* | 24 | 22 | 24 | $63 |

Dupont Circle | 1990 M St. NW (bet. 19th & 20th Sts.) | 202-659-1990 | www.vidaliadc.com

"Highbrow Low Country cooking" coupled with an "impressive wine list", servers who "remember you and your needs" and a "bright, airy" space make diners "instantly forget" they've "stepped underground" at this "stellar" Dupont New American; true, a few naysayers suggest it's "living on its reputation", but they're vastly outnumbered by those who say it's "worth the splurge" (tip: a "three-course lunch special" trims tabs); P.S. "leave room for dessert."

Westend Bistro by Eric Ripert *American* | 21 | 19 | 21 | $58 |

West End | Ritz-Carlton | 1190 22nd St. NW (M St.) | 202-974-4900 | www.westendbistrodc.com

Partisans proclaim "they've pulled it off" – i.e. the "trend where big-name chefs with formal restaurants go downscale" – at this West End New American, citing "refined" bistro fare with a "unique Eric Ripert twist" (e.g. "ethereal" fish burgers), "professional" but "friendly" service and a "who's-who" bar scene; still, contrarians who expect "exponentially more given all the hype" and its Ritz-Carlton branding gripe about a "hotel-restaurant feel", "unmanageable noise" and "hit-or-miss" fare at "high prices."

Zaytinya ● *Mediterranean/Mideastern* | 25 | 23 | 21 | $42 |

Penn Quarter | Pepco Bldg. | 701 Ninth St. NW (G St.) | 202-638-0800 | www.zaytinya.com

Foodies "worship" at José Andrés' "cathedral of Eastern Mediterranean" flavors in the Penn Quarter, a "sleek", "airy" space "oozing hipness" and offering a "dazzling array" of "fascinating small plates" covering "Greece to Lebanon with all stops in between"; it's "loud, brash" and "always crowded", but staffers who "keep it real", a "user-friendly wine list" and tabs that "won't suck the money out of your wallet" help make it the Most Popular restaurant in the DC Survey – and render reservations "indispensable."

Westchester/Hudson Valley

TOP FOOD RANKING

	Restaurant	Cuisine
29	Xaviars at Piermont	American
28	Freelance Cafe	American
	Serevan	Mediterranean
	Il Cenàcolo	Italian
	Blue Hill at Stone Barns	American
	Ocean House	Seafood
27	Johnny's Pizzeria	Pizza
	Sushi Nanase	Japanese
	Zephs'	American/Eclectic
	La Panetière	French
	X2O Xaviars	American
	Caterina de Medici	Italian
	Restaurant X/Bully Boy	American
	Twist	American
	Escoffier	French
26	Azuma Sushi	Japanese
	Il Barilotto	Italian
	Iron Horse Grill	American
	La Crémaillère	French
	Arch	Eclectic

OTHER NOTEWORTHY PLACES

Restaurant	Cuisine
Artist's Palate	American
Bedford Post	American
Beso	Eclectic
Buffet de la Gare	French
Cookery	Italian
Crabtree's Kittle House	American
42	American
Glenmere	American
Harvest on Hudson	Mediterranean
Mercato	Italian
Mulino's	Italian
Nina	Eclectic
Plates	American
Sapore	Seafood/Steak
Sonora	Nuevo Latino
Swoon Kitchenbar	American
Tarry Lodge	Italian
Terrapin	American
Union	American/Pan-Latin
Wasabi	Japanese

Arch, The Ⓜ Eclectic
26 | 25 | 26 | $71

Brewster | 1292 Rte. 22 (end of I-684) | 845-279-5011 |
www.archrestaurant.com

You'll be "pampered from start to finish" at this "classy" Brewster "legend", where "simply superlative", "classical" Eclectic cuisine and "dessert soufflés to die for" are served in a "graceful stone house" exuding "old-world elegance"; sure, tabs are a tad "hefty" (though "Sunday brunch is a steal"), but "put on a coat and tie and spend a few bucks" – "if this doesn't conjure up romance, there's no hope."

Artist's Palate Ⓩ American
24 | 24 | 22 | $47

Poughkeepsie | 307 Main St. (bet. Catharine & Market Sts.) |
845-483-8074 | www.theartistspalate.biz

"Hip has come to Poughkeepsie" in the form of this "upscale" New American "oasis", where culinary couple Charlie and Megan Fells "work magic in the open kitchen", creating "ambitious" "original" concoctions like the "must-try lobster mac 'n' cheese"; a "courteous" staff works the "cutting-edge cool" space – a "rehabbed" 19th-century department store where even the "bathrooms are fabulous."

Azuma Sushi Ⓜ Japanese
26 | 15 | 19 | $47

Hartsdale | 219 E. Hartsdale Ave. (bet. Bronx River Pkwy. & Central Park Ave.) |
914-725-0660

"Sushi purists" tout this "small", "Tokyo-style" Hartsdale Japanese where there are "no gimmicks" just "clean flavors" thanks to an "impeccable" selection of raw fish sliced by "authentic hands"; maybe the "chilly" atmosphere "should be avoided by those on antidepressants" and there's "too much attitude" for nonregulars, but overall it's "about the best around" – even if the "prices are tough to swallow."

Bedford Post, The Barn American
24 | 22 | 19 | $61

Bedford | Bedford Post | 954 Old Post Rd./Rte. 121 (bet. Indian Hill Rd. & Rte. 137) | 914-234-7800 | www.bedfordpostinn.com

This "bustling" Bedford cafe and bakery co-owned by Richard Gere earns praise for its "inventive" New American breakfasts and lunches based on "local, organic" ingredients and set down in fashionably rustic quarters; yet while the "food is always on the mark", "amateurish" service can be a sore spot, especially given such "pricey" tabs.

Beso Eclectic
25 | 21 | 22 | $49

New Paltz | 46 Main St. (Chestnut St.) | 845-255-1426 |
www.beso-restaurant.com

"You'll eat well" at this "laid-back" "slice of Manhattan" in New Paltz, "a beacon" of "fine dining" where chef Chad Greer's "imaginative" seasonal Eclectic dishes and "memorable" desserts provided by pastry chef spouse Tammy Ogletree all come "presented with flair"; a "thoughtful staff" takes the edge off somewhat "tight seating" in the small two-story space, so even if it's "pricey" for the neighborhood, ultimately, it's "worth it."

Blue Hill at Stone Barns Ⓜ American
28 | 28 | 27 | $124

Pocantico Hills | Stone Barns Ctr. | 630 Bedford Rd. (Lake Rd.) |
914-366-9600 | www.bluehillfarm.com

"Locavore meets urban sophisticate" at Dan Barber's "tranquil" New American, a "trendy-rustic" converted barn on the Rockefeller estate in Pocantico Hills producing "fresh-as-the-morning" ingredients for "breathtaking" eight-plate prix fixes; a staff that's "passionate about food" sees you through the "amazing adventure" that's "a must for any foodie", and if a few moan about the "pre-recession prices", less expensive meals with three or five courses were added post-Survey; P.S. on weekends you can "walk the grounds" and eat lunch at the cafe.

Buffet de la Gare 🅜 French
26 | 21 | 24 | $66

Hastings-on-Hudson | 155 Southside Ave. (Spring St.) | 914-478-1671
"Passionate" owners are at the helm of this "charming" French bistro in Hastings, a "sophisticated" nexus where the food is "sublime", the service "superlative" and the interior "romantic" (indeed, the "only thing missing is the Eiffel Tower"); most agree you "could not ask for more – except for someone else's credit card" when the "expensive" bill arrives – but ultimately this "first-class" dining experience is "well worth it"; P.S. it's "small" so "book well ahead."

Caterina de Medici 🅢 Italian
27 | 27 | 24 | $53

Hyde Park | Culinary Institute of America | 1946 Campus Dr. (Rte. 9) | 845-471-6608 | www.ciachef.edu
"It's amazing what these kids can do" declare the dazzled at this "outstanding" student-staffed restaurant at the Hyde Park cooking school where "everything is special", from the "stunning", "Tuscan-inspired" surroundings to the "fantastic" Italian cuisine; given such a "delightful experience", no one minds the limited hours (closed Saturdays and Sundays) or occasional "glitches" from "nervous" servers.

Cookery, The 🅜 Italian
- | - | - | M

Dobbs Ferry | 39 Chestnut St. (Main St.) | 914-305-2336 | www.thecookeryrestaurant.com
This Dobbs Ferry find features a seasonal menu of stylish Italian comfort food such as house-cured meats and fresh pastas, plus affordable wines and an intriguing lineup of cocktails; the decor mixes industrial elements like exposed brick and ductwork with homey ones, such as a snug bar and a well-worn wooden table that once belonged to chef David DiBari's grandmother.

Crabtree's Kittle House American
25 | 24 | 24 | $66

Chappaqua | Crabtree's Kittle House Inn | 11 Kittle Rd. (Rte. 117) | 914-666-8044 | www.kittlehouse.com
"Like dining in a rich uncle's country home", this "charming" Chappaqua inn is "first-rate in all respects", from the "fine service" to the "scrumptious" New American cuisine backed by an "inexhaustible" wine list that "would make Robert Parker jealous"; despite some whispers that it's "showing its age", for most it remains a local "treasure" that "never fails to lift the spirits" – just be prepared for equally lofty tabs; P.S. the Food score does not reflect a post-Survey chef change.

Escoffier Restaurant 🅢🅜 French
27 | 25 | 26 | $62

Hyde Park | Culinary Institute of America | 1946 Campus Dr. (Rte. 9) | 845-471-6608 | www.ciachef.edu
You'll be reminded of the days when "haute" was hot at this Hyde Park cooking school's "crown jewel", a "classic French" restaurant where "beautifully plated" fare "prepared by students" "gets all As"; though a few find the "elegant" room "a tad stuffy", "endearing servers" who

make the "occasional blunder" add an "amusing" note; in sum, "it's lovely", so reserve "in advance and splurge."

42 Ⓜ American
22 | 26 | 22 | $87

White Plains | Ritz-Carlton Westchester | 1 Renaissance Sq., 42nd fl. (Main St.) | 914-761-4242 | www.42therestaurant.com

The "knockout views" are "something to behold" at this aerie atop the Ritz-Carlton in White Plains, a "luxurious", "modern" setting showcasing chef-owner Anthony Goncalves' "forward-thinking" New American creations; however, many express "disappointment" at the "inconsistent quality", not to mention service that's sometimes "below what you would expect" at these prices.

Freelance Cafe & Wine Bar Ⓜ American
28 | 20 | 26 | $54

Piermont | 506 Piermont Ave. (Ash St.) | 845-365-3250 | www.xaviars.com

"Of course it's wonderful, it's Peter Kelly" purr patrons of this "foodie's mainstay" in Piermont, a "low-key version of upscale Xaviars" next door offering "a taste" of the same "sublime" New American fare at more "modest prices"; a "well-trained" staff "welcomes" regular folks and "local celebs" in the small, "minimalist" space that's "part NYC, part Paris, with a touch of LA", so the "only flaw is no reservations" (read: "long waits", unless you "eat late" or "go midweek").

Glenmere American
– | – | – | E

Chester | Glenmere | 634 Pine Hill Rd. (Glenmere Rd.) | 845-469-1900 | www.glenmeremansion.com

Sumptuous sums up this Chester New American addition set in a beautifully restored 1911 Italianate mansion–cum-hotel; luxury priced, elegant plates are served by candlelight in the Supper Room, resplendent with painted mirrored panels and chandeliers, Thursday–Saturday evenings and for Sunday brunch; meanwhile, simpler fare and gentler tariffs are on offer every day in the cozy Frog's End Tavern, which features a hand-carved walnut bar.

Harvest on Hudson Mediterranean
22 | 26 | 22 | $56

Hastings-on-Hudson | 1 River St. (Main St. off Southside Ave.) | 914-478-2800 | www.harvest2000.com

"Terrific food" and a "stunning setting" meet cute at this Hastings "keeper" (aka "Westchester's answer to Tuscany") that's equally celebrated for "inventive" Mediterranean cooking sourced from "locally grown" items and "over-the-moon" vistas of the Hudson and the Palisades; the "massive fireplace", "country club" mood and "Manhattan prices" draw in droves of "special-occasion crowds", and if a minority sees a victory of "style over substance", it's still "hard to beat for drinks in the garden with the river flowing by."

Il Barilotto Ⓩ Italian
26 | 23 | 24 | $48

Fishkill | 1113 Main St. (North St.) | 845-897-4300 | www.ilbarilottorestaurant.com

They "know what fine dining means" at this "upscale", "upbeat" Fishkill Italian offering "phenomenal", "modern cuisine" with "scrumptious" specials and a "top-shelf wine list"; the "nicely refinished" 1800s carriage house, with its exposed brick, vintage posters and mahogany bar, exudes "style", so with "impeccable service" you've got "Manhattan quality without the commute or expense."

Cenàcolo Italian
28 | 22 | 25 | $63

Newburgh | 228 S. Plank Rd./Rte. 52 (bet. I-87 & Rte. 300) |
845-564-4494 | www.ilcenacolorestaurant.com

"Cancel the trip to Tuscany, the food's better" at this Newburgh "gem"
serving "sensational" Northern Italian cuisine with a "mind-boggling list
of specials" (so "ignore the menu"), and such a "terrific antipasti assortment" that "you can make a meal" of that alone; add "incredible" wines
and "fantastic service" in the "romantic" setting and who cares about
"luxe prices" – it's the "perfect splurge" and "too good to miss"; "bravo!"

Iron Horse Grill ⌦Ⓜ American
26 | 22 | 25 | $60

Pleasantville | 20 Wheeler Ave. (bet. Bedford & Manville Rds.) |
914-741-0717 | www.ironhorsegrill.com

"Charming" chef-owner Philip McGrath "warmly greets each guest
like a regular" at this Pleasantville New American that "stands out" for
its "superb" seasonal cuisine and "thoughtful" wine selections; a
"dedicated" staff and "quaint" setting in a converted railway station
boost the appeal; in short, it's a "class act" worth the "splurge."

Johnny's Pizzeria ⌦Ⓜ⇓ Pizza
27 | 7 | 14 | $21

Mt. Vernon | Lincoln Plaza | 30 W. Lincoln Ave. (bet. Rochelle Terrace &
5th Ave.) | 914-668-1957

There's "no better pie north of the Bronx" proclaim purists who "can't
live without" the "perfectly made" pizzas (some of the "thinnest in the
county") at this longtime Mt. Vernon parlor also turning out Neapolitan
entrees; maybe it's "not the friendliest place", but even "run-down"
quarters and "major parking hassles" don't deter faithful fans who swear
such "heavenly" 'za is "worth suffering for"; P.S. no slices, cash only.

La Crémaillère Ⓜ French
26 | 26 | 26 | $82

Bedford | 46 Bedford-Banksville Rd. (Round House Rd.) | 914-234-9647 |
www.cremaillere.com

"La crème de la crème" of Bedford, this longtime "charmer" pampers
guests with "professional" service and "delectable" "classic French"
feasts set down in an "enchanting" country-elegant setting; prices
aren't recession-friendly, but "rich" regulars and "special-occasion"
celebrators find it "worth every penny"; P.S. jackets suggested.

La Panetière French
27 | 27 | 27 | $80

Rye | 530 Milton Rd. (Oakland Beach Ave.) | 914-967-8140 |
www.lapanetiere.com

"Impeccable" sums up this "refined" Rye "grande dame" where "exquisite" New French creations are backed by a "voluminous" (900-
label) wine list; "meticulous attention to detail" shows in its "superior"
service that "never fails to impress" and "gracious" flower-filled setting, so "if you want to break the bank for a memorable dinner", don a
jacket and do it here.

Mercato Ⓜ Italian
26 | 18 | 21 | $46

Red Hook | 61 E. Market St./Rte. 199 (Cherry St.) | 845-758-5879 |
www.mercatoredhook.com

A "fixture" with a "loyal, devoted following", this "always packed" Red
Hook venue is known for "delicious", "down-to-earth" Northern Italian
fare "prepared with finesse" by "passionate chef" Francesco Buitoni
("he "wine list is pretty fab too"); service is "attentive", so even though

FOOD | DECOR | SERVICE | COST

tables are "close" and the "small", "noisy" "old house" has "bare-bones decor", most don't mind given such "memorable" meals.

Mulino's of Westchester ●☒ *Italian*   25 | 23 | 24 | $65

White Plains | 99 Court St. (Quarropas St.) | 914-761-1818 | www.mulinosny.com

"Power-lunchers" and "special-occasion" celebrants convene at this "glitzy" White Plains Italian for "ambitious, upscale" meals served by a staff that's always "a whisper away"; granted, it's "expensive", but "worth paying the extra cash" given touches like "complimentary antipasti" and a "waterfall"-equipped garden.

Nina *Eclectic*   25 | 24 | 23 | $47

Middletown | 27 W. Main St. (bet. Canal & North Sts.) | 845-344-6800 | www.nina-restaurant.com

"Terrific from beginning to end", chef Franz Brendle's "excellent" Eclectic fare is "the best reason to come" to Middletown aver the sleek weekenders who "flock" to it; the "lively", "New York City" vibe remains after an expansion added "a really nice lounge" and alleviated "tables on top of each other", leaving the "well-trained waiters" more room to "cosset" customers; it's "a bit expensive", but "worth it."

Ocean House ☒ *Seafood*   28 | 16 | 24 | $44

Croton-on-Hudson | 49 N. Riverside Ave./Rte. 9A (Farrington Rd.) | 914-271-0702

Loyalists "hate to give away the secret" of this Croton "gem" sending out "superbly fresh" seafood "cooked to perfection" in "matchbox" sized digs set in an old diner; a "wonderful" staff adds a "warm" touch and its BYO policy "keeps costs low", so the only downside is the "no reservations policy" ("get there early" or "prepare to wait").

Plates ☒ *American*   24 | 21 | 22 | $62

Larchmont | 121 Myrtle Blvd. (Murray Ave.) | 914-834-1244 | www.platesonthepark.com

"Imaginative" chef-owner Matthew Karp is behind this Larchmont "gem" where his "whimsical" New American creations – e.g. whiskey-glazed chicken and "homemade Ring Dings" – are matched with "boutique wines" in an "inviting" setting that oozes "sophistication"; the staff is "eager to please", so while some raise eyebrows at "pricey" tabs, most maintain "it'll set you back, but it's worth it."

Restaurant X & Bully Boy Bar ☒ *American*   27 | 24 | 25 | $61

Congers | 117 N. Rte. 303 (bet. Lake Rd. & Rte. 9W) | 845-268-6555 | www.xaviars.com

A "step below Xaviars", but still "outstanding" declare disciples of Peter Kelly's Congers "conquest" where staffers "willing to go that extra mile" serve "scrumptious" New American fare in "pretty" rooms with a "country" vibe; sure, it's "expensive", but "worth every dollar", particularly the "bargain" $25 prix fixe lunch or Sunday's "amazing", "18 course eating extravaganza" (aka "brunch").

Sapore *Seafood/Steak*   26 | 22 | 23 | $51

Fishkill | 1108 Main St. (North St.) | 845-897-3300 | www.saporesteakhouse.com

"If you're hankering for prime, aged beef", this "grown-up" steakhouse in Fishkill "is the place", with "phenomenal" meats and "amazing sea food" served by a "prompt", "attentive" staff; the "good wine selection" and "traditional" rooms "full of good-looking patrons seeking urbane food" are other clues it's best on "an expense account", but "you get what you pay for."

Serevan *Mediterranean*   28 | 24 | 25 | $55

Amenia | 6 Autumn Ln. (Rte. 44, west of Rte. 22) | 845-373-9800 | www.serevan.com

Amenia gourmands "can't say enough" about "genius" chef-owner Serge Madikians and his "exceptional" Med boîte where "vegetarians, carnivores" and "even picky NYers" are kept "happy" via "memorable" meals crafted with "exotic" "Middle Eastern" touches; yes, it's a bit "expensive", but a "well-trained" staff presides over the "inviting" dining room and the "beautiful garden" come summer.

Sonora *Nuevo Latino*   24 | 22 | 22 | $51

Port Chester | 179 Rectory St. (Willett Ave.) | 914-933-0200 | www.sonorarestaurant.net

"Everything clicks" at this "vibrant" Nuevo Latino "winner" parked in a "hard-to-find" Port Chester address, where top toque Rafael Palomino cooks up "creative", "flavor-filled" dishes that are "plated beautifully"; the bi-level setting is "calmer upstairs" and "trendier downstairs", but no matter where you sit you can expect "attentive" service, "great energy" and "pricey" tabs – though the lunchtime prix fixe is an "incredible bargain."

Sushi Nanase *Japanese*   27 | 17 | 21 | $67

White Plains | 522 Mamaroneck Ave. (DeKalb Ave.) | 914-285-5351

"Master" chef-owner Yoshimichi Takeda "rules" this "tiny" White Plains Japanese turning out "pristine" sushi "made the traditional way" for those who abide his "finicky" reservations policy that yields little grace for lateness; it's "not for amateurs" (i.e. "no California rolls") and it is "expensive", although acolytes agree such "sublime" fare is "worth every penny"; P.S. no walk-ins allowed; call ahead for the omakase.

Swoon Kitchenbar *American*   24 | 23 | 21 | $45

Hudson | 340 Warren St. (bet. 3rd & 4th Sts.) | 518-822-8938 | www.swoonkitchenbar.com

What with chef Jeffrey Gimmel's "tantalizing" savory fare and wife Nina's "divine desserts", they are one "dynamic duo", declare "foodies" getting a "frisson" at Hudson's "sweetheart" of a New American; add "elegant" decor with "gorgeous" "floral displays" and most are swept away enough to find sometimes "absentminded service" easily "forgivable" and tabs "on the pricey side" "worth it."

Tarry Lodge *Italian*   24 | 24 | 20 | $50

Port Chester | 18 Mill St. (Abendroth Ave.) | 914-939-3111 | www.tarrylodge.com

Chef-superstar Mario Batali and partner Joe Bastianich have "knocked it out of the park" with this much-"hyped" revamp of a beloved Port Chester tavern, now showcasing their brand of "true Italian" cooking like wood-fired pizzas and "exceptionally crafted" pastas, all served with "superb" wines in a "lively" (some say "deafening") gold-hued setting; throw in surprisingly "reasonable prices", and it makes a "tempting" suburban "alternative to Babbo" – "if you can ever get in."

	FOOD	DECOR	SERVICE	COST

Terrapin *American*

| | 24 | 23 | 21 | $47 |

Rhinebeck | 6426 Montgomery St./Rte. 9 (Livingston St.) | 845-876-3330 | www.terrapinrestaurant.com

Everything's "divine" at Josh Kroner's "upscale" Rhinebeck New American "hot spot" set in a "gorgeous converted church"; there's a "hushed", "fancy side" serving "flavorful", "adventurous dishes" that match the "grandeur of the space" and a "cheaper", "bustling bistro" with "fantastic tapas" and "design-your-own sandwiches"; the staff is "terrific", and in summer, you can "sit outside and watch the street scene."

Twist ☑ *American*

| | 27 | 18 | 26 | $46 |

Hyde Park | 4290 Albany Post Rd. (bet. Crumwold Pl. & Fuller Ln.) | 845-229-7094 | www.letstwist.com

"Don't be fooled" by the "unassuming" strip-mall location, because there's "exceptional" cuisine to be had at chef Benjamin Mauk's "always packed" Hyde Park New American "welcoming gourmands and kiddies alike"; the "memorable" meals come via "spry servers" bopping around the colorful room, although "chef wannabes" prefer to sit at the "high counter overlooking the kitchen" and "watch the action"; P.S. sidewalk seating "is a plus in good weather."

Union Restaurant &
Bar Latino ☑ *American/Pan-Latin*

| | 25 | 23 | 23 | $51 |

Haverstraw | 22-24 New Main St. (bet. B'way & Maple Ave.) | 845-429-4354 | www.unionrestaurant.net

It "bodes well" for Haverstraw's "revival" declare those dispensing "kudos" to chef David Martinez and host Paulo Feteira ("former members of the Xaviars group") for "doing everything right" at their "exciting" New American; "creative" cuisine with dashes of "Latin flair" comes served by an "attentive" "young staff" in an old brick building made "festive" with a "pretty" hacienda motif, while "fair" prices and "cool cocktails" cap off the "dining adventure."

Wasabi *Japanese*

| | 26 | 22 | 22 | $54 |

Nyack | 110 Main St. (bet. Cedar & Park Sts.) | 845-358-7977

Wasabi Grill *Japanese*

New City | Town Plaza | 195 S. Main St. (3rd St.) | 845-638-2202 www.wasabichi.com

"Local celebrities" can be found mingling with mere mortals at Nyack's Japanese "hot spot" (aka "Nobu on the Hudson"), where "artistic" chef-owner Doug Nguyen dispenses "outrageously original" dishes and takes sushi "to a higher plane"; the "hip, urban" atmosphere is "sexy" and "sleek" and service is "capable", so the "only challenge is getting a table"; yes, your "wallet takes a beating", but don't be surprised if "by the end of the evening, you're planning your return"; P.S. the New City addition, also offering hibachi, opened post-Survey.

Xaviars at Piermont ☑ *American*

| | 29 | 25 | 28 | $91 |

Piermont | 506 Piermont Ave. (bet. Ash & Gerhardt Strasse Sts.) | 845-359-7007 | www.xaviars.com

"A true class act", chef-owner Peter Kelly's Piermont New American is the "jewel in the crown" of his mini-empire – and of our Westchester/ HV Survey, which it tops for Food; "beguiling" cuisine comes served or

the "finest china" by a "top-level" staff in the "tiny", "tastefully decorated" room, providing a "magical" "respite from a hectic world"; it's
"a little on the expensive side" (the minimum option: an $80 prix fixe),
but devotees declare "the only time I've been disappointed is when I
couldn't get a table."

X2O Xaviars on the Hudson ⓜ *American*　　27　28　25　$70

Yonkers | Historic Yonkers Pier | 71 Water Grant St. (Buena Vista Ave.) |
914-965-1111 | www.xaviars.com

Smitten surveyors say Peter Kelly "has done it again" with this "spectacular" waterside venue in Yonkers – voted Westchester/Hudson
Valley's Most Popular – that "more than delivers on the hype" with
"knock-your-socks-off" "adventurous" New American cuisine
matched with "magnificent river views"; add in a "stellar" wine selection, "seamless service" and a "stunning" room, and even if a handful
huff "overpriced", for most it's a "triumph" all around; P.S. "try the prix
fixe lunch – it's quite a bargain", as are the small plates in the lounge.

Zephs' Ⓢ ⓜ *American/Eclectic*　　27　20　25　$54

Peekskill | 638 Central Ave. (bet. Union Ave. & Water St.) | 914-736-2159 |
www.zephsrestaurant.com

From the "adventurous appetizers" through the "exquisite entrees" to
the "decadent desserts", a "true celebration of food" is served up by
chef Victoria Zeph at this "lovely" New American–Eclectic restaurant
staffed by "pleasant but unobtrusive" servers; the "simply furnished
dining room" is in an "out-of-the-way spot" in Peekskill ("bring your
GPS!"), but between "gracious host Mike Zeph" and the "unhurried atmosphere", you're in for a "beautifully executed" "night of dining."

Menus, photos, voting and more – free at ZAGAT.com

ALPHABETICAL
PAGE INDEX

Abacus | Dallas/Ft. Worth 87
Abattoir | Atlanta 15
ABC Kitchen | New York City 200
Abe & Louie's | Boston 39
Abe & Louie's | Palm Beach 223
Absinthe | Naples, FL 177
Acacia | Tucson 296
Accanto | Portland, OR 243
Acme Oyster House | New Orleans 191
Acquerello | San Francisco Bay Area 268
Ad Hoc | San Francisco Bay Area 268
Adour at the St. Regis | Washington, DC 302
Aji 53 | Long Island 141
Ajihei | New Jersey 182
Akai Hana | Columbus 73
Alana's Food & Wine | Columbus 73
Alan Wong's | Honolulu 114
Alba Osteria & Enoteca | Portland, OR 242
Al Di La | New York City 200
Alex | Las Vegas 132
Alinea | Chicago 54
Alizé | Las Vegas 132
Alma | Minneapolis/St. Paul 172
Amada | Philadelphia 229
Amanda's | New Jersey 182
Ame | San Francisco Bay Area 268
American Restaurant, The | Kansas City 126
Américas | Houston 119
Amici | Dallas/Ft. Worth 87
Anchovies & Olives | Seattle 278
Andina | Portland, OR 242
André's | Las Vegas 132
André's | New Jersey 182
Angelini Osteria | Los Angeles 150
Angelo's Barbecue | Dallas/Ft. Worth 87
Annie Gunn's | St. Louis 286
Annisa | New York City 200
Anthony's Coal Fired Pizza | Ft. Lauderdale 109
Antonio's Cafe & Deli | Orlando 215
Antonio's La Fiamma Ristorante | Orlando 215
Antonio's Sand Lake | Orlando 215
A.O.C. | Los Angeles 150
Apizza Scholls | Portland, OR 242
Aquagrill | New York City 200
Aquarelle | Austin 28
Arch, The | Westchester/Hudson Valley 312
Area 31 | Miami 159
Argyll | Denver & Mountain Resorts 96
Aria | Atlanta 15
Arizona Inn | Tucson 296
Armani's | Tampa/Sarasota 291
Arthur Bryant's | Kansas City 126

Artist Point | Orlando 215
Artist's Palate | Westchester/Hudson Valley 312
Arun's | Chicago.. 54
A.R. Valentien | San Diego 262
Asanebo | Los Angeles 150
A16 | San Francisco Bay Area 268
Assaggi Bistro | Detroit 104
Atlanta Fish Market | Atlanta 15
Atlas Bistro | Phoenix/Scottsdale 237
Atlas Global Bistro | Detroit 104
Atlas Restaurant | St. Louis 286
Atmosphere | Atlanta 15
Auden's Kitchen | San Antonio 257
August | New Orleans 191
Au Petit Paris | Houston 119
Aureole | Las Vegas 132
avec | Chicago 54
Avenue | New Jersey 182
Avenues | Chicago 54
Azul | Miami 159
Azuma Sushi | Westchester/Hudson Valley 312
Azure | Honolulu 114
Babbo | New York City 200
Babette's Cafe | Atlanta.. 15
Babita Mexicuisine | Los Angeles 150
Bacchanalia | Atlanta... 16
Bacchus | Milwaukee... 167
Bacco Ristorante | Detroit 104
Backstreet Café | Houston 119
Baleen | Naples, FL... 177
Balthazar | New York City 200
Bambara | Salt Lake City & Mountain Resorts 252
B&B Ristorante | Las Vegas 132
Bankers Hill | San Diego 262
Barcelona | Columbus 73
Barcelona Restaurant & Wine Bar | Connecticut................... 78
Barclay Prime | Philadelphia 229
Bar La Grassa | Minneapolis/St. Paul............................ 172
Bar Masa | New York City 205
Barney's | Long Island 141
Barolo Grill | Denver & Mountain Resorts 96
Barrington's | Charlotte.. 48
Barrio Cafe | Phoenix/Scottsdale 237
Bartolotta | Las Vegas 133
Barton G. The Restaurant | Miami 159
Basho Japanese Brasserie | Boston............................... 39
Basi Italia | Columbus 74
Basilic | Orange County, CA 209
Bay Avenue Trattoria | New Jersey 182
Bayona | New Orleans 191
Bazaar by José Andrés, The | Los Angeles........................ 150
Beach Bistro | Tampa/Sarasota 291

ALPHA INDEX

Beachhouse at the Moana | Honolulu 114

Beast | Portland, OR 243

Bedford Post, The Barn | Westchester/Hudson Valley 312

Bellagio Buffet | Las Vegas 133

Bencotto | San Diego 262

Bentley's on 27 | Charlotte 48

Benu | San Francisco Bay Area 268

Bern's Steak House | Tampa/Sarasota 291

Bernard's | Connecticut 78

Besito | Long Island 141

Beso | Westchester/Hudson Valley 312

Beverly Hills Grill | Detroit 105

Biba | Sacramento 247

Bibou | Philadelphia 229

Bidwell Street Bistro | Sacramento 247

Biga on the Banks | San Antonio 257

Bijoux | Dallas/Ft. Worth 87

Binkley's Restaurant | Phoenix/Scottsdale 238

Birch & Barley/Churchkey | Washington, DC 302

Birchrunville Store Cafe | Philadelphia 229

Bisato | Seattle 278

Bistro Alex | Houston 119

Bistro Bonne Nuit | Connecticut 78

Bistro Daisy | New Orleans 191

Bistro 88 | Austin 28

Bistro 5 | Boston 39

Bistrot La Minette | Philadelphia 229

Bistro Vatel | San Antonio 258

Bizou Grill | Los Angeles 151

Blackbird | Chicago 54

Black Cat | Denver & Mountain Resorts 96

BlackSalt | Washington, DC 302

Bleu Provence | Naples, FL 177

BLT Steak | Atlanta 16

BLT Steak | Honolulu 115

BLT Steak | Miami 159

Blue Bottle Cafe | New Jersey 182

Blue Door at Delano | Miami 159

Blue Duck Tavern | Washington, DC 302

Blue Ginger | Boston 39

Blue Hill | New York City 201

Blue Hill at Stone Barns | Westchester/Hudson Valley 312

Blue Moon Fish Co. | Ft. Lauderdale 109

Blue Point Grille | Cleveland 68

Blue Restaurant & Bar | Charlotte 49

Blue Sage Vegetarian Grille | Philadelphia 230

Bluefin | Orange County, CA 209

Bluefin | Philadelphia 230

Bluefin | Tucson 297

BluePointe | Atlanta 16

Bluestem | Kansas City 126

Boathouse at Saugatuck | Connecticut 78

Boat Street Cafe | Seattle 278
Bobby Flay Steak | Atlantic City 24
Boca | Cincinnati 63
Bohanan's Prime Steaks & Seafood | San Antonio 258
Bolsa | Dallas/Ft. Worth 87
Boma – Flavors of Africa | Orlando 215
BonBonerie | Cincinnati 63
Bonefish Grill | Ft. Lauderdale 110
Bonefish Grill | Palm Beach 223
Bonefish Grill | Tampa/Sarasota 292
Bone's Restaurant | Atlanta 16
Bonnell's | Dallas/Ft. Worth 87
Bosphorous Turkish Cuisine | Orlando 215
Botero | Las Vegas 133
Boucherie | New Orleans 191
Bouchon | Las Vegas 133
Bouchon | Los Angeles 151
Bouchon | San Francisco Bay Area 269
Boudro's on the Riverwalk | San Antonio 258
Boulevard | San Francisco Bay Area 269
Boulevard Bistro | Sacramento 247
Bouley | New York City 201
Bourbon Steak | Miami 159
Bourbon Steak | Washington, DC 302
BP Oysterette | Los Angeles 151
Branch Water Tavern | Houston 119
Brandywine | Los Angeles 151
Brasserie by Niche | St. Louis 287
Bravo Nader! | Long Island 141
Bread Line | Washington, DC 303
Brennan's | Houston 119
Brigtsen's | New Orleans 192
Bristol Seafood Grill | Kansas City 127
Brown Dog Cafe | Cincinnati 63
Bryant & Cooper Steakhouse | Long Island 141
Buckhead Diner | Atlanta 17
Buckhorn Steak & Roadhouse | Sacramento 248
Buddakan | Atlantic City 24
Buddakan | New York City 201
Buddakan | Philadelphia 230
Buffet de la Gare | Westchester/Hudson Valley 313
Burger Bar | Las Vegas 133
Busy Bee Cafe | Atlanta 17
Cacharel | Dallas/Ft. Worth 88
Café & Bar Lurcat | Naples, FL 178
Café Atlántico/Minibar | Washington, DC 303
Cafe Bink | Phoenix/Scottsdale 238
Café Bizou | Los Angeles 151
Café Boulud | New York City 201
Café Boulud | Palm Beach 224
Cafe Brazil | Denver & Mountain Resorts 96
Café Castagna | Portland, OR 243

Café Chardonnay | Palm Beach 224
Café Cortina | Detroit 105
Café du Parc | Washington, DC 303
Cafe Juanita | Seattle 278
Café L'Europe | Palm Beach 224
Café Levain | Minneapolis/St. Paul 172
Cafe Martorano | Ft. Lauderdale 110
Cafe Matisse | New Jersey 183
Cafe Maxx | Ft. Lauderdale 110
Café Pacific | Dallas/Ft. Worth 88
Cafe Panache | New Jersey 183
Cafe Poca Cosa | Tucson 297
Cafe Ponte | Tampa/Sarasota 292
Café Rabelais | Houston 120
Caffe Casta Diva | Philadelphia 230
Caffè Molise | Salt Lake City & Mountain Resorts 252
Cakes & Ale | Atlanta 17
California Grill | Orlando 215
Cameron's American Bistro | Columbus 74
Campagne | Seattle 278
Campiello Ristorante | Naples, FL 178
Canlis | Seattle 278
Canoe | Atlanta 17
Canteen | San Francisco Bay Area 269
Cantinetta | Seattle 279
Canyon | Ft. Lauderdale 110
Canyon Ranch Grill | Miami 160
Capital Grille, The | Charlotte 49
Capital Grille, The | Detroit 105
Capital Grille, The | Ft. Lauderdale 111
Capital Grille, The | Kansas City 127
Capital Grille, The | Orlando 216
Capital Grille, The | Philadelphia 230
Capital Grille, The | Tampa/Sarasota 292
Capriccio | Atlantic City 24
Captain Charlie's Reef Grill | Palm Beach 224
Cardwell's at the Plaza | St. Louis 287
Carillon, The | Austin 28
Carlos' | Chicago 55
Carmelita | Seattle 279
Carole Peck's Good News Cafe | Connecticut 78
Carpe Diem | Charlotte 49
Casa D'Angelo | Ft. Lauderdale 111
Casa D'Angelo | Palm Beach 224
Casa Vicente | Tucson 297
Castagna | Portland, OR 243
Catalan Food and Wine | Houston 120
Caterina de Medici | Westchester/Hudson Valley 313
Cavey's Restaurants | Connecticut 79
Central Michel Richard | Washington, DC 303
Chachama Grill | Long Island 142
Chalk Food + Wine | Cincinnati 64

Chameleon Cafe | Baltimore/Annapolis. 33
Charleston | Baltimore/Annapolis 33
Charlie Palmer at Bloomingdale's | Orange County, CA 209
Charlie Palmer at the Joule | Dallas/Ft. Worth 88
Charlie Trotter's | Chicago 55
Chatham's Place | Orlando 216
Cheesecake Factory | Connecticut 79
Cheesecake Factory | Long Island. 142
Cheesecake Factory | New Jersey. 183
Chef Mavro | Honolulu 115
Chef Vola's | Atlantic City 25
Chego! | Los Angeles 151
Chez François | Cleveland 68
Chez Jean-Pierre Bistro | Palm Beach. 225
Chez Nous | Houston. 120
Chez Panisse | San Francisco Bay Area 269
Chez Panisse Café | San Francisco Bay Area 269
Chez Roux | Houston 120
Chez Shea | Seattle 279
Chima Brazilian Steakhouse | Ft. Lauderdale. 111
China Gourmet | Cincinnati. 64
Chinato | Cleveland 69
Chinois on Main | Los Angeles 152
Chops City Grill | Naples, FL 178
Chops Lobster Bar | Atlanta 17
Chops Lobster Bar | Palm Beach 225
Christini's Ristorante Italiano | Orlando. 216
Churrascos | Houston 120
Chuy's | Austin 29
Cinghiale | Baltimore/Annapolis. 34
Cítricos | Orlando. 216
Citronelle | Washington, DC 303
Citrus | San Antonio. 258
CityZen | Washington, DC 304
Clancy's | New Orleans 192
Clementine | Baltimore/Annapolis. 34
Clio/Uni | Boston 39
Clyde Common | Portland, OR 243
Cochon | New Orleans. 192
Cochon Butcher | New Orleans. 192
Colt & Gray | Denver & Mountain Resorts 96
Columbia | Orlando 216
Columbia | Tampa/Sarasota 292
Columbia Café | Tampa/Sarasota 293
Columbus Fish Market | Columbus. 74
Columbus Park Trattoria | Connecticut 79
Commander's Palace | New Orleans 192
Common Grill | Detroit 105
Community Table | Connecticut 79
Continental | Atlantic City. 25
Cookery, The | Westchester/Hudson Valley 313
Coppa | Boston. 40

Copper Onion, The | Salt Lake City & Mountain Resorts 252
Coquette | New Orleans 193
Coquette Cafe | Milwaukee 167
Corduroy | Washington, DC 304
Cork | Washington, DC 304
Coromandel | Connecticut 79
Corson Building | Seattle 279
Cosmos | Minneapolis/St. Paul 173
Crabtree's Kittle House | Westchester/Hudson Valley 313
Craft | Atlanta 18
Craft Dallas | Dallas/Ft. Worth 88
Craftsteak | Las Vegas 134
Craigie on Main | Boston 40
Crop | Cleveland 69
Crossing, The | St. Louis 287
Crush | Seattle 279
Cucharamama | New Jersey 183
Cucina Toscana | Salt Lake City & Mountain Resorts 253
CulinAriane | New Jersey 183
Cumin | Cincinnati 64
Cyclo | Phoenix/Scottsdale 238
Cypress | New Orleans 193
Cyrus | San Francisco Bay Area 270
Da Campo Osteria | Ft. Lauderdale 111
Dahlia Lounge | Seattle 280
Dakota, The | New Orleans 193
Da Marco | Houston 121
Damian's Cucina Italiana | Houston 121
D'Amico Kitchen | Minneapolis/St. Paul 173
Daniel | New York City 201
Dante | Cleveland 69
DaPietro's | Connecticut 80
Dario's | Long Island 142
Daveed's at 934 | Cincinnati 64
Dave's Grill | Long Island 142
David Burke Fromagerie | New Jersey 184
DC Coast | Washington, DC 304
DeepWood | Columbus 74
Degustation | New York City 201
Delancey | Seattle 280
Delfina | San Francisco Bay Area 270
Delfino | Boston 40
Del Frisco's Double Eagle Steak House | Dallas/Ft. Worth 88
Del Frisco's Double Eagle Steak House | Denver & Mountain Resorts 96
Del Frisco's Double Eagle Steak House | Houston 121
Del Frisco's Double Eagle Steak House | Las Vegas 134
Del Frisco's Prime Steak & Lobster | Orlando 217
Della Femina | Long Island 142
Delmonico Steakhouse | Las Vegas 134
DeLorenzo's Tomato Pies | New Jersey 184
Delphine | Los Angeles 152
Del Posto | New York City 202

Dewey's Pizza | Cincinnati 64
Di Fara | New York City 202
Din Tai Fung | Los Angeles. 152
di Paolo | Atlanta 18
Di Pasquale's Italian Market | Baltimore/Annapolis 34
Dish, The | Tucson 297
Dmitri's | Philadelphia 231
Doc Ford Fort Myers Beach | Naples, FL 178
Doc Ford's Sanibel Rum Bar & Grille | Naples, FL 178
Dock's Oyster House | Atlantic City 25
Dogwood | Atlanta. 18
Dogwood | Baltimore/Annapolis 34
Dolce | Charlotte 49
Dolce de Palma | Palm Beach 225
Dolce Vita Pizzeria Enoteca | Houston. 121
Dominic's | St. Louis 287
Dominic's Trattoria | St. Louis 287
Donatello | Tampa/Sarasota. 293
Donovan's Steak & Chop House | San Diego 263
Dough | San Antonio 258
Dovetail | New York City 202
Downtown 140 | Cleveland 69
Driskill Grill | Austin 29
Duke's Canoe Club | Honolulu 115
Duo | Denver & Mountain Resorts 97
Earle, The | Detroit. 105
Eastern Standard | Boston. 40
Ebbitt Room | New Jersey 184
Ecco | Atlanta 18
Eddie Martini's | Milwaukee 168
Eddie Merlot's | Columbus 74
Eddie V's Prime Seafood | Austin 29
Eddie V's Prime Seafood | Dallas/Ft. Worth 89
Eddie V's Prime Seafood | Houston 121
Eddie V's Prime Seafood | Phoenix/Scottsdale 238
Eduardo de San Angel | Ft. Lauderdale. 111
Eiffel Tower | Las Vegas 134
El Bizcocho | San Diego 263
El Charro Café | Tucson 297
elements | New Jersey. 184
1111 Mississippi | St. Louis. 287
Eleven Madison Park | New York City. 202
11 Maple Street | Palm Beach. 225
Elizabeth's Cafe at Perfect Parties | Connecticut 80
Ella Dining Room & Bar | Sacramento. 248
Ellerbe Fine Food | Dallas/Ft. Worth 89
Elway's | Denver & Mountain Resorts 97
Emeril's | New Orleans 193
Emeril's Orlando | Orlando 217
Emeril's Tchoup Chop | Orlando. 217
Enzo's Restaurant on the Lake | Orlando 217
Eos | Miami. 160

Visit ZAGAT.mobi from your mobile phone

Equinox | Washington, DC 304
Erna's Elderberry House | San Francisco Bay Area 270
Escargot 41 | Naples, FL 178
Escoffier Restaurant | Westchester/Hudson Valley 311
Euphemia Haye | Tampa/Sarasota 293
Eve | Detroit 106
Everest | Chicago 55
Eve, Restaurant | Washington, DC 305
EVOO | Boston 40
Extra Virgin | Kansas City 127
Fahrenheit | Cleveland 69
Faidley's Seafood | Baltimore/Annapolis 34
Farmhaus | St. Louis 288
Fascino | New Jersey 184
Fearing's | Dallas/Ft. Worth 89
Feast | Houston 121
Feast | Tucson 298
Feng Asian Bistro | Connecticut 80
Ferraro's | Las Vegas 134
Fiamma | Charlotte 49
Fig Tree | Charlotte 49
Fiorella's Jack Stack | Kansas City 127
Firebox | Connecticut 80
Firefly | Las Vegas 135
Fire Food & Drink | Cleveland 70
Firehouse | Sacramento 248
FireLake | Minneapolis/St. Paul 173
fish | Philadelphia 231
Five Crowns | Orange County, CA 210
Five Sixty Wolfgang Puck | Dallas/Ft. Worth 89
Flagstaff House | Denver & Mountain Resorts 97
Floataway Cafe | Atlanta 19
Flying Fig | Cleveland 70
Flying V | Tucson 298
FnB Restaurant | Phoenix/Scottsdale 238
Fond | Philadelphia 231
Fonda San Miguel | Austin 29
Forage | Salt Lake City & Mountain Resorts 253
Forté | Palm Beach 225
42 | Westchester/Hudson Valley 314
Fountain Restaurant | Philadelphia 231
Four Rivers Smokehouse | Orlando 217
Four Seasons – The Restaurant | Palm Beach 226
410 Bank Street | New Jersey 185
4th & Swift | Atlanta 19
Frances | San Francisco Bay Area 270
Francesco | Miami 160
Frank Fat's | Sacramento 248
Frank Pepe Pizzeria | Connecticut 80
Frank Pepe's The Spot | Connecticut 81
Frasca Food and Wine | Denver & Mountain Resorts 97
Fratelli Lyon | Miami 160

Frederick's | San Antonio. 258
Frederick's Bistro | San Antonio 258
Freelance Cafe & Wine Bar | Westchester/Hudson Valley. 314
French Laundry, The | San Francisco Bay Area 270
French Room | Dallas/Ft. Worth. 89
Frog and the Peach | New Jersey. 185
Frontera Grill | Chicago 55
Fruition | Denver & Mountain Resorts 98
Gabbi's Mexican Kitchen | Orange County, CA. 210
Galatoire's | New Orleans 193
Gargoyles on the Square | Boston. 41
Gari | New York City 202
Gary Danko | San Francisco Bay Area. 271
Gautreau's | New Orleans 194
Genoa | Portland, OR. 243
George's California Modern | San Diego 263
George's Ocean Terrace | San Diego 263
Gian-Tony's | St. Louis 288
Gibsons Bar & Steakhouse | Chicago 56
Gilmore's | Philadelphia. 231
Ginger Park | Boston 41
Girasole | Atlantic City 25
Glass Wall | Houston. 122
Glenmere | Westchester/Hudson Valley 314
G. Michael's Bistro & Bar | Columbus 74
Good Food on Montford | Charlotte. 50
Gorbals, The | Los Angeles 152
Gotham Bar & Grill | New York City 203
Gotham Steak | Miami. 160
Grace | Dallas/Ft. Worth. 89
Gramercy Tavern | New York City 203
Grange | Sacramento. 248
Graziano's Restaurant | Miami 161
Greenhouse Tavern | Cleveland 70
Green Leaf | Seattle. 280
Green Zebra | Chicago. 56
Grill at Hacienda del Sol | Tucson 298
Grill at Leon Springs | San Antonio. 259
Grille 66 | Ft. Lauderdale 112
Grocery, The | New York City 203
Grouper & Chips | Naples, FL 179
Grouse Mountain Grill | Denver & Mountain Resorts. 98
Gumbo's | Austin 29
Guy Savoy | Las Vegas 135
GW Fins | New Orleans 194
Hakkasan | Miami 161
Hal's on Old Ivy | Atlanta 19
Hamersley's Bistro | Boston 41
Hana Japanese Restaurant | San Francisco Bay Area 271
Harvest | St. Louis 288
Harvest on Fort Pond | Long Island. 143
Harvest on Hudson | Westchester/Hudson Valley 314

ALPHA INDEX

Harvest Supper | Connecticut 81
Harvest Vine | Seattle.. 280
Hatfield's | Los Angeles 152
Hattie's | Dallas/Ft. Worth....................................... 90
Haven | Houston 122
Hawks | Sacramento 249
Heartland | Minneapolis/St. Paul 173
Heathman Restaurant, The | Portland, OR 244
Helena's Hawaiian Food | Honolulu............................. 115
Hell's Backbone Grill | Salt Lake City & Mountain Resorts 253
Herbfarm | Seattle... 280
Herbsaint | New Orleans 194
Higgins Restaurant & Bar | Portland, OR......................... 244
High West Distillery | Salt Lake City & Mountain Resorts 253
Hinterland Erie Street Gastropub | Milwaukee.................... 168
Hiro's Yakko San | Miami 161
Hiroshi Eurasion Tapas | Honolulu............................... 115
Hobbit, The | Orange County, CA 210
Hoku's | Honolulu 115
Holeman and Finch | Atlanta 19
Honey Pig Gooldaegee Korean Grill | Washington, DC 305
Hong Hua | Detroit 106
Horizons | Philadelphia.. 232
Hot Doug's | Chicago 56
Hudson's on the Bend | Austin................................... 30
Hue | Orlando 218
Hugo's | Houston.. 122
Hungry Mother | Boston.. 41
Hyde Park Prime Steakhouse | Columbus 75
Hy-Vong | Miami... 161
Ibiza | Connecticut 81
Ibiza | Houston.. 122
Il Barilotto | Westchester/Hudson Valley 314
Il Barone Ristorante | Orange County, CA 210
Il Capriccio | Boston 41
Il Casale | Boston.. 42
Il Cenàcolo | Westchester/Hudson Valley 315
Il Gabbiano | Miami.. 161
Ilios Noche | Charlotte 50
Il Mulino | New York City 203
Il Mulino New York | Atlantic City 25
Il Mulino New York | Long Island 143
Il Sogno | San Antonio... 259
Il Terrazzo Carmine | Seattle 280
I M Tapas | Naples, FL.. 179
Indika | Houston 122
Inn at Little Washington | Washington, DC 305
In-N-Out Burger | Los Angeles................................... 152
In-N-Out Burger | Orange County, CA............................ 210
Iris | New Orleans 194
Iron Horse Grill | Westchester/Hudson Valley 315
izakaya | Atlantic City... 25

Izakaya Den | Denver & Mountain Resorts 98
Jacques-Imo's Café | New Orleans. 194
Jake's Famous Crawfish | Portland, OR 244
Jake's Fine Dining | Milwaukee 168
James | Philadelphia 232
J&G Steakhouse | Washington, DC 305
Janos | Tucson 298
Jardinière | San Francisco Bay Area 271
Jasper's | Dallas/Ft. Worth. 90
Jasper's | Kansas City 128
Jax Fish House | Denver & Mountain Resorts 98
Jax Kitchen | Tucson 298
J BAR | Tucson 299
JCT. Kitchen & Bar | Atlanta 19
Jean Georges | New York City. 203
Jean-Louis | Connecticut 81
Jeff Ruby's Carlo & Johnny | Cincinnati 65
Jeff Ruby's Precinct | Cincinnati 65
Jeff Ruby's Steakhouse | Cincinnati 65
Jiko – The Cooking Place | Orlando. 218
Joel Palmer House | Portland, OR. 244
Joël Robuchon | Las Vegas 135
Joe's Seafood, Prime Steak & Stone Crab | Chicago 56
Joe's Stone Crab | Miami. 162
Joe T. Garcia's | Dallas/Ft. Worth 90
Johnny's Bar | Cleveland 70
Johnny's Half Shell | Washington, DC 306
Johnny's Pizzeria | Westchester/Hudson Valley 315
John's Roast Pork | Philadelphia 232
Josef's | Ft. Lauderdale 112
Joule | Seattle. 281
Justus Drugstore: A Restaurant | Kansas City. 128
Kai | Phoenix/Scottsdale. 238
Kanomwan | Houston 122
Karen Krasne's Extraordinary Desserts | San Diego 264
Karen Krasne's Little Italy | San Diego 263
Karl Ratzsch's | Milwaukee 168
Katsu Japanese | Chicago 57
Kaygetsu | San Francisco Bay Area 271
Kee Grill | Palm Beach 226
Ken's Artisan Pizza | Portland, OR 244
Kevin Rathbun Steak | Atlanta 20
Keystone Ranch | Denver & Mountain Resorts 98
Kincaid's | Minneapolis/St. Paul. 173
Kiran's | Houston 123
Kisaku Sushi | Seattle. 281
Kitchen, The | Denver & Mountain Resorts 99
Kitchen, The | Sacramento 249
Kitchen A Bistro | Long Island. 143
Kith & Kin | Chicago. 57
Kokkari Estiatorio | San Francisco Bay Area. 272
Komi | Washington, DC 306

ALPHA INDEX

Korma Sutra | Kansas City 128
Kotobuki | Long Island. 143
K-Paul's Louisiana Kitchen | New Orleans. 195
K Restaurant | Orlando 218
Kru | Sacramento. 249
Kuma's Corner | Chicago 57
Kyma | Atlanta. 20
La Belle Vie | Minneapolis/St. Paul 174
La Boca | New Orleans 195
La Bonne Soupe Café | Sacramento. 249
La Brochette Bistro | Ft. Lauderdale. 112
La Campania | Boston 42
La Carta de Oaxaca | Seattle 281
La Condesa | Austin 30
La Crémaillère | Westchester/Hudson Valley 315
Lacroix at The Rittenhouse | Philadelphia. 232
La Folie | San Francisco Bay Area. 272
La Frite | San Antonio 259
La Gloria Ice House | San Antonio 259
La Grenouille | New York City. 203
La Grotta | Atlanta 20
La Grotta Ravinia | Atlanta 20
Lake House | Long Island 143
Lake Park Bistro | Milwaukee 168
L'Albatros | Cleveland. 70
La Luce | Orlando 218
Lambert's | Dallas/Ft. Worth 90
La Mer | Honolulu 116
La Merenda | Milwaukee 168
L'Angolo | Philadelphia 232
L'Antibes | Columbus 75
Lanny's Alta Cocina Mexicana | Dallas/Ft. Worth 90
La Nuovo Cucina | Orlando. 218
La Panetière | Westchester/Hudson Valley 315
La Plage | Long Island 144
La Provence | New Orleans. 195
Lark, The | Detroit 106
Lark | Seattle 281
LaSpada's Original Hoagies | Ft. Lauderdale. 112
L'Atelier | Denver & Mountain Resorts 99
L'Atelier de Joël Robuchon | Las Vegas 135
L'Atelier de Joël Robuchon | New York City 204
La Toque | San Francisco Bay Area. 272
La Tour | Denver & Mountain Resorts 99
L'Auberge Chez François | Washington, DC 306
L'Auberge Provençale | Washington, DC 306
Laurelhurst Market | Portland, OR. 244
Lazy Ox Canteen | Los Angeles 153
Le Bar Lyonnais | Philadelphia 233
Le Bec-Fin | Philadelphia. 233
Le Bernardin | New York City 204
Le Bistro | Honolulu. 116

Le Cellier Steakhouse | Orlando 219
Le Cirque | Las Vegas.................................... 136
Le Coq au Vin | Orlando.................................. 219
Le Farm | Connecticut 81
Le Fou Frog | Kansas City................................ 128
Legal Sea Foods | Boston 42
Le Gourmand | Seattle................................... 281
Leila's | Los Angeles..................................... 153
Le Meritage | New Orleans 195
Le Midi | San Antonio 259
Le Mistral | Houston 123
Lemon Grass | Sacramento 249
Le Petit Cafe | Connecticut 82
Le Pigeon | Portland, OR 245
Le Rendez-Vous | Tucson................................ 299
Le Rêve Patisserie & Café | Milwaukee.................... 169
Les Nomades | Chicago 57
L'Escalier | Palm Beach 226
Le Soir | Long Island.................................... 144
L'Espalier | Boston 42
Le Virtù | Philadelphia 233
Libby's | Tampa/Sarasota 293
Liberty, The | Charlotte 50
Liberty House Restaurant | New Jersey 185
Lidia's | Kansas City.................................... 128
Lilette | New Orleans.................................... 195
Limani | Long Island.................................... 144
Lincoln | New York City 204
Lindey's | Columbus..................................... 75
Linwoods | Baltimore/Annapolis.......................... 35
Little Moir's Food Shack | Palm Beach 226
Little Moir's Leftovers Café | Palm Beach 226
Little Saigon | Atlantic City 26
Lodge Restaurant of Castle Hills, The | San Antonio........ 259
Logan | Detroit 106
Log Haven | Salt Lake City & Mountain Resorts 253
Lola | Cleveland 71
Lolita | Cleveland 71
Lolita | Philadelphia 233
Lonesome Dove Western Bistro | Dallas/Ft. Worth 90
Lon's at the Hermosa | Phoenix/Scottsdale................. 239
Lorena's | New Jersey 185
Lotus of Siam | Las Vegas 136
Lou Malnati's Pizzeria | Chicago.......................... 57
L2O | Chicago 58
Luca d'Italia | Denver & Mountain Resorts 99
Luce | Charlotte 50
Lucia's | Minneapolis/St. Paul 174
Lucques | Los Angeles................................... 153
Lula Cafe | Chicago 58
Luma on Park | Orlando................................. 219
Lumière | Boston 43

Luxe Kitchen | Cleveland 71
M | Columbus 75
Magnolia Pancake Haus | San Antonio 260
Makoto | Washington, DC 306
Mandarin, The | Salt Lake City & Mountain Resorts 254
Manny's Steakhouse | Minneapolis/St. Paul 174
Manresa | San Francisco Bay Area 272
Mansion, The | Dallas/Ft. Worth 91
Marcello's La Sirena | Palm Beach 226
Marcel's | Washington, DC 307
Marché Moderne | Orange County, CA 211
Marco's Coal-Fired Pizzeria | Denver & Mountain Resorts 99
Marea | New York City 204
Marinus | San Francisco Bay Area 272
Mariposa, The | Salt Lake City & Mountain Resorts 254
Mark, The | New York City 204
Market | Boston 43
Market Restaurant & Bar | San Diego 264
Market Street Grill | Salt Lake City & Mountain Resorts 254
Mark's American Cuisine | Houston 123
Maroni Cuisine | Long Island 144
Martine | Salt Lake City & Mountain Resorts 254
Martinique Bistro | New Orleans 196
Mas | New York City 205
Masa | New York City 205
Masa's | San Francisco Bay Area 273
Mashiko | Seattle 282
Mason Street Grill | Milwaukee 169
Masraff's | Houston 123
Mastro's City Hall Steakhouse | Phoenix/Scottsdale 239
Mastro's Ocean Club | Orange County, CA 211
Mastro's Ocean Club | Phoenix/Scottsdale 239
Mastro's Steakhouse | Los Angeles 153
Mastro's Steakhouse | Orange County, CA 211
Match | Connecticut 82
Matsuhisa | Denver & Mountain Resorts 100
Matsuhisa | Los Angeles 154
Matsuri | Miami 162
Matyson | Philadelphia 233
Max Downtown | Connecticut 82
Max's Oyster Bar | Connecticut 82
Mayflower Inn & Spa | Connecticut 82
Maynards Market & Kitchen | Tucson 299
Mazza | Salt Lake City & Mountain Resorts 254
McKendrick's Steak House | Atlanta 20
McNinch House | Charlotte 50
Meat Market | Miami 162
Mehndi | New Jersey 185
Meigas | Connecticut 82
Mélisse | Los Angeles 154
Mercat a la Planxa | Chicago 58
Mercato | Westchester/Hudson Valley 315

Meritage | Boston 43
Meritage | Milwaukee 169
Meritage | Minneapolis/St. Paul 174
Mesón 923 | New Orleans........................... 196
Métro Bis | Connecticut............................ 83
Metropolitan Grill | Seattle 282
MF Buckhead | Atlanta 21
MF Sushibar | Atlanta 21
Mi Cocina | Dallas/Ft. Worth 91
Mi Nidito | Tucson 299
Mia | Atlantic City 26
Mia's | Dallas/Ft. Worth 91
Michael | Chicago 58
Michael Mina | Las Vegas 136
Michael's Genuine Food & Drink | Miami 162
Michael Smith | Kansas City 129
Michel's | Honolulu 116
Michy's | Miami 162
Mikuni | Sacramento 250
MiLa | New Orleans................................ 196
Mille Fleurs | San Diego........................... 264
Milos, Estiatorio | New York City 205
Mirabelle, Restaurant | Long Island 144
Mira Mare Ristorante | Naples, FL 179
Mirko's | Long Island 144
Mise en Place | Tampa/Sarasota 293
Mission, The | Phoenix/Scottsdale 239
Mistral Kitchen | Seattle 282
Mitchell's Steakhouse | Columbus 75
Mix | Las Vegas 136
Mizuna | Denver & Mountain Resorts 100
mk | Chicago...................................... 59
Mockingbird Bistro Wine Bar | Houston 123
Modern, The | New York City 205
Modern Cafe | Minneapolis/St. Paul 174
Modo Mio | Philadelphia........................... 234
Momocho | Cleveland 71
Momofuku Ko | New York City 205
Montagna | Denver & Mountain Resorts 100
Montgomery Inn | Cincinnati 65
Moretti's of Arlington | Columbus 76
Morimoto | Philadelphia........................... 234
Morimoto Napa | San Francisco Bay Area 273
Mori Sushi | Los Angeles 154
Morton's The Steakhouse | Atlantic City........... 26
Morton's The Steakhouse | Chicago................ 59
Morton's The Steakhouse | Cincinnati.............. 66
Morton's The Steakhouse | Houston 123
Morton's The Steakhouse | Orlando 219
Morton's The Steakhouse | San Diego.............. 264
Mosaic | Long Island 145
Mosca's | New Orleans............................. 196

ALPHA INDEX

Mozaic | Tampa/Sarasota 294
Mr. Bill's Terrace Inn | Baltimore/Annapolis 35
Mr. B's Bistro | New Orleans.................................. 196
Mr. John's Ristorante | New Orleans 197
Mulino's of Westchester | Westchester/Hudson Valley 316
Mulvaney's B&L | Sacramento 250
Muss & Turner's | Atlanta.................................... 21
M Waterfront Grille | Naples, FL 179
Myers + Chang | Boston 43
Nada | Cincinnati.. 66
Nagahama | Long Island 145
Naha | Chicago 59
Nana | Dallas/Ft. Worth 91
Nan Thai Fine Dining | Atlanta 21
Naoe | Miami... 163
Napa & Co. | Connecticut 83
Napa Rose | Orange County, CA 211
Naples Tomato | Naples, FL 179
Neighborhood Services | Dallas/Ft. Worth...................... 92
Nell's | Seattle 282
Neptune Oyster | Boston 43
New York Prime | Atlanta 21
New York Prime | Palm Beach 227
Niche | St. Louis.. 288
Nicholas | New Jersey....................................... 185
Nick & Sam's | Dallas/Ft. Worth 92
Nick & Toni's | Long Island 145
Nicola's | Cincinnati 66
Nina | Westchester/Hudson Valley............................. 316
Ninety Acres at Natirar | New Jersey 186
Nisen Sushi | Long Island 145
Nishino | Seattle 282
Nisi Estiatorio | New Jersey 186
Nobhill Tavern | Las Vegas 136
Nobu | Las Vegas... 137
Nobu | New York City.. 206
Nobu 57 | New York City 206
Nobu Miami Beach | Miami 163
Nobu, Next Door | New York City 206
Nobu Waikiki | Honolulu...................................... 116
Noca | Phoenix/Scottsdale.................................... 239
Noir Food & Wine | Los Angeles 154
NoMI | Chicago 59
No. 9 Park | Boston 44
Nopa | San Francisco Bay Area................................ 273
Norman's | Orlando 219
North Fork Table & Inn | Long Island 145
Nuestra Cocina | Portland, OR 245
Obelisk | Washington, DC 307
Oceanaire Seafood Room | Minneapolis/St. Paul 175
Oceanaire Seafood Room | Orlando 220
Ocean House | Westchester/Hudson Valley 316

Oceanique | Chicago 60
Oceano Bistro | St. Louis 288
Ocean Prime | Orlando 220
Ocean Prime | Tampa/Sarasota 294
O'Connell's Pub | St. Louis 288
Oishii | Boston 44
Oishii Boston | Boston 44
Oklahoma Joe's Barbecue | Kansas City 129
OLA | Miami 163
Old Homestead | Atlantic City 26
Old Vine Café | Orange County, CA 211
Oleana | Boston 44
Olivéa | Denver & Mountain Resorts 100
Olivia | Austin 30
One Restaurant & Lounge | New Orleans 197
one sixtyblue | Chicago 60
OneSpeed | Sacramento 250
112 Eatery | Minneapolis/St. Paul 175
Opus | Denver & Mountain Resorts 100
Orchids | Honolulu 116
Orchids at Palm Court | Cincinnati 66
Orient, The | Long Island 146
Ortanique on the Mile | Miami 163
Osteria | Philadelphia 234
Osteria del Mondo | Milwaukee 169
Osteria del Teatro | Miami 163
Osteria Mozza | Los Angeles 154
Owen's Fish Camp | Tampa/Sarasota 294
O Ya | Boston 44
P.F. Chang's China Bistro | Atlantic City 26
P.F. Chang's China Bistro | Charlotte 51
P.F. Chang's China Bistro | Phoenix/Scottsdale 240
Paci | Connecticut 83
Paesanos | San Antonio 260
Paesanos Riverwalk | San Antonio 260
Paesanos 1604 | San Antonio 260
Paggi House | Austin 30
Pago | Salt Lake City & Mountain Resorts 255
Painted Lady | Portland, OR 245
Palace, The | Cincinnati 66
Palace Arms | Denver & Mountain Resorts 101
Palena | Washington, DC 307
Paley's Place Bistro & Bar | Portland, OR 245
Palm, The | Atlantic City 26
Palm, The | Miami 163
Palm, The | Orlando 220
Palme d'Or | Miami 164
Palomino | Cincinnati 67
Pamplemousse Grille | San Diego 264
Panama Hatties | Long Island 146
Pane Rustica | Tampa/Sarasota 294
Panzano | Denver & Mountain Resorts 101

Pappadeaux | Houston 124
Pappas Bros. Steakhouse | Dallas/Ft. Worth 92
Pappas Bros. Steakhouse | Houston 124
Pappy's Smokehouse | St. Louis 289
Paragary's Bar & Oven | Sacramento 250
Parallax | Cleveland. 71
Park Ave | Orange County, CA 212
Park Kitchen | Portland, OR 245
Pascal's on Ponce | Miami 164
Paseo | Seattle 282
Pasta Nostra | Connecticut 83
Pastiche | Milwaukee 169
Pastiche Modern Eatery | Tucson. 299
Patois | New Orleans. 197
Paul Manno's | St. Louis 289
Paul's Homewood Café | Baltimore/Annapolis. 35
Pazzo! Cucina Italiana | Naples, FL 179
Peacock Inn | New Jersey 186
Pelagia Trattoria | Tampa/Sarasota. 294
Pelican Club | New Orleans 197
Perbacco | San Francisco Bay Area 273
Perla's | Austin 30
Per Se | New York City 206
Peter Luger | Long Island 146
Peter Luger Steak House | New York City 206
Peter's Inn | Baltimore/Annapolis 35
Petit Louis Bistro | Baltimore/Annapolis 35
Petit Robert Bistro | Boston 45
Picasso | Las Vegas 137
Piccola Italia | New Jersey 186
Piccolo | Long Island 146
Picholine | New York City 206
Pineapple Room | Honolulu 117
Ping Pang Pong | Las Vegas 137
Piropos | Kansas City 129
Pizzeria Bianco | Phoenix/Scottsdale 240
Pizzeria Mozza | Los Angeles. 155
Pizzeria Ortica | Orange County, CA 212
Pizzeria Paradiso | Washington, DC 307
Pizzeria 712 | Salt Lake City & Mountain Resorts. 255
Plates | Westchester/Hudson Valley. 316
Plaza Cafe | Long Island 146
Pluckemin Inn | New Jersey 186
Pok Pok | Portland, OR 246
Pomme | St. Louis 289
Por Fin | Miami 164
Prado at Balboa Park | San Diego. 265
Prezza | Boston 45
Pricci | Atlanta. 22
Primavera Ristorante | San Diego 265
Prime One Twelve | Miami 164
Prime Rib | Baltimore/Annapolis 36

Prime Rib | Philadelphia...234
Prime Rib | Washington, DC 307
Prime Steakhouse | Las Vegas...137
Primo | Orlando 220
Primo | Tucson 300
Prospect | San Francisco Bay Area 273
Providence | Los Angeles..155
Publican, The | Chicago..60
Pumpkin | Philadelphia 234
Punch Neapolitan Pizza | Minneapolis/St. Paul 175
Pura Vida | Atlanta..22
Quiessence Restaurant & Wine Bar | Phoenix/Scottsdale...........240
Quince | San Francisco Bay Area 274
Quinones Room at Bacchanalia | Atlanta............................22
Raglan Road Irish Pub & Restaurant | Orlando 220
Rainbow Palace | Ft. Lauderdale......................................112
Raku | Las Vegas 137
Ralph's on the Park | New Orleans 197
Ramos House Café | Orange County, CA............................212
Ram's Head Inn | New Jersey 187
Rancho Pinot | Phoenix/Scottsdale 240
Rasika | Washington, DC...308
Rathbun's | Atlanta 22
Rat's | New Jersey 187
Rattlesnake Club | Detroit..106
Ravenous Pig, The | Orlando 221
Ray's Hell Burger | Washington, DC.................................308
Ray's Hell Burger Too | Washington, DC 308
R Bar & Restaurant | Kansas City 129
RDG + Bar Annie | Houston...124
Rebeccas | Connecticut 83
Red Iguana | Salt Lake City & Mountain Resorts 255
Red Iguana 2 | Salt Lake City & Mountain Resorts 255
Red Light | Miami..164
Red O | Los Angeles...155
Red The Steakhouse | Cleveland.......................................72
Reef | Houston 124
Refectory | Columbus 76
Rendezvous | Boston 45
Restaurant Alba | Philadelphia 235
Restaurant Insignia | San Antonio 260
Restaurant Latour | New Jersey 187
Restaurant X & Bully Boy Bar | Westchester/Hudson Valley 316
Restaurant Zoë | Seattle 283
Rialto | Boston 45
Rialto | Long Island..147
Rigsby's Kitchen | Columbus...76
Rioja | Denver & Mountain Resorts 101
RioMar | New Orleans...198
RIS | Washington, DC 308
Ristorante Bartolotta | Milwaukee 170
Ritz-Carlton Dining Room | San Francisco Bay Area 274

ALPHA INDEX

River Café | New York City 206
River Lane Inn | Milwaukee. 170
River Palm Terrace | New Jersey 187
RN74 | San Francisco Bay Area 274
Roast | Detroit. 107
Roberto | New York City 207
Romeo's Cafe | Miami. 165
Room 39 | Kansas City 129
Roots Restaurant & Cellar | Milwaukee. 170
Roppongi | San Diego 265
Rosemary's | Las Vegas 138
Rover's | Seattle. 283
Royal China | New Orleans. 198
Roy's | Honolulu 117
Roy's | Naples, FL 180
Roy's | Orlando 221
Roy's | Tampa/Sarasota 295
Rudy's Country Store and Bar-B-Q | San Antonio. . . 260
Rugby Grille | Detroit 107
Ruth's Chris Steak House | Atlantic City. 27
Ruth's Chris Steak House | Naples, FL. 180
Ruth's Chris Steak House | New Jersey 187
Ruth's Chris Steak House | Orlando 221
Saam at The Bazaar by José Andrés | Los Angeles. . . . 155
Saddle Peak Lodge | Los Angeles 155
Saddle River Inn | New Jersey 188
Saffron Restaurant & Lounge | Minneapolis/St. Paul. . . 175
Sagami | New Jersey 188
Sage | Las Vegas 138
Saint-Emilion | Dallas/Ft. Worth 92
Sala da Pranzo | Milwaukee 170
Salt | Baltimore/Annapolis 36
Salt Lick | Austin 30
Salt Rock Grill | Tampa/Sarasota. 295
Saltwater | Detroit. 107
Salumi | Seattle 283
Sammy's Woodfired Pizza | San Diego 265
Samos | Baltimore/Annapolis. 36
Sam's | Boston. 45
Sanaa | Orlando. 221
Sandbar Fish House & Market | San Antonio 260
Sanford | Milwaukee 170
Sansei | Honolulu 117
Sapore | Westchester/Hudson Valley 316
Sapori | San Diego 265
Sardinia | Miami 165
Sasabune | New York City. 207
Savona | Philadelphia 235
Scalini Fedeli | New Jersey 188
Scalini Fedeli | New York City 207
Scarpetta | Miami 165
Schoolhouse at Cannondale | Connecticut 84

Schwa | Chicago 60
SeaBlue | Atlantic City 27
Sea Change | Minneapolis/St. Paul 176
Seafood Buffet | Salt Lake City & Mountain Resorts 255
Sea Salt | Naples, FL. 180
Seasons 52 | Orlando. 221
Sel de la Terre | Boston 46
Serenade | New Jersey. 188
Serevan | Westchester/Hudson Valley 317
Sérgio's in University Circle | Cleveland. 72
Serious Pie | Seattle 283
1789 | Washington, DC 308
1770 House Restaurant & Inn | Long Island. 147
Shade | Houston. 124
Shanghai Terrace | Chicago. 60
Shinsei | Dallas/Ft. Worth. 92
Shiro | Los Angeles. 156
Shiro's Sushi | Seattle 283
SHO Shaun Hergatt | New York City. 207
Siam Lotus Thai | Long Island 147
SideBern's | Tampa/Sarasota 295
Sidney Street Cafe | St. Louis 289
Sierra Mar | San Francisco Bay Area. 274
Silk Road | Las Vegas 138
Silo | San Antonio. 261
Silo 1604 | San Antonio. 261
Simon Prime Steaks & Martinis | Atlantic City 27
Simon Restaurant & Lounge | Las Vegas 138
Sitka & Spruce | Seattle. 284
Six89 | Denver & Mountain Resorts 101
Slanted Door, The | San Francisco Bay Area 274
Smyth | Milwaukee 171
Sola | Philadelphia 235
Sonoma Modern American | Charlotte 51
Sonora | Westchester/Hudson Valley 317
Sorellina | Boston. 46
Sotto Sotto | Atlanta 22
Soul Gastrolounge | Charlotte. 51
Source, The | Washington, DC 308
Sovana Bistro | Philadelphia 235
Spago | Los Angeles. 156
Spiaggia | Chicago. 61
Spiga | Miami 165
Spinasse | Seattle. 284
Splendido at the Chateau | Denver & Mountain Resorts 101
Spring | Chicago. 61
Spring Hill | Seattle 284
Spruce | Salt Lake City & Mountain Resorts 255
Spruce | San Francisco Bay Area. 275
Squeaky Bean | Denver & Mountain Resorts 102
Sra. Martinez | Miami 165
Sripraphai | New York City 207

Staple & Fancy Mercantile | Seattle 284
Starker's Restaurant | Kansas City 129
Starr Boggs | Long Island 147
Steak 954 | Ft. Lauderdale 113
Stella! | New Orleans 198
Stellina Pasta Cafe | St. Louis 289
Stephan Pyles | Dallas/Ft. Worth 93
Sterling Brunch | Las Vegas 138
Still River Café | Connecticut 84
Stone Creek Inn | Long Island 147
Stonehenge | Connecticut 84
Streetside Seafood | Detroit 107
Strip House | Las Vegas 139
Strip House | Naples, FL 180
Studio | Orange County, CA 212
Sugarcane Raw Bar Grill | Miami 166
Sugiyama | New York City 207
Sullivan's Steakhouse | Charlotte 51
Sushi Den | Denver & Mountain Resorts 102
Sushi-Don Sasabune Express | Los Angeles 156
Sushi Nanase | Westchester/Hudson Valley 317
Sushi Nozawa | Los Angeles 156
Sushi of Gari | New York City 202
Sushi of Gari 46 | New York City 202
Sushi Ota | San Diego 266
Sushi Ran | San Francisco Bay Area 275
Sushi Sasa | Denver & Mountain Resorts 102
Sushi Sasabune | Honolulu 117
Sushi Sasabune | Los Angeles 156
sushi wabi | Chicago 61
Sushi Yasuda | New York City 208
Sushi Zo | Los Angeles 156
Sushi Zone | San Francisco Bay Area 275
Swann Lounge | Philadelphia 235
Sweet Basil | Denver & Mountain Resorts 102
Switch Steak | Las Vegas 139
Swoon Kitchenbar | Westchester/Hudson Valley 317
SW Steakhouse | Las Vegas 139
Tableau | Las Vegas 139
Tables | Denver & Mountain Resorts 102
Tabu Grill | Orange County, CA 212
t'afia | Houston 125
TAG | Denver & Mountain Resorts 103
Takashi | Salt Lake City & Mountain Resorts 256
Tallgrass | Chicago 61
Talula's Table | Philadelphia 236
Tanoreen | New York City 208
Taormina | Honolulu 117
Tapenade | San Diego 266
Taranta | Boston 46
Tarbell's | Phoenix/Scottsdale 240
Tar Pit, The | Los Angeles 157

Tarry Lodge | Westchester/Hudson Valley 317
Tasting Room | Baltimore/Annapolis 36
Tavolino | Tucson 300
T. Cook's | Phoenix/Scottsdale 241
Tei An | Dallas/Ft. Worth 93
Tei Tei Robata Bar | Dallas/Ft. Worth 93
Telepan | New York City 208
Tellers American Chophouse | Long Island 147
Ten Tables | Boston 46
Teppo Yakitori & Sushi Bar | Dallas/Ft. Worth 93
Terrapin | Westchester/Hudson Valley 318
Thai Arroy | Baltimore/Annapolis 36
Thai Place | Kansas City 130
Thai Spice | Ft. Lauderdale 113
Thali | Connecticut 84
Thali Too | Connecticut 84
3660 on the Rise | Honolulu 117
3030 Ocean | Ft. Lauderdale 113
32 East | Palm Beach 227
Thomas Henkelmann | Connecticut 85
Three Birds | Cleveland 72
Tierra | Atlanta 23
Tiffin | Philadelphia 236
Tillman's Roadhouse | Dallas/Ft. Worth 93
Tilth | Seattle 284
Timo | Miami 166
Tinto | Philadelphia 236
Todd English's Bluezoo | Orlando 222
Todd's Unique Dining | Las Vegas 139
Toku | Long Island 148
Tony Mandola's Gulf Coast Kitchen | Houston 125
Tony's | Houston 125
Tony's | St. Louis 290
Topolobampo | Chicago 61
Top Steak House | Columbus 76
Torchy's Tacos | Austin 31
Toro | Boston 46
Toro Bravo | Portland, OR 246
Tosca | Washington, DC 309
Toscana | Charlotte 51
Tosoni's | Seattle 284
Tower Café | Sacramento 250
Towne | Boston 47
Tradition by Pascal | Orange County, CA 213
Trattoria L'incontro | New York City 208
Trattoria Marcella | St. Louis 290
Tree Room | Salt Lake City & Mountain Resorts 256
Tre Figlio | New Jersey 188
TRIO | Austin 31
Trio | Cincinnati 67
Troquet | Boston 47
Tru | Chicago 62

ALPHA INDEX

Truluck's | Naples, FL 180
Truluck's | Palm Beach 227
Tuli Bistro | Sacramento 251
2941 Restaurant | Washington, DC.............. 309
20.21 | Minneapolis/St. Paul 176
Twist | Westchester/Hudson Valley 318
2 Amys | Washington, DC 309
Uchi | Austin 31
Uchiko | Austin 31
Umami Moto | Milwaukee 171
Union League Cafe | Connecticut............... 85
Union Restaurant & Bar Latino | Westchester/Hudson Valley 318
Union Square Cafe | New York City 208
Upperline | New Orleans 198
Uproot | New Jersey 189
Upstream | Charlotte 52
Valencia Luncheria | Connecticut 85
Valentino | Houston 125
Valentino's Cucina Italiana | Ft. Lauderdale 113
Veloce Cibo | Las Vegas 139
Venue | Denver & Mountain Resorts 103
Veranda, The | Naples, FL...................... 180
Vernona | Tampa/Sarasota 295
Versailles | Miami 166
Vespaio | Austin 31
Vesta Dipping Grill | Denver & Mountain Resorts 103
Vetri | Philadelphia 236
Via Vite | Cincinnati 67
Vic & Anthony's | Houston..................... 125
Victoria & Albert's | Orlando 222
Vidalia | Washington, DC....................... 309
Vie | Chicago 62
Vincent | Minneapolis/St. Paul 176
Vincent's on Camelback | Phoenix/Scottsdale ... 241
Vines Grille & Wine Bar | Orlando.............. 222
Vine Street Café | Long Island 148
Vintage Prime Steakhouse | Long Island 148
Virgilio's Pizzeria Napoletana | Denver & Mountain Resorts 103
Vivace | Tucson 300
Vizard's | New Orleans 198
Volt | Baltimore/Annapolis..................... 37
Wa | Los Angeles 157
WA Restaurant | Orlando....................... 222
Wallsé | New York City 208
Wasabi | Westchester/Hudson Valley 318
Wasabi Grill | Westchester/Hudson Valley 318
Washington Inn | New Jersey................... 189
Waterbar | San Francisco Bay Area 275
Waterboy | Sacramento 251
Water Grill | Los Angeles 157
Waterloo & City | Los Angeles 157
Watershed | Atlanta 23

Wayfare Tavern | San Francisco Bay Area 275
Webster House | Kansas City 130
Westend Bistro by Eric Ripert | Washington, DC 310
West End Grill | Detroit 107
Whispers | New Jersey 189
White House | Atlantic City 27
Whitney, The | Detroit 108
Wildfire | Chicago 62
Wildfish Seafood Grille | Orange County, CA 213
Wild Ginger | Seattle 285
WineSellar & Brasserie | San Diego 266
Wink | Austin 32
Winvian | Connecticut 85
Wolfgang Puck American Grille | Atlantic City 27
Woodberry Kitchen | Baltimore/Annapolis 37
Woodfire Grill | Atlanta 23
Woodward House | Connecticut 85
Worthington Inn | Columbus 76
WP24 | Los Angeles 157
Xaviars at Piermont | Westchester/Hudson Valley 318
XOCO | Chicago 62
X2O Xaviars on the Hudson | Westchester/Hudson Valley 319
Yachtsman Steakhouse | Orlando 222
Yao Fuzi Cuisine | Dallas/Ft. Worth 94
York Street | Dallas/Ft. Worth 94
Yutaka Sushi Bistro | Dallas/Ft. Worth 94
Zahav | Philadelphia 236
Zaytinya | Washington, DC 310
Z Cucina | Columbus 76
Z Cuisine A Côté | Denver & Mountain Resorts 103
Zebra Restaurant & Wine Bar | Charlotte 52
Zelko Bistro | Houston 125
Zephs' | Westchester/Hudson Valley 319
Zingerman's Delicatessen | Detroit 108
Zorba's Bar & Grill | Baltimore/Annapolis 37
Zuni Café | San Francisco Bay Area 276

Wine Vintage Chart

This chart is based on our 0 to 30 scale. The ratings (by U. of South Carolina law professor **Howard Stravitz**) reflect vintage quality and the wine's readiness to drink. A dash means the wine is past its peak or too young to rate. Loire ratings are for dry whites.

Whites

	95	96	97	98	99	00	01	02	03	04	05	06	07	08	09
France:															
Alsace	24	23	23	25	23	25	26	23	21	24	25	24	26	25	25
Burgundy	27	26	22	21	24	24	24	27	23	26	27	25	26	25	25
Loire Valley	-	-	-	-	-	-	26	21	23	27	23	24	24	26	
Champagne	26	27	24	23	25	24	21	26	21	-	-	-	-	-	-
Sauternes	21	23	25	23	24	24	29	24	26	21	26	24	27	25	27
California:															
Chardonnay	-	-	-	-	22	21	25	26	22	26	29	24	27	25	-
Sauvignon Blanc	-	-	-	-	-	-	-	-	-	26	25	27	25	24	25
Austria:															
Grüner V./Riesl.	22	-	25	22	25	21	22	25	26	25	24	26	25	23	27
Germany:	21	26	21	22	24	20	29	25	26	27	28	25	27	25	25

Reds

	95	96	97	98	99	00	01	02	03	04	05	06	07	08	09
France:															
Bordeaux	26	25	23	25	24	29	26	24	26	25	28	24	23	25	27
Burgundy	26	27	25	24	27	22	24	27	25	23	28	25	25	24	26
Rhône	26	22	23	27	26	27	26	-	26	25	27	25	26	23	26
Beaujolais	-	-	-	-	-	-	-	-	-	-	27	24	25	23	27
California:															
Cab./Merlot	27	25	28	23	25	-	27	26	25	24	26	23	26	23	25
Pinot Noir	-	-	-	-	-	-	25	26	25	26	24	23	27	25	24
Zinfandel	-	-	-	-	-	-	25	23	27	22	24	21	21	25	23
Oregon:															
Pinot Noir	-	-	-	-	-	-	-	26	24	26	25	24	23	27	25
Italy:															
Tuscany	25	24	29	24	27	24	27	-	25	27	26	26	25	24	-
Piedmont	21	27	26	25	26	28	27	-	24	27	26	25	26	26	-
Spain:															
Rioja	26	24	25	-	25	24	28	-	23	27	26	24	24	-	26
Ribera del Duero/Priorat	26	27	25	24	25	24	27	-	24	27	26	24	26	-	-
Australia:															
Shiraz/Cab.	24	26	25	28	24	24	27	27	25	26	27	25	23	-	-
Chile:	-	-	-	-	25	23	26	24	25	24	27	25	24	26	-
Argentina:															
Malbec	-	-	-	-	-	-	-	25	26	27	25	24	-		

Menus, photos, voting and more - free at ZAGAT.com